A·M·E·R·I·C·A·N
MILITARY LEADERS

A·M·E·R·I·C·A·N
MILITARY LEADERS

Roger J. Spiller, *Editor*
Joseph G. Dawson III, *Associate Editor*
Charles R. Shrader, *Photograph Researcher*

PRAEGER

New York
Westport, Connecticut
London

Library of Congress Cataloging-in-Publication Data

American military leaders / Roger J. Spiller, editor ; Joseph G.
  Dawson III, associate editor ; Charles R. Shrader, photograph
  researcher.
      p.   cm.
  Bibliography: p.
  Includes index.
  ISBN 0-275-93139-0 (alk. paper)
    1. United States—Armed Forces—Biography—Dictionaries.
  2. Generals—United States—Biography—Dictionaries. 3. Admirals—
  United States—Biography—Dictionaries. 4. Military biography—
  Dictionaries. I. Spiller, Roger J. II. Dawson, Joseph G., 1945- .
  U52.A44   1989
  355'.0092'2—dc19   88-32344
  [B]

Copyright © 1989 by Roger J. Spiller and Joseph G. Dawson III

All rights reserved. No portion of this book may be
reproduced, by any process or technique, without the
express written consent of the publisher.

Library of Congress Catalog Card Number: 88-32344
ISBN: 0-275-93139-0

First published in 1989

Praeger Publishers, One Madison Avenue, New York, NY 10010
A division of Greenwood Press, Inc.

Printed in the United States of America

10 9 8 7 6 5 4 3 2 1

The cover photograph is a reproduction of Norman Rockwell's painting, "To Make Men Free," U.S. Army Art Collection, U.S. Army Center of Military History, Washington, D.C., photo no. CC-25024.

Contents

Introduction	vii
Photo Essay	xiii
Biographical Essays	1
Appendix: Chronology of American Military Developments	353
Index	401
Contributors	411

Introduction

Springtime—the third spring of the war: the commander had long since proved his ability and audacity in leading major field armies, but now he was faced with his gravest challenge.

From his vantage point overlooking a small river town, the commander observed part of the enemy's forces, but they were formidable in their own right. Reports indicated that the enemy general, only a few miles distant, had moved forward with an even larger force which threatened to envelop the commander's position. Should he retreat? His army would then be vulnerable to pressure on both flanks by the ever more powerful enemy. Or should he turn his army to meet the greater threat to the rear of his positions?

The commander reached a decision, as unconventional as it was audacious: violating one of the cardinal rules of positional warfare, he divided his forces in the face of the enemy, left a token force to block the enemy to his front, and turned the bulk of his forces toward the major threat behind him. As his forces approached the main enemy army, the commander saw it was poorly disposed. He took another risk, divided his army yet again, and ordered his boldest subordinate to assault the enemy's flanks.

All the risks paid off more handsomely than anyone might have imagined. The commander's maneuvers won a stunning tactical victory, a setback for the enemy that eventually brought about the downfall of the opposing general. The victory confirmed the commander's place as one of his nation's most respected, revered military leaders.

Students of military history will recognize this episode from the American Civil War. The commander was Robert E. Lee, leading his Army of Northern Virginia at the Battle of Chancellorsville in 1863 against Joseph Hooker's Army of the Potomac. The stark contrasts between Lee and Hooker, played out on the Virginia countryside, underscored for history to see the greatness of one commander and the mediocrity of the other.

Three-quarters of a century and half a world away, another commander received word in the early morning hours of an intercepted radio broadcast, indicating that enemy aircraft had launched a devastating surprise attack on a distant friendly base, an attack that plunged his nation once more into war. Logic demanded that the commander look to his own defenses and prepare for the war that would surely turn his way. Yet, more than eleven hours after the war began, enemy air forces struck the commander's unprotected, vulnerable bombers parked at an airfield, destroying or damaging most of them. Somehow, the commander had lapsed, had failed to issue orders to his subordinates, and had failed to produce even the most elementary defensive plans.

The commander in this case was General Douglas MacArthur, then at his headquarters in Manila, the Philippine Islands, in December, 1941, in one of the most peculiar episodes in the war between the United States and Japan. How could a general with MacArthur's vast experience allow his bombers to be caught in the open and destroyed on the ground? How, so many hours after the Japanese attacked Pearl Harbor, could MacArthur and his Air Force commander, Lewis Brereton, have been surprised by the Japanese air strike? Indeed, what is one to make of this episode when one sees MacArthur go on to be one of the top commanders during World War II, and, during the Korean War, conceive and command the brilliant strategic stroke at Inchon?

After the battle of Fredericksburg, Robert E. Lee told a companion, "It is well that war is so terrible—we would grow too fond of it." Notwithstanding the general's melancholic observation, people never tire of studying war, sitting in judgment on those who have been charged to conduct it, and especially arguing who were the great commanders and what qualities made them so. But what makes a great military commander—a Lee over a Hooker, the MacArthur of Inchon rather than the MacArthur of Manila? Unfortunately for kings, prime ministers, or presidents, no formula guides one to mark the difference between a Ulysses S. Grant and a George B. McClellan, or to measure with precision the qualities required to make a great general or admiral.

Perhaps because the foundations of military leadership are so elusive, theorists and scholars have never tired of attempting to reduce those foundations to understandable terms. The great military theorists of the nineteenth century, Antoine Henri Jomini and Carl von Clausewitz, had very different visions of warfare, but they agreed that successful commanders will possess a collection of traits called "character."

Character in a military commander transcends education, intelligence, experience, and a sense of professionalism. Many officers have possessed these fundamental qualities, but few will be remarkable at the higher levels of command. Great military leaders must also have a particular visceral combination of qualities—good health and reserves of stamina, mental toughness and physical stamina that fortify them in the face of the succession of crises that inevitably make up battle. The pressures of battle on land or sea over several hours or days can exhaust the most robust officers, making them anxious, distracted, unsure of themselves and their resources. Abraham Lincoln put it best when he said of his leading general-in-chief, "The great thing about Grant, I take it, is his perfect coolness and persistency of purpose. I judge he is not easily excited—which is a great element in an officer."

"Coolness and persistency of purpose" in a commander always have been great elements in an officer, but the times in which a leader fought framed his actions on the battlefield and the larger role he was expected to play as a military commander. In the American Revolution, George Washington, as commander-in-chief of the American armies, often moved dangerously close to the battle lines. This was the age of linear tactics and smoothbore cannon and muskets, where enemies drew close for combat—often as close as one hundred yards or less—and leadership by personal example made heroes of those who survived the cauldron of war. At the battles of Trenton and Princeton, Washington virtually acted as the direct field commander of his small army rather than using two or three generals as division or wing commanders to direct troops in actual contact with the enemy. Washington was not typically at the forefront of his troops, however. His personal leadership at Trenton and Princeton helped to rally the troops, but as the senior general he could rely upon subordinates to direct major units in combat. Benedict Arnold and Nathanael Greene, among other generals, were expected as divisional or small field force leaders to place themselves in battle where they could see the enemy's maneuvers and personally influence events on the field. At any event, military leadership was still a highly personal art that entailed highly personal as well as military risks.

Even in the late eighteenth and early nineteenth centuries, the question of the degree to which a senior commander should hazard himself was debatable. The loss of a highly respected and popular officer could have serious consequences for his own soldiers' morale or, correspondingly, lift the fighting spirit of the enemy if they learned that a renowned enemy had been killed. Balancing the roles of "director" of combat and actual combatant was difficult in those days when personal demonstrations of courage were thought to inspire or renew confidence among the troops. The directing brain of an army, as Winfield Scott demonstrated in his brilliant campaign against Mexico City in 1847, could be worth thousands of soldiers. His value to the war effort was as a planner and director of the campaign, and in any case Scott had more than established his credentials as a warrior against the British in the Battles of Chippewa and Lundy's Lane during the War of 1812.

During Winfield Scott's active service, from the first few years of the nineteenth century until the Civil War, vast technological changes overtook the conduct of warfare. By the 1860s, the railroad, field telegraph, armorclad ships, and steam power had done much to alter habits of strategy grown comfortable during the past several centuries of conflict. At the tactical level, rifled cannon and muskets greatly increased the range, accuracy, and firepower of those who still contested with one another on the field of battle itself. The art of managing troops in combat tended to lag behind these changes, however: signals by bugle call or drum roll, and orders transmitted by voice or messenger—the techniques of command and control still required operational leaders, brigade, division, and sometimes corps commanders—were still used so leaders could be close to their troops and the line of battle.

At least by the time of the Civil War, a shift in expectations about where a commander should be in the zone of battle had been made. While naval commanders were still in personal danger, as Flag Officer David G. Farragut was at the battles of New Orleans and Mobile, it no longer seemed logical or necessary for important national army commanders such as Lee or Joseph E. Johnston to lead infantry assaults. The death of Confederate General Albert Sidney Johnston on Shiloh battlefield in April, 1862, seemed to confirm the new imperatives of command. Johnston's death was a severe blow to the Confederacy and removed a widely-respected leader whose skills would be sorely missed later in the war. Despite this deadly example, some Civil War commanders surrendered to the dramatic attractions of forces locked in mortal combat, though increasingly it was by virtue of accident or extraordinary turn of event that brought such leaders as Jeb Stuart, James McPherson, and Joseph Hooker directly under enemy fire. That both James Longstreet and Stonewall Jackson were shot accidentally by their own soldiers later in the war was unusually bad luck for the Confederate Army, but these accidents called into question why such important leaders were so unmindful of their larger responsibilities in the first place. So much had the values of courage changed that the severe wounds of Generals John Bell Hood and Richard S. Ewell merely cast doubt upon their wisdom, for which no degree of courageousness could compensate.

At least in the United States, the experiences of the Civil War brought to an end the old romantic notion—always bankrupt—that all a battle captain need bring to a war was a chivalrous spirit. If the new firepower of armies was not sufficient to overturn these romantic ideas, the new dimensions of warfare itself forced different habits upon future commanders. Increasingly, technical and managerial skills were required from those who would oversee vast military machines whose work was done at points far beyond the vision and immediate control of their leaders. By the time of the Spanish-American War in 1898, few expected expeditionary leaders William Shafter and Nelson Miles to be with leading combat troops, although top naval squadron or fleet commanders such as Winfield S. Schley or William T. Sampson could still come under direct fire from enemy ships or shore batteries.

Thus, by the twentieth century, the requirements of military leadership had become highly stratified: certainly at the tactical level, perhaps at the operational level, one could still argue that "character" was a requisite. But what of the higher levels, at the heights of army, army groups, air force, or naval task force? Looking back at the Civil War from the vantage points of the Western Front in 1917, or the global operations of 1942–1945, the risks that Grant, Lee, and their colleagues had taken were no longer acceptable. National political and military leaders understood, and often insisted, that officers of high importance should not travel with field armies; taking advantage of new communications technology, they could direct and manage the war effort from a distant headquarters near the nation's political leaders. Therefore, Army Chief of Staff Peyton C. March made invaluable (but not well publicized) contributions to the American war effort in World War I from Washington, while John J. Pershing at times was almost as much a diplomat as a molder and leader of the American Expeditionary Force in France. Officers below Pershing in the chain of command, Robert Bullard and Hunter Liggett, for instance, were much more removed from the front lines than those who held corresponding posts in earlier wars. By 1942, it would have been preposterous for George C. Marshall to take the field; he was obviously too valuable to the Allied cause as Chief of Staff of the U.S. Army. Overseas, management of far-flung military resources had become the chief task confronting Dwight D. Eisenhower, Douglas MacArthur, and Chester Nimitz. The transformation of the higher military commander from warrior to manager may have been completed on that day in 1944 when Eisenhower, with only few options open to him, had to decide when to launch the Allied invasion of Normandy.

Thus, the changing shape of warfare itself has changed the shape of military leadership. No longer could talented amateurs reckon on assuming command of complex forces who were fighting for unprecedentedly higher stakes than ever before. Armies and navies were much less susceptible to command by the "youthful geniuses" that populated the military adventures of bygone years, and although wars still offer opportunities for the emergence of truly romantic figures such as George Patton or the paratroop commander James Gavin, one does not have to look far into such lives to see that they were first, thoroughgoing military professionals who were more than equal to the new technical and tactical challenges they faced.

Those who continue to search for the secret keys to successful military leadership, or imagine that they have found them, will perhaps be disappointed by the biographical essays that follow. What they show, above all, is that military leaders, like the wars that call them forth, are creatures of their particular time and place, and as such, serve as the keys not to secret ways but to a broader understanding of this nation's military past.

American Military Leaders is an abridgement of the three-volume *Dictionary of American Military Biography*, originally published by Greenwood Press in 1984. The original *Dictionary* was unprecedented: never in this country had so many military historians—more than 240—cooperated in a venture of such magnitude. The idea was to write original biographical essays on four hundred of the most important military figures in American history. Each of the essays was to incorporate the latest scholarship on the life under study, and each was to venture an appraisal of its subject. This approach was meant not only to advance our knowledge of this country's leading military figures, but also to contribute to an understanding of the nation's military history in general.

The scope of the original *Dictionary* suggested by the nature of its entries that American military history was made by a much wider range of people than soldiers alone—politicians, certainly, but also scientists, inventors, explorers, physicians, and humanitarians. In fact, some of the most interesting and illuminating essays in the *Dictionary* were not about soldiers—or soldiering—at all.

And yet, it is battle, the prospect of it, the conduct and consequences of it, that most vividly separates military affairs from all other sorts of history. Enterprises and actions that in other circumstances seem ordinary enough take on a unique characteristic when they occur in war. One writer has suggested recently that logic itself may fall victim to peculiar influences which have no corollary in normal life, and more than a century and a half ago, Carl von Clausewitz, the only philosopher war has ever produced, wrote in his classic, *On War*, that in warfare "the light of reason is refracted in a manner quite different from that which is normal in academic speculation."

The same is no less true of the men who have commanded in war. Intimate acquaintance with war, even genius in war, is no guarantor of a generally successful life. The essays collected here demonstrate the fickle nature of military greatness, and the uncertain roads military leaders have taken to reach it.

Leaders in War and Peace...

General George Washington takes command of the Continental army at Cambridge, 1775 *(National Archives, Washington, D.C., NA 148-GW-178)*.

General Andrew Jackson commands at New Orleans, 1815 *(United States Army Military History Institute, Carlisle Barracks, Penn., SC 96970)*.

... from Mexico ...

General Winfield Scott commands at Churubusco, 1847 *(United States Army Military History Institute, SC 320459).*

A

B

C

D

A. General Ulysses S. Grant, United States Army *(United States Army Military History Institute, MOLLUS Mass 91-4686).*

B. General William T. Sherman, United States Army *(United States Army Military History Institute, MOLLUS Mass 11-526L).*

C. Lieutenant General Thomas J. Jackson, Confederate States Army *(United States Army Military History Institute, MOLLUS Mass 87-4400).*

D. General Robert E. Lee, Confederate States Army *(United States Army Military History Institute, MOLLUS Mass 13-622).*

... to Appomattox ...

...with Cutlass...

Admiral David G. Farragut *(United States Army Military History Institute, MOLLUS Mass 15-714).*

Admiral David D. Porter *(United States Army Military History Institute, MOLLUS Mass 64-3182).*

Civil War cavalrymen campaigning against the Plains Indians (L. to R.: Wesley Merritt, Philip Sheridan, George Crook, James Forsyth, George Custer). *(United States Military Academy Library, Special Collections Division, West Point, N.Y.)*

...and Saber

A New Generation Rises . . .

"The Class the Stars Fell On": The United States Military Academy Class of 1915 visits Gettysburg, 3 May 1915 (*United States Military Academy Archives*).

...on Land...

Lieutenant Colonel William J. Donovan, United States Army *(United States Army Military History Institute, SC 25158)*.

Major Holland M. Smith, United States Marine Corps *(United States Army Military History Institute, SC 13131)*.

...at Sea...

Vice Admiral William S. Sims, United States Navy *(United States Army Military History Institute, US 13657)*.

...and in the Air...

Brigadier General William Mitchell, United States Army *(United States Army Military History Institute, SC 86985)*.

. . . Learning from Their Mentors . . .

General John J. Pershing and Colonel George C. Marshall, France, 1918 *(United States Army Military History Institute, SC 91374).*

. . . and Each Other . . .

L. to R.: Generals Hap Arnold, Dwight Eisenhower, George Marshall, and Omar Bradley with Admiral Ernest King, France, 1944 *(United States Army Military History Institute, SC 192610).*

... a Variety of Styles

Major General George S. Patton, Jr., Fort Knox, Kentucky, 1941 *(United States Army Military History Institute, Sig. Sec., Fort Knox).*

Generals Patton, Eisenhower, and Bradley, Bastogne, Belgium, 1945 *(United States Army Military History Institute, ETO HQ 45-1491T).*

L. to R.: Generals Alfred M. Gruenther, Mark W. Clark, George C. Marshall, Lucian K. Truscott, Edward M. Almond, Joseph T. McNarney, and Willis D. Crittenberger, Via Reggio, Italy, 1945 *(United States Army Military History Institute, SC 438970).*

And in the Pacific...

a Loss...

General Douglas MacArthur greets General Jonathan Wainwright on his release from a Japanese POW camp, 1945 *(United States Army Military History Institute, SC 210621-S)*.

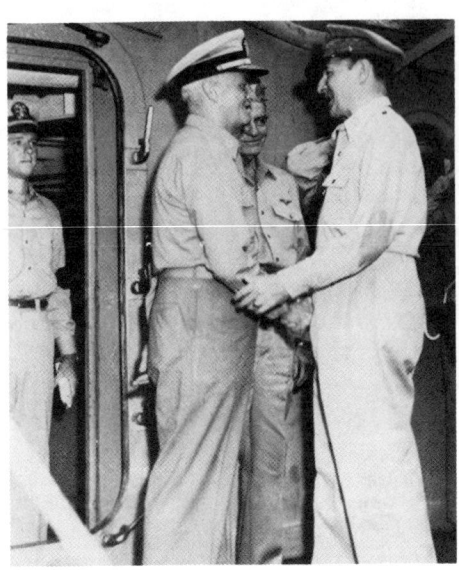

Admirals Chester W. Nimitz and William F. Halsey welcome General MacArthur aboard the USS *Buchanan* in Tokyo Bay, 1945 *(United States Army Military History Institute, SC 210650-S)*.

a Win...

Generals Courtney Whitney and Matthew B. Ridgway, an unidentified battalion commander, and General of the Army Douglas MacArthur, Korea, 1951 *(United States Army Military History Institute, SC 356736)*.

and a Draw...

... Prepare the Way for a New Generation of Asian Warriors

General William C. Westmoreland faces the press *(United States Army Military History Institute, USA 12-066-3305-AL70).*

General Creighton W. Abrams in the field *(United States Army Military History Institute, USA RGS 123S).*

The Old Army...

General Winfield Scott, Commanding General, United States Army, 1841-1861 *(National Archives, Washington, D.C., US 111-BA-1664)*.

...and the New Look

Major General Maxwell D. Taylor, 1944, Chief of Staff, United States Army, 1955-1959 *(United States Army Military History Institute, SC 195369)*.

A·M·E·R·I·C·A·N
MILITARY LEADERS

Biographical Essays

ABRAMS, Creighton Williams, Jr. (b. Springfield, Mass., September 15, 1914; d. Washington, D.C., September 4, 1974), Army officer; commander, U.S. Military Assistance Command, Vietnam.

Creighton Abrams spent his boyhood in rural Massachusetts, graduating from Agawam High School, where he was captain of its undefeated football team and valedictorian of his senior class. Inspired by a lecture delivered at Agawam by a West Point graduate, Abrams successfully sought appointment to the U.S. Military Academy and matriculated there in 1932. At West Point he excelled in horsemanship and lettered in football. In 1936 he graduated 185th of 276 in his class and was commissioned a second lieutenant of cavalry.

The next four years Abrams spent as a troop officer in the 1st Cavalry Division at Fort Bliss, Texas, receiving regular promotions to first lieutenant (1939) and captain (1940). During 1940 he served with the old 1st Armored Division, but in 1941 he was transferred to the newly activated 4th Armored Division, located in California. Following his promotion to major in February 1942, he took command of a battalion of the 37th Armored Regiment. Only a few months later he was promoted to lieutenant colonel. He served as executive officer of the regiment until he assumed command of the 37th Tank Battalion at Camp Bowie, Texas.

Abrams and the 37th Tank Battalion went into action in Normandy in July 1944, and subsequently they participated in all campaigns of the 4th Armored Division. A serious student and practitioner of modern mobile combat, Abrams built a deserved reputation as one of the best tank commanders of the war, earning the respect and compliments of his comrades and superiors. General George Smith Patton, Jr.* commended Abrams, saying that "I'm supposed to be the best tank commander in the Army, but I have one peer—Abe Abrams."

After his distinguished battlefield service in World War II, Abrams received numerous and challenging postwar assignments in the United States and abroad, as well as completing courses of instruction at the Command and General Staff College (1949) and the Army War College (1953). For two years (1946–1948) Abrams served as director of tactics at the Armor School, Fort Knox, Kentucky, where he revised the Army's manual on armor tactics. Some years later (1954–1956), he was chief of staff at the Armor Center. During the early 1950s he commanded the 63d Tank Battalion and the 2d Armored Cavalry Regiment in Europe. During the Korean War, Abrams gained valuable experience at the corps level, serving successively as chief of staff of I Corps, IX Corps, and X Corps. In these positions he planned defenses against the last major Communist offensives of the Korean conflict. Subsequently, Abrams was promoted to brigadier general (1956) and major general (1960). For three years (1956–1959) he held the position of deputy assistant chief of staff for Reserve Components, General Staff, Department of the Army.

In the early 1960s Abrams usually found himself at or near points of crisis. He was assistant division commander and commander of the 3d Armored Division in Europe during the Berlin crisis (1962). In September 1962 he was placed in charge of federal soldiers deployed at Oxford, Mississippi, to quell rioting that had occurred over the admission of a Negro, James M. Meredith, to the University of Mississippi. In May 1963 Abrams commanded troops that had been alerted in case it became necessary for them to intervene in Birmingham, Alabama, during racial unrest there.

In July 1963 he became commanding general of V Corps, one of the two corps-sized American ground combat forces in Europe. He was promoted to lieutenant general (1963) and general (1964), and then became vice chief of staff, U.S. Army, in Washington, D.C. These and other important assignments all were prelude to the greatest challenge of Abrams' career: his service in Vietnam.

In April 1967 President Lyndon B. Johnson assigned Abrams as the deputy commander of the U.S. Military Assistance Command, Vietnam. His principal responsibility was to improve the fighting capabilities of the South Vietnamese forces. During the Tet Offensive of 1968, Abrams supervised allied military operations in northern Vietnam, specifically ordering the recapture of Hue.

In July 1968 he assumed command in Vietnam following the North Vietnamese psychological victory in the Tet Offensive of 1968. For the next four years, Abrams' mission required the reduction of direct U.S. military involvement and the training of the South Vietnamese forces to assume increasing responsibilities for defense of their country. He departed Vietnam in June 1972 following the North Vietnamese Easter Offensive.

While serving in Vietnam, Abrams was nominated to be chief of staff, U.S. Army. The Senate confirmed his appointment on October 12, 1972, by a vote of eighty-four to two. For two years, until his death from lung cancer on September 4, 1974, Abrams worked diligently to rebuild the Army which had suffered the traumas of a rapid reduction in size, repositioning of forces occasioned by the end of military operations in Vietnam, and the political effects of the war itself in the United States.

He was interred at Arlington National Cemetery on September 6, 1974.

As a battalion commander in World War II, Abrams established a reputation that would follow him for the rest of his career. Throughout the Army he was known for aggressive, fearless leadership in combat. During the American Army's advance across France and into Germany, Abrams' battalion was the point battalion of General Patton's Third Army.

On December 26, 1944, Abrams' battalion was the first American unit to reach the 101st Airborne Division, which had been surrounded at Bastogne, Belgium, during the Germans' Ardennes Offensive (the "Battle of the Bulge"). On the way to Bastogne, when a concealed German antitank gun held up the advance of his armored task force, Abrams went forward in his command tank to destroy the gun and keep the advance moving to Bastogne. He was awarded his second Distinguished Service Cross for valor for that action.

Although Abrams held important and sensitive positions following his World War II service, he did not become well known outside the Army until he assumed command of the U.S. Army Military Assistance Command, Vietnam. Alert to the problems of the presidency during the difficult post-Tet period, Abrams also understood the internal and external political characteristics of the war and prompted quick changes in American military tactics. At Abrams' direction, the Army placed greater emphasis on defense of populated areas and deemphasized the massive sweep operations used under General William Childs Westmoreland.* Search and destroy tactics were replaced by tremendous numbers of small patrols and ambushes. Abrams' tactics were to get inside the enemy's system and, in his words, to "hound and harass and drive the enemy's influence from the land." Allied cross-border operations into Cambodia in 1970 and Laos in 1971 were conducted to push the enemy away from South Vietnam's borders, ensure the security of the American withdrawal, and give the South Vietnamese additional time to develop the Vietnamization program.

In his advisory role, Abrams' efforts rearmed and trained the Army of the Republic of Vietnam, including its militia—the provincial and district forces. A measure of his success came when the South Vietnamese Army withstood and eventually repulsed a massive North Vietnamese invasion in the spring of 1972 with only American advisors and air power in South Vietnam for assistance. Furthermore, Abrams instituted the nation-building pacification programs, which were designed to improve the educational, medical, transportation, and agricultural systems in South Vietnam. He was particularly sensitive to the war's impact on the hapless Vietnamese people and constantly stressed cooperation with local Vietnamese authorities.

Abrams' command of the U.S. Army Military Assistance Advisory Command from 1968 until 1972 was one of the most difficult tasks in American military history. The Nixon administration's policy of giving the South Vietnamese a chance for survival after America's military participation ended was achieved. While in Vietnam, Abrams' remarkable character and complete candor enabled him to achieve the respect of the virtually uncensored American news media, which was often hostile towards the Army.

As chief of staff of the U.S. Army, Abrams guided the rebuilding of the Army's professional and ethical standards in the bitter period following the American withdrawal from Vietnam in January 1973. He directed the introduction of a voluntary enlistment system, although he stated publicly that if the volunteer Army became racially and intellectually nonrepresentative of America, "then it's not an Army of the United States." He stressed modernization of the reserve forces and began implementing a reserve reorganization plan.

Abe Abrams is one of the unsung military figures of American history. He was inspirational, brave, bold, and wise. As division commander of the 3d Armored Division, Abrams was rated by his superiors as being "the outstanding armor commander of his generation." He was considered to be the "number one fighting general in the Army" according to General Bruce C. Clark. Aside from his combat prowess, Abrams excelled as an advisor to America's top civilian leaders, whether in the Department of Defense, Congress, or the White House. His success in this difficult role for a military officer was the crowning achievement of his illustrious career.

BIBLIOGRAPHY

Johnson, Lyndon B. *The Vantage Point*. New York: Holt, Rinehart, and Winston, 1971.
Millett, Allan R. *A Short History of the Vietnam War*. Bloomington: Indiana University Press, 1978.
Palmer, Dave R. *Summons of the Trumpet*. San Rafael, Calif.: Presidio Press, 1978.

VAN M. DAVIDSON, JR.

ALMOND, Edward Mallory (b. Luray, Va., December 12, 1892; d. Washington, D.C., June 11, 1979), combat commander in three wars.

Edward Mallory Almond was graduated from the Virginia Military Institute in 1915 and was commissioned a second lieutenant of infantry in the U.S. Army on November 30, 1916. In World War I he commanded the 12th Machine Gun Battalion of the 4th Division in France, where he participated in the Aisne-Marne and the Meuse-Argonne offensives. For his actions in World War I, Almond was promoted to major and was awarded the Silver Star and the Purple Heart medals. He remained in Europe with the Army of Occupation until July 1919.

Upon his return to the United States, Almond was assigned to Marion Institute, Alabama, as professor of military science and tactics. Postwar reductions in the Army cost Almond his majority, and he reverted to the rank of captain until his promotion to major in 1928. He attended the Infantry School and was retained there as an automatic weapons instructor until he was selected to attend the Command and General Staff School. In 1930 he joined the 45th Infantry Regiment in the Philippine Islands, where he commanded a battalion of Filipino troops.

In 1933 Almond attended the Army War College and was then detailed to the Latin American Section of the Military Intelligence Division of the War Department General Staff. He was promoted to lieutenant colonel in 1938 and attended both the Air Corps Tactical School and the Naval War College before returning to the General Staff. In 1941 he became the assistant chief of staff (G–3) for the VI Corps, was promoted to colonel, and then became chief of staff for VI Corps.

Almond's service in World War II really began with his promotion to brigadier general and his assignment as assistant division commander of the 93d Infantry Division. In September he received his second star and command of the 92d Infantry Division. After organizing and training the division, Almond commanded it in combat in Italy in 1944 and 1945. For his World War II service, General Almond was awarded the Distinguished Service Medal, an Oak Leaf Cluster to the Silver Star, the Legion of Merit, the Bronze Star, the Air Medal, and the Army Commendation Medal with two Oak Leaf Clusters.

General Almond returned to the United States to command the 2d Infantry Division but in 1946 was ordered to Japan as assistant chief of staff (G–1) for Army Forces, Pacific. He soon became deputy chief of staff and in 1949 was assigned as chief of staff for both Army Forces, Pacific, and Far East Command. In 1950 his duties were expanded to include chief of staff, United Nations Command.

When hostilities were initiated in Korea in 1950, Almond, as the American and United Nations chief of staff, was responsible for implementing the decisions of General Douglas MacArthur,* the supreme commander, United Nations Command. In September 1950 General Almond was named commander of the X Corps for the Inchon-Seoul Campaign. He continued in command of the X Corps during the advance into North Korea, the retreat to Hungnam, and the subsequent operations in South Korea until July 1951. He was promoted to the rank of lieutenant general in February 1951. For his service in the Korean conflict, he was awarded the Distinguished Service Cross with Oak Leaf Cluster, an Oak Leaf Cluster to the Distinguished Service Medal, the Distinguished Flying Cross with two Oak Leaf Clusters, the Bronze Star with "V" device, and fifteen Oak Leaf Clusters to the Air Medal. In August 1951 General Almond was designated commandant of the Army War College, a position he held until his retirement from active service on January 1, 1953.

"Ned" Almond, as he was known, was the son of Walter Coles and Grace Pophan Almond. He married Margret Crook in 1917, and they had a son and a daughter. Both his son and his son-in-law were killed in action in World War II in Europe. After leaving the Army, General Almond became an executive of the Life Insurance Company of Alabama. He was active in numerous civic and charitable organizations, particularly the Boy Scouts of America. He was a member of the Board of Visitors of the Virginia Military Institute from 1960 to 1968, serving as president of the board in 1968.

General Almond's reputation, as any commander's, must be determined by his accomplishments as a commander in the field. He distinguished himself as a machine gun battalion commander in World War I. Between the wars he was selected to attend all the schools necessary for advancement to the higher levels of command. His performance at those schools and in command and staff assignments rightly drew the favorable attention of his superior officers. Almond impressed many observers as the embodiment of the courtly Southern soldier. Another view of Almond expressed by a contemporary stated that "when it pays to be aggressive, Ned's aggressive, and when it pays to be cautious, Ned's aggressive, and he wouldn't step two paces to the rear for the devil himself."

General George Catlett Marshall* personally selected Almond to command the 92d Infantry Division in World War II. This command was one of the most controversial of the war because the 92d was a Negro unit. From the initial organization, through its training period and deployment in the Italian campaigns, this division, the only black division committed to combat as a division, was subjected to extraordinary scrutiny by the military and the American public. As a Southern, white Regular Army officer, Almond was certainly justified in describing this command as the most difficult of his career. Almond's personal opinion of his role, and that of his division in World War II, may be deduced from the title given to the history of the 92d Division's operations in Italy: *A Fragment of Victory*.

In 1950, as chief of staff to General Douglas MacArthur, Almond was responsible for developing Operation CHROMITE, the plan for the Inchon invasion. MacArthur then named Almond to command the X Corps which was to carry out CHROMITE. Almond has described his command of the X Corps as the most rewarding assignment of his career because it afforded him the opportunity of independent command. The redeployment of the X Corps to the northeast coast of North Korea, the advance to the Yalu River, and operations in the Chanjin (Chosen) Reservoir against Chinese "volunteers" once again made Almond a figure of controversy, but his skillfully executed withdrawal of X Corps and thousands of Korean refugees by sea from Hungnam earned him a third star. In Korea Almond made extensive use of the Marine Corps' helicopters and became a strong advocate of organic Army aviation units. He was also instrumental in instituting studies for improving tactical air support techniques based upon his Korean experiences.

General Almond's military service to his country spanned thirty-seven years and three wars. His accomplishments at each level of his career clearly indicated that he was an officer of exceptional ability. His military reputation will always be judged, however, by the accomplishments of his two major combat commands, the 92d Infantry Division in Italy and the X Corps in Korea.

BIBLIOGRAPHY

Appleman, Roy E. *South to the Naktong, North to the Yalu (June–November, 1950).* Vol. 2. *U.S. Army in the Korean War.* Washington, D.C.: U.S. Government Printing Office, 1961.
Fisher, Ernest F., Jr. *Cassino to the Alps.* Vol. 4. *Mediterranean Theater of Operations* Subseries; *U.S. Army in World War II.* Washington, D.C.: U.S. Government Printing Office, 1977.
Goodman, Paul. *A Fragment of Victory in Italy During World War II: A Special Study.* Carlisle Barracks, Pa.: Army War College, 1952.
Lee, Ulysses. *The Employment of Negro Troops.* Vol. 8. *Special Studies* Subseries; *U.S. Army in World War II.* Washington, D.C.: U.S. Government Printing Office, 1966.
Schnabel, James F. *Policy and Direction: The First Year.* Vol. 1. *U.S. Army in the Korean War.* Washington, D.C.: U.S. Government Printing Office, 1972.

DAVID CHILDRESS

ARNOLD, Benedict (b. Norwich, Conn., January 14, 1741; d. London, England, June 12, 1801), Army officer. Arnold's name is synonymous with military treason.

Benedict Arnold was the product of an old and distinguished New England family. His great-grandfather, named Benedict, had been a governor of Rhode Island. But his father, also Benedict, failed as a merchant and was known as the town drunkard in Norwich. Arnold's mother, Hannah Waterman King, raised her energetic and athletic son with a stern hand. Declining family financial circumstances forced the decision to withdraw young Benedict from school and to apprentice him to the Lathrop brothers, family cousins who operated one of the most successful apothecary shops in eastern Connecticut.

Arnold took to the apothecary's trade and became a prosperous merchant. He purchased shares in commercial ships and, on numerous occasions, captained vessels in which he was a heavy investor. In 1767, Arnold married Margaret Mansfield, the daughter of the sheriff of New Haven, Connecticut. Before her untimely death in 1775, she bore him three sons. The first demonstrable signs of Arnold's combative character also become manifest during the New Haven years. He fought a duel with a ship captain in the Bay of Honduras over a slight matter of honor. Likewise, as one who engaged in smuggling activities, not uncommon among successful New England merchants in the late colonial period, he was active in organizing the local populace against informers to local British customs agents.

Clearly in the forefront of Connecticut citizens who advocated extreme measures in resisting king and Parliament, Arnold was anxious to attain military rank. In March 1775 he became a captain in the Governor's Second Company of Guards, a newly formed militia unit. After Lexington and Concord, Arnold marched the company to Massachusetts where it joined the forces penning up General Thomas Gage in Boston. Arnold convinced the Massachusetts Committee of Safety to entrust him with the capture of Fort Ticonderoga, one of the keys to controlling the vital Hudson Highlands corridor and an easy source of artillery for the people's army back east. Arnold rushed westward, only to confront Ethan Allen and the Green Mountain Boys, who had been authorized by Connecticut to reduce Ticonderoga. The sorry state of British defenses made the fort's capture a foregone conclusion; yet it was marred by squabbling between Arnold, Allen, and others over such issues as command privileges, proper credit for the victory, and the post-campaign settlement of accounts.

The contention at Ticonderoga was another source of Arnold's developing reputation for belligerence, but that did not deter George Washington* from urging the Continental Congress to name Arnold a colonel in the regular service and to put him in charge of one of the two small armies that invaded Canada. His march to Quebec remains a legendary story of the human will to survive. But the final assault (under cover of a driving snowstorm late on the evening of December 30, 1775), ended in chaos after the commander in charge, Richard Montgomery, was killed and Arnold was seriously wounded in his leg.

Named a brigadier general shortly after the battle at Quebec, Arnold supervised the hasty construction of a "fleet" of boats and prepared to defend Lake Champlain against General Guy Carleton's advancing forces. On October 11 Carleton's fleet attacked Arnold's well-chosen defensive position between Valcour Island and Lake Champlain's western shore. A furious battle ensued during which Arnold once again displayed his intrepid ability to command. The fury of Arnold's stand convinced Carleton not to press his advantage so late in the campaign season and effectively delayed the British at a time when American forces in northern New York were quite weak. Arnold's blocking action helped to set the stage for General John Burgoyne's defeat at Saratoga in 1777.

Meanwhile, Arnold became bogged down in petty disputes, including charges of slandering other officers, mismanaging public funds, and using confiscated goods for private purposes, most of which arose during the retreat from Canada. These allegations no doubt played a role in the decision of Congress to pass over Arnold for promotion to major general. In February 1777 Congress promoted five brigadiers, all Arnold's junior in service and none even close to possessing his record in accomplishments. Naturally, Arnold considered the incident a grave slap at his honor. Washington, an admirer of Arnold's battlefield grit, urged him not to act hastily. Arnold was on the verge of taking his case directly to Congress, but a British raid on Danbury, Connecticut (April 1777) intervened. Arnold rallied the local militia and drove the invaders away. The Danbury raid at last led Congress to recognize his battlefield merits and to name him major general, but without a restoration of seniority. Out of pique and disgust, Arnold resigned in late July 1777.

Fate then took a strange twist. Washington had just recommended Arnold as an officer capable of rallying revolutionary support for the Continental Army's Northern Department in its challenge to Burgoyne's invasion. Ever ready for combat, Arnold asked for a suspension of his resignation and raced northward.

He led a successful relief expedition into the Mohawk Valley to free rebel forces trapped in Fort Stanwix by Colonel Barry St. Leger. But this signal achievement did not avert contention with General Horatio Gates,* who had just taken over command of the Northern Department. Gates, more cautious than Arnold, wanted to defend entrenched positions; his subordinate wanted to carry the fight to the British. At Freeman's Farm on September 19, Gates refused to send troops ahead of American lines to assist Arnold. Despite the American victory that day, Gates did not mention Arnold's important role in official reports. Heated words between the two officers resulted in Gates' decision to relieve Arnold of command of the American left wing. At the second Saratoga engagement (Bemis Heights, October 7), the sulking subordinate could not be restrained. When Arnold learned that the tide of battle was not going well, he rushed to the front, personally rallied several companies, and turned the tide. But he once again sustained a serious wound in his leg—the same that had been mangled at Quebec. Arnold refused amputation, but his well-known physical agility was gone for life.

While Gates became the hero of Saratoga, a thankful Congress restored Arnold's seniority, but that belated action did not improve his shattered health or abate the growing bitterness in his mind. The series of slights and general contention surrounding his military career led Arnold to question the merits of the Revolutionary cause. Like many other officers, he was particularly angry about civilians who profiteered from the war while he was rebuffed and accused of financial chicanery when trying to settle accounts with Congress and other civil agencies. His alienation was ripening when Washington, trying to reward Arnold in his period of physical convalescence, appointed him to command in Philadelphia in June 1778.

Washington's sense of humanity and generosity backfired. Arnold lacked the evenhandedness of a dispassionate administrator and soon made enemies all over the city. He chose to rule by pomp and circumstance and ingratiated himself with the wealthiest families, many of whom had been all but openly loyal to the British during Sir William Howe's occupation. His romance with Margaret Shippen, the youngest of neutralist Edward Shippen's three daughters, and his under-the-table business dealings irked the local republicans. Consequently, several prominent patriots mounted a campaign to get rid of Arnold and smeared him openly with a list of eight alleged abuses of authority. Arnold insisted upon a congressional investigation, which dragged on until January 1780, when a military court exonerated him on all but two charges—those of allowing a vessel in which he was a heavy investor to clear port when all others could not, and of using public wagons for private purposes. Ultimately, Congress ordered Washington to reprimand Arnold, which the commander in chief did in stern but compassionate terms.

The reprimand hurt Arnold deeply, but it was not a factor leading to initial communications with the British. The treasonous correspondence was six months old when the military court issued its decision. Far more important was Arnold's sense that human frailty had ruined the republican cause. Furthermore, in marrying Margaret Shippen (April 8, 1779), he moved closer to the British. His nineteen-year-old bride had been a favored belle among the younger British officers during their stay in Philadelphia. One in particular, Major John André, was at the center of the plot that developed. By the time Washington offered his rebuked officer the command at West Point in August 1780, Arnold was fully committed to allowing the British to seize that strategically vital fort. Only the fortuitous capture of André (September 23) and Arnold's hasty flight down the Hudson River (September 25) saved the Americans from what could have been a disastrous military blow, if Sir Henry Clinton had had the opportunity to follow up on the plans that Arnold and André had devised.

Arnold's traitorous course has biased most accounts of his life and military exploits. But that career, at least until after Saratoga, was invaluable to the success of the American War for Independence. Washington early recognized Arnold's resourcefulness and raw courage in the face of overwhelming military obstacles. The soldiers who served under Arnold clearly respected him. In battle, Arnold was a masterful tactician. But his defiant, impetuous temperament hurt him over and over again in relations with fellow officers. Rather than rising above petty disputes, he wallowed in them.

André's bravery in facing hanging as a common spy, as opposed to Arnold's seeming cupidity, made Arnold seem just that much more of a scoundrel to contemporaries. In popular lore, he quickly became the cursed general who had sold his soul to the devil for filthy lucre (the British paid him handsomely for his treason). Arnold had hoped that other disillusioned rebels would follow him and give up on the military effort, but the very name "Arnold" became a rallying cry for renewed vigor and commitment to the languishing American cause. The traitor received a commission in the Regular British Army as a brigadier general and led savage attacks against Virginia and Connecticut before he and Peggy sailed for London in 1782. In London, Arnold at first held celebrity status, even meeting with King George III. But soon the war's end led the British to treat him with circumspection. They never fully trusted him, and a few openly showed disrespect, which resulted in at least one duel.

Until his death in 1801, Arnold struggled as a merchant to bring in income for his growing family—Peggy bore him four sons and one daughter. But there was no escape from the past. Friendships were few, and he died in obscurity. The excellence of his military record simply could not outweigh his treason.

BIBLIOGRAPHY

Arnold, Isaac N. *The Life of Benedict Arnold: His Patriotism and His Treason.* Chicago: Jansen, McClurg and Company, 1880.

Flexner, James T. *The Traitor and the Spy: Benedict Arnold and John André.* New York: Harcourt, Brace, 1953. Reprint, Boston: Little, Brown and Company, 1975.

Roberts, Kenneth, ed. *March to Quebec: Journals of Members of Arnold's Expedition* . . . New York: Doubleday, Doran and Company, 1938.

Van Doren, Carl C. *Secret History of the American Revolution: An Account of the Conspiracies of Benedict Arnold and Numerous Others* . . . New York: Viking Press, 1941.
Wallace, Willard M. *Traitorous Hero: The Life and Fortunes of Benedict Arnold.* New York: Harper and Brothers, 1954.

JAMES KIRBY MARTIN

ARNOLD, Henry Harley (b. Gladwyne, Pa., June 25, 1886; d. Sonoma, Calif., January 15, 1950), Army Air officer. Arnold is considered the father of the modern U.S. Air Force.

Henry H. ("Hap") Arnold was one of five children born to Dr. Herbert Alonzo Arnold and Adna Louise (Harley) Arnold. Both families traced their roots to pre-Revolutionary America, and Arnold's father served briefly as a medical officer in the Spanish-American War. Henry attended public schools in Lower Merion and entered West Point in 1903 after considering medicine and the clergy as alternatives. Disappointed upon graduation at his assignment to the infantry rather than his choice of the cavalry, he was first assigned to the Philippines where he served with the 29th Infantry until his return to Governor's Island, New York, in 1909. In 1911, motivated primarily by the opportunity for promotion, Arnold took the qualifying examination for the Ordnance Department, but before learning of results, he accepted a War Department invitation to volunteer for flight training with the Wright Brothers in Dayton, Ohio. After having accumulated 3 hours and 48 minutes in the air, Arnold was designated one of the first military aviators in the United States. Assigned to College Park, Maryland, he established a world altitude record of 6,540 feet and as a consequence of this and other feats was awarded the first Mackay Trophy in 1912, presented annually thereafter for the most meritorious accomplishment in military aviation. As a result of crashes in which he was involved or witnessed or in which close friends were killed, Arnold did not fly from 1912 to 1916. His marriage in September 1913 to Eleanor A. Pool, daughter of a Philadelphia banker, was followed by reassignment to the Philippines in 1913–1916, where he served with the 13th Infantry along with fellow Lieutenant George Catlett Marshall.* Arnold volunteered for duty with the Air Service upon his return to the United States in 1916, and after several final months with the infantry at Madison Barracks, New York, he was promoted to captain and designated supply officer of the Aviation School at Rockwell Field, North Island, San Diego, California, where he returned to flying duty. On the eve of America's entrance into World War I, Arnold was posted to Panama where he commanded the 7th Aero Squadron. With the United States' entry into the war, Arnold was recalled to Washington where he headed the information office of the Aviation Section of the Signal Corps. He rose quickly in rank and as a colonel in August 1917 became assistant director of military aeronautics with responsibility for training as well as acquisition of most American flying bases in the United States. His success in

Washington prevented his acquiring the combat assignment he desired, and he did not reach France until the Armistice.

In the postwar years, Arnold, now reduced to his permanent rank (captain, promoted to major in 1921), served in a variety of assignments in California from January 1919 through the summer of 1924 and did not participate directly in the early controversy surrounding William ("Billy") Mitchell.* Arnold attended the Army Industrial College in 1925–1926, served briefly as information officer for the Air Service, and supported Mitchell with testimony at Mitchell's court-martial trial. Beginning that same year, he found time to begin authoring or co-authoring five books he would write on the subject of military aviation.

In his own words, he was "exiled" to Fort Riley, Kansas, in the aftermath of Mitchell's court-martial, but after attendance at the Command and General Staff School at Fort Leavenworth, Kansas, he served briefly at Fairfield Air Depot and Wright Field in the Dayton, Ohio, area, earning promotion to lieutenant colonel in 1931 and reassignment to California. For the next four years, he commanded March Field, Riverside, California, where he experimented with materiel and tactics associated with the transformation of the base from a training to operational one with both pursuit and bombing aircraft assigned. He worked closely with the embryonic motion picture industry, seeking publicity and support for air power. His rapport with members of the scientific community at the California Institute of Technology was to begin an association that stressed scientific assessment of air forces. While at March Field he supervised the Civilian Conservation Corps personnel assigned there and in 1934 became responsible for the western air mail zone in that ill-fated experiment.

Later that same year Arnold was chosen to lead a flight of B-10 bombers from Washington, D.C., to Juneau, Alaska, and return. This feat earned Arnold his second Mackay Trophy, contributing to his promotion to brigadier general and in March 1935, a new assignment as commander of the First Wing, General Headquarters Air Force, located at March Field. Less than a year later he was recalled to Washington as assistant chief of the Air Corps, a position he held until September 1938, when he succeeded Major General Oscar Westover, chief of the Air Corps, who was killed in a plane crash. Arnold was to head the Air Corps from this time until his retirement in March 1946.

At the threat of war, Arnold found sympathy for expansion of the air arm from President Franklin D. Roosevelt, who in the spring of 1940 following the defeat of France issued a presidential call for fifty thousand aircraft for the defense of the Western Hemisphere. Arnold's efforts to strengthen the Army Air Corps (redesignated the Army Air Forces in July 1941) resulted in congressional appropriations of over $2.1 billion for Army aviation in 1941.

De facto recognition of Arnold's role as spokesman for Army aviation was indicated by his presence at the August 1941 Atlantic Charter Conference in Argentia, Newfoundland, with Roosevelt, Churchill, and the combined British and American military staffs. From then through the end of the war, Arnold served as a member of the British-American Combined Chiefs of Staff and its American counterpart, the U.S. Joint Chiefs of Staff. Except for the Yalta Conference when he was absent because of hospitalization following a second heart attack, Arnold was the spokesman for Army aviation at wartime meetings and conferences. He enjoyed the confidence of Roosevelt, Churchill, and Marshall and at the same time earned the suspicion of American naval aviators who were concerned over Arnold's views and powers as the precursors of a separate American air arm. Arnold wisely deferred the struggle for autonomy to the postwar period. He was promoted to lieutenant general in December 1941, general in March 1943, and five star general of the Army in December 1944.

An advocate of strategic bombing, Arnold sent officers to Europe within six weeks of Pearl Harbor to develop and plan the strategy of bombing the European Continent, at the same time realizing that the bombing of Japan would have to be delayed until aircraft were developed and bases were acquired within range of such operations. Traveling extensively during the war, Arnold became familiar with the problems and difficulties of Army Air Forces units throughout the entire world.

Arnold's reputation properly rests on his having built the greatest air force the world has seen. Out of a struggling institution which at the time of the September 1938 Munich Agreement possessed but a handful of B–17s Arnold created an organization which, at its zenith, had approximately 2.5 million personnel, organized into 243 combat groups operating more than sixty-three thousand aircraft from airfields worldwide. Although neither a superb organizer nor a formulator of strategic thought, Arnold was best known as an innovator with a ready smile and a dedication to hard work. Dissatisfied with explanations, he demanded results from his staff. He had vision and an appreciation of the role of technology in air power; he solicited and received the cooperation of Dr. Theodore von Karman and other leaders of the nation's scientific community in air force experimentation and development. Concerned with the future, he rotated his most promising staff officers between staff and combat assignments, thus seeking a cadre of versatile leadership for the postwar force. Impetuous, volatile, dedicated, and outwardly friendly, Arnold was truly the father of the U.S. Air Force.

BIBLIOGRAPHY

Arnold, H. H. *Global Mission.* New York: Harper and Brothers, 1949.
Coffey, Thomas. *Hap: General of the Air Force Henry Arnold.* New York: Viking, 1982.
Copp, DeWitt S. *A Few Great Captains: The Men and Events That Shaped the Development of U.S. Air Power.* Garden City, N.Y.: Doubleday and Company, 1980.

Huston, John W. "The Wartime Leadership of Hap Arnold." In *Air Power and Warfare; Proceedings of the Eighth Military History Symposium*. Washington, D.C.: Office of Air Force History, 1979.

JOHN W. HUSTON

BEAUREGARD, Pierre Gustauve Toutant (b. May 28, 1818, Contreras Plantation, St. Bernard Parish, La.; d. February 18, 1893, New Orleans, La.), Army officer. Beauregard held Confederate commands at Fort Sumter, Manassas, and Shiloh during the Civil War.

The third child of a scion of Louisiana's bayou delta country, P.G.T. Beauregard attained a fame befitting his distinguished Gallic lineage. After three years at a private school in New Orleans and four in the French School in New York City, Beauregard entered West Point in March 1834. A gifted student, already well grounded in mathematics, Beauregard did well at the Military Academy, graduating second in a class of forty-five and receiving his commission as an engineer.

He spent the next eight years at various coastal posts on the Atlantic and the Gulf of Mexico, honing the engineering skills that were to be his hallmark as a soldier. As an engineer on the staff of Winfield Scott* during the Mexican War, Beauregard performed several valuable reconnaissance surveys and was twice wounded. His greatest triumph, however, was in arguing Scott into choosing the Chapultapec route into Mexico City over the objections of the rest of the staff. For this service he was brevetted to major, his second brevet commission of the war.

Until the outbreak of the Civil War, Captain Beauregard (he had been promoted in 1853) spent most of his time in his home state at a variety of activities: superintending construction of forts on the lower Mississippi, as well as that of the New Orleans Customs House; improving navigation at the mouth of the river; and dabbling in New Orleans politics. In 1858 he ran an unsuccessful campaign for mayor of that city on a reform ticket against the local Know-Nothing machine.

Thanks to his powerful Louisiana political connections (U.S. Senator John Slidell was a brother-in-law), Beauregard received the coveted post of superintendant of West Point on January 23, 1861. But because he had made no secret of his pro-Southern sentiments, Beauregard's tenure at the Academy set a record for brevity. It lasted four days.

In early March, after resigning his commission in the U.S. Army, Beauregard was commissioned a brigadier general in the Confederate Army and assigned to the command of the forces in and about Charleston, South Carolina. His command of the attack on Fort Sumter earned him overnight fame, and on June 3, 1861, the "Hero of Sumter" assumed command of the main Confederate Army in Virginia. Together with General Joseph Eggleston Johnston,* who spirited reinforcements to the field, Beauregard directed this army to victory at the First Battle of Manassas in July. His star had reached its apogee; he was promoted to full general.

Beauregard soon fell into disfavor with President Jefferson Davis, however, and in early 1862 he was ordered to the western theater as second-in-command to General Albert Sidney Johnston.* Beauregard planned the Confederate attack on the Union Army under Ulysses Simpson Grant* at Shiloh, Tennessee, in April 1862, and he assumed command of the army after Johnston's death on the battlefield. Beauregard's retreat from the field at Shiloh and his subsequent evacuation of Corinth were skillfully conducted. Nevertheless, Davis relieved Beauregard of his command shortly thereafter for failing to secure permission before leaving the army on sick leave. Placed in command of the Department of South Carolina, Georgia, and Florida, Beauregard returned to Charleston in September. There he successfully managed the defense of the city against several Union assaults until late April 1864, when he took over command of the Department of North Carolina and Southern Virginia.

His new department included all of Virginia south of the James River, and in this command Beauregard performed his greatest service to the Confederacy. He arrived at Petersburg on May 10, brimming with plans to save Richmond and confronted by an immediate threat, the twenty thousand-man Army of the James, under General Benjamin Franklin Butler. Beauregard's overly ambitious plan to destroy Butler's army went awry at the Battle of Drewry's Bluff on May 16, but he did succeed in immobilizing the enemy in his peninsula entrenchments, thus removing a serious threat south of the capital and freeing badly needed reinforcements for the main Confederate Army under Robert Edward Lee.* Beauregard once again rose to the occasion in mid-June. Correctly divining the shift of Grant's army to the south of Richmond, he conducted a brilliant three-day defense of Petersburg with a badly outnumbered force. His quick action held the city just long enough to enable Lee's army to arrive.

After the fall of Atlanta, Beauregard was placed in command of the Military Department of the West, a figurehead post. He spent the waning days of the war attempting to stem the surge of a Union Army under William Tecumseh Sherman,* who led his troops through Georgia and the Carolinas. On February 22, 1865, Beauregard relinquished command to General Johnston.

Following the war, Beauregard returned to New Orleans, where for the remainder of his life he figured prominently in the business and political affairs of the city and state: as president of two railroads, as adjutant general of Louisiana for ten years, as supervisor of drawings for the infamous Louisiana Lottery Company from 1877 to 1893, and, briefly, as New Orleans' commissioner of public works. Beauregard was the author of several books and articles on Civil War military affairs. His chief works include *A Report on the Defense of Charleston* (1874) and *A Commentary on the Campaign and Battle of Manassas* (1891).

As large in ego as he was small in stature, and with a touchy pride to accompany his soldierly appearance, P.G.T. Beauregard never realized his potential as a first echelon military commander. Of excellences he had more than his share: he was a confident and personally courageous leader, respected by his men.

Lacking neither pugnacity nor imagination, he often demonstrated masterly defensive skills. His defense of Petersburg in 1864 with a patchwork force of about ten thousand against the better portion of two Union army corps was classic, as was his use of deception against Henry Wager Halleck* at Corinth. His engineering skills were formidable, as the disposition of his troops and guns during the defense of Charleston during 1863–1864 proved. And on more than one occasion—in Virginia in 1861 and again in northern Mississippi in early 1862—Beauregard evinced noteworthy organizational talents.

Unfortunately, Beauregard's virtues paled in comparison to his weaknesses. A better-than-average field commander, competent enough in handling situations he could see, he could not make war on a map. But how he loved to try! Undeterred by an unbroken record of overly complex battle plans that failed, Beauregard insisted upon seeing himself as a superior strategist, and he frequently pressed his ideas upon the government. What sound strategical sense he had, however, was rendered invisible by his penchant for formulating grand plans wherein fantasy and grandiose promises of victory predominated. Captivated by his study of Napoleon's campaigns and by the textbook principles of French military theorist Antoine Henri Jomini, Beauregard planned in ethereal realms, as unconcerned by the realities of his own situation and the capabilities of Confederate logistics as he was disregardful of the enemy's intentions. Even so, Beauregard had a firm grasp of the importance of the military principle of concentration, and he urged it repeatedly upon his superiors.

He might have gained a more respectful hearing for his ideas but for another, more serious, failing. For a full general, in the public eye from the very outset of the war, Beauregard displayed a shocking lack of political savvy. And like it or not, high-ranking soldiers must number this quality among their virtues to be effective. Beauregard never did. Soon after the Battle of Manassas he began to consort with the Davis administration's enemies in the Confederate Congress and to make public his distrust and disdain for the government. Too proud and vain to accept his limits as a subordinate, Beauregard swiftly earned the enmity of President Davis.

Exalting one's self at the expense of the commander in chief could have only one result: Beauregard spent the rest of the war in a series of second-rate assignments. Like many another in the large cadre of Davis-haters, Beauregard allowed his own pride, sensitivity, and suspicions to blind him to his own shortcomings. Indeed, by 1864 the relationship between the two men had become so corrosive that Beauregard dawdled about sending reinforcements from his department to Lee, a man Davis trusted.

Had he been given the chance Beauregard might have developed into an excellent commander. And perhaps the fault was not his alone. Jefferson Davis, a petulant and petty man himself on occasion, once characterized Beauregard as "forever driving on possibilities." The characterization was unfair. To his credit, Beauregard at least *saw* possibilities. To his detriment, he never saw how to translate vision into reality.

BIBLIOGRAPHY

Basso, Hamilton. *Beauregard: The Great Creole.* New York: Charles Scribner's Sons, 1933.
Davis, William C. *Battle at Bull Run: A History of the First Major Campaign of the Civil War.* Garden City, N.Y.: Doubleday and Company, 1977.
Roman, Alfred. *Military Operations of General Beauregard.* 2 vols. New York: Harper and Brothers, 1884.
Sword, Wiley. *Shiloh: Bloody April.* New York: William Morrow and Company, 1974.
Williams, T. Harry. *P.G.T. Beauregard: Napoleon in Gray.* Baton Rouge: Louisiana State University Press, 1954.

THOMAS E. SCHOTT

BLISS, Tasker Howard (b. Lewisburg, Pa., December 31, 1853; d. Washington, D.C., November 9, 1930), military diplomat, educator, staff officer, chief of staff. Bliss was the founding president of the Army War College and one of the five American commissioners at the Paris Peace Conference of 1919.

Tasker H. Bliss was the son of a Baptist clergyman, a professor at Lewisburg Academy, forerunner of Bucknell University. His father, George Ripley Bliss, was a nationally respected expert in classical languages who trained his son in Greek and Latin. The combination of a large family and a small income led to Bliss's interest in the service academies.

Graduating from the Military Academy eighth in the class of 1875, Bliss joined the 1st Artillery in Savannah, Georgia, but he was destined to spend very little time with his regiment. In 1876 he returned to West Point for four years' service as an instructor of modern languages. While there, his interest in military history brought him to the attention of Major General John McAlister Schofield, the superintendent.

After another three years of regimental duty, Bliss attended the Artillery School at Fortress Monroe, graduating with honors in 1884 and serving the following year on the school's staff. His growing intellectual reputation led to Bliss's appointment to the fledgling Naval War College in 1885, where for three years he lectured on military science. In connection with the duty, he was sent to Europe to study the military education systems of Britain, France, and Germany.

When Schofield became commanding general of the Army in 1888, he chose Bliss as an aide de camp. Appointed inspector of small arms and artillery target practice, Bliss became involved in the Army's cult of target shooting, but more to his taste were the efforts of the coast artillery to adjust to the new technology of rifled weapons and indirect fire. During this period, he also secured a transfer to the Commissary Bureau, which brought with it promotion to captain.

In 1897, Bliss went to Spain as military attaché. When war broke out, Bliss was ordered home to serve on the staff of General James H. Wilson, commanding the 1st Corps at Chickamagua Park, Georgia. A division under Wilson served in the brief Puerto Rican Campaign, where Bliss distinguished himself by attempting to negotiate the surrender of the Spanish troops opposing Wilson's force.

January 1, 1899, found Bliss serving as collector of customs for Cuba and the port of Havana. Over the next three and one-half years, Bliss worked hard to eliminate the atmosphere of casual corruption that had permeated the Customs House under Spain. He trained Cubans to replace the American personnel, while at the same time rebuilding the Customs House to improve its sanitation. His knowledge of tariffs had to be acquired on the job, but the War Department's respect of his newfound knowledge made his opinions important in the revision of American tariffs on Cuban products. After the American withdrawal, Bliss returned to negotiate a treaty of reciprocity with the Cuban government.

His outstanding work in Cuba earned Bliss his first star in 1902. He reported to Washington, D.C., for service on the Army War College Board, which Secretary of War Elihu Root was using as a *de facto* general staff. When the General Staff Corps came into being on August 15, 1903, Bliss became president of the Army War College. For the first year, it was a school without students, while Bliss prepared his faculty for what he considered the proper role of the institution. He sought a college in the Latin sense, a group of men working together on matters of common concern. Thus, Bliss's War College served as the planning arm of the General Staff, with the students forming committees to study the likely campaigns in various geographic areas, under the supervision of General Staff officers. A plan consisted largely of the orders for the first few days of a campaign; when complete, it was filed for possible future use. It was one of these War College plans that was used during the second occupation of Cuba in 1906.

By that time, Bliss was in the Philippines. He left Washington in 1905, as part of Secretary of War William Howard Taft's diplomatic mission to Japan. In late 1905 Bliss arrived in the Moro Province as military governor. He served briefly, in 1909, as commanding general of the Philippine Division.

Bliss returned to Washington in 1909 for another four months' duty as president of the War College, followed by command of the Department of California. The Mexican Revolution made this another assignment with diplomatic overtones. It was followed by two years as the head of the Department of the East, until in 1913 Bliss went back to border duty, commanding the Southern Department.

In 1915 Bliss became assistant chief of staff and a major general, in charge of the Mobile Army Division, where he once again had a hand in war plans. Still in this position when the United States entered World War I, Bliss was not particularly successful in dealing with the problems of mobilization. He did, however, play a large role in shaping American strategy to concentrate the war effort in France. With Chief of Staff Hugh Lenox Scott's departure for Russia in May 1917, Bliss became acting chief of staff, succeeding to the position on September 23, 1917. Bliss remained chief officially until May 18, 1918, though most of that time he was out of the country.

Bliss reached retirement age at the end of 1917, but the Congress continued him on active duty, while also making him a brevet full general. In January 1918 he arrived in Europe to take up new duties as the American military representative on the Supreme War Council, a body recently formed to bring unity to Allied strategy. In this position, Bliss worked to concentrate Allied efforts on the defeat of the German armies in France, opposing tangential efforts for strategic reasons and always worrying that the Allies were fighting an imperialistic war to divide up the world.

President Woodrow Wilson chose Bliss as one of the five American commissioners heading the delegation to the Paris Peace Conference of 1919. Although Bliss was an ardent supporter of Wilson's Fourteen Points, he felt that the president ignored him during the conference. Bliss did influence the technical military portions of the German treaty, and perhaps he modified the conference's policy toward Soviet Russia by strongly and eloquently opposing schemes for large-scale military intervention.

Bliss returned to the United States to face retirement, but he continued to be active in many areas. He served two terms as governor of the Soldiers' Home in Washington, D.C., and he helped to found the Council on Foreign Relations in New York City. In numerous speeches and articles until his death, he continued to advocate American membership in the League of Nations, as well as the cause closest to his heart, international disarmament.

There are many officers whose careers demonstrate the changing nature of the Army between 1877 and 1917: Leonard Wood, Robert Lee Bullard,* and Henry Tureman Allen are three good examples. Bliss's career certainly illustrates the new duties of the Army that came with world power: he served as an educator, colonial administrator, diplomat, and staff officer. Bliss was probably the leading strategic thinker in the Army from 1903 through World War I. But his career is more than just a representation of these changes; Bliss played a major role in the creation of the modern American Army.

As a young lieutenant and captain, he was active in the Army's professional society, the Military Service Institution, and he was one of the organizers of the Army and Navy Club in Washington, D.C. His duties as an aide to the commanding general involved him in the technological modernization of the artillery, as well as the changes in drill techniques necessary to adjust to that modernization.

Of special importance are the three years Bliss spent in Washington as one of the organizers of the General Staff. The Army War College Board began the efforts to create long-range policies in such areas as mobilization planning and education, as well as preparing the way for the General Staff Corps. As president of the Army War College, Bliss chose to make the institution a functioning part of the General Staff, writing the first comprehensive group of contingency plans for the Army. These plans may appear primitive when compared to the products of the European general staffs, but in view of America's political isolation, they were generally appropriate. Another of his duties, as its chief planner, was to represent the army in the sessions of the Joint Army and Navy Board. Bliss reformed the Army's educational system, creating a progressive structure beginning with post schools for junior officers and culminating in the Army War College. Thus, Bliss shaped the Army's organization to deal with its new tasks as the army of a great power, but also, more than any other officer, he prepared the Army intellectually to face this new situation.

During the Great War, Bliss's service on the Supreme War Council was of great importance to the American war effort. Enjoying the respect and trust of his colleagues, Bliss quickly became a reconciler of differences, a task that suited his personality. At the same time, however, he helped to achieve two major American goals, the acceptance of an Allied supreme commander in France and the concentration of Allied effort on the defeat of the German armies in France.

A reflective man greatly influenced by his study of Greek and Roman history, Bliss saw the destructiveness of modern war as a threat to the entire progress of Western civilization. As he wrote in 1921, "a war of the nations in arms is in reality one of life and death. . . . [Thus] for the first time in modern history, we are confronted by a war of a nature which threatens the continuity, if not the existence, of our civilization." Thus, Tasker Bliss, because of his knowledge of warfare and its role in history, became a leading advocate of the League of Nations and of disarmament, two means to limit the need for war.

BIBLIOGRAPHY

Challener, Richard D. *Admirals, Generals and American Foreign Policy, 1898–1914.* Princeton, N.J.: Princeton University Press, 1973.
Coffman, Edward M. *The War to End All Wars: The American Military Experience in World War I.* New York: Oxford University Press, 1968.
Millett, Allan R. *The General: Robert L. Bullard and Officership in the United States Army, 1881–1925.* Westport, Conn.: Greenwood Press, 1975.
Palmer, Frederick. *Bliss, Peacemaker: The Life and Letters of General Tasker Howard Bliss.* Freeport, N.Y.: Books for Libraries Press (reprint edition), 1970.
Trask, David F. *The United States in the Supreme War Council: American War Aims and Inter-Allied Strategy, 1917–1918.* Middletown, Conn.: Wesleyan University Press, 1961.

THOMAS R. ENGLISH

BRADLEY, Omar Nelson (b. Clark, Mo., February 12, 1893; d. New York City, N.Y., April 8, 1981), military commander; the "GI's General" in World War II.

Omar Nelson Bradley was born on February 12, 1893, in Clark, Missouri. Upon the death of his father, John Smith Bradley, a schoolmaster, in 1908, Bradley and his mother, Sarah Elizabeth Bradley, a seamstress, moved to Moberly, Missouri. Bradley won a congressional appointment to the U.S. Military Academy at West Point in 1911. He graduated forty-fourth in the class of 1915, the class upon which general's stars later fell in profusion.

While serving in various posts in the United States and Hawaii, Bradley came under the eye of General George Catlett Marshall when Bradley became chief of the Weapons Section while Marshall was assistant commandant of the Infantry School at Fort Benning, Georgia. As Marshall organized the Army, he made Bradley assistant secretary of the General Staff and, in February 1941, commandant of the Infantry School. The commandant's position brought to Bradley the first general's star of the class of 1915. Marshall then gave Bradley stateside command experience with the 82d Infantry (later Airborne) and then the 28th Infantry Division. Bradley received his second star.

From Marshall, Bradley moved into the orbit of Dwight David Eisenhower,* the man who would lead Marshall's organization in Europe. Marshall suggested that Bradley be Eisenhower's "eyes in North Africa." Eisenhower agreed, and Bradley landed in Algiers on February 24, 1943, to assist his former West Point classmate. Eisenhower shortly ordered General George Smith Patton, Jr.,* to assume command of II Corps in the theater, and Bradley and Patton would be together for most of the war. Patton, not comfortable with Bradley's "looking over his shoulder," had Bradley appointed his assistant corps commander. When Patton left the command to prepare for the invasion of Sicily, Bradley led the II Corps to a successful conclusion of the North African Campaign. Bradley then led II Corps in the invasion on July 10, 1943, of Sicily. After slapping some soldiers during the campaign cost Patton his chance to command the American ground forces for OVERLORD, the invasion of Normandy, France, Bradley in October 1943 got the assignment. The assignment would culminate in a command that comprised 1.3 million troops, the largest American field command in history, and Bradley would have Patton as one of his Army commanders. Bradley's First Army landed in France on June 6, 1944. After failing at one attempt, the First Army broke through at St. Lô on July 26. Bradley then assumed overall command of American ground forces in the Twelfth Army Group. In this capacity, Bradley would confront Britain's Field Marshal Bernard L. Montgomery.

Bradley and Montgomery had disagreements over command and strategy. Montgomery wanted to continue as overall ground commander and to concentrate on a single thrust into Germany instead of a broad advance. Bradley agreed with Eisenhower's decisions of no overall ground commander and of a broad advance. Tactically, he felt that Montgomery's failure to move quickly to affect a linkup between the Canadians and elements of Patton's army had resulted in the escape through Falaise of too many Germans.

Bradley restrained Patton from going beyond Montgomery's orders in closing the gap at Falaise, but he gave Patton permission to prepare an offensive in late December while allowing Courtney Hicks Hodges'* First Army to continue its offensive. Even though the front stalemated, Bradley did not shift forces to build up the Ardennes area which had been depleted for troop building in the other areas. The subsequent German thrust on December 16, 1944, through the Ardennes Forest made a shambles of American optimism as it was initially quite successful. Although this Battle of the Bulge was settled within a short time, the Allied victory was a costly one. One cost was an estrangement between Eisenhower and Bradley, brought about by Eisenhower's giving Montgomery command of part of Bradley's forces.

Although Eisenhower's plans for the drive into Germany assigned the leading role to Montgomery's forces, Bradley exploited his own successes to cross the Rhine before Montgomery. Eisenhower then decided to have Bradley's forces link up with the Russians. During the last week of April, the First and Ninth Armies met the Russians at the Elbe River while Patton moved south and took Czechoslovakia. Eisenhower decided not to mount a drive on Berlin or Prague, and the European war ended in May.

After the war ended, Bradley became Veterans Administrator, where he tried to ease the return for millions of veterans. On February 7, 1948, he became chief of staff. On January 16, 1949, he became the first chairman of the Joint Chiefs of Staff, earning a fifth star in September 1950. Bradley's years on the Joint Chiefs of Staff were hectic ones, as both internal fights and actions by other nations created a constant sense of crisis. From the Berlin Blockade to the formation of the North Atlantic Treaty Organization to the rearmament of Western Europe, from the flush deck carrier to the funding of NSC 68, from reliance on nuclear deterrents to reliance on a deterrent of nuclear and conventional readiness, from agreement to a ground war in Asia to a clarification that the involvement had to be limited, from an unsuccessful attempt to stop a landing at Inchon, to defense of the president's removal of the American commander in Korea—Bradley was at his post.

On August 15, 1953, Bradley left full-time active service, forty-two years after his entry into West Point. After that time, he served in a variety of public and private positions and was frequently called upon for military advice. He died in New York City on April 8, 1981.

Although not nearly as colorful as many of his contemporaries, the general who seemed so democratic, self-effacing, and concerned that he became the "GI's General" was in fact as controversial as his more flamboyant peers. Bradley's professional life involved him directly with Marshall, Eisenhower, Montgomery, Patton, and Douglas MacArthur,* as well as many others. Much of American military history revolves around the decisions of these men and those whom they opposed. The period from the beginning of World War II was a critical turning point for the United States, including the military. During the war Bradley was at the center of decisions that did not lose the war and may indeed have helped to win it. But there remains intense debate both over many of those decisions and over their consequences for the postwar world. After the war, military technology seemed to have robbed the United States of any time to decide whether or not a conflict would involve this nation, and yet, to many the atomic bomb promised security on the cheap. Many felt that communism was a mortal threat, but did not want to pay for defense and thus sacrifice the good life to higher taxes, especially after fifteen years of Depression and then war.

The Army's position was especially precarious, for the Army now seemed obsolete in a world which, if it went to war, would destroy itself in a nuclear holocaust. The Korean War did bring enormously increased defense spending as well as acceptance of the notion of a limited war, but the policy of containment as well as the emphasis on European defense brought new division in the wake of President Harry S. Truman's firing of MacArthur.

Bradley's imprint during all these years was that of a stabilizer. He was not a bloodless patsy above bureaucratic battles. There is no study in depth of Bradley, although Charles Whiting's highly critical *Bradley* is an effective beginning. All the same we do know some things. Bradley used Patton as well as any commander could have; he helped to shape much of the strategy in Europe by personal influence and by allowing his commanders tactical flexibility, often turning a potential liability into an asset; despite differences with Montgomery, he avoided an open break; he commanded at various levels throughout the war and, despite the Ardennes scare, suffered no great defeats and at times capitalized on opportunities for tactical success. After the war, he, like Eisenhower before him, kept some semblance of an army in being during a perilous period in which the Army fought for its existence, discovered limited war, and saw its most famous general fired. Through all of this, Bradley's personal prestige remained high and this in turn helped the Army.

Omar N. Bradley was a lieutenant colonel at the beginning of 1941; four years later he was a five star general. Most of the advancement came for leadership of men in combat. Whatever the mix of motivation or wisdom of various decisions, Bradley did much more than hold his own in the company of giants. If he had done nothing more, this alone would merit his full inclusion in the ranks of those commanders.

BIBLIOGRAPHY

Ambrose, Stephen E. *The Supreme Commander*. Garden City, N.Y.: Doubleday and Company, 1970.
Bradley, Omar N. *A Solider's Story*. New York: Holt, Rinehart and Winston, and London: Eyre and Spottiswoods, 1951.
———, and Blair, Clay, Jr. *A General's Life*. New York: Simon and Schuster, 1983.
Manchester, William. *American Caesar*. Boston, Toronto: Little, Brown and Company, 1978.
Pogue, Forrest C. *The Supreme Command: U.S. Army in World War II*. Edited by Kent Roberts Greenfield. Washington, D.C.: Office of the Chief of Military History, U.S. Department of the Army, 1954.
Whiting, Charles. *Bradley*. New York: Ballantine Books, 1971.

JOSEPH P. HOBBS

BRAGG, Braxton (b. Warren, N.C., March 22, 1817; d. Galveston, Tex., September 26, 1876), Army officer. Bragg commanded the Army of the Tennessee, the principal Confederate field army in the western theater during the Civil War.

Braxton Bragg was born into the family of a moderately successful North Carolina contractor, Thomas Bragg, who had been able to acquire more than twenty slaves. Bragg's father did all in his power to instill ambition into his sons, and young Braxton received his early education at Warrenton Male Academy. Although a fine horseman, Bragg showed little interest in the recreational activities pursued by his peers as they took time away from more serious duties. He entered the U.S. Military Academy at West Point, New York, in 1833 at the age of sixteen. He proved to be an excellent student, graduating number five in a class of fifty.

Commissioned second lieutenant, 3d Artillery, as of July 1, 1837, he served in the frustrating Florida War against the Seminole Indians at various times from 1838 to 1843. Early in his military career, he developed a quarrelsome character, often tangling with his peers, superiors, and even himself, as the following anecdote illustrates. Ulysses Simpson Grant,* in his *Memoirs*, recalled a story about Bragg when he was both company commander and the company quartermaster: "As commander of the company he made a requisition upon the quartermaster—himself—for something he wanted. As quartermaster he declined to fill the requisition, and endorsed on the back his reasons for so doing. As company commander he responded to this, urging that his requisition called for nothing but what he was entitled to, and that it was the duty of the quartermaster to fill it. As quartermaster he still persisted that he was right." He then referred the matter to his commanding officer, who remarked: "My God, Mr. Bragg, you have quarreled with every officer in the army, and now you are quarreling with yourself." During the Mexican War, Bragg fought with distinction during the defense of Fort Brown, Texas (May 3–9, 1846), and the battles of Monterrey, Mexico (September 21–23, 1846), and Buena Vista (February 22–23, 1847). For his battlefield performance, he was brevetted captain, major, and lieutenant colonel. After the war, Bragg served on garrison duty at Jefferson Barracks, Missouri, and on frontier duty before declining promotion to major, 1st Cavalry, as of March 3, 1855, and resigning from the U.S. Army as of January 3, 1856.

Bragg purchased and operated a sugar plantation in Louisiana in 1856, and, on the eve of the Civil War, he owned 109 slaves and had a net profit of $30,000. He was also elected a commissioner of the Board of Public Works in Louisiana, serving in that office from 1859 to 1861.

With the outbreak of the Civil War, Bragg accepted an appointment as brigadier general, Confederate States Army, as of February 23, 1861, and was assigned to the command of coastal defenses between Pensacola and Mobile. Promoted to major general, he commanded a corps in the Army of the Mississippi (later named the Army of the Tennessee). As a subordinate of Albert Sidney Johnston* and Pierre Gustauve Toutant Beauregard* during the Battle of Shiloh (April 6–7, 1862), Bragg conducted an aggressive attack on the first day of the battle that brought initial success to the Confederate forces. After the Confederate retreat from Shiloh, Bragg was promoted to general to rank from April 6 and placed in command of the army on June 27.

In late August, Bragg moved his army into central Kentucky in what began as a brilliant campaign. The purpose of the move was to bring Kentucky into the Confederacy, but Bragg soon became bogged down in politics, allowing the Union forces to escape from a precarious position. After the indecisive Battle of Perryville, Kentucky, on October 8, Bragg withdrew into Tennessee. On December 31, Bragg attacked a Union force led by Major General William Starke Rosecrans* at Murfreesboro, Tennessee, inflicting heavy casualties. Bragg, however, did not exploit his immediate tactical successes, and on January 3, 1863, withdrew his forces from the field. Subject to severe criticism for his withdrawal, Bragg was able to retain his command because of his friendship with Confederate President Jefferson Davis. But during the next six months Bragg became involved in a series of bitter disputes with his subordinates, and his army was curiously inactive. He neither sought out the enemy nor prepared adequate defensive positions. Defensive positions were of particular importance because Bragg's army was growing smaller as it sent reinforcements to Mississippi while the opposing Union force was growing stronger. Consequently, William Rosecrans,* in a brilliant summer campaign, maneuvered Bragg out of Chattanooga on September 9, 1863.

Reinforced by a corps under James B. Longstreet,* Bragg attacked Rosecrans south of Chattanooga in the Battle of Chickamauga, September 19–20. Only the heroic stand of Major General George Henry Thomas* prevented the destruction of the Union forces. Even so, Bragg missed an opportunity by not again attacking the disorganized enemy forces, and, instead, he besieged Chattanooga. Perhaps overconfident because of a seemingly impregnable defensive position, Bragg detached Longstreet for a campaign against Union forces in east Tennessee. As a result, General Grant was able to defeat Bragg decisively in the Battle of Chattanooga, November 23–25, and shortly thereafter, Bragg was relieved of his command.

After his defeat at Chattanooga, Bragg never again held an important field command. He spent most of the remainder of the war as a military advisor to Davis with the impressive, but ineffective, title of general in chief. He was captured by Union forces in Georgia on May 9, 1865, while accompanying Davis in his flight from Richmond. After the war, Bragg served as a commissioner of public works in Alabama, and at the time of his death in Galveston, Texas, he was chief engineer of the Gulf, Colorado, and Sante Fe Railroad.

Bragg is perhaps the most harshly criticized Confederate commander of the Civil War. Yet, at the beginning of the war, few had doubts about his military abilities. A genuine hero of the Mexican War, he appeared to be one of the more distinguished officers to support the Southern cause. And he was without doubt an excellent organizer and disciplinarian. Although his sternness was not always an asset in dealing with volunteer troops, he built the Army of the Tennessee into an efficient and effective fighting force.

At crucial moments, however, Bragg's nerve failed him and he was unable to make decisions, thereby greatly weakening his effectiveness as a commander.

This trait during his campaign in Kentucky during 1862 after an impressive start cost the Confederacy dearly in missed opportunities. After tactical success against Rosecrans at Murfreesboro, Bragg failed to renew the battle even though he was in a favorable situation, and his notable victory over Rosecrans at Chickamauga was canceled by an unwillingness to follow up his success. By settling for a siege of Union forces in Chattanooga, Bragg missed one of the real opportunities that the Confederacy had to strike a severely damaging blow at the Union.

To make matters worse, Bragg had a series of recurring illnesses that were probably psychosomatic. Under intense pressure, he became ill. His rigid thought patterns and inability to make decisions support the contention of mental illness. In modern terms, the evidence suggests that Bragg had a mental and physical breakdown during the summer of 1863. It had a real, if unmeasurable, impact on Bragg's performance and was probably reflected in his relationships with his officers.

Bragg's inability to get along with his subordinates was seriously debilitating. He was constantly involved in prolonged (and often petty) arguments with his officers. These disputes destroyed command unity in the Army of the Tennessee which was so essential for success. While he was a good planner and organizer, he did not work in a vacuum. His indecision on the field coupled with his quarrelsome nature makes credible the harsh criticisms of Bragg by both his contemporaries and later historians.

BIBLIOGRAPHY

Connelly, Thomas L. *Army of the Heartland: The Army of Tennessee. 1861–62*. Baton Rouge: Louisiana State University Press, 1967.

———. *Autumn of Glory: The Army of Tennessee, 1862–65*. Baton Rouge: Louisiana State University Press, 1971.

Horn, Stanley F. *The Army of Tennessee: A History*. New York: Bobbs-Merrill Company, 1941.

McWhiney, Grady. *Braxton Bragg and Confederate Defeat*. Vol. 1. New York: Columbia University Press, 1969.

Tucker, Glenn. *Chickamauga*. Indianapolis, Ind.: Bobbs-Merrill Company, 1961.

DAVID L. WILSON

BULLARD, Robert Lee (b. Yongesborough, Ala., January 15, 1861; d. New York City, N.Y., September 11, 1947), lieutenant general, U.S. Army. Bullard became one of the most successful field commanders of the Army during World War I.

Tall, slender and athletic in appearance, Robert L. Bullard served forty-four years in the U.S. Army, commanded every type of combat unit from platoon to field army, and fought foes from the Apaches in the Southwest to Germans on the Western Front. Once when asked to describe his career, he answered that "my job as an officer was to make my men fight." A fellow officer thought that Bullard's "outstanding characteristic as a soldier was a constant drive to get into the thick of things—always to go to the sound of the guns and get into the fight, no matter where the fight was taking place...and he always got there." Another, however, recalled that Bullard's aggressiveness applied only to military operations: "His common sense and simplicity, the stories he told so well, his keen sense of humor and warmth of friendship endeared him to all who were privileged to know him."

The eleventh of twelve children and second son of Daniel Bullard and Susan Mizell, Bullard was born on his father's farm in Lee County, Alabama. Christened William Robert, he changed his name to Robert Lee after the Civil War. His father, descended from English mariners, came from North Carolina. Bullard's mother was of French Huguenot ancestry. Daniel and Susan Bullard were pioneer settlers in eastern Alabama, where Daniel raised cotton, sold cotton gins, and speculated in land. The family was part of an industrious, ambitious, education-oriented rural elite that supported its own church and school. Bullard showed such academic promise as a boy that he attended the Agricultural and Mechanical College of Alabama (now Auburn University) for one year and then won a competitive appointment to the U.S. Military Academy, which he entered in 1881. His motive for going to West Point was to finish college without going into debt.

Bullard's academic record at West Point was undistinguished, and he finished twenty-seventh of thirty-nine in the class of 1885. Like other graduates of low standing, he was assigned to the infantry. Joining the 10th Infantry in New Mexico, Bullard spent most of the next thirteen years with his regiment. In 1886 he participated in the campaign against Geronimo. In 1888 he married Rose Douglass Brabson, the daughter of a Tennessee congressman and stepdaughter of an Army surgeon. They had four children. Weary of frontier duty and disturbed by his stagnant career, Bullard, still a first lieutenant at thirty-seven, arranged a transfer to the Subsistence Department in 1898.

When the war with Spain began, Bullard accepted command of a black Alabama infantry regiment, an assignment for which he lobbied vigorously. As colonel of the 3d Alabama Volunteers, he earned a deserved reputation as an effective troop trainer and disciplinarian. Bullard was then appointed colonel of the 39th U.S. Volunteer Infantry regiment, a unit raised to fight in the Philippine Insurrection. Bullard commanded this regiment in combat in southern Luzon in 1900 and 1901. The regiment was noted for its aggressiveness and determination—the qualities of its colonel. When his regiment mustered out, Bullard stayed in the Philippines as a commissary but arranged a transfer back to the infantry in 1902 at his regular rank of major, thus "jumping" more than a hundred of his peers in seniority. To answer his critics, he volunteered for more combat service against the Moros on Mindanao, where he served as a battalion commander and district governor until 1904.

Between 1904 and 1917, Bullard enhanced his reputation with varied service. Between 1906 and 1909, he was an official in the Provisional Government of Cuba; in 1910 he went to Mexico to search for Japanese naval bases. He instructed the California and Hawaiian National Guard. Graduating from the Army War

College in 1912 and promoted to colonel, he took command of the 26th Infantry. Bullard turned his unit into a combat-ready part of the 2d Division, a force organized for possible intervention in Mexico. In 1915 Bullard's regiment helped pacify the lower Rio Grande Valley, which was plagued with Anglo-Mexican guerrilla war. In 1916 Bullard commanded a brigade of National Guard regiments from Louisiana, South Dakota, and Oklahoma. The guardsmen found Bullard a demanding but personable officer.

When the United States entered World War I, Bullard first commanded an officer training camp, but he was reassigned in June 1917 to the 2d Brigade of the 1st Division, sent to France to boost French morale. He was finally promoted to brigadier general, a rank for which he had lobbied for fifteen years. In France General John Joseph Pershing* made Bullard commandant of the American Expeditionary Force's (AEF's) infantry officer and specialist schools, a post he held until December 1917. Pershing then returned Bullard to the 1st Division to replace a commander who did not meet Pershing's standards for personal leadership. Under Bullard's command, the 1st Division staged the successful attack on Cantigny (May 28–31, 1918) that demonstrated to the Germans and Allies the AEF's offensive ability. An able division commander, Bullard made many inspection trips to the frontlines and was popular and respected by his men. He also gathered an exceptional group of officers, including three future chiefs of staff and many future generals. Because he spoke French and knew European history, Bullard also got along well with his French superiors.

In July 1918 Bullard assumed command of the III Corps, which took over a sector along the Vesle River during the Aisne-Marne counteroffensive. Until early September 1918, the III Corps attacked the German defenses but advanced only after the Germans retreated to the Aisne. The III Corps then moved to the Meuse-Argonne sector where Pershing's First Army attacked on September 26. The progress of the offensive was disappointing, but the III Corps did well enough to convince Pershing to assign Bullard to command the new Second Army. This force saw serious combat for only two days before the Armistice, but would have mounted an offensive on Metz if the war had continued. Promoted to lieutenant general, Bullard received the Distinguished Service Medal and several foreign decorations for his service in France.

Bullard's last assignment before his compulsory retirement at sixty-four in 1925 was as commanding general of the II Corps Area at Fort Jay, Governors Island, New York. He had no major impact on military policy, but he publicized military affairs by writing articles, making speeches, and stimulating interest in the ROTC, the Reserve, and the National Guard. He continued this work as president of the National Security League and by writing articles on military affairs for the Hearst newspaper chain. His memoir, *Personalities and Reminiscences of the War* (1925), was a candid analysis of the AEF. His other books, *Fighting Generals* (1944) and *American Soldiers Also Fought* (1936), were anecdotal narratives about World War I designed to counter claims that the AEF played no major role in the Allied victory. Bullard was also active in New York society and veterans' organizations during his retirement. The general died of a cerebral hemorrhage in 1947 and is buried at West Point.

Little known outside the Army and the veterans of World War I, Bullard served during the Army's transition from a frontier constabulary to a modern force of citizen-soldiers, commanded by professional officers and designed for war with other industrialized world powers. Like most of his contemporaries in the AEF, Bullard served in relative anonymity, a characteristic of the professionalized Army officer corps of his era. Bullard was an accomplished officer who built his reputation on his ability as a field commander, his loyalty to both superiors and subordinates, and his thorough knowledge of tactics, logistics, administration, communications, and unit organization. He was especially effective in building troop morale. Although he remained skeptical of academic military education and the virtues of centralized management, he supported the wide-ranging military reforms of his era since he appreciated the value of staff planning, merit promotion, and continuing military education.

Throughout his career, Bullard cultivated the image of Alabama "country boy" and "Old Army" Indian-fighter, but he was a sophisticated, cosmopolitan officer who consistently demonstrated his intelligence, adaptability, and industriousness in a variety of challenging assignments. His personal motto was "wherever you are, do as much as you can." In his later years, Bullard became a nativist, isolationist, philosophical conservative, and critic of the New Deal. His post-retirement literary career, however, did not reflect those personal qualities that made him a successful officer. Instead, he successfully responded to a series of demanding changes in the U.S. Army and proved over a period of twenty years (1898–1918) that he could command American field forces of growing size and complexity. Like other officers of his Army, Bullard helped define the role of modern American general.

BIBLIOGRAPHY

Chase, Joseph Cummings. *Soldiers All: Portraits and Sketches of the Men of the A.E.F.* New York: George H. Doran Company, 1920.
Millett, Allan R. *The General: Robert L. Bullard and Officership in the United States Army, 1881–1925.* Westport, Conn.: Greenwood Press, 1975.

ALLAN R. MILLETT

BURKE, Arleigh Albert (b. Boulder, Colo., October 19, 1901), naval officer. Burke served a record three terms as chief of naval operations from 1955 to 1961.

Arleigh Burke, who was of Swedish descent (his grandfather's name was Björkgren), was raised in the hard-working rural environment of post-frontier Colorado. His interest in a military career developed early, and in 1919 he won appointment to the Naval Academy. Industrious and ambitious, he overcame the handicap of a modest education in Boulder and was graduated seventieth in a class of 412 in 1923. His early career was characteristic of that of junior naval officers in the interwar period. After five years at sea in the battleship *Arizona*, Burke chose a career specialty. He studied ordnance explosives at the Navy Postgraduate School in Annapolis and then earned an M.S.E. degree in chemical engineering from the University of Michigan in 1931, thereby joining the prestigious "Gun Club" of the Bureau of Ordnance. Burke's service in destroyers began in 1937, following a series of ordnance-related assignments. In 1939, as a lieutenant commander, he took command of the *Mugford* and led his ship to the coveted Destroyer Gunnery Trophy for that year.

The attack on Pearl Harbor found Burke serving as a gun mount inspector at the Naval Gun Factory in Washington. He immediately applied for sea duty, but his request was not granted until January 1943, when he was sent to command a destroyer division in the Solomon Islands. His innovative concepts for use of destroyers in night actions, as well as his impressive performance as commander of Destroyer Squadron 23 in the battles of Empress Augusta Bay and Cape St. George in November 1943, established Burke as a top tactician and combat commander, and won him the Distinguished Service Medal, the Navy Cross, and the Legion of Merit. In March 1944 Captain Burke became chief of staff to Vice Admiral Marc Andrew Mitscher,* commander, Fast Carrier Task Force 58, and in that post coordinated the operations of the largest naval striking force in history in the battles of the Philippine Sea, Leyte Gulf, and Okinawa.

Burke's subsequent career was closely linked with the Navy's struggle to preserve itself as a modern fighting force in the face of the unification of the armed forces, rapid technological change, and the Cold War between the United States and the Soviet Union. A year-long tour as Mitscher's postwar chief of staff introduced Burke to these problems, as he helped to organize the Navy's first postwar striking fleet. After Mitscher's death in 1947, Burke was appointed to the General Board, the group of officers that advised the secretary of the Navy on high policy questions. In this post he prepared a major report on the Navy's future role in national security, which was the most comprehensive and influential study of its kind produced during this period. In 1949 Burke became head of the Organizational Reseach and Policy Division of the Office of the Chief of Naval Operations, which developed the Navy's position on the National Security Act Amendments of 1949 and then coordinated the Navy's presentations during the controversial B-36 investigation and unification and strategy hearings. Temporarily removed from the flag officer selection list as a result of his role in the so-called Admirals' Revolt, Burke was reinstated by President Harry Truman and became a rear admiral in 1950.

When the Korean War broke out, Burke was immediately dispatched to serve as deputy chief of staff to the commander, U.S. Naval Forces, Far East, and in July 1951 began six months of service on the United Nations Truce Negotiating Team. This experience, which he found intensely frustrating, sharpened his understanding of the Communist threat facing the United States, and helped shape his emerging strategic philosophy. After his return to Washington, Burke served for two years as director of the Navy's Strategic Plans Division, tackling such problems as the Navy's place in the American rearmament program begun in 1950, and the implications of the Eisenhower administration's "New Look" at U.S. defense policy taken in 1953.

In June 1955, while Rear Admiral Burke was serving as commander, Destroyer Force, Atlantic Fleet, President Dwight David Eisenhower* promoted him to chief of naval operations (CNO) over ninety-two more senior admirals. He was reappointed to the Navy's top uniformed post in 1957 and again in 1959. After retiring from the Navy in 1961, Burke served on the board of directors of a number of large corporations and public service organizations, until his second retirement in the early 1970s.

Arleigh Burke is best known for his exploits in destroyers and his service with Admiral Mitscher during World War II, but his greatest historical significance lies in his contributions to postwar naval strategic planning and policymaking. As chief of naval operations, Burke was committed above all to improving the combat capability of the U.S. Navy and applied his technological training, his operational experience, as well as his considerable leadership abilities to this task. President Eisenhower had appointed him as CNO in hopes that he would speed up the Navy's assimilation of new technology, appoint younger, more vigorous officers to positions of responsibility, and provide inspiration to a somewhat demoralized fleet. All three expectations were realized.

Burke was particularly effective in bringing new technology into the navy. He accelerated programs for construction of nuclear-powered submarines and surface ships and, building on the work of preceding CNOs, brought guided missiles into widespread use through the fleet. He also promoted innovations in aircraft design, communications systems, and antisubmarine warfare. His proudest accomplishment as CNO was his sponsorship in 1955 of the fleet ballistic missile development program which produced the Polaris submarine-launched nuclear deterrent system.

Taking office at a time when the Navy's role in national defense was eclipsed by public emphasis on nuclear weapons and massive retaliation, Burke focused attention on the unique characteristics and capabilities of naval forces. He identified limited war as the primary task facing the Navy of the future. Furthermore, Burke prepared the service to confront that challenge, with emphasis on the need for a balanced, versatile fleet.

The value of Burke's efforts to prepare the Navy for limited conflicts was proven during the 1958 crises in Lebanon and the Taiwan Straits and subsequent tensions in Berlin and the Congo. The Navy that undertook the quarantine of Cuba in the 1962 missile crisis owed much of its success to Burke's preparations. Burke was less successful in his opposition to increased centralization of American defense organization. His fight to maintain an independent, modern Navy and introduce greater flexibility into defense planning received a series of setbacks with the 1958 amendments to the National Security Act, the 1960 establishment of a centralized, joint targeting agency for strategic nuclear weapons, and the introduction in 1961 under the Kennedy administration of Robert Strange McNamara's Planning, Programming, and Budgeting System.

Despite such setbacks, Arleigh Burke was an able and even inspiring spokesman for his generation of naval officers. His efforts to maintain the strength of American sea power established a standard for naval leadership in the post-World War II era.

BIBLIOGRAPHY

Davis, Vincent. *The Admirals Lobby*. Chapel Hill: University of North Carolina Press, 1967.
Hewlett, Richard G., and Francis Duncan. *Nuclear Navy, 1946–1962*. Chicago: University of Chicago Press, 1974.
Jones, Ken, and Hubert Kelley, Jr. *Admiral Arleigh (31–Knot) Burke, the Story of a Fighting Sailor*. Philadelphia: Chilton Books, 1962.
Kinnard, Douglas. *President Eisenhower and Strategy Management, A Study in Defense Politics*. Lexington: University of Kentucky Press, 1977.
Rosenberg, David Alan. "Arleigh Albert Burke." In *The Chiefs of U.S. Naval Operations*. Edited by Robert William Love, Jr., Annapolis, Md.: Naval Institute Press, 1980.

DAVID ALAN ROSENBERG

CLARK, Mark Wayne (b. May 1, 1896, Madison Barracks, N.Y.; d. Charleston, S.C., April 17, 1984), soldier, statesman, author, educator.

Mark Wayne Clark, a 1917 graduate of the U.S. Military Academy, was rapidly promoted and sent to France for World War I. In France he commanded a battalion of the 11th Infantry Regiment and served on the staff of the First Army. After the war he served with the Third Army on occupation duty in Belgium and Germany.

Upon his return to the United States, Clark was sent on the Chautauqua circuit as a speaker. He then was assigned to the Office of the Assistant Secretary of War. In 1925 he graduated from the Infantry School, was assigned to the 30th Infantry Regiment, and from 1929 to 1933 was an instructor with the Indiana National Guard. In 1935 Clark, now a major, was assigned to duty with the Civilian Conservation Corps. Upon graduation from the Army War College, he was posted to Fort Lewis, Washington, and in 1940 was appointed an instructor at the Army War College and promoted to lieutenant colonel. Within months he was ordered to the General Headquarters of the Army to serve as assistant chief of staff for operations. In August 1941 he was promoted to the grade of brigadier general. In early 1942 he was assigned to Army Ground Forces, first as deputy chief of staff and then as chief of staff.

In June 1942 Clark went to Great Britain as commander of Army Ground Forces in Europe, and in October, after promotion to major general, he was named deputy commander in chief of Allied Forces in North Africa. In January 1943 Clark, now a lieutenant general, assumed command of the Fifth Army, which in September 1943 landed in Italy to begin its long and bloody approach march towards Rome, which fell to Clark in June 1944. In December Clark assumed command of the 15th Army Group in Italy, a position he occupied until the cessation of hostilities in Europe. In March 1945 Clark received his fourth star, and in June he was appointed U.S. commander in chief of Occupation Forces in Austria and U.S. high commissioner of Austria. In 1947 Clark assumed command of the Sixth Army and in 1949 became chief of Army Field Forces. In May, 1952 General Clark was sent to Korea as commander in chief, United Nations Command, and U.S. commander in chief, Far East Command. In October 1953 General Clark returned from Korea and retired from active duty to become the president of The Citadel in March 1954. He held this position until July 1965 when he became president emeritus.

As a military commander General Clark's reputation of necessity is based upon his role as commander of two of the more controversial operations in American military history: the Italian campaigns of World War II and the final years of the Korean conflict. Clark's selection for both of these commands was obviously the result of the favorable impressions created by years of diligent work in school, command, and staff assignments. He was promoted from lieutenant colonel to brigadier general in thirteen months, bypassing the rank of colonel, before America entered World War II. His close relationship with both Generals George Catlett Marshall and Dwight David Eisenhower,* combined with his diplomatic demeanor, made him the ideal choice to establish the American logistical and training program in the European theater. General Clark managed to escape the coils of staff work prior to the invasion of North Africa by leading a clandestine mission to negotiate with French officers in North Africa.

In 1943 Clark was given command of the Fifth Army for the conquest of Italy, which Winston Churchill described as "the soft underbelly of the Axis." Clark's experiences in Italy proved Mr. Churchill wrong, and Rome fell, for only the second time in history, to Clark's forces two days before the Normandy invasion in June 1944. The long and bloody Italian Campaign from Salerno, by way of Cassino, Anzio, and Rome, to the Alps is still one of the more misunderstood operations of World War II. Clark, in his book *Calculated Risk*, relates that after Normandy, Italy was the "forgotten front." He aptly compares his army's role to that of guards and tackles in football who block and tie up the enemy's line, an unglamorous but vital function. Clark's achievements earned for him command of the 15th Army Group and a fourth star, but he was still in Italy, and the primary focus of the war had long since shifted to the North.

Clark's postwar experiences as high commissioner of Austria enhanced his reputation as a soldier-diplomat, and in 1947 he was named as deputy to the U.S. secretary of state to participate in the London and Moscow conferences of the Council of Foreign Ministers. Here Clark demonstrated his abilities in negotiation with the Communists. This experience would be invaluable to him a few years later in Korea.

In 1952 General Clark, as commander in chief of United Nations Command in Korea, found himself once again fighting a determined enemy on a mountainous peninsula. As had been the case in Italy, he was given limited resources to achieve a limited objective. Clark remained committed to the concept of victory, but again, as in Italy, military considerations were secondary. Denied the means to achieve victory by his government and ordered to negotiate an armistice with the Communists, Clark put aside his own personal feelings and called upon his past experiences to attempt to reach a fair and honorable truce in Korea. In that endeavor Clark was successful, but as he stated, "In carrying out the instructions of my government, I gained the unenviable distinction of being the first United States Army commander in history to sign an armistice without victory."

General Clark requested retirement from active service in October 1953. In 1954 his second book, *From the Danube to the Yalu*, was published. He accepted the position of president of The Citadel, and during a tenure of eleven years he guided the academic and military training of 4,046 graduates of that institution.

General Clark has in his lifetime earned repute as a soldier, diplomat, author, and college president. Few Americans have had the opportunity to make the contributions to this nation that General Clark has had, and fewer still have been as successful.

BIBLIOGRAPHY

Blumenson, Martin. *Salerno to Cassino*. Vol. 3: *Mediterranean Theater of Operations* Subseries; *U.S. Army in World War II*. Washington, D.C.: U.S. Government Printing Office, 1969.
Clark, Mark W. *Calculated Risk*. New York: Harper and Brothers, 1950.
———. *From the Danube to the Yalu*. New York: Harper and Brothers, 1954.
Fisher, Ernest F., Jr. *Cassino to the Alps*. Vol. 4: *Mediterranean Theater of Operations* Subseries; *U.S. Army in World War II*. Washington, D.C.: U.S. Government Printing Office, 1977.
Hermes, Walter G. *Truce Tent and Fighting Front*. Vol. 4: *U.S. Army in the Korean War*. Washington, D.C.: U.S. Government Printing Office, 1966.

DAVID CHILDRESS

CLARK, William (b. Caroline County, Va., August 1, 1770; d. St. Louis, Mo., September 1, 1838), explorer, territorial governor, Indian superintendent. Clark was one of the nation's greatest explorers and Indian superintendents.

Clark belonged to an old Virginia family. His ancestors migrated from Scotland to Jamestown in the late seventeenth century. Although born in Virginia, William moved with his family to a new plantation at the Falls of the Ohio (Louisville) in Kentucky in 1785, when he was only fourteen years old. At that time the Kentuckians were carrying on desultory warfare with the hostile Indians living north of the Ohio, and young Clark participated as a militiaman in a number of filibustering expeditions against these tribes in the 1780s and early 1790s. In 1794 he fought as a second lieutenant in the Regular Army under General Anthony Wayne* in the famous Battle of Fallen Timbers. Clark remained in the

Army until July 1, 1796, when he resigned his commission as a first lieutenant in order to return home and manage the family plantation in Kentucky.

It was while in Kentucky managing the family plantation that Clark received and quickly accepted the invitation of Meriwether Lewis, then a captain in the 1st U.S. Infantry Regiment, to join him in leading a military expedition to explore a commercially feasible route from the mouth of the Missouri River across the continent to the Pacific Ocean. Clark had become acquainted with Meriwether Lewis a few months before his resignation from the Army, and perhaps earlier. In late 1795 or early 1796 Ensign Lewis was assigned to the "Chosen Rifle Company" which Clark commanded. The two men maintained at least occasional contact in the ensuing years.

Clark joined Lewis in October 1803 with several young recruits for the expedition as Lewis descended the Ohio River from Pittsburgh in a keelboat. The expedition spent the winter of 1803–1804 at Camp Wood River, Illinois, opposite the mouth of the Missouri, preparing for the journey. While there, Clark was primarily in charge of the camp and the training of the men. Although promised a captaincy in the Corps of Engineers, when it arrived just before the expedition's departure up the Missouri, Clark's commission was as a second lieutenant in the Corps of Artillerists. Nevertheless, on the expedition Clark was treated as a captain—equal in every respect to Lewis. Of the two officers Clark was the more expert waterman, and whenever the Corps of Discovery was traveling by water, he usually stayed with the boats while Lewis walked on shore. He was also the expedition's cartographer and made nearly all of the expedition's maps. A big, bluff, warm-hearted redhead, Clark was the more skilled of the two officers in dealing with the Indians, and he enjoyed a closer relationship with the enlisted members of the party than Lewis.

Following the return of the expedition, as part of the reward for his services, in 1807 Clark became principal Indian agent for Louisiana Territory and brigadier general of its militia. His main duties were to keep the Indians of the Missouri and upper Mississippi at peace and to protect the frontiers of Louisiana in case of Indian attack. To strengthen the defenses of the territory, Clark helped Acting Governor Frederick Bates reorganize its militia, and in 1808 he and Governor Lewis arranged for the establishment of two new frontier military posts—one on the Lower Missouri and one on the upper Mississippi. Through his agents and spies, Clark gathered and relayed to the governors of Louisiana and Illinois, as well as the secretary of war, information on the intentions and activities of the tribes in and near those territories.

As Louisiana's principal Indian agent, Clark received, counseled, and sometimes made agreements with many different delegations of Indians that visited St. Louis. He also escorted a number of delegations of chiefs and principal men to Washington so that they might see the evidence of the great wealth and power of the United States and confer with important federal officials.

In June 1813 Clark became governor of Missouri Territory (as Louisiana was renamed the year before), in which capacity he also served as *ex-officio* superintendent of Indian affairs and commander in chief of the territorial militia. Clark estimated the Indian population under his authority at that time at about sixty-four thousand. There were an additional one hundred thousand or more Indians living farther to the west and north over whom he had only nominal control. Clark became governor of Missouri when the United States was in the middle of the War in 1812, and one of his principal responsibilities was to protect the territory from attack by the hostile tribes of the upper Mississippi. To this end, he had gunboats constructed to patrol the Mississippi above St. Louis, he relocated several hundred friendly Sauk and Fox Indians away from the war zone, and he ordered the erection of a chain of blockhouses along the north side of the Missouri River. In the spring of 1814, then, he led a force of regulars and volunteers up the Mississippi and seized Prairie du Chien, Wisconsin, from the British and their Indian allies, but the Americans were able to hold it for only a short time. He also sent agents to the tribes of the upper Missouri to try to induce those Indians to send war parties out against the pro-British tribes on the upper Mississippi.

After the war, Clark was one of the three commissioners appointed by President James Madison to conclude peace treaties with those hostile tribes. That accomplished, his chief concern was to keep all the tribes friendly and promote trade with them both for the economic benefits to be enjoyed by the American traders and as a means of controlling the Indians.

Soon after the admission of Missouri to the Union as a state, in May 1822 Clark became superintendent of Indian affairs at St. Louis, a post newly created by Congress. In this position he continued to have responsibility for the tribes of the Missouri and upper Mississippi. While trying to keep the Western tribes at peace, during the ensuing decade and a half Clark was mainly concerned with the removal of Indians living east of the Mississippi River and in Missouri to reservations in present eastern Kansas. As the Indians moved westward, the importance of Clark's post gradually declined. His administrative powers were somewhat reduced by the terms of the Indian Administration Act of 1834, and the area of his jurisdiction was made smaller by the creation of Wisconsin Territory in 1836. By this time Clark was in failing health. On August 1, 1838, he celebrated his sixty-eighth birthday, and one month later he died.

Clark's fame depends first and foremost on his achievements as co-leader of the Lewis and Clark Expedition. His early experience growing up on the Virginia and Kentucky frontiers and participating as a junior officer in campaigns against the Indians of the Old Northwest equipped him superbly for joint command of the Corps of Discovery. His steadfastness of character, calm determination, unusual understanding of the Indians, and concern for the welfare of his men, together with his frontier experience, all contributed significantly to the success of that historic enterprise. His genial, extroverted, and humane qualities complemented ideally Lewis's intense, introspective nature.

Besides being a great explorer, Clark was one of the United States' most able and successful Indian agents and superintendents. He enjoyed to a remarkable degree the trust and confidence of thousands of Indians living on the upper Mississippi and on the Missouri and its tributaries. By his advice and wise counsel he contributed greatly to reducing the violent resistance of the Indians living in those vast areas to the inexorable push of the whites into their country. Although not a policymaking official, because of his vast experience and great integrity his superiors frequently asked Clark for advice and help in formulating measures for the management of Indian affairs. The recommendations which he and Governor Lewis Cass of Michigan Territory made in 1828, for example, significantly influenced the framing of the sweeping Indian reorganization and intercourse acts which Congress passed in 1834.

While serving his government ably and conscientiously, Clark sought also to promote the best interests of the Indians as he understood them. In the judgment of his contemporaries, he succeeded exceptionally well in doing so. In 1833, Pierre Menard, the Kaskaskia merchant-trader and Indian subagent, wrote Clark upon resigning his commission in the Indian Department: "The poor remnant (in this region at least) of those who once covered the greatest portion of our quarter of the Globe, are more indebted to your active and humane exertions, for the comparative happiness which they have in prospect, than to any other individual within my knowledge." Although Clark's attitude toward and treatment of the Indians may be considered by modern standards to have been paternalistic and patronizing, by the standards of his own time and place they were enlightened, fair, and often humane.

BIBLIOGRAPHY

Bakeless, John. *Lewis and Clark: Partners in Discovery.* New York: William Morrow and Company, 1947.
Jackson, Donald, ed. *The Letters of the Lewis and Clark Expedition.* Urbana: University of Illinois Press, 1962.
Osgood, Ernest S., ed. *The Field Notes of Captain William Clark, 1803–1805.* New Haven, Conn.: Yale University Press, 1964.
Steffen, Jerome O. *William Clark: Jeffersonian Man on the Frontier.* Norman: University of Oklahoma Press, 1977.
Thwaites, Reuben G., ed. *The Original Journals of the Lewis and Clark Expedition, 1804–1806.* 7 vols. and atlas. New York: Dodd, Mead, 1904–1905.

JOHN L. LOOS

COLLINS, Joseph Lawton (b. New Orleans, La., May 1, 1896; d. Washington, D.C., September 12, 1987), World War II division and corps commander; chief of staff, U.S. Army.

Joseph Lawton Collins, son of an Irish-born father, entered the U.S. Military Academy in June 1913 at the age of seventeen. He graduated in April 1917, ranked thirty-fifth in a class of 139. He was commissioned a second lieutenant of artillery, and his first assignment was with the 22d Infantry at Fort Hamilton, New York. Despite stateside assignments in a time of war, Collins won rapid promotions. In less than four months he was a temporary captain; he won his major's leaves in September 1918 when he returned to the 22d Infantry as supply officer.

Collins then spent twenty-six months in Germany, initially commanding a battalion of the 18th Infantry at Coblenz and then serving as assistant chief of staff, G–3, American Forces in Germany. He was promoted to permanent captain in June 1919, a rank he reverted to from temporary major in the following March. He returned to the United States in the summer of 1921 for a four-year assignment as instructor in the Chemistry Department of the U.S. Military Academy. In fact, Collins' career from 1921 to 1933 was entirely devoted to education—student in the Company Officers Course at the Infantry School and in the Field Artillery School's Officers Advanced Course; Infantry School instructor; and student at the two-year Command and General Staff School, Fort Leavenworth. This twelve-year academic stint ended in 1933 with assignment to the 23d Brigade (Philippine Scouts), followed by duty as assistant chief of staff, Intelligence, in the Philippine Division. He was promoted to major in 1932.

Collins returned to the United States in June 1936. He graduated from the Army Industrial College in 1937 and from the Army War College in 1938. From July 1938 until the approaching war forced the institution to close in June 1940, Collins taught at the Army War College. He then served as assistant secretary of the War Department General Staff, with promotion to lieutenant colonel coming in June 1940. The following January found Collins in Alabama as chief of staff of the VII Corps.

Five days after Pearl Harbor, the VII Corps received orders to move to California. Collins soon learned that he was to be chief of staff of the Hawaiian Department, a position which he held from December 1941 until May 1942 and which earned him temporary promotion to brigadier general and a Distinguished Service Medal.

On May 6, 1942, Collins assumed command of the 25th Infantry Division. He took his unit to Guadalcanal the following December where it relieved the 1st Marine Division. Major General Collins also commanded the 25th in the New Georgia Campaign. While in the Pacific, he earned a second Distinguished Service Medal, the Silver Star, and the Legion of Merit. He also picked up the nickname "Lightning Joe," a reference to the lightning bolt depicted on the shoulder patch of the 25th Infantry Division. December 1943 saw his transfer to the European Theater of Operations where, in the following February, Collins assumed command of the VII Corps in England preparing for the invasion of Normandy.

The VII Corps landed on Utah Beach on D-Day, June 6, 1944. Collins came ashore on D plus 1 and led his corps in the capture of the port of Cherbourg. He continued to lead the VII Corps throughout the European fighting until the April 1945 linkup with the Russians on the Elbe River. In the course of the European Campaign, Collins won his third Distinguished Service Medal, his second Silver Star and Legion of Merit, and a Bronze Star Medal. His foreign decorations included the Legion of Honor and Croix de Guerre with Palm (France); Companion Order of Battle (Great Britain); two presentations of the Order of Suvarov (USSR); and the Grand Officer Order of Leopold II and the Croix de Guerre with Palm (Belgium). By April 1945 he had received the three stars of a lieutenant general.

Collins became deputy commanding general and chief of staff, Headquarters, Army Ground Forces, Washington, D.C., in August 1945. Three and one-half months later he became director of information, U.S. Army, followed in June 1946 by assignment as chief of public information. His appointment as deputy chief of staff, U.S. Army, in September 1947 was followed by service as vice chief of staff in November 1948. On August 16, 1949, Joseph Lawton Collins became the eighteenth chief of staff of the U.S. Army. He had been promoted to general in January 1948.

Collins served as chief of staff until August 14, 1953. These four years encompassed the Korean War, a period made more difficult by the disconcerting disagreement between President Harry S. Truman and General Douglas MacArthur.* Service as chief of staff won for Collins his fourth Distinguished Service Medal.

President Dwight David Eisenhower* requested Collins, upon termination of his four-year term as Army chief of staff, to remain on active duty as the U.S. Representative on the Military Committee and Standing Group of NATO. Then in October 1954, Eisenhower asked Collins to interrupt this duty in order to serve as special representative of the United States in Vietnam with personal rank of ambassador. Collins was to recommend a program of assistance aimed at reinforcing the political and economic stability of President Diem's government, as well as improving the internal security of the country. This thankless assignment was beset by endless difficulties. At its termination a year and a half later, Collins remarked to President Eisenhower and Secretary of State John Foster Dulles that he hoped he had not let them down. Dulles replied that when Collins went to Vietnam there was a 10-percent chance of saving that country from communism. "You have raised that figure to at least 50 percent." Collins returned to his NATO assignment until March 31, 1956, when he retired from military service.

In April 1957 General J. Lawton Collins joined Charles Pfizer and Company as vice-chairman of its international division. He held that position until retirement in April 1969. Meanwhile, he had served as vice-chairman and director of the President's Committee for Hungarian Refugee Relief, chairman of the Foreign Student Service Council of Greater Washington, and member of the Board of Trustees of the Institute for International Educators.

The 1917 and 1918 edition of the *Howitzer*, the yearbook of the U.S. Military Academy, said this about the attitude and characteristics of Cadet Lieutenant Joe Collins: "first, concentration and decision, second, rapid and hearty action." The writers of yearbook blurbs seldom are so prescient. This description aptly

describes Collins' entire military career. He was short, feisty, and ruggedly handsome. His confidence and enthusiasm were unbounded; he seldom seemed discouraged. General Omar Nelson Bradley* called Collins one of the most outstanding field commanders in Europe and certainly the most aggressive. Having picked the "nervy and ambitious" Collins as corps commander for Operation COBRA in France, Bradley told Collins that he had given him all possible support, except his pistol. Collins held out his hand for the pistol.

Bradley also wrote of Collins' "unerring tactical judgment with just enough bravado to make every advance a triumph." To his energy, Bradley continued, "he added boundless self-confidence. Such self-confidence is tolerable only when right, and Collins, happily, almost always was."

This was the man who led the U.S. Army VII Corps from Normandy to the Elbe, the corps that spearheaded the First Army's breakthrough at St. Lô, blocked the German counterattack at Mortain, and broke through the Siegfried Line and captured Aachen. Later, the VII Corps drove to the Rhine, captured Cologne, and led the First Army attack that enveloped the Ruhr. Collins' admirers were not restricted to fellow Americans; Bernard L. Montgomery said that he was the First Army's most aggressive corps commander.

Collins' postwar positions as deputy chief of staff and vice chief of staff essentially were the same—principal assistant to the chief of staff, U.S. Army. He was, in fact, the author of the headquarters reorganization plan that prompted this change. Combining these jobs with his tour as chief of staff meant that J. Lawton Collins served almost six years in the two top positions of Army leadership.

In addition to his prowess as a combat commander, Collins was an educator, a superb administrator, a diplomat, and a humanitarian. His literary bent resulted in two fine books—*War in Peacetime* and *Lightning Joe, An Autobiography*.

J. Lawton Collins—Lightning Joe—has been called a soldier's general. He was also a general's general which, parodoxically, might be an even greater accolade.

BIBLIOGRAPHY

Blumenson, Martin. *Breakout and Pursuit: U.S. Army in World War II*. Washington, D.C.: U.S. Government Printing Office, 1961.
Collins, J. Lawton. *Lightning Joe, An Autobiography*. Baton Rouge: Louisiana State University Press, 1979.
———. *War in Peacetime, The History and Lessons of Korea*. Boston: Houghton Mifflin Company, 1969.
Harrison, Gordon A. *Cross Channel Attack: U.S. Army in World War II*. Washington, D.C.: U.S. Government Printing Office, 1951.
MacDonald, Charles B. *The Last Offensive: U.S. Army in World War II*. Washington, D.C.: U.S. Government Printing Office, 1973.
———. *The Siegfried Line Campaign: U.S. Army in World War II*. Washington, D.C.: U.S. Government Printing Office, 1963.

BROOKS E. KLEBER

CROOK, George (b. Taylorsville, Ohio, September 8, 1828; d. Chicago, Ill., March 21, 1890), Army officer. Crook was a noted Union general in the Civil War and very prominent in the Indian Wars after 1865.

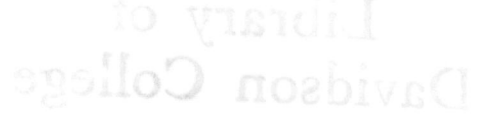

George Crook was the son of a prosperous farming family that had originally emigrated to the American colonies from Scotland in the late seventeenth century. During the War of 1812, Crook's father had fought in defense of Fort McHenry. Crook attended school in Dayton, Ohio, and entered West Point on July 1, 1848. He compiled an unenviable academic record at the Military Academy, and in July 1852 he was graduated thirty-eighth in a class of forty-three. Crook was the lowest ranking cadet ever to achieve the rank of major general, U.S. Army. Even as a cadet Crook reflected the laconic, taciturn, and stoical personality that became so well known to his staff and the press in later years.

Crook spent most of the pre-Civil War years of his career fighting hostile Indians in California and Oregon. The rapid settlement of California brought about by gold strikes and a booming economy created conflict between the gold seekers and the Indians. Crook began his life-long study of Indians, their environment, cultures, languages, and ways of warfare. Crook, the cadet who had been at the bottom of his French class at West Point, learned some of the West Coast Indian languages. He preferred field duty to garrison life and was appalled at the drunkenness and dullness of many of his fellow officers. While fighting the Pit River Indians in 1857, Crook was wounded and carried the arrowhead to his grave.

Crook saw extensive action during the Civil War. In September 1862 he was promoted to brigadier general of volunteers and after commanding a division at Antietam (September 1862), he served in West Virginia for several months. In 1863 he took part in the Tullahoma Campaign (June 1863) and fought at Chickamauga (September 1863). Subsequently, he engaged in a brisk chase of Confederate cavalry under General Joseph Wheeler.* In 1864 Crook was assigned to command first the Department of West Virginia and later the VIII Corps in the Army of the Shenandoah under General Philip Henry Sheridan.* Crook and his corps performed in exemplary fashion in the important battles of Winchester and Fisher's Hill (September 1864), but in October they were routed out of their positions at Cedar Creek by a Confederate attack planned by General Jubal Anderson Early.* In February 1865 Crook was captured by Confederate raiders and spent some time in Richmond's Libby Prison. After being exchanged, he assumed command of the Cavalry Corps of the Army of the Potomac. By the end of the war, he had been cited for gallant and meritorious service on several occasions and had been promoted to major general of volunteers and brevet major general in the Regular Army.

As a lieutenant colonel in the regulars, Crook returned west in 1866. He continued to build his reputation as an innovative Indian campaigner in Idaho, Oregon, and California, but he earned his greatest laurels when pitted against the Apaches of the Southwest. As commanding general of the Department of Arizona from 1871 to 1875, Crook utilized Apache auxiliaries, established a famous logistics service using mule pack trains, and brought peace to that troubled territory. For his brilliant work he was promoted to the rank of brigadier general in 1873. In addition to his organized innovations, a great part of Crook's success with the Apaches lay in his attempt to deal openly and honestly with them.

In 1875 Crook became commanding general of the Department of the Platte and was a principal architect of the vigorous and unrelenting campaign that finally broke the back of Sioux and Northern Cheyenne military resistance. He personally commanded his force of thirteen hundred soldiers and Indian allies against a slightly larger force of hostiles led by Crazy Horse, the astute warchief of the Oglala Sioux. In a controversial battle at the Rosebud River in Montana on June 17, 1876, Crook and his troops were handled roughly by Crazy Horse and the Sioux, but held the battlefield at the end of the fight. Eight days later at the Little Big Horn, the same warriors destroyed a large portion of the 7th Cavalry under Lieutenant Colonel George Armstrong Custer.* After the 1876 campaign, Crook made it a central part of his policy to protect the Indians from corrupt Indian agents and hostile frontiersmen, and to deal equitably with the various tribes.

Corrupt government agents, a corrosive factional strife between the Indian Bureau and the Army, and white encroachment on Indian lands had undone much of Crook's earlier work in the Southwest. In 1882 Crook was reassigned to the Department of Arizona. The hostile Chiricahua, led by the chiefs Geronimo, Chato, and Nana, presented the Army with a serious problem. Enlisting Western Apache auxiliaries and taking a few soldiers, Crook plunged into the Sierra Madre of Mexico and successfully apprehended the hostiles in 1883. For two years Indian affairs in the Southwest were peaceful under Crook's stern and watchful eyes. Disgruntled with reservation life, Geronimo and some Chiricahuas left the reservation in 1885. In the spring of 1886 Crook and a handful of men again crossed into Mexico and convinced the hostiles to surrender, but the chary Geronimo again fled. Because of his evenhanded treatment of the Chiricahua and the Western Apaches, Crook was the target of vilification in the frontier press. Furthermore, General Sheridan doubted the wisdom of Crook's using Apaches to fight other Apaches. Other generals, especially Nelson Appleton Miles,* were critical of Crook's tactics. Relations between Crook and Sheridan reached the breaking point, and Crook asked to be relieved of command in Arizona. Crook was reassigned to the Department of the Platte until May 1888. Promoted to major general, Crook moved to Chicago and assumed command of the Division of the Missouri in 1888. Although he was far removed from the frontier, Crook continued to work for Indian rights. Crook never retired, and nearing his thirty-eighth year of active duty, he died in Chicago.

Following important service in the Civil War, General Crook became a central figure in the military history of the American West. He and other soldiers faced the turmoil caused by thousands of settlers spilling into the Indian lands of the Trans-Mississippi. Crook believed that pacification of the West depended upon two factors, military success and equitable treatment of the Indians, whom he believed were often unjustly treated. Crook concluded that white injustice to the Indians lay at the bottom of most of the Indian wars.

To ensure military success against the Indians, Crook stressed innovation and mobility. He scrapped the cumbersome supply wagon trains and developed the mule pack train to such a degree of proficiency that his methods were still utilized in World War II. The soldiers of the Regular Army were seldom able to meet the unique and rigorous demands of fighting the Indians, and, whenever possible, Crook enlisted Indian auxiliaries and scouts. Crook knew that using Indian auxiliaries often demoralized the hostiles, hastened surrender, and saved countless lives. Using mule pack trains and Indian allies, Crook's forces achieved a mobile striking ability denied to traditional army units. His most phenomenal success with his methods came against the Apaches of the Southwest who had defied and defeated the Europeans since the sixteenth century.

Crook realized that winning battles was only a part of maintaining peace between the Indians and settlers. He believed that the only guarantee for any peace was an honest, humane, and consistent Indian policy. Through his long association with the Indians in many parts of the West, he learned that deceitful and corrupt government officials, both civilian and military, caused the terrible wars that resulted in so many deaths. Crook's views on Indian management rankled the Indian Bureau and many residents of the Western states. The use of Indian auxiliaries earned him the animosity of many fellow officers, including General Philip Sheridan (once Crook's friend) and General Nelson Miles, who subsequently found himself forced to use Crook's methods when all else had failed.

The Indians perhaps gave the greatest testimony to the validity of the work of General Crook. He won the friendship and respect of many Indians and their chiefs at the same time he was being abused in the frontier press. Towards the end of his life, Crook became a severe critic of government Indian policy and took his crusade for Indian rights to the public; the shy, quiet general addressed audiences on behalf of the Indians. By the time of his death, the sixty-one-year-old Crook could look back on a career that embraced the settlement of the last American frontier.

BIBLIOGRAPHY

Bourke, John G. *On the Border with Crook*. New York: Charles Scribner's Sons, 1891.
King, Charles. *Campaigning with Crook*. New York: Harper and Brothers, 1890.
Schmitt, Martin, ed. *General George Crook: His Autobiography*. Norman: University of Oklahoma Press, 1960.
Thrapp, Dan L. *The Conquest of Apacheria*. Norman: University of Oklahoma Press, 1967.
Utley, Robert M. *Frontier Regulars: The United States Army and the Indian, 1866–1891*. New York: Macmillan Company, 1973.

JOSEPH C. PORTER

CUSTER, George Armstrong (b. New Rumley, Ohio, Dec. 5, 1839; d. Little Big Horn River, Montana, June 25, 1876), Army officer.

Although the son of an Ohio blacksmith, Custer spent much of his childhood in the home of a half-sister in Monroe, Michigan. He received an appointment to West Point in 1857 and graduated four years later as the goat of his thirty-four member class. In his last year at the academy he displayed the inclination to disregard military rules that later would win him both fame and death when, as officer of the guard, he failed to stop a fight between cadets. Courtmartialed and found guilty, he was saved from punishment by the urgent need for officers to command the rapidly expanding army.

Appointed a second lieutenant in the 2d Cavalry, Custer participated in the campaigning around Washington and came to the attention of General George B. McClellan,* who appointed him as an aide on his staff in June 1862. After McClellan's replacement Custer moved onto the staff of General Alfred Pleasonton, who assumed command of the Army of the Potomac's cavalry corps in June 1863. In an effort to bring more aggressive leadership to the moribund Union cavalry, Pleasonton secured brigadier's stars in the volunteers for three of his young aides; Wesley Merritt, Elon Farnsworth, and Custer. The latter was but twenty-three at the time of his promotion.

At Gettysburg, in his first test as a brigade commander, Custer proved the soundness of his promotion by distinguishing himself in the great cavalry battle on July 3. A tenacious, fierce fighter, Custer was utterly fearless but was as careless with the lives of other men as he was with his own. But as the Union army leaders grew more concerned with results than casualties Custer's reputation would continue to rise. When Philip Sheridan* took command of the Army of the Potomac's cavalry in the spring of 1864 he recognized in Custer a kindred spirit and soon came to regard him as one of his most trusted officers. Custer impressed Sheridan with aggressive performances at Yellow Tavern in May, where one of his men killed Jeb Stuart,* and at Trevillian Station in June, where he extricated his men from a Confederate trap.

In the Shenandoah campaign Custer was given command of the 3d Cavalry Division and promoted to brevet major general of volunteers. Sheridan often gave Custer's division the advance and the "Boy General" repeatedly won distinction as Jubal Early's* Confederates were swept from the valley. Even the glory of the Shenandoah was soon overshadowed as Custer's division took a prominent part in cutting off Lee's army in the Appomattox campaign. Custer, always in the front, received the Confederate flag of truce. During the last six months of the war, Custer's division had captured 111 pieces of artillery, 65 battle flags, and nearly 10,000 Confederate soldiers. An appreciative Sheridan purchased the table on which the surrender terms were written and presented them to Custer's wife, declaring that "there is scarcely an individual in our service who has contributed more to bring this about than your very gallant husband." Along with the praise came promotions to brevet brigadier and brevet major general in the regulars and major general of volunteers.

With the disbandment of the volunteer army Custer returned to his regular rank of captain in the 5th Cavalry, but in the army reorganization of 1866 he was commissioned lieutenant colonel of the new 7th Cavalry. Custer held that rank until his death, but since the regiment's colonel remained on detached duty Custer actually commanded the 7th.

Custer saw his first Indian fighting in the unsuccessful 1867 campaign against the southern Cheyennes and their allies led by General W. S. Hancock. The dismal campaign ended with Custer found guilty by court-martial for being absent from duty to visit his wife. Custer, who felt he was being made a scapegoat for the failure of the ill-planned campaign, was suspended from the army for a year. Sheridan, who replaced Hancock as commander of the Department of the Missouri soon after the court martial, was in complete agreement with Custer on the trial and soon recalled Custer to duty against the Cheyennes. Custer's regiment formed the major strike force of Sheridan's winter campaign of 1868–1869, and on November 27 the Seventh destroyed the village of Black Kettle on the Washita River in Indian Territory. It was an important victory over a band of Indians that the government had clearly branded as hostiles, but the deaths of numerous Indian women and children and the abandonment of a seventeen-man detachment of the 7th on the field clouded the battle in controversy.

Custer served in Kansas and then on Reconstruction duty in Kentucky before being ordered to the northern plains in 1873. He participated in the 1873 Yellowstone expedition, where he got his first taste of battling the Sioux, and the following year led a 1,200 man expedition to explore the Black Hills of South Dakota. Custer's expedition discovered gold in the Black Hills and the ensuing influx of prospectors helped bring on war with the non-reservation Sioux.

Custer was to have commanded the expedition ordered out in 1876 to force the hostiles onto their reservations, but his testimony before Congress concerning fraud in the management of post sutlerships and Indian traderships won him President Grant's enmity. He was stripped of his command and only the intercession of Generals Alfred Terry and Sheridan permitted him to accompany the expedition in command of his regiment. The campaign's plan called for three columns to move into the hostile country from different directions: General George Crook* to move north from Fort Fetterman in central Wyoming; Colonel John Gibbon to move east down the Yellowstone River from Forts Ellis and Shaw in Montana; and General Terry to move west from Fort Abraham Lincoln on the Missouri River. It was hoped that these movements would disconcert the hostiles and drive them into one of the columns.

Unknown to the others, Crook was defeated by Crazy Horse at the Rosebud on June 17 and forced to retire to his supply base. Meanwhile, Terry's column joined Gibbon on June 21, and a plan was devised whereby Custer would follow an Indian trail up Rosebud Creek while Gibbon moved up the Big Horn and Little Big Horn rivers. Terry would go with Gibbon and the two columns would meet on the Little Big Horn.

Custer, with 655 men, marched rapidly up Rosebud Creek and then crossed to the Little Big Horn where he discovered a large hostile encampment on the morning of June 25. Custer planned to wait another day to give Gibbon's column time to close in, but, discovered by Indian scouts, he decided to attack immediately before the hostiles could escape. Without knowing the size of the enemy force he unwisely divided his command into four parts: Captain Frederick Benteen with three companies was sent off to the left to block the Indians' escape; Major Marcus Reno with three companies was sent up the center to attack the Indian village; Captain Thomas McDougall was detailed with a company to guard the pack train; and Custer with five companies was to support Reno's attack by striking the village from the right. The Indian fighting force, variously estimated at from 1,500 to 5,000, proved larger than anyone had dreamed possible. Reno's attack was repulsed with heavy losses, and he sought safety on some bluffs above the Little Big Horn where he was soon reinforced by Benteen and McDougall. Custer and his five companies, some 212 men, were surrounded and killed. Terry and Gibbon arrived on June 27 and rescued Reno's men. Much of the blame for the disaster must be placed on Custer, whose rashness and overconfidence led him to split his command in the face of a numerically superior army so that it was defeated in detail. It can be argued in his defense, however, that his attack was justified under the circumstances since no one expected the Indians to be so numerous or so willing to stand and fight.

"Custer's Last Stand" has overshadowed the rest of Custer's career and has become one of the best-known battles in American history despite its lack of military importance. Custer quickly emerged as the symbolic hero of the Army in the West and was lionized throughout the following fifty years. Recent shifts in the popular mood regarding the plight of the Indians have led to Custer, still ever the symbol, becoming identified as a villainous figure. Despite this shift in popular opinion, Custer and his last battle continue to fascinate the public.

While still alive Custer nurtured this public fascination. He realized the usefulness of dramatic flair to impress soldiers and civilians alike, and so during the Civil War sported a uniform of black velvet trimmed with gold braid. On the western plains he adopted the fringed buckskin suit of the frontiersman, but kept the crimson scarf and shoulder-length, reddish-blonde hair from his Civil War days. Custer was one of the most flamboyant officers ever to serve in the Army, and most observers failed to understand him, blinded by either the gallant cavalier or the eccentric egomaniac. Those who served with him in the Civil War tended to remember him with "a pistol in his boot, jangling spurs on his heels, and a ponderous claymore swinging at his side—a wild daredevil of a general, and a prince of advance-guards, quick to see and act." But to many who rode with him on the western plains he was "an incarnate fiend" and a "complete example of a petty tyrant," who spared neither man nor beast in his search for glory. Sheridan, who perhaps knew him best, fondly remembered that "if there was any poetry or romance in war Custer could develop it." He saw in Custer the aggressiveness and blind courage so essential in an effective cavalry officer. But Sheridan also recognized the volatile side of Custer's character, feeling him "too impetuous, without deliberation; he thought himself invincible and having a charmed life." According to Sheridan, Custer was a man-child who "was as boyish as he was brave and always needed someone to restrain him." At Little Big Horn there was no one to offer a restraining hand.

BIBLIOGRAPHY

Custer, Elizabeth B. *Boots and Saddles, or Life in Dakota with General Custer*. New York: Harper & Brothers, 1885.
Custer, George Armstrong. *My Life on the Plains or, Personal Experiences with Indians*, Edgar I. Stewart, ed. Norman: University of Oklahoma Press, 1962.
Graham, W. A. *The Custer Myth: A Source Book of Custeriana*. New York: Bonanza Books, 1957.
Jackson, Donald. *Custer's Gold: The United States Cavalry Expedition of 1874*. New Haven: Yale University Press, 1966.
Merington, Marguerite, ed. *The Custer Story: The Life and Intimate Letters of General George A. Custer and His Wife Elizabeth*. New York: Devin-Adair, 1950.
Monaghan, Jay. *Custer: The Life of General George Armstrong Custer*. Boston: Little Brown, 1959.
Stewart, Edgar I. *Custer's Luck*. Norman: University of Oklahoma Press, 1955.
Utley, Robert M., ed. *Life in Custer's Cavalry: Diaries and Letters of Albert and Jennie Barnitz 1867–1868*. New Haven: Yale University Press, 1977.

PAUL A. HUTTON

DEVERS, Jacob Loucks (b. York, Pa., September 8, 1887; d. October 15, 1979), Army officer, military administrator, and World War II commander.

Jacob L. Devers was the eldest of four children born to Ella and Philip Devers, a York jeweler. After distinguishing himself as a leader in his high school class, he enrolled to study engineering at Lehigh University. At the last moment he decided instead to attend the U.S. Military Academy when he received an appointment there in the fall of 1905. He graduated in 1909 (thirty-ninth out of a class of 103) and began his forty-year military career as a field artillery officer. Following two assignments in the Western United States, he returned to West Point in 1912 as a mathematics instructor and became an excellent polo player as well as coaching basketball and baseball in his spare time.

He was stationed in Hawaii when the United States entered World War I. In December 1917 he was posted to Fort Sill, Oklahoma, and served there in various positions related to artillery training throughout the war. Gravely disappointed that he had not been sent to France during the conflict (in fact, he felt it had ruined his career), he received some solace by being ordered to Europe in May 1919, attending a French artillery school, and then serving in the Army of Occupation in Germany for several months.

During the interwar years, he was given assignments primarily at West Point, Fort Sill, and Washington, D.C., and he devoted a good deal of his seemingly boundless energy seeking improvements in artillery techniques and tactics. Like many officers at midcareer, he attended the Command and General Staff School at Fort Leavenworth, Kansas (graduating with distinction) and the Army War College in Washington. His efforts were rewarded during this third tour of duty at the Military Academy (between 1936 and 1939), when he was promoted to the permanent rank of colonel.

When World War II broke out in Europe, Devers was serving as chief of staff in the Panama Department. In May 1940 President Franklin D. Roosevelt named him the senior Army member of a military board to locate suitable bases in the bases-for-destroyers deal with Great Britain. He accomplished this taxing assignment by flying and sailing from Newfoundland to Trinidad in almost every imaginable type of air and naval craft. After a short tour of duty in Washington, in October 1940 he became commander of the 9th Division at Fort Bragg, North Carolina. During Brigadier General Devers' nine-month stay, the number of personnel handled at Fort Bragg rose dramatically, and he was responsible for directing an extensive building program along with streamlining training procedures for draftees and National Guard troops.

His ability to get things done led General George Catlett Marshall,* the acting Army chief of staff, in July 1941 to select Devers to head the armored forces training center at Fort Knox, Kentucky. With the situation in Europe and Asia becoming more ominous, the armored forces were also expanding rapidly and undergoing numerous changes. Devers' dynamism and his advocacy of improved techniques in mobile warfare and weaponry went a long way in shaping the armored units into a modern force considered capable of fighting the vaunted Wehrmacht on equal terms.

In May 1943, with America's presence in the European theatre growing and with the untimely death of Lieutenant General Maxwell Andrews in an airplane crash, Devers was named overall commander of American forces in Europe. From his headquarters in London, he was responsible for much of the organizing and training of U.S. divisions which were arriving in Britain for the projected cross-Channel attack.

Nevertheless, Devers, now fifty-six years old and a lieutenant general, still longed for a combat command. Originally, he hoped the Normandy invasion would provide him with the chance, but at the end of 1943 he was named deputy supreme commander in the Mediterrancan theater instead. In July 1944, however, he was finally given an opportunity to command Army formations in the field. He was appointed head of 6th Army Group, which was being formed to direct U.S. and French units once they had invaded southern France, advanced northward, and established contact with General Dwight David Eisenhower's* forces as Eisenhower pushed across France. The junction was effected much sooner than expected, and Devers took over active command on September 15.

While not gaining the notoriety of the other army groups in the West, Devers' group did participate in a number of important operations, including the clearing of Alsace and the reduction of the Colmar pocket in early 1945. On March 26, 1945, his twelve American and eleven French divisions proceeded to cross the Rhine River and started moving across central and southern Germany and into Austria at a rapid rate. Nuremberg fell on April 20, and Hitler's retreat at

Berchtesgarten on May 4. On May 6, Devers, representing the Allies, accepted the surrender of German forces in western Austria.

With the war in Europe over, Devers was named commanding general of Army Ground Forces, a job which, after the defeat of Japan, consisted of the almost thankless tasks of training and administrating the army units that remained. He served in this capacity until his retirement in 1949. After assuming several civilian and military advisory positions in the 1950s, he lived for a number of years in Washington.

In assessing Devers' long and illustrious military career, four personal characteristics stand out: his enthusiasm, energy, dependability, and devotion to the armed services and country he loved. These traits are quite evident in the way he handled the many tasks he was asked to perform.

His most significant contribution was his appreciation of the possibilities of twentieth-century warfare and his good fortune to serve in positions that allowed him to make many of these possibilities become a reality. He was fascinated by innovative ideas. At Fort Sill in the 1920s, for instance, he developed techniques that allowed artillery units to fire for effect much sooner than had been the case previously. While at Fort Knox, he fostered the increased use and development of self-propelled artillery, more and better medium tanks, and improved tank engines, suspension systems, and design. He also advocated extensive air support for mobile formations, thus calling for tactics that resembled those used by Germany's *blitzkrieg* forces. And even though certain of his ideas were never implemented, others that were initially turned down, such as the attachment of tank destroyer battalions to divisions, became accepted practice by the end of the war.

Devers was further impressed by the possibilities of air power. Not only did he understand its application for armored warfare; he also appreciated how it could be utilized in amphibious and airborne operations. After the war his belief in the importance of air power continued, and he strongly backed guided missile and atomic research for both land and aerial weapons.

In addition, Devers was an outstanding organizer, and his hard work and dedication produced impressive results. At Fort Bragg and again at Fort Knox, he oversaw important construction projects, expanded greatly the number of troops being trained, and improved training methods. His organizational ability also allowed him to deal successfully with the myriad of duties he performed in 1943 in Great Britain and later in Italy, where he was overall commander of U.S. forces. And his last active military assignment, as head of Army Ground Forces (later Army Field Forces), was singularly suited to his administrative talents.

Despite his reputation as an administrator, Devers always wanted to be considered a fighting man. While his command of 6th Army Group in 1944 and 1945 was not as distinguished as it might have been (he was decisive, but at times impulsive and inaccurate in the evaluations he sent to his superiors), it was sufficient to earn him the acclaim of his fellow citizens at war's end. He rightly deserved the fourth star he received in March 1945.

Another contribution made by General Devers (and one too often overlooked) was his effectiveness in dealing with the other services and with foreign leaders. Whether he dealt with naval representatives in Panama, air force commanders in Italy, or British or French generals in Europe, his firm, yet fairminded, approach to problems gained him their respect.

Although not as flamboyant as some of the other American generals, he enjoyed good relations with the press. No doubt, part of the reason stemmed from his infectious smile, almost boyish appearance, and amiable manner. But besides being likeable, the reporters also recognized that General Devers was an extremely competent, thoroughly professional military leader. His competence and professionalism are well exemplified in his understanding of how technology could be applied effectively to modern warfare.

BIBLIOGRAPHY

Blumenson, Martin, ed. *The Patton Papers.* 2 vols. Boston: Houghton Mifflin Company, 1972–1974.
Chandler, Alfred D., Jr., ed. *The Papers of Dwight David Eisenhower: The War Years.* Vols. 3–4. Baltimore: Johns Hopkins University Press, 1970.
Lattre de Tassigny, Jean de. *The History of the First French Army.* Translated by Malcolm Barnes. London: Allen and Unwin, 1952.
MacDonald, Charles B. *The Last Offensive. (United States Army in World War II. European Theater of Operations.)* Washington, D.C.: U.S. Government Printing Office, 1973.
Pogue, Forrest C. *George C. Marshall: Organizer of Victory.* New York: Viking Press, 1973.
Seventh U.S. Army. *Report of Operations in France and Germany 1944–1945.* 3 vols. Heidelberg: Aloys Gräf, 1946.

ALAN WILT

DEWEY, George (b. Montpelier, Vt., December 26, 1837; d. Washington, D.C., January 16, 1917), naval officer. Dewey is renowned as the victor at Manila Bay during the Spanish-American War, and for his service as president for seventeen years of the Navy's General Board.

Dewey claimed descent from a French Huguenot family that settled briefly in Kent, England, before Thomas Duee emigrated to Massachusetts in 1634. Dewey's father, Julius Yemans Dewey, was a prominent physician who built a small fortune as president of the National Life Insurance Company. Dewey won appointment to the Naval Academy in 1854 and ranked fifth among the fifteen graduates in 1858. After a cruise with the European Squadron in the steam frigate *Wabash*, Dewey passed his final examination and on April 19, 1861, was the third in his class to receive his commission as lieutenant.

Because of the scarcity of naval officers at the outbreak of the Civil War, Dewey won the billet of executive officer in the steam frigate *Mississippi* shortly before the old side-wheeler joined the blockading squadron under David Glasgow Farragut* in Gulf waters. Dewey later claimed that his service under Farragut was far better training than any schooling he had received at Annapolis, and he always regarded Farragut as the model naval officer—"urbane, decisive, and indomitable." As Melancthon Smith, the *Mississippi*'s skipper, suffered from poor night vision, he trusted Dewey to navigate his ship during the dash by Farragut's squadron on April 24, 1862, past Forts Jackson and St. Philip, the defenders of New Orleans. The following year, when Farragut attempted a similar run past Port Hudson, the *Mississippi*'s inept civilian pilot grounded her on a mud bank, but Dewey won high praise for his cool-headed direction of the small boats that removed the crew from the stranded ship under heavy enemy fire. Subsequently, Dewey served as executive officer in the steam frigate *Colorado* during the attack led by David Dixon Porter on Fort Fisher in 1865. Dewey emerged from the war with the rank of lieutenant commander.

After a tour with the revived European Squadron in the sloop-of-war *Kearsarge*, Dewey returned to the United States to marry Susan Boardman Goodwin, the daughter of the former New Hampshire governor, and to serve five years at the Naval Academy under a reforming superintendent, David D. Porter. Susan Dewey died in 1872, just five days after giving birth to a son, George Goodwin Dewey.

Dewey's naval service during the three decades after the Civil War was honorable but without special distinction. He was saddened by the Navy's postwar decline, but he was not sufficiently moved to join such reformers as Stephen Bleeker Luce, Alfred Thayer Mahan,* and Bradley Allen Fiske to demand improvements. Among his duties during the 1870s and 1880s, Dewey led a survey of the waters of the Gulf of California on the third-class sloop *Narragansett*, acted as lighthouse inspector with an office in Boston (1875–1877), and was secretary of the Lighthouse Board in Washington (1878–1882).

Dewey employed political influence in 1889 to win appointment as chief of the Bureau of Equipment; in this post he was much concerned with providing coal for the "New Navy" of steam and steel. From Equipment he moved in 1893 to the presidency of the Lighthouse Board and two years later to the presidency of the then prestigious Board of Inspection and Survey. It was in the latter capacity that he observed the trials of the early battleships *Texas, Maine, Iowa, Indiana*, and *Massachusetts*. In 1896, at the age of fifty-nine, he was finally promoted to the rank of commodore, which rank entitled him to command a squadron and to fly a single starred pendant. The following year, encouraged by Assistant Secretary of the Navy Theodore Roosevelt,* Dewey again employed political influence to achieve position, command of the Asiatic Station.

Dewey raised his pendant at Yokohama in January 1898 as the United States moved toward war with Spain. He was already assembling the scattered ships of the Asiatic command when, ten days after the sinking of the *Maine*, Roosevelt cabled the commodore the famous order: "Keep full of coal. In event of declaration of war with Spain, your duty will be to see that the Spanish Squadron does not leave the Asiatic Coast, and then offensive operations in the Philippines." Dewey had his squadron concentrated at Mirs Bay near Hong Kong when on April 24 the Navy Department directed him to use his "utmost endeavors...to capture or destroy" the Spanish Squadron in the Philippines.

The four cruisers and two gunboats that Dewey, in the manner of Farragut, led into Manila Bay in the early hours of May 1 were far superior in tonnage, guns, and general fighting efficiency to the pathetic squadron of the Spanish commander, Rear Admiral Don Patricio Montojo. Once Dewey spotted the Spanish ships drawn up in crescent formation before the old arsenal at Cavite, he led his force into battle standing on the unprotected bridge of the protected cruiser *Olympia*, his flagship. Firing at ranges of two thousand to three thousand yards, Dewey's squadron passed the Spanish thrice to the west and twice to the east before withdrawing to the center of the bay at 7:30 AM for breakfast and to count ammunition. At 11:16 Dewey returned to complete the destruction of Montojo's remaining vessels.

Dewey thereafter occupied and controlled Manila Bay, awaiting the arrival from the United States of Army units sufficient to hold Manila. During the summer, Dewey encouraged the Philippine insurgents under Emilio Aguinaldo to rise against Spanish rule and assumed a stern attitude toward the German Vice Admiral von Diederichs, who for unexplained reasons assembled his squadron in the bay. Dewey also engaged in secret negotiations with the Spanish governor general that paved the way for the city's surrender on August 12 after only token resistance to attacks by the American Army and Navy. Dewey was deeply impressed by the strategic importance of Subig Bay to the north of Manila, but he was ambivalent as to whether the United States should retain the Philippines. In recognition of his war achievements, Congress in 1899 bestowed on Dewey the rank of Admiral of the Navy with proviso that he could not be retired except by his own request.

Dewey returned to the United States in the summer of 1899 at the height of his extraordinary popularity. His public image was shortly dimmed, however, by circumstances attending his marriage to a wealthy Washington socialite, Mildred MacLean Hazen, and by his rather awkward bid for the presidency.

From 1900 until his death in 1917 Dewey served as the first (and only) president of the General Board of the Navy, the senior body established by Secretary of the Navy John D. Long to advise on high-level naval policy. In 1902–1903 Dewey commanded the widely publicized fleet maneuvers in the Caribbean, which have been regarded as a warning to Germany during the second Venezuelan Crisis. And in 1903 he assumed the chairmanship of the new Joint Army and Navy Board, the predecessor of the Joint Chiefs of Staff.

During his last eighteen years George Dewey was the unchallenged elder statesman of the U.S. Navy with a public reputation comparable to that of his great foreign contemporaries: John Arbuthnot Fisher of Britain, Alfred von Tirpitz of Germany, and Marquis Heihachiro Togo of Japan. It was his spectacular victory at Manila Bay that catapulted Dewey to first place in the Navy. Although accomplished with exemplary dispatch in the heroic manner of a Farragut, his May Day victory was really a foregone conclusion given the overwhelming superiority of the American squadron over the Spanish. Indeed, the battle was significant chiefly for its political consequences. But for Manila Bay, it is hardly likely that the United States would have acquired the Philippines or so rapidly assumed a major role in East Asian affairs.

Dewey's contributions to the Navy as leader of the General Board, although largely unknown to the public, were probably as significant to the Navy as was his victory at Manila Bay. Under his direction, the General Board debated strategies for war against Germany (Plan Black) and Japan (Plan Orange), proposed the 1903 building program to complete a fleet of forty-eight battleships by 1920, recommended the development of naval bases commanding a naval route from the Atlantic seaboard via the Caribbean and an isthmian canal to the Pacific and China, and generally supported the maintenance of a single battlefleet concentrated in the Atlantic. Dewey supported the all-big-gun *Dreadnought*-type battleship in opposition to the more conservative Alfred Thayer Mahan, and he fought hard for a naval base at Subig Bay against General Leonard Wood and Army strategists, who wanted to concentrate Philippine defense at Manila.

Dewey sought with considerable success to hold himself above naval factional politics. His success is demonstrated by the fact that he was idolized by both Secretary of the Navy Josephus Daniels and Daniels' bitter critic, Rear Admiral Bradley Fiske. During the preparedness campaign prior to the United States' entry into World War I, Dewey publicly defended the Navy's efficiency against the critics of the Wilson administration even as he supported the General Board's program for a Navy second to none. Far more than to brilliance or to intellectual originality, Dewey's success must be attributed to a combination of fortuitous accident, extraordinary dignity, sound common sense, and skillful personal diplomacy during nearly three decades of practically unbroken tenure on the Washington scene.

BIBLIOGRAPHY

Dewey, George. *Autobiography of George Dewey, Admiral of the Navy*. New York: Charles Scribner's Sons, 1916.

Sargent, Nathan. *Admiral Dewey and the Manila Campaign*. Washington, D.C.: Naval Historical Foundation, 1947.

Spector, Ronald. *Admiral of the New Navy: The Life and Career of George Dewey*. Baton Rouge: Louisiana State University Press, 1974.

West, Richard S. *Admirals of Empire: The Combined Story of George Dewey, Alfred Thayer Mahan, Winfield Scott Schley, and William Thomas Sampson*. Indianapolis: Bobbs-Merrill Company,1948.

WILLIAM R. BRAISTED

DONIPHAN, Alexander William (b. Mason Couny, Ky., July 9, 1808; d. Richmond, Mo., August 8, 1887), lawyer; Doniphan was a commander of the expedition that wrested the American Southwest from the Mexicans in 1846.

Alexander W. Doniphan was born into the family of Joseph Doniphan and Anne Smith, both Virginians. Joseph had gone to Kentucky with one of Daniel Boone's parties and had taught school there for perhaps a year, then returned to Virginia sometime before 1779 to enlist in the Continental Army. He was present at Yorktown for the surrender of Lord Charles Cornwallis. After the Revolution, he married Anne Smith and returned with her to Kentucky in about 1790. When Joseph died in 1813, Anne decided that Alexander needed an education that she could not provide and sent the boy to school in nearby Augusta, Kentucky, where he resided with his elder brother, George. His tutor, Richard Keene, was a graduate of Trinity College and a fugitive of the Irish rebellion of 1798. Keene's influence proved very great to the boy; Keene forced him to study the major poets and the classics, developing in him a zest for oratory and a concern for political liberty. At age fourteen Alexander enrolled in the new Methodist academy, Augusta College, from which he graduated at age eighteen with distinction in the classics. His mother encouraged him to study the law and helped him to find a place in the office of Martin Marshall of Augusta in the manner of the times. Marshall required the lad to continue his study of the classics for six more months; then Doniphan studied U.S. and English history with emphasis on Anglo-Saxon legal history before turning to law texts. After three years of this work, Doniphan was admitted to the bar of both Kentucky and Ohio.

In 1830 Doniphan moved to Lexington, Missouri, and began the practice of law, his chief occupation for the next thirty years. He acquired an outstanding reputation in unpopular causes and served as defense attorney in virtually every major criminal case tried in western Missouri during those decades. The demand for his services undoubtedly was based as much on his renowned eloquence as on his knowledge of the law.

Some of Doniphan's law practice came about as a result of the large migration of Mormons into western Missouri; in one instance Doniphan defended a church leader charged with conspiracy to commit the murder of the state governor. Even though most of the region disliked the Mormons and sought revenge, Doniphan got the accused off with a punishment of only five minutes in jail.

In 1833 Doniphan moved from Lexington to Liberty and made that his home for the rest of his life. It was there that in 1837 he met and married Elizabeth Jane Thornton, described by a friend as a very intelligent, cultured lady. The couple had two sons, both of whom died in accidents while yet young. And it was from Liberty that Doniphan was elected three times to serve in the Missouri State General Assembly.

During the so-called Mormon War of 1838, Doniphan was appointed commanding officer of the 1st Brigade of Missouri militia. His reputation as a responsible state leader was enhanced greatly by his conduct in this affair. Ordered by his commander to put to death some Mormon leaders, including Joseph Smith, Doniphan refused, calling the proposed action murder. Although he took a very unpopular stand and at the same time disobeyed a direct military order, Doniphan saved the lives of the men and added considerably to the public estimate of his courage and integrity.

Missourians remembered these characteristics, and in 1846 when war broke out with Mexico, Doniphan received the recognition of his neighbors and the state. The War Department created the Army of the West at Fort Leavenworth, using Colonel Stephen Watts Kearny's 1st Dragoons as the nucleus, fleshed out with eight companies representing as many counties in Missouri. These companies combined into a unit classified as the 1st Regiment of Missouri Volunteers. Into the Clay County company Alexander Doniphan enlisted as private. Shortly thereafter, Kearny ordered the troops to elect their own field grade officers. Assembled on the parade grounds at the fort, the Missouri volunteers were addressed by the candidates before conducting the balloting. Aided by his appearance, oratory, military experience, and some free meals provided by residents of Liberty, the six foot-four inch Doniphan was the overwhelming choice for commander of the regiment with the rank of colonel in the volunteers.

Under the overall command of Colonel Kearny, the Army of the West left Fort Leavenworth for Santa Fe, New Mexico, in June 1846. This portion of the campaign was uneventful in a military sense. But with the army spread out for many miles over the Santa Fe Trail, Doniphan's portion—roughly half of the men—gradually changed from an undisciplined mob of boys, farmers, German immigrants, and unemployed into a tough military unit. Five weeks and 850 miles later, Doniphan and his regiment entered Santa Fe, accepting it from the Mexicans without a fight. At this point, Kearny, now a brigadier general, critically divided the Army of the West. His own mission was to take California from the Mexican government, leaving Doniphan the combined tasks of capturing the rest of New Mexico, subduing Navajos, Utes, and Zuñis and invading northern Mexico at least to Chihuahua, where he was "to link up with General Wool." All of this was to be done with less than nine hundred volunteers completely cut off from their government during the entire campaign.

In the heart of enemy country, Doniphan's own command was now weakened by the necessity of coercing the three tribes into accepting the jurisdiction of the United States and, more importantly, keeping the Utes and Navajos from kidnapping Mexicans and running off their livestock. Some of the Missourians struggled nearly one thousand miles, often in blizzard conditions, to track down the tribes, who fled as far as Canyon de Chelly in what is now Arizona. By this prodigious feat, Doniphan brought temporary peace among the Southwestern tribes and could feel that his right flank and rear were protected before he plunged into old Mexico.

Already beaten up by weather and the effect of long marches, Doniphan's regiment started toward Mexico. On Christmas Day 1846 they were attacked at El Paso by about twelve hundred Mexican dragoons. The Mexican forces seriously underestimated the morale of the Americans; their bold cavalry charge was sharply turned away by Doniphan's defensive tactics. The Mexicans lost forty to fifty killed and 150 wounded; the Americans lost only seven wounded.

Doniphan occupied El Paso with certain feelings of insecurity, but he took the proper steps to gain the friendship of the Mexicans before he dared resume his march south. He gradually realized that the natives feared the American occupying force less than they did their neighbors, the Apaches, who behaved toward them just as did the Navajos and Utes further north. Thus, Doniphan used more of his precious time and supplies pursuing the Apaches to teach them to let the citizens of El Paso alone. Only then did he dare resume his march to Chihuahua, another 270 miles of pitiless desert away.

Just north of Chihuahua along the Sacramento River, the Mexicans set up their last defense against the Missouri Volunteers. Through superior artillery tactics, the Americans drove the Mexicans from their entrenchments and opened the door to Chihuahua and the entire Mexican northwest. Incredibly, three hundred Mexicans but only two Americans were killed. Doniphan's orders had been to help Brigadier General John Ellis Wool capture Chihuahua, then await further instructions. Without help or even knowledge of Wool's whereabouts, Doniphan had taken the province and the city. Some of his men wanted to continue on to Mexico City, but most were ready to go home. Their one-year enlistments had ended. They were completely isolated and unsupported in a foreign land; they were ragged, filthy, and broke. A messenger to General Zachary Taylor* finally cleared matters; Doniphan learned for the first time of Winfield Scott's* campaign aimed at Mexico City; the war in the north was nearly over, and Doniphan was to join Taylor prior to letting his men go home. Three more weeks of desert marching brough Doniphan to Taylor, who had not moved since his victory at Buena Vista in February. Some men reenlisted, but the majority made one more long march to Matamoros and then took ship to New Orleans and home.

After the war Doniphan resumed his law practice. In 1861 he went to Washington to represent Missouri in an attempt to prevent civil war; then he was offered command of the Missouri state guard but declined because the death of his two sons had undermined the health of his wife. He continued law practice in Liberty until his death.

Alexander Doniphan represented the finest type of American pioneer and civilian soldier, helping to bring law and stability to his state in the most trying of times. Pressed into military duty, he exhibited great leadership and skill in commanding the Missouri Volunteers. Virtually unaided by their government, they fought their way across thirty-six hundred miles of prairie and desert, land as unknown and unfriendly as the Mexicans and Indians whom they fought. Doniphan's military victories were complete and unquestioned; just as important was his judicious manner of managing the conquered, not only adding vast terrain to the American nation, but also bringing the first taste of American law to thousands of people who would now be citizens and wards of the United States.

BIBLIOGRAPHY

Bauer, K. Jack. *The Mexican War, 1846-1848*. New York: Macmillan, 1974.
Connelley, William E. *Doniphan's Expedition*. Topeka, Kans.: By the author, 1907.
George, Isaac. *Heroes and Incidents of the Mexican War*. Greensburg, Pa.: Review Publishing Company, 1903.
Hughes, John T. *Doniphan's Expedition*. Cincinnati: J. A. and U. P. James, 1848.
Karnes, Thomas L. *William Gilpin, Western Nationalist*. Austin: University of Texas, 1970.

THOMAS L. KARNES

DONOVAN, William Joseph (b. Buffalo, N.Y., January 1, 1883; d. Washington, D.C., February 8, 1959), World War I combat hero, lawyer, World War II strategic intelligence chief. Donovan is considered the father of American intelligence by some.

William "Wild Bill" Donovan was born into an Irish immigrant family in New York. His father was a railroad man. A devout Roman Catholic, William attended church schools until entering Niagara University for three years before transferring to Columbia College where he continued in the law school of Columbia University. At Columbia he was a contemporary of Franklin D. Roosevelt, although they moved in separate circles, and he was quarterback of the football team. He received the LL.B. degree in 1907 and returned to Buffalo at the age of twenty-four to practice law.

By 1912 Donovan had formed his own law firm (specializing in corporate law) and was instrumental in organizing the Buffalo Cavalry Troop I in the New York National Guard. In this unit he saw duty during the Depew railroad strike and along the Texas border as part of John Joseph Pershing's* expedition against Pancho Villa. On July 15, 1914, he married Ruth Rumsey, a member of an old and wealthy Buffalo family. The first of many overseas missions began in 1915 when he went to Poland as a representative of the Rockefeller Foundation's American War Relief Commission.

With the U.S. entry into World War I, Donovan joined the 69th Regiment of the 27th New York National Guard Division. Although this unit continued to call itself the Old 69th, it became the 165th Infantry of the 42d Rainbow Division. Some accounts claim that the strenuous training program which he developed as battalion major for the 165th gave him the nickname "Wild Bill"; other accounts indicate that the name came from his football days or from the Mexican Campaign. At any rate the nickname was widely known by the end of the war.

Donovan emerged from World War I as a national hero, having seen action at Champagne-Marne, St.-Mihiel, and Argonne. Wounded twice, he was promoted to colonel and given command of the regiment. He was the first to receive the triple honors of Congressional Medal of Honor, Distinguished Service Cross, and Distinguished Service Medal, along with numerous foreign decorations. In 1957 when he received the National Security Medal, he became the first to hold all four decorations. The poet Joyce Kilmer was also a member of the 165th and was killed while with Donovan.

Mustered out in 1919, Donovan and his wife traveled privately to Japan, which resulted in a brief official trip to Siberia to evaluate the Kolchak government. He returned to Buffalo as an attorney and entered Republican politics. In 1922 he was appointed U.S. district attorney for western New York. He developed a reputation as a crime-fighter, cracking down on narcotics, burglary rings, both labor and corporations, and vigorously enforcing the Volstead Act. In 1924 he was the Republican nominee for lieutenant governor. He lost the election but did considerably better than his running mate who lost to Al Smith.

Following his defeat in 1924, Donovan moved to Washington, D.C., where President Calvin Coolidge appointed him head of the Justice Department's Criminal Division. The next year he became assistant attorney general, leading the important Anti-Trust Division. In 1928 he became chairman of a commission on studying the problem of water rights related to the Rio Grande River. As a leader in the Republican party, Donovan was a strong supporter of Herbert Hoover. With Hoover's election as president in 1928, many assumed that Donovan would become attorney general. He did not receive the appointment, perhaps because he was both a "wet" and a Catholic, two major issues in the 1928 election.

In 1929 Donovan returned to private life and opened a law office in New York City. During the Depression, he worked with the American Legion on behalf of unemployed veterans. He made an unsuccessful bid for the New York governorship in 1932, which was a bad year for Republicans generally. The 1930s saw considerable foreign travel for Donovan, as he was fascinated by events in Europe. He amazed foreign affairs experts in 1935 by gaining an audience with Mussolini and receiving unprecedented permission to observe the Italian Army action in Ethiopia. The following year he traveled to Spain to see the civil war.

The advent of hostilities in Europe saw President Franklin Roosevelt rely increasingly on Donovan for foreign intelligence. In 1940 he went on a series of secret missions for the president, including Africa, South America, the Middle East, and the Pacific, as well as Europe. He covered some twenty-five thousand miles, and his confidential reports to Roosevelt convinced the president, despite their political differences, of Donovan's great worth. On March 26, 1941, Donovan made a report to the nation, over national radio, on the dangers of Nazism. On July 11, Roosevelt appointed him to head the new Office of the Coordinator of Information (COI), with a staff of 250 experts in various fields.

After the United States entered World War II, Roosevelt created the Office of Strategic Services (OSS) with Donovan in charge. The public information component of the old COI became a separate agency, the Office of War Information, under playwright Robert Sherwood. As OSS chief, Donovan reported to the Joint Chiefs of Staff.

The American intelligence and counterintelligence posture at the beginning of the war was extremely limited, and most of the successes later achieved must be credited to Donovan and his fledgling OSS. Except for Latin America and the Far Eastern Command, Donovan's mandate included the entire world. In addition to responsibility for gathering and evaluating strategic intelligence, the OSS also planned and executed special operations and services. Donovan, by virtue of his personality and his leadership, must be credited with the broad definition of "strategic services" which came to encompass counterintelligence, sabotage, and espionage, as well as behind-the-lines operations with partisans, propaganda, and psychological warfare. He was made brigadier general in 1943 and major general the following year.

The basic organization of the OSS included secret intelligence (operatives in the field), morale operations (propaganda), and research and analysis (intelligence estimates and analyses), as well as documentation and map components. Donovan recruited into the OSS a wide variety of people, including a number of well-known personalities. These familiar names, along with their romantic exploits, are no doubt in part responsible for the reputation the OSS achieved—not that there was any ambivalance in the American mind as to the techniques used. "Oh So Secret" was a popular nickname for the organization.

Looking forward to the end of the war, Donovan proposed to Roosevelt that a peacetime agency similar to OSS be developed. Roosevelt died before approving the plan, and President Harry Truman disbanded the OSS immediately after the Japanese surrender. After serving briefly as assistant chief counsel for the prosecutor at the Nuremberg trials, Donovan returned to private law practice in New York where he continued to lobby for a central intelligence agency.

Eventually, much of what Donovan had recommended was achieved by the National Security Act of 1947 which established the Central Intelligence Agency as a separate organization. Although Donovan was not chosen to head the new CIA, as some had expected, his influence was undoubtedly felt in it since many OSS personnel joined the CIA, notably Allen Dulles and Richard Helms who served as CIA directors.

In 1946 Donovan sought but did not get the Republican nomination for U.S. senator from New York. In 1953, at the age of seventy, he was appointed ambassador to Thailand; he served until 1954. Throughout this period he was an elder statesman in the legal field, and as late as 1956 he visited Europe to work for refugees from the Hungarian rebellion, for whom he raised $1.5 million. He received the National Security Medal in 1957. He suffered a stroke in 1956 and upon his death in 1959 was buried in Arlington Cemetery with full military honors.

Although Donovan established a solid reputation for himself as a soldier in World War I, he is best known as head of the OSS in World War II. The OSS suffered its share of failures and was criticized for wastefulness and costly errors, but by comparison to any wartime intelligence effort and especially to other contemporary agencies, the OSS must be rated a significant success. Donovan's role is almost unanimously appreciated by historians. Although Donovan personally regretted that he was not appointed to head the new CIA, it may be fortunate for his standing in history that he was not. His position rests securely on the now romantic days of World War II, and the subsequent criticisms of intelligence agencies, especially the CIA, beginning in the late 1960s have not sullied that reputation. The role, techniques, and even desirability of intelligence and counterintelligence continue to be debated, but "Wild Bill" Donovan remains an American hero.

BIBLIOGRAPHY

Alsop, Stewart, and Thomas Braden. *Sub Rosa; O.S.S. and American Espionage.* New York: Reynal and Hitchcock, 1948.
Duffy, Francis P. *Father Duffy's Story.* New York: George H. Doran Company, 1919.
Ford, Corey. *Donovan of OSS.* Boston: Little, Brown, and Company, 1970.
Ransom, Harry Howe. *The Intelligence Establishment.* Cambridge, Mass.: Harvard University Press, 1970.
Rowan, Richard Wilmer, and Robert G. Deindorfer. *Secret Service; Thirty-Three Centuries of Espionage.* New York: Hawthorn Books, 1967.
Seth, Ronald. *Encyclopedia of Espionage.* Garden City, N.Y.: Doubleday and Company, 1972.
Smith, R. Harris. *OSS: The Secret History of America's First Central Intelligence Agency.* Berkeley: University of California Press, 1972.
Wilhelm, Maria. *The Fighting Irishman: The Story of "Wild Bill" Donovan.* New York: Hawthorn Books, 1964.

ROY TALBERT

EARLY, Jubal Anderson (b. Franklin County, Va., November 3, 1816; d. Lynchburg, Va., March 2, 1894), Army officer. Early was a division and corps commander in the Confederacy's Army of Northern Virginia.

Although "Old Jube" Early graduated from the U.S. Military Academy at West Point (in 1837, eighteenth in a class of fifty), he never intended to become a career soldier. The third of ten children, he lived and studied around his western Virginia home until he was sixteen and his mother died. Since West Point provided a suitable and respectable change of scene for the grief-stricken youth, his father secured an appointment for him in 1833.

Early's short-lived service as an artillery officer was undistinguished: garrison duty at Fortress Monroe in 1837, brief service in the Seminole War of 1837–1838, and then resignation of his commission on July 31, 1838. Eighteen months later, he successfully passed the bar and began practicing law at Rocky Mount, Virginia. Politically the staunchest of Whigs, Early won a seat in the Virginia House in 1841 but was soundly defeated for reelection. In 1842 he was appointed commonwealth attorney, a post he held for the next ten years. Only his voluntary service in the Mexican War and two more unsuccessful runs for office (for delegate to the state constitutional convention in 1850 and for the legislature in

1853) interrupted Early's moderately prosperous law business before the Civil War.

Appointed a major in the 1st Virginia Volunteers on January 7, 1847, Early went with it to northern Mexico. Zachary Taylor* had already fought his great battles. Only occupation duty and a two-month stint as military governor of Monterrey remained for Early—this, and a severe case of rheumatism that stooped his back for life.

Mustered out in April 1848, Early returned to Virginia. In 1861 he served as a delegate to the state convention where he vehemently opposed and voted against secession. At the onset of hostilities, however, he volunteered for Confederate service and was appointed colonel of the 24th Virginia Infantry. Commanding a brigade at First Manassas, Early performed well enough to earn a promotion to brigadier general.

For the next two years Early showed steady growth as a soldier. Wounded at Williamsburg in May 1862, he was forced to relinquish his brigade. By July he had another. In the corps of Thomas Jonathan "Stonewall" Jackson* he served with distinction in the Second Manassas Campaign. His sterling performance at Sharpsburg—a savage counterattack at a critical moment on the left of the Confederate line and skillful performance as a stand-in for his wounded division commander—earned him the commendation of Robert Edward Lee,* Jackson, and James Ewell Brown Stuart.* But no promotion. This would come on January 17, 1863, after another timely counterpunch on the right at Fredericksburg the previous month.

Now commanding a division, Early held Fredericksburg despite having an inferior force and receiving garbled orders while Lee crushed Joseph Hooker* at Chancellorsville in May 1863. At Gettysburg Early's division saw action late on July 1 and participated in the fruitless dusk assault on Culp's Hill the next day. Twice during the next several months Early assumed temporary corps command, first replacing Richard Stoddert Ewell during the Mine Run Campaign of late 1863 and then replacing Ambrose Powell Hill* during the Wilderness Campaign. Promoted to lieutenant general, on May 31, 1864, Early took over command of the II Corps after Cold Harbor and Ewell's retirement.

Ordered to the Shenandoah Valley in June 1864, Early's fourteen thousand-man army chased one Federal force from the lower Valley and another from Harper's Ferry, and advanced on Washington, defeating a third Union force under Lewis Wallace* at Monocacy, Maryland, on July 9, 1864. Encountering VI Corps veterans from the army of Ulysses Simpson Grant* on the capital's outskirts, Early skirmished and then retired to Virginia.

Early remained in the Valley, disrupting communications and launching a series of destructive cavalry forays, one of which burned the town of Chambersburg, Pennsylvania, until confronted by a formidable Federal force under Philip Henry Sheridan* in September. Early then sustained a series of crippling defeats: at Winchester, at Fisher's Hill, and, on October 19, 1864, at Cedar Creek. In March, 1865 George Armstrong Custer* obliterated what was left of

Early's force at Waynesborough. Bowing to public outcry, Lee reluctantly relieved Early of command.

After Appomattox, Early fled to Mexico and from there to Canada where he stayed until 1869, when he returned to his law practice in Lynchburg, Virginia. In 1877 he began a long, lucrative association with the Louisiana Lottery Company as a director. Prominent in the formation of the Southern Historical Society in 1869, Early served as its president and guiding spirit until his death. As a champion of Lee and Jefferson Davis and a bitter, unforgiving critic of James B. Longstreet,* Early contributed prolifically to the Society's *Papers* and to a wide range of journals, newspapers, and magazines. His apologetic but scrupulously accurate *Autobiography*, published posthumously in 1912, is still regarded as a model of its kind and perhaps his finest achievement. Early was unreconstructed to the last. He died a bachelor.

Of men's affections Jubal Early earned very little. Sarcastic, outspoken, profane, irreligious, and caustic, Early was a born scrapper, both on and off the battlefield. Little love was lost between Early and his subordinates, but his superiors—Lee, Jackson, and Ewell—all recognized his considerable talents as a soldier. Early fought as hard as any general in the Army of Northern Virginia. Not really a professional soldier, despite his West Point education, he learned the art of war quickly and grew in stature as the war progressed.

Unfortunately for the Confederacy this growth was uneven. Until Gettysburg, Early's star had risen steadily; afterwards, with the notable exception of his campaign in the Valley and march on Washington it shone with its former brilliance only sporadically. On many fields until then, he had exhibited the kind of aggressiveness and pluck in battle clearly distinguishing a warrior of self-reliant grit. Early specialized in timely, tactically decisive counterattacks. At First Manassas the arrival of his brigade on the left of Pierre Gustave Toutant Beauregard* turned the tide of battle. Early performed even more spectacularly at Sharpsburg by pitching into Hooker's corps and repulsing it just as Lee's left was being overrun. A similar slashing counterpunch corked a breech on Lee's right at Fredericksburg. By the time of Chancellorsville, Lee had enough confidence in him to entrust Early with protecting his rear at Fredericksburg. Early accomplished this job admirably, despite an almost disastrous mixup in orders that caused him to abandon his position temporarily.

Early also had talents as a planner: on his own in the Valley, he carried out operations during the summer of 1864 that strategically accomplished all that Lee could have hoped. In addition to gathering vast quantities of stores, he established the Valley as a second front, preserved Lee's supply source, and kept communications open to the West. And his basic plan of attack at Cedar Creek, so successful at first, miscarried only because of Early's failure to press his advantage, though his subordinates warned that such delay courted disaster. This curious hesitancy was also evident at Gettysburg. It was Early rather than Ewell who remonstrated so strongly with Lee against further attacks on the Union right on July 1, an attack that had it been delivered might have proven decisive.

Several shortcomings limited Early as a commander. His natural aggressiveness sometimes degenerated into recklessness and impetuosity, as at Williamsburg in 1862. By late 1864 Early's self confidence had actually become a liability: he underestimated Sheridan—to his cost. Indeed, almost all of Early's weaknesses came into play during that final inglorious campaign. His tendency to commit his forces piecemeal—a tactic that had succeeded at Monocacy—ruined him at Winchester where he lost almost 40 percent of his twelve thousand-man force. Several times before the Battle of Fisher's Hill on September 22, 1864, Early had proven a poor judge of terrain. (He had gotten hopelessly lost at Malvern Hill; had launched an ill-fated, badly coordinated attack without proper reconnaissance at Bethesda Church on May 30, 1864; and had once, in December 1863, muffed an opportunity to bag a sizable enemy cavalry unit by dispatching his own troopers in the wrong direction.) This time, however, he disposed his small force so badly—in a line much too long to defend—that Sheridan easily routed it.

For a commander of combined arms, Early also evinced severe deficiencies in his employment of cavalry. He never respected the mounted force anyway, and so he neglected its training and alienated its commanders. Inefficiencies in the cavalry contributed heavily to the Fisher's Hill defeat: Early had invited disaster by dismounting a lackluster unit and using it as an anchor for his flank. And at Cedar Creek a month later, Early irreparably weakened himself by detaching a large portion of his cavalry.

A superb brigadier and an excellent division commander, Early faltered only in corps command—and then only on occasion. Lee, it should be noted, always thought highly of his abilities, and more often than not Early justified the confidence of his superiors. The last six months of the Civil War enhanced the reputations of very few Confederate commanders, and Early's miserable showing against Sheridan in the Valley has clouded his reputation, perhaps unfairly. It can be argued that no Confederate general could have succeeded there against the kind of power that was brought to bear. Until then, Jubal Early ranked among the finest soldiers in the Army of Northern Virginia. It is an accolade he still deserves.

BIBLIOGRAPHY

Bushong, Millard K. *Old Jube: A Biography of General Jubal A. Early.* Boyce, Va.: Carr Publishing Company, 1955.

Early, Jubal A. *Autobiographical Sketch and Narrative of the War Between the States.* Philadelphia: J. B. Lippincott Company, 1912.

Freeman, Douglas S. *Lee's Lieutenants: A Study in Command.* 3 vols. New York: Charles Scribner's Sons, 1942–1944.

Vandiver, Frank L. *Jubal's Raid: General Early's Famous Attack on Washington in 1864.* New York: McGraw-Hill Book Company, 1960.

THOMAS E. SCHOTT

EICHELBERGER, Robert Lawrence (b. Urbana, Ohio, March 9, 1886; d. Asheville, N.C., September 26, 1961), Army officer; commander, U.S. Eighth Army in the Pacific, 1944–1945. Eichelberger's crowning achievement was his role in the liberation of the Philippines.

The youngest of five children of a prominent lawyer who was a Union veteran, and a former Southern girl who could remember the ravages of the Vicksburg Campaign, Robert Eichelberger grew up on a farm near Urbana, Ohio. After two years at Ohio State University, he entered the U.S. Military Academy at West Point in 1905, graduating sixty-eighth in a class of 103 in 1909. Twenty-seven of his classmates ultimately became general officers.

Lieutenant Eichelberger's first assignment was with the 10th Infantry at Fort Benjamin Harrison, Indiana. He accompanied his regiment to Texas in 1911 when it was part of the Maneuver Division hastily assembled to keep a watchful eye on Mexico. Six months later the 10th was sent to Panama, where Eichelberger met and married Emma Gudger, daughter of the chief justice of the Canal Zone. Miss Em, as she was affectionately called, became his life-long companion, confidante, and ardent champion. In 1915 Eichelberger served on patrol duty on the Mexican border with the 22d Infantry. The following year he became professor of military science and tactics at Kemper Military School in Boonville, Missouri. After a brief stint as instructor at the Third Officers' Training Camp in Camp Pike, Arkansas, Captain Eichelberger joined the War Department General Staff in Washington.

There he served Major General William Sidney Graves as executive assistant to the chief of staff, and when General Graves left to command the American Expeditionary Force sent to Siberia in 1918 as part of a joint allied military action, Eichelberger, now a major, went along as assistant chief of staff and later as chief intelligence officer. For Eichelberger the Siberian experience was a crash course in leadership; he admired Graves for his integrity, courage, and honesty, and he learned much from the candid discussions that animated their daily walks. Eichelberger also learned to respect the Japanese soldier while distrusting the militarism and motives of the Japanese leaders. "Some of the biggest liars and crooks in the world are assembled here," he confided to Miss Em, "and they are all knocking us.... It is a great life for a poker player."

After leaving Siberia in 1920, Eichelberger continued in military intelligence in China, the Philippines, and with the War Department. During the Washington Disarmament Conference in 1922, he was the liaison officer with the Chinese delegation, and in 1924 he transferred to the Adjutant General's Department. His name was at the top of the 1926 list of "Distinguished Graduates" of the Command and General Staff School at Fort Leavenworth, where he remained for three more years as an instructor, and in 1930 Eichelberger graduated from the Army War College. From 1931 to 1935 he served at the Military Academy as adjutant and secretary of the Academic Board, after which he spent three years as secretary to the War Department General Staff, first under General Douglas MacArthur* and then General Malin Craig. When war clouds darkened over Europe, he transferred back to the infantry. After attending the Infantry School at Fort Benning, Colonel Eichelberger assumed command of the 30th Infantry at the Presidio of San Francisco.

In October 1940 Eichelberger was promoted to brigadier general and soon afterwards was named superintendent of the Military Academy, where his reforms brought greater realism to training—and greater success to the football team. He successfully fought to preserve the four-year course of instruction in the face of demands to accelerate the program to meet wartime needs.

Soon after the Japanese attacked Pearl Harbor, Eichelberger was given command of the 77th Division, which was being organized at Fort Jackson, South Carolina. The smart performance of his troops in a demonstration staged for the benefit of Sir Winston Churchill helped to persuade Britain's wartime leader of the ability of the United States to raise an army capable of pulling its weight in Europe. In June Eichelberger was given command of I Corps, which was being trained in amphibious warfare; by late August 1942 he and part of his staff reached Australia, where MacArthur was organizing his counteroffensive against the Japanese in New Guinea.

Ordered "to take Buna, or not come back alive," Eichelberger assumed command of the American forces that were bogged down in the New Guinea jungle, and by January 1943 he had won the first Allied victory over the enemy in the Pacific. In April 1944 Eichelberger commanded RECKLESS Task Force in the seizure of Hollandia; two months later he was sent to straighten out the nasty situation on the island of Biak, where another American offensive was stalled. His success in these operations contributed to his selection as commander of the newly formed Eighth Army, and in the Philippines the "Amphibious Eighth" planned and executed fifty-two landing operations. While the Sixth Army bore the brunt of the early fighting on Leyte and the conquest of Luzon, elements from the Eighth Army did participate in the dash for Manila in February 1945. After the war Eichelberger's Eighth army was charged with the military occupation of Japan.

Eichelberger spent three years in Japan supervising the demobilization of the Japanese Army, the processing of some 6 million repatriots, the destruction of military supplies and equipment, the trial of Japanese war criminals, and the execution of MacArthur's policies in maintaining order and reshaping Japanese society. He retired from the Army on December 31, 1948, to write his recollections of the war, *Our Jungle Road to Tokyo*. In 1950 he was awarded his fourth star. General Eichelberger spent most of his retirement years in Asheville, where Miss Em felt most at home.

Eichelberger's first triumph, in his own estimation at least, was his greatest. At Buna, he first demonstrated his skill as a combat leader. Before his arrival, the American forces had become bogged down in the swamps and were falling victim to the mosquitoes and the Japanese. His arrival, according to his Australian superior, "was a very pure breath of fresh air." He quickly reorganized his forces, improved supplies, and provided dynamic leadership that infused his troops with new life. For many years Buna served as a case study of the modern corps commander in the leadership course at the U.S. Army Command and General Staff College, Fort Leavenworth.

At Hollandia, where MacArthur's strategy achieved a tactical surprise, Eichelberger's speedy construction of bases and airfields necessary to support forthcoming operations was regarded as "a logistical miracle," and at Biak he put life into a sagging offensive to capture a vital site for heavy bomber fields.

Eichelberger's most spectacular achievement was the part played by his new Eighth Army in the liberation of the Philippines. MacArthur considered the Visayan operations "a model of what a light but aggressive command can accomplish in rapid exploitation," and General George Catlett Marshall wrote of the "lightening speed" of the amphibious thrusts at Panay, Cebu, and Mindanao.

Although his Eighth Army seldom got the recognition Eichelberger craved, it was slated for a leading role in the projected invasion of Japan, and MacArthur's appreciation is a matter of record. "No army of this war," he proclaimed, "has achieved greater glory and distinction."

BIBLIOGRAPHY

Eichelberger, Robert L. *Our Jungle Road to Tokyo*. New York: Viking Press, 1950.
Fleming, Thomas J. *West Point: The Men and Times of the United States Military Academy*. New York: William Morrow and Company, 1969.
James, D. Clayton. *The Years of MacArthur*. 2 vols. Boston: Houghton Mifflin Company, 1975.
Luvaas, Jay, ed. *Dear Miss Em: General Eichelberger's War in the Pacific, 1942–1945*. Westport, Conn.: Greenwood Press, 1972.
Milner, Samuel. *Victory in Papua*. Washington, D.C.: Office of the Chief of Military History, 1957.
Smith, Robert Ross. *The Approach to the Philippines*. Washington, D.C.: Office of the Chief of Military History, 1953.
———. *Triumph in the Philippines*. Washington, D.C.: Office of the Chief of Military History, 1963.

JAY LUVAAS

EISENHOWER, Dwight David (b. Denison, Tex., October 14, 1890; d. Washington, D.C., March 28, 1969), general of the Army; thirty-fourth president of the United States.

"Ike" Eisenhower was descended from German immigrants ("Pennsylvania Dutch") who had moved west after the Civil War. When he was one year old, his father, a semiskilled worker, moved the family to Abilene, Kansas, where Ike grew up. Although the family lived on the "wrong side of the tracks," his mother Ada, a strong-willed, intelligent woman, filled Ike and his five brothers with ambition, often saying that America was full of opportunity for those who would seize it.

Ike seized it. He passed a competitive examination that gained him admittance to West Point in 1911; he graduated in 1915 with a good, if not outstanding, record. The next year he courted and won the hand of Mamie Dowd; they remained happily married for fifty-three years. Unfortunately for Eisenhower's career, however, he did not get to France to command men in combat in World War I, which had a depressing effect on both his promotion rate and his ego. He spent the interwar years on various staff assignments, especially in Washington, or attending the postgraduate schools of the Army, where he always stood first in his class. On the eve of World War II he was fifty years old, still a lieutenant colonel, unknown to the public. But Douglas MacArthur* thought him the best officer in the army, and General John Joseph Pershing* had recommended him to Chief of Staff George Catlett Marshall.*

Four days after Pearl Harbor, Marshall called Eisenhower to Washington, to serve as his chief planner in the War Plans Division (later the Operations Division). There Ike, working under Marshall's guidance, sketched out the strategy the United States would follow in World War II, basically a holding, defensive action in the Pacific, with an all-out offensive in Europe, capped by an invasion of Nazi-occupied France and a drive on into Germany. Marshall then selected Ike as the ideal officer to execute the plan. In May 1942 Ike went to England to take command of the American Army in the European Theater of Operations.

The Eisenhower-Marshall strategy of an immediate invasion of France, however, was vetoed by the British, who persuaded President Franklin D. Roosevelt of the wisdom of an Allied invasion of French North Africa instead. Eisenhower, already on the spot, was given the command. In November 1942 he launched the first Allied offensive as Anglo-American forces under his command captured Algiers, Casablanca, and Oran. By May 1943, following a temporary setback at Kasserine Pass, Eisenhower's forces had destroyed all Axis resistance in North Africa. In July Ike commanded the invasion of Sicily, and in September his forces hit the beaches of Salerno, on the Italian mainland. Although they did not reach Rome before winter, Ike had managed to drive the Axis from the Mediterranean. In the process he had welded together a team of British and American officers, unequaled in the annals of warfare for its cooperation.

In January 1944 Eisenhower left the Mediterranean to go to London, where he took command of Operation OVERLORD, the long-postponed invasion of France. His response to that challenge, especially the tough decision he had to make on June 5 about whether or not weather conditions would permit the invasion, is one of the most famous stories of the war. A period of stagnation followed the success of OVERLORD, as the Germans pinned down Ike's men in Normandy, but on August 1 the Americans broke through and General George Smith Patton, Jr.'s* Third Army began the process of running the Germans out of France. By October France had been liberated, but the war was not over, according to Ike's senior British officer on the Continent, Field Marshall Bernard L. Montgomery, because of Ike's cautious strategy. Instead of advancing into Germany on a broad front, Monty advocated a single narrow thrust along the North German Plain on into Berlin. Ike refused, on military as well as political grounds, and insisted on advancing with all armies abreast. After hurling back the German last-ditch counterattack of December 1944 (Battle of the Bulge), Eisenhower's forces drove into Germany, crossed the Rhine in March 1945, and by early May brought all resistance to an end. Eisenhower emerged from the war as one of the great generals of modern times and one of the two or three most popular Americans of his age.

His popularity was so great that he was inevitably a candidate for the presidency. But in 1948, after a short hitch as chief of staff, he retired from the Army, turned down offers from both parties for the nomination, and instead took up duties as president of Columbia University. In 1950 he returned to active duty when President Harry S.Truman made him the first commander of the National Atlantic Treaty Organization (NATO) forces, which were just being formed. In 1952 the Republicans convinced him that it was his duty to run for the presidency, which he did with great success, winning a decisive victory in November, the first for a Republican since 1928.

As President, Eisenhower's emphasis was on peace and a balanced budget. He had been elected on a violent anti-Communist platform that denounced Truman's policy of containment and called instead for the liberation of Communist-enslaved countries. But that was rhetoric; in practice, Ike's policy was also containment, which was shown immediately in Korea, where he negotiated a cease-fire and armistice with the Chinese without liberating North Korea, much less China. The next year, 1954, Eisenhower spurned numerous opportunities to enter the war in Vietnam on the French side. And in 1956, when the Hungarian revolt offered him a chance to drive the Russians from at least one Central European satellite, he stayed out. Similarly, he turned down opportunities to get involved in a shooting war with China over the islands of Quemoy and Matsu.

Ike insisted on peace because he believed that war, or an all-out arms race, would bankrupt the United States. A fiscal conservative, he was the last president to have a balanced budget (inflation averaged one and one quarter percent per year during his eight years in power), brought about by extensive cuts he made in the Department of Defense. He cut the Army, Navy, and Air Force, and refused to spend money on missile development or the building of nuclear weapons at anything like the rate demanded by the Pentagon and by hawkish Democratic senators, led by John Kennedy and Lyndon Johnson. Instead, Ike introduced the "New Look," which relied on the nuclear bomb to deter the Russians from any aggressive adventures. Reporters called the policy "More bang for a buck," while three Army chiefs of staff denounced it as an "all-or-nothing" posture and resigned in protest against Ike's cuts in the Army budget. Eisenhower continued to hold down the expenditures, based on his knowledge—gained from the CIA's U–2 flights—that the United States was comfortably ahead of the Russians in military affairs.

In November 1956 Eisenhower was reelected in a landslide. In his second term he continued to pursue peace and a balanced budget. He turned his back on the civil rights revolution, which was just getting underway, although he did set a crucial precedent in 1957, when he sent U.S. Army paratroopers to Little Rock, Arkansas, and federalized the Arkansas National Guard to enforce a desegregation court order. In general, however, his was never a reform administration. What was important about his eight years in power was that the Republicans accepted the New Deal reforms, such as social security. His best known innovation was the interstate highway system.

Ike responded to Fidel Castro's coming to power in Cuba with equanimity, saw no reason to panic when the Russians tried to force the West out of Berlin, and shrugged off Russian threats after Francis Gary Powers' U–2 was shot down deep inside the Soviet Union in 1960. This opened him to charges of having neglected the nation's defenses. In the 1960 presidential campaign, John Kennedy made a major issue out of the so-called missile gap and bomber gap, and defeated Richard Nixon in a tightly contested race. In his farewell address, Ike warned the nation about the influence, sought or unsought, of the military-industrial complex. He retired to his farm in Gettysburg, Pennsylvania, where he wrote and enjoyed the role of elder statesman.

Although never a battlefield commander, Ike was nevertheless a great general, perhaps the best of his century. His breadth of view and strategic vision were unmatched. He had, as MacArthur once said and Churchill repeated, the gift of being able to see the whole problem. He was especially good at getting the best out of his subordinates, be they staff officers or field commanders. And he had the ability to make a decision and make it stick.

Eisenhower was never a war president. Indeed, his proudest boast was that for eight years he kept the peace; his next boast was that he balanced the budget. His critics called him a do-nothing president, but by the end of the 1960s many of those critics would like to have seen Ike back in office.

BIBLIOGRAPHY

Ambrose, Stephen E. *The Supreme Commander: The War Years of Dwight D. Eisenhower.* New York: Doubleday, 1970.

Chandler, Aldred D., Jr., and Stephen E. Ambrose, eds. *The Papers of Dwight David Eisenhower: The War Years.* 5 vols. Baltimore: Johns Hopkins University Press, 1970.

Eisenhower, Dwight D. *Crusade in Europe.* New York: Doubleday, 1948.

———. *The White House Years.* 2 vols. New York: Doubleday, 1963 and 1965.

Parmet, Herbert S. *Eisenhower and the American Crusades.* New York: Macmillan Company, 1972.

Pogue, Forrest C. *The Supreme Command.* In *United States Army in World War II.* Edited by Kent Roberts Greenfield. Washington, D.C.: U.S. Department of the Army, 1954.

STEPHEN E. AMBROSE

ELLIS, Earl (b. Iuka, Kan., December 19, 1880; d. Koror, Palau Islands, Western Caroline Island Group in the Central Pacific, May 12, 1923), Marine Corps officer. Ellis was one of the Marine Corps' early articulators of amphibious doctrine.

Earl "Pete" Ellis was one of eight children of Augustus W. and Katherine E. Ellis. His maternal grandfather, Andrew Axline, a Presbyterian minister, led a group of parishioners, including Ellis' parents, from Iowa to "dry" Kansas in 1877. These pioneers founded the town of Iuka (named after a Civil War battle) in Pratt County, "where they could raise their children free from the influence of liquor." Augustus Ellis joined his father, John, in the family real estate business in the city of Pratt, not far from Iuka. Young Earl Ellis attended the Pratt public schools and graduated from the local high school in 1900. With his parents' consent, Earl Ellis enlisted in the Marine Corps that September in Chicago.

The motivation underlying Ellis' decision to join the Corps remains a matter of speculation. Youthful rebellion against the narrow strictures of his upbringing may have been a reason for his enlistment. Moreover, the romantic appeal of the sea, faraway places, and patriotism probably all played their part.

In any event, Ellis did very well as a Marine enlisted man. Promoted rapidly, he became a corporal in February 1901, a scant five months after his enlistment. The Marine Corps further recognized the young corporal's ability later in the year when it commissioned Ellis as a second lieutenant on December 21, 1901.

Ellis' early assignments conformed to the usual pattern for a career Marine officer of that period. He completed his officer training at the Boston Navy Yard in 1902, and then joined the 1st Marine Brigade in the Philippines. In 1903 Lieutenant Ellis became one of the officers of the Marine guard serving in the battleship *Kentucky*, flagship of the Asiatic Fleet. He received his promotion to first lieutenant in 1904.

Beginning with a second tour in the Philippines in 1908, Ellis became identified with the Marine Corps Advance Base Force, which was the forerunner of the modern Fleet Marine Force. In the event of war, the Navy's General Board had assigned to the Marine Corps the task of seizing and defending advanced bases in support of the fleet. In 1908 the emphasis was on defense of such a base, and the only existing Marine Advance Base Force was the Marine brigade in the Philippines. Captain Ellis, promoted to that rank in December 1908, served as the Advance Base officer and was responsible for the defenses of Grande Island in Subic Bay. Despite occasional eccentric behavior and heavy drinking, Ellis impressed his immediate superiors in the Philippines, Major John Archer Lejeune* and Lieutenant Colonel Joseph Henry Pendleton, both of whom praised the young captain for his ability and devotion to duty.

Returning from the Philippines in 1911 with a reputation for brilliance, Ellis attended the Naval War College at Newport, Rhode Island. After completing the course, he remained at the Naval War College as a member of the permanent staff until September 1913. While at the college, Ellis wrote a seminal study on advance base theory.

After leaving the War College, Ellis served as the intelligence officer of the Advance Base Brigade which carried out the first major advance base maneuver in conjunction with the Atlantic Fleet. Ellis made a reconnaissance of the island of Culebra, near Puerto Rico, where the brigade landed in January 1914 and set up extensive defenses.

With the successful completion of the exercise, Ellis, at the request of the Navy, was sent to Guam, where he supervised the establishment of the permanent defenses on that island. While on Guam, Ellis suffered the first of his physical and emotional collapses which were to reoccur periodically throughout the remainder of his career. After being hospitalized, Ellis returned from Guam in December 1915, in apparent good health and still enjoying the confidence of senior Marine officers.

From early 1916 until mid–1917 Ellis remained at Headquarters, Marine Corps in Washington as the personal aide to the commandant, Major General George Barnett, who, as a colonel, had commanded the Advance Base Brigade on Culebra. Ellis and two other junior officers made up the nucleus of the Headquarters planning staff under the direction of the assistant to the commandant, Colonel Lejeune. This staff was largely responsible for the development of plans for the expansion of the Marine Corps which occurred during this period in response to the growing possibility of American involvement in World War I. The pressures on the small staff increased even more after the American entry into the war in April 1917. Overwork, an excess of alcohol, and nervous exhaustion all took their toll on Ellis, who had been promoted to major. During this period, he suffered two relapses, one in 1916 and a more serious breakdown in 1917. Upon releasing Ellis from the hospital after the last collapse, his doctor blamed the sick officer's condition partially on the close confinement of office work and recommended that he be reassigned to more active duty.

Obeying his new orders, Ellis made a liaison visit to France to study Allied training procedures and then returned to Washington in early 1918. In May 1918, at his request, he returned to France, becoming the adjutant of the 4th Marine Brigade, which formed part of the U.S. 2d Division under General Lejeune's command. Serving with distinction, Ellis was credited with developing a plan that resulted in driving the German lines back some thirty kilometers in October 1918, during the Battle of Blanc Mont Ridge. After the Armistice, the Marine Brigade moved into Germany and finally returned to the United States in August 1919.

Upon his return, Ellis continued his unorthodox career. Almost immediately, he combined a leave home to Pratt with a secret mission to Mexico, where he visited the oilfields in Tampico. Coming back to Washington, he suffered another emotional breakdown. Following a three-month sick leave, Ellis, in April 1920, became the intelligence officer of the 2d Marine Brigade stationed in the Dominican Republic. In December 1920 General Lejeune decided to assign Ellis to the newly created Operations and Training Section at Headquarters, Marine Corps. Prompted by renewed attention to the potential threat of war with Japan in the Pacific, the Marine Corps commandant ordered Ellis to revise Marine Corps war plans. Working day and night, Ellis developed the important Operation PLAN 712, entitled "Advanced Base Operations in Micronesia," which foreshadowed the Marine campaign in the Central Pacific during World War II. During the writing of the plan, he suffered several relapses and began checking himself into the hospital every morning. Nevertheless, he completed his work by the end of May 1921. General Lejeune approved the plan in July.

Following the completion of the Micronesia Plan, Ellis' career took a most bizarre turn. He convinced Marine and naval authorities to send him on a sensitive intelligence mission to determine the extent of Japanese fortifications, if any, in the mandated islands that Japan had recently acquired from a defeated Germany. Traveling as a tool manufacturing representative, Ellis, recently promoted to lieutenant colonel, obtained a visa from the Japanese consul general in Sydney, Australia. Unable to find a direct steamer to the Carolines, Ellis went via the Philippines to Yokohama, Japan, in hopes of finding passage to the Pacific Islands. While in Japan, Ellis collapsed from nephritis, a kidney disease, and from alcohol poisoning. Confined to the U.S. Naval Hospital at Yokohama, Ellis escaped from the hospital on the night of October 6, 1922, when he learned that the American authorities in Japan planned to send him home. The American officials were not to learn about Ellis' whereabouts until the Japanese informed them that Ellis had died on the island of Koror in May 1923.

The circumstances surrounding Ellis' death caused much speculation that the Japanese may have killed him. These suspicions were strengthened when a U.S. sailor, Chief Pharmacist Lawrence Zembsh, who was sent to the Carolines to pick up Ellis' ashes, returned in a catatonic state. Zembsh continued to suffer from amnesia until his death in September 1923, during the earthquake that destroyed the U.S. Naval Hospital in Yokohama. Nevertheless, the evidence, including interviews conducted with the inhabitants of Koror following World War II, would indicate that Ellis died a natural death, although the Japanese were suspicious of him and had him watched and followed. General Lejeune's assessment in a letter to Ellis' brother Ralph was probably correct: "I am personally of the opinion that Earl's death was due to disease, which probably was aggravated by intemperance. Of course, there are rumors, but there is no evidence that these rumors are true."

Ellis made important contributions to the development of American war planning for the Pacific and the articulation of amphibious doctrine. His writings on the Advance Base Force reflected the evolutionary change in Marine Corps and naval thought from an emphasis on the defense of the advanced base to the seizure of such a base in an amphibious assault.

In his 1913 study of the advanced base, Ellis provided a synthesis of existing advance base doctrine developed by the Navy's General Board, the Naval War College, and the Marine Corps Advance Base School, which had been founded in 1910. He focused on the need of the Marine Corps to secure bases in time of war in support of the fleet and to deny the same to the enemy as well as the location and defense of such bases. Although Ellis stressed the defensive aspect of the advance base mission, he implied that it could also be offensive. He observed that "In a war with Japan, the U.S. would assume the strategic offensive. The U.S. Navy must proceed to the Far East and gain command of the sea."

Although writing on other aspects of advance base work, it was not until his Micronesia Plan in 1921 that Ellis addressed the full ramifications of seizing advanced bases defended by a determined enemy. He predicted that the Japanese would probably initiate the war and that an American counteroffensive would require the capture of the Japanese-controlled islands in the Central Pacific. He described at considerable length the geography and physical characteristics of Micronesia and then detailed the organization, tactics, air, and naval gunfire that would be required to take these islands. Ellis made a distinction between the assault forces with its infantry and field artillery and what he called the Base Defense Force of heavy artillery, antiaircraft guns, and technical troops which would come in later and hold the base.

Ellis was in the forefront of those Marine planners during the 1920s and 1930s who were responsible for making the terms "Marines" and "amphibious assault" synonymous.

BIBLIOGRAPHY

Heinl, Robert D., Jr. *Soldiers of the Sea: The U.S. Marine Corps, 1775–1962.* Annapolis, Md.: Naval Institute Press, 1962.

Hough, Frank O., et al. *Pearl Harbor to Guadalcanal.* Washington, D.C.: U.S. Government Printing Office, 1958.

Isely, Jeter A., and Philip A. Crowl. *The U.S. Marines and Amphibious War.* Princeton, N.J.: Princeton University Press, 1951.

Millet, Allan R. *Semper Fidelis: The History of the U.S. Marine Corps.* New York: Free Press, 1980.

Reber, John J. "Pete Ellis: Amphibious Warfare Prophet." U.S. Naval Institute *Proceedings* 103 (November 1977): 53–64.

JACK SHULIMSON

FARRAGUT, David Glasgow (b. Campbell's Station, near Knoxville, Tenn., July 5, 1801; d. Portsmouth, N.H., August 14, 1870), naval officer. Farragut was the most successful officer of the Union Navy during the Civil War (1861–1865).

Originally named James Glasgow Farragut, the U.S. Navy's future first admiral became the ward of Master Commandant David Porter in 1808 after the lad's mother died of yellow fever. Two years later the boy accepted an appointment as a midshipman. Out of devotion to his benefactor, he changed his name from James to David. Porter assumed command of the 32-gun frigate *Essex*, and young Farragut learned the routine of a man-of-war under his tutelage. During the War of 1812, *Essex* successfully operated against British merchantmen in the Atlantic and preyed on English whalers in the Pacific. Porter showed his confidence in Farragut by giving him command of a prize. Porter's intrepidity and seamanship ever served as an inspiration to Farragut.

After the war with England, Farragut had a variety of assignments. In 1815 he was sent to the 74-gun ship-of-the-line *Independence*, flagship of a squadron formed under Commodore William Bainbridge to defend American rights against pirates in the Mediterranean. He later served in Porter's "mosquito fleet" fighting piracy in the West Indies. There he fell ill with yellow fever which badly impaired his health. In 1823 the young officer married Susan C. Marchant of Norfolk, Virginia. In ill-health, she became an invalid for life. In 1825 Farragut got his promotion to lieutenant. After a cruise to Europe and duties at Norfolk, in 1828 he reported to the 18-gun sloop-of-war *Vandalia*, being fitted out for service along the coast of South America. A year later serious trouble with his eyes compelled him to return home; he was inactive until 1832. In the spring of 1833, once more in *Vandalia*, Farragut sailed for South America.

After his return, almost four years ashore elapsed before Farragut embarked in the 38-gun frigate *Constellation* at Pensacola, Florida. Next, he was selected to command the 20-gun sloop *Erie* to the coast of Mexico. This mission enabled him to observe operations of French warships against Mexico. His reports to Washington concluded that properly used men-of-war could be extremely effective against shore fortifications. In 1839 Farragut returned to Norfolk and remained there until his wife died in 1840. He welcomed orders in 1841 assigning him to the *Delaware*, and while that 86-gun ship-of-the-line was being refitted for service on the Brazil Station, was promoted to commander (September 1841). On the Brazil Station, Farragut was placed in command of the 16-gun sloop *Decatur* and brought her back to Norfolk in 1843. That December he married and remained devoted to another Norfolk girl, Virginia Loyall. In 1845 he became second-in-command of the Norfolk Navy Yard. Much to his disappointment, Farragut saw no important action in the Mexican War (1846–1848).

During the early 1850s, Farragut filled administrative assignments in Washington and Norfolk. In 1854 he helped establish and then commanded the Mare Island Navy Yard near San Francisco, California. Farragut received his captain's commission in September 1855. After returning east, he took command of the new screw sloop-of-war *Brooklyn* in January 1859. In *Brooklyn*, Farragut became familiar with the type of vessels that would be the capital ships of the Union Navy during the Civil War.

Following the Confederate attack on Fort Sumter, the state of Virginia seceded, forcing Farragut to choose between his nation and his adopted state. Without hesitation, he elected to remain loyal to the Old Flag that he had served for half a century. Farragut sailed from Norfolk to New York and requested active duty in defense of the Union. He remained involuntarily idle for most of the first year of the Civil War.

In the autumn of 1861, President Abraham Lincoln and his advisors began planning a seaborne attack on New Orleans to match a drive down the Mississippi River by Union forces. Farragut was selected to lead the thrust from the sea. He had extraordinary successes against the forts below New Orleans (April 1862) and the defenses of Mobile, Alabama (August 1864). In addition, forces under his command had operated against Vicksburg, Mississippi (1862–1863). While he was near Vicksburg, Congress created the rank of rear admiral, and Farragut was the senior of the four officers who got the new title (July 1862). He was given the newly created rank of vice admiral (December 1864) and was further elevated to admiral in July 1866.

The admiral was placed in command of the European Squadron in 1867. With his flag in the five thousand-ton screw frigate *Franklin*, Farragut began a triumphal cruise in the waters of the Old World. Europe's royalty welcomed and entertained him. He returned home in November 1868. The admiral died in Portsmouth Navy Yard on August 14, 1870.

In late 1861 Farragut was chosen to lead the attack on New Orleans. He sailed for the Gulf of Mexico in February 1862. After reaching Ship Island, Mississippi, he labored for almost two months getting his deep-draft warships in position to attack the downriver forts that protected the Crescent City. On April 18, a flotilla of mortar schooners opened fire on the Southern works and kept up the barrage for six days. When this cannonade failed to make the Confederates surrender, Farragut demonstrated his decisiveness, ordering his steamers to dash upstream by the Rebel guns. On April 24 his warships ran the gauntlet past the batteries and found New Orleans helpless. The city surrendered on April 25, and the forts struck their colors on April 28. The capture of New Orleans meant that the Confederacy had lost its largest city—the home of many banks, industries, and shipbuilding facilities.

Subsequently, Farragut pushed up the Mississippi to meet the gunboats of the Western Flotilla. Farragut twice ascended the river from New Orleans to Vicksburg. On his second run, he actually ran past the Vicksburg batteries and joined the Western Flotilla, but his actions contributed no lasting benefit to the Union cause. The unexpected foray of the Confederate ironclad *Arkansas* forced Farragut to retire below Vicksburg, leaving a few gunboats to guard Baton Rouge. After responding to a Confederate strike on Baton Rouge, Farragut returned to blockade duty in the Gulf.

In the autumn, Farragut went back up the Mississippi to help the Army wrest the last stretch of the river—from above Vicksburg to below Port Hudson—from Confederate hands. Meanwhile, Major General Ulysses Simpson Grant* and Rear Admiral David Dixon Porter (Farragut's foster brother) were laboring to take Vicksburg. Farragut decided to run past Port Hudson with or without Army support. On the night of March 14, 1863, Farragut led a flotilla of seven ships upriver. Each of his heavier ships was lashed to the inboard or fort side of a gunboat. Thus, while the gunboat protected the smaller warship from the Southern guns, her consort's masked machinery was available to provide additional propulsion. The *Albatross* was paired with the *Hartford*, Farragut's flagship, which led the Union advance. Despite a fearful cannonade and a hairbreath escape from grounding, these two ships fought their way upstream; but, for various reasons, none of the others were able to follow. Nevertheless, the two successful Union ships blockaded the mouth of the Red River and cut the communications line which was feeding Vicksburg and Port Hudson, as well as the army of Robert Edward Lee* in the East. In May vessels of David Dixon

Porter's squadron moved south of Vicksburg, and Farragut returned to New Orleans. Port Hudson surrendered in July.

Ordered north for a rest, Farragut reached New York in August 1863, devoting the remainder of the year to regaining his strength. *Hartford* then departed for the Gulf and anchored in Pensacola Harbor in January 1864. The admiral devoted ensuing months to overseeing the blockade of his part of the Gulf coast while awaiting troops and ironclads to reduce Forts Morgan and Gaines which guarded the entrance to Mobile Bay.

On August 5 Farragut's squadron of eighteen ships fought its way into Mobile Bay. In this operation, Farragut again tied a gunboat to the port or lee side of each of his heavier wooden ships. The guns of the forts, a large group of submerged torpedoes (or, in modern terms, a minefield) which narrowed the deep-water channel, and the Confederate squadron led by the ironclad ram *Tennessee* awaited the Federal fleet. Southern vessels were under the command of Admiral Franklin Buchanan. Eager to engage the South's most powerful ship, the monitor *Tecumseh* headed straight for *Tennessee*, but struck a torpedo and sank. *Brooklyn*, the Union's leading wooden ship, began backing to clear the torpedoes and thus threw the entire column into confusion. In *Hartford*, Farragut—lashed to the rigging so that he might see the action from above the smoke of battle—boldly directed his ships to steer right through the minefield. "Damn the torpedoes," he was quoted, "full speed ahead." The flagship, followed by the rest of the fleet, raced past *Brooklyn* through the mines; fortunately for Farragut and his ships, no more torpedoes exploded. A wild melee ensued in which several Federal ships rammed the *Tennessee* and forced her to strike her colors. This victory left the Union squadron in control of the waters approaching Mobile and closed the South's last important Gulf port.

The many virtues that were happily blended in Farragut's personality enabled him to become a master of his profession. His excellent grasp of the strategic realities of the Civil War enlightened the planning and execution of his operations on the Gulf and on the Mississippi. His tactical skill and decisiveness enabled him to lead his squadron through the unpredictability of battle to victory against dedicated opponents—especially at Mobile. Farragut's signal accomplishments were over land fortifications, which he considered vulnerable, and his attitudes toward shore forts and batteries had been developing since the time of his observations on the Mexican coast. All of these factors combined to make Farragut the most noteworthy American naval officer between the heroes of 1812 and World War II.

BIBLIOGRAPHY

Anderson, Bern. *By Sea and by River: The Naval History of the Civil War*. New York: Alfred A. Knopf, 1962.
Jones, Virgil C. *The Civil War at Sea*. 3 vols. New York: Holt, Rinehart, and Winston, 1960–1962.
Lewis, Charles A. *David Glasgow Farragut: Admiral in the Making*. Annapolis, Md.: U.S. Naval Institute, 1941.

———. *David Glasgow Farragut: Our First Admiral*. Annapolis, Md.: U.S. Naval Institute, 1943.
Mahan, Alfred Thayer. *Admiral Farragut*. New York: University Society, 1905.
———. *The Gulf and Inland Waters*. New York: Charles Scribner's Sons, 1883.

JAMES L. MOONEY

FLETCHER, Frank Jack (b. Marshalltown, Iowa, April 29, 1885; d. Bethesda, Md., April 25, 1973), naval officer. Fletcher was carrier task force commander in the Battles of the Coral Sea and Midway in World War II.

Appointed from Iowa, Frank Jack Fletcher entered the U.S. Naval Academy in 1902 and graduated in 1906. His first command (1910) was the destroyer *Dale* in the Asiatic Torpedo Flotilla. In 1914 while serving as an aide to his uncle, Rear Admiral Frank Friday Fletcher, he earned the Medal of Honor for gallant service during the occupation of Vera Cruz. As a lieutenant commander, Fletcher saw active service during World War I as captain of the destroyer *Benham*, operating on convoy escort and patrol duty in British and French waters, and received the Navy Cross. Subsequently, he remained with destroyers, then commanded a submarine tender and the susbmarine base at Cavite, Philippine Islands.

In 1929 Fletcher attended the Naval War College, received his promotion to captain (1930), and was posted to the Army War College. These assignments prepared him to become, in 1931, chief of staff of the Asiatic Fleet under Admiral Montgomery M. Taylor. His tour coincided with the Japanese invasion of Manchuria and the fighting in Shanghai. In 1933 Fletcher joined the Navy Department as aide to the secretary of the navy, Claude A. Swanson. After sea duty (1936–1937) as captain of the battleship *New Mexico*, he returned to the Navy Department and later served as assistant chief, Bureau of Navigation. Attaining flag rank in November 1939, Rear Admiral Fletcher proceeded to the Pacific, first as commander of Cruiser Division Three. Then in June 1940 he took over the four heavy cruisers of Cruiser Division Six, the post he held when war broke out on December 7, 1941.

Fletcher's first major assignment was command of Task Force 14 with the aircraft carrier *Saratoga*. His mission was to reinforce the Wake Island garrison. Ordered to reach Wake on December 24, Fletcher was recalled on the morning of December 23 because Wake had fallen to Japanese atack. On December 31, 1941, he received the administrative posts of commander, Cruisers, Scouting Force, Pacific Fleet, and also commander, Cruiser Division Four. In early January 1942 Fletcher formed Task Force 17 around the carrier *Yorktown* and later that month escorted a convoy bound for Samoa. On February 1, 1942, Task Force 17, in concert with forces led by Vice Admiral William Fredrick Halsey, Jr.,* executed air strikes against Japanese bases in the Marshall and Gilbert islands.

In late February 1942 Fletcher took Task Force 17 into the South Pacific and joined Vice Admiral Wilson Brown's Task Force 11 in the Coral Sea. Together on March 10 they launched an air attack on Japanese ships at Lae and Salamaua in New Guinea. After Brown's departure, Fletcher remained on patrol in the Coral Sea area guarding the line of communication between the Hawaiian Islands and Australia. Meanwhile on April 19, he became commander, Cruisers, Pacific Fleet. Coming under his control in May was Task Force 11 (Rear Admiral Aubrey W. Fitch), centered around the carrier *Lexington*. In response to Japanese invasion threats against Port Moresby, New Guinea, and the Solomon Islands, Fletcher led his carrier force in the Battle of the Coral Sea (May 4–8), which forced the Japanese to withdraw while the Americans lost the carrier *Lexington*.

Arriving at the end of May at Pearl Habor, Task Force 17 then sortied to help oppose the Japanese attack on Midway Island. At sea, Fletcher assumed tactical command of the three American carriers, *Yorktown, Enterprise,* and *Hornet*. On June 4, American carrier aircraft secured decisive victory by sinking four Japanese carriers, but Fletcher's flagship *Yorktown* was crippled (and sank on June 7) which compelled him to relinquish command to Rear Admiral Raymond Ames Spruance.* For Fletcher's service at Coral Sea and Midway, he was promoted to vice admiral (to date from June 26, 1942) and received the Distinguished Service Medal. During the initial phase of the Guadalcanal operation, Fletcher acted as commander of the Expeditionary Force and the carrier task forces. His carriers on August 24, 1942, fought the Battle of the Eastern Solomons and helped repulse a Japanese attempt to retake Guadalcanal. Wounded on August 31 when his flagship *Saratoga* was torpedoed, Fletcher returned to the United States.

After a well-deserved rest, Fletcher in November 1942 became commandant of the Thirteenth Naval District and also the Northwestern Sea Frontier. His efforts to return to a sea command were unavailing despite the recommendation of his commander in the Pacific, Admiral Chester William Nimitz.* Relinquishing the naval district post in October 1943, Fletcher assumed command of the North Pacific Area which was responsible for combat operations in Alaskan and Aleutian waters. His North Pacific Force, by means of air strikes and warship raids, tied down significant Japanese forces in the Kurile Islands and northern Japan and prepared for the invasion of Paramushiro in the event the Soviet Union entered the war against Japan. In August and September 1945 Fletcher conducted the occupation of northern Honshu and Hokkaido in the Japanese home islands. That December he joined the Navy's General Board which acted in an advisory capacity to the secretary of the navy, and in May 1946 became its chairman. On May 1, 1947, Fletcher was promoted to admiral and retired from the Navy. He died on April 25, 1973, after a long illness.

Frank Jack Fletcher's importance in U.S. naval history centers around his role as commander of fast carrier task forces which fought their Japanese counterparts in several of the classic carrier actions in 1942. Indeed, of the six actual carrier-versus-carrier duels that took place during the Pacific War, Fletcher led American flattops in three: the battles of the Coral Sea (May 1942), Midway (June 1942), and the Eastern Solomons (August 1942). The Battle of the Coral Sea marked a milestone in naval history because it was the first occasion in which opposing task forces relied solely on carrier-borne aircraft for the decisive attacks instead of closing to within gun and torpedo range of each other.

All three of Fletcher's carrier battles resulted in Allied strategic victories, earned at a time when the Japanese menace in the Pacific was paramount and Allied strength had fallen to its lowest point. This, however, has not spared Fletcher from considerable criticism by some naval historians. They consider his command decisions in the Wake Island relief attempt, at the Battle of the Coral Sea, and during his brief participation in the Guadalcanal Campaign to be distinctly controversial. According to these historians, Fletcher at crucial times was unaggressive or timid, with an obsession for refueling his ships when the situation supposedly did not justify diverting them from the mission at hand. These criticisms largely have not survived detailed examination in light of the latest available documentary sources. Especially held against Fletcher was his lack of aviation experience. This was a common trait, however, among most of the early war carrier task force commanders who obtained their posts by virtue of their status as senior flag officers in the Pacific Fleet.

Fletcher never forfeited the respect and confidence of Admiral Nimitz, who entrusted him with the Pacific Fleet's precious carriers during the crucial early months of the war. Despite his recent introduction to carrier aviation, Fletcher secured important victories under extremely difficult conditions in a new form of naval warfare waged against skilled and determined opponents. It was once said of Admiral Sir John Jellicoe in World War I that he was one person who could have lost the war in an afternoon. The same injunction could be equally applied to Fletcher for the spring and summer of 1942. Indeed, his Japanese counterpart at Midway, Vice Admiral Chuichi Nagumo, just may have doomed Japan's chances for victory in the Pacific War through the destruction of his four carriers by Fletcher and Spruance.

BIBLIOGRAPHY

Dyer, George C. *The Amphibians Came to Conquer: The Story of Admiral Richmond Kelly Turner*. 2 vols. Washington, D.C.: U.S. Government Printing Office, 1971.
Lundstrom, John B. *The First South Pacific Campaign: Pacific Fleet Strategy, December 1941–June 1942*. Annapolis, Md.: Naval Institute Press, 1976.
Morison, Samuel Eliot. *History of United States Naval Operations in World War II*. 15 vols. Boston: Atlantic, Little, Brown and Company, 1947–1962.
Potter, E. B. *Nimitz*. Annapolis, Md.: Naval Institute Press, 1976.
Sweetman, Jack. *The Landing at Vera Cruz: 1914*. Annapolis, Md.: Naval Institute Press, 1968.

JOHN B. LUNDSTROM

FORREST, Nathan Bedford (b. Chapel Hill, Tenn., July 13, 1821; d. Memphis, Tenn., October 29, 1877), Confederate cavalry leader. Forrest is considered the greatest American cavalryman, a natural military genius.

Nathan B. Forrest was the eldest son of a blacksmith who moved his family in 1834 to north Mississippi, then a wild frontier. On his father's premature death, young Forrest was left, at sixteen, as the breadwinner for a large and destitute family. Although almost totally without formal education, Forrest survived and then prospered. By 1861, he was a millionaire; having made his fortune first by trading horses, then as a slave dealer, and finally from cotton plantations. Widely respected around Memphis where he settled, Forrest was known for his integrity, his kind treatment of slaves, and his courage; he once thwarted a three thousand-man lynch mob with a small pen knife. In 1861 Forrest was authorized to raise a regiment of cavalry which he equipped at his own expense.

Moving into Kentucky with an army under Albert Sydney Johnston*, Forrest quickly distinguished himself in several skirmishes. Serving at Fort Donelson when Ulysses Simpson Grant* attacked, Forrest refused to surrender and slipped out of the besieged garrison with his regiment. At Shiloh, Forrest, without orders, moved to the Confederate extreme right where his men, fighting as infantry, helped win the initial Southern success. Later, Forrest blocked a Union pursuit by conducting a brilliant rearguard action as the Confederate Army returned to Corinth.

Forrest was ordered into middle Tennessee by General Braxton Bragg,* and in July 1862, in the type of startling, strategic raid behind enemy lines that became his hallmark, captured the Union garrison at Murfreesboro. Promoted to brigadier general, Forrest continued to bedevil Union communications until September 25, when Bragg, who viewed Forrest as a mere guerrilla, stripped him of his forces and ordered him with only a small escort to go behind enemy lines to recruit and equip a new army. Forrest was successful in raising, mounting, and equipping his forces at Union expense in west Tennessee and in fighting his way through superior enemy forces pursuing him. He rejoined the Army of the Tennessee in January 1863. Soon he was raiding behind enemy lines again, destroying supplies and railroads, defeating detached garrisons, and defeating or eluding every force sent to contain him.

In April 1863 a Union cavalry column of two thousand men under Colonel Abel Streight struck across the Tennessee River into northern Alabama aiming to disrupt Confederate industry and communications in northern Georgia. Moving fifty miles in thirty-six hours, Forrest was quickly on Streight's trail. Although badly outnumbered, he unremittingly pressured Streight's rearguard day and night for three days through mountainous terrain, driving him nearly 140 miles. Carefully husbanding the strength of his own forces, Forrest rotated those attacking to allow his troops to rest. Constantly driven without rest, Streight's command collapsed and surrendered without a fight almost within sight of their prime objective, Rome, Georgia.

At Chickamauga, Forrest, commanding infantry as well as his own forces, performed brilliantly and was partially responsible for the Southern victory. Bragg, however, stripped Forrest of his command once more. Forrest angrily quit the Army only to be personally mollified by Jefferson Davis and given an independent command in northern Mississippi. Allowed more latitude to show his genius, Forrest, now a major general, recruited a new army from behind enemy lines in Tennessee and Kentucky.

Forrest commanded cavalry that never numbered more than four thousand, and he kept the Confederate granary of northern Mississippi free of Union control until the dying days of the war. He repelled four major invasions and three times raided deep into Tennessee and Kentucky, twice reaching the Ohio River. Destroying railroads and supply bases, interrupting river communications, overrunning isolated garrisons, and defeating any force with the temerity to fight him, Forrest quickly became a legend. In the process he inflicted nearly fifty thousand casualties and tied down important Union forces. When they overran Fort Pillow, Tennessee, Forrest's men fought so ferociously that they were accused of massacring the Negro garrison. At Brice's Crossroads, in June 1864, with twenty-nine hundred men and four guns he attacked and nearly annihilated General Samuel D. Sturgis' eighty-two hundred man, twenty-two gun force invading Mississippi. Forrest first drew the Union cavalry away from the infantry, attacked and defeated it, then drove it back on to the weary, hurrying infantry which in turn was defeated. Then pursuing until men and horses literally collapsed in the road, Forrest captured all of Sturgis' guns, wagons, and seventeen hundred men; there were five hundred others wounded or dead and the remnant was mostly disarmed fugitives.

All of Forrest's successes could not prevent major invasions of the South such as that led by William Tecumseh Sherman.* Pleading vainly to be turned loose on Sherman's supply lines, the very thing the Northerners feared most, Forrest was denied his chance largely because of Bragg's interference. Belatedly promoted to lieutenant general, Forrest was never given a good opportunity to fully demonstrate his genius. Blinded by prejudice against cavalry raiders and Forrest's slave-trading, uneducated background, the high Confederate leaders never gave him a major command.

In December 1864 Forrest moved into middle Tennessee to support John Bell Hood's* offensive against well-equipped and overwhelming Union forces under George Henry Thomas.* Forrest arrived in time to cover the retreat of the Army of the Tennessee after the disastrous Battle of Nashville. In his finest moment, Forrest commanded the hard-pressed rearguard of infantry and cavalry and succeeded in getting Hood's starving, ragged, barefoot, freezing, and almost disarmed army safely across the flooded Tennessee River. Unable to prevent large-scale invasions in 1865 and hearing of Appomattox, Forrest surrendered his few remaining forces at Gainesville, Alabama, on May 5, 1865.

The transition from war to peace was difficult for Forrest, whose fortune had been destroyed and who was accused of heinous crimes by the North. Urging his soldiers to be "good citizens as they had been good soldiers," Forrest at first set an example of peaceful acceptance of Northern domination. Later in the heated politics of Reconstruction Tennessee, Forrest became the head and moving spirit of the Ku Klux Klan. Originally created as an answer to the legal terrorism of Governor William Brownlow whose partisans acted under the color of martial law, the Klan quickly and violently spread to other states where it proved an ideal vehicle for the restoration of white rule. Forrest officially dissolved the Klan in January 1869. By then it had served its purpose in Tennessee and was out of his control elsewhere. Forrest never admitted his role in the Klan.

War's end found Forrest broken in health and finances. Efforts to recoup his fortune involved Forrest in an unsuccessful railroad venture that led to bankruptcy and to endless litigation. Typically, Forrest assumed the debts as a personal burden. Before his death, he had paid off most debts and had maintained a generous charity for the families of his ex-soldiers. Successful in reestablishing cotton plantations, Forrest was making another fortune when he died in 1877 of a lingering, wasting disease, first contracted in 1865 and diagnosed as "chronic dysentery."

Completely ignorant of military tactics and untrained in any aspect of war, Forrest devised his own system of warfare. His primary targets were Union lines of communication, which he struck in sudden and forceful strategic raids, foreshadowing the *blitzkrieg* of a later day. Tactically, Forrest's system was based upon seizing and holding the initiative under almost all conditions. Even on the defensive, Forrest's men charged to meet an attack. Asked to describe his method of making war, Forrest said that he generally tried to "get there first with the most men" and that he would trade "fifteen minutes of bulge [initiative] for three days of tactics." Once he had the initiative he held it, never relaxing the pressure as long as it was physically possible to maintain it, even if only a handful of troops were available to him. Forrest's offensive thrusts fell first on the front and then on the flanks and rear of his foes. Once he had beaten his enemies, Forrest pursued them with a brutal relentlessness that was extraordinary in military history. This relentlessness was based upon Forrrest's concept of battle as a means to an end, the destruction of the enemy force, and not an end in itself. "War means fighting and fighting means killing," he said; and he wondered, "What does he fight battles for?" of a superior who failed to pursue a beaten foe. His troops, incredibly mobile cavalry, often fought on foot as infantry in battle. Later in the war, some Union cavalry commanders began to adopt Forrest's successful dragoon tactics. Artillery played a major role in Forrest's system, and he worked hard to master its technicalities. Occasionally used at long range, more commonly, Forrest's guns were double shotted with canister and, moving with the front ranks, were used as assault weapons. Original and brilliant in his use of improvisations, Forrest won many victories because of his fertile imagination. Repeatedly, his commands were able to cross flooded rivers, twice on grapevine bridges, dominated by enemy gunboats while pursued by larger armies. Several Union units surrendered to Forrest without fighting; he tricked them into believing they were outnumbered, a deception aided by Northern propaganda which painted Forrest as a bloodthirsty monster. Richly varied ruses, deceptions, ambushes, and a quietly efficient scouting and intelligence system were key parts of Forrest's tactical method. He made himself the best informed Confederate general about Union strength and intentions in his region.

A superb quartermaster, Forrest recruited, equipped, and largely subsisted his forces behind enemy lines and mostly with captured goods. His meticulous care for men and horses paid rich military dividends, for Forrest could move his forces faster and farther than any other officer on either side. A stern disciplinarian, the big (six foot-two inch) Forrest often enforced discipline with his fists and unhesitatingly shot down his own men who broke under the stress of battle. He carefully guarded their lives from unnecessary loss and quarreled with several superiors over wasting his men. But in combat he could be ruthless in sacrificing them when it was necessary. Always in the thick of fighting, Forrest led by personal example. Wounded four times, he had twenty-nine horses killed under him and personally killed enemy soldiers in hand-to-hand combat during the war. Forrest is considered to be one of the greatest horse soldiers of his—or any—age.

BIBLIOGRAPHY

Henry, Robert Selph. *As They Saw Forrest*. Jackson, Tenn.: McCowat-Mercer Press, 1956.
———. *"First With the Most" Forrest*. New York: Bobbs-Merrill Company, 1944.
Jordan, General Thomas, and J. P. Pryor. *The Campaign of Lieut.-Gen. N.B. Forrest, and of Forrest's Cavalry*. New York: Blelock and Company, 1868; reprint, Dayton, Ohio: Morningside Bookshop, 1977 (original 1867).
Morton, John W. *The Artillery of Nathan Bedord Forrest's Cavalry*. Nashville, Tenn.: Publishing House of the Methodist Episcopal Church, 1909.
Wyeth, John Allen. *That Devil Forrest*. New York: Harper and Brothers, 1959 (original edition, 1899).

WALTER E. PITTMAN

GATES, Horatio (b. Maldon [?], England, April [?] 1728; d. New York City, N.Y., April 10, 1806), Army officer. Gates' major achievement was the victory at Saratoga in October 1777.

Horatio Gates was born to working-class parents in England and seemingly was fordoomed to a life of menial labor. Yet, for some reason he came under the protection of Horace Walpole and, possibly, Thomas Osborne, duke of Leeds. Thus, in 1749, at the age of twenty-one, he entered the officer corps of the British Army. Serving in America until the end of the Seven Years' War, he saw extensive service and was promoted to major in 1762. As the Army reverted to a peacetime footing, the young officer found himself cut off from advancing to a lieutenant colonelcy because of his lower class social origins. Hence, he retired from the Army and in 1773 moved his family (his wife Dorothy and son Robert) to Virginia, where he settled into a comfortable life on a quiet farm named "Travellers Rest."

When war broke out between Britain and America, Gates quickly made known his support of the patriot party. Having long ago evinced Whiggish political views, he was welcomed into rebellion and on June 17, 1775, Congress appointed him adjutant general with the rank of brigadier general in the Continental Army. During the siege of Boston in the winter of 1775–1776, his extensive knowledge of Army organization helped George Washington* bring order and regularity to the raw troops in Massachusetts. Gates' service led Congress on May 16, 1776, to promote him to major general and to appoint him one month later commander of a patriot Army that had invaded Canada in the previous year. Arriving in New York to assume his new position, he found that the Army was no longer "in Canada" but had retreated into Philip Schuyler's Northern Department. Since both generals asserted control over these troops, they agreed that Congress must clarify the command problem—which it did in favor of Schuyler. Gates accepted this situation with little grace but was mollified when Schuyler appointed him commander of upstate New York. Thus, he worked closely with Benedict Arnold* in the summer and fall of 1776 to repel Guy Carleton's thrust from Canada up Lake Champlain towards Fort Ticonderoga. In December he led six hundred Continentals to Washington's assistance, after which he assumed command of Philadelphia. He retained this post for only two months before being ordered by Congress on March 25, 1777, back to Ticonderoga to supersede Schuyler.

The continual bickering between congressional proponents of Gates and Schuyler profited no one except John Burgoyne, who threatened invasion of New York in the spring of 1777. But the quarrel had one more round to go before it ceased. On May 15 Schuyler managed to get Congress to restore him to office, only to have Gates maneuver against him in that body and on August 4 be ordered for the final time to take charge of the Northern army. With the command situation at last clarified, Gates could concentrate upon defeating the enemy; in the battles of Freeman's Farm (September 19) and Bemis Heights (October 7), the American general, ably assisted by Arnold and Daniel Morgan,* fought Burgoyne to a standstill and forced him on October 17 to sign a convention, which provided that his Anglo-German troops would be returned to Europe and not serve again in the war. Although Gates has often been charged with being too hasty in accepting these terms, as well as being dilatory in reporting his victories to Washington, both charges are largely unsubstantiated. Also not proven are arguments by many historians that Gates, as chairman of the Board of War, participated during the winter of 1777–1778 in the so-called Conway Cabal, a supposed scheme by Thomas Conway to replace Washington with Gates as commander in chief.

After a useful tenure on the Board of War, Gates was ordered by Congress on April 15, 1778, to command once more in the Hudson River Valley. His only "accomplishment" during that summer was a ridiculous duel (the second in six months) with James Wilkinson, an ex-aide, in which Wilkinson fired at him three times with no effect. On October 22 Congress sent Gates to Boston to command the troops of the Eastern Department, and in the spring of 1779, after surlily turning down Washington's offer to command an Indian expedition (the one John Sullivan would accept), he was posted in Providence. After the British evacuated Newport in October, he requested from Washington, and was granted, leave to retire to "Travellers Rest."

On June 13, 1780, Congress asked Gates to take control of the Southern army—or what was left of it—after Benjamin Lincoln's surrender of Charleston on May 12. "An Army, without Strength," was the way Gates described his new command on July 3; but he quickly organized a little force at Coxe's Mill, North Carolina, and set out toward the enemy to the south. On the night of August 15, he marched from Rugeley's Mill with his half-starved and bone-tired army toward Camden, only to encounter a British expedition under Charles, Lord Cornwallis, moving toward him. The next day, August 16, the two armies clashed in the Battle of Camden. Gates' poorly disposed militiamen were routed, and his Continentals, commanded by Johann de Kalb, were so decimated that it took the American general three months to reorganize and rebuild at Hillsborough.

When Congress learned of Gates' debacle, the legislators turned upon their erstwhile favorite and voted to allow Washington to appoint Nathanael Greene* in his stead, until a court of inquiry could make a study of Gates' conduct in the South. Not until August 14, 1782, did Congress rescind its earlier resolution and give the general leave to rejoin the army. With his self-respect belatedly restored, he served as Washington's second-in-command at Newburgh in the winter of 1782–1783 and had some role in fomenting officer unrest during the final, unquiet months of the Continental Army's existence. In late March 1783 he left camp for the last time and went home to the bedside of his ailing wife, who died on June 1.

After the war, Gates lived an active life. He served as president of the Virginia State Society of the Cincinnati and supported the movement toward a stronger national constitution. Since his only son had died in 1780, he was without a family and lonely, but in 1786 he married a rich widow named Mary Vallance; four years later, he sold his Virginia farm and settled on Manhattan. In vigorous old age, he emerged as a Jeffersonian in politics and was elected in 1800 to a term in the New York state legislature. But soon his health began to decline; in 1803 he informed his old friend, Benjamin Rush, that he was so "Lean" that he looked like "a Skeleton." Less than three years later, he was dead at the age of seventy-eight.

To assess Gates' importance in American military history, it is necessary to analyze both his relationship with Washington and his qualities as an Army officer. In fact, these two facets of the man's career cannot be separated, for each contributed to, and modified, the other in important ways. A crucial thing to keep in mind about Gates' career is that it was greatly advanced, especially after 1776, by the support of strongly Whiggish congressmen such as Samuel

Adams and James Lovell. These men were for political reasons not inclined to be strongly pro-Washington because they viewed him as being too conservative and militaristic; after 1777 the commander in chief reciprocated their distrust, for he became convinced that his position was endangered by their support of Gates. Therefore, in all likelihood he used the events of the so-called Conway Cabal, including his attacks on Gates, more as a political device to secure his own position than to destroy any real attempt by his critics to have him removed from command of the Army. That he succeeded can be seen in the fact that after 1778 the power of the radical Whigs in Congress was so reduced that the legislature became more supportive of a Regular Army and that Gates' reputation was afterward stained with the unmerited charge of being an enemy of Washington.

Even if his controversy with the commander in chief had not colored men's assessments of Gates' military career, he would be regarded as only a modestly talented man whose greatest martial gift lay in his ability to organize and administer large military forces. As adjutant general at Boston, as commander of the much weakened patriots at Ticonderoga and Crown Point in 1776, as reinvigorator of Schuyler's shaken men on the upper Hudson a year later, and as rebuilder of the shattered American force in the South after Camden, he showed uncommon talents as a restorer of morale and a builder of armies. Against Burgoyne, Gates displayed no flashes of brilliance, but he did show common sense in taking a strongly defensive position on his antagonist's route of march and forcing the British Army to fight on his own terms. He realized that time was on the Americans' side; that Morgan's riflemen could be better used in a static, defensive position; that Burgoyne was an impetuous gambler who "might risque all upon one Throw"; and, finally, that the course of the war to that time confirmed that patriot troops performed better in battle when behind defensive fortifications. All the foregoing, plus Gates' own caution, led him to perform against Burgoyne in such a way as to deserve credit for the American victory.

At Camden, Gates was neither as shrewd nor as lucky as he had been three years earlier. He planned to employ the same strategy against Cornwallis as had worked against Burgoyne: to march his army into a strong, defensive position near the British and force them to attack at disadvantage. However, in attempting this maneuver, he made a series of mistakes that assured his defeat—especially since his latest antagonist refused to follow the script. Marching an underequipped and underfed army too hastily toward the enemy, Gates exhausted his men and left behind in North Carolina a much needed cavalry force that had been weakened at Charleston and was rebuilding. Dividing his forces on the eve of battle by sending a reinforcement of four hundred troops to Thomas Sumter, he set out towards the British with the remainder of his army on a *night march* without adequate cavalry for scouting. Relying too heavily on raw militiamen in the battle itself, he disposed them against regulars and then, remarkably, ordered them to charge into British bayonets—practically a guaranteed formula for disaster. Forced to leave the field of battle while his Continenals under de Kalb were engaged with the enemy, he threw himself open to sarcastic denunciations by his calumniators and did irreparable harm to his reputation.

After Camden, however, Gates' critics would have derided his military talents in any case, for they had eagerly awaited such an opportunity. As Rush declared, "His defeat... gave more pleasure than pain to thousands." Thus, they took advantage of the general's discomfiture to "prove" that he was not responsible for Burgoyne's defeat (the credit was given largely to Arnold), and his reputation was fixed for a century and a half. Yet, the historical record indicates that for all his faults and missteps, Gates still deserves laurels for his administrative talents and his victory at Saratoga.

BIBLIOGRAPHY

Billias, George A. "Horatio Gates: Professional Soldier." In *George Washington's Generals*. Edited by George A. Billias. New York: William Morrow, 1964.
Knollenberg, Bernhard. *Washington and the Revolution, a Reappraisal: Gates, Conway, and the Continental Congress*. New York: Macmillan Company, 1940.
Nelson, Paul David.*General Horatio Gates: A Biography*. Baton Rouge: Louisiana State University Press, 1976.
Patterson, Samuel White. *Horatio Gates: Defender of American Liberties*. New York: Columbia University Press, 1941.
Shipton, Clifford K., ed. *Sibley's Harvard Graduates*. Vol. 12, Boston: Massachusetts Historical Society, 1962.

PAUL D. NELSON

GAVIN, James Maurice (b. New York City, N.Y., March 22, 1907). Army officer, airborne commander, military strategist and tactician.

James Maurice Gavin entered the Army at the age of seventeen in 1924 as a private and retired at the age of fifty-one in 1958 as a lieutenant general. His rise in the Army was meteoric, and his retirement deliberately premature. Along the way he acquired the reputation of being one of the military's finest, boldest, and most independent analytical minds.

Gavin, orphaned at age two and unable to find a challenging job after being raised in the coal mining town of Mount Carmel, Pennsylvania, did not let modest beginnings deter his rise to the top of his chosen profession. From private in April of 1924 he rose to private first class and then corporal before entering the U.S. Military Academy at West Point in July 1925. Upon graduation in 1929, he was commissioned a second lieutenant of Infantry. It would be five years before he made first lieutenant and five more years before he made captain, but the World War II years saw him rapidly advance. He was promoted to major in October 1941, lieutenant colonel in February 1942, and colonel in September 1942. He received his brigadier general's star in September 1943 and in October 1944 made major general. In March 1955 he was promoted to lieutenant general, the rank with which he retired in 1958.

In his first dozen years of commissioned service, Gavin served in the usual variety of posts for a young infantry officer at home and abroad. After three months duty as a flying student at Brooks Field, Texas, he had tours successively with the 25th Infantry at Camp Harry S. Jones, Arizona; the Infantry School at Fort Benning, Georgia; the 38th and 29th Infantries at Fort Sill, Oklahoma; the 57th Infantry (Philippine Scouts) at Fort William McKinley, Philippine Islands; and the 7th Infantry at Vancouver Barracks, Washington. In August 1940 he became an instructor in the Department of Tactics at the U.S. Military Academy.

After one year at the Academy, Gavin made the decision that would set him on the road to fame—he became a paratrooper. The Army was experimenting with a Parachute School at Fort Benning, and Gavin saw the possibilities of airborne warfare. In August 1941 he obtained a transfer to the Provisional Parachute Group at Benning and, upon graduation from the training school, was assigned to the 503d Parachute Battalion. In December he was named plans and training officer of the group. From February to April 1942 he attended the Command and General Staff School at Fort Leavenworth, and, upon graduation, returned to duty with airborne troops at Fort Bragg, North Carolina. In July 1942 he assumed command of the 505th Parachute Infantry Regiment which in January 1943 was assigned to the 82d Airborne Division. Gavin and the 82d would be together for almost the entire remainder of World War II.

Gavin would go with the 82d from Sicily to Salerno to Normandy to Nijemegen, Holland, to the Ardennes to the Elbe and, finally to Berlin. Gavin led the 505th Parachute Combat Team in a night drop into Sicily on July 9, 1943, that spearheaded that invasion. He commanded the regiment in a parachute landing on Salerno Bay, Italy, on September 14 to reinforce the American beachhead. In October Gavin became assistant division commander of the 82d. From November 1943 until February 1944 he served as airborne advisor to the supreme commander in London before returning to the division to prepare for the Normandy invasion. In that invasion on the night of June 5–6, 1944, he commanded the parachute assault section of the division. Upon the return of the 82d to England, Gavin on August 15 assumed command of the division. He commanded the division in the airborne operations in the vicinity of Nijmegen, Holland, in September 1944, as part of the ill-fated MARKET-GARDEN, a combined airborne and ground offensive that was designed to get across the Rhine and clear the way to victory over Germany by the end of 1944. The 82d then fought alongside regular infantry troops during the Battle of the Bulge, the German offensive in the Ardennes in December. The division next fought through central Germany until the surrender of the German Army in May 1945. In July the 82d took up station in Berlin, and Gavin assumed the additional duty of American representative on the City Kommandantura. In December he and the division returned to Fort Bragg, North Carolina.

In March 1948 Gavin left his airborne command for tours of duty in the United States and abroad in various high-level command and staff positions. He was chief of staff of the Fifth Army at Chicago until April 1949, when he became the Army member of the Weapons Systems Evaluation Group in the Office of the Secretary of Defense in Washington, D.C. In June 1951 he became chief of staff of allied forces in Southern Europe and, in December 1952 commanding general of the U.S. VII Corps in Germany. In March 1953 he returned to Washington, D.C., to serve as G–3, Department of the Army. In March 1955 he became deputy chief of staff for plans and research and in October chief of research and development. While serving in Washington, Gavin found himself directly opposed to the "new look" in defense policy whereby the administration of President Dwight David Eisenhower* stressed strategic nuclear retaliatory power at the expense of conventional weapons. Rather than provide lip-service to a policy with which he disagreed, Gavin retired in 1958 in order to tell "the American people directly what I thought was wrong with the U.S. Defense picture." A few months later Gavin published *War and Peace in the Space Age*. In the book, he outlined his ideas on the need of a flexible response to world crises, a response that should include the means to fight a limited war.

Gavin proved to be a prolific writer on military affairs. In 1947 he had published *Airborne Warfare*, which for some time was a standard text for paratroopers. Among his other books are *Crisis Now*, a 1968 study of the Vietnam problem, and *On to Berlin*, a 1978 account of his experiences with airborne troops during World War II.

In addition to writing and speaking on matters of national security, Gavin interrupted his highly successful business career to serve as ambassador to France for eighteen months during the administration of President John F. Kennedy. He left his position as chairman of the board of Arthur D. Little, Inc., in 1977, to become a consultant to that firm. He currently resides in Cambridge, Massachusetts.

As with the 82d itself, Gavin won combat decorations with good cause for his airborne leadership both in theory and practice. He was a pioneer in developing airborne operations, especially in the use of small unit attack groups, and remained the airborne's champion in the larger strategic arena. In combat, he led brilliantly and courageously, receiving the Distinguished Service Cross for his actions under fire in Sicily and a Bronze Oak Leaf Cluster to the Distinguished Service Cross for his actions in Normandy. Even though MARKET-GARDEN failed, Gavin's unit did well, despite the fact that their operations, as all others, did not go as planned. Indeed, after the 82d's efforts at Nijmegen, Lieutenant General Miles C. Dempsey, the commander of the British Second Army ground forces in the operation, told Gavin: "I'm proud to meet the commanding general of the greatest division in the world today." Throughout Gavin's combat leadership of airborne troops, he implemented his belief that successful airborne combat required boldness, courage, and speed of movement—in short, the emulation of cavalry troops. Gavin was known for his calmness under fire. Perhaps one veteran put it best: "He could jump higher, shout louder, spit farther and fight harder than any man I ever saw."

Gavin's leadership and courage were also sorely tested in peace. He believed that the Army had to be able to fight limited wars, especially by using a highly mobile airborne cavalry force. Gavin saw many of his proposals for developing the capacity to fight limited wars accepted and developed by the Army during the administrations of Presidents Kennedy and Lyndon B. Johnson. The fact that the war in Vietnam went badly for the United States does not mean that the strategy of flexible response was proved inadequate. Rather, the American failure in Vietnam stemmed from a misunderstanding of the civil dimensions of that conflict and from various specific decisions along the way.

What emerges, then, is a soldier of courage and imagination who in the end left his beloved army to serve his country in a way he thought he must—by speaking to the national security issues of his time.

BIBLIOGRAPHY

Buchanan, Albert Russell. *The United States and World War II.* 2 vols. New York: Harper and Row, 1964.
Gavin, James M. *On to Berlin: Battles of an Airborne Commander, 1943–1946.* New York: Viking Press, 1978.
———. *War and Peace in the Space Age.* New York: Harper and Row, 1958.
———, and Hadley, Arthur T. *Crisis Now.* New York: Random House, 1968.
Marshall, S.L.A. *Night Drop.* Boston: Little, Brown and Company, 1962.
Ridgway, Matthew B. *Soldier.* New York: Harper, 1956.
Ryan, Cornelius. *A Bridge Too Far.* New York: Simon and Schuster, 1974.

JOSEPH P. HOBBS

GEIGER, Roy Stanley (b. Middleburg, Fla., January 25, 1885; d. Bethesda, Md., January 23, 1947), Marine Corps officer. Geiger was a pioneer Marine aviator and commanded troops in amphibious operations during World War II.

Born to the large family of a county school superintendent, Roy Geiger developed into a strapping young man. He made enough money for tuition at Florida State Normal School at Deland and in 1904 enrolled as a law student in the John B. Stetson University, earning the bachelor of laws in 1907. Geiger passed the bar examination but practiced law only briefly. He enlisted in the Marine Corps in November 1907.

Geiger served for more than a year as an enlisted man before he was commissioned a second lieutenant in 1909. Following two years of shipboard assignments, he was sent to Nicaragua as a part of the constabulary force. Promoted to first lieutenant (1915), he opted for pilot training the next year. He completed the aviator's course at the Navy Flying School in Pensacola, Florida, and pinned on wings soon after he was promoted to captain.

The United States entered World War I in April 1917. Preparing to go to Europe, Captain Geiger trained an aviation detachment at Coconut Grove Naval Air Station near Miami, Florida. In July 1918 the provisional 1st Marine Aviation Force, under the command of Major Alfred Cunningham, deployed to France, where British pilots and mechanics trained them in the use of Britain's DH-4 two-seater bomber. Cunningham's Marines operated four DH-4 squadrons, one of them commanded by Geiger. During October and November the Marines flew fourteen major missions and dropped twenty-seven thousand pounds of bombs on German targets.

In 1920 Geiger was promoted to major, and during the next two decades he gained valuable experience and education. He flew planes in Haiti (1919–1921) and led the 1st Aviation Group of the 3d Marine Brigade at Quantico, Virginia (1921–1924). Geiger distinguished himself at the U.S. Army Command and General Staff School at Fort Leavenworth, Kansas (1924–1925). After commanding the air station at Quantico, he attended the Army War College in Washington, D.C. (1928–1929). He returned to Quantico as commander of Aircraft Squadrons, East Coast Expeditionary Force. In November 1931 Geiger became director of Marine Corps Aviation in Washington. He was promoted to lieutenant colonel in 1934 and held the directorship until May 1935. For the next four years he was stationed at Quantico and had charge of Marine Air Group One, 1st Marine Brigade of the Fleet Marine Force.

In 1939 Geiger began studying at the Naval War College and by March 1941 had finished the requirements of the senior and advanced courses. He was promoted to colonel (1936) and brigadier general (1941). Late in 1941 he returned to Quantico to lead the 1st Marine Aircraft Wing, Fleet Marine Force.

During World War II Geiger held a number of important commands. In September 1942 he took his pilots to Henderson Field on Guadalcanal in the Solomon Islands. Geiger's airmen helped the Navy to beat back the Japanese, making significant contributions to the first Allied victory in the Pacific. From May to October 1943 Geiger again served as director of Marine Corps Aviation in Washington, D.C., but returned to the Pacific to take part in the campaign on Bougainville. Subsequently, Geiger directed the III Amphibious Corps through several campaigns. The first of these returned Guam to American control (July–August 1944). Second, he participated in the controversial invasion of Peleliu (September–October 1944). Geiger's field service climaxed in the battle for Okinawa (April–June 1945), where he temporarily commanded the Tenth Army. This was the first time a field army had come under the command of a Marine general or an aviation officer.

With the war all but over, Geiger was posted to Pearl Harbor as lieutenant general and commander of the Fleet Marine Force, Pacific. In 1946 he observed the American atomic test on Bikini Island and made recommendations on the organization of the postwar Marine Corps. He had been suffering for some time with problems in his circulatory system and died in 1947.

By 1942 Roy Geiger had built a reputation as a top-flight pilot who believed that Marine infantrymen would benefit directly from the close support of Marine aviation. Geiger set down on Guadalcanal (codenamed "Cactus") about a month after the initial American landings. Geiger's amalgam of Marines, Army aviators, and ship-less Navy carrier pilots was dubbed the "Cactus Air Force." Japanese pressure against Guadalcanal mounted steadily. In October, during the showdown in the air over "Cactus," shortages of spare parts, fuel, ammunition, and bombs were normal at Henderson Field. Geiger's pilots flew in any available aircraft—fighters, torpedo-bombers, and dive bombers, once using the general's PBY Catalina Flying Boat on a bombing run. At the height of the fighting, Geiger commanded more than one thousand men, including pilots, mechanics, and support personnel. Geiger sent his men against enemy aircraft as well as troop transports and warships. Furthermore, Cactus pilots hit the Japanese on the ground, assisting the 1st Marine Division (under Major General Alexander Archer Vandegrift*) and various U.S. Army units. Geiger's losses were heavy; on some days less than twenty planes were fit to fly. Geiger lost more than one hundred planes and pilots. Two hundred airmen were wounded. But the Cactus Air Force shot down four hundred Japanese aircraft, sank ten ships, and damaged several others. Geiger and his men were instrumental in capturing Guadalcanal from the Japanese.

Subsequently, the American strategy was to "island-hop" toward Japan, taking some islands for the use of airfields and ports, but bypassing and isolating others. This approach used plans developed in part by Major Earl H. Ellis* during the 1920s. On Bougainville, Geiger served for a month as deputy commander of the I Marine Amphibious Corps under General Vandegrift. He took command of "IMAC" in November, 1943 (when Vandegrift was made commandant of the Marine Corps) and gained valuable experience in conducting jungle warfare. Geiger changed the direction of his career from aviation to ground combat.

Under the direction of Lieutenant General Holland McTyeire Smith,* Geiger participated in the campaign for the Marianas Islands and was the senior commander ashore on Guam. Prior to that assault, however, the fight for Saipan provided lessons for Geiger. There had not been enough accurate pre-invasion naval gunfire against Saipan. In twenty-nine days of fighting on Saipan, the Americans lost more than three thousand killed and over thirteen thousand wounded. After fourteen days of naval shelling delivered by ships under Admiral Richard L. "Close-in" Conolly and bombing by naval and Marine air units, Geiger's III Amphibious Corps landed on Guam. The pre-invasion preparations against Guam served as a model of such bombardments. In twenty-one days of fierce combat Geiger's forces suffered fourteen hundred killed and more than five thousand wounded, about half the casualties Americans sustained on Saipan. The entire Guam operation serves as one of the best examples of cooperation among the Navy, Marines, and the Army during World War II.

The assault on Peleliu (in the Palau Islands) had been planned as a stepping stone to the recapture of the Philippines, aiming toward a landing on Mindinao. By September 1944, however, the Japanese had sustained severe losses; the Americans boldly decided instead to strike directly to Leyte. The American high command, including General Douglas MacArthur,* Admiral Chester William Nimitz,* and the Joint Chiefs of Staff, approved the change of plans, but after some discussion, the assault on Peleliu proceeded, though the need for it had been reduced by changing the main line of approach on the Philippines. The fighting in the Palaus was overshadowed by the spectacular successes around Leyte.

Geiger's principal subordinate, Marine Major General William Rupertus, predicted that Peleliu would be taken in four days. After a week of fighting with no immediate end in sight, Rupertus declined Geiger's suggestion to bring in a regiment of the Army's 81st Infantry Division to reinforce the 1st Marine Division. Evidently, Rupertus wanted Peleliu to be an all-Marine campaign. The fighting was bitter, especially against the fortified caves and bunkers of Peleliu's Umurbrogol Ridge. The 1st Marine Regiment (under Colonel Lewis Burwell Puller*) suffered 50 percent casualties and was replaced on Geiger's order and over Rupertus' objections. Eventually, the island was secured but at great cost (more than nine thousand American casualties) and after two months of combat.

Taking Peleliu remains a controversial step in the Pacific War. Admiral William Frederick Halsey, Jr.,* believed that the invasion was unnecessary because of the move toward Leyte. Admiral Jesse Barrett Oldendorf, whose ships inflicted little damage on Japanese emplacements, thought that the assault on Peleliu should not have been made. Furthermore, Geiger and Rupertus did not see eye to eye on use of the 81st Infantry. Geiger should have committed Army regiments to battle earlier, despite Rupertus' ill-conceived opposition. Nevertheless, as the authors of the official Marine Corps history point out, the capture of the Palaus did yield some positive points. American bombers flew from Angaur and inflicted damage on Japanese positions on Luzon. Holding the Palaus reduced the number of air and submarine bases from which the Japanese could interdict America's supply line. Finally, Ulithi Atoll became a major American base for the invasion of Okinawa.

Okinawa lies only four hundred miles from Japan, and the Americans intended to use it as a base for several airfields. To take Okinawa the Allies delivered the heaviest pre-invasion barrage of the island war, under the supervision of Admiral Richmond Kelly Turner. Command of the invasion force was unusual in that it was to be led by an Army officer, Lieutenant General Simon B. Buckner, rather than a Marine.

The invasion of Okinawa commenced on April 1, 1945. After two weeks the Marines and soldiers had made little gains in yard-by-yard advances against the stout Japanese defenses. Japanese kamikazes pounded the U.S. Navy, inflicting fearful losses in men and ships. Despite sound advice from Geiger and other Marines (including Vandegrift), Buckner rejected a plan to make an amphibious landing to flank the Japanese. Instead, the infantrymen slugged slowly in a grinding campaign that resulted in the highest casualties of an American amphibious battle. The Tenth Army sustained more than sixty-five thousand casualties of all types (killed, wounded, missing, accident, disease); almost ten thousand sailors were killed and wounded; the Japanese sunk thirty-six American ships and shot down 763 U.S. airplanes (April–June 1945).

Okinawa was the culmination of all that the Marine Corps had trained and fought for. Without attempting a flanking amphibious assault, there appeared to be no choice other than a campaign of attrition. Naval officers and Marines criticized Buckner for his handling of the Okinawa fighting. Repercussions of his refusal to order a second amphibious assault reached all the way to Admiral Nimitz, who squelched the criticism temporarily by supporting Buckner's tactical choice. The Marines' criticism of Buckner added to the enmity between the Army and the Marine Corps after the war, and casts doubt on conclusions that the Okinawa Campaign was any model of interservice harmony.

On June 18, 1945, Buckner was killed by Japanese artillery fire. Geiger succeeded to the command of the Tenth Army for five days, until relieved by Lieutenant General Joseph Warren Stilwell.* Although officially Geiger was the only Marine general to command a field army, previously Holland Smith had charge of a force comprising about six divisions in the Marianas Campaign. Unofficially, American procedures limited Marines to corps commands in the field.

Geiger served as a Marine for nearly forty years. During that time he saw the Corps grow from a colonial constabulary to a mighty amphibious strike force. He participated in several significant Pacific campaigns, bringing a pilot's keen eye to amphibious operations.

BIBLIOGRAPHY

Heinl, Robert D. *Soldiers of the Sea: The U.S. Marine Corps, 1775–1962*. Annapolis, Md.: Naval Institute Press, 1962.

Millett, Allan R. *Semper Fidelis: The History of the United States Marine Corps*. New York: Macmillan Company, 1980.

Shaw, Henry I., et al. *History of U.S. Marine Corps Operations in World War II*. 5 vols. Washington, D.C.: U.S. Government Printing Office, 1958–1971.

Sherrod, Robert. *History of Marine Corps Aviation in World War II*. Washington, D.C.: Combat Forces Press, 1952.

Willock, Roger, *Unaccustomed to Fear: A Biography of General Roy S. Geiger, USMC*. Princeton, N.J.: Privately printed, 1968.

JOSEPH G. DAWSON III

GRANT, Ulysses Simpson (b. Point Pleasant, Ohio, April 27, 1822; d. Mount McGregor, N.Y., July 23, 1885), Army officer. Grant is considered a "Great Captain" by military historians.

Grant was the first of six children born to Jesse Root and Hannah Simpson Grant. His father was a tanner, a Whig in politics, a Methodist, and Mason. The Grants christened their first-born Hiram Ulysses, but the name was subsequently reversed. Grant was educated in local schools and helped in the family tannery, farmed, and hauled wood.

In the winter of 1838–1839, Jesse Grant secured an appointment to the U.S. Military Academy for his son. Entertaining no plans for a career in the military, Grant reluctantly entered the class of 1843. Because of an error by the appointing congressman, he was registered as Ulysses Simpson Grant, and he had to retain the name. At West Point, he failed to distinguish himself academically and collected his share of demerits. He was graduated twenty-first in a class of thirty-nine, which included thirteen other future Civil War generals, ten who fought for the North and three the South.

Grant was ordered to Jefferson Barracks, Missouri, near St. Louis, where as a brevet second lieutenant he reported to the 4th Infantry Regiment. In 1845 he joined the army of General Zachary Taylor* at Corpus Christi, Texas. Although he had little sympathy with his nation's goals in the Mexican War, Grant served with distinction in Taylor's campaign through the Battle of Monterrey (1846), and as a regimental quartermaster in the army of General Winfield Scott* on his campaign inland from Vera Cruz to Mexico City. By the end of the war, Grant was a first lieutenant with brevets for gallantry at Molino del Rey and Chapultepec (1847).

In August 1848 he married Julia Dent, sister of a West Point classmate. The couple had four children—three boys and a girl. After tours of duty in New York and Michigan, in 1852 Grant was assigned to the Far West and left his wife and first-born son in St. Louis. He was stationed at Fort Vancouver, Washington Territory, until promoted to captain in 1853 and then ordered to Fort Humboldt, California. Humboldt was a dreary post commanded by a martinet, Captain Robert C. Buchanan. Lonely, bored, and disenchanted with the Army, Grant drank too much. After a reprimand by Buchanan, Grant resigned from the service in 1854.

Grant rejoined his family near St. Louis. A trying six years ensued—years of privation, menial pursuits, limited prospects, and despondence. He successively sought to earn a livelihood as a farmer, firewood salesman, real estate agent, bill collector, candidate for county engineer, and customhouse clerk. He was unsuccessful in these ventures. In 1860 he moved to Galena, Illinois, to work in obscurity as a clerk in a leather-goods store managed by two of his brothers. The next year the Civil War started.

In the weeks following the firing on Fort Sumter and the call by President Abraham Lincoln for seventy-five thousand volunteers, Grant drilled a company of Galena volunteers and then clerked in the office of the Illinois adjutant-general. His applications for field duty elicited no response. But on June 17, 1861, the governor of Illinois named Grant colonel of the 21st Illinois Volunteer Infantry. After a few weeks in a camp of instruction, Grant's regiment was ordered to Missouri. There he was made a brigadier general of volunteers and placed in command of the District of Southeast Missouri, headquartered at Cairo, Illinois.

Grant secured permission from his reluctant superior, General Henry Wager Halleck,* to make an amphibious thrust up the Tennessee River against Fort Henry. The Confederate fort fell to Union gunboats on February 6, 1862. Grant exploited this success by marching on nearby Fort Donelson, on the Cumberland, which was captured on February 16, along with its more than fourteen thousand defenders. These victories had immediate and far-reaching repercussions—the Confederates were compelled to abandon southern Kentucky, and much of middle and west Tennessee, including the Nashville industrial complex. ''Unconditional

Surrender" Grant became a household word in the North, while a grateful President Lincoln appointed Grant a major general of volunteers.

On April 6, 1862, the Confederate Army under General Albert Sidney Johnston* surprised Grant at Pittsburg Landing, Tennessee, near Shiloh Church. Although the Federals were driven from their camps and back on the landing, Grant did not panic. When darkness closed in, the Union lines had stabilized. Reinforced by troops under General Don Carlos Buell, Grant counterattacked the next day, recovered the initiative, and forced the Confederates to retire in Corinth, Mississippi.

Bloody Shiloh had been a costly victory, and Grant's conduct before the battle became a subject of controversy. General Halleck hastened to the front and assumed command as the army closed in on Corinth; Grant became Halleck's second-in-command. But in July Halleck was called to Washington to become general in chief, and Grant resumed command of the Army of the Tennessee.

In November Grant's columns marched south, and his objectives were to capture Vicksburg, Mississippi, and secure control of the 240 miles of the Mississippi River between Vicksburg and Port Hudson, Louisiana. During the winter, on four occasions he sought to bypass Vicksburg but failed, and it appeared he might be replaced. On March 20, 1863, Grant made a fateful decision. He started his army on a march southward through the Louisiana parishes. In mid-April Rear Admiral David Dixon Porter passed the Vicksburg batteries with his gunboats and transports, rendezvousing with Grant's army thirty river-miles south of the city. On April 30 Grant crossed the Mississippi with twenty-four thousand men and sixty cannon. During the next eighteen days Grant conducted one of history's great campaigns. Striking rapidly inland, he met and defeated the Confederates in five battles. One Southern army under General John C. Pemberton was invested in Vicksburg, while a second under General Joseph Eggleston Johnston* was scattered. Grant's efforts to storm Vicksburg failed. But cut off from supplies and reinforcement, Pemberton surrendered, along with 29,500 Confederates and large quantitites of war material, to General Grant on July 4, 1863, after a harrowing forty-seven day siege. Port Hudson fell to General N. P. Banks on July 9, and the Union again controlled the Mississippi from Cairo to the Gulf. Grant was hailed in the press and on the street, and was promoted to major general in the Regular Army.

That autumn Grant was placed in command of the Division of the Mississippi and ordered to relieve the army of General William Starke Rosecrans,* beleaguered in Chattanooga following its mid-September defeat at Chickamauga. After replacing Rosecrans with General George Henry Thomas,* Grant implemented a plan for supplying and reinforcing the army holed up in Chattanooga. Upon the arrival of four divisions under General William Tecumseh Sherman* from Vicksburg, Grant took the offensive. On November 23 the attack opened, to be climaxed by the surge up Missionary Ridge two days later. The Confederate Army under General Braxton Bragg* was swept from the field.

On March 2, 1864, Grant was promoted to lieutenant general and soon after was placed in command of the armies of the United States. Realizing that the way to victory was to crush the two major Confederate armies, Grant made his plans. In Virginia there would be a coordinated thrust by three Union armies directed at the Army of Northern Virginia, commanded by Robert Edward Lee,* while in northwest Georgia, General Sherman would hammer the Army of the Tennessee, commanded by General Joseph E. Johnston. Grant established his headquarters, not in Washington, but with the Army of the Potomac, then commanded by General George Gordon Meade.*

The Union armies took the offensive in the first week of May 1864. At the Wilderness (May 5–6) Meade's Army of the Potomac suffered frightful casualties, but unlike his predecessors Grant did not recoil. He directed Meade's columns to pass around Lee's right flank. Lee won that race, and after being successively fought to a standstill at Spotsylvania, the North Anna, and Cold Harbor, Grant employed his superior numbers to turn Lee's right and inch his way closer to Richmond. Union losses were staggering and by mid-June equaled Lee's strength at the beginning of the campaign. The North could replace its casualties, however; the South could not.

Stealing a march on Lee, the Army of the Potomac crossed to the south side of the James River and moved against Petersburg. A terrible four-day battle (June 15–18) ensued, but the Confederates held and Grant was unable to slip in Richmond's back door. This led to nine months of siege warfare, during which time the Union armies south of the James slowly extended their rifle-pits and forts westward to cut or threaten the railroads and roads over which Lee supplied his army. North of the James, the Federals inched their way toward Richmond.

Besides initiating and coordinating these movements, Grant maintained contact with his other army commanders to ensure that his strategic goals were implemented and proper priorities were given to the allocation of reinforcements and supplies. Especially significant was his decision to place General Philip Henry Sheridan* in charge of an army with the mission of destroying the Confederacy's economic resources and military power in the Shenandoah Valley.

Sheridan's victory at Five Forks (April 1, 1865) proved decisive, and the next day Grant hurled the armies of the Potomac and the James against Lee's attenuated and undermanned Petersburg lines, scoring massive breakthroughs. On the night of April 2 the Confederates evacuated Petersburg and Richmond and retreated to the west in hopes of rendezvousing with Johnston's army in North Carolina.

At Appomattox Court House, Lee found his route blocked by Sheridan's cavalry, while the Army of the Potomac slashed at his rear. On Palm Sunday, April 9, in the parlor of the Wilmer McLean House, Lee surrendered his army to General Grant. Grant's terms were generous and well received by the Confederates. Before another seven weeks passed, the other Southern armies laid down their arms and America's bloodiest war was history.

Universally esteemed, Grant continued as head of the Army, and in 1866 President Andrew Johnson named him General of the Army, a rank unused since 1799. At first, Grant sought to maintain a neutral stance in the increasingly acrimonious quarrels over Reconstruction policies between President Johnson and Congress, controlled by the Radical Republicans. Grant gradually shifted his position and became linked with the Radicals.

Nominated by the Republicans for the presidency in 1868, he defeated Democrat Horatio Seymour by a whopping electoral vote, though his margin in the popular vote was surprisingly small. Grant was easily reelected to a second term in 1872, thumping Horace Greeley. Grant was well trained for the military but ill-prepared for the White House. He looked to important congressmen and senators for guidance. Personally honest but politically naive, Grant made several unfortunate choices for cabinet officers and other advisors; a number of these men proved to be corrupt or incompetent, and a series of scandals rocked his administration.

Grant retired from public office in 1877, but in 1880 he again sought the Republican presidential nomination. He lost out to James A. Garfield. Two years later, Grant joined a New York brokerage firm, Grant and Ward, in which his name was exploited. In mid-1884 the enterprise failed, throwing Grant into bankruptcy.

Grant was now stricken with cancer of the throat. To provide for his family, in a race against death Grant wrote his *Personal Memoirs*. A classic military account, his memoirs were a financial success, earning for his heirs more than $450,000. In July 1885, a few days after laying aside his pen, the pain-wracked and speechless old soldier died.

Ulysses S. Grant certainly merits inclusion on any roll of the "Great Captains." In February 1862 he first demonstrated his abilities as a strategist and tactician, a rare combination. Although others had earlier pointed to the Tennessee and Cumberland rivers as the vulnerable point in the Confederate front, it was Grant who proceeded against Fort Henry and then exploited the subsequent breakthrough, closing in on Fort Donelson. At a key moment in the Donelson fighting, on February 15, he made decisions that turned apparent defeat into victory.

At Shiloh, Grant demonstrated other facets of his character—a bulldog-like determination and nerves of steel. He arrived on the field at midmorning on April 6 to find his army in disarray. Some units were grimly contesting the Confederate surge, others had not yet engaged, and many soldiers had panicked. Grant kept his nerve. He encouraged his troops and formed new lines; the Confederate onslaught slowed, and the tide turned.

The Vicksburg Campaign was Grant's masterpiece. His strategic concept was bold. Appreciating the value of the Navy, he employed it to give a new dimension to riverine warfare. Securing his bridgehead across the Mississippi at the Battle of Port Gibson (May 1, 1863), Grant marched his columns northeast rather than north. His object in taking the indirect approach was twofold—the capture of Vicksburg *and* the destruction of Pemberton's army. He made no effort to hold the countryside as his army struck inland. Instead, at frequent intervals until mid-May, large, heavily guarded wagon trains left Grand Gulf on the Mississippi to reinforce Grant's columns as they outmaneuvered and beat the Confederates in detail.

At Chattanooga, Grant carefully built up a superior striking force and then dealt Bragg's Confederates a fearful blow. As at Vicksburg, victory in this campaign called for an appreciation by Grant of the logistics involved in supplying and reinforcing tens of thousands of soldiers.

Upon assuming command of the Union armies, Grant demonstrated a keen strategic insight and a strength of will that brought victory to the North. His relations with his principal subordinates, particularly General Meade, with whose army he traveled, are lessons in the art of command. Grant established goals, oversaw logistics, and coordinated movements, while the Army leaders were responsible for tactical control and day-to-day operations of their commands. He did intervene, on occasion, if the situation warranted. Although terrible in attack and relentless in pursuit, Grant at Vicksburg and Appomattox was magnanimous in victory.

BIBLIOGRAPHY

Catton, Bruce. *Grant Moves South*. Boston: Little, Brown and Company, 1960.
———. *Grant Takes Command*. Boston: Little, Brown and Company, 1968.
Fuller, J. F. C. *The Generalship of Ulysses S. Grant*. New York: Dodd, Mead, and Company, 1929; reprint, Bloomington: Indiana University Press, 1958.
Grant, Ulysses S. *Personal Memoirs of U.S. Grant*. 2 vols. New York: J. J. Little and Company, 1885.
Lewis, Lloyd. *Captain Sam Grant*. Boston: Little, Brown and Company, 1950.
McFeely, William. *Grant: A Biography*. New York: W. W. Norton and Company, 1981.
Woodward, William E. *Meet General Grant*. New York: Horace Liveright, 1928.

EDWIN C. BEARSS

GREENE, Nathanael (b. Warwick, R.I., July 27, 1742 OS; d. Mulberry Grove, Savannah, Ga., June 19, 1786), general in the War of Independence.

Little in Green's earlier years suggested he would one day have a prominent role in a revolution. Because his Quaker parents, Nathanael and Mary Mott Greene, favored hard work and minimal education, he went to work early in the family-owned forge and mills, learning each job—from anchorsmith to merchant. Largely self-educated, he read widely and later became a fluent letter writer.

Until England closed the port of Boston in 1774, Greene showed slight interest in public affairs. Then, repudiating his Quaker pacifism, he helped found the Kentish Guards. Prevented by a slight limp from being elected an officer, he consented to serve as private, using his spare time to study military treatises. Six months later, in May 1775, for obscure reasons, the Assembly bypassed veteran officers of the French and Indian War to appoint Greene brigadier general of the Rhode Island Army of Observation. Within weeks he had three regiments uniformed, equipped, and encamped near Boston. When his brigade was taken into the Continental Army in June 1775, he became, at thirty-two, the army's youngest general.

The stalemate at Boston and Long Island in 1775–1776 provided Greene an opportunity to learn from veteran soldiers as well as from books and to adapt his practical knowledge to military needs. His career before December 1776, however, was not impressive. After preparing Long Island's defenses, he was made major general in August 1776, but he fell ill before British General William Howe attacked. At Harlem Heights in September he acquitted himself well, but two months later, as commander of Forts Washington and Lee, he watched across the Hudson (with George Washington*) as Howe's army overran Mount Washington, taking twenty-eight hundred prisoners. It was a bitter lesson; never again would he be caught without an avenue of retreat.

The stigma was largely erased in December 1776 by General George Washington's* daring attack on Trenton, which Greene helped to plan and execute. At Brandywine in September 1777, Greene's division marched four miles in forty-five minutes to check the British in a fierce engagement after they turned Washington's flank. During the night offensive at Germantown in October, Greene's column penetrated enemy lines before realizing that Sullivan had had to retreat in fog. Willard Wallace called his disengagement and retreat "remarkable achievements."

At Valley Forge in February 1778, a congressional committee urged the quartermaster post on Greene. Reluctant to leave the "line of splendor" for a chaotic department, he did so finally because of Washington's desperation and his own fear for the patriot cause. Although he offered to accept a general's salary, his assistants insisted on traditional commissions, and Congress set a 1 percent commission for the three.

As head of the sprawling department of three thousand employees, Greene made enormous improvements in the face of shortages and rapidly depreciating currency. Depreciation also brought criticism of Greene and his assistants as commissions in Continental dollars rose astronomically and some people irrationally blamed them for high prices. Even more damaging was the profiteering of some agents, whose misdeeds smeared the entire department. Greene's relations with Congress became increasingly strained, and in August 1780 he resigned.

During Greene's tenure as quartermaster, Washington often sought his advice and occasionally assigned him active duty: in June 1778 near the end of the Battle of Monmouth he repulsed a column under Cornwallis; in August 1778 in Rhode Island he defended John Sullivan's right against strong attacks; and in June 1780 at Springfield, New Jersey, he turned back Baron Knyphausen's five thousand men with half the number.

In October 1780, with Charles Cornwallis controlling Georgia and South Carolina after defeating Horatio Gates* at Camden, Congress approved Washington's choice of Greene to command the Southern army. En route south, he was promised Henry ("Light-horse Harry") Lee's* legion, and in Maryland and Virginia he pleaded for more men and supplies. He left a subordinate, Baron Frederic William Steuben,* in Virginia to raise men. En route he also familiarized himself with the South through maps. His ability to imprint the topography of a region in his mind from maps or observation was part of his genius. His quartermaster experience helped him keep a constant assessment of each region's supply potential.

At Charlotte, North Carolina, on December 3, 1780, he took command from Gates of a hungry, ragged, ill-equipped army of one thousand Continentals and twelve hundred militiamen. Although Greene remained in the South until August 1783, he won his military laurels in the first nine months. Tactical victories eluded him, but with an inferior army he adopted a successful strategy of mobility, of doing with what he had, of using finesse where he lacked strength, of strategic retreats to save his army for another day. He became especially adept at winning the cooperation of partisan leaders. Above all, he never gave in to discouragement. "We fight," he wrote, "get beat, rise, and fight again."

The one tactical victory of his Southern campaign was Daniel Morgan's* destruction of Guy Carleton's legion at Cowpens on January 17, 1781. Greene had prepared the way by the unorthodox move of dividing his small army. With supplies exhausted around Charlotte, he had accompanied eleven hundred men to a more bountiful and defensible area seventy miles southeast at Cheraw, South Carolina. He sent Morgan westward with six hundred men to attract militia and to watch Cornwallis' army of four thousand men, which lay between them. After Cowpens, Greene headed north to rendezvous with Morgan, who was now in retreat before Cornwallis. In Greene's and Morgan's race to cross the Dan River (where Greene had ordered boats built), they not only eluded Cornwallis but also caused him to destroy most of his wagons and supplies in fruitless pursuit. Greene soon recrossed the Dan to encourage North Carolina patriots.

Despite the loss of Morgan (from ill-health) and many militiamen, additional troops brought Greene's numbers to forty-two hundred. That scarcely a fifth of these men had seen action did not deter him from confronting Cornwallis' two thousand veterans. Although Cornwallis had not replaced his wagons and baggage, he accepted Greene's challenge. On a hill near Guilford Court House, North Carolina, Greene deployed his men in three lines as Morgan had done at Cowpens, the militia in front to fire several times before retreating. At noon on March 15, Cornwallis attacked across an open field. Unfortunately, the North Carolina militia fired only once and ran, but Virginia militia and Continental infantry and cavalry fought furiously—until Greene withdrew rather than risk further loss. Cornwallis kept the field, but 30 percent of his men lay dead or wounded as compared with only 6 percent of Greene's. Cornwallis' army was finished as a fighting force. He stumbled toward the coast at Wilmington, whence he later departed for Virginia—and Yorktown.

Greene, reduced to fifteen hundred Continentals by militia withdrawals, headed south, where eight thousand British held nine interior posts plus Charleston and Savannah. Although he was defeated by Lord Rawdon at Hobkirk's Hill on April 19 and was forced to abandon the siege of Fort 96 in June, he succeeded in four months—with the help of partisans under Francis Marion,* Thomas Sumter, and Andrew Pickens—in clearing the British from the interior. His men covered nine hundred miles in the sweltering heat.

On September 8, with twenty-two hundred men, Greene made a surprise attack on Colonel Alexander Stewart's army at Eutaw Springs. Seasoned veterans declared it the hardest fought battle of the war. Greene was near victory when one of his regiments, in overrunning the British camp, found food and rum. At the same time, Stewart's right, ensconced in a thicket and a brick house, took a heavy toll of Greene's cavalry. When Stewart's retreating column turned and made a stand, Greene withdrew. Both sides were near exhaustion. A fourth of Greene's troops and a third of Stewart's were casualties. The battle was a draw, but the campaign was Greene's when Stewart withdrew to Charleston. For Eutaw Springs, Greene's praises were sung North and South.

Victory at Yorktown did not bring peace to the South. The British still held Charleston and Savannah and gave indications of strengthening them. Moreover, the Whigs and Tories continued regularly to plunder and kill each other. As important as Greene's military achievements were his efforts to reconcile the warring factions and to restore civil government.

In gratitude, South Carolina and Georgia gave him estates, while North Carolina gave him western land. In June 1782 his wife joined him and was with him when he entered Charleston after the British evacuation in December 1782.

The following months were trouble-filled. No sooner had he coped with mutiny than he was accused of profiteering, charges that arose when two former aides were discovered to be partners of John Banks, whose firm had provided Greene's army with food and uniforms. To bolster his credit, Banks had hinted that Greene was to become a partner. Although vindicated by associates (and later by Alexander Hamilton), Greene suffered from the charges. Even worse was Banks' bankruptcy, which left Greene owing thousands of dollars—a debt that shortened his life. Ten years after his death, Congress reimbursed his family.

Greene returned north in August 1783 to a hero's acclaim. Two years later he moved to Georgia and was struggling to make his estates profitable, when he died suddenly on June 19, 1786. He was survived by Catharine and five children under eleven years of age.

Greene's early death denied him a place in the popular pantheon of Revolutionary heroes, although he was fully appreciated by his contemporaries. Many would have applauded Alexander Hamilton when, in his eulogy of Greene, he spoke of his "universal and pervading genius." Not all military historians would agree, but none would deny his genius. British historian J. W. Fortescue called Greene a "very noble character [who] seems to me to stand little if at all lower than Washington as a general in the field." Douglas Southall Freeman thought that next to Washington, Greene had done "the most in the field to achieve Independence." Another historian, Christopher Ward, called him Washington's "right arm" and said that "in the opinion of some well qualified judges he was Washington's superior, both as a strategist and as a tactician."

BIBLIOGRAPHY

Greene, Nathanael. *The Papers of General Nathanael Greene.* Edited by Richard K. Showman, Robert E. McCarthy, and Margaret Cobb. Chapel Hill: University of North Carolina Press, 1976–.
Thayer, Theodore. *Nathanael Greene: Strategist of the American Revolution.* New York: Twayne Publishers, 1960.
Treacy, M. F. *Prelude to Yorktown: The Southern Campaign of Nathanael Greene, 1780–81.* Chapel Hill: University of North Carolina Press, 1963.
Wallace, Willard M. *Appeal to Arms: A Military History of the American Revolution.* New York: Harper and Brothers, 1951.

RICHARD K. SHOWMAN

HALLECK, Henry Wager (b. Westernville, N.Y., January 16, 1815; d. Louisville, Ky., January 9, 1872), Army officer and military intellectual. Halleck served as general in chief and chief of staff of the Union armies during the Civil War.

Born in Oneida County of generally prosperous, old New York farming families, Halleck disliked farming and to escape it ran away to live with his maternal grandfather, Henry Wager. Wager, a friend of Frederic William Steuben* (Baron von), adopted the boy and financed his schooling at Hudson Academy. Halleck went on to Union College, where he was elected to Phi Beta Kappa and received the A.B. degree in 1837, two years after he left the college for West Point. In 1839 Halleck was graduated from the Military Academy third in a class of thirty-one and was commissioned second lieutenant in the Corps of Engineers. As the favorite student of Dennis Hart Mahan,* Halleck had taught classes while still a cadet and after graduation was appointed assistant professor of engineering. The next year he became an assistant to the Board of Engineers for Atlantic Coast Defences, contributing a *Report on the Means of National Defence* (28th Congress, 2d Session, *Senate Executive Document No. 85*). Following this acquaintance with the overall planning of coastal fortifications, Halleck did practical work on the defenses of New York Harbor, where he served from 1840 to 1844. He toured European fortifications, returning to resume his work at New York in 1845.

Halleck united to his growing mastery of military engineering a broad study of European literature on military policy, strategy, and tactics. While still a first lieutenant—he was commissioned in that rank on January 1, 1845—he was invited to deliver a series of lectures on military topics before the Lowell Institute of Boston late in 1845. In 1846 the lectures were published as *Elements of Military Art and Science; or, Course of Instruction in Strategy, Fortification,*

Tactics of Battles, &c. This book, which was to appear in 1862 in a third edition with comments on the Mexican and Crimean Wars during the Civil War, would alone assure Halleck a major place in the history of American military thought. It was the first comprehensive study of the military art by an American author, encompassing in addition to the subjects enumerated in the title a moral apology for war, logistics, military education, and American military policy, all approached from a historical perspective. Although Halleck disclaimed originality and critics have sometimes dismissed the book as a mere paraphrase of Antoine Henri Jomini, the work surpasses its author's modest assessment. Halleck's *Elements of Military Art and Science* is an early flowering of the professional and intellectual approach to officership nourished by the West Point of Sylvanus Thayer and Dennis Hart Mahan.

After the outbreak of the war with Mexico, Halleck left New York for Monterey, California. He occupied the six-month sailing trip translating Jomini's *Vie politique et militaire de Napoléon*; the translation was published in four volumes in 1864. Halleck and his fellow passengers, including Lieutenant William Tecumseh Sherman,* reached California too late to participate in the conquest of the territory. Halleck prepared defensive works against counterattacks as far south as the Mexican west coast port of Mazatlán, and he was sufficiently involved in the backwash of the fighting to win a brevet as captain. His meritorious service included administrative achievements as secretary of state to the military government of California. Halleck also participated in the 1849 convention that drew up the constitution under which California was admitted to statehood. Following various staff postings in California, Halleck in 1853 returned to his first expertise to plan and construct Pacific Coast fortifications. He was commissioned captain on July 1, 1853.

Halleck had begun reading law early in his military career, and his involvement in creating civil government in California stimulated his interest in the law. A legal career in the new state, where he was an influential figure, obviously offered more encouraging prospects for advancement than the peacetime Army. In 1849 he helped found the San Francisco law firm of Halleck, Peachy and Billings, and on August 1, 1854, he resigned his commission to give full time to the firm. On April 10, 1855, he married Elizabeth Hamilton, grand-daughter of Alexander Hamilton. A scholar as well as a practitioner in the law as in the Army, Halleck established a major reputation as a jurist with his synthesis, *International Law, or Rules Regulating the Intercourse of States in Peace and War* (1861; new edition 1908).

It testifies to the eminence of "Old Brains" Halleck as a citizen as well as a soldier that President Abraham Lincoln appointed him on August 19, 1861, as one of the few full major generals of the Regular Army at the beginning of the Civil War. Two months later, on November 18, Halleck succeeded John Charles Frémont in command of the Department of the Missouri, with headquarters at St. Louis and encompassing Illinois, Iowa, Minnesota, Wisconsin, Missouri, and Arkansas, as well as Kentucky west of the Cumberland River. The administrative capacity that Halleck had displayed in California served well to restore good order to the command which Frémont had left in an administrative shambles. Halleck probably arrived too late to be successful in restoring a larger kind of law, order, and loyalty to the Union in Missouri. He received partially merited credit, however, for the successes of his subordinate Ulysses Simpson Grant* at Forts Henry and Donelson. In March 1862 the credit became tangible with the extension of his command, as the Department of the Mississippi, to include in addition to his old department the Department of Kansas to the west and the area eastward as far as a north-south line through Knoxville, Tennessee. Halleck coordinated the movement of the armies under Grant and Don Carlos Buell in the offensive that led to the Battle of Shiloh. Halleck then took personal command of these armies, and another under John Pope, for the campaign to complete the conquest of western Tennessee down to the Memphis and Charleston Railroad by taking Corinth, Mississippi. Corinth fell to Halleck on June 10, 1862.

The cautious pace that characterized the drive against Corinth after Halleck took the field might have raised doubts about "Old Brains' " vigor and resolution in the face of direct responsibility for combat. Nevertheless, Union victories in Halleck's department so exceeded progress elsewhere that on July 11, 1862, Lincoln appointed Halleck general in chief of the armies of the United States. Halleck chose to make this command mainly one for the exercise of his administrative talents, rather than a strategic headquarters. He coordinated communications between the widespread Union armies and the War Department, and served as a useful liaison between President Lincoln and Secretary of War Edwin McMasters Stanton on the one hand and the generals in the field on the other. Knowing at first hand both the military and the political worlds, he could better make the wishes and anxieties of each understandable to the other. But Halleck did not produce the coherent direction of the war for which Lincoln had hoped. Whenever possible, he avoided responsibility for decisions that might involve risks.

Coherent strategic direction awaited Halleck's supercession by Grant on March 9, 1864. Because Grant desired to campaign with the Army of the Potomac while also commanding the overall war effort, he retained Halleck in Washington in the new post of chief of staff of the Army to continue serving as coordinator of communications. This post of administration without pressing responsibility was altogether appropriate to both the strengths and the weaknesses Halleck had demonstrated throughout the war, as well as to his scholarly knowledge of military procedures.

After Robert Edward Lee* surrendered in April 1865, Grant transferred Halleck to another appropriate post, command of the Military Division of the James with charge over the initial reconstruction of Virginia. Halleck offended Sherman and to some degree Grant by his brusque intervention from Richmond to overrule Sherman's initially generous surrender terms to Joseph Eggleston Johnston.* In August Halleck was shifted to the less sensitive Division of the Pacific, where The remained far from the turmoil of Reconstruction for four years. In July 1869 he returned east to head the Division of the South. By this time, the vindictiveness toward the South that had influenced Halleck's quarrel with Sherman had cooled, and Halleck was inclined to believe that using military force in the South simply stirred up resentments creating an occasion for yet more application of force. Halleck died in 1872 with the issues of Reconstruction still unresolved.

An unprepossessing, paunchy, rather pop-eyed man without personal warmth, Halleck had few friends and could readily emerge from the Civil War a scapegoat for all sorts of things that went wrong during the nearly two years when he commanded the Union armies or even in his year as chief of staff. His reputation as a Civil War military commander is probably lower than it ought to be. Despite his shying away from responsibility, certain strategic achievements stand to his credit. He helped conceive the Henry-Donelson Campaign and generally encouraged Grant throughout it, Grant's later testimony to the contrary notwithstanding. The larger conception of moving up the Tennessee River as an avenue toward breaking the Confederacy's best lateral line of communication, the Memphis and Charleston Railroad, was to a major degree Halleck's. He displayed moral courage when he first assumed the office of general in chief by deciding promptly to withdraw George Brinton McClellan's* army from the Virginia Peninsula, on the ground that nothing more could be expected from it there; this decision meant accepting at least the appearance of a severe setback at the outset of Halleck's command. Despite the tendency of his writings toward a conservative, limited style of war, Halleck contributed to the design of campaigns led by Sherman and Philip Henry Sheridan* in Georgia, the Carolinas, and the Shenandoah Valley to destroy Confederate economic resources and morale, reaching for decisive objectives beyond the enemy armies.

Meanwhile, Halleck's administrative accomplishments remained consistently impressive, though it is misleading to interpret him as a forerunner of the twentieth-century Army chiefs of staff. His offices and his conduct of them were different from the chief professional post as designed by Elihu Root. The Civil War command system among Stanton, Grant, and Halleck functioned not as a model of military organization in a democracy but as a triumph of individuals over illogical organization charts.

Halleck was not always as generous and adaptable as when he stepped down from command of the armies to be chief of staff under Grant. His pettiness toward Sherman had been foreshadowed by his jealous efforts to slow Grant's rise to prominence during and just after the Shiloh Campaign. His moral qualities did not consistently equal his military brain. But in the scholarly products of his brain, he left enduring monuments. His *Elements of Military Art and Science* makes Halleck, along with Dennis Hart Mahan, one of the two founders of American professional military scholarship and thought.

BIBLIOGRAPHY

Ambrose, Stephen E. *Halleck: Lincoln's Chief of Staff*. Baton Rouge: Louisiana State University Press, 1960.

Grant, Ulysses S. *Personal Memoirs of U. S. Grant.* 2 vols. New York: Webster, 1885.
Thomas, Benjamin P., and Harold M. Hyman. *Stanton: The Life and Times of Lincoln's Secretary of War.* New York: Alfred A. Knopf, 1962.
Weigley, Russell F. *Towards an American Army: Military Thought from Washington to Marshall.* New York: Columbia University Press, 1962.
Williams, Kenneth P. *Lincoln Finds a General: A Military Study of the Civil War.* 5 vols. New York: Macmillan Company, 1950–1959.

RUSSELL F. WEIGLEY

HALSEY, William Frederick, Jr. (b. Elizabeth, N.J., October 30, 1882; d. Fishers Island, N.Y., August 16, 1959), naval officer. Halsey was a fleet commander in the Pacific during World War II.

William F. Halsey, Jr., came from a long line of seafarers. Halsey's father, a Naval Academy man, class of 1873, retired from the service with the rank of captain. Young Halsey entered the Academy in 1900, stood in the middle of his class academically, and played football on an often defeated Navy team. Following graduation in 1904, Ensign Halsey served in the battleship *Kansas* when it steamed around the world as part of President Theodore Roosevelt's* Great White Fleet. In December 1909 he married Frances Cooke Grandy.

Soon after the United States entered World War I, Commander Halsey joined the American Destroyer Force based at Queenstown, Ireland, commanding the *Benham* and then the *Shaw*. For his services during the war, Halsey was awarded the Navy Cross. After World War I, Halsey held various assignments, including stints at the Naval War College at Newport, Rhode Island, and the Army War College in Washington, D.C., spending most of his sea time on destroyers.

Subsequently, Halsey's career was oriented toward aircraft carriers. After training at Pensacola and qualifying as a pilot in the spring of 1935 at the age of fifty-two, he commanded the carrier *Saratoga*. He then became commandant of the Pensacola Naval Air Station and later, alternately commanded both U.S. Navy carrier divisions. In the spring of 1940, the Navy Department designated Halsey as commander, Aircraft Battle Force, with the rank of vice admiral, commanding all the carriers of the Pacific Fleet.

On December 7, 1941, Halsey with his force, including the *Enterprise*, three cruisers, and nine destroyers, was 150 miles west of Oahu when the Japanese struck Pearl Harbor. Refueling at Pearl Harbor, the *Enterprise* sortied before dawn on December 9 with orders to hunt down enemy submarines. Meanwhile, Admiral Chester William Nimitz* had relieved Admiral Husband Edward Kimmel* as commander in chief, Pacific Fleet. In late January 1942 Nimitz decided to send a carrier force, commanded by Halsey, to strike the Japanese bases in the Marshall Islands. Although the results proved meager, the carrier force gained valuable combat experience. After leading his campaign against the heart of the Japanese defenses in the Central Pacific, Halsey was suddenly acclaimed the nation's first naval hero of the war.

Soon after returning to Pearl Harbor, Halsey's force was ordered to carry the B-25 bombers of Colonel James Harold Doolittle across the Pacific to within striking range of Tokyo. Doolittle and his men delivered their blow on April 18, 1942, causing little damage, but the news that Tokyo had actually been bombed lifted American morale.

Halsey fell ill in May 1942, and, much to his disgust, he was unable to command the American forces against the Japanese in the Battle of Midway. Instead, Raymond Ames Spruance* served as commander. Fully recovered in early fall, Halsey became commander of the South Pacific Force in mid-October 1942.

Although the U.S. Marines had landed on Guadalcanal in August, the Japanese Navy still commanded the sea in the southern Solomon Islands. Halsey infused the American forces in the South Pacific with new confidence, and after several battles, his ships became more adept at night fighting and destroying enemy planes. Simultaneously, Marine and Army units on Guadalcanal began consistently defeating the enemy. The Japanese evacuated Guadalcanal on February 9, 1943.

As a part of the push toward the Philippines, three naval actions in the Solomons during July 1943 won control of surrounding waters, and on August 5, 1943, the XIV Corps captured Munda Field in New Georgia. The essence of Halsey's strategy had been to bypass the principal Japanese strongpoints, including Rabaul, sealing them off with sea and air power, leaving their garrisons stranded, while the Allies constructed new air and naval bases in some less strongly defended spots several hundred miles nearer to Japan. Subsequently, on November 5 and 11 carrier-based planes pounded Rabaul, and, day by day, bombers based on Bougainville continued the work of wearing away the enemy air forces. By March 25, 1944, Rabaul was neutralized. The war in the South Pacific had ended.

After conferring with naval brass in Pearl Harbor, San Francisco, and Washington, Halsey and his Third Fleet steamed out of Pearl Harbor on August 24, 1944, to cooperate with the forces under General Douglas MacArthur* and Admiral Thomas Cassin Kinkaid in the invasion of the Philippines. On October 20 American forces sloshed ashore on Leyte Island. In response, the Japanese high command decided to commit the entire Imperial Fleet to defeat American naval forces at Leyte and isolate MacArthur. Japan divided its fleet into three separate units. The Southern Force of battleships and cruisers was to maneuver through Surigao Strait, break into Leyte Gulf at daybreak on October 25, and rendezvous with the powerful Center Force, which was to move through San Bernardino Strait and come around Samar from the north. The Japanese Northern Force, built around four carriers, was to lure Halsey's Task Force 38, the American carrier force, northward, away from Leyte Gulf.

As the battle was joined, Kinkaid deployed almost every battleship, cruiser, and destroyer to catch the Southern Force as it came through Surigao Strait in the early hours of October 25. The high-caliber fire of the American unit sank several enemy ships and sent the rest of the Southern Force fleeing. Japan's massive Center Force had been damaged and delayed by American aircraft in the Sibuyan Sea on October 24. Halsey overestimated the damage that his bombers had inflicted. After his search planes discovered the Northern Force of carriers coming down from Japan, Halsey chose to move his force north and sink the carriers, not even leaving a destroyer to guard San Bernardino Strait.

The Center Force left the strait unopposed and approached the northern entrance of Leyte Gulf undetected. Off the island of Samar the Japanese attacked Kinkaid's escort carriers. The ensuing battle was perhaps the most gallant action in naval history, and the bloodiest. As the Japanese had no air support, the Americans were able to defeat a fleet that had more than ten times their firepower.

Up north in the battle off Cape Engano, Halsey's planes sank all four enemy carriers. The battle for Leyte Gulf on October 25, 1944, left the U.S. Navy in command of Philippine waters. Never again could the Japanese fleet mount an effective offensive. However, Halsey was severely criticized for dividing his forces and leaving Leyte beachhead open to enemy naval attack. Controversy has continued to surround Halsey's handling of his force at Leyte Gulf.

In the last months of the war, Halsey's forces launched strikes over other Philippine islands, Formosa, Okinawa, and Japanese installations on the China coast. In the summer of 1945 Halsey's Third Fleet conducted air raids against Tokyo and nearby naval installations. In August 1945 American bombers dropped atomic bombs on Hiroshima and Nagasaki with devastating effect. Japan's leaders, recognizing that their country faced certain destruction, surrendered unconditionally on August 14. The official surrender took place on September 2 on board Halsey's flagship, *Missouri*, anchored in Tokyo Bay.

In November 1945 at San Pedro, California, Halsey hauled down his four star flag and turned over command of his fleet to Rear Admiral Howard Kingman. A month later Halsey was promoted to five star rank, fleet admiral of the U.S. Navy.

After retiring in 1947, Halsey refought the Battle of Leyte Gulf with his critics, managed the University of Virginia's Development Fund, and made goodwill tours to South America and Australia.

Halsey was a risk-taker who welcomed hazardous missions. For years before World War II he had been an apostle of naval air power, touting its importance, its effectiveness, its flexibility. He argued that airplanes could bring the battleground into "streets and gardens far removed from the scene of a formalized surface engagement." In the kind of war that the vast expanses of the Pacific dictated, strong, fast carrier forces were indispensable since they could strike at long range. Halsey displayed a shrewd confidence in the extremely mobile fast carrier task force, appraising it as a force that could gain command of the air at a required time and place to establish the conditions necessary for amphibious operations.

To this day students of naval history have refought the Battle of Leyte Gulf. Was Halsey right in steaming off to destroy enemy carriers, or did he leave Admiral Kinkaid in the lurch? Halsey insisted that his decision to move north was correct. If the Center Force did steam through San Bernardino Strait, it could at best, Halsey believed, "merely hit and run."

Admiral Halsey was not one of the Navy's intellectuals. His official reports are couched in the commonplace. His speeches, private correspondence, and reports reveal that he often thought in clichés and that his vocabulary was narrow. Despite his shortcomings, he had the knack of appointing extremely intelligent officers to his staff upon whom he relied for decision-making. Only on rare occasions did he overrule them.

"Another of Halsey's traits," remembered a staff member, "was the fierceness with which he defended his staff, even his men. He gave them credit for the victories won, he blamed himself for the losses."

"Halsey possessed to a magnificent degree," said a naval commander, "the intuition that let him know just how to get the best out of his people under any conditions."

"Admiral Halsey's strongest point," wrote another staff officer, "was his superb leadership. While always the true professional and exacting professional performances from all his subordinates, he had a charismatic effect on them which was like being touched by a magic wand. Anyone so touched was determined to excel."

Admiral Raymond Spruance described Halsey as "a grand man to be with," a "splendid seaman," able to "smack them [the enemy] hard every time he gets a chance."

Halsey may well have been America's most colorful and most famous admiral.

BIBLIOGRAPHY

Halsey, William F., and J. Bryan III. *Admiral Halsey's Story*. New York: McGraw-Hill, 1947.
Merrill, James M. *A Sailor's Admiral: A Biography of William F. Halsey*. New York: Thomas Y. Crowell, 1976.
Morison, Samuel E. *History of United States Naval Operations in World War II*. 15 vols. Boston: Atlantic, Little, Brown, 1947–1962.
Potter, E. B., ed. *Sea Power: A Naval History*. Englewood Cliffs, N.J.: Prentice-Hall, 1960.

JAMES M. MERRILL

HILL, Ambrose Powell (b. Culpeper County, Va., November 9, 1825; d. near Petersburg, Va., April 2, 1865), Army officer. Hill was a Confederate division and corps commander during the Civil War.

Ambrose Powell Hill was born into the family of a prosperous Virginia merchant and politician. In his youth, he engaged in many outdoor activities and became an excellent horseman. He also developed an intense admiration for the exploits of Napoleon. He received his early education at a neighborhood school and then attended Simms' Academy (Black Hill Seminary) before being accepted at the U.S. Military Academy at West Point, New York, in 1842. Because of illness and deficiencies in chemistry and philosophy, he had to repeat his third year, graduating fifteenth in a class of thirty-eight in 1847. Commissioned second lieutenant, 1st Artillery, as of August 26, 1847, he hastened to join his regiment in Mexico.

Arriving during the final stages of the Mexican War, Hill participated in some of the engagements leading to the capture of Mexico City. After the war, he was stationed briefly at Fort McHenry, Maryland. His regiment was next ordered to Florida to participate in unsuccessful campaigns against the Seminole Indians (1850–1851, 1853–1855). He was promoted to first lieutenant in 1851. Hill contracted yellow fever in 1855, and after recuperating, transferred to the U.S. Coast Survey office in Washington, D.C., serving from November 23 until obtaining a leave of absence on October 26, 1860.

Hill opposed slavery on moral grounds, but he was such a firm supporter of states' rights on the eve of the Civil War that he felt obliged to support his native state. Consequently, he resigned from the U.S. Army as of March 1, 1861, and was commissioned colonel, Virginia Volunteers, as of May 9, commanding the 13th Virginia Infantry. After brief service in western Virginia, he was present at the First Battle of Manassas (Bull Run), but his regiment was not engaged. Hill was appointed brigadier general as of February 26, 1862, and placed in command of the 1st Brigade, 2d Division, commanded by Major General James Longstreet.* Hill fought his brigade well at Williamsburg, Virginia, on May 5, but it suffered 326 casualties, which were more than any other Confederate brigade engaged that day.

Promoted to major general as of May 26, Hill was assigned to command a newly constituted division near Richmond which he named the Light Division. Presumably, Hill meant the name to imply a force organized for rapid movement, and the name caught the imagination of the Southern press (which he also may have intended). Hill opened the Battle of the Seven Days at Mechanicsville, Virginia, on June 26, attacked first at Gaines' Mill the following day, and participated in the attack on Union lines at Frazier's Farm on June 30. His division suffered heavy losses during these fights.

Because of friction that developed between Hill and Longstreet, General Robert Edward Lee* sent Hill to reinforce Lieutenant General Thomas Jonathan ("Stonewall") Jackson* in the Shenandoah Valley. Hill, however, became involved in a bitter dispute with Jackson too. Yet, he was invaluable to Jackson during the battles of Cedar Mountain and Second Manassas. During the Maryland Campaign, Hill received the surrender of the Union garrison at Harper's Ferry on September 14. He saved the Army of Northern Virginia from disaster at the Battle of Antietam by making a forced march from Harper's Ferry on September 17 to arrive on the field just as the Confederate lines were collapsing.

Returning to action with Lee's army on December 13, Hill fought in the battle of Fredericksburg, where a gap between his units allowed the only Union penetration of Confederate lines. At the Battle of Chancellorsville, Hill participated in the flanking movement that smashed the Union lines. He assumed command of the II Army Corps when Jackson was mortally wounded, only to be severely wounded himself shortly thereafter. For his skill as a division commander, Hill was promoted to lieutenant general as of May 23, 1863, and was given command of the III Army Corps of the newly reorganized Army of Northern Virginia.

As a corps commander, Hill committed Confederate forces to battle at Gettysburg without orders or a clear understanding of the situation, suffering heavy casualties on July 1. He made some gains on the first day of the battle, but his attacks on July 2 were poorly organized and uncoordinated, and, as a result, unsuccessful. On the third day of the battle, most of his troops were placed under Longstreet's command for the unsuccessful assault on Cemetery Ridge. On October 14, Hill launched another poorly organized and uncoordinated attack on Union positions at Bristoe Station, Virginia, resulting in heavy Confederate losses without any positive results.

Hill's corps was heavily engaged during the Battle of the Wilderness, May 6–7, 1864, and his line was collapsing when saved by reinforcements from Longstreet. He then took a leave of absence due to illness, returning on May 21 to participate marginally in the battles of North Anna and Cold Harbor. After Union forces crossed to the south side of the James River, Hill's corps was involved in the defense of Petersburg during the final months of the war. He was killed by Union soldiers near Petersburg on April 2, 1865, trying to rejoin his troops after the Confederate line had been shattered.

Hill's reputation as a soldier is based on his performance as a division commander. His Light Division was extremely well trained and effective on the battlefield. He could move his troops with astonishing speed and was an aggressive officer with a good sense of timing, but often at heavy cost in casualties. His finest hour as a commander was the forced march of his division from Harper's Ferry to Antietam on September 17. Without his timely arrival, Lee's army would have been destroyed on that bloody day. His inability to get along with Jackson and Longstreet somewhat limited his effectiveness, but as a division commander, he was without peer, and Lee described him in May 1863 as "the best soldier of his grade with me."

While Hill was a first-class division commander, his performance as a corps commander was uneven at best. At both Gettysburg and Bristoe Station, Hill's unplanned and poorly organized attacks came at heavy cost to the Army of Northern Virginia. During the Battle of the Wilderness, his corps was nearly overwhelmed, and his effectiveness as a commander deteriorated thereafter. He was plagued by constant illnesses. Self-doubt and failure deeply affected his performance, and the evidence suggests that his illnesses were psychosomatic.

Ambrose Powell Hill can best be described as a brilliant division commander who was promoted beyond his ability.

BIBLIOGRAPHY

Freeman, Douglas Southall. *Lee's Lieutenants: A Study in Command*. 3 vols. New York: Charles Scribner's Sons, 1942–1944.
Hassler, William Woods. *A. P. Hill: Lee's Forgotten General*. Richmond: Garrett and Massie, 1957.
Schenck, Martin. *Up Came Hill: The Story of the Light Division and Its Leaders*. Harrisburg, Pa.: Stackpole Company, 1958.

DAVID L. WILSON

HODGES, Courtney Hicks (b. Perry, Ga., January 5, 1887; d. San Antonio, Tex., January 16, 1966), World War II commanding general of the U.S. First Army in Europe.

The son of a small-town newspaper publisher, Courtney Hodges entered West Point in 1904 but was dismissed after his first year, having failed in geometry. Overcoming parental reluctance, he enlisted in the infantry in 1906 and three years later gained a commission through competitive examination. In World War I Hodges commanded a battalion in the 5th Infantry Division, earning a Distinguished Service Cross for seizing and holding a key bridgehead across the Meuse River. Because of a "hump" of wartime officers granted regular commissions, Hodges remained a permanent major from 1920 to 1934. Nevertheless, the interwar period was for him one of significant professional development. Besides attending the usual General Staff and War College courses, Hodges graduated from the Field Artillery School at Fort Sill and taught infantry tactics at Langley Field, experiences that made him keenly aware of the vital role of artillery and tactical air support in ground warfare. From 1929 to 1933 he was stationed at Fort Benning, where he won the friendship of Omar Nelson Bradley* and the confidence of George Catlett Marshall,* then assistant commandant of the Infantry School.

As the Army's chief of staff in 1940, Marshall promoted Hodges to brigadier general and commandant of the Infantry School. Early in 1941 he brought Hodges to the War Department as the major general in charge of its Infantry Bureau. Following the massive departmental reorganization of March 1942, Hodges headed briefly the Army's new Replacement and School Command. Regarded professionally as a leading expert on infantry training, equipment, weapons, and tactics, in each of the foregoing assignments Hodges significantly influenced the preparation of the American citizen-army for overseas ground combat.

From mid-1942 to the end of 1943 Hodges successively commanded the X Corps and Third Army, both of which were training organizations. As commander of a field army he advanced to lieutenant general. For the invasion of Europe, however, he relinquished the Third Army to George Smith Patton, Jr.,* a proven master of exploitation and pursuit. Still highly esteemed by both Marshall and Bradley (to be the senior American ground commander in the invasion), Hodges went to England early in 1944 as deputy head of Bradley's First Army. Once the Third Army had followed the First into the Normandy battle, Bradley would supervise both formations from a new command echelon: the 12th Army Group. Hodges would replace Bradley at the First Army.

Hodges took over as planned on August 1, 1944, directing the First Army on a swift drive across France to the German border. During the autumn months his troops fought a series of costly, inconclusive battles of attrition along the Siegfried Line in the Aachen and Huertgen Forest region. Just before Christmas of 1944, an unforeseen German offensive erupted from the Ardennes Forest, rolling back the First Army's right wing. Absorbing the main weight of the massive German attack, Hodges counterattacked on January 3, 1945. During much of the Battle of the Bulge, his First Army was directed by Field Marshal Sir Bernard L. Montgomery's 21st Army Group. Returning on January 17, 1945, to Bradley's control, Hodges' command battled into the Rhineland. In March at Remagen it seized a vital bridge across the Rhine. The First Army, together with the Ninth to its left, then encircled more than three hundred thousand German troops in the Ruhr Valley and drove into the heart of Germany. Less celebrated than Patton's Third, Hodges' was nevertheless the first Allied army to pass the German border, breach the Siegfried Line, capture an important German city, cross the Rhine, and make contact with the westward-moving Soviet Army at the Elbe River.

Promoted to full general in April 1945, Hodges was reassigned with First Army headquarters to General Douglas MacArthur's* Pacific command. Had the war lasted until March 1946, the First would have been one of two American armies assaulting Honshu in the Japanese home islands. After the Japanese surrender, the First resumed its peacetime role as an area-defense and training-army headquarters at Governor's Island in New York Harbor. From there Hodges retired early in 1949 to San Antonio, Texas, where he died seventeen years later.

At forty-one Hodges had married Mrs. Mildred Lee Buchner, a widow who, like her new husband, was an expert shot. The general was renowned throughout his long career as a trap shooter and big-game hunter.

Asked once to compare his own First Army with Patton's Third, Courtney Hodges responded by saying, "We were a zonal army. We just slugged.... Some people [like Patton] just naturally attract attention, and all my friends tell me I look more like a school teacher than a general." Hodges remained a comparatively obscure figure during and after the war, despite heading a command with a peak strength over half that of the Union Army in the Civil War. Although Hodges was the subject of several wartime magazine feature articles, after 1945 he did not bother to justify his record by publishing his memoirs. By V-E Day few American generals had more battleline experience than Hodges, nor had any Allied army on the Western Front fought harder or more successfully than the First. Yet he had no nickname. Even the sober, methodical Bradley was celebrated widely as "the GI's General," whereas of Hodges the *New York Times* could say only that "most of the troops under him would be at a loss to describe him or even give you his full name."

Up to a point, Hodges' reticence commended him to his superiors, who understandably became weary of Patton's childish posturing and Montgomery's overweening vanity. According to General Dwight David Eisenhower,* the Allied supreme commander, Hodges was "sturdy and steady." Without knowing Hodges well, Eisenhower nevertheless accepted him as a prospective Army commander in December 1943, after Marshall had praised the Georgian as being "exactly [the] same class of man as Bradley.... [Hodges is]...quiet [and] self-effacing." After the war Bradley described his friend Hodges as "a military technician whose faultless techniques made him one of the most skilled craftsmen of my entire command." Charles B. MacDonald, one of the Army's official historians, refers to Hodges as an Army commander "of the first rank," although MacDonald is severely critical of Hodges' handling of the Battle of the Huertgen Forest. To clear the dense forest First Army troops struggled for many weeks. So rugged was the Huertgen that it denied to the Americans effective exploitation of their air and artillery superiority. Hodges, who normally did not visit subordinate headquarters below the divisional level, failed to see the atrocious conditions with which his men had to contend. Moreover, neither he nor any other Allied senior commander was quick to grasp the overriding strategic importance of certain dams controlling the floodwaters of the Roer River. Pinching out the dams ought to have been the First Army's principal objective from the beginning of the Siegfried Line Campaign. Even after losing the Huertgen Forest, the Germans continued to cling to the Roer Reservoirs.

In December 1944 all of the Allied commanders and their intelligence officers were painfully surprised by the German Ardennes counteroffensive. From Adolph Rosengarten, a liaison officer, Hodges had received frequent briefings on German wireless communications intercepted and deciphered by ULTRA, but even this priceless source failed to betray the planned German attack. Then, when the First Army came under the direction of the 21st Army Group, Montgomery was apparently put off by Hodges' lack of outward charisma. The field marshal considered changing Army commanders, but was dissuaded by Eisenhower, who pointed out that "Hodges is the quiet...type and does not appear as aggressive as he really is. Unless he becomes exhausted he will always wage a good fight." Caught between Montgomery, who wished to make tactical withdrawals in order to build up his reserves, and his subordinate commanders, who insisted on launching immediate counterattacks, Hodges somehow fought his share of the Battle of the Bulge with considerable skill. Eisenhower did not at once realize how effectively Hodges had performed, however. On a confidential evaluation he ranked Hodges below several American generals with comparable responsibilities and experience, and even behind two First Army corps commanders. By the end of March 1945 Eisenhower had come to understand the magnitude of

Hodges' achievements, hailing the First Army commander as "the spearhead and the scintillating star" of the climactic thrusts across the Rhine.

Throughout his active command of the First Army, Hodges worked harmoniously with the efficient staff he had inherited from Bradley. He and his headquarters officers kept close track of all the Army's units down to the platoon level. In contrast, Patton's Third Army plotted nothing lower than regiments. At times Hodges' subordinate commanders chafed under his tight leash. Hodges neither overawed his corps and divisional commanders with the egocentric, but magnetic, personality of a Patton, nor won their affection with the warmth of a Bradley. It was widely known that Hodges invariably entrusted the First Army's most important missions to Joseph Lawton Collins'* VII Corps, an understandable preference in view of Collins' exceptional abilities.

In short, Hodges directed the First Army after the fashion of a business executive: objective, detached, and personally colorless—and quick to scrutinize statements of profit and loss. Whatever his personality shortcomings, as commander of the First Army the trim, silver-haired, mild-mannered general with the close-cropped mustache and plastic cigarette-holder oversaw a remarkably successful military organization. Near the end of the war Eisenhower concluded that "by and large" he would find it "difficult to choose" the best of his several exceptionally capable Army commanders. Unlike Patton, Hodges would have been well satisfied by his chief's fairminded assessment.

BIBLIOGRAPHY

Bradley, Omar N. *A Soldier's Story*. New York: Henry Holt, 1951.
Eisenhower, Dwight D. *The Papers of Dwight David Eisenhower*. Edited by Alfred D. Chandler, et al. Vols. 3 and 4. Baltimore: Johns Hopkins University Press, 1970–.
Hill, Gladwin. "For Hodges History Repeats." *New York Times Magazine* (March 25, 1945): 8, 34–35.
MacDonald, Charles B. *The Siegfried Line Campaign*. Washington, D.C.: U.S. Government Printing Office, 1963.
———. *The Mighty Endeavor: American Armed Forces in the European Theater in World War II*. New York: Oxford University Press, 1969.
Murray, Patrick. "Courtney Hodges." *American History Illustrated* (January 1973): 12–25.
"Precise Puncher." *Time* (October 16, 1944): 28–31.

RICHARD G. STONE, JR.

HOOD, John Bell (b. Owingsville, Ky., June 1, 1831; d. New Orleans, August 30, 1879), Army officer. John Hood is best known as the commander of the Texas Brigade during the Civil War.

Born to a well-to-do Kentucky family, John Hood enjoyed an unbridled childhood until entering West Point in 1849. The Spartan simplicity of the Military Academy clashed with young Hood's spirit; he was almost dismissed for excessive demerits. Not caring much about academics, John Hood was graduated forty-fourth in a class of fifty-five in 1853. Hood's graduation order of merit gained him a first assignment with the 4th Infantry Regiment in California. For the next fifteen months Hood's most exciting task was surviving on a lieutenant's pay in Gold Rush country. His next duty station, however, gave him much more valuable experience. Posted to the 2d Cavalry Regiment, commanded by Colonel Albert Sidney Johnston* and Lieutenant Colonel Robert Edward Lee,* Hood worked very closely with both men, gaining their respect for his personal courage and aggressiveness in fighting the Comanches.

Unlike Lee, Hood never hesitated when it came time to choose between the Union or the Confederacy. He resigned from the U.S. Army in April, 1861 and, because his native Kentucky stayed with the Union, adopted Texas as his new home. Accepting a Confederate commission, Hood first commanded the cavalry forces in the Virginia Peninsula.

Hood's association with the cavalry soon ended when President Jefferson Davis appointed him the commander of the 4th Texas Regiment. This unit had arrived in Virginia without a qualified commander, and Davis, who desired to have native sons leading state units, gave the adopted Hood his chance. The new commander spent the next few months establishing a rapport with the rowdy Texans by always explaining why training and discipline were necessary and by developing a deep sense of unit pride. Davis recognized Hood's talent with the frontiersmen and in March 1862 gave the young colonel command of the entire Texas Brigade. In their first fight two months later, the Texans established a reputation for steadiness under fire. At Eltham Landing in May 1862, Hood's unit repulsed a Federal attempt to turn the Confederate position. Performing like veterans, the Texans demonstrated the value of Hood's training and discipline.

In the remaining months of 1862 Hood and his troops performed gallantly. Robert E. Lee called Hood one of his most promising officers, while the Texas Brigade became the South's shock troops—always being placed where the hardest fighting was about to occur. At Gaines' Mill, in June, Hood led his soldiers in a decisive frontal assault against the entrenched Union infantry and artillery forces, breaching the Northern lines and routing the blueclad troops. Although not requiring a great deal of tactical brilliance, Hood's assault was highly praised by Lee, who described it as one of the most courageous acts he had ever witnessed.

Hood and his brigade again proved their mettle at Antietam. Positioned on Lee's left flank, Hood's unit prevented the Confederates' early defeat by repelling the attacks of two Union corps, thereby buying the required time for Lee to feed his reserves into the battle. The Texas Brigade was shattered, but Lee, praising Hood for his stubborn defense and audacious counterattack, promoted him to major general and gave him command of the division which included his Texans.

The next summer, Lee again marched north, this time to Gettysburg. Receiving the assignment of taking Little Round Top, Hood, after pleading unsuccessfully to be sent further south and around the Federal left, led a frontal assault—the tactic for which he had become so famous. This time not even Hood's inspiration could move his men up that hill. Suffering a terrible arm wound, Hood left the field and missed the remainder of this disastrous battle.

After less than ten weeks of medical care, Hood rejoined the division, his now paralyzed arm strapped to his body. Once again luck abandoned the young general; in September 1863 he lost a leg at Chickamauga leading a charge against the Union center. Convalescing in Richmond, Hood became the darling of Confederate society. Having suffered grievous losses, the South needed heroes to bolster morale, and the adopted Texan gallantly accepted his new role. Gaining political support by serving as an advisor to President Davis, Hood soon gained command of a corps in the Army of the Tennessee under Joseph Eggleston Johnston,* who was defending Atlanta. Promoted to lieutenant general, the aggressive Hood was soon at odds with Johnston, the master of the defense. Hood believed that Johnston, by his constant retreat, had given up excellent opportunities to strike at the Federal army under William Tecumseh Sherman* and had thereby lost men and territory without gaining any benefits. President Davis agreed and gave command of the army to Hood.

With Sherman's army slowly closing on Atlanta, the offensively minded Hood made two audacious attacks that achieved initial surprise. Failing to coordinate his forces, however, Hood could not achieve decisive results and did not check Sherman's advance. Threatened with the envelopment of his entire force inside Atlanta by Sherman's southward moving troops, Hood evacuated the city and attempted a desperate gamble. He intended to march north and, by cutting Sherman's supply lines from Nashville, force a Union withdrawal from Atlanta.

Slipping away from Sherman's troops, Hood, who had to be strapped on his horse, began the bold attack on the Federal supply lines. After an initial effort to catch the elusive Confederates, Sherman cut himself off from his supply base and headed for the sea. The job of stopping Hood fell to General George Henry Thomas.* Failing again to coordinate and control his corps commanders, Hood was unable to strike at the scattered Union forces and allowed them to fall back on Franklin, Tennessee, where they entrenched. After a futile frontal assault in which the Army of the Tennessee suffered tremendous casualties, Hood marched his force to Nashville, hoping for a miracle. There General Thomas, using a series of flanking movements, crushed the last remaining troops in the Army of the Tennessee. Hood asked to be relieved after this defeat. He learned of Lee's surrender on his way back to Texas to recruit another army.

John Bell Hood spent his remaining fourteen years in New Orleans. Failing at a variety of business endeavors, he struggled hard to support his wife and eleven children. When yellow fever swept New Orleans in 1879, it claimed the gallant Hood.

Hood's finest quality was his ability to lead men in combat. The shot and shell which made other men apprehensive never seemed to affect him. His coolness under fire was legendary and became an inspiration to all around him. The chief beneficiary of this leadership was the Texas Brigade—a group of rowdy frontiersmen to whom the word discipline meant absolutely nothing. Hood was able to harness their spirit and match it to his own. By explaining the reasons for training and discipline, he gained their respect and trust. In the crucible of combat this respect was soon transformed into genuine mutual admiration. Hood and the Texas Brigade became the same, with the unit acquiring his personality— courageous, aggressive, and possessing an indomitable will to fight. Their performance earned them the title "Grenadier Guards of the Army of Northern Virginia" and Hood the reputation as one of the bravest men in the Confederacy. John Bell Hood never commanded the Texas Brigade; he led it.

This form of leadership, absolutely vital at the brigade and division level, was of less value when Hood became a corps and later an army commander. Too far removed from the troops to exert his charisma, Hood lacked the capability to command the entire Army of the Tennessee. His failure to coordinate among his corps cost him victories outside Atlanta and Nashville. At a time when the South needed a brilliant strategist, all Hood could offer was a well-worn tactician. His greatest flaw lay in his utter dependence on the unimaginative frontal assault. Determined to let courage and will instead of maneuver decide the issue, he weakened his army before Atlanta and then destroyed it at Franklin and Nashville.

Hood's career mirrored the major problem that plagued the Confederacy as the war dragged on. The qualities for brigade and division command were not always the same as those required for higher command. John Bell Hood was a fighter, not a strategist; but when the battle flags were unfurled and the drums began to beat, there was no better assault force than Hood and his Texas Brigade.

BIBLIOGRAPHY

Dyer, John P. *The Gallant Hood*. New York: Bobbs-Merrill Company, 1950.
Freemen, Douglas Southall. *Lee's Lieutenants*. New York: Charles Scribner's Sons, 1943.
Hood, John B. *Advance and Retreat*. Bloomington: Indiana University Press, 1959.
O'Conner, Richard. *Hood: Cavalier General*. New York: Prentice-Hall, 1949.
Simpson, Harold B. *Hood's Texas Brigade: Lee's Grenadier Guard*. Waco, Tex.: Texian Press, 1970.

ROBERT E. WOLFF

HOOKER, Joseph (b. Hadley, Mass., November 13, 1814; d. Garden City, N.Y., October 31, 1879), Army officer. Hooker was commander of the Union Army of the Potomac at Chancellorsville during the Civil War.

The grandson of a captain in the American Revolution, Joseph Hooker received his early education at the Hopkins Academy in Hadley, Massachusetts. He was graduated twenty-ninth out of fifty in the West Point class of 1837. Following service in the Second Seminole War and along the Canadian border, he returned to the Military Academy as adjutant.

In the War with Mexico, Hooker participated heroically in the campaigns of both Zachary Taylor* and Winfield Scott,* winning three brevets for meritorious conduct at Monterrey, the National Bridge, and Chapultepec. His record was marred, however, when, at a court of inquiry, he testified unwisely and inaccurately on behalf of schemer Gideon Johnson Pillow against Scott, thereby incurring Scott's permanent enmity.

Restless and ambitious, and faced with slow promotions after the Mexican War, Hooker resigned from the Army in 1853 and farmed without conspicuous success near Sonoma, California. He was later superintendent of military roads in Oregon in 1858–1859 and a colonel of California militia in 1859–1861. While on the West Coast, he gained the hostility of Henry Wager Halleck* that would follow him in the Civil War.

When Fort Sumter was bombarded by the Confederates in mid-April 1861, Hooker offered his services to the Union. When no high commission was tendered him, he journeyed to Washington, D.C., and was a civilian observer at the First Battle of Bull Run in July. He finally secured an interview with President Abraham Lincoln, during which he proclaimed that he was a better general than any the Federals had at Bull Run. Lincoln apparently liked his self-assurance and named him a brigadier general of volunteers. He commanded successively a brigade and division in the Army of the Potomac that George Brinton McClellan* was organizing near Washington.

Hooker was at this time a fine figure of an officer—tall, robust, and of soldierly bearing. He had a florid complexion, a great shock of graying hair, and penetrating blue eyes. Immensely self-confident, he could savagely denounce superiors as well as subordinates, although he was well liked by most of the men in the ranks and the officers under him. Possessed with lion-hearted courage, he was exhilarated by personally experiencing mortal combat in the field. While preeminently the officer of action and dash, he could ably plan military operations and, up to a point, execute them dexterously. Hooker played a prominent part in the Battle of Williamsburg on the Peninsula, May 5, 1862, as well as in several of the heavier engagements of the Seven Days' Battle in late June. His combativeness won for him the sobriquet "Fighting Joe," although the actual words resulted from a journalistic error and he was never proud of the nickname.

At South Mountain on September 14, 1862, in command of the I Corps, Hooker played a leading role in driving the Southerners from Turner's Gap, thereby helping significantly to force Robert Edward Lee* and his Army of Northern Virginia back into a cramped defensive position along the Antietam Creek near Sharpsburg, Maryland. In the Battle of Antietam, on September 17, while impetuously leading his troops forward early in the day on the northern end of the field, he was wounded in the foot and borne from the field. In the Fredericksburg Campaign of Ambrose Everett Burnside in December, Hooker commanded a grand division of two corps. While his spirited attacks against the stonewall were abortive, Hooker's advice to Burnside to desist from such suicidal assaults was sound and should have been heeded.

When Burnside was relieved of his command, Hooker was named commander of the Army of the Potomac in January 1863, although Lincoln felt impelled to write him a remarkable letter. In it, the president said, accurately and bluntly,

"... you have taken counsel of your ambition.... I have heard... of your recently saying that both the army and the Government needed a dictator. Of course, it was not for this, but in spite of it, that I have given you the command. Only those generals who gain successes can set up dictators. What I now ask of you is military success, and I will risk the dictatorship." Hooker was profoundly moved by the letter.

Hooker's stewardship of the Army of the Potomac began auspiciously in the winter of early 1863 when he capably instituted a number of needed administrative reforms. He then turned toward planning a campaign against the Confederate Army still ensconced at Fredericksburg. Fighting Joe would have some one hundred and thirty-two thousand men compared to Lee's sixty-two thousand. The Federal commander would dispatch his cavalry to operate on the enemy's line of communications between Fredericksburg and Richmond while Hooker, leaving John Sedgwick with some forty thousand men opposite Lee, would move the bulk of the national army up the north bank and cross the Rappahannock and Rapidan rivers and come in from the west against Lee's rear at Fredericksburg. It was a brilliant and feasible plan. But Hooker damaged his good reputation as head of the army by his loud and bombastic overconfidence.

The campaign began well enough in late April 1863, despite the ineffectiveness of the Federal cavalry, when, in a masterfully executed maneuver, Hooker crossed the rivers and reached Chancellorsville, just ten miles to the west of Lee's army, still in position at Fredericksburg facing Sedgwick. On the morning of May 1 Hooker pushed his large force eastward, the advance elements of it emerging from the tangled Wilderness onto open ground, where the superior Union artillery could play to good effect. But Hooker was astonished to see Lee, now apprised of the Federal threat, actually moving westward to confront him, the Confederate chieftain leaving Jubal Early* with some ten thousand men to contain Sedgwick at Fredericksburg. Losing his nerve, and uncharacteristically refusing to fight offensively, Hooker, against the advice of all of his top generals, recoiled back into the Wilderness and deployed his army in a defensive arc about the crossroads at Chancellorsville. This enabled Lee to send Thomas Jonathan ("Stonewall") Jackson* on the latter's famous turning movement and flank attack of May 2 against Hooker's exposed right (west) wing, which was shattered by Jackson's sledgehammer blow and sent reeling backward. But nightfall and the mortal wounding of Jackson halted the Confederate advance.

The next day in a resumption of the fighting, Hooker was injured but would not relinquish command, and he still insisted that the army fight passively on the defensive. After Sedgwick had driven Early away from Fredericksburg, Sedgwick was bettered by Lee at the Battle of Salem Church and forced to the north side of the river via Banks Ford. Near Chancellorsville, Hooker's lines were forced back slowly, the Union commander refusing to use two of his best corps which had remained unengaged. Despite the recommendation of a majority of his corps commanders to stay and fight it out, the demoralized Hooker retreated back to his starting point opposite Fredericksburg after having lost some 17,287 men at Chancellorsville, as against Lee's 12,463. With Lee launching his second invasion of the North in June 1863, Hooker maneuvered his army well in the early stages of the Gettysburg Campaign; but, having incurred the loss of confidence of Lincoln, Secretary of War Edwin McMasters Stanton, and General in Chief Halleck, he was replaced in command of the Army of the Potomac by George Gordon Meade.*

After the battle at Gettysburg, Hooker was later given command of the newly formed XX Corps, made up of the remnants of the XI and XII Corps, and he again showed his high ability as a corps commander under Ulysses Simpson Grant* at the fighting around Chattanooga—especially at Lookout Mountain—in late 1863 and with the armies under William Tecumseh Sherman* in Sherman's advance upon Atlanta in the spring and summer of 1864. But Hooker resigned his command when a junior officer—Oliver Otis Howard—was given command of one of Sherman's armies instead of himself.

From September 28, 1864, to July 5, 1865, Hooker headed the Northern Department; from July 8, 1865, to August 6, 1866, the Department of the East; and from August 23, 1866, to June 1, 1867, the Department of the Lakes. He had been married in 1865 to Olivia Groesbeck. Owing to partial paralysis stemming from his old Chancellorsville injury, he retired from the Army as a major general on October 15, 1868.

Except for exceptionally meritorious service rendered in the Mexican War, Joseph Hooker's career up to the Civil War was largely an unrewarding one. Possessing self-confidence, high physical courage, audacity, and administrative abilities of a high order, Hooker was fatally flawed by his lack of self-control, mercurial temperament, and sharp tongue. Even more serious were his lack of subordination and his talk of a military dictatorship.

But Hooker was graced with real military talents, and, up through the level of corps or grand division (wing) commander, he was one of the ablest of all Civil War generals. He was incapable of sustained mental concentration, however, and he lacked the intellect and character to command a great army, as shown at Chancellorsville. This operation was masterfully planned and, in its initial stages, brilliantly executed. Hooker, however, could not make war on the map or successfully command troops that he could not actually see with his own eyes, nor could he improvise adequately. Even after Stonewall Jackson's successful flank attack, Hooker would still have been master of the situation had he counterattacked with his thirty-seven thousand fresh troops. That he refused to do so shows that Lee had regained the initiative and had reasserted the moral ascendancy over Fighting Joe.

Hooker had started out the Chancellorsville Campaign determined to remain on the strategic and tactical offensive. He was convinced that Lee would have to retreat, and he was astounded and stunned into mental paralysis when Lee daringly refused to withdraw and instead turned upon the Federals. The Union commander acknowledged in his official report that he "could not get his men in position" to employ all of them in the combat. Some argue that Hooker, said to have been "a three-bottle man," suddenly stopped his drinking and that this helped cause his loss of nerve at the climax of the operations at Chancellorsville. When he resumed his habit, he again performed excellently as a corps commander under Grant and Sherman.

Some historians believe that Lincoln should never have named Hooker to the army command in the first place and that the president's own remarkable letter to the general contains within it ample reasons why so reckless a person as one who talked of a dictatorship should never have been entrusted with a position of such great military responsibility.

BIBLIOGRAPHY

Bigelow, John, Jr. *The Campaign of Chancellorsville: A Strategic and Tactical Study.* New Haven, Conn.: Yale University Press, 1910.
Dodge, Theodore A. *The Campaign of Chancellorsville.* Boston: J. R. Osgood, 1881.
Hassler, Warren W., Jr. *Commanders of the Army of the Potomac.* Baton Rouge: Louisiana State University Press, 1962.
Hebert, Walter H. *Fighting Joe Hooker.* Indianapolis: Bobbs-Merrill Company, 1944.
Williams, T. Harry. *Lincoln and His Generals.* New York: Alfred A. Knopf, 1952.

WARREN W. HASSLER, JR.

INGERSOLL, Royal Eason (b. Georgetown, D.C., June 20, 1883; d. Bethesda, Md., May 20, 1976), naval officer. Ingersoll commanded the Atlantic Fleet and Western Sea Frontier in World War II.

Royal Eason Ingersoll liked to date his entry into the Navy from the time he was "carried into the Naval Academy in the arms of [his] nurse" when his father, then Lieutenant and later Rear Admiral Royal Rodney Ingersoll, became an instructor there in the fall of 1883. His mother was Cynthia Eason of La Porte, Indiana, where he attended public schools during his father's long deployments at sea. He also attended private schools in Annapolis along with William Frederick Halsey, Jr.,* and made practice cruises with the Academy midshipmen. Ingersoll won a competition for the appointment from Indiana's Thirteenth Congressional District and entered the Academy in May 1901 along with Chester William Nimitz.* He graduated with distinction in 1905, standing fourth in a class of 114.

Ingersoll's first tour after graduation was in the old battleship *Missouri*, with Halsey as a roommate and Lieutenant (later Admiral) Thomas Charles Hart as a senior shipmate. Then as a boat officer he ferried delegates to the Russo-Japanese Peace Conference around Portsmouth Harbor and served in the gunboat *Marietta*, the transport *Hancock*, and (until felled by appendicitis after six days) the presidential yacht *Mayflower*. Ingersoll made part of the world cruise of the Great White Fleet in its flagship *Connecticut*. Commissioned ensign in 1907 and lieutenant (both grades) in 1910, he married Louise Van Harlingen, a La Porte friend, in 1910. He soon taught seamanship and English at the Academy, and in 1913 he went to the protected cruiser *Saratoga*, flagship of the Asiatic Fleet, at the height of the Chinese revolution. He held various staff jobs, including fleet engineer and flag secretary, before going to another Asiatic Fleet ship, the protected cruiser *Cincinnati*, as her executive officer.

In 1916 Ingersoll came home to head, as a lieutenant commander (and temporary commander after February 1918), the communications office at Navy Department headquarters. In Paris he organized communications for the American delegation to the Peace Conference. After successive tours as the executive officer in the battleships *Connecticut* and *Arizona*, he received the permanent rank of commander in 1921 and took over the Japanese espionage desk at the Office of Naval Intelligence in Washington for three years. There he worked with projects that helped with the subsequent cryptographic breakthrough known as MAGIC. In 1924 he missed the chance for a destroyer as his first command; offered the choice of a transport, a cargo ship, or the converted yacht *Nokomis*, he chose the *Nokomis* and hydrographic survey duty in the Caribbean.

In July 1926 Ingersoll began the full-year course at the Naval War College in international law, strategy and tactics, problem-solving, and situation estimates, after which the college president, Admiral William V. Pratt, brought him onto the staff for a year. Then Pratt became commander, Battle Fleet, and took Ingersoll, a captain since June 1927, as his assistant chief of staff. When Pratt became commander in chief, U.S. Fleet, in 1929, Ingersoll accompanied him. In 1930 Pratt became chief of naval operations (CNO) and took Ingersoll to head the Fleet Training Division. Pratt gave high priority to the post-World War revision of tactical and war instructions, and this task consumed Ingersoll's time until 1933.

In May 1933 Ingersoll took command of the heavy cruiser *Augusta*, flagship of the Scouting Force and based in the Pacific; in October he went to Mare Island Navy Yard to supervise the fitting out and commissioning of the new heavy cruiser *San Francisco*, which he commanded until June 1935. There followed three years as director of war plans in the CNO's office, where Ingersoll worked extensively with "Plan Orange" and served also as a technical advisor at the London Naval Conference of 1935–1936. As of July 1, 1937, he was thirty-fifth on the list of 271 captains, sixteen numbers below Husband Edward Kimmel,* ten below Halsey, and two above Nimitz; he was the most junior of the seven captains on the current promotion list for rear admiral, a rank that took effect on May 1, 1938. Flag rank brought him command of Cruiser Division Six in the Pacific, and in the summer he became assistant to the CNO, Admiral Harold Raynsford Stark.

Stark, calculating potential wartime assignments in the autumn of 1941, expected to leave Ernest Joseph King* in command of the Atlantic Fleet, send Nimitz to the Asiatic Fleet in place of Hart, and give Ingersoll the Pacific command, leaving Kimmel with the superior post of commander in chief, U.S. Fleet. Pearl Harbor changed things. Kimmel lost both his positions, King went to Washington as Fleet commander in chief, and Secretary William Franklin

Knox picked Nimitz for the Pacific Fleet. Hart kept the Asiatic Fleet, a command approaching closer to oblivion with every passing day. Stark finally agreed to give up his chief deputy, and thus, with the temporary rank of vice admiral, Ingersoll became commander in chief, Atlantic Fleet, on December 30, 1941. On July 1, 1942, he received the rank of admiral, also a temporary wartime commission. He gave up the flagship *Augusta* to patrol and escort duty and shifted to the ancient frigate *Constellation*, permanently moored at Newport, thus becoming the only American admiral to fight a war from a commissioned flagship nearly 150 years old. Later, in the converted yacht *Vixen*, he could move up and down the coast to visit ports.

In November 1944 Ingersoll went to San Francisco to command the Western Sea Frontier, which embraced all installations in the ten Western states. Unquestioned control over all aspects of mobilization, logistics, training, and manpower for the final assault on Japan required the additional titles of deputy commander in chief, U.S. Fleet, and deputy CNO. "I was like Pooh Bah in The Mikado," he recalled. "If I couldn't accomplish what I wanted under one head, I could accomplish it under another." On April 10, 1946, he gave up all active duty, and on August 1, 1946, he retired with the permanent rank of admiral to date from July 1, 1942. For the duration of the war after mid-1942, Ingersoll was the fourth ranking officer on the active list (other than recalled retirees), Stark, King, and Nimitz being senior in the grade of admiral. The five star rank of fleet admiral, created in December 1944 and limited to four officers, went immediately to William Daniel Leahy, who had been recalled from retirement in 1942 to chair the Joint Chiefs of Staff, King, and Nimitz; the fourth slot remained vacant until December 1945 when Halsey was promoted over Stark and Ingersoll. At the time of his death, Ingersoll was the senior officer on the Navy retired list.

During his forty-year career, Royal Eason Ingersoll experienced most of the major events of naval history. Three contributions deserve special evaluation. First, Ingersoll performed well a vital function of the commanding officer: teaching juniors. Ensigns and lieutenants who served under him in *San Francisco*, and themselves retired as captains and admirals, still recall him as fair and effective. When observing junior officers on watch, he did not publicly berate them for errors but instead made mental notes, let the junior bail himself out of trouble, went to his cabin, rang up on the bridge phone, and began an even-tempered conversation with "Well, now, that little maneuver didn't work very well, did it?" The same skills underlay his work on instructions and manuals at the Fleet Training Division. As commander in chief, Atlantic Fleet, he was responsible for preparing thousands of men and hundreds of new ships for combat in one of the largest, most complex, and most demanding wartime training programs ever undertaken.

A second contribution was Ingersoll's extremely keen ability at staff work, particularly operations and planning. His work in naval intelligence and war plans kept him versed in major issues of international relations, and by Pearl Harbor, because highly placed admirals valued his work, he had reached the highest policymaking and executive levels of the Navy.

Ingersoll's third contribution was his command of the Atlantic Fleet and later of the Western Sea Frontier. The Atlantic Fleet position involved staggering responsibilities and often insufficient resources to carry them out. The Atlantic Fleet's principal early tasks of protecting shipping in the North Atlantic and controlling ocean approaches to the Western Hemisphere were well underway upon Ingersoll's arrival. While the battle of the Atlantic against surface raiders and submarines raged from Greenland to Brazil, and Ingersoll had to respond to subordinates, "I wish I could give you a few more destroyers but the 'musts' keep us living from hand to mouth to satisfy demands," the Atantic Fleet had to train and prepare ships built in East Coast yards but scheduled for the Pacific. In addition, Ingersoll had to train, transport, land, and supply the amphibious forces of the Western Task Force in the North African landings of November 1942. The 1943 invasion of Sicily occasioned similar duties, and the responsibilities of the twelve months prior to Normandy dwarfed anything that had gone before. At a press conference on June 6, 1944, Admiral King introduced Ingersoll and praised him for never saying he could not do the job. "He has gone ahead and done it—just how, I don't quite understand."

Although Ingersoll was a fleet commander, his duties were administrative rather than combat. Nor did his personality and style match those of a Halsey. Unassuming, modest, and even a bit shy, the pipe-smoking, stamp-collecting Ingersoll did his job quietly, with the aid of a remarkably small staff, a famous little black notebook full of facts and figures, and a keen intellect. Among his American decorations was one for World War II service, of which he characteristically said, "I always regarded that decoration as the 'croix de chair' for commanding an LMD—a large mahogany desk."

BIBLIOGRAPHY

Administrative History of the U.S. Atlantic Fleet in World War II: Vol. 1. *Commander-in-Chief, U.S. Atlantic Fleet*. 2 vols. Washington, D.C.: U.S. Naval History Division, 1946.

Administrative History of Western Sea Frontier During World War II. 7 vols. Washington, D.C.: U.S. Naval History Division, 1946.

Furlong, William Rea, ed. *Class of 1905, United States Naval Academy*. Annapolis, Md.: U.S. Naval Academy, 1930.

Ingersoll, Royal E. "The Reminiscences of Admiral Royal E. Ingersoll." Oral History Research Project, Columbia University, 1965.

Morison, Samuel E. *History of U.S. Naval Operations in World War II*. 15 vols. Boston: Atlantic, Little, Brown and Company, 1947–1962.

JAMES E. SEFTON

JACKSON, Andrew (b. Waxhaw, S.C., March 15, 1767; d. Nashville, Tenn., June 8, 1845), lawyer, politician (U.S. representative, senator, and president), judge, major general. Jackson was the first person to give his name to an era of American history.

Andrew Jackson was the youngest of three sons of Scotch-Irish immigrants. His father died shortly before Andrew's birth. Both of his brothers and his mother died during the Revolutionary War. Jackson himself, as a fourteen-year-old captured partisan, was slashed with a sabre on his hand and forehead when he refused to polish a British officer's boots.

After studying law, Jackson went to Nashville in 1788 and quickly became successful. In 1796 he was elected U.S. representative. Appointed to the Senate in 1797, Jackson resigned the next year to accept a judgeship on the Tennessee Supreme Court. He was elected major general of the Tennessee militia in 1802. Jackson took his military duties seriously. He studied a translation of French Army regulations and applied the principles he learned to his men.

When war with England came in June 1812, Jackson offered the services of his command. The government accepted but did not call him to active duty because President James Madison disliked Jackson and had no intention of using the Tennessean if he could help it.

By the autumn, however, the administration was contemplating an attack on east Florida, so Jackson was commissioned a major general of U.S. volunteers and ordered to New Orleans where the Tennesseans would be under the overall command of one of Jackson's old enemies, General James Wilkinson. When Jackson reached Natchez, he was told to halt. Fuming over the delay, Jackson was astounded to get a letter from the secretary of war in March 1813 which informed him that the expedition was canceled and that he and his men were dismissed.

Realizing that his men probably would join Wilkinson, Jackson decided to lead them personally back to their homes in Tennessee. On this return march, Jackson's strength in adversity revealed itself clearly for the first time. Noting it, his men nicknamed him, affectionately, "Old Hickory."

Back in Tennessee, Jackson became involved in a brawl with Thomas and Jesse Benton. Jackson was shot in the shoulder and gravely wounded. While recovering, he heard that the Creeks had killed over four hundred people at Fort Mims. Forcing himself out of his sick bed, Jackson ordered volunteers to assemble.

The general moved rapidly to the upper Coosa River, where he built his main base. Two successful battles were fought in November 1813, but they did not break Creek power. Jackson's men became rebellious when vital supplies failed to arrive and disputes erupted over terms of enlistment. Jackson prevented mutiny, but the sullen mood remained.

In February reinforcements began arriving, including the welcome addition of a regular infantry regiment which Jackson knew could be used against refractory militia. By March 1814 Old Hickory had approximately five thousand men and was ready to hit the Indians decisively at one of their fortified camps at the Horseshoe Bend of the Tallapoosa River. This battle, fought on March 27, broke the power of the Creek Nation forever.

To show its gratitude, the government on May 28 appointed Jackson major general in the U.S. Army and assigned him to command the Seventh Military

District in the South. On August 9, 1814, he concluded the Treaty of Fort Jackson with the Creeks by which they ceded twenty-three million acres of land.

He then raced to Mobile and defended it in September against a small British force. Jackson pursued the British to Spanish Pensacola and captured the town on November 7. Jackson was planning to attack the British in a nearby fort when they blew it up and departed. Fearing another attack on Mobile, Jackson hurried back. Waiting there, he decided that New Orleans was the target. He arrived there on December 2.

Despite Jackson's energetic preparations for various possible British lines of advance, one bayou south of the city was not blocked. The British discovered this open waterway and were within seven miles of the city by December 23. Jackson was shocked but immediately ordered a night attack. After a confused engagement, Jackson withdrew.

Jackson prepared a defensive position along the Rodriguez Canal. The line ran from the levee over to a cypress swamp. Jackson also had a battery of heavy guns on the west bank to prevent a flanking attack.

When a show of force on December 28 and an artillery duel on January 1 failed to dislodge the Americans, the British commander, Lieutenant General Sir Edward Pakenham, decided to make a massive frontal assault on January 8. As a prelude, one of his four brigades was to cross the river and capture the American guns on the west bank, thus outflanking Jackson's position. When this was delayed, Pakenham ordered the main attack to begin anyway at dawn. The American artillery made a shambles of the advancing British columns. Within a half hour it was over. Pakenham was dead, and his army had suffered almost two thousand casualties, against six killed and seven wounded on the American side.

In the meantime, the British attack on the west bank had succeeded, but Pakenham's successor was so sickened by the destruction of the main force that he decided to retreat and so ordered the troops back to the east bank. In early March word arrived finally that the war had been concluded by the Treaty of Ghent on December 24, 1814.

Jackson returned to Nashville in April, the greatest hero of the war. The army was reorganized into two divisions, a southern and northern, each commanded by a major general. Jackson was given command of the southern division with headquarters at the "Hermitage," his home in Nashville.

In November 1817 the Seminoles in Spanish Florida were provoked into attacking an American troop boat on the Apalachicola River. The next month, Secretary of War John Caldwell Calhoun ordered Jackson to chastise them, and the First Seminole War had begun.

Jackson invaded in March 1818. He captured the Spanish town of St. Marks, then headed east toward a large Seminole village on the Suwannee River. On the way, he destroyed all Indian villages in his path. He burned his objective and then went back to St. Marks, where he ordered the execution of two British subjects he had captured. He was convinced they were inciting the Indians; he was half right. Jackson next moved west to Pensacola which he captured on May 24.

During this whirlwind campaign, Jackson had completely demoralized the Indians by destroying their homes and executing several of their prominent leaders. By the end of May, the Hero was returning home, again the center of controversy and admiration. Spain protested Jackson's actions violently, but it did see that it could not hold Florida and ceded the area to the United States.

In 1821 Congress reduced the size of the Army. One of the two major generals, Jackson or Jacob Jennings Brown, would have to be demoted, but both were powerful men with influential friends. By persuading Jackson to take the governorship of Florida and thus to quit the Army, President James Monroe avoided an embarrassing dilemma. Jackson was appointed governor in March and resigned his Army commission on June 1, 1821. He resigned the governorship in October to return to Nashville where some friends were already beginning to use his military fame to push him for president.

Unsuccessful in 1824, Jackson was elected president in 1828. During his two terms, he created the modern presidency through his use of executive power with the veto and his misguided but powerful attack on the Bank of the United States. During the Nullification Crisis with South Carolina, Jackson threatened to take to the field again, as commander in chief, before the controversy was resolved. He retired to the "Hermitage" in 1837.

Jackson did not contribute anything new to the art or science of war, but he did give the American people confidence and pride in themselves. He was an amateur soldier, but like George Washington,* another amateur, he had enormous battlefield presence. It is noteworthy that a third amateur soldier-president, Theodore Roosevelt,* admired Jackson immensely.

Jackson was capable of error. It was his fault, ultimately, that the bayou south of New Orleans was not obstructed as he had ordered. He erred in failing to realize until too late the crucial importance of the American position on the west bank of the Mississippi. Under different circumstances, this could have cost him the Battle of New Orleans.

Jackson also had an unfortunate tendency to overreact; his execution of errant militiamen during the War of 1812 and the execution of the two Britons during the Seminole War are good examples. A related shortcoming was his habit of taking everything that went wrong as a personal attack on him. For instance, the Madison administration canceled the invasion of Florida by Jackson's Tennesseans in 1813 because of congressional opposition, but Jackson believed it to be the machinations of evil men out to destroy him. Similarly, a public feud which Jackson had with the War Department during the first months of Monroe's presidency grew out of bureaucratic blundering, not, as he supposed, as a conscious effort to undermine his authority.

His shortcomings were more than compensated by his achievements. His defeat of the Creeks at Horseshoe Bend may not have shown brilliant generalship, but the battle was carefully planned and boldly executed. His next effort, the rapid march from Mobile to Pensacola and back in the autumn of 1814, was truly inspired. Capture of Pensacola made success at New Orleans more certain. Furthermore, if Jackson made mistakes at New Orleans, he did many things right. His concept of a flexible defense until the British revealed their intentions, his daring night attack once they had done so, his ability to get a motley crew to work together effectively at the Rodriguez Canal, and his refusal to pursue the British after January 8—all had the hallmark of professionalism. His lightning thrusts during the First Seminole War were faultless in a strictly military sense. He also had a professional's appreciation of the importance of a regular source of supply and ensured he had such during the Seminole Campaign.

Indeed, even though Jackson gained entree to the military through the militia, his actions and attitudes always were more like those of a regular than a militia general. James Parton was wrong when he described Jackson as being wholly ignorant of the art of war. He studied military writings and tried to instill professional precepts in his Tennesseans. He was a rigid disciplinarian who never tried to court popularity with his men. He valued regular troops in his command principally as a check against mutiny by his militiamen. He was contemptuous of the New York militia who justified their refusal to invade Canada in 1812 on constitutional grounds. He insisted that his own militiamen would not be allowed such scruples over an invasion of Florida.

Along with this undeniable military talent, Jackson also had his share of good luck. As Robert Remini has observed, much of Jackson's success in the War of 1812 was "a matter of his being in the right place at the right time," but every successful general needs good fortune occasionally.

Ultimately, what made Andrew Jackson the most famous and successful general of his generation—more than talent and luck—was his iron resolution to succeed no matter what the odds or price. His will kept his army together after the aborted invasion of Florida in 1813; his will kept an army in the field during the nadir of the Creek War; his will stiffened the resolve of the Louisianans to do their utmost to resist British invasion.

His fortitude is even more remarkable when one realizes that during his campaigns in 1813–1815, he was a very sick man. When he took the field he was still enfeebled from his wound in the Benton fight. To this was soon added dysentery which kept him dangerously weak through the New Orleans Campaign. There were times when only his unconquerable spirit kept him in action.

The ferocity of his nature, his determination to avoid defeat at all costs, is illustrated also in his comments on the defeat of a man he admired—Napoleon Bonaparte. Jackson said that the emperor should have done what he would have done, burned Paris to the ground rather than let it fall to the enemy. There are indications that Jackson would have done this if necessary at New Orleans. In his faults (overreacting and taking everything personally) and his virtues (rapidity of movement and a resolve never to be defeated), Jackson resembles General George Smith Patton, Jr.,* more than any other American general.

BIBLIOGRAPHY

Coles, Harry L. *The War of 1812*. Chicago: University of Chicago Press, 1965.
James, Marquis. *Andrew Jackson: The Border Captain*. Indianapolis, Ind.: Bobbs-Merrill, 1933.
Mahon, John K. *The War of 1812*. Gainesville: University of Florida Press, 1972.
Parton, James. *General Jackson*. New York: Appleton, 1897.
Reilly, Robin. *The British at the Gates: The New Orleans Campaign in the War of 1812*. New York: G. P. Putnam's Sons, 1974.
Remini, Robert. *Andrew Jackson: And the Course of American Empire, 1767–1821*. New York: Harper and Row, 1977.
Ward, John W. *Andrew Jackson: Symbol for an Age*. New York: Oxford University Press, 1955.

JOHN M. WERNER

JACKSON, Thomas Jonathan (b. Clarksburg, Va., January 21, 1824; d. Guiney's Station, Va., May 10, 1863), Army officer. "Stonewall" Jackson was commander of the 2d Corps, Army of Northern Virginia, during the American Civil War.

Thomas Jackson's Scot-Irish father, Jonathan, brought his son into a mountain world characterized by poor-land poverty. Thomas was the second son and third of four children. Following the death of his parents, Thomas lived with his uncle Cummins Jackson. As a young man, Thomas worked in various capacities, including a term as constable, and battled a tendency toward bad health. In the spring of 1842 he obtained an appointment to the U.S. Military Academy at West Point.

Jackson struggled as a student, his deficiencies making the stiff course of study at West Point seem insurmountable at times. His classmates and instructors thought him "slow," and his awkwardness and insecurity produced demerits. But the fragile-looking, wiry frame hosted a soul of steel, and gradually his dogged determination won admirers, friends, and respect. In 1846 he was graduated seventeenth in a class of fifty-nine, among them George Brinton McClellan* and Ambrose Powell Hill.*

War began with Mexico in 1846, and Jackson distinguished himself at Vera Cruz, Cerro Gordo, and Chapultepec. By war's end he had become a brevet major.

In February 1851 Jackson received an inquiry from the superintendent of the Virginia Military Institute (VMI) at Lexington, who wished to know Jackson's interest in an appointment as professor of natural and experimental philosophy. At the time Jackson was involved in an argument with his post commander (Major W. H. French at Fort Meade, Florida) over a technical point of command. Consequently, Jackson applied for the professorship, was selected to fill it, and resigned from the Army in February 1852. When Jackson reported as a teacher at VMI, he was twenty-seven years of age, frail, and already considered eccentric. Jackson's skills as a teacher were limited, but he worked diligently. The cadets played practical jokes on him, and some of them tried to get him dismissed. But the superintendent admired Jackson and successfully defended his professor.

Jackson's social life in Lexington was at first limited to the austere military opportunities at the campus, but eventually they broadened to include an active and devoted relationship with the Presbyterian church. Becoming a famed keeper of the Sabbath, he dutifully attended church meetings, even if he slept through them; and he insisted on taking his turn in oral prayer, although his inarticulateness made these experiences painful for him, for his auditors, and, some said, for the Lord. Church activity brought Jackson increased social invitations. Miss Elinor Junkin, daughter of a Presbyterian minister, set her cap for Major Jackson, and they were wed in August 1853. Their brief time together ended with her death on October 22, 1854, evidently from complications arising from her pregnancy. Jackson despaired at Ellie's death, but he was wed again in July 1857, to Mary Ann Morrison, another daughter of a Presbyterian minister. For the remainder of the 1850s Jackson continued to teach at VMI. In 1859 he commanded the cadet corps which attended the hanging of abolitionist leader John Brown.

When Virginia seceded in April 1861, Jackson received a commission as a colonel of infantry and in June was promoted to brigadier general. He drilled his troops to high efficiency and moved under the command of Joseph Eggleston Johnston* to the field at Manassas Junction (Bull Run), where the first major battle of the Civil War occurred. At a critical moment in the battle, General Bernard Bee rallied his own troops by shouting, "There is Jackson standing like a stone wall." The name stuck. Jackson received promotion to major general in October and in November assumed command in the Shenandoah Valley, a part of the Department of Northern Virginia.

The battles in the spring of 1862 brought Jackson lasting fame. Johnston evacuated Manassas in early March, forcing Jackson to abandon Winchester. He thus began the famous Shenandoah Valley Campaign, rated by many historians as one of the most remarkable in military history. Marching up the Valley, Jackson attacked General James Shields at Winchester on March 23. Shields' superior numbers prevailed, and the Union forces turned back the Confederates. But strategically, Jackson's bold attack proved to be a success, alarming the Federal high command, which shifted troops intended to assist General George Brinton McClellan* in his attack on Richmond. From mid-April until mid-May Jackson operated under the supervision of General Robert Edward Lee* because Johnston was before Richmond facing McClellan. Lee allowed Jackson to remain in the Valley and act independently instead of ordering him to reinforce Johnston. Moving up and down the Valley, Jackson attacked various Federal units, which altogether numbered more than sixty thousand men; but with the Federals separated into parts, Jackson's force of seventeen thousand matched them in action after action, always alarming the Union command that he might break out of the Valley and attack Washington, which seemed ill-defended with so many soldiers engaged in the Richmond Campaign. Thus, actions against Generals

N. P. Banks at Front Royal, May 23–25, John Charles Frémont at Cross Keys on June 8, and James Shields the next day held thousands of Federal troops in the Valley which McClellan required, at least for his own confidence, miles to the east.

Owing to a wound he received in the defense of Richmond, Johnston was replaced by Lee, who thereafter commanded Jackson's troops. Lee brought Jackson to the Richmond area to help relieve the capitol in the Seven Days' Campaign. In action at White Oak Swamp, on unfamiliar grounds, and without the aid of his usual cartographer, Jedediah Hotchkiss, Jackson's actions lacked sharpness.

In July Lee and Jackson advanced on the base of General John Pope at Manassas Junction. Jackson's men covered fifty-one miles in only two days, engaged the enemy, and then joined other Confederate forces for the Second Battle of Manassas, pushing Pope's army nearly to Washington's defenses. This rapid marching gave Jackson's command a new name: the foot cavalry. These actions made Jackson a Southern hero. Now thirty-eight years of age, his eccentricities, such as holding his arm in the air to improve circulation, became endearing instead of amusing.

In the fall of 1862 Jackson moved into Maryland with Lee, and one of his divisions, under A. P. Hill, helped to stop a desperate Union attack in the Battle at Sharpsburg (Antietam). Later that year, at Fredericksburg, Jackson's men fought well beside those of James Longstreet* to repulse the crossing of the Rappahannock River by General Ambrose Everett Burnside. In the spring Lee and Jackson faced the Federals, now commanded by Joseph Hooker,* at Chancellorsville. Lee employed a plan he and Jackson had used before; Jackson marched rapidly to flank Hooker, and together a two-pronged and coordinated attack caught the Union Army in a vice. The fighting went well at first, but at nightfall (May 2, 1863), while on reconnaissance, Jackson was wounded by men of his own command who mistook his staff for Union cavalrymen. He was taken to Guiney's Station, suffered the amputation of his left arm, and on May 10, died of pneumonia and complications from the wounds. "I know not how to replace him," said Robert E. Lee, and "I have lost my good right arm." As Jedediah Hotchkiss observed: "I was in no great battle subsequent to Jackson's death in which I did not see the opportunity which, in my opinion, he would have seized, and have routed our opponents."

Jackson's significance to the Confederate military cause rests on a broad base. First, he seemed always at his best in independent command. Actually, he worked well *with* his commanders, Johnston and especially Lee, and they needed only to give him an outline of intended actions. He could be relied upon to fill in the details of the action, and, always keeping his own counsel, execute the plan with swiftness and skill. Early in the war Jackson's secretive nature led many to think him a glory-seeker or at least uncooperative. In time it became his trademark and worked remarkably well as long as he had Lee, and Lee had him, in a kind of partnered command in which each understood the other's role. Lee could never rely on Jackson's successors this way, and thereafter his army became more of a single unit, and also less successful.

Second, Jackson's significant Valley Campaign in the spring of 1862, more than any other factor, spared Richmond's capture. The Army of the Potomac drew almost within the city's limits, but McClellan's own fearful character, much affected by the absence of the extra soldiers he expected to have with him but who instead had been detained in the Valley to oppose Jackson, doomed his campaign to fail. Meanwhile, Jackson handled his small Valley army brilliantly in what became a classic military campaign.

Third, Jackson's acceptance of his own limitations, and the ability to assemble and coordinate a brilliant staff, made him a successful general. With Colonel A. S. Pendleton as assistant adjutant general and coordinator, and others including Captain Jedediah Hotchkiss, his cartographer, to draw upon, Jackson used his staff to greatest advantage by assigning each man his duty and granting him autonomy to perform it. For example, Jackson would draw his mapmaker aside and in complete secrecy order him to select a route to a camp or rendezvous. Jackson had no real facility for grasping the lay of the land, routes, or directions, but Hotchkiss did and the commander used his engineer's skills. He also used Pendleton's skills at organization in the same way. The other staff members performed well, and when the troops arrived at Hotchkiss' chosen spot, everything was usually in readiness.

Fourth, Jackson's keeping of his own council is something of a miracle. Coupled with his loyalty to and confidence in Lee, this made him the ideal subordinate commander. In this role he had no peer in the American Civil War, and it qualified him for this final significance: Jackson became one of the great heroes of the Confederacy. His death martyred him, and his loss was enormous. Soldiers who followed Jackson blindly moved more cautiously behind Richard Stoddert Ewell or later successors. Duty remained, and the Confederates performed it, but like Hotchkiss and Lee, they always missed Jackson.

BIBLIOGRAPHY

Chambers, Lenoir. *Stonewall Jackson*. 2 vols. New York: Morrow and Company, 1959.
Douglas, Henry Kyd. *I Rode with Stonewall*. Chapel Hill: University of North Carolina Press, 1940.
Henderson, G.F.R. *Stonewall Jackson and the American Civil War*. New York: Longmans, Green, 1898.
McDonald, Archie P. *Make Me a Map of the Valley: The Civil War Journal of Stonewall Jackson's Cartographer*. Dallas: Southern Methodist University Press, 1973.
Vandiver, Frank E. *Mighty Stonewall*. New York: McGraw-Hill, 1957.

ARCHIE P. McDONALD

JOHNSTON, Albert Sidney (b. Washington, Ky., February 2, 1803; d. Shiloh, Tenn., April 6, 1862), Army officer. Johnston was a general in the service of three republics.

Albert Sidney Johnston was descended from New Englanders, but he was Southern by birth and association, and he died defending the South against the land of his ancestors. After two years of schooling at Transylvania University in Lexington, Kentucky, Johnston in 1822 accepted an appointment to the U.S. Military Academy. He was graduated in 1826, standing eighth in his class and having served his senior year in the most prestigious assignment in the Corps of Cadets, that of adjutant of the Corps.

Johnston had an unusually versatile military career. In 1832 he participated in the Black Hawk War as adjutant to the commanding general. Two years later he resigned his commission, and after another two years he went to the infant Republic of Texas, where he soon became the ranking general of the army and later the secretary of war. In the Mexican War he was elected colonel of a regiment of volunteers from his adopted state, Texas, and after the expiration of their enlistments he distinguished himself as a staff officer in the Battle of Monterey. In 1849 President Zachary Taylor* appointed him to the rank of major in the U.S. Army as paymaster of troops on the Texas frontier.

After a long drudgery as paymaster, Johnston in 1855 received a promotion to the rank of colonel in command of the newly formed 2d Cavalry Regiment. More than a dozen officers in that organization would one day be Union or Confederate generals in the Civil War. Among these, in addition to Johnston, were such outstanding figures as Robert Edward Lee,* William Joseph Hardee, and George Henry Thomas.*

In 1857 Johnston was ordered to lead the military expedition against the so-called Mormon Rebellion in Utah. This duty brought him another promotion, to brevet brigadier general, and paved the way to his being appointed in 1860 to command the Department of the Pacific. He was in this position when the seven states of the lower South seceded from the Union.

Johnston's strongest loyalties lay with Texas; when it left the Union he resigned his commission, though he opposed secession in principle. In June 1861 he joined a company of other Southerners who marched cross-country from California to offer their services to the Confederacy. "It seems like fate," he was quoted as saying, "that Texas has made me a Rebel twice." By now Johnston had the reputation, along with Robert E. Lee, of having been one of the foremost active officers in the U.S. Army. Moreover, Johnston was a close personal friend of Confederate President Jefferson Davis, who immediately appointed him to command the western theater of Confederate operations, with the rank of general, second in seniority only to the elderly Confederate Adjutant General Samuel Cooper.

Johnston's line of defense stretched from the Appalachians on the eastern flank to Indian Territory on the western flank. He made his headquarters at Bowling Green, Kentucky. He was at great disadvantage in numbers and arms, and in naval power on the rivers that threaded his front, the Mississippi, Tennessee, and Cumberland. His first critical test came in February 1862 when Union forces under Brigadier General Ulysses Simpson Grant* attacked and captured Forts

Henry and Donelson on the Tennessee and Cumberland rivers, thus breaching the Confederate position. Johnston failed either to concentrate his forces for a determined blow against Grant or to extricate all of them by a prompt abandonment of the forts. Instead, he gave up the Kentucky-Tennessee line but belatedly ordered nearly one-third of his troops into Fort Donelson where most of them were captured. A loud public outcry now arose against him, but Davis supported him and said: "If [Johnston] is not a general...we have no general."

With a Herculean effort Johnston now gathered his scattered forces at the town of Corinth in northern Mississippi, an important rail center. On April 6 he struck Grant's unsuspecting army at Pittsburg Landing (near Shiloh church) on the Tennessee River in Tennessee, seventeen miles from Corinth. The Confederate attack came within an inch of destroying the Union Army. But Johnston was killed early in the afternoon at the climax of the battle. General Pierre Gustave Toutant Beauregard,* second-in-command, took his place and, late in the afternoon, halted the attack until the following morning. That night Grant was heavily reinforced with troops under Don Carlos Buell; the next day Grant defeated the Confederates and drove them back to Corinth.

Because Johnston died so early in the Civil War, in the first great battle of that conflict, his true promise as a commander must remain in question. His indecisiveness in the loss of Forts Henry and Donelson and his subsequent reticence in contrast to the assertiveness of his brilliant and flamboyant subordinate, Beauregard, have caused many students of the Civil War to rate Johnston mediocre at best. Grant later wrote that Johnston was bold in design but vacillating and faltering in execution. T. Harry Williams, the preeminent biographer of Beauregard, expressed doubt that Johnston was capable of exercising high command effectively. J.F.C. Fuller, a British analyst of Civil War military leadership, dismissed Johnston as a "brave but stupid" man.

Yet in the Shiloh Campaign Johnston succeeded in achieving what Napoleon said was one of the most difficult feats in warfare, that of turning a general retreat into an advance. Johnston clearly outdid Grant in bringing together the wings of his army under Grant's very eyes and in staging against him one of the most remarkable surprise assaults in military history. Johnston stood above Beauregard also when at the last moment—Carl von Clausewitz's "moment of truth"—Johnston ordered the attack to proceed over the objection of his unnerved second-in-command.

Finally, although the effect of Johnston's death on the outcome at Shiloh is a point of endless controversy and cannot be determined with certainty, without question he demonstrated in a superb manner a number of the most important qualities of battlefield command. These included presence of mind in the heat of combat, steadfastness in pressing the attack toward its objective, and charisma in arousing his troops to an utmost effort. Weighing everything, one may reasonably suppose Johnston would have been an outstanding source of strength to the Confederacy if he had lived to develop his talents fully.

BIBLIOGRAPHY

Connelly, Thomas H. *Army of the Heartland: The Army of Tennessee, 1861–1862*. Baton Rouge: Louisiana State University Press, 1967.
McDonough, James Lee. *Shiloh: In Hell Before Night*. Knoxville: University of Tennessee Press, 1977.
Roland, Charles P. *Albert Sidney Johnston: Soldier of Three Republics*. Austin: University of Texas Press, 1964.
Sword, Wiley. *Shiloh: Bloody April*. New York: Morrow, 1974.
Williams, T. Harry. *P.G.T. Beauregard: Napoleon in Gray*. Baton Rouge: Louisiana State University Press, 1954.

CHARLES P. ROLAND

JOHNSTON, Joseph Eggleston (b. "Cherry Grove," Prince Edward County, Va., February 3, 1807; d. Washington, D.C., March 21, 1891), Army officer. Johnston held various Confederate commands during the Civil War.

Johnston was of Scottish descent, and his father, Peter Johnston, had served in the Revolution under Henry ("Light-Horse" Harry) Lee. Johnston's boyhood was spent near Abington, where he received his early education at the Abington Academy. In 1825 he enrolled at West Point, graduating in 1829, ranking thirteenth in a class of forty-six.

Resigning from the Army after eight years as a second lieutenant of artillery, having served on the Black Hawk Expedition and in the Seminole War, Johnston became a civil engineer in Florida. In 1837, he returned to the Army as a first lieutenant of topographical engineers. On July 10, 1845, Johnston married Lydia McLane, of Maryland.

Promoted to captain in 1846, he fought in the Mexican War, and was wounded twice at Cerro Gordo and three times at Chapultepec. After the war Johnston was chief of topographical engineers in Texas and served as lieutenant colonel of the 1st Cavalry from 1855 to 1860 on the frontier. In 1860 he was promoted to brigadier general and became quartermaster general of the U.S. Army.

When Virginia seceded from the Union, Johnston immediately resigned his commission and became first a major general in Virginia's state troops, and later a brigadier general in the Confederate service.

Johnston played a major role at the Battle of Manassas (Bull Run), July 21, 1861. Slipping away from a superior Union force in the Shenandoah Valley, Johnston rapidly moved his troops to join the army of General Pierre Gustave Toutant Beauregard* at Manassas. As the ranking officer, Johnston approved Beauregard's plans for the battle, but the engagement began with a Federal assault on the Rebel left which almost carried the Union to victory. Johnston was then at the right of the line, where the Confederates intended to launch an attack. At once he rode to the sound of the guns, arriving in time to help rally the first companies that had been driven back by the enemy onslaught. He then left the Henry Hill, hastened to a vantage point at Portici, about a mile to the southeast where he could see a good portion of the field, and assumed overall direction of the Confederate effort. Johnston exerted a dominant influence on the battle, calling up regiments and brigades, dispatching them to those sections of the front where they were most needed, and finally driving the enemy back in a rout. Although widely complimented for his role at Bull Run, Johnston received far less publicity than the more colorful and dramatic Beauregard, who, ironically, seemed not to have had a clear understanding of the general battle situation at the time decisive action was required.

Johnston next saw major action in the spring of 1862, when a Union army moved to Fortress Monroe. He transferred the bulk of his army east of Richmond to the peninsula between the James and York rivers, recommending that it be concentrated near the Confederate capital. President Jefferson Davis, concurring with the advice of General Robert Edward Lee,* directed that the Confederates should not retreat. Nevertheless, Johnston eventually fell back to defenses on the outskirts of Richmond. Moving up the peninsula, General George Brinton McClellan* split his army, with three corps on the northeast bank of the Chickahominy River and two corps on the south side. Grasping this opportunity, Johnston attacked the Federals south of the stream on May 31, in the Battle of Fair Oaks (Seven Pines). The Confederate attack, planned for dawn, did not get underway until after noon, and then in disorganized fashion. Johnston was never in the area of the main attacking force but was twice wounded. His plan had been good, and because some results were achieved, Johnston's reputation was further enhanced. Because of his wounds, however, Lee replaced him as the Army's commander.

By November 1862 Johnston had sufficiently recovered to report for duty, and he was assigned to command all the territory between the Appalachians and the Mississippi River. His authority was vague, with department heads reporting directly to Richmond rather than to Johnston. Realizing that he was not in good favor with Davis, Johnston suspected he had been given a nominal command with little power and heavy responsibilities to make him look bad. Therefore, Johnston asked to be relieved. Davis refused to comply with the request. But Johnston would not have been without power, if he had been more willing to accept responsibility and take action. For example, in the aftermath of the Battle of Stones River, when the Rebel high command reeked with dissension, Johnston stood by General Braxton Bragg* even when Davis finally ordered him to replace that general.

Another crisis occurred when General Ulysses Simpson Grant* crossed into Mississippi to attack Vicksburg. General John Pemberton requested reinforcements, and Johnston instructed him to unite all forces against Grant. Still suffering from his wound received at Seven Pines, Johnston was not in good physical condition, which may explain why he took no further action until ordered by Davis to assume command in Mississippi. Arriving at Jackson, Johnston found that Grant was between him and Pemberton, and ordered Pemberton to advance upon Grant's rear. Although he replied affirmatively, Pemberton did nothing for hours. Responding to a second order, Pemberton again indicated that he would act, but once more did nothing, until it was too late. Grant drove Pemberton back at Champion's Hill and the Big Black River. Johnston ordered him to pull out of the Vicksburg defenses immediately before Grant trapped him in the river fortress. Once more Pemberton disobeyed and was soon completely invested by Grant's army. Perhaps even more enigmatic than Pemberton's behavior was Johnston's failure to relieve that incompetent commander and either assume command himself or substitute some other general who would obey orders.

In December 1863 Johnston was assigned to command the Army of the Tennessee, then before Chattanooga. He was reinforced to a strength of about sixty-two thousand but refused to attack on the ground of insufficient forces. In early May 1864 the Federals advanced, one hundred thousand strong, led by General William Tecumseh Sherman.*

Johnston hoped that the Union Army would attack his strong defensive position in north Georgia, but Sherman marched around the Confederate Army, forcing it to retreat. Johnston dropped back skillfully, and again Sherman threatened to envelop his position, thus forcing another Confederate withdrawal. The Fabian policy created a tide of protest from Richmond and much of the Southern populace. With Sherman advancing on a broad front, Johnston concentrated around Cassville, hoping to fall upon an isolated enemy flank. Planning to personally lead an attack, he boosted his soldiers' morale, but the assault did not materialize and Johnston became embroiled in controversy with one of his major subordinates, General John Bell Hood.* Whatever the reason, Johnston withdrew from Cassville without fighting a pitched battle. On July 17, in front of Atlanta, he was relieved from command, on the ground that he had failed to stop the advance of the enemy. Hood succeeded him and soon lost a major part of the army in unsuccessful attacks.

Reassigned to the Army of the Tennessee on February 23, 1865, Johnston signed an armistice with Sherman in North Carolina on April 18, surrendering on April 26.

After the war Johnston engaged in the insurance business. He also served one term in the U.S. Congress, after which he settled in Washington, D.C., and was appointed a federal railroad commissioner. Johnston also developed a close friendship with General Sherman. He died of pneumonia, contracted while standing hatless in the winter rain at Sherman's funeral.

Johnston was fifty-four years old and in his prime when the Civil War began. His prewar record seemed to promise a highly successful service with the Confederacy. The small, slight general, distinctively marked by a goatee projecting from a slender face, was conscious of his reputation, perhaps to a fault. He never fully measured up to expectations, although there are several positive factors when his military service is evaluated.

Johnston enjoys the enviable distinction of having never lost a battle. Undoubtedly, he possessed outstanding tactical ability and a talent for grasping an overall battle situation. Furthermore, he had the ability to inspire the soldiers he led. His strategic sense is a moot point; and because his best fighting, as well as most of his fighting, was done from a defensive stance, he appears cautious to a fault. The circumstances never seemed satisfactory to Johnston for an offensive movement.

In spite of outstanding ability, the general was frequently unwilling to shoulder responsibility for major decisions, tended to despondency and depression, did not enjoy a good relationship with President Davis (in fact, his contentious personality earned him many enemies), and too often refused to communicate with Richmond and explain his plans and actions. His failure to communicate was especially detrimental in the north Georgia Campaign.

The only important attack Johnston launched was at Seven Pines, which was badly managed. In all his other campaigns he avoided the offensive. The lack of aggressiveness may have reflected a basic personality trait, or perhaps the general felt great pressure to protect the reputation he had built before the war. Whatever the reason, an unwillingness to risk offensive warfare relegates Johnston to the stature of a second-rank commander.

BIBLIOGRAPHY

Connelly, Thomas L. *Autumn of Glory*. Baton Rouge: Louisiana State University Press, 1971.
Davis, William C. *Battle at Bull Run*. New York: Doubleday, 1977.
Govan, Gilbert E., and James W. Livingood. *A Different Valor: The Story of General Joseph E. Johnston*. New York: Bobbs-Merrill, 1956.
Horn, Stanley F. *The Army of Tennessee*. Indianapolis, Ind.: Bobbs-Merrill, 1941.
Johnston, Joseph E. *Narrative of Military Operations*. New York: D. Appleton and Company, 1874.

JAMES LEE McDONOUGH

JONES, John Paul (b. Kirkbean Parish, Scotland, July 6, 1747; d. Paris, France, July 18, 1792), naval officer. Jones is considered the father of the American Navy.

The fifth child of John Paul, gardener at "Arbigland," John Paul, as he was known then, received only a rudimentary education before being apprenticed to a Whitehaven shipowner. When his master went bankrupt, John Paul received his release from apprenticeship and signed on a slaver for two voyages before returning to the merchant service. By age twenty-one he had become a shipmaster, and by age twenty-five he formed a partnership with a merchant-planter in Tobago. In 1773 John Paul's crew mutinied, and he was forced to kill the ringleader in self-defense. Friends in Tobago advised him to "retire incognito to the continent of America" until a court of admiralty could be formed to hear his case. Jones took their advice, fled to Virginia, and adopted a new surname as a precaution.

At the outbreak of the American Revolution, Jones was commissioned the senior lieutenant in the Continental Navy (December 7, 1775). He refused to accept command of the 12-gun sloop *Providence*, choosing instead to serve aboard the 30-gun frigate *Alfred* in the hope that he could expand his knowledge of ship handling and fleet maneuvering. In this capacity he took part in the New Providence raid and the squadron's engagement with HMS *Glasgow* (20 guns). In the shuffling of positions which followed that skirmish, Jones was posted to command the *Providence* (May 10, 1776).

With this, his first independent command, Jones took sixteen prizes and destroyed local fishing fleets in Nova Scotia. Promoted in rank to captain (October 10, 1776) and transferred to command of the *Alfred*, he led a second successful cruise to the Grand Banks, taking seven prizes.

Upon return to port, Jones learned that he had been placed eighteenth on the seniority list established by Congress and that he had again been assigned to the *Providence*. Incensed, he wrote letters of complaint charging in one that several men placed senior to him were "altogether illiterate and utterly ignorant of marine affairs." Jones was partly vindicated in 1777 when he was posted to command the 18-gun sloop-of-war *Ranger* then under construction, and was subsequently ordered to Europe with the promise of command of a frigate under construction in Holland.

When he arrived in France and found that the promised ship had been transferred to France, Jones sought and obtained from the American commissioners discretionary orders that allowed him to set sail for the Irish Sea in April 1778. Within a month Jones took two merchantmen as prizes and destroyed several others; descended on Whitehaven where he spiked the fort's guns and set fire to the colliers in the harbor; landed at St. Mary's Isle in an attempt to capture the earl of Selkirk, whom Jones hoped to exchange for American seamen held in British prisons; and captured the British sloop-of-war *Drake* (20 guns).

Upon his return to France, plans were laid for future assaults on the British coast in which Jones would command some naval forces and the Marquis de Lafayette* an army. When these plans aborted, Jones settled on a cruise around the British Isles in an old East Indiaman, the *Duc de Duras*, which he renamed the *Bonhomme Richard* in honor of his patron, Benjamin Franklin.

On August 14, 1778, he put to sea from L'Orient with five naval vessels and two privateers and proceeded clockwise around the British Isles, taking seventeen prizes before reaching Scotland's east coast. Jones' control of his subordinates was tenuous at best; the two privateers deserted him, and the captains of the remaining ships refused to support his proposed landing at Leith. Jones next proposed a raid to destroy the Newcastle-on-Tyne coal yards, but again his subordinates refused to follow him.

On September 23, a fleet of forty-one sail was intercepted off Flamborough Head, and after hours of maneuvering there ensued one of the hottest naval engagements of the Age of Sail. Both the 42-gun *Richard* and HMS *Serapis* (44 guns) opened fire almost simultaneously, two of the *Richard*'s largest guns burst, and quickly it became clear that Jones' only hope of victory lay in boarding the more powerful ship. After his attempt at boarding was repulsed, the ships jockeyed for position and finally became entangled. For two hours the *Serapis* poured deadly cannon fire into the *Richard*'s topsides while the seamen and French marines of the *Richard* swept the enemy's deck with small arms and swivels. At 10:00 PM a grenade ignited powder charges on the *Serapis* killing a score of men. Becoming desperate, Captain Richard Pearson of the *Serapis* ordered his men to board the *Richard*. When they were thrown back, he sought to continue the battle, but within a half hour his mainmast began trembling and, seeing no hope of victory, he surrendered. Both commanders lost almost half their crews; Jones also lost the *Richard* which sank two days later.

Subsequently, Jones went to Paris where he was accorded a hero's reception, was entertained lavishly, and was presented with a gold-hilted sword by Louis XVI. In June 1779 he planned to return to America, but he was outmaneuvered for command of the frigate *Alliance* and was forced to remain in France until December when he took command of the *Ariel*, a French ship on loan, to carry war supplies to America.

Upon Jones' arrival in Philadelphia, Congress considered a public investigation of his involvement "relative to the detention of the clothing and arms belonging to these United States, in France," but then decided that the Board of Admiralty should examine the captain privately on the matter. He skillfully answered the board's questions in such a way as to give a detailed account of his triumphs and to lay blame for any delays on others. Governmental restraint soon turned to acclaim as France's ambassador decorated Jones with the *Ordre du Merite Militaire* (which brought with it the title chevalier), and Congress voted "that the thanks of the United States in Congress assembled, be given to Captain John Paul Jones, for the zeal, prudence and intrepidity with which he has supported the honor of the American flag." More importantly, Congress voted unanimously to appoint him to command the 74-gun *America*, the Continental Navy's only ship-of-the-line, then building at Portsmouth. After a frustrating year spent in grappling with problems of obtaining supplies and skilled workmen, Jones was able to get the ship launched only to see it turned over to France. Unable to procure another command, he sought and was given permission to join a French fleet for a cruise to the Caribbean in order to view at first hand the handling of a large fleet.

After the war, the chevalier, as he was known in France, cast about for future employment. He considered several commercial ventures, invested in a few, and sought service in the French Navy. When there was no response to his overtures, Jones traveled to the United States where he defended his financial accounts presented to Congress and tried unsuccessfully to obtain promotion to rear admiral. In 1788 he left America for the last time and traveled to Denmark, where he unsuccessfully pressed claims for prize money due him there.

In mid-April Jones received and accepted Catherine the Great's formal offer of a command in the Russian Imperial Navy. Attracted to Russian service chiefly by the promise of adventure and the opportunity to gain experience in commanding a fleet, Jones left for St. Petersburg where he tarried only briefly before reporting to the Black Sea to take command of a squadron of sailing ships under the direction of Prince Potemkin, commander in chief of all forces in the region. Although plagued by jealous rivals, Jones took a leading part in defeating the Turkish fleet in the Liman Campaign of June 1789. There followed four months of political intrigue and bickering over credit for the victory. Jones emerged the loser, and in November he received orders to report to St. Petersburg under the pretense of reassignment to the Baltic fleet. For several months he languished in the capital, devoting much of his time to compiling a "Narrative of the Campaign of the Liman" and to answering the attacks of his enemies. In April 1790 a trumped-up scandal linking Jones to a young girl ended any chance for a recall to command and led to his decision to leave Russia.

Jones returned to Paris (May 1790) to live out his final days writing letters to friends in America and to Catherine in hope of being restored to command. Short of funds, he sought and received a commission from the American government naming him "commissioner with full powers to negotiate with the Dey of Algiers concerning the ransom of American citizens in captivity." Jones' health had been in decline since his winter journey to Russia four years before, and the broken sailor died before receiving news of his new position. He was almost alone during his last days. Gouverneur Morris, America's minister to France, accepted his will, listing considerable assets, but he ordered that Jones be buried cheaply in order to minimize any personal financial responsibility. When informed of Morris' intentions, the French National Assembly assumed charge of the funeral arrangements and dispatched a detachment of grenadiers to take part in the ceremonies. Jones was buried in the Protestant cemetery outside the city gates of Paris where he lay until 1905 when his remains were transferred to the Naval Academy in Annapolis, Maryland.

Jones' reputation rests on his exploits of 1778 and 1779 which brought the war home to the British people and strengthened American morale at a time when the war appeared to be deadlocked. Jones generated strong feelings in others. As an individual he was always jealous and vain. A man of strong opinions, he resented anyone not up to his standard who was in a position to control his affairs. Robert Morris, Benjamin Franklin, and Thomas Jefferson respected his abilities, but none could be called his close friend. He often quarreled with subordinates and others with whom he had to work. That he was a man of talent cannot be denied, nor can his patriotism be questioned. His disappointments in terms of recognition and command rivalled those of Benedict Arnold,* but his reaction differed sharply. His courage under fire and his solicitude for his men's welfare brought him their respect, but his violent temper cost him their affection.

Jones was continually guided by a high sense of professionalism which led him to seek opportunities to further his own education and to write extensively on naval matters. His plans for the administration of the Navy, his design for an academy to train officers, and his treatises on tactics and strategy show him to have been a man of vision.

Jones never fully adjusted to peacetime. His success as a diplomat was no compensation for his failure to obtain a suitable command and for his disappointment in Russian service. His prophetic plans for American naval power were rejected in his time. His legacy rests not so much on what he did but on how he did it. As the inscription on his tomb asserts: "He gave our navy its earliest traditions of heroism and victory."

BIBLIOGRAPHY

De Koven, Mrs. Reginald. *The Life and Letters of John Paul Jones*. 2 vols. New York: Charles Scribner's Sons, 1913.
Golder, F. A. *John Paul Jones in Russia*. Garden City, N.Y.: Doubleday, Page and Company, 1927.
Lorenz, Lincoln. *John Paul Jones, Fighter for Freedom and Glory*. Annapolis, Md.: Naval Institute Press, 1943.
Morison, Samuel Eliot. *John Paul Jones: A Sailor's Biography*. Boston: Little, Brown and Company, 1959.
Walsh, John E. *Night on Fire: The First Complete Account of John Paul Jones's Greatest Battle*. New York: McGraw-Hill, 1978.

JAMES C. BRADFORD

KIMMEL, Husband Edward (b. Henderson, Ky., February 26, 1882; d. Groton, Conn., May 14, 1968), naval officer. Kimmel was serving as commander in chief, U.S. Fleet, and commander in chief, Pacific Fleet, at the time of the Japanese attack on Pearl Harbor on December 7, 1941.

Husband Edward Kimmel—the son of Major Marius M. Kimmel, a West Point graduate—attended Central University in Richmond, Kentucky, before he received an appointment to the U.S. Naval Academy from Kentucky in June 1900. On February 1, 1904, he graduated thirteenth in a class of sixty-two and, after the two years of sea duty then required by law, received his ensign's commission. He joined the new pre-dreadnought battleship *Virginia* in 1906.

Kimmel spent his tours of duty in the years preceding World War I principally in the fields of gunnery and ordnance. After engineering instruction at the Bureau of Ordnance in Washington, he served in the battleships *Georgia, Wisconsin*, and *Louisiana*, in succession, participating in the dramatic round-the-world cruise of the Great White Fleet commanded by Admirals Robley Dunglison Evans and Charles Sperry. Kimmel then served ashore as assistant to the director of target practices and engineering performances before he returned to sea as ordnance officer in the armored cruiser *California* and later served as fleet gunnery officer for two commanders of the Pacific Fleet.

After a tour as aide to Assistant Secretary of the Navy Franklin D. Roosevelt—an important association in light of the future—Kimmel served a second stint as assistant to the director of target practices and engineering performances at a key time—when the United States entered World War I. He received orders to

London in October 1917 and served as an instructor with the Royal Navy, imparting recent developments in gunnery spotting. He also went to sea as a naval observer and witnessed the Battle of Heligoland Bight. Kimmel became gunnery officer on the staff of Rear Admiral Hugh Rodman, who commanded Battleship Division Nine of the Atlantic Fleet, after the arrival of that group of American dreadnoughts in British waters in December 1917. He remained on Rodman's staff into 1919, when he became executive officer in the battleship *Arkansas*.

Subsequently serving as production officer at the Naval Gun Factory in Washington, Kimmel returned to sea in December 1923, journeying to the Asiatic Station where he commanded, in succession, the destroyers *Preble* and *Tracy*, and concurrently served as commander of two destroyer divisions. Coming back to the United States in the spring of 1925, Kimmel attended the Naval War College, where he excelled in strategy and tactics, and completed the senior course in 1926.

As in the earlier phases of his career, Kimmel alternated tours ashore and afloat, in billets of increasing responsibility into the 1930s. As he advanced up the ladder toward flag rank, Kimmel worked, successively, in the policy and liaison division of the office of the Chief of Naval Operations (CNO) at the time of the Nicaraguan intervention in 1927; commanded Destroyer Squadron 12, Battle Force; served as director of ship movements, office of the CNO; commanded the battleship *New York*; served as chief of staff to Vice Admiral T. T. Craven, commander, Battleships, Battle Force; and was budget officer for the Navy Department.

He achieved flag rank in November 1937, while budget officer, and subsequently broke his flag at sea for the first time in the spring of 1938, in the heavy cruiser *San Francisco* as commander, Cruiser Division Seven. Upon the conclusion of Fleet Problem XX in the spring of 1939, Kimmel led Cruiser Division Seven on a good-will voyage around South America. Kimmel was given the concurrent responsibilities of commander of Cruiser Division Nine and commander of Cruisers, Battle Force, shortly before the outbreak of war in Europe in the summer of 1939.

Within a year of Kimmel's assuming command of the Battle Force cruisers, President Franklin D. Roosevelt—hoping to deter the Japanese from further aggressive steps in the Far East—made a move that ultimately affected the admiral's future. After the end of Fleet Problem XXI, the president directed that the Fleet remain in Hawaiian waters, basing on Pearl Harbor, until further notice. The decision irritated the incumbent commander in chief, U.S. Fleet, Admiral James O. Richardson, who, in two ensuing visits to Washington, unsuccessfully attempted to dissuade the president from his course. Roosevelt ultimately relieved Richardson and picked Kimmel to succeed him over the heads of forty-six more senior officers.

Kimmel relieved Richardson on February 1, 1941, and from that time to early December of that pivotal year, he energetically prepared the Pacific Fleet for war. Less than a year later, however, a Japanese carrier task force—the largest, most powerful unit of its kind in the world—steamed in secrecy from the fog-shrouded Kuril Islands and descended, undetected, upon Oahu on December 7, 1941. Japanese planes from six carriers attacked the ships of the Pacific Fleet at Pearl Harbor early that Sunday morning, and, in less than two hours, sank or damaged eighteen ships, including the bulk of American battleship strength in the Pacific.

Removing the Pacific Fleet as a deterrent at the outset gave the Japanese an early victory and assured the success of their southern operation into British, Dutch, and American Far Eastern possessions. Although the Japanese attack of December 7 caught Oahu's defenders unawares, Kimmel soon set in motion the United States' first offensive—an attempt to relieve Wake Island. Unfortunately for that island outpost, defended bravely by Marines, delays and Kimmel's untimely relief prevented a successful conclusion to that effort. Kimmel was relieved on December 17, 1941, by Vice Admiral W. S. Pye, who was in turn relieved by Admiral Chester William Nimitz* on December 31. Wake fell shortly before Christmas. After testifying at the initial inquiries into the Pearl Harbor disaster, Kimmel retired from the Navy, with the rank of rear admiral, on March 1, 1942, to face ensuing inquiries that lasted into 1946.

After a brief civilian career with the engineering consulting firm of Frederick R. Harris, Inc., in 1947, Kimmel retired from public life to Groton, Connecticut. There he lived out the rest of his days fighting relentlessly and ceaselessly to clear his name; during that time he wrote *Admiral Kimmel's Story* (Chicago, 1955), an uncompromising book in which he set forth his account of what happened on Oahu before December 7, 1941.

Husband Edward Kimmel was a career naval officer who spent the better part of his life preparing for high command; he reached the top of the Navy ladder and then plummetted to the bottom, retired in disgrace and deprived of a chance to redeem himself in uniform. He should rightly have been relieved, but he should not have been disgraced. The Pearl Harbor issue is still lively, and partisans of Admiral Kimmel remain quite vociferous in their criticisms of those in Washington on the eve of hostilities in the Pacific. Yet the blame must be leveled equally upon those in Washington who failed to appreciate Kimmel's need for intelligence data available to them but not to him (and evaluating that data imaginatively); and upon Kimmel himself for failing to properly evaluate the information he did possess.

Kimmel had proved, as Admiral Henry Kent Hewitt pointed out in his inquiry into Pearl Harbor, "indefatigable, energetic, resourceful, and positive" in preparing the Pacific Fleet for war. From the outset, he showed an appreciation of the security of the fleet at anchor in Pearl Harbor, but at the same time maintained—even into the last critical week before the Japanese attack—a rigorous and unbending training schedule for the fleet. The maintenance of that training resulted in the Fleet settling into a predictable routine that made it relatively easy for the Japanese to predict ship movements.

Kimmel allowed himself to become hamstrung by relying upon Washington for prior warning of an impending break in diplomatic relations between the United States and Japan. Such a signal could presage war. Despite the last-minute indecision of Admiral Harold Raynsford Stark, the CNO, and even without the special intelligence (the "MAGIC" intercepts) that he later claimed were crucial, Kimmel had enough information available to him by December 7, 1941, to indicate a situation of unusual severity. He had the "War Warning" message of November 27; the information of December 3 in which the Japanese were destroying their codes; and the information of December 6 in which outlying bases in the Pacific were instructed to destroy their confidential publications. In addition, the monitoring of Japanese naval radio traffic had revealed two key call sign changes, leading to the "loss" of the Japanese carriers on December 1. Kimmel should have judged more accurately the gravity of the situation confronting him, and of the danger to which Oahu, and specifically Pearl Harbor, was exposed. He could have instituted long-range reconnaissance of areas already recognized as probable routes for a Japanese carrier air strike, and he also could have rotated his fleet's "in-port" periods, producing a less predictable routine for the Japanese to anticipate correctly. However, hindsight obscures the fact that the situation looked different to the men in charge at the time. The prevailing attitude evident among Kimmel, his opposite number, General Walter Campbell Short,* and most high government, naval, and military officials in Washington was that the Japanese would strike first somewhere in the Far East, not at Oahu.

Schools of thought for Kimmel's responsibility for what happened on December 7, 1941, are divided. The Navy Board of Inquiry concluded that Kimmel, on the basis of the information available to him, neither committed any offense nor incurred any blame for the disaster. On the other hand, Admiral Ernest Joseph King* believed that Kimmel's errors were those of omission, not commission, and opined that Kimmel lacked superior judgment necessary for his post.

In the final analysis, then, Kimmel is a tragic figure. He kept his mind almost microscopically focused on the probabilities of Japan's courses of action rather than on his enemy's capabilities. Despite working diligently and energetically to be ready for war when it came, he was not prepared for it when it confronted him on December 7, 1941.

BIBLIOGRAPHY

Lord, Walter. *Day of Infamy*. New York: Henry Holt and Company, 1957.
Melosi, Martin V. *The Shadow of Pearl Harbor: Political Controversy over the Surprise Attack, 1941–1946*. College Station: Texas A&M University Press, 1977.
Millis, Walter. *This Is Pearl!* New York: Morrow and Company, 1947.
Morison, Samuel E. *The Rising Sun in the Pacific*. Vol. 3 of *United States Naval Operations in World War II*. Boston: Little, Brown and Company, 1958.

Prange, Gordon. *At Dawn We Slept: The Untold Story of Pearl Harbor.* New York: McGraw-Hill, 1981.

Wohlstetter, Roberta. *Pearl Harbor: Warning and Decision.* Stanford, Calif.: Stanford University Press, 1962.

ROBERT J. CRESSMAN

KING, Ernest Joseph (b. Lorain, Ohio, November 23, 1878; d. Portsmouth, N.H., June 25, 1956), naval officer. King is noted for being commander in chief, U.S. Fleet, and chief of naval operations, 1941–1945.

Ernest J. King had but one aim in life during his first forty years of naval service: he wanted to become the chief of naval operations (CNO). He sought that goal with zealous ambition and unswerving determination; his aspirations were common knowledge throughout the Navy. His family had been literate, industrious working-class Scots and Englishmen who had emigrated to northern Ohio in the late nineteenth century. Young King had brains and talent, and he was a popular student who graduated as valedictorian of his small high school class. When he decided to attend the Naval Academy, the people of Lorain were proud and delighted.

King excelled at Annapolis, rising to the top leadership position as battalion commander. While still a naval cadet, he saw action in the Spanish-American War. King graduated fourth in the class of 1901. During the fifteen years following graduation he served as often on staffs as on ships, shrewdly seeking enhancing assignments that would most rapidly advance his career. When World War I began, he was a staff officer for Admiral Henry T. Mayo, commander in chief, Atlantic Fleet, the Navy's most influential flag officer. As a Mayo protégé, by war's end King had received a meritorious promotion to captain at the youthful age of thirty-nine, together with a Navy Cross.

After the war the Navy entered an inevitable decline owing to peacetime disarmament, and King was an impatient junior captain with nowhere to go. Despairing of getting a major warship command within a reasonable time, King volunteered in 1922 for the submarine service which he hoped would offer better opportunities. Although he never qualified as a submariner, he nevertheless commanded a submarine division and then the Submarine Base at New London, Connecticut. King achieved recognition in 1925 when he salvaged the submarine *S–51*, which had been sunk off Block Island in Rhode Island Sound.

Naval aviation was a developing branch of the naval service in the late 1920s. Federal law required commanding officers of carriers and air stations to be fliers or aviation observers. Most Navy pilots were too junior for such assignments. To remedy the problem, King was among a number of older surface officers who volunteered for flight training in order to qualify for major aviation commands. At age forty-nine King won his wings and subsequently commanded the carrier *Lexington*, which earned him a promotion to rear admiral in 1932.

Owing to the death of Rear Admiral William A. Moffett in the crash of the dirigible *Akron*, King succeeded to command of the Navy's Bureau of Aeronautics in 1933. Despite the austere appropriations caused by the Depression, King's well-run bureau continued to contribute to the advance of naval aviation. King returned to sea in 1936 to command the Navy's patrol plane squadrons; he maintained high standards of combat readiness and established bases throughout the Pacific. In 1938 he was promoted to vice admiral and took command of all carriers and associated aircraft in the fleet. During his tenure, the carrier forces developed advanced doctrine that became standard practice during World War II. When Admiral William Daniel Leahy retired as chief of naval operations in 1938, King entertained hopes that he would succeed Leahy. But Harold Raynsford Stark got the job, and in the summer of 1939 King went to the General Board to pass time until his mandatory retirement in November 1942.

World War II changed everything. King's experience and competence were again in demand, and he returned to sea in early 1941 as commander in chief, Atlantic Fleet. Wearing four stars, he took charge of the unofficial American involvement in the Battle of the Atlantic and personally transported President Franklin D. Roosevelt to the Atlantic Charter Conference at Argentia, Newfoundland. The president and Secretary of the Navy William Franklin Knox frequently sought his counsel, and King so won their confidence that they elevated him to commander in chief, U.S. Fleet, immediately after the attack on Pearl Harbor. In March 1942 Roosevelt sent Stark to London, and King assumed the title of chief of naval operations as well. Throughout the war King served on both the Joint Chiefs of Staff (JCS) and the Combined Chiefs of Staff as one of the principal shapers of Allied grand strategy. Under King's urging, the Allies decided upon a limited offensive against Japan despite the official policy of "Germany first." King concurrently shaped the U.S. Navy into the most powerful naval force in the history of the world.

After the war King retired in Washington, D.C. Following a stroke in 1947 his health declined, and he died at the Portsmouth Naval Hospital in 1956. He was survived by his wife, Martha Lamkin Egerton, six daughters, and a son.

King had a reputation for outspoken bluntness that went to extremes, owing to his sense of self-righteousness and an undisciplined temper. Tact and discretion too often lost out to emotional excesses, especially in his early years. Together with his intellectual arrogance and lack of humility, King simply considered that he had more brains than anyone else in the Navy and acted accordingly. Older officers often felt intimidated in his presence, and they resented the way King made them feel inferior. King also loved parties, chased women, and drank too much, but he never suffered from hangovers owing to his extraordinary stamina.

King vowed that he would become a flag officer solely through professional merit, so he refused to ingratiate himself either with influential cliques or with Franklin D. Roosevelt, who loved the Navy and could make or break a naval career. Consequently, King avoided Washington duty for thirty-two years—until he was promoted to rear admiral. His hope of becoming CNO was wishful thinking, because in 1938 he was an outcast. He was a stranger to the president, and he had too many enemies after years of feuds, fights, and insults.

Following his 1941 resurrection as commander of the Atlantic Fleet, King became a frequent visitor to the White House and Hyde Park, allowing opportunities for FDR to evaluate King at first hand. The president was perceptive enough to recognize in King the indefatigable strength, the moral courage, and the fighting spirit needed to resurrect the Navy from the defeat and shambles of Pearl Harbor.

But commanding the Navy was not King's sole contribution. King had studied strategy for a lifetime, and he was intellectually superior to his colleagues on the Joint Chiefs of Staff. His only equal on the British Chiefs of Staff was Air Chief Marshal Sir Charles Portal of the Royal Air Force. Roosevelt relied more on King than on any other member of the Joint Chiefs for strategic advice, especially in the first eighteen months of the war. King recognized the danger of ignoring Japan while concentrating upon Germany, for if left undisturbed Japan would have consolidated its conquests and would have become impregnable. The war would have lasted years longer if King had not gotten his way for a limited offensive in the Pacific.

On the negative side, King was too much a single-minded professional warrior, thinking solely about how to defeat the Axis by overwhelming force. Other wartime considerations were secondary: he loathed the press, spurned the Congress, and was indifferent to public opinion, logistics, and industrial mobilization. He was a poor public speaker and was content to let General George Catlett Marshall serve as the principal spokesman for the armed forces. He resented civilian authority and tangled frequently with Frank Knox and James Vincent Forrestal. Roosevelt was the only supreme authority to whom King would respectfully defer. Given King's aversion to wartime publicity, the Army Air Force's public relations program was far superior to that of the Navy. Furthermore, Air Force leaders planned for a postwar reorganization while King rarely thought beyond the Axis surrender. By early 1945 the strategy for ending the war had been well established, and King and his JCS colleagues were rarely consulted in the political considerations that dominated the Big Power conferences at Yalta and Potsdam.

King is remembered as brilliant, ruthless, irascible, cold, and arrogant. There is a legend that he would have preferred to have made only one statement about the war: at the proper time he would simply announce, "We won." Another apocryphal legend is that when summoned by FDR to lead the Navy in December 1941, King remarked, "Whenever they get into trouble, they always call for the sons-of-bitches." Indeed, he was delighted with his reputation for toughness and was pleased when a friend sent him a miniature blowtorch from Tiffany's to use for "shaving." Among his friends, however, he was a man of great warmth, sensitivity, and charitableness. Like most great men, his was a complex and fascinating personality.

BIBLIOGRAPHY

Buell, Thomas B. *Master of Seapower: A Biography of Fleet Admiral Ernest J. King.* Boston: Little, Brown and Company, 1980.
Graybar, Lloyd. "Admiral King's Toughest Battle." *Naval War College Review* 32 (February 1979): 38–45.
King, Ernest J., and Walter M. Whitehill. *Fleet Admiral King: A Naval Record.* New York: Norton, 1952.
Morison, Samuel E. *Two Ocean War: A Short History of the U.S. Navy in the Second World War.* Boston: Little, Brown and Company, 1963.
Reynolds, Clark. "Admiral Ernest J. King and the Strategy for Victory in the Pacific." *Naval War College Review* 28 (Winter 1976): 57–67.

THOMAS B. BUELL

LAFAYETTE, Marquis de Marie Joseph Paul Yves Roch Gilbert du Motier (b. Auvergne, France, September 8, 1757; d. Paris, France, May 20, 1843), military officer, political leader.

A distinguished family, the Lafayettes had great wealth but less social prestige. Lafayette's father was killed in battle with the English before his son's second birthday. Young Lafayette enlisted in the French Army at thirteen and at seventeen was a captain of dragoons. In April 1777, armed with the promise of a high commission, he sailed secretly for America. On July 31 Congress commissioned him a major general, without pay or independent command.

Lafayette served with distinction at the Battle of Brandywine, receiving a superficial wound. On December 1 Congress gave him command of a Virginia division. That winter he shared the privations of Valley Forge, warned Washington of the machinations of Thomas Conway, and in January was given command of a proposed invasion of Canada, a visionary scheme that never got off the ground.

With news of the French alliance, in the spring of 1778 Lafayette became a hero and a celebrity, the center of attention. Five feet-nine inches tall, with sandy red hair and hazel eyes, a receding forehead and sharp nose, Lafayette made up in vitality, ambition, dash, and verve what he may have lacked in physical beauty. In May, at Barren Hill, he skirmished with the British and avoided defeat by skillful maneuver. At Monmouth, near the end of June, he was deprived of what might have been a brilliant victory by the jealousy and ineptitude of Charles Lee,* but still merited George Washington's praise. That summer he was active in preparation for John Sullivan's abortive attack on Newport. In October Congress granted him a furlough to return to France.

During a year in France, Lafayette received a hero's welcome, rendered unique and impressive service in his liaison with the king and his ministers, and formulated schemes for French aid to America. "The thought of seeing England humiliated and crushed makes me tremble with joy," he wrote. At the end of April 1780, he was back in America, eager to rejoin Washington's army and to help prepare for the arrival of French forces. For nearly a year Lafayette served as a frequent intermediary with Rochambeau and sometimes as a trusted emissary to the Congress. With George Washington at West Point when Benedict Arnold's* treason was discovered, Lafayette served on the court that voted the death penalty to Major John André. In the spring of 1781, at the head of twelve hundred New England troops, he marched south to Virginia. For the next six months he marched and countermarched, fought sharp skirmishes while avoiding a probably disastrous all-out engagement, frequently outwitted Cornwallis, cooperated with Anthony Wayne,* and eventually played a major role in bottling up Cornwallis and the final victory at Yorktown. That December he returned to France.

In August 1784 he made a triumphant six-month return to his adopted land. He was entertained by Washington at Mount Vernon and was enthusiastically received wherever he went. In 1824 he returned once more to the United States. Invited by President James Monroe, generously rewarded by Congress, he was given a hero's welcome throughout a year-long tour that Senator Sumner said "belongs to the poetry of history." Never has a visitor to America been accorded such demonstrations of gratitude and affection.

Lafayette's career in his native land deserves more space than is available. As a liberal philosopher, a would-be reformer, and a devotee of republicanism, he was important from 1787 until his death. In the early years of the French Revolution he played a leading role; in the 1820s he was a significant figure. Dreaming of a republic in the mould of his beloved United States, he accepted constitutional monarchy as a step in that direction. In his last great public speech he attacked the reactionary policies of Louis-Philippe whom he had helped to power. Always he was a friend, frequently an important friend, to his second country, the United States. When he was buried, in Picpus Cemetery in Paris, soil from Bunker Hill was spread on his grave.

No one questions Lafayette's psychological contribution to the winning of American independence. In November 1777 Baron Johann de Kalb noted that "No one deserves more than he the esteem which he enjoys here. He is a prodigy for his age, full of courage, spirit, judgment, good manners, feelings of generosity and zeal for the cause of liberty on this continent." Lafayette's zeal for liberty, his unbounded energy, his deference and charm, all contributed to the high esteem in which he was held. He constantly urged his government to send more aid to America, and he became the symbol of that assistance. His courage in battle and his desire to be in the thickest fighting endeared him to the soldier in the ranks.

What of his military skill? his leadership in action? Was this "boy," with little military training and no battle experience, able to make a significant contribution to the American cause? Not yet twenty when he landed on our shores, he was not devoid of military knowledge. Howard H. Peckham noted that "He probably did a great deal of reading . . . in the military field. Otherwise it is impossible to explain the ease with which he exercised a major general's command in the Continental army." We know that he was diligent. In December 1777 he wrote his father-in-law, "I read, I study, I examine, I listen, I think, and out of all that I try to form an idea into which I put as much common sense as I can."

Central to Lafayette's excellence as a staff officer were his devotion and loyalty to the commander in chief. "Our General," Lafayette wrote only a few months after his arrival, "is a man truly made for this revolution, which could not succeed without him." Peckham believes that few of the American generals were "more devoted" to Washington than was Lafayette. Louis Gottschalk gives Lafayette primary credit for destroying the "cabal" aimed at replacing Washington.

Lafayette's administrative ability and his concern for the troops under his command cannot be overstressed. Gottschalk wrote, "Greater credit than he has often received . . . is due to Lafayette for the extraordinary efforts to move impoverished, incompetent, and lethargic commissary agents of Virginia and Maryland to effective measures." Peckham wrote, "Lafayette scrupulously looked after his men, spending his own money when Congress failed to provide them necessities."

Lafayette's contemporaries respected him as an officer as well as a human being. When Lafayette commanded troops in Virginia, Washington wrote, ". . . it is my opinion, the command of the troops in that State cannot be in better hands than the Marquis." In June 1781 General Nathanael Greene* wrote Jefferson, "I have the highest opinion of the Marquis's abilities and zeal."

How may the twentieth century regard his military leadership? At Brandywine, under fire for the first time, Lafayette showed physical courage and desire for action. When the British struck Washington's right flank, Lafayette jumped off his horse, urged the men around him to charge the British, and remained at the front after he was wounded. As Washington's men retreated, near dusk, Lafayette rallied troops at the stone bridge across Chester Creek and helped prevent the retreat from becoming a rout.

Lafayette next saw important action on May 18, 1778, when he made camp on Barren Hill with a reconnaissance force of twenty-two hundred men. He selected an excellent defensive position and posted militia at Whitemarsh to protect two fords. These militia did not retain their post; Howe learned from a deserter of the militia's withdrawal and attacked. Lafayette avoided Sir William Howe's trap, outmaneuvered the older general, and forced the British to withdraw to Philadelphia. Lafayette had made mistakes: posting untrained militia in a key spot, failing to check to make sure they retained their position, and remaining two nights in the same camp. Yet, he had outmaneuvered Howe, and he had inflicted more casualties than he had received.

In February 1781, in command of twelve hundred Continentals, Lafayette successfully defended Richmond. In mid-May Cornwallis, determined to wipe out the patriot bases in Virginia, arrived from North Carolina with seventy-two hundred men. On May 24 Lafayette wrote Washington, "I am . . . determined to scarmish [skirmish], but not engage too far. I am not strong enough even to get beaten."

For several weeks Lafayette maneuvered brilliantly, protecting supply bases and keeping open routes for possible reinforcement. In early June, Anthony Wayne* joined him with nine hundred Continentals; William Campbell came with six hundred mounted riflemen, and Frederick William von Steuben* added four hundred and fifty men. By the end of June Lafayette commanded five thousand. At Green Springs, on July 6, Cornwallis outwitted Wayne. Wayne fought stubbornly; Lafayette came up with the main body of his troops, had two horses shot from under him, and suffered rather heavy casualties.

With the exception of that one engagement, Cornwallis steadily retreated; Lafayette followed. Cornwallis was bottled up, Yorktown was brilliantly planned and fought, and independence was guaranteed. Lafayette merits high praise for his role in the Virginia Campaign. He demonstrated boundless energy, strong determination, a genius for administration and public relations, and superior ability to command and lead.

BIBLIOGRAPHY

Gottschalk, Louis. *Lafayette: A Guide to the Letters, Documents & Manuscripts in the United States.* Ithaca, N.Y.: Cornell University Press, 1975.

———. *Lafayette and the Close of the American Revolution.* Chicago: University of Chicago Press, 1974.

———. *Lafayette Joins the American Army.* Chicago: University of Chicago Press, 1937.

Idzerda, Stanley J., et al. *Lafayette in the Age of the American Revolution; Selected Letters and Papers, 1776–1790.* Ithaca, N.Y.: Cornell University Press, 1977.

Loveland, Anne C. *Emblem of Liberty; The Image of Lafayette in the American Mind.* Baton Rouge, La.: Louisiana State University Press, 1971.

RALPH ADAMS BROWN

LAWRENCE, James (b. Burlington, N.J., October 1, 1781; d. off Halifax, Nova Scotia, June 5, 1813), naval officer. Lawrence enjoyed a short, brilliant career, participating in the Quasi-War with France, the Barbary Wars, and the War of 1812.

John Lawrence, James' father, was mayor of Burlington in 1775, a staunch Loyalist during the American Revolution, and was jailed for his sympathies. While imprisoned, John Lawrence befriended fellow inmate Lieutenant Colonel John G. Simcoe, commander of the Queen's Rangers. After the war, Simcoe became lieutenant governor of Canada and invited the Lawrences to live in Canada, which they did until John Lawrence's death in 1796. Returning to New Jersey, James Lawrence entered grammar school in Burlington to prepare for a career in law, according to his father's wishes, but chose instead to follow the sea. For three months, he studied navigation under a Mr. Griscomb and entered the U.S. Navy on September 4, 1798.

That year also marked the beginning of hostilities between the United States and France. Midshipman Lawrence was ordered to the 26-gun frigate *Ganges*

(Captain Richard Dale). On May 23, 1800, Lawrence was transferred to the 36-gun frigate *New York*, under Captain Thomas Robinson, who took Lawrence with him when he assumed command of the 28-gun frigate *Adams*. At the war's end, Lawrence survived the personnel reductions made by the Peace Establishment Act of March 3, 1801, and on September 1, he was reassigned to the frigate *New York*, then laid up at the Washington Navy Yard.

The outbreak of the Barbary Wars necessitated an increase in the number of officers, men, and ships stationed in the Mediterranean. Lawrence reported on board the 12-gun schooner *Enterprise*, under Andrew Sterett, was made acting first lieutenant, and sailed from Baltimore on February 12, 1802. He was promoted to lieutenant on April 6, 1802. Lawrence was one of the men who volunteered to sail under Lieutenant Stephen Decatur on board the ketch *Intrepid* to burn the frigate *Philadelphia*. The *Philadelphia* had grounded on an uncharted reef and fell into Tripolitan hands on October 31, 1803. She was being refitted for action against the American fleet when Commodore Edward Preble* decided to destroy her. With Lawrence as Decatur's first lieutenant, the crew surprised the Tripolitans, boarded, set fire to the *Philadelphia*, and escaped without a man being killed. For his leadership of this exploit, Decatur was awarded a sword by Congress and made a post-captain, while Lawrence and other officers were rewarded with two months' pay. Lawrence thought this to be a "paltry" sum and declined his share.

Between August 3 and September 3, 1804, Lawrence took part in five attacks on the port of Tripoli, and during the fourth attack, he commanded *Gunboat No. 5*. Later that month, Lawrence was appointed first lieutenant of the 28-gun frigate *John Adams*, under Isaac Chauncey, which departed the Mediterranean in February 1805. Shortly after his return to the United States, Lawrence was called upon to command *Gunboat No. 6* which had been ordered to the Mediterranean with six other gunboats to oppose the "mosquito fleet" of Tripoli. The Tripolitan War ended on June 5, 1805, with the signing of a peace treaty, but Lawrence remained in command of *No. 6* and did not return to the United States until July 1806, when he put his gunboat out of commission at Baltimore.

During the next six years, Lawrence served as inspector of gunboats at Portland, Maine, was appointed a member of the court-martial trial that tried Captain James Barron for his role in the *Chesapeake-Leopard* affair, served as first lieutenant on board the 44-gun frigate *Constitution*, and was appointed commanding officer of the brigs *Vixen* (12-guns), *Argus* (18 guns), and *Hornet* (20 guns), successively. He received his promotion to master commandant on November 3, 1810. On the domestic side, in 1808 he married Julia Montaudevert, the daughter of a French sea captain, who bore him two children, a son who died in infancy and a daughter, Mary, who married Lieutenant William Preston Griffin of the U.S. Navy.

During the early months of 1812, when pressures for war with Great Britain were increasing, Lawrence's *Hornet* made a rapid passage to Europe carrying diplomatic dispatches to France and Britain. He returned before the declaration of war of June 18, and the *Hornet* was then attached to the squadron of Commodore John Rodgers,* including the 44-gun frigates *President* and *United States*, and the 36-gun frigate *Congress*, and *Argus*. Rodgers sortied from New York on June 21. During the cruise, the *Hornet* took three prizes for the squadron and participated in the chase of the British frigate *Belvidera* (36 guns).

Lawrence's next assignment was to sail in the *Hornet* with the *Constitution*, under Commodore William Bainbridge, and the 32-gun frigate *Essex*, under David Dixon Porter,* with orders to attack commerce en route to Britain from the West Indies and South America. The *Essex* never joined the squadron, however, and upon reaching Salvador, Brazil, the *Constitution* and *Hornet* went their separate ways. Lawrence tried to provoke an engagement with the British sloop *Bonne Citoyenne* (18 guns), whose captain refused to leave port, much to Lawrence's frustration. He blockaded the port until the arrival of HMS *Montagu* (74 guns) and then sailed northward for the Guianas. On February 24, 1813, Lawrence attacked the British brig *Peacock* (18 guns) off Pernambuco. The *Hornet* was victorious in a brief but devastating engagement that resulted in the surrender of the *Peacock* in fifteen minutes and her sinking shortly afterward. Lawrence was humane in his treatment of his prisoners, and when the news of his battle arrived in the United States, he was hailed as the latest of a new breed of young naval heroes, tenacious in battle and gracious in victory. Lawrence was promoted to captain on March 4, 1813, and despite his preference for the *Hornet* was ordered to command the 36-gun frigate *Chesapeake* at Boston.

Lawrence reported on board the *Chesapeake* in the middle of May, only to discover her crew in a mutinous state due to a dispute with the previous captain over prize money. Almost one-third of the officers and men were new to the ship, though not to the Navy. During late May Lawrence was busy preparing his ship for sea. He had received orders to cruise to the northward toward the Gulf of St. Lawrence where he could intercept supplies and reinforcements for British forces in Canada. By the end of May the *Chesapeake* was ready for sea but not for battle. She was in dire need of a shakedown cruise. During his few weeks on board, Lawrence had exercised the men at General Quarters frequently but the guns had not once been fired.

At dawn on June 1, the British frigate *Shannon* (38 guns), Captain Philip Vere Broke, sailed into Boston Bay near the mouth of the harbor and fired a cannon, offering ship-to-ship combat. Lawrence felt personally provoked and undertook to defend his honor and that of the United States. Within hours the *Chesapeake* was underway, but Lawrence was seemingly unaware of the odds he was facing. Captain Broke had commanded his ship and crew for six years and enjoyed a reputation as an expert in naval gunnery. His crew fought their guns like clockwork and with great accuracy. In the ensuing engagement, the *Chesapeake* followed *Shannon* out to a point eighteen miles east of Boston Light where the *Shannon* waited, sails aback. Lawrence was thereby given the weather gauge, an initial advantage which he immediately relinquished. Rather than rake across the *Shannon*'s stern, Lawrence put down his helm, came alongside, and exchanged broadsides. Broke then had the upper hand, considering *Chesapeake*'s lack of gun drill. Great guns and musketry soon took their effect, wounding Lawrence and damaging *Chesapeake*'s rigging so that she became unmanageable. Lawrence was taken below decks as the fight turned against him. Realizing this, he cried out "Don't give up the ship," urging his officers and crew to resist to the utmost. But British boarding parties soon controlled the decks. A heavy toll in killed and wounded was taken on both sides. The *Shannon* lost thirty-three who died instantly or from their wounds, while the *Chesapeake* suffered sixty-one killed or mortally wounded. Captain Broke received a severe headwound in hand-to-hand fighting and never fully recovered, but Lawrence died on board the *Shannon* en route to Halifax Harbor.

Much has been written on the battle, but it remains clear that Lawrence's hasty decision to accept combat before his ship and crew were ready and his romantic sense of honor led to the undoing of not only the man but also those who sailed with him. His mission, of raiding the Gulf of St. Lawrence, was of greater importance than the possible defeat of a single British frigate. Far more was lost than might have been gained had the *Chesapeake* defeated the *Shannon*.

Despite his defeat, Lawrence's plucky fight has been seen as a stirring example in the annals of the U.S. Navy. His physical courage and nobility of spirit were inspiring to his contemporaries. His death was widely and deeply felt, for he was one of the most popular officers in the Navy and had just reached the peak of his career when he died.

BIBLIOGRAPHY

Knox, Dudley W. *A History of the United States Navy*. New York: G. P. Putnam's Sons, 1936.

Mahan, Alfred Thayer. *Sea Power in Its Relations to the War of 1812*. 2 vols. Boston: Little, Brown and Company, 1905.

Poolman, Kenneth. *Guns Off Cape Ann: The Story of the Shannon and the Chesapeake*. London: Evans Brothers, 1961.

Pullen, Hugh F. *The Shannon and the Chesapeake*. Toronto: McClelland and Stewart, 1970.

Roosevelt, Theodore. *The Naval War of 1812*. New York: G. P. Putnam's Sons, 1882.

WILLIAM S. DUDLEY

LEE, Charles (b. Chester, England, January 26, 1731/2; d. Philadelphia, Pa., October 2, 1782), major general in the Continental Army. Modern authorities believe Lee was politically the most radical American general during the early years of the War for Independence.

Many members of Lee's family served in the British Army, and his father, who commanded the 44th Regiment of Foot, decided early in his son's life that the boy would continue this tradition. When Charles was fourteen, Colonel Lee purchased him a commission in the 44th. Charles began his active service in

1748 and, after seven years of garrison duty in Ireland, went with the regiment to North America in 1755.

By the end of the Seven Years' War, Lee had extensive experience as a combat officer. He fought in every major campaign in America from 1755 to 1760, with the single exception of James Wolfe's conquest of Quebec. In addition, he took part in the defense of Portugal in 1762. He was, by all accounts, a courageous, intelligent officer in the field. On two occasions, his superiors showed their confidence in him by trusting him with important missions. In 1759 Lee was ordered to take fifteen men and search the wilderness between Niagara and Fort Pitt for signs of a French force. In 1762 he led a small force on a surprise raid on a Spanish camp at Villa Velha and destroyed large quantities of munitions and supplies.

Lee analyzed his wartime experiences carefully, reached thoughtful conclusions, and stuck to them in the face of the prevailing wisdom. He felt that the war had amply proven the great effectiveness of light infantry tactics against regular troops, particularly in rugged, sparsely populated countries like America and Portugal. The major reason for their effectiveness was obvious to Lee. An army's logistical systems, so essential to its existence as a fighting force, were peculiarly vulnerable to accident or attack in such areas, and light infantry tactics helped an opposing army take maximum advantage of its opportunities. The difficulties of supplying an army in America had brought home another lesson to Lee: the paramount importance of civilian support. The enthusiastic aid of civilian society could ease logistical burdens considerably and replenish the Army's manpower. Moreover, another advantage of light infantry tactics would appear as recruits entered the service. Since these tactics required less rigorous training and discipline, new recruits could be integrated into the force more quickly. In Lee's opinion, his theories were fully justified by the outcome of the war in America. Unlike most British officers, and despite his own occasional quarrels with civilians over supply contacts and recruiting, Lee believed that Americans' civil and military support had ultimately been crucial to victory. He liked the people and respected them as soldiers. During 1774–1776 these ideas and affections would guide his actions.

Life in England during 1763–1773 frustrated and infuriated Lee. His hot temper, caustic wit, and impolitic fondness for public disputes made for him powerful civilian and military enemies who kept him on half-pay and unpromoted until the general upgrading of the Army in 1772. By that time, he had thoroughly imbibed the principles of the radical, "Real Whig" opposition. Convinced that corrupt ministers had bribed, deceived, and coerced the British people into yielding most of their liberties, certain that that "despicable . . . dolt" George III was no patriot king, Lee decided that America was the last refuge of liberty in the world. Early during the decade of peace, Lee's dissatisfactions and restlessness had carried him to Eastern Europe, where he observed the sporadic fighting there and became in 1769 a major general in the Polish Army. In 1773 those same feelings encouraged him to make a business trip to North America to inspect his extensive land grants and to scout the possibility of moving there. He arrived two months before the Boston Tea Party and the beginning of the imperial crisis.

Since Lee had a public reputation as an opponent of the taxation and coercion of the colonies that preceded him to America, and since he had military experience that might prove necessary, prominent patriots like Patrick Henry, George Washington,* and the Adamses received him enthusiastically during 1774. Lee was equally enthused. He warned them that they must stand firm, or their liberties would be lost. He also encouraged them by scoffing at the notion that British regulars, "the refuse of an exhausted nation," could conquer two hundred thousand "active, vigorous yeomanry, fired with noble ardor, . . . all armed, all expert in the use of arms." He devised a simplified training manual, and he promised that three months of drill would make the militia able to deal effectively with any invader. By December 1774 he was putting his preaching into practice by drilling patriotic forces in Maryland.

In June 1775, after receiving Congress' assurance that he would be compensated for any confiscation of his English property, Lee accepted appointment as major general and resigned his British commission. A summary of his service record for the next year reveals his importance to the American cause. From June until December 1775 Lee commanded the left wing of the army besieging Boston, and he oversaw the training of troops and the construction of entrenchments. From December through March 1776, Washington and Congress made him responsible for encouraging the civilians and preparing the defenses of Rhode Island and New York City. In February Congress, reasoning that he was the only officer who could "speak and think in French," gave him the Canadian command. Then, on March 1, these orders were rescinded, and he was assigned the command of the Southern Military District. From late March through August, he organized defenses from Virginia to Georgia. In June, he commanded the forces that repelled the British invasion of Charleston, and he earned popular acclaim as "The Palladium of American Liberty."

Lee began this year certain that he could conduct the war better than anyone else; he ended it even more certain. At Boston, he tried to avert further fighting by secretly establishing, in direct contradiction to the orders of the Massachusetts provincial congress, contacts with British officers. He was among the first to advise Congress openly to declare independence. Then, having dispensed political advice, he urged Congress to put all militia under Continental control and to draft regular soldiers out of those units. In Rhode Island, New York, Maryland, and Virginia, he was publicly and harshly critical of what he felt was the local patriots' timidity in handling suspected Tories and their former governors. To his mind, the time for persuasion had passed; lenient measures would only guarantee that a British army would have vital civilian support. On his own authority, and frequently in opposition to the wishes of local committees, Lee harassed Loyalists, forcing them to take oaths, threatening them in some areas with prison and loss of property, and in Virginia actually sequestering men, destroying homes, and forcing families to move away from the coast. In South Carolina, Lee discovered that local patriots had ignorantly sited their defenses and lazily left them uncompleted. The Carolinians also obstinately refused to place their militia under his command, although they did follow his technical advice on finishing the forts and on using their ordnance effectively. Lee praised their bravery but realized that the victory was largely due to the harbor's winds and tides and "a most unaccountable languor and inertness on [the enemy's] part." Charleston confirmed to him again that the political timidity and military ignorance of Congress and local committees drastically weakened the war effort. It also reinforced his determination to disobey or modify the politicians' orders whenever he felt it was necessary.

In August, Congress ordered Lee to return to Washington's army. He rejoined it in New York in mid-October and insisted on an immediate retreat into New Jersey. But Washington, under pressure from Congress, kept troops on Manhattan too long and lost twenty-nine hundred men and large quantities of stores. Furious that his commander had listened to "the cattle" in Congress, Lee concluded that he did not have the sense or courage to resist erroneous advice. As a result of this conclusion, Lee essentially stopped obeying Washington. When ordered to bring his forces across the Delaware quickly, Lee moved slowly and advised Washington to return to New Jersey. The local militia "seemed sanguine," he wrote, and the British lines were overextended and vulnerable. Clearly, Lee thought he could duplicate his triumph at Villa Velha, force the British back toward New York, and "re-conquer the Jerseys." Before he could do that, however, he carelessly dawdled at a tavern in Basking Ridge on December 13, 1776, and a British patrol captured him.

Unquestionably, this turn of events, which Lee blamed on the "rascality" of his guards, demoralized him. Perhaps Sir William Howe's obvious desire to try him for desertion and treason disturbed him too. Even if it did not (and Howe soon realized that a court-martial was probably illegal and certainly unwise), the seeming slowness of Congress and Washington to threaten reprisals must have angered Lee. Such was his emotional state when he reflected on the past eighteen months and concluded that America could not win the war, and would only accomplish the weakening of itself and Britain. He discussed his intellectual reason for reaching this conclusion in a plan for militarily ending the war which he sent to Howe in March 1777. Conquer ports in Maryland, issue a proclamation of pardon, and wait for settlers in Maryland and Pennsylvania to declare their loyalty, he advised Howe. The wait would not, he promised, be long. The Germans in particular had been "the most staunch assertors of the American cause," but they were "so remarkably tenacious of their property and apprehensive of the least injury being done to [it]" that they would choose peace before their land became battlefields. This statement exposes the depths of Lee's disenchantment with the American cause. The American people, he now believed, were not merely poorly led. They suffered also from their own unwillingness to make necessary major sacrifices. They were not virtuous enough to win independence.

Lee acted on this conclusion. In February 1777 he cooperated in efforts to open informal peace negotiations. When Congress refused to send agents, he told Howe that seizing the Chesapeake would end the war with a minimum of bloodshed. For the rest of his captivity, and even for two months after his exchange in April 1778, Lee continued to explore ways of negotiating peace. Lack of success resigned him to fighting on. When he returned to the American lines, he coolly told Congress that the Continental Army was inferior to the British in every respect, including morale, and opined that it should never take the offensive. He was probably skeptical of its defensive capacity as well, for he advised Congress to strengthen the cavalry and convert infantry units into light infantry, changes that would force any commander in the direction of harassment and away from confrontation on the battlefield. In May 1778, when he resumed active duty, he urged Washington to be cautious. When the British retreated toward New York in June, Lee was prominent among those who advised a "partial attack" only if a "general action" could be avoided.

Washington agreed with this advice but then increased the size of the attacking force to the point that Lee felt obliged to assume command of it at Monmouth. Because of difficult terrain, torrid heat, poor communications, and unexpectedly strong resistance, the attack foundered. A disorganized retreat began. Fearful that his troops would be trapped and slaughtered, Lee ordered his officers to withdraw to stronger defensive positions. At this time, Washington arrived on the battlefield. Before he fully grasped the situation, he angrily accused Lee in public of disobeying orders. After the British counterattack was fought off, Lee demanded in insulting terms a court-martial to clear his name. Washington responded with charges of disobedience, "making an unnecessary, disorderly, and shameful retreat," and disrespect to a superior officer.

In retrospect, Lee seems innocent of the first two charges and clearly guilty of the third. At the time, however, abstract questions of guilt or innocence mattered little to the court or Congress. Both bodies felt they had to support Washington's authority, and the only way to do that was to find Lee guilty as charged. He was suspended from the Army for a year. After fruitless appeals to Congress and, through the press, to the public for justice, he indulged himself in vicious attacks on Washington and the American people, who "have always a god of the day, whose infallibility is not to be disputed." He never served again in the Army. Lee died convinced that he had unwittingly helped establish an arbitrary government in America.

As John Shy has noted, Lee's contributions to the American Revolution were substantial but difficult to measure. Without doubt, his energy, example, and experience were valuable in 1775–1776. Without doubt, too, had Lee, not Washington, been the hero of the times that tried men's souls in December 1776, the relationship of the military to civil authorities during the crucial years that followed would have been different. This last thought suggests one significance of his career for military historians. An examination of his acts and plans may well reveal what the War for Independence could have been. Equally important, an examination of the causes and progress of his disillusion and tragedy may well reveal what it was.

BIBLIOGRAPHY

Alden, John R. *General Charles Lee: Traitor or Patriot?* Baton Rouge: Louisiana State University, 1951.
Higginbotham, Don. *The War of American Independence.* New York: Macmillan, 1971.
Shy, John. "American Strategy: Charles Lee and the Radical Alternative." In John Shy, *A People Numerous and Armed: Reflections on the Military Struggle for American Independence.* Oxford: Oxford University Press, 1976, pp. 133–62.
Thayer, Theodore. *The Making of a Scapegoat: Washington and Lee at Monmouth.* Port Washington, N.Y.: Kennikat Press, 1976.

JOHN L. BULLION

LEE, Robert Edward (b. Stratford, Westmoreland County, Va., January 19, 1807; d. Lexington, Va., October 12, 1870), Army officer. After serving for more than thirty years in the U.S. Army, Lee commanded the Army of Northern Virginia for the Confederacy during the Civil War.

Robert E. Lee was a man in search of place. He was born, in 1807, into a famous Virginia family. His father, Henry ("Light-Horse Harry") Lee, a hero of the American Revolution, managed to fritter away both his reputation and the family fortune. This circumstance necessitated that Robert seek his education at West Point, where he was graduated in 1829, second in his class of forty-six. (The number one graduate, Charles Mason of New York, resigned from the Army two years later and did not serve in the Civil War.) In 1831 Lee married Mary Custis, the daughter of another distinguished Virginia family and heiress to "Arlington," a great estate in northern Virginia.

Lee, in keeping with his high rank in his graduating class, spent several years in the engineers. In 1847 he was assigned to the staff of General Winfield Scott* (at Scott's request) in Mexico. Lee did not command troops in Scott's campaign against Mexico City, but he distinguished himself for his military acumen, timely advice regarding terrain, and great personal bravery.

In 1852 Lee was named superintendent at West Point, an office that he distinguished. Lee stressed high academic standards, curriculum reform, and stringent military discipline. With all that, he was almost a father to the young men under his tutelage.

In 1855 Lee was posted as lieutenant colonel to Texas, to serve with the 2d Cavalry Regiment (commanded by Albert Sidney Johnston*). He remained with the 2d Cavalry until 1858 when he took an extended leave to "Arlington," which came under his care (but not ownership) upon the death of his father-in-law. In early 1860 he was dispatched to San Antonio to take command of the

Department of Texas. It was the spiritual nadir for Lee, exacerbated by the absence from his family, his despair over his military career, and deep misgivings over the open talk of secession among Southern officers and politicians. Lee opposed disunion, regretted slavery, and wished to serve no flag other than the "Star Spangled Banner." (As if to demonstrate that fact, while on leave at "Arlington" Lee had led the soldiers and Marines who helped to quell John Brown's fanatical raid on Harper's Ferry in 1859.) Yet, as war approached, and in spite of the near-pleading General Scott, Lee resigned from the Army of the United States on April 20, 1861. He could not bring himself to lead that army against the South, and especially Virginia.

The first year of the Civil War was not auspicious for Lee, although he clearly was in the confidence of President Jefferson Davis. Lee had his opportunity in the late spring of 1862 when he assumed command of the Army of Northern Virginia after Joseph Eggleston Johnston* (his classmate at West Point) was severely wounded at Seven Pines. Lee faced a formidable Union Army under George Brinton McClellan.* To submit to McClellan's siege tactics would, in Lee's mind, end in the capture of Richmond and, in any case, such was against his inclinations. He proposed to take the offensive, encouraged by the success of Thomas Jonathan ("Stonewall") Jackson* in the Shenandoah Valley and the apparent vulnerability of McClellan's right wing, practically isolated north of the Chickahominy River. Thus, on June 26, Lee launched his first campaign, a series of bloody, if inconclusive, battles called the Seven Days. His penchant for the attack emerged, as well as his propensity for holding only a slack rein on subordinates, and his reliance upon the frontal assault, which caused such carnage at Malvern Hill. He did force the intimidated McClellan to withdraw from in front of Richmond, however; this was no insignificant feat, even given McClellan's mishandling of his magnificent army.

In August Lee followed his success on the Peninsula with a strike against John Pope at Manassas, where he thoroughly befuddled and thrashed that vainglorious incompetent. These victories encouraged Lee to invade Maryland, a decision of great military and political consequence. But he allowed his army to advance in dispersed order, and thus in mid-September, at Sharpsburg, Maryland (on Antietam Creek), with some twenty-five thousand men he faced a force three times that number under the resurrected McClellan. Discretion would have suggested retreat, but Lee stood. After a day's vicious fighting, marked by inept Union leadership and the providential arrival of Confederate reinforcements under Ambrose Powell Hill,* Lee managed to save his army. President Abraham Lincoln, manifestly disappointed, replaced McClellan with Ambrose Everett Burnside, who responded with the infamous attack against Lee at Fredericksburg, a fight that left Lee at a moral, if not military, advantage in Virginia.

Lee's next adversary was Joseph Hooker* who concentrated his reorganized army near Chancellorsville. Lee moved the bulk of his army to meet the threat (leaving ten thousand men under Jubal Anderson Early* to guard his rear at Fredericksburg). And at Chancellorsville he effected his greatest victory. Jackson's strike against Hooker's right and rear confused the Union forces and most assuredly demoralized their commander. When Lee turned back to confront John Sedgwick, who had broken through with his corps at Fredericksburg, Hooker remained in position, intimidated by Lee and confused even more by a near concussion from a Confederate shell. During the night of May 5–6, the Army of the Potomac retreated, beaten more by the character of the enemy army and its commander than by military circumstances. It was a brilliant victory for Lee, but costly in casualties and the great individual loss of Jackson, mortally wounded by his own men.

Lee now proposed a more ambitious move, this time into Pennsylvania. An invasion of the North would free Virginia from the immediate threat of the still powerful Union Army and would give Lee access to sorely needed supplies. Moreover, he believed that a battle won on Northern soil would be of considerable political effect. Thus Gettysburg.

The Gettysburg Campaign was not Lee's finest. He did not use his cavalry to best advantage; James Ewell Brown Stuart* blazed his own trail northward, Lee could not know the precise disposition of the Union forces, even after the first contact west of Gettysburg. When Richard Stoddert Ewell (Jackson's replacement) did not press his apparent advantage on July 1, it was at least partly because Lee had not issued precise orders to him. The inconclusive second day was the responsibility of James Longstreet,* obstinate to the point of insubordination, but also the responsibility of Lee who could not bring himself to press his senior corps commander. The failure of the infamous assault on July 3 (the so-called Pickett's charge, led by George Edward Pickett*) was, as Lee said, his fault. Perhaps it was Malvern Hill revisited; he did not know what else to do. He did once again rescue his army, aided by the inactivity of his opponent, George Gordon Meade,* who appeared to be stymied and did not or could not follow up his advantage after July 3.

The Virginia campaigns of 1864–1865 are often personalized as a duel between Lee and Ulysses Simpson Grant,* with Grant inexorably wearing down the outmanned Lee until the final meeting at Appomattox Court House. Grant made Lee's army the focus of his campaign, to hold Lee while William Tecumseh Sherman* effected his advance into Georgia. Lee anticipated this tactic and urged a concentration, one that would strengthen him and allow him to make even better use of his geographical ally, the area of trees, briers, and ravines called the Wilderness. The first battles, in early May, had the effect of "fixing" Lee, that is, Grant had made his contact with the Army of Northern Virginia and would not let go. From the Wilderness until the end of the war, Lee was, practically speaking, on the defensive. His often brilliant defensive tactics severely bloodied the enemy, but he lost in terms of men and initiative. Even the old ploy of a threat on Washington failed. When Jubal Early approached the capital in June, Grant had already resolved to move on Petersburg. Lee seemed almost bemused. Perhaps, as J.F.C. Fuller has noted, he may have doubted that Grant was capable of such imagination. Lee could only consolidate at Petersburg and absorb punishment until his army was worn away by casualties and, increasingly, desertions.

In assessing Robert E. Lee, the temptation is to distinguish between the man and the general, a division that is basically artificial and unhistorical. Lee, the man, was by all accounts an admirable figure, possessed of all the virtues of Southern manhood and few of the faults. Some of his virtues—a certain forbearance, even diffidence—led him to slight his duty as a military advisor to his president and on occasion to fail to impress upon his subordinates the need for forceful, coherent action. His undeniable personal courage and devotion to duty led him to expect the same of others; similarly, his devotion to Virginia, the land and the idea, led him to demand much of his soldiers, even when such entailed sacrifices greater than his. His penchant for the audacious offensive made him almost reckless of the cost of lives. Perhaps his early successes, through Chancellorsville, reinforced his low regard for his opponents, "those people" as he patronizingly referred to them. He adopted Winfield Scott's policy of planning the general operation and then leaving the execution to his corps commanders, a failing, if it was such, shared by many generals of the war. As long as he could depend on Stonewall Jackson, his lack of exact orders seemed to make little difference. With Jackson gone, and less bold or less understanding commanders leading his corps, the absence of more precise directives made a considerable difference. Lee knew the efficacy of flanking maneuvers in terms of casualties avoided and strong positions rendered untenable; yet on two notable occasions he ordered assaults on fixed artillery and with disastrous results.

Occasionally, sometimes because of ill-health (as at North Anna), Lee seemed almost bemused, possessed by inertia, when plans did not materialize. Or he attacked, with elan and imagination at Chancellorsville, with a certain fatalism at Gettysburg. His intellect was a curious blend of intuition and reason, vagueness and precision. He appeared to understand the strategic importance of the middle South, yet preoccupied himself with Virginia. That he seldom brought his keen intelligence and imposing personality to bear on broad questions of strategy remains an enigma, unless one accepts his natural preoccupation with his native state, his place.

Lee emerged from the war as the most admired general even after close analysis suggests that others may have been his superior, Grant and Sherman in particular. The profound graciousness of Lee during the negotiations at Appomattox, his heart-rending farewell to his soldiers, and his restrained and decorous postwar career as president of Washington College (renamed Washington and Lee University in 1871) added to his host of admirers and confirmed for them that their admiration was deserved. But the manner in which Lee accepted defeat obscures the extent to which he contributed to that defeat, and that of the commanders of the Civil War; his army absorbed casualties beyond those incurred by his major opponents. The adulation accorded him by his advocates, by fellow officers and historians, remains a monument to the Lee mystique.

BIBLIOGRAPHY

Connelly, Thomas L. *The Marble Man: Robert E. Lee and His Image in American Society.* New York: Alfred A. Knopf, 1977.
Freeman, Douglas Southall. *R. E. Lee: A Biography.* 4 vols. New York: Charles Scribner's Sons, 1936.
Fuller, J.F.C. *Grant and Lee: A Study in Personality and Generalship.* London: Eyre and Spottiswoode, 1933.

JOHN T. HUBBELL

LEJEUNE, John Archer (b. "Old Hickory" Plantation, Raccourci District, Pointe Coupee Parish, La., January 10, 1867; d. Baltimore, Md., November 20, 1942), Marine Corps officer. Lejeune was commandant of the Corps (1920–1929) and supervised its modernization.

John Archer Lejeune was the younger of the two children of Ovide and Laura Archer Turpin Lejeune and grew up in genteel poverty in Reconstruction Louisiana. His father, of Acadian stock and a Confederate officer, had lost all of his extensive landholdings immediately after the Civil War. Through hard work, the elder Lejeune bought back his original plantation but was able to retain only seventy-five acres. John received his primary education from his mother at home. At age thirteen, Lejeune left Louisiana and attended for a year a boarding school run by his uncle James Archer near Natchez, Mississippi.

Influenced at a young age by the martial exploits of his father and his own reading, in September 1881 the young Lejeune entered Louisiana State University (LSU), which at the time was a combination of military preparatory school and college. Although he wanted to go to West Point, Lejeune remained at LSU until 1884, when he accepted an appointment to the Naval Academy, the only vacancy at a service school open to him. He completed his class work at the Academy in 1888, becoming a passed midshipman, and shipped on board the ill-fated cruiser *Vandalia*, which sank off Apia in Samoa during a hurricane in 1889. Surviving the sinking, Lejeune returned to Annapolis in 1890 to take his final examinations. Ranking sixth in a class of thirty-seven, Lejeune elected to enter the Marine Corps. He later explained that he arrived at his choice through a process of elimination; he did not want to be an engineer, and he did not want to spend the greater part of his life at sea.

In October 1890 Lejeune began his first duty assignment at the Marine Barracks at Norfolk, Virginia, where he served for a year. Lejeune next was assigned to the Marine guard in the cruiser *Bennington*. Shortly after Lejeune's arrival, the *Bennington* steamed for South American waters to rendezvous with the American fleet awaiting developments in the crisis with Chile. Once the war scare with Chile was resolved diplomatically, the *Bennington* departed for Europe. Lejeune returned to the United States in 1893 and was once more assigned to the Norfolk Barracks, remaining there for the next four years. In October 1895 he married Ellie Harrison Murdaugh, a daughter of a local judge. In 1897 Lejeune assumed command of the Marine guard in the cruiser *Cincinnati*. With the outbreak of the Spanish-American War in April 1898, the *Cincinnati* participated in the blockade of Cuba but saw relatively little action.

Following the war and the expanding American responsibilities in the Caribbean and the Pacific, Congress in March 1899 authorized a Marine Corps of more than six thousand men, nearly double its prewar strength. After several years of stagnation, the officer corps expanded and promotions, based on seniority, were relatively rapid. A first lieutenant since 1892, Lejeune became a captain in 1899 and a major in 1903. During this period, Lejeune commanded the Marine guard in the battleship *Massachusetts* (1899–1900), served as the recruiting officer in Boston and New York, and commanded the Marine Barracks at Pensacola, Florida.

In the summer of 1903 Lejeune assumed command of the Marine "floating" battalion, which was eventually put aboard the transport *Dixie*. Formed to seize and defend advance bases in support of the fleet, a mission given to the Marine Corps by the Navy General Board in 1900, the battalion was an early precursor of the modern Marine battalion landing team. While at sea in November, the *Dixie* received orders to land Lejeune's battalion in Panama, which had declared its independence from Colombia. President Theodore Roosevelt,* whose canal treaty had been rejected by the Colombian Senate, seized the opportunity to recognize the new Panamanian government and landed the American Marines to prevent the Colombians from putting down the revolution. Lejeune's battalion remained on the Isthmus until December 1904, when it was relieved by another battalion.

Lejeune commanded the Marine Barracks in Washington (1905–1907) and then joined the Marine brigade in the Philippines, which at the time was considered the Marine Pacific Advance Base Force. Upon his arrival, Lejeune took charge of the Marine Barracks at Cavite and later assumed command of the brigade. During the Japanese war scare in the summer of 1907, the Marines in the Philippines received orders to defend Subic Bay and fortify Grande Island which guarded the entrance to the bay. Although the crisis ended quickly, the exercise provided the Marines with valuable experience in the advance base mission. Returning from the Philippines as a lieutenant colonel in the summer of 1909, Lejeune became the first Marine officer to attend the Army War College (1909–1910), where he received his first formal education since leaving the Naval Academy. After leaving the War College, Lejeune received the coveted post of commander of the Marine Barracks in the New York Navy Yard (1910–1913).

In November 1913 Lejeune assumed command of the Mobile Regiment of the newly formed Advanced Base Brigade which was completing its plans for participation in the Atlantic Fleet's winter maneuvers. In January 1914 the brigade landed on the small Caribbean island of Culebra and repulsed a mock attack by an "enemy" landing force. Following the maneuver, Lejeune, recently promoted to colonel, received command of the brigade since its former commander, George Barnett, had become major general commandant of the Marine Corps.

Shortly afterward, Lejeune and the brigade landed at Vera Cruz in April 1914, as a result of the Tampico affair which had exacerbated American relations with the Huerta regime in Mexico. Reinforced by other units, Lejeune relinquished command of the brigade to a more senior colonel and reassumed command of his old regiment.

After his departure with the Marine forces from Mexico in December 1914, Lejeune's next assignment was in Washington as assistant to the commandant, in effect the headquarters chief of staff. During this eventful period (1915–1917), the Marine Corps became involved in both Haiti and the Dominican Republic and began planning for expansion as a result of the outbreak of war in Europe and the growing preparedness movement in the United States. In 1915 and 1916, Lejeune was a member of a personnel board headed by the assistant secretary of the Navy, Franklin D. Roosevelt. The recommendations of this board provided much of the basis for provisions of the Navy Act of 1916 which increased the Marine Corps by five thousand men to a peacetime strength of nearly fifteen thousand men and created six Marine brigadier general slots. Lejeune became a brigadier general in January 1917. Following the U.S. entry into World War I in April 1917, a Marine regiment departed for France in May.

In September Lejeune took command of the Marine base at Quantico, Virginia, which had become the Marine Corps overseas training and staging center, and in May 1918 he departed for France. Although General John Joseph Pershing* rejected his plea for a Marine division in the American Expeditionary Force, Lejeune received command in June of the Army's 64th Brigade. In July Lejeune became the commanding general of the 2d Division, the first Marine officer to command an Army division. Under Lejeune, now a major general, the 2d Division, which included the Marine 4th Brigade as well as Army units, won a series of victories in the late summer and fall of 1918 including the battle of St. Mihiel, Blanc Mont Ridge, and the Meuse-Argonne. Following the Armistice in November, the 2d Division occupied the Coblenz sector of Germany east of the Rhine River. After his return from Europe with the 2d Division in August 1919, Lejeune again took over the Quantico base.

In June 1920 Secretary of the Navy Josephus Daniels, in a controversial move, asked for the resignation of Major General Commandant George Barnett and selected Lejeune to fill the position. Lejeune served as commandant from 1920 to 1929, under three presidents (Woodrow Wilson, Warren Harding, and Calvin Coolidge). Lejeune voluntarily stepped down from the commandancy in 1929 and retired from the Marine Corps on November 12, 1929.

Upon his retirement, Lejeune assumed the superintendency of the Virginia Military Institute. He retired from his second career in 1937 at the age of seventy. He was promoted to lieutenant general in February 1942, under the provisions of new legislation, but he died of cancer in November of the same year in Baltimore. The large Marine base on the eastern coast in North Carolina, Camp Lejeune, was named after the general.

Lejeune was one of the architects of the modern Marine Corps. Although he attained national prominence as a wartime division commander in a land war in Europe, throughout his career Lejeune insisted on the Marine Corps' close relationship to the Navy. He saw the mission of the Marine Corps "to provide the Navy with an efficient expeditionary force habituated to ship life, accustomed to being governed by Navy laws, and regulations, and officered by a personnel whose members have been closely associated with the officers of the Navy officially and unofficially throughout their naval careers."

During the first decades of the twentieth century, Lejeune was closely associated with the Marine Corps Advance Base Force. Although the Advance Base Force was largely defensive, it was the predecessor of the modern Marine Expeditionary and Fleet Marine Force. As early as 1915, Lejeune defined the advance base mission in both defensive and offensive terms. In a presentation at the advance base school, he made the distinction between the Marine role in a war with a naval power and in a war with a land power. In a war with a naval power, the mission of the Marines would be traditional: to seize and defend a base for the fleet while awaiting the decisive naval engagement which would determine the course of the war. In a war with a nonnaval power, on the other hand, Lejeune foresaw a more aggressive role for the Marine Corps. He wrote: "Our duties if organized into regiments and brigades, would be that of the advance guard of an Army. The Marine Corps would be first to set foot on hostile soil in order to seize, fortify, and hold a port from which, as a base, the Army would prosecute its campaign."

Despite the above lecture, in which Lejeune acknowledged his debt to Marine Captain Earl H. Ellis,* Lejeune's strengths lay as a field commander and an administrator rather than as a military theorist. At Vera Cruz and especially in France, Lejeune proved to be an effective combat leader. As assistant to the commandant from 1915–1917, Lejeune pushed for congressional legislation to increase the size of the Corps and organized an informal staff at Headquarters, Marine Corps, that completed much of the prewar planning for the expansion of the Corps.

It was as commandant of the Marine Corps from 1920 to 1929 that Lejeune made his greatest contribution. His political adeptness permitted the Marines to maintain both a stable strength (approximately twenty-one thousand) and their share of the military budget during a period of retrenchments and cutbacks. Based on his association with the Army War College and his experience in France, Lejeune introduced several reforms. He instituted a modern staff system at headquarters, established the Marine Corps Schools (which provided a general program of officer education, extending from young lieutenants to senior field officers), and made Marine aviation an integral part of the Corps' organization. Despite the commitment of the Corps during his commandancy to various missions, from guarding the mails to intervening in Caribbean republics and China, Lejeune maintained the integrity of the Marine Expeditionary Force, which held landing maneuvers with the Fleet. Marine headquarters prepared various war plans, including the Ellis Micronesia plan which foreshadowed the Marine Central Pacific Campaign against Japan.

Lejeune prepared the pathway for the development of modern amphibious doctrine which took place at the Marine Corps Schools in the 1930s and came to fruition in the Pacific during World War II.

BIBLIOGRAPHY

Heinl, Robert D., Jr. *Soldiers of the Sea*. Annapolis, Md.: Naval Institute Press, 1962.
Lejeune, John A. *The Reminiscences of a Marine*. Philadelphia: Dorrance and Company, 1930.
Lewis, Charles L. *Famous American Marines*. Boston: L. C. Page and Company, 1950.
Millett, Allan R. *Semper Fidelis: The History of the U.S. Marine Corps*. New York: Free Press, 1980.
Simmons, Edwin H. *The United States Marines 1775–1975*. New York: Viking Press, 1976.

JACK SHULIMSON

LEMAY, Curtis Emerson (b. Columbus, Ohio, November 15, 1906), Air Force combat commander and chief of staff. LeMay is considered the architect of the Air Force's Strategic Air Command.

Curtis LeMay entered World War II as a promising young major with special knowledge in aerial navigation and bombardment. He emerged from that conflict as a highly successful combat commander and major general. General Carl A. Spaatz,* first Air Force chief of staff, described LeMay as the greatest air combat commander of the war. Often blunt in his manner, LeMay based his success on innovation, ability to lead men, and perseverance which he learned in his youth.

Curtis LeMay was born in Columbus, Ohio, the eldest child of Erving LeMay and Arizona Carpenter, descendants of Ohio farm families. The family moved frequently as LeMay's father worked on various railroad and construction jobs. After living in Pennsylvania, Montana, and California, young Curtis returned to Ohio, graduated from high school in Columbus, and began working his way through Ohio State University. He studied civil engineering and completed his Reserve Officers Training Corps (ROTC) training as an honor graduate. LeMay left college early, however, and joined the National Guard in order to secure a flight school appointment. After training at March and Kelly Fields, he received his pilot's wings on October 12, 1929. LeMay then joined the 27th Pursuit Squadron at Selfridge Field, Michigan.

While assigned to Selfridge, LeMay completed his college degree, worked with local Civilian Conservation Corps (CCC) camps, and participated in the controversial air mail operation of the Air Corps in 1934. In that year, he married Helen Maitland and soon transferred to Hawaii where he established a full-time navigation school designed to aid crew members flying over water. By late 1936 LeMay concluded that bombers would have a more decisive impact than fighters on the outcome of future war, and he requested transfer to a bombardment unit.

In 1937 he joined the 305th Bombardment Group at Langley Field, Virginia, where he continued to develop aerial navigation techniques and trained others in the art of navigation. Acknowledged as the best navigator in the Air Corps, he participated in a number of exercises demonstrating the capability of aircraft to intercept ships at sea—first finding the USS *Utah* in 1937 and then locating the Italian liner *Rex* the following year under very well-publicized circumstances. While at Langley, LeMay was among the first to fly the new B–17s and navigated a flight of those bombers on a good-will tour to South America in 1937 and 1938. Shortly after, LeMay left his bomb group to attend the Air Corps Tactical School at Maxwell Field, Alabama, and by the end of the 1930s his faith in the future of aerial bombardment was deeply rooted.

In late 1940 the Air Corps undertook a rapid expansion and from the 34th Bomb Group Captain LeMay received command of a squadron assigned to Westover Air Base, Massachusetts. He spent part of his time at Westover flying with Canadians and transporting personnel across the North Atlantic to England. Then in May 1942, as a new lieutenant colonel, LeMay was given command of the 305th Bomb Group and was sent to various Western bases where he began training his units for bombing operations against the Axis powers. Shortages of equipment and time made his task exceedingly difficult; still, he realized they would soon be entering combat, and he won the nickname "Iron Ass" for driving his men so hard. These experiences left an indelible mark on his mind—after the war he would strive above all else to insure that his airmen would be properly equipped, trained, and ready to enter combat. LeMay's 305th Bomb Group joined the American forces in England by the fall of 1942, and he quickly won a reputation as an innovative tactician. Before his arrival, aircrews flew evasive actions while trying to bomb their targets, and their accuracy suffered. Crew members believed that any aircraft holding the same heading for more than ten seconds in a combat zone would be shot down. LeMay disputed this contention with a mathematical analysis showing a bomber could fly straight and level for an extended period without additional losses. To prove his point, LeMay led a bombing attack in a new box formation and during the seven minutes preceding bomb release flew without evasive action. No aircraft was lost to ground fire, and the bombing scores improved dramatically. LeMay also instituted the practice of target study by his crew members before flying combat missions, and soon they doubled the number of bombs placed on target. In June 1943 Colonel LeMay became the commander of the 3d Bombardment Division based in England and in August led the famed shuttle bombing raid on Regensburg, Germany, landing in North Africa. He became a brigadier general a month later.

In August 1944 Major General LeMay was transferred to the China-Burma-India theater to head the 20th Bomber Command. After "flying the Hump" to support forward bases and bombing selected targets in China, LeMay was given command of the 21st Bomber Command based on Guam in January 1945. From the Marianas LeMay began his strategic bombing attack on Japan, once again using unconventional tactics. To reduce fuel requirements and thereby deliver heavier bomb loads against weak Japanese defenses, he stripped his B–29s of defensive armament and removed the guns, gunners, and ammunition. LeMay ordered his airmen to attack their targets singly, not in formation, and at low levels. Disbelieving crews found these techniques worked extremely well and without any additional aircraft losses. In March 1945 the 21st Bomber Command devastated four strategic cities in Japan before temporarily exhausting its supply of incendiary weapons. The end of the Pacific war came six months later after two B–29s from LeMay's command dropped atomic bombs on Japan.

Following V-J Day, LeMay temporarily left operational command and became deputy chief of staff for research and development. After launching an active R & D program for the Air Force, Lieutenant General LeMay assumed command of the U.S. Air Forces in Europe on October 1, 1947. The next spring, the Soviet Union blockaded Berlin, and LeMay played a key role in keeping the Western Allies in the city. Under his command, air transports supplied the military and civilian population, and to the surprise of friend and foe, the airlift was able to support the beleaguered city during the winter months. Within a year, the Soviets ended their blockade.

The Berlin crisis of mid-1948 uncovered serious weaknesses in the Strategic Air Command (SAC), the nation's strategic bombing force, and General Hoyt Sanford Vandenberg, the Air Force chief of staff, ordered LeMay back to the United States in October 1948 to rebuild the command. LeMay immediately instituted realistic training and worked to expand the number of planes and men available to SAC. By the time the Korean War erupted in June 1950, the foundation for a modern deterrent force was established. While head of SAC, LeMay adopted the first jet bombers (B–47s and B–52s) and tankers (KC–135s) into his command and accomplished the preliminary work of incorporating intercontinental ballistic missiles into the deterrent force. In 1951 LeMay became the youngest four star general in American history since Ulysses Simpson Grant.*

After commanding SAC for nine years, LeMay became Air Force vice chief of staff under General Thomas White, and from 1961 to 1965, he served as chief of staff. At the Pentagon, he recommended a greater U.S. military role during the 1962 Cuban missile crisis and urged an expansion of strategic bombing against the North in the early years of the Vietnam War. Always concerned about American military strength and readiness, he frequently argued against the defense decisions of the Secretary of Defense, Robert Strange MacNamara.

After his retirement on February 1, 1965, LeMay became an executive for an electronics manufacturing firm. Concerned that America was drifting toward socialism and hoping to stop the trend, he accepted the vice-presidential candidacy of the American Independent party led by Governor George Wallace of Alabama in 1968. In the presidential election, Wallace and LeMay garnered 13 percent of the popular vote and collected forty-six electoral votes.

Although LeMay made many important and lasting contributions to U.S. military aviation, his most important work occurred between 1948 and 1957 when he developed a strong strategic bombing force. The procedures and the state of preparedness he instituted in his organization set standards for other Air Force commands. In those years, American foreign policy increasingly depended upon the nuclear deterrent held by the Strategic Air Command LeMay had created.

LeMay's brilliance lay in his common sense approach to leadership. He could quickly analyze the critical elements of every problem and devise practical solutions. Journalists have typically depicted LeMay as a tough-minded, cigar chomping, no nonsense commander, but they usually have overlooked his ability to understand and to motivate men. LeMay realized, above all else, that a unit was only as good as its men; therefore, he always directed his first concerns toward people and as a commander operated on three principles. LeMay believed each man had to understand the importance of his job, however small. Next, he believed a commander needed to establish clear goals for his unit and, in order to maintain high morale, insure some progress was made toward reaching those objectives. Finally, he believed a commander must recognize and demonstrate sincere appreciation to those who accomplished their tasks. When commanders practiced these considerations, he argued, men would follow and perform beyond the call of duty. In large measure, these leadership principles justified the rich praise of General Spaatz and accounted for LeMay's continued success after World War II.

BIBLIOGRAPHY

Anders, Curt. *Fighting Airmen*. New York: Putnam, 1966.
Borowski, Harry R. "Capability and the Development of Strategic Air Command, 1946–1950." Unpublished Ph.D. dissertation, University of California, Santa Barbara, 1976.
LeMay, Curtis E. "U.S. Air Leadership in World War II." Proceedings, Eighth Military History Symposium, *Air Power and Warfare*. Edited by Alfred F. Hurley and Robert C. Ehrhart. Washington, D.C.: U.S. Government Printing Office, forthcoming.
——— (with MacKinlay Kantor). *Mission with LeMay*. Garden City, N.Y.: Doubleday and Company, 1965.
Sturm, Ted R. "The Man and the Strategist." *Airman* (February 1965).

HARRY R. BOROWSKI

LIGGETT, Hunter (b. Reading, Pa., March 21, 1857; d. San Francisco, Calif., December 30, 1935), infantry officer. Liggett rose to command the First Army of the American Expeditionary Force during World War I.

Hunter Liggett was the son of James and Margaret (Hunter) Liggett. His father was a tailor by vocation but a politician by avocation; he served a brief term, 1879 to 1882, in the Pennsylvania legislature. Although there was no family pressure for him to pursue an Army career—his father was not even a Civil War veteran—Liggett entered the U.S. Military Academy in 1875. He graduated forty-first out of sixty-seven in the class of 1879. For the next thirteen years he served in Montana, Dakota, and Texas, commanding troops in garrison and the field. Although Liggett did not participate in any of the major Indian campaigns, he was involved in several smaller skirmishes that entitled him to the Indian Campaign Badge. One such incident in March 1880 consisted of a thirty-hour, 120-mile pursuit of an Indian band, culminated in a brief skirmish, and resulted in casualties on both sides. The regimental commander commended Liggett's leadership during the action.

From the time he was commissioned until the Spanish-American War, Liggett served with a single regiment, the 5th Infantry. As with most officers of this era, his promotions came slowly; he made first lieutenant in 1884 and captain in 1897. When the regiment left the frontier in 1892 Liggett became regimental adjutant, the unit's principal staff and administrative officer, stationed initially at St. Francis Barracks, Florida, then Fort McPherson, Georgia. It was his first assignment as a staff officer, the first time he was not directly in command of troops.

With the Spanish-American War came a promotion, diversified assignments, but also disappointments. Liggett accepted a volunteer commission as a major and assistant adjutant general. He was a division adjutant in Florida, Alabama, and Georgia from June 1898 to April 1899. But he missed the Santiago Campaign in 1898 and got to Cuba only briefly in 1899. Liggett began a period of service in the Philippines in December 1899. As a volunteer major he commanded a subdistrict on Mindanao for a year. In October 1901 he rejoined the 5th Infantry, at his permanent grade of captain, and commanded troops in Abra Province on Luzon. From the end of 1901 to mid-1902 he returned to a staff assignment as brigade adjutant at Dagupan.

Liggett received his promotion to major in May 1902, which necessitated a transfer from the 5th Infantry to the 21st Infantry and departure from the Philippines for Fort Snelling, Minnesota. He was with his new regiment at that post for one year before becoming the adjutant general of the Department of the Lakes with headquarters at Chicago. He held that staff position for the next four years until September 1907. In that month he again transferred, this time to become a battalion commander with the 13th Infantry at Fort Leavenworth, Kansas.

The next six years were crucial in the development of Liggett's career. Promotions came more rapidly: to lieutenant colonel in 1909, to colonel in 1912, and to brigadier general in 1913. He received instruction at the Army's most advanced schools. Although not officially a student, while at Fort Leavenworth Liggett participated in Staff College conferences, exercises, and wargames. During 1909–1910 he attended the Army War College. Important assignments in policymaking positions also came Liggett's way. After graduation from the War College, he stayed on as a director (1910–1913) and eventually president (1913–1914) of the institution. Concurrently, he served as chief of the War College Division, the principal planning agency of the War Department General Staff. In these posts, Liggett not only held positions of importance, but also made significant contributions to the Army as well. As a director and president of the

War College, he helped reshape the curriculum, giving structure to the course and adding considerable work in military history, operational planning, and general staff duties. He also sought to improve the admission standards so that only officers well-prepared academically could attend the college. From his position on the General Staff, Liggett worked hard to improve the Army's entire system of educating officers, prepared war plans for interventions in Mexico and the Caribbean, and sought means to improve American defenses in the Philippines.

Upon promotion to brigadier general in 1913, Liggett left the War College and the General Staff to assume command of the Department of the Lakes. He remained in important command positions for the next eight years, until his retirement in 1921. From the Lakes command in Chicago he went next to Texas City, Texas, in 1914 to command the 4th Brigade of the 2d Division and then to the Philippines as a brigade commander. He remained there until early 1917, in April 1916 becoming commander of the Philippines Department (at the time the Army's largest overseas command). On March 4, 1917, he reached the pinnacle of military success when he was promoted to major general, only one of seven then in the Army. One month after America's entrance into World War I, Liggett returned to the United States as commander of the Western Department in San Francisco. He remained at that post until September when he assumed command of the 41st Division, composed largely of National Guard troops from Western states.

Liggett took the 41st Division to France in October 1917. Shortly after arriving overseas he toured the Western Front. The purpose was to observe the organization and operations of the French and British armies but also to be observed and assessed by the more experienced Allies. Liggett did not make a good first impression. He was portly, had been recently troubled by rheumatism, and at sixty was somewhat older than most Allied commanders. One English general reported that Liggett was "too old" and "not active enough" for an active field command. General John Joseph Pershing* disagreed. Upon completing his tour of the front in November 1917, Liggett returned to command the 41st Division. Two months later Pershing selected him as commander of the I American Army Corps. Liggett took command on January 20, 1918.

It was a signal honor for Liggett because the I Corps was to have tactical control of the first American divisions operating together in combat in France. Pershing recognized that despite physical limitations Liggett possessed command experience, professional knowledge, strong character, and a sense of proportion found in few other senior American officers. That Liggett was highly respected throughout the officer corps made Pershing's decision that much easier. The I Corps did not immediately become an active operational headquarters. During the winter and spring of 1918, American divisions entered the front piecemeal and participated only in limited actions. Liggett's headquarters did retain administrative control and supervised the training of the American divisions then in France. On July 4, 1918, the corps (consisting of the 2d and 26th U.S.

Divisions and the 167th French) finally took over a portion of the Sixth French Army front. Liggett commanded those divisions in the defensive action near Chateau-Thierry where the German spring and summer offensive was finally halted.

Despite difficulties, Liggett's corps played an important role in the ensuing Aisne-Marne counteroffensive. Inexperienced American troops and commanders made mistakes, suffered unnecessary casualties, and sometimes failed to achieve assigned objectives. Liggett tolerated the mistakes made by the troops but was critical of some of his subordinate commanders. In hard fighting and constant pressure, the I Corps succeeded by early August in driving the Germans back twenty miles to behind the Ourcq and Vesle rivers. For the remainder of August and into September Liggett's corps was on the defensive, first in Champagne and then in Lorraine where it prepared for the first major American offensive of the war.

As one of the four corps in the newly formed First Army, the I Corps assisted in the rapid reduction of the St. Mihiel Salient, long an objective of American planners. Immediately following this operation, which lasted from September 12 to 16, the First Army began a second, more difficult offensive against determined German resistance. Liggett's leadership during the Meuse-Argonne Campaign (September 26-November 11) justified Pershing's faith in him. The I Corps anchored the Army's left flank, advancing north through the treacherous terrain in the Argonne Forest. Liggett pushed his assault divisions (the 77th, 28th, and 35th) relentlessly, but they made only slow progress. To break the stalemate Liggett and the operations section at First Army headquarters simultaneously conceived of an attack westward through the forest against the flank of the German defenders. Liggett assigned the task to the fresh 82d Division which attacked on October 7. By October 10 the Argonne was in American hands. Although Liggett's plan succeeded in clearing the forest, he was disappointed that many German troops escaped to establish another strong defensive position. But Liggett had little time to reflect on the attack.

On October 12, he relinquished command of I Corps to Joseph Theodore Dickman; on October 16 Liggett replaced Pershing as First Army commander. Characteristically, he used the period from October 12 to 16 to visit various units, accumulate information, and assess the condition of his new command. After more than two weeks of sustained fighting and several major assaults, the condition of the First Army was not good. For the next two weeks Liggett "tightened up" the First Army. While there was a lull in the fighting, Liggett brought depleted divisions up to strength, talked with his commanders to improve tactical procedures, ensured better coordination within First Army headquarters by instituting daily meetings among the senior staff, and promoted a former protegé, George Catlett Marshall,* to be chief of operations. Meanwhile, Pershing had relieved several division commanders and one corps commander who had not performed adequately. When the First Army resumed the offensive with an all-out attack on November 1, the assault divisions were more experienced, the logistics support more substantive, and the immediate corps objectives more realistic than for the initial September 26 attack which began the Meuse-Argonne operation. The measures which Liggett instituted to improve the effectiveness of his army before the battle and his operational leadership during the battle contributed significantly to the success of the November 1 attack. That attack broke German defenses along most of the First Army front, permitting the most rapid American advance since the start of the Meuse-Argonne operation. The Armistice of November 11 halted Liggett's First Army.

Following the Armistice, Liggett continued as First Army commander until the unit disbanded on April 20, 1919. On May 2 he became commander of the Third Army, which then consisted of all American occupation forces in the Rhineland. When the Third Army disbanded on July 2, 1919, he returned to the United States where he assumed command of the Western Department, the position he held just before going to France. On March 21, 1921, Liggett retired from the Army as a major general at age sixty-four. By act of Congress he advanced to the retired rank of lieutenant general in 1930. In retirement he wrote two books about his war experiences: *Commanding an American Army: Recollections of the World War* (1925) and *A.E.F.: Ten Years Ago in France* (1928). He died at San Francisco on December 30, 1935.

During World War I Hunter Liggett held perhaps the two most important operational commands in the American Expeditionary Force. As I Corps commander he trained and led the first divisions to fight under independent American command. As commander of the First Army, he led nearly one million men in the concluding offensive of the war. Liggett's managerial ability, tactical sense, and compassion for his troops (one of the few criticisms of his leadership was that on occasion he was "too much influenced by a kind heart") were important factors in the success of American arms in France. His wartime leadership was clearly his most significant contribution to the Army; yet his prewar career had an influence on the service as well. Liggett helped foster the professionalization of the officer corps by bridging the gap between older officers who were products of the Indian-fighting Army and younger, school-trained men who were often Staff College or War College graduates. He influenced the older generation to appreciate the need for a more systematic, intellectual approach in solving military problems. While he encouraged the professionalism of the younger officers, his concern for personal leadership and understanding of human nature tempered their often overintellectualization of the art of war. Liggett's style of leadership as well as his thoughtful, analytical approach epitomized the changing concept of military professionalism of this era.

BIBLIOGRAPHY

Coffman, Edward M. *The War to End All Wars: The American Military Experience in World War I*. New York: Oxford University Press, 1968.

Liddell-Hart, Basil H. *Reputations Ten Years After*. Boston: Little, Brown and Company, 1928.

Liggett, Hunter. *A.E.F.: Ten Years Ago in France*. New York: Dodd, Mead and Company, 1928.

———. *Commanding an American Army*. Boston: Houghton Mifflin Company, 1925.

Millett, Allan R. *The General: Robert L. Bullard and Officership in the United States Army, 1881–1925*. Westport, Conn.: Greenwood Press, 1975.

Pogue, Forrest C. *George C. Marshall: Education of a General, 1880–1939*. New York: Viking Press, 1963.

TIMOTHY K. NENNINGER

LONGSTREET, James (b. Edgefield District, S.C., January 8, 1821; d. Gainesville, Ga., January 2, 1904), Army officer. Longstreet is considered one of the leading Confederate commanders of the Civil War.

The Longstreets, apparently of Netherlands stock, had been established in New Jersey until the general's grandfather moved to Georgia. James Longstreet's first years were spent on a plantation near Gainesville, and at an early age he was taken by his parents to the neighborhood of Augusta, Georgia. His father, also James, died in 1833. Longstreet's uncle, Augustus Baldwin Longstreet, a jurist, literary figure, minister, editor, politician, and educator, had a major role in James' upbringing. The family then moved to Somerset, Morgan County, Alabama.

In 1838 Longstreet was admitted to the U.S. Military Academy from the Huntsville area of Alabama. Attending West Point at the same time were William Tecumseh Sherman,* Richard Stoddert Ewell, George Henry Thomas,* William Starke Rosecrans,* Ulysses Simpson Grant,* Henry Wager Halleck,* and many other future Civil War commanders. Academically, Longstreet was not a great success; he was graduated in 1842, fifty-fourth in a class of fifty-six.

Brevetted second lieutenant, Longstreet joined the 4th Infantry at Jefferson Barracks near St. Louis where he became an even better friend of Grant. He later served at Natchitoches, Louisiana, and with the 8th Infantry at St. Augustine, Florida.

During the Mexican War, Longstreet, under Zachary Taylor,* was at Palo Alto, Resaca de la Palma, and Monterrey. During the advance of Winfield Scott* to Mexico City, he was at Vera Cruz, Cerro Gordo, Churubusco, and Molino del Rey. He was brevetted captain after Churubusco and major after Molino del Rey. He was seriously wounded at Chapultepec.

Longstreet then served on the frontier, before becoming a major in the Paymaster's Department in 1858. There was no question where his loyalty lay during the secession crisis. His resignation from the U.S. Army was effective June 1, 1861. Owing to his sound reputation, he was commissioned a brigadier general in the Confederate forces from June 17, 1861.

Following his able handling of troops at First Bull Run (Manassas) in July 1861, Longstreet was promoted to major general in October. He commanded a division under Joseph Eggleston Johnston* in Virginia and was at Yorktown in April of 1862, before skillfully conducting the rearguard action at Williamsburg on May 5 during Johnston's retreat toward Richmond.

At Seven Pines (Fair Oaks) on May 31, he was charged with being slow and misinterpreting orders. He is credited with competent leadership in the Seven Days' battles near Richmond, June 25 to July 1, 1862. He was now under Robert Edward Lee,* who had taken over from the wounded Johnston. With over half of Lee's infantry, Longstreet followed Thomas Jonathan ("Stonewall") Jackson* north from Richmond and, with Lee and Jackson, was instrumental in defeating General John Pope at Second Bull Run (Manassas) on August 30.

Continuing to advance with Lee's army into Maryland, Longstreet performed well at Antietam (Sharpsburg) in September. Recommended by Lee, he was promoted to lieutenant general on October 11, 1862, and was formally given command of the I Corps of the Army of Northern Virginia. On December 13 at the Battle of Fredericksburg, Longstreet's corps successfully held firm on the Confederate left in Lee's defensive victory. In Longstreet's first independent command he was detached from Lee and sent to the Suffolk area of Virginia. Thus, he and most of his troops were absent from the Battle of Chancellorsville in early May 1863.

With the death of Jackson following Chancellorsville, Longstreet was undoubtedly Lee's leading corps commander. Commanding the right flank of Lee's army on July 2 at Gettysburg, Longstreet led the famous assault on the Federal left, and men of his corps were also involved in the famed Charge of George Edward Pickett* on July 3. Gettysburg was the most controversial of Longstreet's battles.

After a masterful move by railroad to Georgia, Longstreet arrived just in time to have his corps play a major role under Braxton Bragg* in the Confederate victory at Chickamauga in September. Detached from Bragg, Longstreet was not successful in another independent command at Knoxville in the fall of 1863.

Moving with his men back to Virginia, Longstreet fought skillfully at the Battle of the Wilderness, rallying the corps of Ambrose Powell Hill* on May 6, 1864. While leading troops in the forefront of the fight, Longstreet was gravely wounded by his own men. Returning to duty in November, he was involved in the later phases of the defenses of Richmond and the Appomattox Campaign of 1865.

Following the war, Longstreet headed an insurance agency and was a cotton merchant in New Orleans. Turning to the Republican party, which he joined, he held a series of political offices from 1869 to his death at Gainesville, Georgia, in 1904. He was surveyor of customs in New Orleans, postmaster of Gainesville, U.S. minister to Turkey, 1880–1881, U.S. marshal for Georgia, and U.S. railroad commissioner.

Longstreet wrote several articles which fueled the fires of controversy over his Civil War leadership, particularly in regard to Gettysburg. He followed these articles with a memoir, *From Manassas to Appomattox*, first published in 1896.

He was married to Maria Louise Garland of Lynchburg, Virginia, in 1848, and after her death in 1889, he married Helen Dortch.

Longstreet became known, properly, as Lee's "old war horse." Despite a storm of criticism after the war, he still must be considered one of the most capable and effective Confederate generals. In recent years historians have generally taken his side in the several controversies and have restored his position as a major American military figure.

Somewhat more than six feet in height, Longstreet was a striking figure in his rough uniform. His endurance was considerable, and his perception remained keen in the face of physical demands. Generally amiable, he was known primarily as a stoic, taciturn, and dependable commander. However, his temper could be roused when someone disagreed with his firmly held, dogmatic opinions. Part of his sparseness in words may have been a result of his partial deafness.

Longstreet is often credited with being tactically a tenacious defensive fighter, and that aspect of his command abilities was superior. Furthermore, he was an excellent organizer. Looking over his entire career, however, one sees that Longstreet was an aggressive, well-prepared, and hard-striking offensive general as well, particularly at Second Manassas, Chickamauga, and the Wilderness. His soldiers had great respect and admiration for him and followed him wholeheartedly. Under adverse conditions he could evince self-reliance and poise and could transfer this attitude to his men, often leading them in person.

In assessing Longstreet and the adverse criticism of his actions, one has to try to determine how much of this attack was caused by the general's turning to the Republican party during Reconstruction, and, in addition, how much was defense of Lee. Longstreet was highly censured for his change in politics, and, on occasion, former friends and associates refused to talk with him. In his own behalf, he explained that the only way constitutional government could be reestablished was to comply with congressional legislation. While Longstreet had been critical of Lee at Gettysburg shortly after the battle, the real imbroglio of words began in 1873, after Longstreet turned Republican. He was attacked by General Fitzhugh Lee, General Jubal Anderson Early,* and others. The primary criticism leveled against Longstreet is that he delayed carrying out Lee's orders to attack with his right flank on July 2, and that this delay to drive toward Little Round Top was a critical factor in the Confederate defeat. Furthermore, Longstreet is accused of not obeying orders on July 3. But the whole idea of Pickett's charge was undoubtedly a mistake. Several contemporary accounts blame Lee, and the commanding general accepted the blame.

Lee never uttered a word in criticism of Longstreet or anyone else for the defeat at Gettysburg. Throughout the war Lee continually called on Longstreet for advice or to carry out actions, and there seems to have been a close personal relationship between the two generals.

Longstreet was never reckless with the lives of his men, but when the necessity arose, he attacked or defended with an energy and drive that usually got the job done. While his position as a very high grade commander and strong tactical fighter now seems secure, most authorities do not credit him with being an outstanding strategist or an independent leader. His stubbornness and unlimited self-confidence in his own judgment may well have been too often expressed.

Any Army commander in history would have been blessed with an associate such as "Old Pete" Longstreet, truly a reliable general whose record will stand long in history.

BIBLIOGRAPHY

Codington, Edwin B. *The Gettysburg Campaign: A Study in Command.* New York: Charles S. Scribner's Sons, 1968.
Freeman, Douglas Southall. *Lee's Lieutenants.* 3 vols. New York: Charles S. Scribner's Sons, 1942–1944.
———. *R. E. Lee.* 4 vols. New York: Charles S. Scribner's Sons, 1934–1935.
Sanger, Donald B., and Thomas R. Hay. *James Longstreet.* Baton Rouge: Louisiana State University Press, 1952.
Tucker, Glenn. *Lee and Longstreet at Gettysburg.* Indianapolis, Ind.: Bobbs-Merrill Company, 1968.

E. B. LONG

MAC ARTHUR, Douglas (b. Little Rock, Ark., January 26, 1880; d. Washington, D.C., April 5, 1964), Army officer, Allied theater, occupation commander.

Douglas MacArthur was the third son of Arthur MacArthur, who was a distinguished commander in the Civil War, Spanish-American War, and Philippine Insurrection and the Army's highest ranking officer in 1906–1909. Douglas graduated from West Point with highest honors in 1903 and was commissioned a second lieutenant of engineers. During the following decade he served as a junior engineering officer in the Philippines, the United States, and Panama; was an aide to his father and to President Theodore Roosevelt*; graduated from the Army Engineer School of Application; and worked in the office of the chief of engineers. He was a member of the War Department General Staff, 1913–1917, his more unusual assignments including an intelligence mission with the Vera Cruz Expedition and service as War Department censor.

Upon America's entry into World War I, he was soon promoted to colonel and became chief of staff of the 42d Division, sailing with it to France in fall 1917. He served with the 42d also as brigade and division commander in the Champagne-Marne, St. Mihiel, and Meuse-Argonne operations, rising in rank to brigadier general, earning numerous decorations for heroism, and receiving two wounds in action. After the Armistice he participated in the German occupation until April 1919.

That summer he began a three-year term as superintendent of the Military Academy, followed in the 1920s by two command assignments in the Philippines, command of two corps areas in the States, duty on the court-martial of Brigadier General William ("Billy") Mitchell,* and head of the American Olympic Committee in 1928. He was promoted to major general in 1925 and five years later to general when he was appointed chief of staff of the Army. Because of the Great Depression his efforts as the Army's military head, 1930–1935, were largely devoted to preserving the establishment's meager strength. In autumn 1935 he went to the Philippines as military advisor to the Commonwealth and spent the next six years organizing Filipino defense forces. In 1936 he was designated field marshal of the Philippine Army; he retired the next year from the U.S. Army.

He was recalled to active duty as a major general in July 1941 and was given command of U.S. Army Forces in the Far East. He was advanced shortly to lieutenant general and in December to general. After the war with Japan started, he commanded a stubborn defense of the Philippines against the Japanese invaders. Before the islands fell, he went to Australia in March and subsequently assumed command of the newly established Southwest Pacific Theater.

In the Papuan Campaign, August 1942–January 1943, his Australian and American forces thwarted a Japanese drive on Port Moresby and then undertook a counteroffensive that drove the enemy out of southeastern New Guinea. In a series of amphibious assaults, September 1943–August 1944, his American Sixth Army captured the rest of New Guinea's strategic coastal points while also seizing the Admiralties and western New Britain. From early 1944 onward he employed Australian units primarily to contain or eliminate bypassed enemy garrisons. His American forces struck north of the Equator in autumn 1944, invading Morotai in the Moluccas and Leyte and Mindoro in the Philippines.

MacArthur's largest campaign of the war began in January 1945 with the Sixth Army's invasion of Luzon; by July most of the island was secured. Meanwhile, he unleashed his Eighth Army to conquer the rest of the Philippines and sent his Australian forces to invade Borneo and Brunei. Promoted to general of the Army in December 1944, he was named commanding general of U.S. Army Forces in the Pacific in April 1945. With the capitulation of Japan he received the additional appointment of Supreme Commander for the Allied Powers to accept the formal Japanese surrender in Tokyo Bay and to command the ensuing Allied occupation of Japan.

Under his efficient, if sometimes autocratic, direction the Japanese occupation, 1945–1951, was marked by success in eliminating militarist, ultranationalist, and feudal vestiges and by vigorous, although not always productive, efforts to reform that nation's political system, economy, labor relations, society, public health and welfare programs, and educational structure. Among the noteworthy achievements were a liberal constitution, land reform, women's rights, and amicable relations between Japan and the United States. In early 1947 MacArthur was given the added responsibility of heading the Far East Command, which comprised all American forces in Japan, Korea (until 1949), the Ryukyus, the Philippines, the Marianas, and the Bonins.

Shortly after the Korean War began in June 1950, he was designated commander in chief of the United Nations Command, which ultimately included units of eighteen nations, although predominantly South Korean and American. After stopping the North Korean offensive along the Naktong River that summer, MacArthur's forces launched a counteroffensive in September, highlighted by a bold amphibious assault at Inchon, that soon produced a virtual disintegration of the North Korean Army. As his troops advanced toward the Yalu River in November, massive Communist Chinese field armies attacked his widely separated Eighth Army and X Corps, forcing their retreat south of the 38th Parallel. By early 1951, however, the United Nations units had returned to the offensive, driving into North Korea again. In April President Harry S. Truman relieved MacArthur of his commands because of serious differences over civil-military relations and strategic direction of the war.

Conservative Republican factions attempted in vain to get MacArthur nominated for the presidency in 1944, 1948, and 1952. He accepted the board chairmanship of Remington Rand (later Sperry Rand) in 1952 and, except for board duties and occasional speeches, retired in seclusion in New York City. His *Reminiscences* was published in 1964. During his long career he received a large number of American and foreign military decorations as well as honorary degrees and special recognition by Congress. He was honored by a state funeral in Washington, D.C., and was buried in Norfolk, Virginia.

It is unlikely that any biographer will probe fully the personality of MacArthur. His was an enormously complex blend of contradictory traits—egotistical yet modest, flamboyant but shy, austere and gracious, aloof but charming, decisive yet hesitant. Opinions of MacArthur the man vary greatly but usually depend on the degree of personal acquaintance with him: most of his staff officers were bound to him by charisma and intense loyalty, while his severest critics generally had little or no personal contact with him. For the researcher, analysis of his personality is complicated by the host of myths that grew about him, many of which have never been separated from reality, and by the paucity and unrevealing nature of his personal papers. Moreover, his elusiveness is compounded by his mastery of role-taking, whereby he could project, often with uncanny skill, the image he desired for a particular occasion or audience. His beliefs ranged from ultraconservative to liberal, depending on the issue. Thus, while gaining the admiration of American rightists for his militant anticommunism, he could also appeal to former New Dealers with his reforms in Japan.

MacArthur's genius showed most lucidly in his leadership as West Point superintendent, wartime theater commander in the Southwest Pacific, and occupation administrator in Japan. Among his most significant, if not best known, achievements were his pioneering reforms at the Military Academy, 1919–1922, that brought the school, then at its all-time ebb, a revitalized and more versatile curriculum, modernized teaching methods, and new standards of excellence. "If Sylvanus Thayer was the Father of the Military Academy," one authority asserts, "then Douglas MacArthur was its savior."

While the formulation of strategy in the Pacific and Korean wars was undertaken primarily by the Joint Chiefs and their planners, MacArthur excelled at implementing strategic directives with imagination, shrewdness, and boldness, exploiting to the fullest the often minimal logistic support he received and achieving objectives with extraordinarily low casualty rates among his forces. British Field Marshals Alan Brooke and Bernard Montgomery, among other leaders of World War II, declared him to be the outstanding Allied commander of that conflict. His mastery at coordinating ground, naval, and air forces of several nations in well-executed amphibious assaults was demonstrated on scores of occasions in the war against Japan, but his most brilliant stroke in amphibious warfare, the Inchon Operation, was carried to success when he was seventy years old. For all his triumphs, however, he also bore the command responsibility for the defeats by Japan in the Philippines, 1941–1942, and by China in Korea in 1950.

Operating his general headquarters in Tokyo with an effectiveness seldom achieved in so large a bureaucratic structure, MacArthur presided over the vast network of occupation programs with dedication, idealism, empathy, and firm control, making his administration in Japan one of the most enlightened of any occupation in history. Indeed, his leadership in occupied Japan may be viewed by future authorities as the most important phase of his career.

To one who studies MacArthur's behavior over his five decades of military service it is unfortunate but predictable that a leader with such monumental gifts and flaws would face a climactic clash such as occurred in his controversy with Truman in 1950–1951. Although they were evident in episodes on a lesser scale previously, that collision made tragically apparent his more serious limitations, namely, an acute sensitivity to criticism, an inability to adjust to limited warfare or to considerations of global strategy, and an attitude of condescension toward superiors that bordered on insubordination.

BIBLIOGRAPHY

James, D. Clayton. *The Years of MacArthur*. 2 vols. to date. Boston: Houghton Mifflin Company, 1970–1975.
MacArthur, Douglas. *Reminiscences*. New York: McGraw-Hill, 1964.
Whan, Vorin E., Jr., ed. *A Soldier Speaks: Public Papers and Speeches of General of the Army Douglas MacArthur*. New York: Frederick A. Praeger, 1965.
Willoughby, Charles A., ed. *Reports of General MacArthur*. 4 vols. Washington, D.C.: U.S. Department of the Army, 1966.

D. CLAYTON JAMES

MC CLELLAN, George Brinton (b. Philadelphia, Pa., December 3, 1826; d. Orange, N.J., October 29, 1885), Army officer. McClellan was the controversial Union Army general in chief in the Civil War, and moulder and early commander of the Army of the Potomac.

Of Connecticut ancestry, George B. McClellan was born in Philadelphia, the son of a prominent physician who founded Jefferson Medical College. Following education at the University of Pennsylvania Preparatory School, young McClellan, by special action, was permitted to enter the U.S. Military Academy at West Point two years before having attained the minimum age. A brilliant cadet, he graduated second in his class of fifty-nine in 1846, during the Mexican War, and was commissioned in the Corps of Engineers.

On the triumphant campaign for Mexico City led by Winfield Scott,* McClellan won two brevets for courageous and exemplary conduct and refused a third as unmerited. This service was followed by a three-year instructorship at West Point, engineering duties that took him across the country on surveys for possible transcontinental railroad routes, and—by then a captain—membership in the American mission in the mid-1850s to observe the siege of Sevastopol in the Crimean War. After his tour, he remained in Europe to study the military practices, institutions, and equipment of a number of nations, which he reported in a lengthy and perspicacious volume published by the Congress. Also emanating from his recommendations was the famous "McClellan saddle," which he brought back to America and which was used by the cavalry as long as the Army had horses.

McClellan resigned from the Army in 1857 to become chief engineer of the Illinois Central Railroad and then vice president of that railway, one of whose lawyers was Abraham Lincoln. McClellan was subsequently named president of the Ohio and Mississippi Railraod.

When the Civil War erupted, McClellan returned to the Federal service as major general of U.S. Volunteers in command of troops from Ohio, Indiana, and Illinois. In this capacity, on his own initiative, he launched a vigorous offensive into the mountains of northwestern Virginia, winning victories in the miniature but significant battles in June and July 1861 at Philippi, Rich Mountain, and Carrick's Ford. These accomplishments went far toward shaping the creation in 1863 of the new pro-Union state of West Virginia. McClellan received warm encomiums from General in Chief Scott, President Lincoln, and the cabinet for his "activity, valor, and . . . successes." Then, following the staggering Union defeat at First Bull Run on July 21, 1861, he was called to Washington, D.C., to assume command of what was soon known as the Army of the Potomac.

Though slightly under medium height, McClellan was a handsome, erect, muscular man with dark red hair, mustache, and touch of a goatee. He was a soldier of commanding presence. This able officer became one of the most popular—and controversial—generals ever to command American troops in war. He took the summer, autumn, and winter of 1861 to organize and build the truly superb Army of the Potomac which, under a number of inept future commanders, proved to be, first, the shield of the Union and, eventually, under George Gordon Mcadc* and Ulysscs Simpson Grant,* the sword that would compel the surrender of the Confederate Army under Robert Edward Lee* in 1865. From November 1, 1861, to March 11, 1862, the thirty-five-year-old McClellan was general in chief of all the Union armies, and he was an imaginative chieftain who early saw the necessity of coordinated action by all the Federal field forces.

Slowed by a severe case of typhoid fever and occasionally by his own magnification of difficulties, McClellan delayed the advance of the Army of the Potomac against the Confederate capital of Richmond until the early spring of 1862. After protracted and at time heated debates with Lincoln and the hostile secretary of war, Edwin McMasters Stanton, over the timing and route of movement, the general landed his army at Fortress Monroe and marched up the historic Peninsula between the York and James rivers through the heaviest rains known there in twenty years. Overly cautious, he laid siege to Yorktown, which fell on May 4, 1862, after a month's investment. When he reached a point some four miles from Richmond, McClellan was attacked by graycoats under Joseph Eggleston Johnston* on May 31 in the two-day Battle of Fair Oaks (Seven Pines), but, after an initial setback, the Federal commander repulsed the enemy assaults and inched closer to Richmond. With Lee now in command of the army of Northern Virginia, heavy Confederate attacks in the great Seven Days' Battle in the last week of June were—except at Gaines' Mill—repelled by McClellan, the fighting culminating in the massive and bloody repulse of the Southerners at Malvern Hill. The Union suffered more than fifteen thousand casualties in the Seven Days compared to more than twenty thousand casualties sustained by the Confederates.

When Lincoln visited the army at nearby Harrison's Landing, McClellan and all of the other generals but one urged that it be reinforced and allowed to continue the operation against Richmond. But, despite "Little Mac's" protestations, the president and the new general in chief, the inept Henry Wager Halleck,* ordered the Army of the Potomac back to Washington, thereby giving up the campaign. A number of its divisions served under the command of John Pope in his disastrous Second Manassas Campaign in August 1862. With Pope badly defeated in that engagement and the demoralized army retreating in rout upon Washington, McClellan was again put at its head. It was one of the most trying assignments given a commander on either side during the war.

In a remarkable feat, McClellan reorganized his army while on the march northwestwardly from Washington to enable it to confront Lee and counter his first invasion of the North. Wresting the vital initiative from the hitherto victorious gray leader in the Battle of South Mountain on September 14, 1862, McClellan gained a triumph that impelled Lee to fight in a cramped defensive position along the Antietam Creek at Sharpsburg, Maryland. There, on September 17, in the bloodiest single-day's battle of the war, McClellan, in fourteen hours of desperate fighting, hurled a series of heavy attacks at the Confederates; but, owing chiefly to the procrastination of Ambrose Everett Burnside on the Federal left, the resulting piecemeal blows, though winning much ground, were unable to smash or rout Lee's army. Although gaining little more than a tactical draw, McClellan had nonetheless won a strategic success of inestimable value; the battle of Antietam had blocked the threat of foreign intervention in the war. When McClellan failed to advance into Virginia as swiftly as the administration wished, and owing also to political factors, he was relieved of his command on November 5, 1862, to be replaced by the least effective of the Union corps commanders, Burnside.

McClellan ran unsuccessfully for the presidency in 1864 on the Democratic ticket. He had resigned from the Army on election day. In the years after Appomattox, Little Mac headed several large engineering enterprises, indulged his tastes in the arts, languages, literature, travel, and mountain climbing, and was an able and popular governor of New Jersey for two terms. McClellan died of heart trouble in 1885, one of the most beloved of Union Army generals. One of his pallbearers was his old Confederate opponent on the Peninsula, Joseph E. Johnston.*

McClellan's reputation as a major figure among Civil War generals is assured. It is based largely on his taking over command of the main Federal army in the East after it had suffered two terrible defeats at Manassas and shaping that massive host into a magnificent fighting machine. His Peninsula Campaign was well conceived and planned, and less direct involvement by the administration might have gone far toward making it more successful than it was. Too, his tactical handling of the Army of the Potomac in the Seven Days battle, culminating in one of Lee's worst defeats, at Malvern Hill, was impressive, as was his whipping of the Army into shape sufficient to gain the all-important initiative at South Mountain and, with heightened morale, to turn back Lee's invasion at Antietam at a time when Great Britain was close to recognizing Southern independence and intervening decisively in the war on behalf of the Confederacy.

On the minus side, McClellan was too much the perfectionist, ever hoping to plan operations down to the last detail without allowing for the inspiration of the moment to cope with imponderables that would inevitably arise. But many of his best efforts were hampered by the hostile and powerful Radical Republicans in Congress, by the belligerent Stanton and the ineffective Halleck, and occasionally by the well-meaning but initially inexperienced Lincoln.

Knowledgeable in the use of the combined arms of infantry, cavalry, and artillery, and possessing an encyclopedic and comprehensive grasp of military art and science, McClellan was flawed by his inability to mesh with the system of civil-military relations inherent in the American polity, a balance which he recognized but with which he found it difficult to accommodate himself. Yet, in the final analysis, his achievements—some of them masterful—outweighed his shortcomings, and the Union was fortunate that, in the early stages of the conflict, a lesser man was not at the helm of their main military effort in the East.

BIBLIOGRAPHY

Hassler, Warren W., Jr. *Commanders of the Army of the Potomac*. Baton Rouge: Louisiana State University Press, 1962.

———. *General George B. McClellan, Shield of the Union*. Baton Rouge: Louisiana State University Press, 1957.
McClellan, George B. *McClellan's Own Story: The War for the Union*. New York: C. L. Webster, 1887.
Myers, William S. *A Study in Personality: General George Brinton McClellan*. C. Appleton-Century, 1934.
Williams, T. Harry. *Lincoln and His Generals*. New York: Alfred A. Knopf, 1952.

WARREN W. HASSLER, JR.

MAHAN, Alfred Thayer (b. West Point, N.Y., September 27, 1840; d. Washington, D.C., December 1, 1914), naval officer, historian, theoretician. Mahan has been called the philosopher of sea power by modern authorities.

Alfred Thayer Mahan was the eldest son of Dennis Hart Mahan,* professor of civil and military engineering at the U.S. Military Academy; his middle name was taken from Sylvanus Thayer, whom his father admired. He entered Columbia College in New York City in 1854; two years later he transferred into the third (sophomore) class at the U.S. Naval Academy and was graduated in 1859, second in the class. During his first class year he earned the enmity of his classmates by putting several of them on report for minor infractions of discipline. They, in turn, "silenced" him.

This was the first of many bitter personal controversies that marked his naval and literary careers. Mahan was a man of enormous ego and temper; he was quick to take offense at real or imagined slights, slow to forgive criticism, unwilling to admit error. Indeed, he went through life with only one close personal friend. As his daughter remembered him, he was "The Cat That Walked By Himself."

From 1859 to 1885 Mahan's naval career was unremarkable and unexciting. He served ingloriously throughout the Civil War on blockade duty and obscurely in various billets ashore and afloat after the war. He was not a skillful seaman. Collisions, groundings, and other nautical mishaps marred his commands at sea. He feared the sea, was unnerved by the responsibility of command, sought assiduously to avoid assignments to sea duty, and was bored and frustrated by his profession. On several occasions he considered resigning his commission.

What Mahan discovered he could do, and do exceedingly well, was write naval history. In 1883, while serving at the Brooklyn Navy Yard, he wrote his first book, a competent account of U.S. naval operations during the Civil War. It caught the eye of Captain Stephen Bleeker Luce, whose protegé he became. At this juncture in his naval career, Commander Mahan was neither an imperialist nor an enthusiast for the modern steam and steel "New Navy" that the nation was belatedly beginning to build. He was not concerned with the foreign policy implications of the New Navy or the technological problems it posed.

The major turning point in Mahan's service career, and in his isolationist view of American foreign policy, came in 1885 when Luce, founder and first president of the new Naval War College in Newport, Rhode Island, secured his assignment to the faculty of the experimental institution. He began teaching naval history at the college in 1886. In 1886–1888 and 1892–1893 he served as its president. Against great opposition from within the Navy, he fought to keep the institution from being absorbed into other naval training facilities, and he worked to install there a curriculum that emphasized consideration of the transcendent historical, theoretical, tactical, and strategical "principles" of naval warfare. He was less concerned that his officer-students study the engineering, ordnance, and architecture of the ships of the New Navy. Mahan's foresight in this regard made the War College the intellectual command center of the reemerging U.S. Navy and defined for it the scholarly mission it has since pursued.

During his first tour as lecturer-president of the War College, Captain Mahan researched and wrote his brilliant, seminal study, *The Influence of Sea Power Upon History, 1660–1783*. Published in 1890, the book was filled with newly discovered imperialist convictions derived from his reading of naval history. It brought its obscure author instant worldwide acclaim and fame. It also brought him into personal association with the leadership of the nascent imperialist movement in the United States, specifically with vigorous Republican party nationalists like Theordore Roosevelt,* Henry Cabot Lodge, and John M. Hay.

These men, and others, were urging the historical, geopolitical, and economic necessity of American commercial, ecclesiastical, and territorial expansion abroad—an expansion that would be sustained strategically and operationally by a revived U.S. Navy and would be effected in diplomatic concert with Great Britain, America's partner in the superior "Anglo-Saxon race" that was destined by God to uplift the world's "backward" peoples spiritually and materially. The new imperialists quickly seized upon Mahan's argument that nations had waxed or waned throughout history in direct relation to their effective acquisition, maintenance, and employment of great navies and merchant marines.

Mahan was seldom, if ever, consulted on major foreign policy decisions by the imperialist leadership of the Republican party in the turbulent years ahead; indeed, they often outdistanced and embarrassed him in the scope, ambition, and crudities of their expansionist activities. But they were as eager to enlist his persuasive pen in their cause as he was pleased and flattered to volunteer it. The more he wrote, the more flamboyantly expansionist he became. As their leading propagandist for American imperialism and navalism, the grateful Republicans protected and rewarded Mahan, whose ranks he formally joined in 1894.

They supported his curricular orientation at the War College, opposed his banishment to sea in 1893 by the anti-imperialist Cleveland administration (he had publicly recommended the annexation of Hawaii), quashed fitness reports critical of his command of the protected cruiser *Chicago* (1893–1895), eulogized him when he retired from the Navy in 1896, called him back to active duty in 1898 to serve on the Naval War Board during the Spanish-American War, placed him on the American delegation to the Hague Peace Conference in 1901, subsidized his writing by ordering him to detached duty at the War College when he needed additional income, and promoted him to rear admiral on the retired list in 1906.

The last two decades of his life were spent almost entirely in writing, a successful second career in which he made considerable amounts of money.

Mahan's lasting reputation rests primarily on his role in defining the cerebral mission of the Naval War College and in clearly explaining to Americans the relationship between naval power, diplomacy, and national security at a time when the competitive state system was girding itself for World War I. His argument from history that nations economically dependent on the sea will perish beneath it unless they marshal and maintain their sea power capability remains a powerful one. A devout Anglican, devoted Anglophile, and sympathetic historian of the Royal Navy and the British Empire, Mahan also contributed positively to the Anglo-American diplomatic rapprochement of 1897–1914.

But as a self-taught historian who became president of the American Historical Association (1902–1903), Mahan's current standing in Clio's retinue is not particularly high. The central idea in his *Influence of Sea Power Upon History*, and in similar books and articles that followed, was not original with him. He never claimed it was, although he did suggest that God had personally revealed the concept to him. Actually, the book was a skillful synthesis of the research and insights of others. Its persuasive influence, at home and abroad, stemmed from the fact that the sea power argument, with its capitalist, colonialist, racist, and militarist overtones, comported nicely with the imperialist urges and ambitions of the world's major industrial nations on the eve of World War I. On the other hand, the thought that the flow of history might have had upon it other influences than sea power made little impression on Mahan. And his conviction that God's mathematically ordered universe was filled with various historical "principles" and "laws" awaiting discovery by divinely inspired historians seems naive in retrospect.

Moreover, Mahan's philosophy of history, which principally sought to justify war as an inevitable and necessary historical phenomenon—glorious, uplifting, civilizing, productive of progress, and wholly Christian—was based largely on the ideas of his uncle, Milo Mahan (1819–1870), an Episcopal clergyman who wrote several books that sought to marry ancient Pythagorean numerology to fundamentalist Anglican theology. The conceptual offspring of this peculiar union was a volatile universe in which sinful mankind was moved toward perfection by the God-directed dialectical clashes of opposing historical forces (thesis, antithesis, synthesis) expressed in numerical terms.

Nor did Mahan's extensive comments on naval tactics, strategy, and technology appear to have much modern applicability. His contribution to the development of battlefleet tactics essentially repeated, in naval terms, Antoine Henri Jomini's (1779–1869) earlier observations on Napoleonic infantry and cavalry tactics which had affirmed the historical "law" that superior concentrated firepower brought skillfully to bear on a lesser segment of an enemy's force would invariably result in victory. Mahan's insistence on the additional historical axiom that a prudent nation must strategically concentrate its naval forces on the outbreak of war made good sense until 1945. Nuclear weaponry would render such concentration virtually suicidal today.

Furthermore, Mahan had little interest in the complex, ever-changing relationships between strategy, tactics, and technology, since he believed that certain immutable military principles (like that of "concentration") were inherent in the universe and that these wholly governed the "art" and "science" of warfare; technological developments, such as airplanes or submarines, had little influence on these larger cosmological determinants.

In fine, Mahan's influence was far greater in his own time than it is now. His insistence, however, that "command of the sea" is important to American security and prosperity, and to the nation's ability to choose peace or war as its overseas interests may require, seems as relevant today as when he wrote it.

BIBLIOGRAPHY

Livezey, William E. *Mahan on Sea Power*. Norman: University of Oklahoma Press, 1947.
Mahan, Alfred Thayer. *From Sail to Steam: Recollections of Naval Life*. New York: Da Capo Press Reprint Series, 1968. (1st ed., New York: Harper, 1907.)
———. *The Influence of Sea Power upon History, 1660–1783*. Boston: Little, Brown and Company, 1890.
Puleston, William D. *Mahan: The Life and Work of Captain Alfred Thayer Mahan, U.S.N.* New Haven, Conn.: Yale University Press, 1939.
Seager, Robert, II, *Alfred Thayer Mahan: The Man and His Letters*. Annapolis, Md.: Naval Institute Press, 1977.
———, and Doris D. Maguire, eds. *Letters and Papers of Alfred Thayer Mahan*. 3 vols. Annapolis, Md.: Naval Institute Press, 1975.

ROBERT SEAGER II

MAHAN, Dennis Hart (b. New York City, N.Y., April 2, 1802; d. by drowning in the Hudson River near West Point, N.Y., September 16, 1871), military educator. As professor of military and civil engineering, and of the science of war at the U.S. Military Academy, Mahan was the principal teacher of the military art to nearly all the West Point graduates who commanded in the Civil War.

The son of Irish immigrants, his father a carpenter, Mahan was a frail youth whose aspiration was to be an artist. He sought appointment to the Military Academy because drawing was a part of the heavily engineering curriculum under Sylvanus Thayer.* Entering West Point in 1820 from Virginia, whither his family had moved and where at Norfolk he had grown up, he discovered a fascination for military subjects. He also revealed a brilliance that immediately caught Thayer's attention. From his second year he was acting assistant professor of mathematics. He graduated first of thirty-two cadets in the class of 1824 and remained at the Academy for two years, first as assistant professor of mathematics, and then as principal assistant professor of engineering. In 1826 he was ordered to Europe to study both military instruction and civil engineering, with emphasis on waterways and roads. While carrying out these broad instructions, he completed a course at the French School of Application for Engineers and Artillery at Metz, probably the leading school in the world in those aspects of military study that West Point was to continue to emphasize. Returning to West Point, he resumed his career as assistant professor of engineering in 1830 and became professor two years later.

Mahan developed a fourth-year course that was the capstone of the Academy curriculum, with a growing quotient of tactics and strategy, entitled by 1843 "Engineering and the Science of War." In both engineering and military subjects, Mahan dealt largely with material about which little had been published in the United States or even in the English language. Therefore, he developed his own texts from his translations of French works, lithographing these versions of materials that often he had brought home with him from Europe on a small press that he had also brought from Europe. Out of his texts developed his published books: *Complete Treatise on Field Fortification* (1836); *Elementary Course of Civil Engineering* (1837); *Summary of the Course of Permanent Fortification and of the Attack and Defence of Permanent Works* (1850); *Industrial Drawing* (1852); *Descriptive Geometry as Applied to the Drawing of Fortification and Stereotomy* (1864); and *An Elementary Course of Military Engineering* (1867). The books on engineering became the foundation of engineering literature in the United States. Mahan's most important book in its impact on military history was *An Elementary Treatise on Advanced-Guard, Out-Post, and Detachment Service of Troops, and the Manner of Posting and Handling Them in Presence of an Enemy, With a Historical Sketch of the Rise and Progress of Tactics, &c., &c.* (1847, 1853, 1863). Its implausible title notwithstanding, this book, especially in its final edition, is a comprehensive survey of tactics and strategy. Along with *Elements of Military Art and Science ...*, written by Mahan's favorite pupil, Henry Wager Halleck,* and in its first edition antedating Mahan's book by a year, *Out-Post* (as it is commonly called) was the foundation of an American professional military literature.

Out-Post assumes a professional level of military officership and a similar competence among the soldiers. Its author not only contributed greatly to professional military study but also helped nurture the disdain of the professional for the military amateur so conspicuous in the attitudes of such a student of his as Emory Upton.* Nevertheless, the title page of *Out-Post* states that the book is "especially for the use of officers of militia and volunteers," and it was in fact widely used for militia and volunteer training before and during the Civil War. To the disgust of the stoutly Unionist author, pirated editions appeared in Richmond and New Orleans during the war. Meanwhile, before the war Mahan had also helped nourish the military tradition of the state from which he had been appointed as a cadet, by encouraging the founding of the Virginia Military

Institute, which used his texts and until 1860 called its summer encampment Camp Mahan.

Mahan was a formidable teacher when invoking the West Point system of frequent enforced recitations; the thought of being caught unprepared by him still terrified William Tecumseh Sherman* in the 1880s. Yet Mahan was also a most unmilitary figure, "the most particular, crabbed, exacting man I ever saw," according to Cadet Tully McCrea. "He is a little slim skeleton of a man and always nervous and cross." Having resigned his second lieutenant's commission on January 1, 1832, when he became a professor, he not only dressed as a civilian but also constantly carried an umbrella. His dedication to West Point was so complete that reaction against it may have helped turn his sons Alfred Thayer Mahan* and the second Dennis Hart Mahan away from the Army to the Navy (though a third son, Frederick A., graduated from West Point). His model of complete dedication to the military profession was also so thorough that it demanded an absolutely apolitical stance, and Mahan never voted. When in 1871 the academic board of the Military Academy decided that Mahan's age required his retirement from the faculty, he soon afterward fell from a boat into the Hudson River. Life without West Point may have lost its meaning for him.

Mahan was first an engineer, but his military teaching did not tie tactics and strategy to the supposedly inherent caution of the engineer. To Mahan, the fortifications erected by the military engineer were useful to the defensive as a temporary expedient, to help exhaust the enemy, and as points of departure and support for the attack. The spade is as important in war as the musket, but the offensive, nevertheless, was Mahan's preferred mode of war, and he instilled in his students the conviction that only the offensive was likely to bring victory in war. Even for the army on the strategic defensive, the attack is the most potent tactical weapon. "Vigor on the field and rapidity of pursuit should go hand in hand for great success." "Carrying the war into the heart of the assailant's country, or that of his allies, is the surest way of making him share its burdens and foiling his plans." "If Fortune is on the side of the heavy battalions, she also frequently grants her favors to superior activity and audacity."

Mahan was not fond of stressing the value of the heavy battalions. His military hero, his prime exemplar of sound strategy, was Napoleon. When faculty and students at West Point founded a Napoleon Club, Mahan was almost inevitably its president. Mahan's Napoleon was not the Napoleon of Carl von Clausewitz's interpretation but the Napoleon of Antoine Henri Jomini, whose writings strongly influenced Mahan and whose thinking was akin to Mahan's. Mahan favored the offensive not of the heavy battalions but of indirection and maneuver. His emphasis on deceptive maneuver accounts in turn for his emphasis, even in the title of his principal military book, on the activities of advanced guards, outposts, and reconnaissances that screen maneuver. To gain information about the enemy and deprive him of information in turn, Mahan recommended that one-fifth to one-third of any force be detailed as reconnaissance parties, advanced guards, and outposts. "There are no more important duties, which an officer may be called upon to perform, than those of collecting and arranging the information upon which the . . . operations of a campaign must be based."

For deceptive maneuver as the essence of the offensive, speed of movement is as important as adequate intelligence and screening. "In this one quality," speed, "reside all the advantages that a fortunate initiative may have procured." "No great success can be hoped for in war in which rapid movements do not enter as an element. Even the very elements of Nature seem to array themselves against the slow and over-prudent general."

Clearly, it was not Mahan's teaching at West Point that encouraged some of the generals of the Civil War to become slow and overprudent. On the other hand, too much of a positive influence should not be claimed for Mahan's teaching of the art of war to Civil War generals. Mahan's concepts of grand tactics and strategy were crammed mainly into a single fourth-year course, in the largely nonmilitary West Point curriculum. To speak either of Mahan's influence, or of Jomini's through Mahan and West Point, as conditioning Civil War generalship can readily make American soldiers of the 1860s appear much more bookish than they were, and far less the military improvisers confronted with new conditions that they had to be.

At the same time, Mahan's insistence on meticulous intelligence, screening, and reconnaissance and on rapid movements underline his call for a high degree of professional competence in officers and similar skill in soldiers. He remains, most centrally, a founder of military study as professional study. What makes the mastery of an occupation a profession is that its education be rooted in historical study, that a series of guiding principles be drawn from historical experience. Such was Mahan's approach to the study required for military officership: "No one can be said to have thoroughly mastered his art, who has neglected to make himself conversant with its early history. . . . It is in military history that we are to look for the source of all military science."

Above all, in military history the student should look to Napoleon. Interpreted by Mahan to a generation and more of West Point cadets, Napoleon left a profound impression upon the American approach to war. Mahan's Napoleon was par excellence the aggressive, offensive-minded commander, the general of swift maneuver against an enemy's exposed flank and rear, and the general who through such maneuver demonstrated "those grand features of the art [of war], by which an enemy is broken and utterly dispersed by one and the same blow."

BIBLIOGRAPHY

Ambrose, Stephen E. *Duty, Honor, Country: A History of West Point*. Baltimore: Johns Hopkins University Press, 1966.
Dupuy, R. Ernest. *Men of West Point: The First 150 Years of the United States Military Academy*. New York: Sloane, 1951.
———. *Where They Have Trod: The West Point Tradition in American Life*. Philadelphia: Lippincott, 1940.

Puleston, W. D. *Mahan: The Life and Work of Captain Alfred Thayer Mahan.* New Haven, Conn.: Yale Univesity Press, 1939.
Weigley, Russell F. *Towards an American Army: Military Thought from Washington to Marshall.* New York: Columbia University Press, 1962.

RUSSELL F. WEIGLEY

MARCH, Peyton Conway (b. Easton, Pa., December 27, 1864; d. Washington, D.C., April 13, 1955), military leader and administrator; Army chief of staff, 1918–1921.

March was a member of a distinguished family. His father, Francis Andrew, was a famous philologist while his mother, Margaret Conway, was related to the great Virginia families. In his generation, four of the five sons were in *Who's Who in America*. After graduation from Lafayette College, March went to West Point where he graduated in 1888. For ten years his was the routine of an artillery officer in a peacetime army dominated by Civil War veterans.

In the Spanish-American War and Philippine Insurrection, March made a brilliant reputation. He completed the two-year course at the Artillery School in March 1898, just in time to take command of the Astor Battery. He led this privately financed unit of volunteers ranging from Ivy Leaguers to veterans of British colonial campaigns into action in the Philippines. His heroism at the Battle of Manila won him a recommendation for the Medal of Honor from Major General Arthur MacArthur.* Later, during the Insurrection, as MacArthur's aide and then as a major and lieutenant colonel in the 33d Volunteer Infantry, he received five more citations for gallantry. As a provincial governor and commissary general of prisoners, he also gained administrative experience. In 1901, General MacArthur wrote about him: "no officer has rendered more efficient or brilliant field service than he in the Island of Luzon."

March spent about half of the next sixteen years with troops, but his most noteworthy assignments were as a member of the first War Department General Staff and of the powerful Adjutant General's Department. The first also afforded him an opportunity to see the Russo-Japanese War as an observer with the Japanese. The second placed him in a position where he could learn thoroughly the intricacies of the Army bureaucracy and brought him to the attention of Secretary of War Newton Diehl Baker.

When the United States intervened in World War I, March was a colonel in command of the 8th Field Artillery. Within a few months, he was a major general and the chief of artillery of the American Expeditionary Force (AEF). In France he supervised the planning and development of the artillery program until February 1918 when Secretary Baker called him back to Washington to be the chief of staff.

During the first eleven months of the war, Hugh Lenox Scott, Tasker Howard Bliss,* and John Biddle attempted to cope as chiefs of staff with the problems of mobilizing and bringing to bear the military effort of the United States. While many of the delays, mistakes, and outright failures could be blamed on lack of proper organization and the necessity to compress the process of changing from peace to war footing in such a brief period, Baker and others saw the need of a more effective administrator in the position of chief of staff.

March took over as acting chief of staff on March 4, 1918. In May he became the chief of staff and received the temporary rank of full general. He saw that his basic task was to get enough men to France to win the war. When he came to power, there were fewer than 1.7 million men in the entire Army with some quarter of a million in the AEF. The measure of his success is in the statistics: the Army more than doubled in total strength, and the AEF expanded to some 2 million in the eight months prior to the Armistice. To achieve this result, March strove consistently for a more efficient and effective General Staff, War Department, and Army.

Within the War Department, he decisively established the primacy of the General Staff by ruthlessly clipping the power of the chiefs of the administrative bureaus and by placing the supply organizations under his assistant chief of staff, Major General George Washington Goethals. In the Army, generally, he sought to increase efficiency by creating new branches which reflected technological innovations: Air Service, Tank Corps, Motor Transport Corps, and Chemical Warfare Service. He also abolished the distinctions between the National Army, National Guard, and Regular Army. His much criticized shortening of the West Point course to one year was perhaps due more to his long-term desire to reform the Military Academy than to the need for a relatively few more wartime lieutenants. As chief of staff, he attempted to eliminate outside political influence in the Army, and, through his institution of regular press conferences, he tried to make information more available. Behind all of these changes was the metamorphosis of the Office of Chief of Staff to a much more powerful position which he spelled out in General Order No. 80 as the "immediate adviser of the Secretary of War on all matters relating to the Military Establishment" with the rank and authority of the nation's senior soldier.

Although General John Joseph Pershing,* the commander of the AEF, was pleased with the primary result of March's actions—namely, the tremendous increase in the troops in the AEF—he was irritated by the fact that March did not subordinate himself as his predecessors in Washington had done. There was friction and one major dispute over the eventual strength of the AEF. Pershing expected March to put his 100 Division Plan into effect without giving full consideration to the domestic capability to sustain this program. Then he refused to accept a lesser strength plan. The surprisingly quick end of the war prevented the situation from getting out of hand.

After the Armistice, March remained in office until June 30, 1921. In this anticlimactic period he supervised the return of the AEF, the demobilization of the emergency Army, and the transition of the Regular Army to peacetime duties. Faced with opposition from Pershing and others as well as the simple fact that Congress and the people wanted to cut the Army to the bone, March failed to get the five hundred thousand strength he wanted. Nor was there a chance for the three-month universal training program which he supported.

In retirement, he lived in Europe, New York, and, finally, Washington and maintained interest in military matters. Deeply hurt by the lack of recognition which Pershing's memoirs gave him and the War Department for their wartime contributions, March responded in 1932 with *The Nation at War*. Not content to describe his and the War Department's activities, March severely criticized Pershing and gave the old controversy a thorough airing. He followed the events of World War II (in which two of his sons-in-law, Joseph M. Swing and John Millikin, became generals) and the Korean War with great interest. Finally, in 1953, President Dwight David Eisenhower* presented him with the thanks of Congress—a tribute that curiously did not refer to his wartime achievements.

March's place in history rests on his role in the American victory in World War I. After the war, Secretary Baker succinctly stated what this soldier did and evaluated his contribution in two letters. In 1919 he explained to the chairman of the Senate Military Affairs Committee:

> The Chief of Staff was the head of the organization at home. His driving power, his high professional equipment, and his burning zeal imparted to our whole machine an impetus which never slackened . . . [as he] organized, expedited and stimulated our mobilization at home, and made effective that support and cooperation upon which, under modern war conditions, the success of the commander in the field depends.

Seventeen years later, in a letter to the former chief of staff, Baker emphatically summed up the importance of his work: "The war was won by days. Your energy and drive supplied the days necessary for our side to win."

A brilliant, decisive, hard man, March had little time for the amenities. This lack of tact and apparent insensitivity caused criticism, contributed to the animosity which many military and political leaders felt toward him, and unquestionably denied him some of the credit and honors his accomplishments deserved. As George Catlett Marshall pointed out, this trait of antagonizing people was a great weakness; yet, General Marshall still considered March "a master administrator." Douglas MacArthur* was more complimentary: "He was that rare combination—a courageous leader and a skilled administrator. . . . A tremendous officer—a tremendous Chief of Staff." What honors could surpass that tribute?

BIBLIOGRAPHY

Coffman, Edward M. *The Hilt of the Sword: The Career of Peyton C. March*. Madison: University of Wisconsin Press, 1966.

———. *The War to End All Wars: The American Military Experience in World War I*. New York: Oxford University Press, 1968.

March, Peyton C. *The Nation at War* Garden City, N.Y.: Doubleday, Doran and Company, 1932.

EDWARD M. COFFMAN

MARION, Francis (b. Berkeley County, S.C., 1732 (?); d. Berkeley County, S.C., February 27, 1795), partisan leader in the American Revolution.

Francis Marion, the enigmatic partisan leader during the American Revolution, was born in 1732 in rural South Carolina rice country and reared at a plantation on Winyah Bay, near Georgetown. In these isolated surroundings, he received only a meager education. His one longing was for adventure at sea. At the earliest possible month, when he was fifteen, Marion enlisted on a schooner to the West Indies. The voyage was a disaster; the ship capsized, leaving Marion adrift for seven days before he was rescued. Chastened, Marion returned to his farm.

He still sought excitement, however, and in 1756, during the French and Indian War, he enlisted in the South Carolina militia as a lieutenant. Soon he was embroiled in fierce fighting against the Cherokees. In his initial encounter two-thirds of his company perished; the pugnacious young officer was characterized by his command as "an active, brave and hardy soldier."

At the age of forty-one Marion purchased his own estate, "Pond Bluff," four miles below Eutaw Springs, on the Santee River. The importunate political troubles with Great Britain gave Marion little opportunity to enjoy his farm. He was elected to his colony's Provincial Congress in 1775, and, when hostilities with the parent state flared, Marion enlisted as one of ten captains in an infantry regiment.

Marion spent the initial year of the War for Independence recruiting and training troops, securing installations in Charleston that Britain chose not to defend, and supervising the construction of new fortifications in and about the harbor of Charleston. In late June 1776 he played an active, though minor, role in aborting General Henry Clinton's attempt to invade the city. During this year Marion was promoted first to the rank of major and then, following the action at Charleston, to lieutenant colonel.

Colonel Marion saw little action during the next thirty-six months. He spent most of the period in garrison duty in Charleston, training his men and earning a reputation as a priggish commander. Late in 1779, however, after British forces seized Savannah, Marion served in the Franco-American Expedition, led by General Benjamin Lincoln* and the Count d'Estaing, to retake the Georgia port. Marion's regiment spearheaded the attack of the South Carolina forces, a bloody foray that was repulsed with the loss of about 20 percent of the troops. With the collapse of the assault Marion was posted at remote Shelton, charged primarily with responsibility for tracking down deserters from the Savannah Campaign. He was recalled to Charleston in January 1780, when it became obvious that Britain again planned an assault on the city.

Marion played no role in the defense of Charleston, however. In March he suffered a broken ankle—the evidence indicates that the accident occurred at a raucous party—and General Lincoln ordered Marion and all other officers "unfit for duty" to evacuate the city. Until July the colonel remained in hiding from marauding Tories; then, his ankle partially mended, Marion joined General Horatio Gates'* Southern Army in North Carolina.

Colonel Marion soon was restive. Without an independent command and intrigued by the partisan activities of Thomas Sumter, Marion requested a leave to direct militia activities in the Williamsburg district, a Whig stronghold in eastern South Carolina. Gates consented, ordering Marion to disrupt the flow of supplies from Camden to General Charles Cornwallis' legions.

At age forty-eight, Marion commenced his guerrilla activities in August 1780. With congenitally malformed ankles and knees, a disability now exacerbated by his slowly healing broken ankle, Marion appeared to many to be incapable of enduring the rigors of a martial life. Contemporaries described him as short and lean, with a high forehead, an aquiline nose, and dark, piercing eyes. Henry ("Light-Horse Harry") Lee, who twice acted in concert with Marion's force, thought the leader was taciturn and modest. He dressed sparsely, and during his two years of partisan strife he lived on an exiguous diet of lean beef, hominy, and potatoes. He disdained alcoholic beverages, preferring a concoction of vinegar and water with each meal. His force generally had no tents and few blankets; the men lived a Spartan existence, concealed in forests and swamps, often moving cryptically several miles each night from camp to camp.

Marion's band quickly became skilled practitioners of irregular warfare. They launched sporadic, rapier raids against the British lines of supply. They struck at British camps to rescue American prisoners, once liberating one hundred and fifty captives of the debacle at Camden. They engaged in the macabre business of stalking and plundering Tories. Frequently, they were ordered to seize supplies, boats, and even slaves for use by American forces. In the fall of 1780 Cornwallis even complained to Clinton that "Col. Marion had so wrought on the minds of the People . . . that there was scarce an Inhabitant between the Santee and the Peedee that was not in arms against us." Banastre Tarleton, the implacable commander of Loyalist partisans, allegedly referred to Marion as a "d—d *old fox*" who could not be apprehended by Satan himself; the "Swamp Fox" nickname grew from the popularization of that acerbic comment.

Marion had hardly assumed command when Britain stepped up its campaign against southern Whigs. In August 1780 fifty-nine prominent Carolinians were dispatched into exile in Florida, and numerous estates were arrogated. The policy of harassment played into Marion's hands, however, giving him—for a brief, euphoric period—sufficient volunteers with which to work. Perceiving the danger, the British, in September, debouched a force through the Cheraws in northeastern South Carolina to extirpate Marion. His mobility limited by cumbersome field artillery pieces, Marion was nearly trapped. He escaped, of course, but he never again traveled with field pieces.

In December 1780 Nathanael Greene* supplanted Gates as commander of the Southern army. Realizing he was unlikely to receive adequate assistance from Congress, Greene turned to the partisans. Marion was placed in charge of the Carolina low country and Sumter of the high country, but Sumter was given overall command. Marion fumed, and at times he deliberately refused to cooperate, prompting Greene to excoriate the commander and to order him to "Cooperate with [Sumter] in any manner he may direct."

The next nine months were perhaps Marion's most active period. He and Lee took Fort Watson in April, reducing a force of one hundred and twenty British. Late in May he seized Georgetown, an important coastal town. Thereafter, the governor provided him with the names of specific Loyalists, and Marion was ordered to arrest the men and confiscate their property.

In September Greene commanded Marion to attach his force to the Southern army, and three days later he fought under Greene at the Battle of Eutaw Springs. Greene adopted the strategy that had been employed successfully by Daniel Morgan* at Cowpens. Militia forces under the command of Marion, Andrew Pickens, and the Marquis Francis de Malmedy were placed in the frontline to take the first shock of the enemy assault; better disciplined Continental troops comprised the second line. After four hours of fierce fighting, during which time each side lost about five hundred men in killed and wounded, the British withdrew. Marion's men gave a good account of themselves, and Greene lauded their "degree of Spirit and firmness" that "would have graced the soldiers of the King of Prussia."

Within a month of this encounter Cornwallis' army surrendered at Yorktown, and the war began to wind down. Marion, however, remained active throughout 1782 hunting down Loyalists and endeavoring to prevent supplies from reaching the British troops holed up in Charleston. He also returned to politics and was elected to the State Senate. In December 1782 his brigade was officially disbanded.

Marion returned to "Pond Bluff," which had been nearly extirpated through neglect and by war. His marriage, at age fifty-four, to Mary Videau, a wealthy forty-nine-year-old spinster, facilitated the restoration of the farm. He lived prosperously, though not happily, for the next dozen years. He continued to serve in the South Carolina Senate, and he was elected to the state's constitutional convention in 1790. Marion died on February 27, 1795.

Francis Marion played a substantive role in thwarting Britain's "Southern Strategy" during the Revolution. Imperial planners believed British armies could drive Continental forces from the region and that Loyalist partisans then would pacify each colony and restore civilian government. Marion's activities hindered and intimidated the Tories. In addition, his tactics of harassment had a pernicious effect on British forces, producing shortages of some supplies and delays in the receipt of other essentials.

Marion was not without fault. Jealous of his independence, he often sullenly refused to cooperate with the other partisan commanders. Yet, overall, this reserved, hirsute, bellicose man was an adroit leader, a commander who controlled his men with light reins. His failings arose more from manpower shortages and from lack of ammunition than from errors of command. His greatest talent was to grasp the real meaning of guerrilla warfare, to acknowledge that his purpose was to destroy and to disrupt his foes, not to seize and hold the territory over which he fought.

BIBLIOGRAPHY

Rankin, Hugh F. *Francis Marion: The Swamp Fox*. New York: Thomas Y. Crowell, 1973.
Simms, William Gilmore. *The Life of Francis Marion*. New York: George F. Cooledge and Brother, 1844.
Weigley, Russell F. *The Partisan War: The South Carolina Campaign of 1780–1782*. Columbia: University of South Carolina Press, 1970.

JOHN FERLING

MARSHALL, George Catlett (b. Uniontown, Pa., December 31, 1880; d. Washington, D.C., October 16, 1959), chief of staff of the Army, secretary of state, secretary of defense, Nobel Laureate.

Originally from Virginia, Marshall's forebears were for three generations residents of Kentucky. He was descended on his father's side from his great great grandfather, the Reverend William Marshall, brother of Chief Justice John Marshall's father. The future general attended private and public schools in Uniontown before entering the Virginia Military Institute in 1897. He graduated in 1901 holding the rank of first captain. He was commissioned as second lieutenant of infantry on February 3, 1902. He was married eight days later to Elizabeth Carter Coles, of Lexington, Virginia.

Marshall arrived in Manila just at the close of the Philippine Insurrection in 1902 and was assigned to duty with the 30th Infantry Regiment on the island of Mindoro. For several months he was the officer in charge of a part of a company in the southern part of the island. After serving for several months in Manila, he returned to the United States in 1903 and was assigned to Fort Reno, Oklahoma, and then sent on a mapping detail in west Texas.

In 1906 he entered the Infantry and Cavalry School at Fort Leavenworth, Kansas, graduating first in his class and remaining for a second year at the Army Staff College. From 1908 to 1910 he was an instructor in the Fort Leavenworth schools. During summers he gained valuable experience by assignments to various maneuvers where he had an opportunity to perform staff duties far in excess of his rank. He became a first lieutenant only in 1907 and a captain in 1916.

He had a number of short assignments in the 1910–1913 period, the longest being to the Massachusetts militia as instructor and the second longest as a company commander in the 4th Infantry Regiment at Fort Logan Roots, Arkansas. He also took part in the Texas maneuvers as an officer in the maneuver division. From 1913 to 1916 he was again in the Philippines. Early in 1914 he won great acclaim for stepping in on a moment's notice to act as chief of staff of an invasion force in the Philippine maneuvers of that year. During this period he served as aide to Major General Hunter Liggett,* the head of the Philippine Department.

He returned to San Francisco in 1916 where he was aide to the commander of the Western Department, Major General James Franklin Bell,* former chief of staff of the Army, who had discovered Marshall at Fort Leavenworth and thereafter did much to push his military experience and education. When Bell moved to the Eastern Department, Governor's Island, New York, in 1917, he took Marshall with him for an assignment overseas.

Marshall accompanied the 1st Division units overseas in June 1917 as training officer. Later, as operations officer, he helped to plan the first U.S. attack in France. In the summer of 1918 after rising to the rank of lieutenant colonel, he was assigned briefly to General Headquarters at Chaumont where he helped to plan operations in the St. Mihiel salient. Later as First Army chief of operations, he helped move hundreds of thousands of troops in and out of the Meuse-Argonne salient, winning the nickname "Wizard" for his grasp of logistics.

Following the war, he worked on occupation plans for Germany as chief of staff of VIII Corps and was assigned in the spring of 1919 to General John Joseph Pershing* as aide. He traveled through Western Europe, taking part in numerous victory parades before returning to Washington in September 1919. For a number of months, he accompanied Pershing and other members of the staff on inspection trips to camps and munitions plants throughout the United States, getting exelent training for future chief of staff duties in wartime. He worked with Pershing on details of the National Defense Act and helped to present it to Congress. He also helped Pershing prepare his reports on World War I. Marshall remained as aide until 1924 when he was assigned to Tientsin, China, as executive officer of the 15th Infantry Regiment. In his three years there he learned something of Chinese language and culture and on two occasions as acting commander had the problem, which he dealt with successfully each time, of coping with marauding members of bands of warlords fighting for control of North China.

In 1927, Marshall was assigned to the staff of the Army War College and was just beginning his teaching when his wife died suddenly. Shortly afterward, he was reassigned as lieutenant colonel in charge of instruction at the Infantry School, Fort Benning, Georgia. In his five years there, he stressed study of World War I lessons and realism about possible future conflict. His staff included Omar Nelson Bradley,* Joseph Lawton Collins,* Joseph Warren Stilwell,* Matthew Bunker Ridgway,* and Walter Bedell Smith.* It is estimated that some 165 future generals attended classes or acted as staff members there in that period. While there, in 1930, he married for a second time, with Pershing acting as his best man. His wife, Katherine Tupper Brown, widow of a Baltimore attorney, was the mother of three children (the younger son was later killed in the fighting at Anzio).

Marshall commanded a battalion of the 8th Infantry Regiment at Fort Screven, Georgia, in 1932–1933, and won promotion to colonel. He then commanded briefly the 8th Infantry Headquarters at Fort Moultrie, South Carolina. Much of his time in the two assignments was spent in developing Civilian Conservation Corps (CCC) camps in Florida and South Carolina. From 1933 to 1936 he was senior instructor of the Illinois National Guard. Promoted to brigadier general at the end of that service, he assumed command of the 5th Infantry Brigade at Vancouver Barracks, Washington. His duties also included supervision of Civilian Conservation Corps camps in that area. During this period he welcomed the first Soviet crew to make a transpolar flight from the Soviet Union to the United States. Bound for Oakland, California, a fuel shortage forced them to land on the parade ground almost in front of Marshall's quarters.

In the summer of 1938 Marshall was appointed to head the War Plans Division in Washington and later in the year to be deputy chief of staff of the Army. In the following spring, he was nominated for the post of chief of staff of the Army. He was sent almost at once on a special good-will tour to Brazil. From July 1 to September, Marshall acted as chief of staff while his predecessor, Malin Craig,* was on terminal leave. On September 1, shortly after Hitler attacked Poland, Marshall was sworn in as a permanent two star general and then as a temporary four star.

During the next two years, Marshall labored to enlarge and train the Army and Army Air Forces, to increase munitions production, and to sell the Army's program to Congress and the public. Meanwhile, he was selecting officers for a possible conflict, injecting war realism into training, striving to get weapons to Britain, China, and the Soviet Union as well as to his own forces. This period saw the adoption and, then, extension of the Selective Service Act, large peacetime maneuvers, and talks with Great Britain about common action in case the United States entered the war. Raising the total Army and Army Air Forces strength to the authorized level of two hundred thousand, he started these services on the way to a wartime high of more than 8 million men and women. With the attack on Pearl Harbor, he reorganized the War Department staff on a wartime basis, establishing the Operations Division as a Washington command post. Marshall was to play a leading role in the various early war conferences as the leading proponent of the cross channel strategy. He was present at all the major meetings beginning with Argentina in the summer of 1941 and including the Washington meetings, two Quebec meetings, Cairo-Tehran, Malta and Yalta and Potsdam, as well as special missions he made to London in April and July 1942 to talk to Winston Churchill and in 1943 with Churchill to Algiers. He also went to the Normandy beaches with other chiefs of staff in June 1944. In late 1943 he flew to the Pacific to talk with Douglas MacArthur* and visited most of the U.S. divisions in the line in Europe in October 1944.

He retired on November 20, 1945, and within less than a week President Harry S. Truman asked him to go to China in an effort to bring peace between the Chinese Nationalists and Communists. After a year of patient effort, he gave up the mission as a failure and returned home to accept the task of secretary of state, succeeding James F. Byrnes.

As secretary of state, Marshall spent much of his time attending Council of Foreign Ministers' meetings in Moscow and London and a meeting of the U.N. General Assembly in Paris as well as U.N. meetings in New York. He also attended Latin American meetings in Brazil and Bogota. His secretaryship was marked by the proclamation of the Truman Doctrine, the recognition of Israel, preliminary negotiations for the treaties leading to the North Atlantic Treaty Organization, and the Berlin airlift. He is best known for the European Recovery Act which followed the address he gave during the Harvard Commencement of 1947. He indicated that various leaders shared the credit for the authorship but believed that his chief role lay in his strong nonpolitical stance which made it possible for him to work with both parties and in his series of speeches and appearances he made throughout the country and before Congress to sell the idea of aid to Europe. Marshall returned from the Paris meeting of the U.N. General Assembly meeting near the end of 1948 for the removal of a kidney. He resigned for reasons of ill-health in January 1949.

Within a few months, Marshall was back as head of the American Red Cross. Before the year had ended, Truman asked him to take over as secretary of defense in order to deal with problems raised by the Korean War. Special legislation was passed waiving, in his case only, the prohibition against a military man serving as head of defense. Agreeing to stay one year, Marshall worked to rebuild the manpower of the Army, to press for increased war production, and to push legislation for universal military service. He resigned in September 1951, terminating service that covered almost the first half of the century.

He had been involved in the recall of Douglas MacArthur earlier that year. Although he initially counseled delay in that action, he approved the president's action and, later, in hearings before a congressional committee, made a strong statement in behalf of strong civilian control over military affairs. Before the end of his secretaryship, he came under heavy attack by Senator Joseph McCarthy, who charged him with being soft on communism. Marshall was defended by members of Congress of both parties but was to undergo several years of attacks for the Army's failure to protect Pearl Harbor, for the failure of his China policy, and for the recall of MacArthur. His alma mater proclaimed a special day in his honor and named one of the barracks arches (the other two are named for George Washington* and Thomas

["Stonewall"] Jackson*) for him, and governor of Virginia gave him-Virginia's highest civilian award.

In December 1953 Marshall was invited to Oslo, Norway, to become the first professional soldier to receive the Nobel Prize for Peace. It was made clear that the award was given for his great contributions to the reconstruction of Europe. Marshall died at Walter Reed Hospital in Washington in 1959 and was buried at Arlington National Cemetery.

BIBLIOGRAPHY

Pogue, Forrest C. *George C. Marshall: The Making of a General, 1880–1939*. New York: Viking Press, 1963.

———. *George C. Marshall: Ordeal and Hope, 1939–1942*. New York: Viking Press, 1966.

———. *George C. Marshall: Organizer of Victory, 1943–1945*. New York: Viking Press, 1973.

FORREST C. POGUE

MEADE, George Gordon (b. Cadiz, Spain, December 31, 1815; d. Philadelphia, Pa., November 6, 1872), Army officer. Meade was commander of the Union Army of the Potomac in the Civil War, and the victor at the Battle of Gettysburg.

George Gordon Meade was born in Cadiz, Spain, his father—an American citizen—being a U.S. naval agent and, until ruined as a result of the Napoleonic Wars, a wealthy businessman. Young Meade's early education was gained in Philadelphia, Washington, and Baltimore. He was graduated from the U.S. Military Academy at West Point in 1835, standing nineteenth in a class of fifty-six. After a year's service in the Second Seminole War, Meade resigned from the Army in 1836 and for six years pursued a livelihood as a civil engineer. In 1840 he was married to Margaretta Sergeant, who bore him six children. Rejoining the Army in 1846, Meade won a brevet in the Mexican War at Monterey. This combat service was followed by routine assignments, including survey work along the Great Lakes and northern border. He was promoted to captain in 1856.

When the Civil War started in 1861, Meade was appointed brigadier general of volunteers and named to the command of one of the brigades in the famous Pennsylvania Reserves. In this capacity he served in the Peninsula Campaign, led by George Brinton McClellan,* in the spring and early summer of 1862. At Glendale Meade was severely wounded. But he returned in time to fight at Second Manassas in August under John Pope and, as a division commander, with McClellan at South Mountain and Antietam in September. In November Meade was promoted to major general of volunteers. At Fredericksburg in December he commanded a division under Ambrose Everett Burnside; Meade's troops temporarily broke through two Confederate defensive lines commanded by Thomas Jonathan ("Stonewall") Jackson.* At Chancellorsville, under Joseph

Hooker,* in April-May 1863, he headed the V Corps, which was not heavily engaged.

In all of these operations, Meade had performed most capably as a combat leader of reliability and sagacity. He was tall and graceful, though slightly stooped, possessed an aquiline nose and quick-moving eyes, and his graying brown hair was thinning. He wore spectacles for nearsightedness, and his regulation army hat brim was pulled down all around. His commanding presence and steady mien were marred only by a sharp, violent temper which cascaded forth in moments of great stress. This made it difficult to approach him even with important matters in the heat of battle. None recognized this irascibility more than Meade himself, and he was swift to make amends. But on occasion he indulged in self-pity and self-deprecation, and he was thin-skinned to criticism.

But Meade's assets bulked large. He was adept at terrain analysis and in the use of the combined arms of infantry, cavalry, and artillery. Though cautious, he was an unrelenting combatant, and he was a man of the highest honor, character, and integrity. These talents and traits were to be fearfully tested within a few weeks after Chancellorsville.

With Robert Edward Lee* launching his second invasion of the North in early June 1863, President Abraham Lincoln and General in Chief Henry Wager Halleck* named Meade to succeed Hooker in command of the Army of the Potomac. This was on June 28, just three days before the greatest battle ever fought in the Western Hemisphere erupted at Gettysburg on July 1—a combat that would rage for three bloody days.

On the first day, neither Meade nor Lee was on the field as portions of their armies collided unexpectedly west and north of Gettysburg. Relying upon such accomplished subordinates as John Buford, John F. Reynolds, Abner Doubleday, and Winfield Scott Hancock, Meade's outnumbered forces held back the attacking Confederates for over eight hours and then fell back in some disorder to a strong position on Cemetery Ridge south of the town. Meade arrived on the battlefield during the night, determined to stay and fight it out on the morrow, and concentrated the rest of his army at Gettysburg. Lee did the same with his grayclad legions, now somewhat outnumbered by the Federals.

On the second day of the battle—July 2—fighting commenced in the late afternoon. After having spent most of the time securing his right wing, Meade, upon hearing the engagement reopen with heavy attacks by James Longstreet* upon the Union left at the Peach Orchard, Wheatfield, Devil's Den, and the key Little Round Top, daringly exposed his right wing by rapidly shifting troops to his threatened left, thereby checking the Southern assaults after they had scored some initial gains. Meade's army repelled a blow against East Cemetery Hill, although the Confederates managed to gain a lodgment on the evacuated lower slopes of Culp's Hill on the extreme Federal right.

Meade called a night-time council of war of his top generals and concurred in their recommendation to remain and fight it out on the defensive at Gettysburg. The National commander grasped the initiative at 4:00 AM on July 3 when he attacked the graycoats on Culp's Hill. In some seven hours of unrelenting combat the Federals pushed the Confederates off the hill, thereby ending their threat to the Union right.

Estimating that Lee would then attempt to overwhelm his center, Meade deployed sufficient infantry and artillery forces to meet such a challenge. In midafternoon, following the heaviest artillery cannonade of the war—lasting an hour and fifty minutes—Lee hurled against the Union center some fifteen thousand Southern troops, under George Edward Pickett,* across nearly a mile of open fields in what comprised one of the greatest infantry charges of history. Despite the gallantry of the attackers, Meade's artillery fire, and then his musketry volleys, tore apart the gray phalanx. A few hundred intrepid Confederates dented the Federal line at "The Angle" of a stonewall near the copse-of-trees objective, only to be enveloped by Meade's supporting infantrymen. The remnants of the assaulting force fell back in confusion to their starting point on Seminary Ridge.

It was probably wise that Meade refrained from trying to mount a counterattack; had he done so, it would most likely have suffered the same fate as Pickett's charge. The National commander had sustained some twenty-three thousand casualties out of about eighty-eight thousand engaged, as against Lee's losses of approximately twenty-eight thousand out of some seventy-five thousand. In Lee's retreat from Gettysburg, Meade pursued circumspectly and rejected the gamble of assaulting the Army of Northern Virginia along the Potomac River near Williamsport, Maryland. When sharply criticized by Lincoln for "permitting" Lee to retire safely into Virginia, Meade asked to be relieved of his command—a proffer that was not accepted by the president. There was only desultory, indecisive fighting between Meade and Lee in the remaining summer, fall, and winter months of 1863, the operations being restricted largely to those of maneuver. The two armies then went into winter quarters near the Rapidan River.

When Ulysses Simpson Grant* was named general in chief of all the Union armies in March 1864 and established his field headquarters with the Army of the Potomac—thus, in effect, reducing Meade to his executive officer—Meade took this occurrence in stride. Although the arrangement made for an awkward command relationship, both generals—so different in characteristics and personality—worked hard to get along together amicably. The major decisions in the costly 1864 battles of the Wilderness, Spotsylvania Court House, Cold Harbor, and Petersburg were made by Grant, and very few and limited successes were gained. At Cold Harbor Meade wisely prevailed upon Grant to desist from ordering further suicidal frontal attacks. And in the final Appomattox Campaign in April 1865, which led to Lee's capitulation on April 9, Meade showed to good advantage.

In the seven years of life remaining to him after the Civil War, Meade was given command of the Third Military District (Alabama, Georgia, and Florida), one of the five military occupation districts in the ex-Confederacy. He won the respect of most Southerners for his firm but fair dealings and policies. From

1869 until he died in 1872, he commanded the Military Division of the East, with headquarters in Philadelphia. On October 31, while taking his daily walk from the office with his wife, he was stricken with a terrible pain in his back, in the area of his old Glendale wound. Pneumonia set in and led to his death.

Posterity has not, perhaps, treated Meade fairly. He was, to a high degree, eclipsed by the very success he scored at Gettysburg, and, as General Francis A. Walker had declared, "There is probably no other battle of which men are so prone to think and speak without a conscious reference to the commanding general of the victorious party, as they are regarding Gettysburg." In addition to skillful tactical handling of his army at Gettysburg, Meade showed the marks of good military leadership when, without trying to handle too many details himself, he entrusted tasks of great importance to such accomplished subordinates as W. S. Hancock, John Reynolds, and Gouverneur K. Warren. For the first time in the Civil War in the Eastern Theater of Operations, the teamwork of the top generals of the Army of the Potomac was of a high order.

Having been in command only three days before the pivotal Gettysburg engagement, Meade approached many of the trying decisions gropingly at first; but, in the final analysis, almost all of his major actions and judgments proved to be unerringly correct. Lee thought that Meade, along with McClellan and Grant, were the most able generals he had faced during the war. In unhesitatingly accepting the command at a crucial moment and successfully meeting the stern challenge at Gettysburg, Meade, in the words of historian James G. Randall, "fulfilled a responsibility unexcelled, unless by Washington, in previous American history."

Despite some limitations, George G. Meade is perhaps entitled to more recognition than he has received as the victor over the redoubtable Robert E. Lee in one of the most critical and decisive battles in which the nation has ever been engaged. The rest of his life may also serve as a model for the professional soldier in a republic such as the United States.

BIBLIOGRAPHY

Cleaves, Freeman. *Meade of Gettysburg*. Norman: University of Oklahoma Press, 1960.
Coddington, Edwin B. *The Gettysburg Campaign: A Study in Command*. New York: Charles Scribner's Sons, 1968.
Hassler, Warren W., Jr. *Commanders of the Army of the Potomac*. Baton Rouge: Louisiana State University Press, 1962.
Meade, George. *The Life and Letters of George Gordon Meade*. 2 vols. New York: Charles Scribner's Sons, 1913.
Pennypacker, Isaac R. *General Meade*. New York: D. Appleton, 1901.

WARREN W. HASSLER, JR.

MILES, Nelson Appleton (b. near Westminster, Mass., August 8, 1839; d. Washington, D.C., May 15, 1925), Army officer. Miles was one of the Army's premier Indian-fighters and the last commanding general of the Army (1895–1903).

Born to an established farming family in Massachusetts, Nelson Miles learned his letters and numbers at a nearby academy. He then went to Boston seeking a job and more schooling. Miles clerked in a crockery store and took classes at night to supplement his education. In 1860 he concluded that a civil war was likely and sought instruction from a retired French Army officer. After the firing on Fort Sumter, he borrowed money to raise a company of volunteers, but only gained a lieutenancy in the 22d Massachusetts Volunteer Infantry Regiment.

Miles fell to his military duties with an ardor that impressed senior officers. He became aide de camp to Brigadier General Oliver Otis Howard and served on Howard's staff during the Peninsula Campaign with the Army of the Potomac under General George Brinton McClellan.* Miles was wounded at the Battle of Seven Pines. Subsequently, his rise up the ranks was rapid: lieutenant colonel of the 61st New York Volunteer Infantry at the Battle of Antietam (September 1862); colonel of the 61st New York at Fredericksburg (December 1862), where he was shot through the throat and praised in dispatches by his division commander, Major General Winfield Scott Hancock. Severely wounded at Chancellorsville, Miles had to miss the Battle of Gettysburg. Promoted to brigadier general of volunteers (May 1864), he led a brigade and fought in the major actions from the Wilderness to Appomattox, earning his brevet as major general for actions at the Battle of Reams' Station (August 1864).

On the strength of his record, Miles sought a commission in the Regular Army. Meanwhile, he was given the controversial task of guarding Jefferson Davis. He ordered that Davis be manacled in a dank cell at Fortress Monroe, Virginia. Miles was made colonel of the newly created 40th Infantry Regiment of black troops stationed in North Carolina. He evidently did not care either for an assignment with black troops or Reconstruction duty. In 1868 he wed Mary Sherman, niece of General William Tecumseh Sherman* and U.S. Senator John Sherman of Ohio, thus linking himself to one of the nation's influential families. In 1869 Miles obtained a transfer to the 5th Infantry and began his service in the Trans-Mississippi.

From 1869 to 1890, Miles led soldiers against the major Western tribes and built a reputation as America's most successful Indian-fighting Army officer. Under the strategic direction of Major General Philip Henry Sheridan,* he led one of four columns in the Red River War (1874–1875) against the Comanche, Kiowa, and Southern Cheyenne in Texas and Indian Territory (Oklahoma). Following the defeat of Lieutenant Colonel George Armstrong Custer* (1876), Miles commanded one of the columns that forced the Sioux and Northern Cheyenne into Canada or onto reservations. In 1877 he got the credit for defeating the Nez Perce under Looking Glass and Chief Joseph, although General Howard, his old mentor, arrived on the field before the tribe surrendered. Meanwhile, in the Department of Arizona, Major General George Crook* had been unable to defeat the Apaches. In 1886 Sheridan relieved Crook and posted Miles to Arizona. Miles defeated the Apaches and captured their charismatic leader Geronimo. Miles was promoted to brigadier general (1880) and major general (1890).

He was in command of the Military Division of the Missouri for the denouement of the Indian Wars—the tragedy at Wounded Knee (1890), where the Sioux, inspired by the Ghost Dance and their legendary leader Sitting Bull, appeared on the verge of taking the warpath. Following an argument over a demand that the Indians surrender all weapons, the Army killed more than two hundred "hostiles"—including women and children.

In 1895, as the senior major general and upon the retirement of John McAllister Schofield, Miles inherited the title and office of commanding general of the Army. Ulysses Simpson Grant* (1865–1869), Sherman (1869–1883), and Sheridan (1883–1888) had previously held the office, and all had found it difficult to function in a command with an ill-defined role vis-à-vis the Army bureau chiefs. Schofield had contented himself with giving advice to the secretary of war and the president. Miles wanted to make the postion one of genuine leadership rather than a ceremonial sinecure. For three years Miles thrashed about in official Washington, dealing abruptly with bureau chiefs who jealously guarded their independence. Matters were made worse by Miles' intense dislike for Secretary of War Russell Alexander Alger. At the outbreak of war with Spain in 1898, Miles was fit, trim, and in very good health, quite capable of acting as either the senior field commander or a top presidential advisor and coordinator of Army training, assignments, and campaign plans, something analogous to a chief of staff. Miles wanted both and got neither. Because of personality conflicts with President William McKinley and Secretary Alger, Miles' effectiveness decreased steadily. The command of the field army in Cuba went to Major General William Rufus Shafter.* McKinley and Alger allowed Miles to plan and lead the successful invasion of the Spanish colony of Puerto Rico (July-August 1898).

After the Spanish war, apparently as a prelude to entering politics, Miles caused a controversy by accusing the War Department of supplying poisoned beef to the Army. He also criticized McKinley's policy of suppressing the Philippine *insurrectos*. Furthermore, Miles disagreed with plans proposed by Secretary of War Elihu Root to reorganize the American Army and create the position of chief of staff. President Theodore Roosevelt* was pleased to force Miles to retire in 1903 at the mandatory retirement age of sixty-four.

During his long retirement, Miles lived uneventfully in Washington, D.C. The general wrote two volumes of memoirs. He died in 1925.

Nelson Miles had a lengthy, distinguished, and controversial career. Commissioned to serve the Union in 1861, he rose from volunteer lieutenant to brevet major general, and subsequently fought against the major Western Indian tribes. He was awarded the Medal of Honor in 1892 for his Civil War exploits and became commanding general of the Army—all very heady for a former crockery clerk.

Miles' reputation rests on his record of accomplishment in the West. Miles developed into an outstanding regimental and independent field force commander. He earned a reputation as a vain, egotistical, ambitious, hard-driving, knowledgeable, skilled, determined, and aggressive officer. He got results. Although he joined the critics—including Sheridan—who disparaged Crook's use of Indians of one tribe to fight their own tribesmen, Miles often used scouts and auxiliaries, especially when he directed the campaign against the Apaches. Miles took pride in trimming his uniform with bear fur (which earned him the sobriquet "Old Bear Coat"), experimenting with the heliograph in the Southwest, and increasing the mobility of his infantrymen by mounting them on captured Indian horses. Miles followed Sheridan's example of destroying captured supplies and ponies to deprive the tribes of their logistic support. Miles deserves recognition for aggressively pursuing the Sioux and Nez Perce, but his victory over the Apaches was gained by use of false flags of truce and made absolute by exiling entire bands to prisons in Alabama and Florida. Grateful politicians pointed out that the removal of the Apaches opened up the Arizona Territory to settlement.

Unlike other prominent American military leaders, Miles did not crown his career with high elective office. His argumentative and sometimes offensive relations with Presidents McKinley and Roosevelt and Secretaries of War Alger and Root spoiled the end of his career. In 1899 Miles' public condemnation of the supply of tinned beef to the army by Secretary Alger and Commissary General Charles P. Eagan resulted in a great scandal and Eagan's and Alger's resignations, but no favorable results for Miles. If Miles had expected to gain the nomination of the Democratic party in 1900, he had badly miscalculated. The "embalmed beef" controversy poisoned the waters between the commanding general and the civilian administration, although McKinley did agree to approve Miles' promotion to lieutenant general in 1901.

Elihu Root replaced Alger in 1899 and designed a plan to revamp the U.S. Army along the lines of the German model. Initially, Root expected Miles to be the first chief of staff under the new system, but Miles, a stickler for tradition and apparently believing that the change was intended to degrade him, bitterly criticized the plan in public congressional hearings. General Schofield, Major General Wesley Merritt, and other officers favored the plan, which would give the chief of staff responsibility to supervise and coordinate the bureaus and field commands under the authority of the secretary of war. Rather than a step down, as Miles saw it, the position of chief of staff later became one of considerable power.

In his last months of active duty, Miles found other ways to aggravate the administration. He needlessly took the side of Admiral Winfield Scott Schley* against Admiral William Thomas Sampson* in their argument over each other's role in the Battle of Santiago. Miles deserved President Roosevelt's official and public censure for making statements detrimental to good conduct and discipline in the services. Furthermore, Miles used an inspection trip through Hawaii, Guam, and the Philippines to publicly condemn the Army's alleged mistreatment of Filipino prisoners and to meet with an *insurrecto* leader. These inopportune acts led Roosevelt to mark Miles' retirement with only a cold and pro forma announcement.

Miles' argumentativeness and use of newspapermen to promote his own image detracted from his contributions during the Spanish war. Among these were his calling attention to the dangers of a premature campaign into Cuba; recommending the need for strengthening Merritt's forces bound for the Philippines; inspecting the training camps in the United States, the port of embarkation at Tampa, Florida, and the frontline positions in Cuba; and masterminding the capture of Puerto Rico before the end of the war. Unfortunately, Miles could not let anyone, be it the secretary of war, the president, or a naval board of inquiry, have the last word if he disagreed with them. Miles was definitely a general of the nineteenth century and would have been completely out of his element trying to act as a coalition commander or senior officer of the American Expeditionary Force in a total war such as World War I.

BIBLIOGRAPHY

Cosmas, Graham A. *An Army for Empire: The United States Army in the Spanish-American War*. Columbia: University of Missouri Press, 1971.
Johnson, Virginia W. *The Unregimented General: A Biography of Nelson A. Miles*. Boston: Houghton Mifflin Company, 1962.
Miles, Nelson A. *Personal Recollections and Observations*. Chicago: Werner and Company, 1896.
———. *Serving the Republic*. New York: Harper, 1911.
Ranson, Edward. "Nelson A. Miles as Commanding General, 1896–1903." *Military Affairs* 29 (Winter 1965–1966): 179–200.
Utley, Robert M. *Frontier Regulars: The United States Army and the Indian, 1866–1890*. New York: Macmillan Company, 1973.

JOSEPH G. DAWSON III

MITCHELL, William (b. Nice, France, December 28, 1879; d. New York City, N.Y., February 19, 1936), U.S. Army officer and pilot. Mitchell was the first major publicist of air power in the United States and a founder of the U.S. Air Force.

William ("Billy") Mitchell, an eighteen-year-old scion of a politically active and once wealthy family in Wisconsin, quickly became a second lieutenant in the Signal Corps of the U.S. Army at the outbreak of the war with Spain in 1898. He was commissioned six weeks after he dropped out of Columbian College (later George Washington University) to enlist in a volunteer regiment. He would not complete his degree work at George Washington until 1919, because the challenges of occupation duty in Cuba and combat service in the Philippines stirred him to accept a career commission in 1901 as a first lieutenant in the Signal Corps. By 1904, Mitchell was a captain.

Assignments to communications work and two years of study (1907–1909) at the Army's School of the Line and its Staff College absorbed his time until 1912. In the next year, a prestigious appointment to the General Staff put him in recurring contact with aeronautics, one of the emerging missions of the Signal Corps. In 1916 Mitchell left the General Staff to direct Army aviation until Lieutenant Colonel George Owen Squier could take charge. Internal squabbles in Army aviation, its failure in Mexico, and the deteriorating international situation were opening new opportunities in aeronautics for officers such as Mitchell. Now a major, he became Squier's deputy, and, at his own expense, he learned to fly in his off-duty hours at a civilian flying school.

The relationship between Squier and Mitchell did not go well. In January 1917 Squier supported Mitchell's transfer to France as an observer. Mitchell reached Paris four days after the United States entered the world war, unsuccessfully tried to take charge of American aeronautical planning in Europe, qualified himself to wear the wings of a U.S. Army pilot, and intensively studied the employment of aviation on the Western Front. After his rival, Brigadier General Benjamin Delahaub Foulois, conceded Mitchell's tactical knowledge and made way for him, he assumed direction, as a colonel, of American Expeditionary Force (AEF) aviation at the front.

Under Mitchell, American airmen enjoyed marked success in supporting the AEF ground forces, most dramatically in striving for a massive use of air power at the Battle of St. Mihiel. When the war ended, Mitchell was a heavily decorated brigadier general, firmly established as the senior American air combat leader.

This wartime success put Mitchell at the head of a group of AEF fliers who campaigned through the press and in Congress for an air force on the model of Britain's Royal Air Force, independent from the Army and Royal Navy. He was undaunted when a separate service was denied the American airmen in 1920. As the assistant chief of the Army Air Service in Washington, D.C., he perceived that the coming of air power had thrown into question the role of a U.S. Navy built around the battleship as the nation's first line of defense. The sinking by Mitchell and his aircrews of the former German battleship *Ostfriesland* in the bombing tests of July 1921 brought him to the peak of his standing with the American people, but no organizational changes resulted.

His superior, Major General Mason Matthews Patrick, tried to keep Mitchell out of further controversy by sending him on temporary assignments away from Washington. In 1924, with the inadequately funded Army air arm deteriorating and his personal commitment to build an air force that would be his monument unflagging, he launched a strident publicity campaign. After voicing exaggerated claims that damaged his credibility in Congress, he lost his Air Service post with its rank as a brigadier general and was transferred to San Antonio, Texas, in March 1925.

His intransigence worsened, and in September 1925 Mitchell deliberately invited a court–martial to focus public attention on his views. He publicly condemned the Navy and War departments for "almost treasonable" neglect of national defense. President Calvin Coolidge gave Mitchell his court-martial, but defused the associated issues with a comprehensive and speedy report from a board of leaders in American aviation, chaired by Dwight Morrow. The seemingly inevitable finding of "guilty" by Mitchell's judges and his sentence, modified by Coolidge to five years' suspension from the Army at half-pay, left him no choice but to resign from the service.

From his Virginia estate, Mitchell renewed his publicity campaigns, publishing some one hundred magazine and newspaper articles and two of his five books in the next decade. His central theme was America's increasing vulnerability to the onset of the air age. Future wars would be decided by strategic bombing attacks on a nation's vital centers, or its material and psychological means of resistance. He anticipated the resurgence of German militarism and believed a war between the United States and Japan was certain. The war would begin with a destructive air attack against an ineffectively defended Hawaiian Islands and could be best deterred by the threat of American bombardment of Japan's highly inflammable cities.

These ideas, Mitchell argued, demanded a reorganization of the nation's military system with a department of defense supervising the activities of coequal land, sea, and air services. He sought a prominent place in such a reorganization through his family ties with the Democratic party. The election of Franklin D. Roosevelt in 1932 raised his hopes, but he soon antagonized the president. The downturn in his fortunes accelerated when the public, beset by worries about the Depression, no longer seemed interested in his ideas. As disappointing as these setbacks must have been, Mitchell still persisted in his uncompromising attitudes until he suddenly died at only fifty-six years of age from influenza complicated by heart trouble.

Mitchell was not an original thinker; his military theories owed much to the ideas of his colleagues in the various Army air operations and those of his associates in the international community of airmen he joined in France during World War I. Rather, his contribution came through his imaginative trail blazing in preparing the American people to understand the implications of those ideas for national security.

His impact on the U.S. military services was far reaching. His leadership assured the Army of sufficient air protection in France in World War I to fight the German ground forces without serious hindrance from their own more experienced air force. The Navy moved more quickly into the air age to find answers to the questions he raised. His combat success in France, earned under extremely difficult circumstances, set an inspiring precedent for American airmen in subsequent wars and was an indispensable dimension to the self-image of the future U.S. Air Force. However many his shortcomings, Mitchell's leadership in the immediate postwar years gave his followers, such as Henry Harley Arnold* and Carl Andrew Spaatz,* a sense of purpose that helped to sustain them until they had attained key appointments just before World War II. Central to that sense of purpose were the ideas that Mitchell identified for them, ideas whose realization he spurred. Those ideas included the global potential of air power; its application to the defense of the United States and its territories, especially those in the Pacific region; the possibilities of strategic bombardment; and the necessity for an air force, a full partner to the Army and the Navy in a department of defense.

In 1946 Congress recognized the realization of nearly all those ideas and Mitchell's other contributions by voting him a special posthumous medal for his "outstanding pioneer service and foresight in the field of American military aviation."

BIBLIOGRAPHY

Davis, Burke. *The Billy Mitchell Affair*. New York: Random House, 1967.
Devine, Isaac Don. *Mitchell, Pioneer of Air Power*. Revised. New York: Duell, Sloan and Pearce, 1958.
Hurley, Alfred F. *Billy Mitchell: Crusader for Air Power*. New ed. Bloomington: Indiana University Press, 1975.
Mitchell, Ruth. *My Brother Bill*. New York: Harcourt Brace, 1953.

ALFRED F. HURLEY

MITSCHER, Marc Andrew (b. Hillsboro, Wisc., January 26, 1887; d. Norfolk, Va., February 3, 1947), naval officer. Mitscher is regarded as one of the premier leaders of American aircraft carriers during World War II.

Raised in Washington, D.C., Mitscher was appointed to the Naval Academy from Oklahoma, where his father had been an Indian agent. Marc was nicknamed "Oklahoma Pete"—later shortened to "Pete"—for his wild antics which got him into disciplinary difficulties. An average student, he graduated 108th in his 1910 class of 131 midshipmen.

Reporting to the Pacific Fleet, he served aboard two armored cruisers. Mitscher moved to the Caribbean in 1912 for consecutive service in the gunboats *Vicksburg* and *Annapolis*, and the armored cruiser *California* (renamed *San Diego*), and he participated in the Vera Cruz incident of 1914. After brief duty on two destroyers, he reported for aviation training aboard the armored cruiser *North Carolina* at Pensacola, Florida, in October 1915.

Upon graduation as Naval Aviator No. 33 in June 1916, Lieutenant, junior grade, Mitscher received advanced flight training at Pensacola, including balloon and catapult experiments aboard the armored cruiser *Huntington*, in which he sailed on convoy duty during the summer of 1917. His subsequent World War I service took place at three naval air stations, Montauk Point and Rockaway on Long Island and Miami, Florida, in command of the latter two. In early 1919 he joined the aviation section in the Office of the Chief of Naval Operations and participated in the trans-Atlantic flights of the NC flying boats. His NC–1, of which he was a pilot, came down short of the Azores, but the achievement of going even that far earned him the Navy Cross.

Mitscher's considerable skills as a pilot then took him to the Pacific Fleet aircraft tender *Aroostook* at San Diego where he also commanded the naval air station (1919–1922); to the Anacostia Naval Air Station, as station commander;

and the plans division of the Bureau of Aeronautics, during which duty he led Navy teams in the International Air Races at Detroit (1922) and St. Louis (1923). Transferred to the Navy's first aircraft carrier, *Langley*, in 1926, he helped to fit out and head the air department of the carrier *Saratoga* (1926–1929). He served as executive officer in the *Langley* (1929–1930) and the *Saratoga* (1934–1935). He landed the first airplane on the *Saratoga* in June 1928.

A leader in the Navy's growing air arm, Commander Mitscher returned to the Aeronautics Bureau (1930–1933) and then to the West Coast as chief of staff to Rear Admiral A. W. Johnson, Base Force air commander. Mitscher commanded the aircraft tender *Wright* (1937–1938) after another tour of duty at the Aeronautics Bureau and then led Patrol Wing 1 at San Diego in the rank of captain. He was assistant chief of the Aeronautics Bureau (June 1939–July 1941), at which time he reported to Newport News, Virginia, as prospective commanding officer of the new carrier *Hornet*, commissioned in October 1941.

In the Atlantic when war with Japan broke out, Captain Mitscher took the *Hornet* into the Pacific to launch Army bombers under the command of Lieutenant Colonel James Harold "Jimmy" Doolittle against Tokyo, which he did successfully in April 1942. Two months later he brilliantly led his ship in the Battle of Midway, where his planes helped to sink four Japanese carriers. Selected for rear admiral the previous December, Mitscher assumed that rank in July as commander, Patrol Wing 2 in Hawaii, shifting in December to Nouméa in the South Pacific, to command Fleet Air in the Guadalcanal Campaign. In April 1943 he commanded Allied air forces in the Solomon Islands Campaign until August, when he took over Fleet Air on the West Coast of the United States.

Rear Admiral Mitscher took command of the Fast Carrier Task Force, Pacific Fleet (Task Force 58), in January 1944 and covered the landings in the Marshall Islands, going on to destroy Japanese naval air forces at Truk in the Caroline Islands and in the Marianas Islands during February, his flag aboard the new carrier *Yorktown*. Promoted to vice admiral in March, he raided the Palau Islands, then supported the landings at Hollandia, New Guinea, and struck Truk again in April. While covering the landings in the Marianas in June, his force defeated the Japanese Fleet in the Battle of the Philippine Sea. His flag was in the new *Lexington*, which he commanded during additional operations in the Marianas and strikes on the Bonin Islands.

Redesignated commander of the 1st Fast Carrier Task Force and Task Force 38 in August 1944, Vice Admiral Mitscher participated in the Philippine Campaign through November, including the battle for Leyte Gulf. His task force (58) covered the Iwo Jima and Okinawa landings between January and May 1945, his planes striking the Japanese homeland and sinking the superbattleship *Yamato*. In battling the deadly kamikazes, Mitscher received damage to his flagships, the carriers *Bunker Hill* and *Enterprise*, and ended up on the carrier *Randolph*.

In July 1945 he reported as deputy chief of naval operations for air in Washington, D.C, where he remained until early the next year. Promoted to the four star rank of admiral in March 1946, Admiral Mitscher spent the rest of his career in the Atlantic. He commanded the Eighth Fleet until September 1946. He died of a heart attack while serving as commander in chief of the Atlantic Fleet.

Mitscher knew no equal in the wartime Pacific Fleet for the respect and love of his men. That he was the complete professional and a fearless leader in battle accounted for part of their loyalty, but an added factor was his well-known, extraordinary efforts to save the lives of his airmen when they were in trouble. The most notable of his lifesaving efforts occurred on the night of June 20, 1944. His pilots, most of whom were inexperienced in night landings, were returning, exhausted and low on fuel with damaged aircraft, after their distant strike against the Japanese fleet. Mitscher ordered that all ships' lights be illuminated so that the pilots could see the flight decks.

A small, slight man, Mitscher spoke in low, barely audible tones and with a strict economy of words. Superbly calm in battle, he nurtured a quiet sense of humor while developing revolutionary carrier tactics before and in the midst of combat. He avoided publicity throughout his career, preferring to let his actions speak for themselves. Prematurely bald since his twenties, save for a thin wisp of light hair, the clear complexion of his youth had turned leathery from years in the open-air cockpits of the Navy's early planes and on the bridges of carriers. Three aircraft crashes had not interrupted his career, but the grueling round-the-clock battles of 1945 took their toll on his health. In all likelihood, he suffered a mild heart attack during that spring, but simply stayed in his sea cabin while his staff continued the fight under the able direction of his chief of staff, Arleigh Albert Burke.*

No officer ever questioned Mitscher's judgment (nor has any historian for that matter), except for Admiral Raymond Ames Spruance* when he rejected Mitscher's plea to attack the enemy fleet earlier in the Marianas operation—which led to a controversy in which Mitscher himself absolutely refused to participate. He was happiest—and most successful—when operating at sea as an independent tactical commander. At the helm of Task Force 58/38, "Pete" Mitscher molded the Fast Carrier Task Force into the most deadly naval force in history to that time which destroyed the Japanese fleet and left the carrier arm as the nucleus of the U.S. Navy for the ensuing generation.

BIBLIOGRAPHY

Deurs, George van. *Wings for the Fleet*. Annapolis, Md.: Naval Institute Press, 1966.
Morison, Samuel Eliot. *New Guinea and the Marianas*. Boston: Little, Brown and Company, 1957.
Reynolds, Clark G. *The Fast Carriers: The Forging of an Air Navy*. Rev. ed. Huntington, N.Y.: Robert Krieger, 1978.

Smith, Richard K. *First Across! The U.S. Navy's Transatlantic Flight of 1919*. Annapolis, Md.: Naval Institute Press, 1973.

Taylor, Theodore. *The Magnificent Mitscher*. New York: W. W. Norton, 1954.

CLARK G. REYNOLDS

MORGAN, Daniel (b. probably in New Jersey, likely 1735; d. Winchester, Va., July 6, 1802), general in the War of American Independence.

Daniel Morgan, who always avoided any discussion of his early life, was a product of the Virginia frontier where he settled in 1753. A teamster with the Braddock Expedition in 1755, later, in the French and Indian War, he served in the Virginia rangers and suffered a wound in a now-unknown skirmish. As a militia officer, he also fought Indians in Lord Dunmore's War in 1774.

In 1775, the forty-year-old Morgan, a veteran frontier fighter, raised one of the companies of backwoods riflemen called for by the Continental Congress. After joining George Washington's* American Army at Cambridge, Massachusetts, Morgan and his company were included in Benedict Arnold's* expedition against British Canada. After an arduous march through the Maine wilderness, Arnold was wounded in the American attack on the city of Quebec, and Morgan took command, but eventually he and his men were captured.

Released from captivity the following year, Morgan received a promotion to colonel and gained from Washington a special corps of light infantry composed of picked Continentals from the western counties of Pennsylvania, Maryland, and Virginia. They were officially known as the Rangers but were more commonly called Morgan's Riflemen, a unit that put together a splendid combat record during its brief existence.

Morgan's rifle regiment played a crucial role in the campaign of 1777, especially after it was detached from Washington's immediate command in New Jersey and sent to upstate New York, where General Horatio Gates'* American Northern army was feebly contesting the southward advance from Canada of British General John Burgoyne. Morgan's frontiersman, dressed in hunting garb and skilled in Indian tactics, so terrorized Burgoyne's redskinned allies that they refused to continue their scouting activities. In the two major battles of the Saratoga Campaign, September 19 and October 7, 1777, Morgan's men pushed forward from Gates' entrenchments and began the action. They helped to throw the British off stride, and they took a heavy toll of the enemy, just as they subsequently led the American advance after the retreating Burgoyne, who later acknowledged the large part Morgan had played in his defeat and surrender.

A strong admirer of Washington, Morgan in the winter of 1777–1778 at Valley Forge spoke out angrily against the critics of the commander in chief, though it is doubtful whether Morgan and like-minded officers were correct in their view that a plot existed to remove Washington in the so-called Conway Cabal. By 1780, however, Morgan's relationship with Washington was strained. Most of Morgan's best rifle companies had been detached for Indian fighting, and afterward his regiment was disbanded. Disappointed because a new, large light infantry unit had been assigned to Anthony Wayne,* and because his promotion to brigadier general was not forthcoming, Morgan took his case to Congress. Although the lawmakers agreed that Morgan had been "Neglected," they felt that nothing could be done for him at the time. Contrary to what some historians have written, Morgan did not resign, accepting instead an "honorable furlough" until a promising assignment opened.

Ever loyal to the cause but nonetheless deeply disturbed, Morgan returned to his home near Winchester, Virginia, where he remained until the summer of 1780. Then he responded to a call from his Virginia neighbor and former commander, Horatio Gates,* now in charge of the American Southern army. Though in ill-health, he joined Gates in North Carolina, soon after Gates' defeat at Camden.

Morgan, now belatedly promoted to brigadier general, assisted Gates in reorganizing the Southern forces, but Gates was soon replaced by General Nathanael Greene,* who recognized that Morgan's talents lay in guerrilla warfare. Moreover, Greene lacked the resources to contest openly with his adversary, British General Cornwallis. Consequently, Greene divided his small command at Charlotte, North Carolina, sending Morgan into western South Carolina while Greene himself moved in a southeasterly direction. Morgan's success at arousing the country people prompted Cornwallis to send Banastre Tarleton's Tory Legion against the veteran frontiersman.

Morgan, falling back toward the border of the Carolinas, made a stand against Tarleton at the Cowpens on January 17, 1781. The location was an open slope with no protection for his flanks, and most of Morgan's men were militia, unaccustomed to formal combat. Even so, Morgan knew his troops, and he was a superb psychologist. Morgan's militia, placed in a long row in front of his regulars, were skilled marksmen who picked off many of Tarleton's men before filing off behind the regulars, according to Morgan's plan. Then, during the heavy exchange between Morgan's regulars and the Legion, Morgan hit the British flanks with his cavalry and reformed militia. The result was a double envelopment of the enemy, who immediately panicked and collapsed. Cowpens was the tactical masterpiece of the war. As Morgan said, he had "entirely Broke up Tarleton's Legion," the "flower" of Cornwallis' army.

After Morgan retreated into North Carolina and reunited with Greene, the American generals, with Cornwallis in close pursuit, retreated into Virginia. His health impaired by the arduous campaign, Morgan returned home and saw only limited service during the remainder of the war.

A farmer and grist mill operator in the postwar years, Morgan in the 1790s returned to public life. He commanded the militia forces that garrisoned Pittsburgh following the collapse of the Whiskey Rebellion in 1794, and he served one term as a Federalist member of the U.S House of Representatives. Convinced that the Jeffersonians were subverting the Constitution, "the envy and wonder of the surrounding world," the stormy old soldier once threatened to call out his Virginia militiamen against the Republicans, whom he denounced as egg-sucking chickens. Advancing age and crippling arthritis confined him to home during his final years.

Although Morgan was not a professional soldier in the modern sense, his life was bound up with things military, from his service in the colonial wars, through the War of Independence, and concluding with a lengthy, postwar career as a major general of Virginia militia, which included a campaign against the Whiskey Rebels. Moreover, though ill-educated, Morgan thought of himself as a military expert, as the Continental Army's leading authority on guerrilla or partisan tactics. His accumulative success with irregular tactics exceeded that of any other American leader, although Wayne, Andrew Pickens, Thomas Sumter, and Francis Marion* also scored achievements with mobile, detached forces.

A splendid leader of men, Morgan—"the old wagoner"—was a warm, colorful leader who cared about his soldiers, and they in return responded to him, as, for example, when he persuaded untried militia to stand and fight at Cowpens. A contemporary correctly wrote of Morgan that no other officer "knew better how to gain the love and esteem of his men." His troops were mainly from frontier regions, where the rifle—with its great range and accuracy—was the preeminent weapon in hunting and Indian-fighting. Morgan, to be sure, would have been out of his element as a military administrator or as the commander of a division or an entire army. Fortunately for him, he was never assigned a post that exceeded his training or talents as were Israel Putnam, Benjamin Lincoln, and any number of other American Revolutionary generals.

Finally, Morgan's advance through the ranks, from humble beginnings to general officer, was unique by the standards of the eighteenth century when, especially in Europe, men of gentle birth and fortune dominated the officer corps. The American Revolution produced a democratic spirit in the land. Morgan, the outstanding combat officer in the Continental Army, symbolized that new day in America.

BIBLIOGRAPHY

Bass, Robert D. *The Green Dragoon: The Lives of Banastre Tarleton and Mary Robinson.* New York: Holt, 1957.

Callahan, North. *Daniel Morgan, Ranger of the Revolution.* New York: Holt, Rinehart and Winston, 1961.

Graham, James. *Life of General Daniel Morgan.* Cincinnati: Derby and Jackson, 1856.

Hart, Freeman H. *The Valley of Virginia in the American Revolution.* Chapel Hill: University of North Carolina Press, 1942.

Higginbotham, Don. *Daniel Morgan: Revolutionary Rifleman.* Chapel Hill: University of North Carolina Press, 1961.

R. DON HIGGINBOTHAM

NIMITZ, Chester William (b. Fredericksburg, Tex., February 24, 1885; d. San Francisco, Calif., February 20, 1966), naval officer. Nimitz served in World War II as commander in chief, Pacific Fleet and Pacific Ocean Areas.

Karl Heinrich Nimitz was one of a group of German immigrants who arrived in Texas in 1846 and founded the town of Fredericksburg. His son Chester Bernard married Anna Henke, the local butcher's daughter. Five months later Anna was a widow and pregnant. The following February she gave birth to Chester William, the future fleet admiral. When Chester was five years old, Anna married his Uncle William, her late husband's younger brother, and the family moved to nearby Kerrville to manage a small hotel.

As he neared the end of his high school career, Chester, desiring further education but lacking the means, applied for an appointment to West Point. None being available, he gladly accepted an appointment to the U.S. Naval Academy and easily passed the entrance examination. Graduating in 1905, he stood seventh in overall achievement in a class of 114.

With the rank of passed midshipman, Nimitz was ordered to duty in the battleship *Ohio*, then the flagship of the U.S. Asiatic Fleet. In 1907, having passed the required examination, he was commissioned ensign and given command of a gunboat, in which he roved the Philippines. A war scare that year brought a number of laid-up warships back into service. Nimitz was ordered to Manila to get the destroyer *Decatur* back into commission and take command of her, an unprecedented responsibility for a twenty-two-year-old ensign. One night in mid-1908, Ensign Nimitz ran the *Decatur* aground, for which he was court-martialed and publicly reprimanded.

Here was a situation that could have ruined a young officer's career, but so flawless was Nimitz's record otherwise that within a few months he was promoted to lieutenant, completely skipping the rank of lieutenant, junior grade. Back in the United States he commanded a series of submarines and made himself an authority on diesel engines. At age twenty-six he became commander of a submarine division, and the following year he addressed the Naval War College on the subject of submarines. During this period, he married Catherine Freeman, who bore him a son and three daughters.

Sent to Europe by the Navy to study diesel engines, he returned to the United States and at the New York Navy Yard superintended the construction of diesel engines in the new oiler *Maumee*, of which he became executive officer and chief engineer. With her commanding officer he invented the system of underway refueling. Upon the entry of the United States into World War I, the *Maumee* proceeded to the mid-Atlantic to refuel U.S. warships en route to Europe.

Promoted to lieutenant commander, Nimitz in August 1917 reported as engineering aide to commander, Submarine Force, Atlantic Fleet, a duty that took him to the Mediterranean and the British Isles. Following the war, he served as senior member, Board of Submarine Design, and then executive officer of the battleship *South Carolina*. In 1920–1922 Nimitz met one of the most formidable challenges of his career by superintending the construction of the submarine base at Pearl Harbor, built mostly with salvaged war materials that he had collected, often without permission, from East Coast shipyards.

In 1922–1923 Nimitz was a student at the Naval War College at Newport, Rhode Island. Then, as tactical officer of the battle fleet, he introduced the circular formation, recently invented at the War College, and was instrumental in integrating the Navy's lone carrier, the *Langley*, into fleet maneuvers.

In 1926 Commander Nimitz was one of six naval officers selected to establish in American universities the first units of the Naval Reserve Officers' Training Corps. He set up, administered, and taught classes in the unit at the University of California at Berkeley. From 1933 to 1935 Captain Nimitz was commanding officer of the cruiser *Augusta*, flagship of the U.S. Asiatic Fleet. The following two years he served in the Navy Department as assistant to the chief of the Bureau of Navigation—as the Bureau of Naval Personnel was called until World War II. Then, attaining the rank of rear admiral, he went to sea again and briefly commanded Battleship Division One with his flag in the battleship *Arizona*. In mid-1939, back in Washington, Nimitz was chief of the Bureau of Navigation, training sailors and assigning them to duty in a navy expanding rapidly under threat of war.

Following the Japanese attack on Pearl Harbor, President Franklin D. Roosevelt relieved Admiral Husband Edward Kimmel* of command of the Pacific Fleet and appointed Nimitz to the post. On the last day of 1941, Nimitz became an admiral in assuming his duties as commander in chief, Pacific Fleet, which, because of the growing complexity of operations and communications, had become a land-based command. Nimitz made his headquarters at Pearl Harbor until 1945, when he transferred to Guam.

In March 1942 General Douglas MacArthur*, on presidential orders, flew from the Philippines to Australia, where he was given supreme command of the Southwest Pacific Area, which included Australia, New Guinea, the Philippines, and adjacent islands. At the same time Nimitz received an additional appointment as commander in chief, Pacific Ocean Areas, in which capacity he commanded all military and naval forces and operations, American and Allied, in the North, Central, and South Pacific Areas. He thus commanded the conquest of Guadalcanal and the drive across the Pacific via the Gilberts, the Marshalls, the Marianas, Iwo Jima, and Okinawa, and he commanded the Pacific Fleet at all times, even when it supported MacArthur's invasions of Hollandia and the Philippines.

Toward the end of 1944 Nimitz received his fifth star as fleet admiral. Following the defeat of Japan, at the surrender ceremony aboard the battleship *Missouri* in Tokyo Bay, September 2, 1945, Admiral Nimitz signed the instrument of surrender for the United States.

The following December, Fleet Admiral Nimitz began a two-year tour as chief of naval operations, succeeding Admiral Ernest Joseph King*. In 1949 Nimitz was engaged by the United Nations to supervise a plebiscite in Kashmir to decide whether it would join Pakistan or India. Prime Minister Nehru blocked the plebiscite, but Nimitz stayed with the United Nations until mid-1952, touring the United States and speaking as the United Nations good-will ambassador.

As fleet admiral, Nimitz theoretically remained on active duty the rest of his life, available for council to the Navy Department. In fact, however, he retired to "Longview," the home he had purchased in Berkeley, California. He refused many lucrative offers from business, preferring to maintain his image as naval commander and symbol of the Old Navy, but he did serve as a regent for the University of California.

Admiral Nimitz's fame, at least among the general public, derives almost exclusively from his command of the Pacific Fleet and Pacific Ocean Areas in World War II. In this capacity, as his biography notes, he "commanded thousands of ships and aircraft and millions of men, amounting to more military power than had been wielded by all the commanders in all previous wars." The British chiefs of staff left control of the Pacific War to the American Joint Chiefs of Staff, and these left operations in the Pacific Ocean Areas largely to Admiral Nimitz and to Admiral King, chief of naval operations and commander in chief of the U.S. Fleet. Nimitz and King, with their staffs, met at intervals in Washington, San Francisco, or Pearl Harbor to plan strategy. Thus, as area commander, Nimitz was not merely carrying out orders from above.

Besides the usual qualities of a successful commader in chief—leadership, judgment, organizational skill, ability to distinguish the essential from the trivial, decisiveness, and readiness to take calculated risks—Nimitz had other attributes that uniquely fitted him for his post. These included serenity, courtesy and consideration, unshakable integrity, and a rare perceptiveness in dealing with people. His famous serenity enabled him to think clearly and make the right decisions during the first four months of 1942, when it seemed that nothing could stop the Japanese advance; and during the Battle of Midway, when he could send out only three carriers and a few cruisers and destroyers to take on the whole Japanese Combined Fleet. All these qualities stood him in good stead in dealing with his fellow officers. Above him was the imperious, often caustic, Admiral King, who never hesitated to blast any officers, including Nimitz, when they failed to produce the results he expected. Below him were such stubborn, opinionated warriors as those whom the press aptly nicknamed "Bull" (William Frederick) Halsey, Jr.,* "Terrible" (Richmond Kelly) Turner, and "Howlin' Mad" (Holland McTyeire) Smith. On his own level was the brilliant but devious General MacArthur, who regarded Nimitz as his competitor for glory and strove to undermine his strategy. Nimitz treated all such officers with courtesy and fairness and with a calm command presence that won their respect and cooperation.

Admiral Nimitz was less well known to the public than were some of his subordinates, such as Admiral Halsey, or his fellow commanders in chief, Generals Dwight David Eisenhower* and MacArthur. His relative anonymity resulted in part from his shunning of publicity. But, in any case, he was not an attractive subject for journalism because there was nothing particularly striking about his appearance, his conduct, or his manner of expressing himself. He had no salient characteristics of appearance or personality. "He was," according to one observer, "impossible to caricature by word or line." Simplicity was his essence.

BIBLIOGRAPHY

Hoyt, Edwin P. *How They Won the War in the Pacific: Nimitz and His Admirals.* New York: Weybright and Talley, 1970.

Matloff, Maurice. *Strategic Planning for Coalition Warfare, 1943-1944.* Washington, D.C.: U.S. Government Printing Office, 1959.

———, and Edward M. Snell. *Strategic Planning for Coalition Warfare, 1941-1942.* Washington, D.C.: U.S. Government Printing Office, 1953.

Morison, Samuel Eliot. *History of United States Naval Operations in World War II.* 15 vols. Boston: Atlantic, Little, Brown, and Company, 1947-1962.

Morton, Louis. *Strategy and Command: The First Two Years.* Washington, D.C.: U.S. Government Printing Office, 1962.

Potter, E. B. *Nimitz.* Annapolis, Md.: Naval Institute Press, 1976.

E. B. POTTER

PATCH, Alexander McCarrell (b. Fort Huachuca, Ariz., November 23, 1889; d. San Antonio, Tex., November 21, 1945), lieutenant general, U.S. Army; organizer of the Americal Division; corps and Army commander.

Alexander M. Patch was the son of Captain Alexander M. Patch. Although he was born in Arizona, young Alexander was raised in Lebanon County, Pennsylvania. He attended St. Luke's Preparatory School near Philadelphia and one year at Lehigh University before entering the U.S. Military Academy at West Point in 1909. Graduating from the Academy in 1913, he was commissioned a second lieutenant of infantry.

Patch was promoted to first lieutenant on July 1, 1916, and served that year with the 18th Infantry Regiment on the Mexican border. He was promoted to captain on May 15, 1917, and was sent to France during World War I with the 18th Infantry Regiment, 1st Division. While overseas, he attended the British Machine Gun School in England and then commanded the Machine Gun Battalion of the 1st Division. From April to October 1918 he was director of the Army Machine Gun School in France.

Returning to the 18th Infantry, he served in France and Germany with the regiment until February 1919, when he was reassigned to the Training Section, General Headquarters, American Expeditionary Force. His final assignment was with the chief athletic officer, Headquarters District of Paris during April and May 1919.

During his service in France, Patch was promoted to major on January 5, 1918, and to lieutenant colonel on October 31, 1918. He participated in the Aisne-Marne, St. Mihiel, and Meuse-Argonne campaigns.

Upon his return to the United States, Patch served for short periods at Camp Benning, Georgia, and with the Reserve Officers Training Corps Section of the Committee on Education and Special Training, Washington, D.C. On March 15, 1920, he reverted to his permanent grade of captain but was promoted to major on July 1. In September he was reassigned as assistant professor of military science and tactics at Staunton Military Academy in Staunton, Virginia, remaining there until August 1924.

In June 1925 he was named the distinguished graduate of his class at the Command and General Staff College, Fort Leavenworth, Kansas. Following his graduation, Patch was assigned to Fort Eustis, Virginia, until August, when he returned to Staunton as professor of military science and tactics.

In August 1928 he was assigned to the 12th Infantry Regiment at Fort Washington, Maryland, where he remained until June 1931. He then became a student at the Army War College, graduated in June 1932, and returned once more to Staunton as professor of military science and tactics. While there, he was promoted on August 1, 1935, to lieutenant colonel.

In July 1936 he became a member of the Infantry Board, Fort Benning, Georgia, where he helped develop and test the three-regiment "triangular" division concept. He became an instructor of the Alabama National Guard in March 1939. The following August 6 Patch was promoted to the temporary grade of colonel and was given command of the 47th Infantry Regiment at Fort Bragg, North Carolina. In December he was ordered to training duty at that post.

Along with promotion to brigadier general, on August 4, 1941, Patch was assigned to command the Infantry Replacement Training Center, Camp Croft, South Carolina.

In early January 1942 he was summoned to Washington, D.C., and was told that he would take command of forces which were to be sent to New Caledonia, in the Pacific. His new command, designated Task Force 6814, included many units of the National Guard 26th and 33d Infantry Divisions which had been made surplus when those commands had reorganized into "triangular" divisions.

The Task Force sailed to the Pacific in late January. It was planned that General Patch should stay in Washington initially and then fly out to join the Task Force in Australia. However, he contracted pneumonia and did not join it until after the force had landed in New Caledonia in early March. He was promoted to the temporary grade of major general on March 10.

Other "surplus" commands joined the Task Force, until the War Department decided to form a division from these formations. Washington authorities suggested the division be named "Necal" (an early code word for the New Caledonia expedition). Patch suggested "Bush" Division. A private in one of the units offered "Americal"—American troops on New Caledonia. "Americal," it was, on May 27, 1942, and Major General Alexander M. Patch became its first commander. The newly formed division underwent intensive training under Patch's direction in order to prepare itself for active combat. He opened a special Officers' Candidate School in June so as to train and commission selected enlisted men from the division. Nearly 385 candidates were finally graduated from the course.

The Americal, under General Patch, relieved the 1st Marine Division on Guadalcanal on December 9, 1942. He was given command of all troops on the island. He was named commander of the XIV Corps, embracing troops on Guadalcanal and neighboring islands, in January 1943 and remained in this assignment until April, when he was recalled to the United States.

That spring, he took command of the IV Corps area, headquartered at Camp Young, California, where he subsequently directed the training of some one hundred thousand men. He was sent to Sicily in March 1944 to command the Seventh Army.

In July Patch moved to Italy with the Seventh and on August 15, this army, along with five French divisions, invaded southern France in Operation DRAGON. On August 18, Patch was promoted to the temporary rank of lieutenant general. The Seventh Army, under his command, advanced rapidly through France, contacting George Smith Patton, Jr.'s,* Third Army north of Dijon on September 11. Becoming part of the 6th Army Group, the Seventh advanced through the Vosges, Alsace, and seized Strasbourg in November. Patch's Seventh saw more hard fighting, as they defeated a heavy German attack in January 1945, closed the Colmar pocket in February, advanced through the Saar, was the first army to reach and cross the Rhine, captured Nuremberg and Munich, finally contacting General Mark Wayne Clarke's Fifth Army at the Brenner Pass on May 4.

Recalled to the United States in June, General Patch was given command of the Fourth Army at Fort Sam Houston, Texas, on July 7. Again, he was training troops, a task in which he was considered a master.

This assignment was short-lived, however, because in October he was named to a special group to study and recommend what the Army's postwar organization and strength should be. The recommendations made by this group were interesting, sometimes imaginative—and controversial. One recommendation was the establishment of a separate air force. The study was barely completed when General Patch contracted pneumonia. He died on November 21, 1945, and was buried in the National Cemetery, West Point, New York, on November 24.

General Patch's decorations included the Distinguished Service Medal with two oak leaf clusters and the French Order of a Commander of the Legion.

Lieutenant General Alexander M. Patch, known as "Sandy," was noted as a disciplinarian with a "temper like the devil before dawn." He was not without a sense of humor, however, for he was also known for his deadpan wit. Less flamboyant than some other generals, he did, nevertheless, wear a scarf, upon which the map of France had been printed when his army invaded that country.

General Lesley James McNair called Patch one of the finest corps commanders in the Army. General Dwight David Eisenhower* characterized him as "one of [America's] outstanding troop leaders." He seemed to have a special rapport with the troops he commanded. Although he was full of nervous energy, he was always mindful of his men and tried to spare them whenever possible. Perhaps he was influenced by his extensive knowledge of Rudyard Kipling's works. At any rate, he was able to chat easily with his men, often while rolling a cigarette from a sack of Bull Durham.

But perhaps the overriding characteristics of General Patch were his superior abilities as a leader and trainer of men. He alone was tasked with organizing and training a division overseas in World War II. The division he fathered—the Americal—earned many accolades later in the war. He alone was recalled to the United States twice during the war to take on the difficult, and vital, task of training large numbers of men for combat. He was one of the few senior officers who commanded large formations in both the Pacific and European theaters. From corps command in the Pacific, he rose to command the Seventh Army in Europe.

It is important to note that, in spite of the numerous reassignments he experienced during the war, he rose in rank and was, finally, entrusted with designing a formula for the postwar American Army.

His philosophy of leadership is aptly expressed in his article, which appeared in *Military Review*, December 1943, entitled "Some Thoughts on Leadership." The essence of this philosophy is that leadership is founded on character and that the greatest attributes of a leader are honesty, courage of purpose, and an unselfish attitude. Lieutenant General Alexander M. Patch epitomized these attributes in his own career.

BIBLIOGRAPHY

Cronin, Francis D. *Under the Southern Cross, The Saga of the Americal Division.* Washington, D.C.: Combat Forces Press, 1951.
Patch, Alexander M. "Some Thoughts on Leadership." *Military Review* 22, (December 1943).

UZAL W. ENT

PATTON, George Smith, Jr. (b. San Gabriel, Calif., November 11, 1885; d. Heidelberg, Germany, December 21, 1945), military commander. Patton, known for his relentlessly aggressive tactics, commanded the U.S. Third Army in World War II.

George Smith Patton, Jr., inherited a warrior's legacy from his father's family dating back to the American Revolution. His mother's family had amassed a considerable fortune in landholdings. Patton would love both war and the good life.

After attending Virginia Military Institute for one year, Patton won an appointment to the U.S. Military Academy. Because of a deficiency in mathematics, he graduated with the class of 1909, not 1908. He chose cavalry as his branch, serving at Fort Sheridan, Illinois, and Fort Myer, Virginia. In 1912 he became the first American to compete in the Olympics in the Modern Pentathlon, an event stressing horsemanship. In 1913 he went to the French Cavalry School to study saber methods and horsemanship. From 1913 to 1915 he attended and taught at the cavalry school at Fort Riley, Kansas. He next joined the 8th Cavalry at Fort Bliss and then Sierra Blanca, Texas. On March 13, 1916, he left the 8th

Cavalry to join the Punitive Expedition into Mexico as aide to General John Joseph Pershing.*

In Mexico Patton saw combat. He killed General Julio Cardenas and his orderly in a firefight. Promoted to captain on May 15, 1917, Patton again joined Pershing in the American Expeditionary Force. In November he became the first member of the Tank Corps and organized the first American tank training center at Langres, France. In August 1918 Patton saw combat as a tank commander. On September 23, during the Meuse-Argonne Offensive, he was wounded, receiving the Purple Heart and Distinguished Service Cross. He left Europe in 1919 as a colonel.

During the interwar years Patton lived well, but professionally he endured the consequences of being in an army reduced in size—he reverted to his rank of captain and did not achieve the rank of colonel again until 1938. He served in various units and attended the Army's advanced schools. He published more than a dozen articles in the *Cavalry Journal*.

As the Army prepared for World War II, Patton assumed greater responsibilities. In July 1940 he went to Fort Benning, Georgia, where he assumed command of the 2d Armored Brigade of the 2d Armored Division; then in April 1941 the division; and, in January 1942 the 1st Armored Corps. In March he organized the Desert Training Center near Indio, California. On the last day of July, he was ordered to Washington to prepare for the Invasion of Africa.

Patton entered combat in command of a thirty-two thousand man force landing on the west coast of Africa on November 8. In the wake of a near-disastrous battle at Kasserine Pass, General Dwight David Eisenhower* named Patton to rejuvenate the II Corps in March 1943. Within two weeks Patton transformed it into an effective unit. He received his third star and in mid-April was pulled out of combat to command the Seventh Army in the invasion of Sicily. He was to provide flank protection for the drive up the north coast to Messina by Montgomery's Eighth Army. Patton chafed at his role, and, from the moment he first went ashore on July 11, 1943, he assumed a more active role. Reacting to Montgomery's stalemate, he got permission to drive toward Palermo. Obtaining that goal on July 22, he wheeled east and captured Messina before the Eighth Army.

Patton's dash brought problems. His forces stalled at Troina for a time, and during this period, he slapped two soldiers in hospitals in separate incidents, contending that they were fit for combat. The controversy resulted in Patton's being left in Sicily in occupation duty, missing any role in the Italian Campaign and losing any possible chance to be the American ground commander in the cross channel invasion of Europe scheduled for mid-1944.

Patton's exile ended in January 1944 when he was brought to England. He went to France on July 6, 1944, a month after D-Day. He initially commanded a corps and then, on August 1, assumed command of the Third Army. Once the breakthrough was made at Avranches, Patton's forces exploited it. Within a week, much of Brittany had been reduced and the Third Army headed east across

France for the Lorraine and Saar campaigns, as prelude to driving up the Palatinate corridor and crossing the Rhine between Mainz and Mannheim. But the weather and heavy fortifications, especially at Metz, forced Patton to halt in late November at the Saar. While he prepared for a fresh offensive, the Germans on December 16 attacked in the Ardennes.

Patton correctly anticipated that his Third Army would shift from its Saar bridgehead to the Ardennes front. This wheeling of men and vehicles in winter was a crucial part in the relief of Bastogne and the defeat of the Germans in the Battle of the Bulge. He made Bastogne more important to the Germans by driving from it into the German flank, forcing the Germans to shift forces to meet that threat. By late January 1945 the Allies returned to the offensive. Patton's role was to be active defense in the area of the Siegfried Line through the Eifel hills past Trier and on down to the Saar. His defense was particularly active, and, despite rough terrain and stiff opposition, his forces captured Trier on March 1. Patton then received orders to move on Koblenz. His armored column struck out, and by March 8 elements of the First and Third had linked up a few miles west of the Rhine. Patton then crossed the Moselle, deep into the Saar. The Third Army then closed the Rhine from Koblenz south to Mannheim. On March 22 Patton's forces crossed the Rhine and began a dash across Germany to clear the Frankfurt Corridor in the direction of Kassel. The Third Army, comprising nearly five hundred thousand men at times, advanced thirty miles a day.

During this campaign, Patton dispatched a tank force sixty miles inside enemy territory to Hammelburg, where his son-in-law was being held. The raid was a complete failure. Patton's final disappointment occurred when he was forbidden to take Prague because of agreements with the Russians.

In September Patton lost his beloved Third Army because of his publicized reluctance to ban former members of the Nazi party from administrative jobs. He was given command of a paper army, the Fifteenth. On December 9, he received a broken neck in a highway accident, and, on December 21, 1945, in a German hospital in Heidelberg, he died in his sleep.

Patton was as complex as he was controversial, both as a person and as a commander. He was the unstable, arrogant, ambitious, detested man of action who loved war. He was also a man who, although proudly believing that he had been many times a warrior, loved beautiful things and was torn by self-doubt. But whatever the mix that made Patton what he was as a person, all these contradictions came together to form one of America's foremost commanders.

Whatever the controversies over Patton as commander, overall and in specific engagements, certain things remain clear. No commander was more audacious, yet Patton never blundered into a major disaster. He at times faced limited opposition, bogged down and fought vainglorious battles, but, commanding more daringly than any other, his forces suffered relatively small losses while gaining great amounts of territory and inflicting substantial losses. Unable to discipline himself, he made his men into martinets and he even inexcusably slapped two of them, but he also molded them into disciplined, effective fighting units. These men mocked and cursed him behind his back and complained, "Our blood, your guts," but they also said they would follow him into Hell. He forced subordinate commanders and men to extend themselves in a way that they might not otherwise have done and to attain the resultant sense of pride and satisfaction. Surely, one of the reasons for this was his personal courage. To the end he remained the commander who personally participated in the battle—anachronistic, perhaps, in a way of war increasingly demanding preparation at a desk, but if so, he was indeed quite a "magnificent anachronism."

Other characteristics of Patton in command reflected this personal touch. He tried hard to ignore limiting orders, often reconnoitering in such a way that his rock soup was started whereby one starts with a rock but the other ingredients change the nature of the soup from the original orders. Thus, he always probed for the lucky break and did not function easily as part of an integrated whole. He, therefore, preferred and was at his best in lightning armored attack. Clearly, few could be indifferent to such a commander, and perhaps that is a prime accolade for leadership.

Through all the controversy, the warrior remained a cavalryman—charge with horse, or charge with tanks, but charge!

BIBLIOGRAPHY

Blumenson, Martin. *The Many Faces of George S. Patton, Jr.* Colorado Springs, Colo.: U.S. Air Force Academy, 1972.
———. *The Patton Papers, 1885–1940* and *1940–1945*. 2 vols. Boston: Houghton Mifflin Company, 1972, 1974.
Codman, Charles R. *Drive*. Boston and Toronto: Litte, Brown and Company, 1957.
Essame, Hubert. *Patton: A Study in Command*. New York: Charles Scribner's Sons, 1974.
Farago, Ladislas. *Patton: Ordeal and Triumph*. New York and Toronto: Ivan Oblensky and George J. McLeod, 1963.

JOSEPH P. HOBBS

PERRY, Oliver Hazard (b. South Kingston, R.I., August 23, 1785; d. near Port of Spain, Trinidad, August 23, 1819), naval officer. Perry is considered the hero of the Battle of Lake Erie, September 10, 1813.

Oliver Hazard Perry was born in the Perry family homestead near Kingston, Rhode Island. His grandfather, Freeman Perry, held prominent judicial rank in the province, owing in part to his marriage into the aristocratic family of Oliver Hazard, and was a Quaker. Perry's father, Christopher R. Perry, with his five brothers, followed the sea as his vocation, thus leaving Perry's schooling largely to his mother, Sarah Wallace Perry, an intelligent woman of Scotch descent. The family made its home in Newport while Oliver was still young, and at the age of fourteen, in 1798, he signed on the 28-gun frigate *General Greene* as a midshipman under the command of his father. Perry reached the rank of lieutenant in 1802 during service on board the 28-gun frigate *Adams* in the Mediterranean.

Following a respite back in the United States, Perry accepted appointment to the crew of the 38-gun frigate *Constellation* which sailed for Tripoli in July of 1803. While blockading the Tripolitan coast, Perry was given the captaincy of the 12-gun schooner *Nautilus* within the squadron of Commodore John Rodgers* and continued service at various Mediterranean ports. In 1805 Rodgers transferred Perry to the 44-gun frigate *Constitution*, and in 1806 they returned home.

Back in Rhode Island and Connecticut between 1807 and 1809, Perry directed construction of President Thomas Jefferson's gunboats and commanded several gunboat squadrons at New York and other ports to enforce the Embargo Act. Perry held command of the 12-gun schooner *Revenge*, patrolling the southern Atlantic coast. In 1811, back in Newport on a mission to survey that harbor, the *Revenge* ran aground. Following an investigation that found the pilot at fault, Perry was acquitted of the charge of negligence in the loss of the sunken vessel. The incident kept him on shore, and on May 5, 1811, he was married to Elizabeth Champlin Mason in Newport.

When war broke out in June 1812, Perry had command of a gunboat flotilla stationed at Newport. In mid-February of 1813 he received orders to report to Lake Erie for service under Commodore Isaac Chauncey. He arrived at Presque Isle, the present site of Erie, Pennsylvania, in March, only to find that no American fleet existed to deter the British from controlling the Lake. Master Commandant Perry spent the spring building vessels. By summer he had ten vessels but lacked officers and men enough to encounter the British force of Captain Robert H. Barclay known to be patrolling in the Lake. When Commodore Chauncey finally sent a crew, which Perry considered a motley bunch, the commander proceeded to the difficult task of getting the vessels over the sandbar at the harbor. This was considered the more dangerous as Barclay's force had been patrolling the area diligently, but, to Perry's surprise, the British force was absent from its post during the American endeavor which took place between August 1 and 4. The task was a tricky as well as a physically difficult one of getting the two 20-gun brigs—*Lawrence* and *Niagara*—and the gunboats over the shallow sandbar at the harbor entrance. The trick was managed by securing "camels" to the frigates' hulls, pumping out the water, and floating the vessels across at a less than normal hull depth. On August 8 Perry received a contingent of eighty-nine men, led by Lieutenant Jesse Elliot, whom Perry placed in command of the second brig, the *Niagara*. By August 12 the fleet was on its way up the Lake in search of Barclay's force. At Seneca Perry conferred with General William Henry Harrison who was having to hold up the movement of his army until the lake was cleared of British forces. At the British land base at Malden, up the Detroit River, Perry found Barclay's fleet at anchor on August 25. The confrontation of fleets was delayed by strong and uncertain winds, the outfitting of the British flagship, the corvette *Detroit* (20-guns) which was just built and launched, and the illness of Perry and much of his crew. Further manpower arrived at the end of August when General Harrison sent Perry about one hundred reinforcements to man the vessels. Perry's fleet was anchored in Put in Bay. On

September 1 Perry returned to Malden where he learned that the *Detroit* was fitted out but that Barclay was still not ready for battle. Perry considered a direct attack on Malden to be too risky to undertake. Ten days later Barclay's fleet approached, and Perry sailed to meet it in the Lake. There, on September 10, 1813, the two fleets joined in battle. Perry's flagship *Lawrence* fought until shattered, whereupon Perry, having proclaimed "Don't give up the ship," transferred his command to the *Niagara* from which he proceeded to devastate the *Detroit* and much of the rest of the British fleet. The laggardness of the *Niagara* prior to Perry's boarding of it led to a bitter dispute between its commander, Jesse Elliott, and Perry, with Elliott claiming he had been treated unfairly in Perry's reports of the battle.

Perry went on shore to join Harrison's army in pursuit of the British Army. He assisted in the Battle of the Thames on October 5, another defeat for the British, and rejoined his fleet at Detroit. By mid-November he was home in Newport.

Perry resigned his command, accepted prize money from Congress, and assisted in defense preparations for coastal towns. In 1814 he assisted in the defense of Baltimore, having been promised command of the 44-gun frigate *Java* under construction there. In command of the *Java* Perry sailed for the Mediterranean in 1816.

During his duty there he struck Marine Captain John Heath in a burst of passion concerning the captain's conduct. This led to a court-martial at which Perry received only a reprimand. Back in Newport in 1818 the dispute with Elliott, which had been festering, worsened to the point that each party asked for a Navy court-martial. Meanwhile (in May 1819), Perry accepted President James Monroe's request that he undertake a diplomatic mission to Venezuela.

In command of the 28-gun frigate *John Adams* and the schooner *Nonsuch*, he sailed to the Orinoco River. Finding its mouth after much expenditure of time and difficulty, Perry was able to take only the smaller vessel up the river the several hundred miles to Angostura, the seat of the new republic. Simón Bolívar was away, but his vice-president received Perry warmly. The mission—to secure Venezuelan payment for captured American vessels—resulted in their agreement to the American demands on August 11. In the meantime, general sickness, probably yellow fever, had broken out among Perry's crew. Eager to leave, Perry nevertheless stayed three days following the agreement out of diplomatic courtesy. During the return jounrey down the river Perry contracted the fever. He died on board the *Nonsuch* at sea just prior to reaching the *John Adams* which was awaiting his return at Port of Spain, Trinidad. Perry was buried on Trinidad, escorted with British military honors. In 1826 his body was brought back to Newport on board the sloop-of-war *Lexington*.

Perry's reputation rests on his victory on September 10, 1813, at the Battle of Lake Erie. By the time of his death at the age of thirty-four, he had shown qualities of industriousness and perseverance that might have led him to even more noteworthy achievements. His victory on Lake Erie allowed the army of General Harrison to pursue and defeat the British army of General Henry Procter and thus secure the Northwest Territory to the United States. This ended all British plans for superiority over the Great Lakes area.

When Perry first arrived at Presque Isle, there was no fleet to command. Within days he had established both construction operations and command procedures. Once the vessels were ready, the commandant persevered in getting them over the bar, a feat many thought to be impossible. Once engaged in combat he fought as long as he had weapons and men: the victory appears to be justly attributed to Perry.

He went unhesitatingly on land where he took a leadership role in the military Battle of the Thames. The Battle of Lake Erie and the Battle of the Thames crushed forever British efforts to dominate the Northwest region. Perry's comment upon the Battle of Lake Erie—"We have met the enemy and they are ours"—might have been repeated in similar form after his successful mission to Venezuela.

The two blurs on Perry's career—the cases of Jesse Elliott and John Heath—do not appear to have diminished his public luster. The record indicates that Elliott did in fact fail to bring the *Niagara* to Perry's aid in the *Lawrence* during the heat of battle and that, therefore, Perry's censure was justified. In the case of the strike at Heath, Perry appears to have been in the wrong, perhaps temperamentally overwrought by inactivity or a complex of problems.

BIBLIOGRAPHY

Dutton, Charles J. *Oliver Hazard Perry*. New York: Longmans, Green and Company, 1935.
Forester, C. S. *The Age of Fighting Sail: The Story of the Naval War of 1812*. Garden City, N.Y.: Doubleday, 1956.
Guttridge, Leonard F., and Jad D. Smith. *The Commodores: The U.S. Navy in the Age of Sail*. New York: Harper, 1969.
Mahon, John K. *The War of 1812*. Gainesville: University of Florida Press, 1972.

FRANK C. MEVERS

PERSHING, John Joseph (b. Laclede, Mo., September[?] 13, 1860; d. Washington, D.C., July 15, 1948), General of the Armies; commander of the American Expeditionary Force (AEF) in World War I.

Shaving a few months off his age so as to qualify for entrance, Pershing entered the U.S. Military Academy in 1882. He was a middling student but a natural leader, being elected president of his class and first captain of cadets. After a stint on the frontier in New Mexico and South Dakota, Pershing served as professor of military science at the University of Nebraska from 1891 to 1895. While there, he had outstanding success with a drill team (the Varsity Rifles), which, when he left in 1895, voted to change its name in his honor, becoming the Pershing Rifles, the first of scores of military companies in America to bear that name.

Pershing returned to West Point as a tactical officer in 1897, where his excessive sternness earned him the nickname "Nigger Jack" or "Black Jack"—a name derived from his service with Negro troops on the frontier. In the Spanish-American War he did exceedingly well; one officer described him as "cool as a bowl of cracked ice" under fire. He served three tours in the Philippines (1899–1903, 1907–1908, 1909–1913), mostly in Mindanao among the fierce, war-like Moros, where he had considerable success in imposing American authority with a minimum of bloodshed.

In 1905 he married Helen Frances Warren, daughter of Senator Francis E. Warren, chairman of the Senate Military Affairs Committee. The following year he was suddenly promoted from captain to brigadier general, leapfrogging 862 other officers and leading to charges that he had been promoted because of senatorial "pull." Hoping to block confirmation of his promotion, some disgruntled colonels circulated rumors that he had fathered illegitimate children in the Philippines during his first tour. Pershing denied the charges, and the Senate confirmed the promotion, Senator Warren helping to ease the matter through committee. Apart from the senator's influence, Pershing's record was such that he undoubtedly would have become a general anyway, although perhaps not as soon.

Because of trouble on the Mexican border, Pershing served there from 1914 to 1916. While absent from home, his wife and three daughters were killed in a fire at the Presidio in San Francisco in 1915. Although his name was connected romantically with many women thereafter, he never remarried.

With his field experience in commanding the Punitive Expedition in Mexico from 1916 to 1917, Pershing was the logical choice for command of the American Expeditionary Force in Europe when America entered World War I. His only possible rival, Leonard Wood, was never seriously considered.

The American buildup in Europe was agonizingly slow. Not until May 28, 1918, over a year after declaring war, did American troops engage in any offensive and that was only on a regimental level, at Cantigny. Because of what the Allies considered America's maddeningly slow participation in the war, and because Russia's exit would soon give the Germans manpower superiority on the Western Front, the Allies pressed vigorously for temporary amalgamation of American troops into French and British units. They contended that American staffs and commanders lacked sufficient experience, and by the time they gained it the war might well be lost. The Allies had well-trained staffs and commanders for divisions, corps, and field armies, but lacked the men to fill them. Hence, they argued, America should furnish the necessary manpower—at least during the spring and summer of 1918 when the enemy outnumbered them—to tide them over in the crisis.

The crisis was very severe, as the Germans manhandled Allied armies in five successive offensives (March, April, May, June, and July 1918). But Pershing, maintaining that the crisis was not as great as the Allies contended, steadfastly refused all Allied attempts at amalgamation. His objections were the loss of national identity, the difficulty of reclaiming American contingents without disrupting Allied divisions, language difficulties with the French, recriminations should Allied generals heap up American casualties, and differences in training methods. Specifically, Pershing objected to what he considered an undue Allied emphasis on training for trench warfare as opposed to open warfare.

The American contribution to victory, although late, was substantial. Highlights were the morale lifter at Cantigny, previously mentioned, the action of the 2d and 3d Divisions in blocking the road to Paris against a German breakthrough in May 1918, the 1st and 2d Divisions' spearhead of the Allied attack against the Marne salient on July 18, the subsequent elimination of that salient during late July and early August (the Aisne-Marne Offensive) involving three hundred thousand American troops, the attack on the St. Mihiel salient in September with five hundred thousand American troops, and the final forty-seven-day Meuse-Argonne Offensive which began on September 26 and broke through on November 1, employing an army of over 1 million men.

In addition, there was the moral contribution: the hope given the Allies by the ever-increasing number of American reinforcements and the discouragement caused Germany by the realization that the manpower ratio would grow steadily worse.

After the war Pershing served as chief of staff from 1921 to 1924, when he retired. His later years were devoted to work as chairman of the American Battle Monuments Commission, which supervised American memorials and cemeteries in Europe, and to his memoirs, *My Experiences in the World War* (1931), which won a Pulitzer Prize.

During the war Pershing had some serious disagreements with Peyton Conway March,* the Army chief of staff in Washington. They differed over promotions, over the number of divisions the Americans should have in Europe in 1919 (Pershing wanted far more than March believed possible), and over whether overseas officers should wear the Sam Browne belt. The most serious disagreement, however, concerned which of the two was supreme in the Army. March contended that, as Army chief of staff, he took "rank and precedence" over every other officer, including Pershing. Pershing looked on the Army chief of staff as merely a messenger boy delivering orders from Pershing's civilian superior, the secretary of war. Pershing considered March's contention that he was supreme as similar to a telegraph wire taking on airs simply because it carried an important message.

Part of the difficulty was due to Secretary of War Newton Diehl Baker's confusion concerning General Staff principles and organization. Although it was quite clear in World War II that Army Chief of Staff George Catlett Marshall* was supreme over the European field commander, Dwight David Eisenhower,* World War I was the first war fought since the creation of the General Staff under Elihu Root in 1903. It was not that clear which officer was supreme in World War I. Since three chiefs of staff had quickly come and gone before General March took office, and since, during that time, Secretary Baker had increasingly deferred to his overseas commander, Pershing, whom he greatly admired and desired to become America's great war hero, it was hard for March to assert his military supremacy. In actual practice, Secretary Baker permitted March to raise himself only to coordinate authority with Pershing, not superior.

As commander of the AEF, Pershing played an important role in the victory. A careful rather than a brilliant commander, he worked hard in planning an army on a scale sufficient to tip the balance. It was largely the tremendous American influx that converted an Allied rifleman deficit of 324,000 on March 21, 1918, to a 627,000 superiority by Armistice Day.

Captain B. H. Liddell Hart wrote in *Reputations Ten Years After*: "It is sufficient to say that there was perhaps no other man who would or could have built the structure of the American army on the scale he planned. And without that army the war could hardly have been saved and could not have been won."

In the amalgamation controversy, he took great risks, for if the Germans had broken through and won in 1918 the name "Pershing" would have gone down in history as a synonym for a man who made grandiose plans for a magnificent future which never came about because of failure to recognize an immediate crisis. Nonetheless, he did guess correctly in estimating that the successive Allied crises in 1918, especially the German breakthroughs in March and May, were not as severe as the Allies represented them and that they could in fact hold without Americans being amalgamated into their units.

For all of Pershing's talk about the advantage of open-warfare training and his indictment of the Allies for their defensive mentality and stress on trench warfare, the fact remains that during the last five months of the war, when the Germans were pushed back all along the front, the British advanced farther and faster than the Americans. In addition, they captured twice as many guns and almost four times as many prisoners.

Confronted with this fact, Pershing would later argue that his Americans were pushing against the most sensitive part of the German line, the pivot which the enemy had to hold lest he lose vital rail communication to his armies in the northwest, compelling him to withdraw all along the front. Since Field Marshal Paul von Hindenburg called the Meuse-Argonne "our most sensitive point" and said that "the American infantry in the Argonne won the war," there is something to be said for this.

Actually, it is questionable how much the AEF engaged in open warfare, so much lauded by Pershing, especially during the Meuse-Argonne Campaign. Day after day, the American First Army butted its head against stubborn German resisitance, inching its way ahead from September 26 until November 1, 1918, when it finally broke through. Had the war ended on October 21, instead of November 11, 1918, Pershing's reputation would have been considerably diminished. One has only to look at a war map dated October 31 to see how little the American First Army had advanced under his leadership in comparison with its Allies. The First Army breakthrough on November 1, under Major General Hunter Liggett,* provided a happy ending to the AEF experience, producing a euphoria similar to that caused by Andrew Jackson's* victory at New Orleans at the end of the War of 1812. People forgot the earlier failures and concentrated on the final success.

Pershing felt the Armistice was a mistake. "We shouldn't have done it," he said. "If they had given us another ten days we would have rounded up the entire German army, captured it, humiliated it.... The German troops today are marching back into Germany announcing that they have never been defeated.... What I dread is that Germany doesn't know that she was licked. Had they given us another week, we'd have *taught* them." He was correct about the German attitude. On Armistice Day, General Karl von Einem, commander of a German army, told his troops, "Firing has ceased. *Undefeated* [italics mine]...you are terminating the war in enemy country." A decade later Adolph Hitler was preaching the same error.

BIBLIOGRAPHY

Bullard, Robert L. *Personalities and Reminiscences of the War*. Garden City, N.Y.: Doubleday, Page, and Company, 1925.
Coffman, Edward M. *The Hilt of the Sword: The Career of Peyton C. March*. Madison: University of Wisconsin Press, 1966.
———. *The War to End All Wars: The American Military Experience in World War I*. New York: Oxford University Press, 1968.
Smythe, Donald. *Guerrilla Warrior: The Early Life of John J. Pershing*. New York: Charles Scribner's Sons, 1973.
Vandiver, Frank E. *Black Jack: The Life and Times of John J. Pershing*. 2 vols. College Station: Texas A & M Press, 1977.

DONALD SMYTHE

PICKETT, George Edward (b. Richmond, Va., February 28, 1825; d. Norfolk, Va., July 30, 1875), Confederate general. Pickett lent his name to the Confederate charge at the Battle of Gettysburg.

George E. Pickett, the eldest son of Robert Pickett, a prosperous planter of Henrico county, Virginia, enjoyed all the advantages accruing to members of the Tidewater aristocracy, not the least of which was an extended family of influential relatives. After completing his early education at Richmond Academy, Pickett read law in the office of one of these relatives, an uncle, Andrew Johnson of Quincy, Illinois; it was from this state and through his uncle's influence that Pickett was appointed to West Point in 1842.

Graduating at the very bottom of a fifty-nine member class in 1846, Pickett was commissioned into the infantry. As a lieutenant during the Mexican War, he participated in every important engagement of the campaign led by Winfield Scott* to capture Mexico City, from the siege of Vera Cruz to the storming of Chapultepec. He was twice brevetted: to first lieutenant for gallantry at Contreras and Churubusco in August, and to captain for similar conduct at Chapultepec on September 13, 1847.

After the war Pickett served at a variety of frontier posts in Texas until 1856, when he was transferred to the Far Northwest to fight Indians. By now a captain, Pickett achieved the modest pinnacle of his pre-Civil War fame in this remote corner of the nation, not against the Indians but against the British in Puget Sound. In 1859 in response to pleas from American settlers on San Juan Island, who feared both a British invasion and further outrages by the Indians, Pickett was ordered to occupy the island. This he did with sixty soldiers, and he continued to hold his ground even when confronted by British threats and the guns of three warships anchored broadside of his camp. Diplomacy later engineered a joint British-American occupation of the island, but for his prompt and firm actions Captain Pickett received both the commendation of his commanding officer and the thanks of the Washington territorial legislature. Pickett continued in command of the American force on San Juan until June of 1861 when he resigned his commission to enter the Confederate Army.

Upon arriving in Virginia, Pickett was commissioned a colonel and assigned to duty on the lower Rappahannock River. There he won the good-will of Brigadier General T. H. Holmes, through whose influence he probably owed his promotion to brigadier general in February 1862. Pickett's command, the "Gamecock Brigade," fought with elan at Seven Pines, Gaines' Mill, and Williamsburg during the Peninsula Campaign. Having sustained a serious shoulder wound at Gaines Mill, Pickett missed the Maryland Campaign, but in October 1862 he was promoted to major general and assigned command of a division in the corps of James Longstreet.* His division saw little action at Fredericksburg. It was detached from the army of Robert Edward Lee* and participated creditably in the Suffolk Campaign during the Battle of Chancellorsville in early May 1863.

Elements of Pickett's division won everlasting, albeit dubious, fame for themselves and their commander on July 3, 1863, at the Battle of Gettysburg. Although most of the troops that assaulted the center of the Union line that day were not Pickett's, the heroic, fruitless, and bloody attack was immortalized as "Pickett's charge." The three brigades of Pickett's division suffered casualties of over 62 percent in the attack.

On September 23, 1863, Pickett was given command of the Department of Virginia and North Carolina. His attempt to capture New Berne, North Carolina, in February 1864 miscarried. He was ordered to Richmond and turned his command over to General Pierre Gustauve Toutant Beauregard* in late April. Before Beauregard's arrival, Pickett directed a sturdy makeshift defense against a Union force under Benjamin Franklin Butler, on the Bermuda Hundred line. Pickett then returned to his old division at Cold Harbor and remained with the Army of Northern Virginia until its surrender. On April 1, 1865, his advance position at Five Forks on the far right of Lee's line at Petersburg was overrun by Union forces under the command of General Philip Henry Sheridan.* Five thousand

Confederate troops, essentially all that was left of Pickett's command, were forced to surrender.

After the war Pickett was offered a brigadier general's commission by the Khedive of Egypt, but he refused foreign service because his wife could not accompany him. Thereafter he made a barely tolerable living as the Virginia agent of a New York life insurance company. In January 1851 Pickett had married Sally Minge of Richmond, who died shortly thereafter. He took a second wife in 1863, LaSalle Corbell, a woman he loved with passionate intensity, and had two children by her.

Unfortunately for his reputation as a soldier, it was Pickett's unhappy fate to have presided over two of the worst disasters ever to befall Confederate arms in the eastern theater, the charge at Gettysburg and the crushing defeat at Five Forks. For the first disaster Pickett bears little responsibility but most of the glory. The assault that bears his name was planned by Lee and was carried out by a force that included three of Pickett's brigades plus elements of two other divisions. Although hardly responsible for the ensuing debacle, Pickett, in a report later suppressed by Lee, attempted to blame the attack's failure on lack of support.

Gettysburg not only shattered Pickett's command, but also appears to have permanently shaken Pickett himself. Prior to this time, Pickett had proven himself a capable, if hardly above average, subordinate commander. During the Seven Days' battles, and especially at Seven Pines, Pickett directed his brigade with energy and dispatch. Even so, as a subordinate he left much to be desired. He performed best only under the closest supervision. Longstreet liked him but was always careful to allow him little latitude. Quick thinking—much less imaginative action—was never Pickett's forte.

Moreover, a whimsical streak in his nature asserted itself often enough to make Pickett unreliable or quixotic under pressure. While in departmental command in North Carolina, for example, he ordered the court-martial and execution of twenty-two Carolina unionists, all of whom were serving in the Federal Army, for "(constructive) desertion." During the Suffolk Campaign he absented himself from his division without orders so as to visit his fiancee. Such "knight-errant doings in the field," commented one of his staff officers, were hardly inspiring to the division.

Five Forks was Pickett's most conspicuous failure. Charged with guarding this crucial crossroads along Lee's escape route from Petersburg and astride the southern approach to a vital rail line, Pickett allowed his force of almost ten thousand to be flanked and overrun. When the surprise blow fell, Pickett was two miles in the rear of his line—enjoying a shad-bake dinner. Barely averting capture, he gallantly attempted to rally his troops, but by the time he reached the field the damage had been done. He had not bothered to inform his subordinate commanders of his absence.

His complete culpability for the defeat is open to question, but his lack of judgment is not. And for it he incurred Lee's wrath: he was relieved of his command, or the pitiful remnant thereof, on April 8, 1865, just one day before Lee surrendered. But even then the luster of the heroic charge at Gettysburg surrounded him. And that luster, which only grew brighter with the passage of time, has often obscured the shortcomings of this dashing figure with the long, perfumed tresses. An average brigadier, George Pickett lacked both the stamina and the ability to handle a larger command.

BIBLIOGRAPHY

Coddington, Edward. *The Gettysburg Campaign: A Study in Command.* New York: Charles Scribner's, 1968.
Freeman, Douglas S. *Lee's Lieutenants: A Study in Command.* 3 vols. New York: Charles Scribner's Sons, 1942–1944.
Stewart, George R. *Pickett's Charge: A Microhistory of the Final Attack at Gettysburg, July 3, 1863.* Boston: Houghton Mifflin Company, 1959.
Tucker, Glenn. *High Tide at Gettysburg.* Indianapolis, Ind.: Bobbs-Merrill, 1958.

THOMAS E. SCHOTT

PREBLE, Edward (b. Falmouth [now Portland], Maine, August 15, 1761; d. Portland, Maine, August 25, 1807), naval officer. Preble commanded the U.S. Mediterranean Squadron, 1803–1804, during the Tripolitan War.

Edward Preble was the ninth child and seventh son of Jedidiah Preble, a prominent provincial military officer, merchant, and political figure in the District of Maine. Educated at local schools in Falmouth and at Dummer School in Byfield, Massachusetts, the latter of which he attended during the early years of the American Revolution, Preble entered the Massachusetts state navy in April 1780 as a midshipman in the frigate *Protector*. Midshipman Preble made two cruises in the *Protector*: during the first of them he participated in the bloody battle between the *Protector* and the privateer *Admiral Duff*; the second ended in the capture of the *Protector* by two British frigates, and Preble was, for a few weeks, held prisoner at New York. Early the following year, 1782, he was appointed first lieutenant of the Massachusetts state sloop *Winthrop*, and served in her till the close of maritime hostilities in April 1783. *Winthrop* was primarily employed in protecting the Maine coasting trade against raiders operating out of the British-controlled Penobscot Bay area. Preble's most famous exploit while serving in the *Winthrop*, and the conspicuous deed that first established his public reputation, was the daring capture—with the aid of only fourteen men—of the Loyalist privateer *Merriam* under the guns of Fort George at Bagaduce (now Castine), Maine.

From 1785 until 1798 Preble served, with excellent reputation but without spectacular financial success, as master or supercargo of merchant vessels sailing from North Carolina and Massachusetts ports and trading to Europe, the West Indies, and Africa, as well as along the North American coast. In 1794, when

Congress first enacted legislation authorizing a Federal navy, he immediately sought an appointment in the new organization, but he did not obtain one until after the outbreak of the Quasi-War with France in 1798, when he was commissioned lieutenant (April 9, 1798). After making one cruise in the West Indies as commander of the brig *Pickering*, Preble was promoted to the rank of captain, May 15, 1799, and took command of the 32-gun frigate *Essex* for an elevenmonth voyage (January-November 1800) to Batavia (now Jakarta), Java. This cruise, undertaken to convoy valuable American merchantmen home from the East Indies, was notable both as the longest voyage yet attempted by a ship of the U.S. Navy and as the first time an American naval vessel had showed the flag beyond the Cape of Good Hope.

In the spring of 1803 President Thomas Jefferson selected Edward Preble as the commander of the third U.S. squadron sent to the Mediterranean during the 1801–1805 war with Tripoli. It is on his activities during the twelve months from September 1803 till September 1804 that Preble's reputation as a military commander principally stands. Commodore Richard V. Morris, Preble's predecessor in the Mediterranean command, had proved unequal to the multiple military and diplomatic demands to which the commander of the U.S. Mediterranean Squadron was subject, and was recalled and subsequently dismissed from the Navy. Preble's vigor and decisiveness were in notable contrast to Morris' inactivity and bewilderment, and immediately won him government approval and widespread public attention.

On his arrival at Gibraltar in the 44-gun frigate *Constitution* on September 12, 1803, Preble found Morocco at war with the United States. Mobilizing the ships of the returning United States Squadron as well as his own, Preble massed such overwhelming force along the coasts of Morocco that the sultan was forced by mid-October to reaffirm the highly favorable 1786 treaty between Morocco and the United States. But scarcely was the Moroccan problem solved, when the only other frigate of Preble's squadron, *Philadelphia*, Captain William Bainbridge, ran aground near Tripoli and was captured. Determined that the *Philadelphia* should never be of any use to the enemy, Preble planned and Lieutenant Stephen Decatur executed a brilliant surprise raid in which the former American frigate was burned at her moorings in Tripoli Harbor during the night of February 16–17, 1804.

Because the small vessels of his own squadron (three brigs and three schooners) were not suitable for attacking the maritime defenses of the city of Tripoli, Preble—acting largely on his own initiative—borrowed from the Kingdom of the Two Sicilies six gunboats and two bomb ketches to supplement his own force, the only vessel of which capable of silencing the Tripolitan fortifications was the *Constitution*. Between August 3 and September 3, 1804, Preble launched a series of six attacks on the city of Tripoli and the shipping in its harbor. Of these, the first—resulting in the capture of three Tripolitan gunboats—was the most successful. Thereafter, the commanders of the enemy gunboats avoided close-range combat, and the firepower available to Preble was unequal to that of the Tripolitan fortifications. Concurrent attempts to end the war by negotiation failed because of Preble's distrust of the French mediator, Bonaventure Beaussier, as well as the American commander's lack of sensitivity to the internal political situation at Tripoli. The arrival of a larger U.S. squadron, sent out as a result of the loss of the *Philadelphia* and unavoidably commanded by a senior officer, terminated Preble's Mediterranean command on September 9, 1804.

Following his return to the United States, Preble was employed in superintending gunboat construction and as a trusted professional advisor to Secretary of the Navy Robert Smith. Although instinctively conservative politically and in earlier years identified with the Federalist party, Preble had gradually and inconspicuously shifted his political loyalties to the Jeffersonian Republicans and was the naval officer to whom President Jefferson turned to command a proposed—but never executed—naval expedition to counter the supposed treasonable designs of Aaron Burr in the Mississippi Valley. Preble died as a result of a chronic stomach or intestinal disorder that had undermined his health since the year 1800.

In the process by which the United States developed, more or less out of nothing, a professional naval officer corps during the years between 1798 and 1812, Edward Preble's place is that of one of the most important role-models for younger career officers. Fortunately, the apogee of Edward Preble's professional life coincided with the tenure in office (1801–1809) of Secretary of the Navy Robert Smith, the civilian official most responsible for, and interested in, the development of that professional officer corps.

A man of violent and ill-controlled temper, and a harsh disciplinarian, Preble earned first the grudging and then the enthusiastic admiration of his subordinates by his decisiveness and vigor, by his unhesitating use of prudent discretion and initiative, by his willingness to delegate important and responsible assignments to promising young men, by his fervent defense of what he held to be the national interests and national honor of the United States, and—most of all—by his refusal to give up in the face of great reverses and depressing odds in the enemy's favor.

Preble was a committed believer in the crucial role of force in the maintenance of international order. At the same time, his sixteen years in the merchant service and his close family and social ties to leading mercantile figures of Massachusetts made him sensitive to the economic needs of the U.S. merchant marine, which the Navy was established to assist and protect. Despite these years of merchant marine experience, Preble thought of himself as a professional naval officer: that is, as he would have expressed the idea, a person whose formative years had been spent in learning to be a military man; who had risen by demonstrated competence through each of the ranks from midshipman to captain; and who, by preference and conscious choice, devoted his mature years to service to his country. By temperament Edward Preble was an administrator and man of action rather than a military intellectual, consumed by an intense desire to leave a famous name; he sought that fame through self-sacrifice in his country's cause.

BIBLIOGRAPHY

McKee, Christopher. *Edward Preble: A Naval Biography, 1761–1807*. Annapolis, Md.: Naval Institute Press, 1972.

Pratt, Fletcher. *Preble's Boys: Commodore Preble and the Birth of American Sea Power*. New York: Sloane, 1950.

CHRISTOPHER McKEE

PULLER, Lewis Burwell (b. West Point, Va., June 26, 1898; d. Hampton, Va., October 11, 1971), Marine Corps officer. Puller is considered to be an outstanding tactical combat leader and was perhaps the most decorated marine of all time.

Lewis "Chesty" Puller was born into one of the old families of Virginia, the family's presence in that state dating from the middle of the seventeenth century. His grandfather died fighting for the South in the Civil War. Growing up steeped in the lore of the Civil War, Puller also was an avid reader of Julius Ceasar's *Gallic Wars*. He enrolled at the Virginia Military Institute in 1917, but growing impatient to enter the World War, he dropped out in 1918 to enlist in the U.S. Marine Corps.

Puller was disappointed to learn that he was among several enlisted men chosen to help train recruits in boot camp at the Marine Barracks, Parris Island, South Carolina. After the war, he was sent to Officers' Training School and was commissioned a second lieutenant in the Marine Corps Reserve in 1919. He was almost immediately placed on the inactive list due to postwar cutbacks in the Marine Corps.

Marine Captain William Rupertus talked Puller into returning to the Marine Corps as a corporal, serving in Haiti as an officer of the *Gendarmerie d'Haiti*. The *Gendarmerie* was a combined army and police established by a Haitian treaty with the United States. Most of its officers were enlisted or commissioned U.S. Marines, while its enlisted personnel were Haitians. Puller arrived in Haiti in 1919 and stayed for five years. He used this tour to learn small-unit tactics and participated in frequent action against the Cacos. In his first assignment he exhibited the drive that marked his entire career. Puller had to take a pack train of ammunition twenty-five miles from Port-au-Prince to Mirebalais and part of the supplies an additional sixteen miles to Los Cohobos. At that time Puller did not speak Spanish, and neither his twenty-five men nor their sergeant spoke English. Not wanting to spend the night on the trail, Puller hurried his men along. At one place, the *Gendarmerie* column rode into an equally surprised column of Cacos. Puller instinctively had his men and pack animals charge. Amidst the thunder and the dust the Cacos retreated. Puller arrived in Mirebalais that night and then pushed on early the next morning for Los Cohobos. He completed that mission so quickly that his department commander doubted at first that Puller had actually gone to Los Cohobos. Thus, in 1919 Puller demonstrated the emphasis on fast marching and aggressive attacks that were to become two of his characteristics. Furthermore, in Haiti he learned the importance of marksmanship and of not only leading his men from the front but also of caring for them in camp. Those concerns also became his life-long hallmarks. The Haitian govenment awarded Puller the *Medaille Militaire* for his services in action after he had been in the country only eight months. That was the first of his many combat decorations.

Puller returned to the United States in early 1924 as a new second lieutenant in the U.S. Marine Corps. During the next two years he served at the Marine Barracks, Norfolk, Virginia, completed the Basic School, required of all Marine lieutenants, and was assigned to the 10th Marine Regiment at Quantico, Virginia. In 1926 Puller became a student naval aviator at Pensacola, Florida. He did not succeed in earning pilot's wings, however. After a two-year tour at Marine Barracks, Pearl Harbor, he spent six months at San Diego before a combat tour in Nicaragua.

In December 1928 Lieutenant Puller was assigned to duty with the Nicaraguan *Guardia Nacional*, serving above his Marine Corps rank, as a captain. In 1930, Puller earned the first of his five Navy Crosses. (Puller was the only marine to earn five of them.) Puller had fought five actions against rebel forces between February and August 1930, routing the rebels each time without casualties to his own forces. In addition, he captured impressive amounts of enemy dispatches, munitions, animals, and food. In 1931, he went to the United States to attend the company officers' course at the Army Infantry School, Fort Benning, Georgia. Puller returned to Nicaragua in July 1932 to be greeted with the news that a price had been placed on his head by the leader of the rebels, Augusto Sandino. That September Puller led his company on a ten-day march of more than one hundred and fifty miles during which he fought four engagements and killed at least thirty rebels. Puller received a second Navy Cross for his aggressive exploits during that patrol.

In January 1933 Puller left Nicaragua for China where, in addition to other duties with the marine detachment guarding the American Legation at Peiping, he commanded the famous "Horse Marines," the mounted detachment that guarded American residences and outlying areas. While in China, he studied the Japanese and Chinese armies and acquired a respect for their endurance, marching, and fighting capabilities. He next commanded the marine detachment aboard the cruiser *Augusta* of the Asiatic Fleet, Captain Chester William Nimitz,* commanding.

In June 1936 Puller returned to the United States to teach at the Basic School in Philadelphia. On November 13, 1937, he married his Virginia sweetheart, Virginia Montague Evans. They eventually had three children. After returning to the command of the *Augusta*'s marine detachment, Puller served as a battalion executive officer and commanding officer with the 4th Marine Regiment at Shanghai, China. He returned to Camp Lejeune, North Carolina, in August 1941 to take command of the 1st Battalion, 7th Marine Regiment, 1st Marine Division.

In September 1942 the 7th Marines went in to reinforce the 1st Marine Division on Guadalcanal. There Puller won his third Navy Cross when his battalion stopped a regiment of veteran Japanese soldiers from seizing the vital Henderson Airfield. His half-strength unit killed more than fourteen hundred enemy on the night of October 24–25, 1942. In the wake of this outstanding action, General George Catlett Marshall* asked Puller to be one of a number of officers to return to the United States to give talks to raise morale and to explain the war effort. Puller, always in inspirational leader, was a success on this tour.

In January 1944 Puller won his fourth Navy Cross as executive officer of the 7th Marines. At Cape Gloucester, New Britain, he took command of two battalions when their commanding officers were wounded. Puller moved through heavy machine gun and mortar fire to reorganize the battalions and led them in taking a strongly fortified enemy position.

He commanded the 1st Marine Regiment during the fight for Peleliu in September and October 1944. He returned to the United States in November 1944 to train recruits. His abilities to lead and his interest in the welfare of the enlisted marine made him a natural officer for the position. He was famous for insisting that enlisted men ate before noncommissioned officers and they in turn ate before officers.

At the outbreak of the Korean War in 1950, Puller bombarded Marine Corps Headquarters with requests for a combat command. He was soon given the 1st Marines, his old regiment, which was then being reactivated at Camp Pendleton, California. He landed with his regiment at Inchon, Korea, that September. Later, he earned his fifth Navy Cross inspiring and directing the actions of his men during the bloody "attack in a different direction," as the Marines fought their way through the Chinese Communist forces to the coast during the withdrawal from the Chosin Reservoir. Puller also received the Army's Distinguished Service Cross for that action. In January 1951 he was promoted to brigadier general and was made assistant division commander of the 1st Marine Division.

Puller returned to Camp Pendleton to command the 3d Marine Brigade in May 1951. While training reinforcements, he continued to preach and practice his principles of physical fitness. To paraphrase his policy: if the enemy marches twenty miles a day, Marines have to march twenty-five. Puller was promoted to major general in 1953. In July 1954 he assumed command of the 2d Marine Division at Camp Lejeune and then served as deputy camp commander until he retired due to ill-health on November 1, 1955. He was promoted to lieutenant general at that time.

Puller served as a Marine officer and enlisted man for thirty-seven years. He held the Navy Cross with Gold Stars in lieu of four additional awards; the Army Distinguished Service Cross; the Army Silver Star Medal; the Legion of Merit with combat "V" and Gold Star; the Bronze Star Medal with combat "V"; the Air Medal with two Gold Stars; the Purple Heart Medal; the Presidential Unit Citation Ribbon with four bronze stars; the Marine Corps good conduct medal with one bronze star; and nineteen other U.S. decorations and seven foreign awards.

"Chesty" Puller's Marine Corps nickname came from the kind of stiffness with which he stood with his barrel chest thrown out. His reputation rests on his combat leadership and on his "Pullerisms." He often said that he owed his successes to his enlisted men and his junior officers. He carried his own pack, ate what his men ate, and walked when they walked. His presence rallied his men in combat, and, as he told them, "You don't hurt 'em if you don't hit 'em." As he was fond of telling the chain of command, the press, and any available audience, "Paperwork will ruin any military force." Upon his return to a combat unit in April 1943, Puller wrote the commandant of the Marine Corps, "It is respectfully requested that my present assignment to a combat unit be extended until the downfall of the Japanese government." His statement to the effect that ice cream and refreshment centers ("canteens") were making American fighting men soft, and his remarks about fighting men who drank whiskey and beer brought down the wrath of the temperance forces on him. But his reputation helped the Marine Corps through a peacetime crisis as well as its wartime needs when he came to the defense of the Corps at the trial in 1956 of Marine Staff Sergeant Matthew McKeon who was being tried for the death of six recruits during a night training march. At the court-martial Puller testified on the importance of rugged training for the marine's ability to survive in combat. His testimony had a strong impact on the court. His reputation at his death was such that the commandant of the Marine Corps and twenty generals came to his funeral in his parish church yard.

BIBLIOGRAPHY

Davis, Burke. *Marine! The Life of General Lewis B. (Chesty) Puller, USMC (Ret.).* Boston: Little, Brown and Company, 1962.

Montross, Lynn, et al. *U.S. Marine Operations in Korea.* 5 vols. Washington, D.C.: U.S. Government Printing Office, 1954–1972.

Schuon, Karl. *U.S. Marine Corps Biographical Dictionary.* New York: Franklin Watts, 1963.

Shaw, Henry I., Jr., et al. *History of U.S. Marine Corps Operations in World War II.* 5 vols. Washington, D.C.: U.S. Government Printing Office, 1958–1971.

MARTIN K. GORDON

RICKOVER, Hyman George (b. Maków, Russian Poland, January 27, 1900; d. Arlington, Va., July 8, 1986), naval officer. Rickover directed the program to develop the world's first atomic submarine.

Hyman G. Rickover was born in Russian-occupied Poland in 1900. Several years later his father Abraham joined the thousands of Jewish immigrants who left Eastern Europe for the United States. The elder Rickover settled in New York, set up a tailor shop, and sent for his family. In 1910 the Rickovers moved to Chicago where young Hyman tried to keep pace with his studies while supplementing the meager family income through a variety of part-time jobs. Unable to afford a college education, he received the support of a local congressman in 1918 for appointment to the U.S. Naval Academy at Annapolis.

Rickover's life at the Naval Academy forecast later experiences as a naval officer. He remained isolated from his more athletic and boisterous classmates, spending his time alone in his room. Each year Rickover fell near the bottom of his class in the subject of military character, and only strong performances in several academic subjects permitted him to graduate 107th out of 540 midshipmen in 1922. For the next five years Rickover served on board the destroyer *La Vallette* and the battleship *Nevada*. On both warships he continued to stay away from his comrades, preferring to study engineering in his quarters. This dedication was not entirely futile since he won the recognition of his superiors for improving the *Nevada*'s wiring and communication systems.

Rickover returned to the Naval Academy in 1927 for additional study and then enrolled at Columbia University where he received his master's degree in electrical engineering in 1929. From Columbia he went to submarine school at New London, Connecticut, and then into the submarine service. Rickover liked duty on the quiet undersea craft and worked tirelessly to upgrade the still primitive and dangerous machinery on the fragile warships. Nevertheless, the Navy Department neglected him for submarine command and in 1934 sent him first to the battleship *New Mexico* and then three years later to command the *Finch*, a dilapidated minesweeper used to tow gunnery targets. Dissatisfaction with the latter assignment probably convinced Rickover in 1937 to apply for permanent shore duty as an "Engineering Duty Only" officer.

Throughout most of World War II Rickover headed the Electrical Section of the Bureau of Ships in Washington where he directed improvements in the design of obsolete electrical equipment and overcame critical wartime supply shortages by extensive contracts with private industry. His aggressive management of the Electrical Section between 1941 and 1945 prompted deputy chief of the Bureau of Ships, Rear Admiral Earle W. Mills, to select Rickover for special assignment in 1946. Mills ordered Rickover to direct a team of naval officers dispatched to the Manhattan District laboratories at Oak Ridge, Tennessee to study developments in the new field of nuclear technology. Rickover enthusiastically visited those labs instrumental in the creation of the atomic bomb. He discussed the latest technology with engineers and read extensively about nuclear physics and engineering. He became convinced that the Navy could at once develop a nuclear reactor to power warships.

Unfortunately for Rickover, few naval officers shared his conviction about the immediacy of nuclear power. Although Chief of Naval Operations Chester William Nimitz* and others agreed that the Navy must develop an atomic submarine, their recommendations in 1947 were for long-term study and development rather than for a crash program. Consequently, Rickover launched a crusade to force reactor development and nuclear propulsion on a cautious naval establishment. Appointment as Navy liaison to the Atomic Energy Commission in 1948 and as head of the newly formed Nuclear Power Branch of the Bureau of Ships in 1949 gave Rickover the platforms to press his plans. Cleverly, he used each agency to prod the other into moving ahead rapidly on nuclear propulsion.

Moreover, he reestablished earlier contacts with civilian industrial contractors and developed valuable relations with congressional committees.

It was the growing fear of Russian nuclear power and the tensions of the Cold War rather than Rickover's agitation, however, which provided the final catalyst for construction of an atomic submarine. In August 1950 the Truman administration authorized development of such a weapon. This decision mobilized Rickover's team of naval and civilian engineers to design a water-cooled nuclear reactor for a submarine. Rickover determined to skip intermediate test stages and build the reactor and submarine hull concurrently. These steps facilitated early completion in 1954 of the world's first nuclear-powered submarine, the *Nautilus*.

While Rickover labored on the *Nautilus* project, he battled a naval establishment intent upon forcing his early retirement from the service. Finally, political and public pressure convinced the Navy to promote him to rear admiral in 1953, while at the same time successful sea trials of the *Nautilus* in 1955 strengthened his hold over the nuclear propulsion program. Now, subsequent changes in reactor design and in personnel selection would require Rickover's personal approval, and characteristically the admiral scrutinized every technical detail and examined every potential candidate for the nuclear navy. Moreover, triumph with the *Nautilus* led to his designation as head of a program to construct the first nuclear power plant in the United States at Shippingport, Pennsylvania. Rickover's nuclear network turned to the civilian project and grafted its rigorous safety standards and technical precision on to private industry. By December 1957 the generating station became operational.

The Shippingport project gave Rickover a reputation as one of the nation's leading nuclear engineers. At the same time he received additional national attention for a crusade to improve American education. Rickover had long stressed the necessity of thorough educational preparation for his engineers and naval officers and had formed nuclear power schools at New London in 1956 and Mare Island in 1958. But it was a trip to Russia in 1959 with Vice-President Richard M. Nixon which prompted Rickover to speak out on the apparent weakness of American education in comparison to that of the Soviet Union. In speeches, essays, and several books, the admiral lashed out at the deficiencies in the entire U.S. school system.

Public recognition brought new stature within the Navy. During the following years Rickover assumed more control over the Navy's nuclear program, observing sea trials of each new atomic warship and screening every officer for command of the expanding nuclear fleet. Yet he still confronted old animosities which surfaced from time to time, such as exclusion from the planning stages of the *Polaris* program to develop nuclear missile submarines. However, Rickover had become something of an institution, and when he reached mandatory retirement age in the early 1960s, he was retained through the next two decades as director of the Division of Naval Reactors.

Rickover's place in American military history will remain subject to heated debate. Interpretations of his contributions seem to generate strong differences of opinion, while uncertainty about the safety of nuclear power adds to the ongoing controversy about Rickover. Admirers call him the father of the nuclear navy, while critics claim that others were equally capable of developing the nuclear navy and with far less friction and high-handed measures. In fact, a number of naval officers did recognize the potential of nuclear powered warships after World War II, and many worked to develop such a program. Only Rickover, however, risked his career and battled the bureaucracy to ram through an immediate and practical program. The early stages of nuclear power development required a gadfly to keep the issue burning as postwar America tried to define its military requirements and priorities.

Rickover was more than a promoter and publicist. He was the force behind the entire naval nuclear program. His dogged perseverance, incessant badgering, and engineering know-how contributed substantially to the successful harnessing of nuclear energy for military purposes. Rickover's reactor program revolutionized naval warfare. Now warships could remain at sea indefinitely without refueling and submarines could circle the globe without surfacing to replenish batteries. Whether less abrasive officers might have eased some of the growing pains of the nuclear navy seems less important than the effective leadership Rickover supplied in the birth of a nuclear fleet.

BIBLIOGRAPHY

Blair, Clay, Jr. *The Atomic Submarine and Admiral Rickover.* New York: Henry Holt, 1954.
David, Heather M. *Admiral Rickover and the Nuclear Navy.* New York: G. P. Putnam's Sons, 1970.
Hewlett, Richard G., and Francis Duncan. *Nuclear Navy. 1946–1962.* Chicago: University of Chicago Press, 1974.
Polmar, Norman. *The Atomic Submarine.* Princeton, N.J.: Van Nostrand Reinhold Company, 1963.
Rickover, Hyman G. *Education and Freedom.* New York: Dutton and Company, 1959.

JEFFERY M. DORWART

RIDGWAY, Matthew Bunker (b. Fortress Monroe, Va., March 3, 1895), Army officer. Ridgway commanded the 82d Airborne Division in World War II and Allied ground forces during the Korean War.

Ridgway was born into the Army, at Fortress Monroe, where his father, a colonel of artillery, was then stationed. The "Army brat" was graduated from West Point in 1917 (along with Mark Wayne Clark* and Joseph Lawton Collins*). Lieutenant Ridgway's first duty assignment was a 3d Infantry border post, Camp Eagle Pass, in Texas. Ridgway spent all of the months of World War I at this fortification, where he eventually rose to command of the regimental headquarters company.

In the fall of 1918 Ridgway returned to West Point as an instructor of French and Spanish and director of athletics. Six years as a teacher at the Military Academy were followed by two years as a student in the Infantry School, Fort Benning, Georgia. The remainder of the 1920s and 1930s were consumed in the peripatetic manner common to peacetime service in the officer corps: constantly changing duty assignments, ranging from northern China (with George Catlett Marshall*), through Texas, Nicaragua, Bolivia, Georgia, Panama, the Philippines, Kansas (Command and General Staff School), Illinois, Washington, D.C. (Army War College), San Francisco (the Presidio), and Brazil (again with Marshall). Finally, as the two-decade journey ended, he was assigned to the War Plans Division of the General Staff in Washington.

Early in 1942, shortly after America entered World War II, Ridgway, by then a two-star general, assumed command of the 82d Infantry Division from Omar Nelson Bradley.* The 82d, which had a distinguished record in World War I, had been reactivated because of the war. Within a few months of his assumption of command, he was asked to convert his division into an airborne unit. The airborne concept of inserting units into combat behind enemy lines—utilizing gliders and paratroopers—was then new to warfare. The first large-scale application was in the German assault on Crete (May 1941), a costly experiment the Nazis never repeated.

Ridgway created one of the Army's first airborne units. He and his command were ordered to North Africa in the spring of 1943. He continued the preparation of his troops in Morocco until July, when part of the 82d made the first large-scale night jump in history as part of the assault on Sicily. Poor ground-air coordination and other factors caused the troopers to be dropped, not in the designated area near the town of Gela, but in small groups dispersed over hundreds of square miles of Sicilian terrain. The error worked out for the best, however, because the reports of American forces coming from so many locales at once threw the German and Italian commanders into a state of confusion. General Karl Student, Germany's authority on airborne operations, said (in 1945) that the troopers of the 82d brought success to the Allied invasion of Sicily, particularly since they blocked the Hermann Goering Armored Division from reaching the beaches being invaded by General George Smith Patton, Jr.* One wag described the Sicilian drop as "the best-executed snafu in the history of military operations." The airborne drop on Sicily did demonstrate that a new tactical tool was available: vertical envelopment.

For a time after Sicily, the high command of the Army was skeptical about the validity of airborne operations, but Ridgway and other advocates persistently supported the concept, and three airborne divisions (the 82d, 101st, and the British 6th) participated in the Normandy D-Day invasion. Ridgway jumped with the 2d Battalion of his 505th Parachute Regiment during the night of June 5, 1944. It was the objective of the 82d to hold the causeways that criss-crossed the flooded areas just beyond Utah Beach. Following the landing of his gliders the next morning, Ridgway's division captured Ste. Mère-Église, the first French city to be liberated. The 82d achieved its primary objective but sustained 46 percent casualties, not uncommon in such operations.

The success of the airborne mission convinced General Dwight David Eisenhower* of the utility of vertical envelopment, and he created the First Allied Airborne Army and named Ridgway to head the XVIII Corps. Command of the 82d was transferred to James Maurice Gavin.* The 101st was led by Maxwell Davenport Taylor.* These two divisions were promptly loaned to the British for Operation MARKET-GARDEN, a scheme by Field Marshall Bernard Montgomery to trap a German army in Holland. A British general (Frederick Browning) was made commander of the operation. The American airborne forces achieved their objectives, but the operation was a failure. Ridgway, who had no command responsibilities in this campaign, believed that it failed because the British high command was much too timid in moving up armor and ground forces in support of the American and British airborne units.

The forces commanded by General Ridgway participated in the bitter six weeks of fighting in the Ardennes, crossed the Rhine at Wesel, fought their way through the Ruhr pocket, crossed the Elbe, and finally made contact with Soviet forces (May 2, 1945), just as the war in Europe ended. In all these operations, Ridgway's forces performed gallantly and well; their commander was always in the forward positions when the going got rough.

Following the war, Ridgway assumed command of the Mediterranean Theater of Operations. In January 1946, however, he was transferred to London as Eisenhower's representative on the Military Staff Committee of the United Nations, an advisory body to the Security Council. Other assignments followed in the pre-Korean War period: chairman, Inter-American Defense Board (1946–1948); commander in chief, Caribbean Command (1948–1949); and, in October 1949, deputy chief of staff for administration and training.

General Walton Harris Walker, commander of the Eighth Army fighting in Korea was killed in an accident on December 23, 1950. Ridgway was designated as his replacement and immediately left Washington for Korea. General Douglas MacArthur,* who had been trying to direct the war from Tokyo prior to Walker's death, turned over complete control of all ground forces to Ridgway. The Eighth Army had been seriously demoralized and physically chewed up by a surprise Chinese Communist offensive that would eventually drive the Eighth well below the 38th parallel. Ridgway began by countermanding a standing order to hold current positions at all costs. He told his commanders to fall back in good order on predetermined phase lines.

A new Communist offensive in January 1951 drove Ridgway's forces some seventy-five miles south of Seoul where the line finally held. Two months earlier, MacArthur had informed the Pentagon that he would need four more divisions to stabilize his line: Ridgway did it with the available forces. Some four weeks after assuming command of an army in retreat against vastly superior forces, he launched a counteroffensive (January 25, 1951). His force—some 365,000 soldiers—surged forward against the 484,000 troops of Lin Piao, falling back briefly in the face of heavy counteroffensives, but always recovering and pressing onward throughout February. By the end of the month Ridgway had regained the 38th parallel and gone beyond it. That line would ebb and flow with the tide of offensives and counters, but the war was to end many months later with the South Korean border essentially *status quo ante bellum.*

President Truman ended a long struggle with the intractable MacArthur on April 11, 1951 by relieving him of all his commands, including commander in chief, Far East, and United Nations commander, and turning them over to Ridgway. Two months later the truce negotiations began that were to drag on interminably, and the major operational phase of the Korean War ended.

In May 1952, President Truman selected Ridgway, by then a four star general, to replace Eisenhower as the head of the North Atlantic Treaty Organization (Supreme Commander, Allied Powers in Europe). In the thirteen months Ridgway directed NATO, he enlarged it from twelve divisions to almost eighty (including active and reserve divisions). He instilled in the NATO forces his conviction that all of free Europe should be defended, not just those areas that were readily defensible.

Ridgway returned to Washington in October 1953 to assume the highest of Army posts, that of chief of staff. His two-year tenure was a time of great conflict. Senator Joseph McCarthy was at the peak of his demagoguery and freely abused Secretary of the Army Robert T. Stevens and many ranking officers. One of Ridgway's achievements during his two-year tenure was to prop up the flagging morale of the officer corps against McCarthy's virulent and largely unwarranted attacks.

The chief of staff also had considerable difficulty in his dealings with Secretary of Defense Charles Wilson. Wilson espoused a reduction of conventional ground forces in favor of the doctrine of massive retaliation. Ridgway repeatedly challenged this so-called New Look for the American military in the belief that it was a serious error to place so much reliance on nuclear weaponry. In 1955, at the age of sixty, he completed his two year tour as chief of staff and resigned from active service.

Matthew Ridgway was a pioneer in airborne warfare. He organized the 82d Airborne into an effective fighting machine. Later, as commander of the XVIII Corps in the First Airborne Army, he devised techniques for the utilization of such forces that were of immeasurable consequence in the conduct of the European Campaign. He trained most of the other senior airborne commanders in World War II. The tactical employment of vertical envelopments as an important weapon in a commander's arsenal owes much to Ridgway's innovative approach.

In Korea he demonstrated that troops properly employed and motivated can triumph over superior numbers and adverse conditions. Furthermore, Ridgway demonstrated that as an off-site tactician, MacArthur was not all that legend made him out to be.

Ridgway's tenure as chief of staff is of profound significance in the history of the American military for three reasons. First, he fought brilliantly and effectively against the doctrine of massive retaliation. He argued that a primary reliance on atomic devices would render America impotent in dealing with conventional wars that did not call for either the strategic or tactical application of nuclear weaponry. He also argued that massive retaliation was morally wrong and could never lead to a durable peace. Second, he developed (along with Gavin and Taylor) the concept of the flexible response in brushfire conflicts. This was a carefully measured and articulated response that would minimize the possibility of escalation into a nuclear Armageddon.

Lastly, as the French were losing their grip on Indochina and President Eisenhower was considering the possibility of American intervention, Ridgway produced what later came to be called the Ridgway Report. The report laid out in specific, documented language the terrible price in men, money, and material which the United States would have to expend if it became involved in Vietnam. Ridgway's report was a prime determinant in Eisenhower's decision not to join the conflict. There is some paradox in a professional soldier arguing against a military solution, but it speaks of Ridgway's character that he considered this to be the most important contribution of his entire career.

Ridgway embodied all the virtues this nation needs in its military leadership. He was brilliant, highly principled, nonpolitical, and courageous. In the pantheon of twentieth-century American soldiers four figures will always stand out from the shadows: George Marshall, Dwight Eisenhower, Douglas MacArthur, and Matthew Ridgway.

BIBLIOGRAPHY

Alberts, Robert C. "Profile of a Soldier: Matthew B. Ridgway." *American Heritage* 27 (February 1976): 4–7, 73–82.
Eisenhower, John. *The Bitter Woods*. New York: Putnam's, 1969.
Halberstam, David. *The Best and the Brightest*. New York: Random House, 1969.
Manchester, William. *American Caesar: Douglas MacArthur, 1880–1964*. Boston: Little, Brown and Company, 1978.
Ridgway, Matthew B. *The Korean War*. Garden City, N.Y.: Doubleday, 1967.
———. *Soldier: The Memoirs of Matthew B. Ridgway*. New York: Harper, 1956.

RICHARD F. HAYNES

RODGERS, John (b. near Havre de Grace, Md., ca. 1771–1773; d. Philadelphia, Pa., August 1, 1838), naval officer. Rodgers was the senior American naval officer during the War of 1812, and he proposed a strategy of fleet action rather than single-ship cruises.

John Rodgers' parents, "Colonel" John Rodgers and Elizabeth Reynolds Rodgers, founded the United States' premier naval family, with flag rank descendants into the twentieth century. "Colonel" Rodgers had emigrated from Scotland in 1760 and had settled in Harford County, Maryland. By 1775 he owned and operated a tavern near modern Havre de Grace. He raised a company of Maryland militiamen for the patriot cause and in 1778 was commissioned a captain. Although he never held a higher rank, he was always known as "Colonel" Rodgers.

John Rodgers was one of the earliest of eight children. Fascinated by the sea, but disliking school and farming, the young man attempted to run away to Baltimore to join a merchantman. Seeing the boy's ardor, his father agreed to sign him up as an apprentice if the youth promised to abstain from alcohol. John took the oath and abstained from alcohol for the rest of his life. Service aboard the merchantman was good for the young man who soon was made a ship's officer. By the time he was twenty Rodgers had his own ship which engaged in general European trade out of Baltimore. Rodgers spent eleven years in the merchant marine where he, like so many other Americans, learned well the practical skills of sailing, navigation, and seamanship.

When the Quasi-War with France began in 1798, Rodgers accepted a commission as second lieutenant aboard the 38–gun frigate *Constellation* under Thomas Truxton.* The first lieutenant resigned shortly after, and Rodgers became the executive officer of the frigate. He was serving in that capacity when the American vessel captured the French frigate *Insurgente* (36 guns) on February 9, 1799. Rodgers was honored for the victory along with the rest of the crew of the *Constellation*, and as a further recognition of his abilities, he was promoted to the rank of captain—the first American officer to be promoted to that rank under the new government. He was given the captured vessel to command. Later Rodgers transferred to the 20–gun corvette *Maryland* in which he sailed to the West Indies. At the end of the war, Rodgers bore the American minister and a new treaty to France.

Unsure of his future with the Navy, Rodgers returned to merchant service for several months. Returning to Baltimore in May 1802, he was recalled to service in the Navy and sailed to the Mediterranean where he participated in the actions against the Barbary pirates until the summer of 1806. As captain of the 28–gun frigate *John Adams*, Rodgers along with Lieutenant Andrew Sterrett commanding the 12–gun schooner *Enterprise* captured and destroyed the largest vessel in the Tripolitan fleet. During his North African service, Rodgers was at times commander of the U.S. fleet in those waters and hence was entitled to be called "commodore." By 1806 Rodgers had succeeded Commodore Edward Preble* as the U.S. commander and negotiated peace terms with Tripoli along with the civilan U.S. minister, Tobias Lear. Rodgers took a hard line in the negotiations, for he never believed that the lives or comfort of the American prisoners in the Tripolitan jails were worth trading for a dishonorable peace backed by tribute. During this period Rodgers took umbrage at the remarks of Captain James Barron and challenged the captain to a duel. Barron declined the challenge.

Returning to the United States in 1806, Rodgers married Minerva Denison of Sion Hill, Maryland. She bore him eleven children, one of whom was Rear Admiral John Rodgers, Jr.

Back in the United States, Rodgers was one of the members of the naval board which found Captain James Barron guilty of failure to do his duty as senior officer aboard the *Chesapeake* when it submitted to the *Leopard* (July 1807). Barron was suspended without pay for five years. From 1807 to 1809 Rodgers enforced the Jefferson administration's embargo north of the Delaware River.

In 1810 Rodgers, as captain of the 44–gun frigate *President*, commanded a fleet in charge of protecting the northern portion of the American coast. On May 16, 1811, the *President* severely damaged the British 20–gun sloop, *Little Belt*. The British captain claimed that Rodgers had used unfair methods, but an American court of inquiry upheld Rodgers' account. Rodgers was hailed as a hero by President Thomas Jefferson and the secretary of the Navy. Rodgers' success was seen as just revenge for the *Leopard*'s earlier humiliation of the *Chesapeake*.

Rodgers was the senior, active duty, naval officer in the War of 1812. On hearing of the outbreak of the war, Rodgers ordered his fleet of three frigates and two lesser ships to sea. He feared that if he delayed, the British would blockade the American coast and prevent his departure. Rodgers was the only American naval captain in the war to recommend concentration and fleet action. He understood that an American fleet's presence would force the British Navy to concentrate its own ships. If the strategy was successful, it meant that the Royal Navy would do less damage to American merchantmen than would more scattered enemy vessels on single-ship cruises.

While the *President* was engaged in a fight with the British frigate *Belvidera* (36–guns), a gun burst and Rodgers suffered a broken leg. His small fleet sailed east to Spain and then north to the British Isles where he failed to sail into the Channel and the Irish Sea, an omission which later strategists have frequently criticized. On this cruise the American fleet took only eight enemy merchantmen. This lack of success, in contrast to the more colorful single-ship duels of other American captains, convinced the administration that fleet cruises were not only unprofitable but dangerous as well since a large portion of the American Navy could be lost in one unsuccessful battle. Rodgers' two other cruises, with smaller fleets, were equally unsuccessful.

In June 1814 Rodgers accepted command of the new 44–gun frigate *Guerriere* which was then being finished in Philadelphia. He never was able to get this vessel to sea during the war. In August 1814 he and his sailors were ordered to Washington and later to Baltimore to defend these cities. During the battle for the cities, his sailors' efforts were decisive in protecting the inner harbor.

After the war Rodgers was appointed head of a Board of Navy Commissioners which Secretary of the Navy William Jones had suggested was necessary for better naval administration. The commissioners ran all the nonpolitical aspects of the Navy from supplies and strategy to personnel and contracts. In 1823 Rodgers served a short time as interim secretary of the Navy. The next year he resumed active command as commodore of the Mediterranean Squadron. His flagship was the 74–gun *North Carolina*, a ship-of-the-line. Rodgers returned to Washington in 1827 where he once again headed the Board of Navy Commissioners. He resigned due to ill-health on May 1, 1837, and died on August 1, 1838, at the Naval Asylum in Philadelphia. He is buried in the Congressional Cemetery in Washington.

Several modern historians consider Rodgers the premier American naval strategist of the War of 1812. His idea to maintain fleet cohesion during the War of 1812 was far ahead of his time and would only be recognized two generations later by the great naval theorist Alfred Thayer Mahan.* Rodgers' fleet, although unsuccessful by contemporary standards, did force the British to concentrate their forces. This permitted American merchantmen to return home safely. Rodgers was disappointed that his own contemporaries failed to recognize the importance of his novel strategic ideas.

He always was more a theorist than a fighter. Several times during the war, Rodgers had the opportunity to place himself near the jugular of British trade but failed to take the necessary risks. He was a methodical leader, disciplined and stern. Never a lovable or colorful sailor, Rodgers nonetheless provided the early American Navy with a worthy heritage of naval strategy and an example of competent leadership.

BIBLIOGRAPHY

Eckert, Edward K. *The Navy Department in the War of 1812*. Gainesville: University of Florida Press, 1973.
Forester, Cecil S. *The Age of Fighting Sail, The Story of the Naval War of 1812*. Garden City, N.Y.: Doubleday and Company, 1956.
Guttridge, Leonard F., and Jay D. Smith. *The Commodores, The U.S. Navy in the Age of Sail*. New York: Harper and Row, 1969.
Mahon, John J. *The War of 1812*. Gainesville: University of Florida Press, 1972.
Paullin, Charles O. *Commodore John Rodgers, Captain, Commodore, and Senior Officer of the American Navy, 1773–1838, a Biography*. Cleveland: Arthur H. Clark Company, 1910.

EDWARD K. ECKERT

ROOSEVELT, Theodore (b. New York City, N.Y., October 27, 1858; d. Long Island, N.Y., January 6, 1919), assistant secretary of the Navy, volunteer Army officer, president of the United States. During his presidency, Roosevelt devoted unusual attention to modernizing the American armed forces, especially the Navy.

Prompted by the actions of his father, a rich New York glass importer, an asthmatic and sickly young Theodore Roosevelt made room in a scholastic schedule devoted to such subjects as ornithology, philately, and biology, adding strenuous physical exercises. By his teenage years, Roosevelt began living the "strenuous life," performing rituals of exercise which included wrestling, boxing, hiking, shooting, swimming, and horseback riding. T.R. studiously sampled the curricula in history and natural science at Harvard College. He began the research that resulted in the first of many books, *The Naval War of 1812* (1882).

Graduating Phi Beta Kappa from Harvard in 1880, Roosevelt entered Columbia Law School but left in 1881 after being elected as a Republican to the lower house of the New York state legislature.

Grief-stricken at the death of his young wife, Roosevelt abandoned the familiar environs of New York in 1884 to become a "cowboy," operating a ranch in Dakota Territory. The change of scene did him good, and, energetically as usual, in 1886 he bustled back to politics, campaigning for the office of mayor of New York City. He lost. Sitting out of politics temporarily, T.R. plunged into writing and produced essays and books, including *Ranch Life and the Hunting Trail* (1888) and the first two volumes of his four-volume opus *The Winning of the West* (1889).

In 1889 Roosevelt returned to politics, taking the appointment of President Benjamin Harrison to a seat on the U.S. Civil Service Commission. After serving enthusiastically for six years on what had been a rather drab panel, T.R. sought the appointive position as president of New York City's Board of Police Commissioners. A crimefighting commissioner, Roosevelt stalked the streets for two years. The Navy had been one of his special interests ever since he heard his uncles Bulloch (James and Irvine) talk about their days in service to the Confederacy. T.R. and friends (including U.S. Senator Henry Cabot Lodge) pressed President-elect William McKinley to make him assistant secretary of the Navy in 1897. Roosevelt made the assistant secretary's traditionally mundane billet into one of influence. Taking an interest in everything in the Navy Department, T.R. interrogated officers, inspected ships and ordnance, and investigated plans at the Office of Naval Intelligence. He naturally joined other scholars, businessmen, politicians, and military officers (including his friend Captain Alfred Thayer Mahan*) who wanted to lead America into the race for colonies. Sensing that war with Spain was in the offing over the matter of Cuba's revolution, T.R. helped to put the Navy on a war footing. Soon after the mysterious destruction of the U.S. battleship *Maine* in Havana, Cuba, America and Spain were at war. Recognizing that the old Spanish Pacific colony of the Philippines was vulnerable to attack, Roosevelt sent a war-warning message to Commodore George Dewey* commanding the U.S. Asiatic Squadron. Dewey took his squadron and struck the Spanish at Manila Bay, winning a great victory.

Meantime, Roosevelt, at age forty and with poor eyesight, used his political connections to obtain a lieutenant colonelcy of volunteers. Resigning as assistant secretary, he dashed around recruiting men into the 1st U.S. Volunteer Cavalry Regiment, popularly known as the "Rough Riders." The regiment's commanding officer, Colonel Leonard Wood, was later promoted, allowing Roosevelt to gain the colonelcy. Roosevelt's Rough Riders, a handpicked one thousand out of twenty-three thousand applicants, hailed from Texas and Harvard, Dakota and Yale, Arizona and Princeton. Cowboys and polo players, businessmen, and Indians volunteered to serve with T.R., who packed twenty pairs of spectacles to take to Cuba. He won no friends in the Army by criticizing his superiors and the War Department's bad rations. The Rough Riders acquitted themselves well, making a national hero out of their colonel. Victory at the battle on San Juan Heights led logically to high political office.

In his Brooks Brothers khaki uniform, Roosevelt returned to New York and was elected governor in 1898. Charging into the governorship as he had up San Juan Hill, he vetoed bills of the legislature, advocated new taxes on businesses, and promoted "Progressive" reforms. Such actions alienated T.R. from the conservative New York Republican machine, which arranged to slide him out of the governorship and into the moribund national vice-presidency. The McKinley-Roosevelt ticket won the election in 1900. On September 6, 1901, President William McKinley was wounded by an assassin at the Pan American Exposition in Buffalo, New York. He died eight days later.

Roosevelt took the oath of office and soothingly pledged to hold to McKinley's policies. Within a few months, however, he began displaying the same political flair that had antagonized conservative New York Republicans. T.R. arbitrated the Coal Strike of 1902, instigated "trust-busting" cases against big corporations, called for Progressive agencies to regulate business, and popularized national parks and environmental conservation, all of which could be seen as departures from McKinley's policies.

Roosevelt was one of America's most active presidents in foreign affairs. Angered that Colombia would not accept a treaty allowing the United States to build a canal through the Colombian province of Panama, T.R struck a bargain with the Panamanians just hours after they revolted against Colombia's government. (Begun in 1904, the Panama Canal was completed in 1914.) In 1904 Roosevelt added to the Monroe Doctrine a controversial corollary which stated that the United States would not let European countries use force to collect debts owed them from Latin American nations. Instead, America would supervise the collection of such debts and police the hemisphere. In 1906 Roosevelt won the Nobel Peace Prize for bringing an end to the Russo-Japanese War. He pushed for an international conference to discuss various claims and disputes in Morocco.

Knowing that diplomacy was ineffective without a strong military force to back it up, Roosevelt devoted much of his time to military matters. Relying on Secretary of War Elihu Root to look after the Army, T.R. focused his attention on the Navy. Under Roosevelt, the U.S. Navy added new ships, increased the number of sailors, and stressed modernized gunnery. He made provisions for concentrating scattered battleships into a fleet. In late 1907 the president sent the U.S. battlefleet around the world on a fourteen-month cruise. By the end of the administration, T.R. had boosted the United States to rank third in naval strength behind Britain and Germany.

Leaving the presidency in 1909, Roosevelt still followed the "strenuous life." His big game hunt to Africa was a grand adventure. Returning to America, he argued with his chosen successor, William Howard Taft, over antitrust and conservation policies. Failing to gain the Republican nomination for president, Roosevelt ran as a third party candidate in 1912, heading the Progressive or "Bull Moose" ticket and promising increased government regulations in his

"New Nationalism" platform. The split among the Republicans gave the election to the Democratic candidate, Woodrow Wilson. Following the election, T.R. pursued his multifaceted interests. He went on a hazardous trip to the Amazon River Basin. He had presented historical lectures at England's Oxford University in 1910 and was president of the American Historical Association in 1913. During the Great War, T.R. criticized the lack of preparedness in Wilson's defense policy. After a German submarine sank the *Lusitania* in 1915, Roosevelt promoted a program called the Plattsburgh Training Camp Movement, designed to give military training to college students. When the United States declared war on Germany in 1917, Roosevelt offered to raise a new Rough Rider-style infantry division, but Secretary of War Newton Diehl Baker declined his services.

While considering the possibility of running for the 1920 Republican presidential nomination, Roosevelt suffered a coronary embolism and died on January 6, 1919, at Sagamore Hill, his home on Long Island.

Theodore Roosevelt serves as an important figure in America's transition from the nineteenth to the twentieth century. He was very knowledgeable in many fields but an expert in none. Whether it was as a legislator or police commissioner, cowboy or big-game hunter, naval secretary (albeit assistant) or volunteer soldier, historian or naturalist, amateur athlete or trust-buster, governor or president—he did well in all his chosen roles, enjoying himself, building his reputation as a man of action and accomplishment.

For the Army, the service in which he spent his hectic Rough Rider days and three quiet years (1882–1884) as a New York National Guard officer, Roosevelt had no great affection or particular interest, beyond modernization. But when Congress declared war on Spain he jumped ship from the Navy Department to become a volunteer Army officer for practical considerations. As a naval observer or supernumerary, he would be unlikely to get the recognition that would come from a battlefield victory. T.R. was like many nineteenth-century volunteer Army officers, expecting that he could quickly pick up the essentials of soldiering, providing inspired leadership but lacking discipline, regarding most Army regulations as mumbo-jumbo, and not getting along well with regimented regulars. In fact, Roosevelt's relations with the Army were stormy, a natural consequence of his criticism of General William Rufus Shafter,* commander of U.S. forces in Cuba, and his assumption that the War Department mishandled supplies and medical services during the Spanish War. (Evidently, T.R.'s public complaints cost him a recommendation for the Medal of Honor, which would have perfectly crowned his active service.) As president, Roosevelt took the side of Secretary of War Elihu Root in the dispute with Commanding General Nelson Appleton Miles* over staff organization. The president relied on Root to carry out the plan of reorganization. (The resulting changes were called the "Root Reforms," not the "Roosevelt Reforms.") Like most nineteenth-century American presidents, T.R. thought that a small Army was capable of winning the battles it might have to fight. Mustering about seventy-seven thousand officers and men in 1908, the Army contained eight thousand fewer soldiers than when he inherited the presidency from McKinley.

When Roosevelt was first inaugurated, he possessed a better understanding of naval matters than any president before or since. His understanding was not as thorough as professionals in such fields as ordnance, for example, but his breadth of knowledge about the Navy was remarkable. As assistant secretary of the Navy, T.R. thought that airplanes might have military utility. He went for a test dive in a submarine prototype. Possessing good strategic sense, Roosevelt conjured up for the Naval War College a theoretical problem of simultaneous crises over Hawaii (involving Japan) and Cuba (involving Spain): T.R. saw the need for a two-ocean navy. However, in the early 1900s the concept of a two-ocean navy had not gained favor among most politicians. In fact, he was president in an era when mammoth military budgets were not politically acceptable.

Roosevelt wanted a large, modern navy with offensive capabilities to shield America's commerce, enforce the Monroe Doctrine, guard the Panama Canal, and protect new island colonies. He envisioned that a navy with such capabilities would actually act as a deterrent to war. Thus, Roosevelt set out to build new ships and replace old ones; reorganize the fleet; increase the number and quality of naval officers and enlisted men; and reform naval administration, training, and gunnery. He tried to resolve a debate over the location of the main U.S. military base in the Pacific. Meanwhile, there was the continuing confusion and concern over strategy: was Britain a future friend or foe? And what of Japan, Britain's ally in the Pacific? To what extent would the German Empire become a rival to the United States in the Pacific and the Caribbean? Roosevelt was not successful in reaching all his goals. Six secretaries of the Navy served in T.R.'s cabinet, indicating that the president was actually his own naval secretary.

T.R. had no doubt how the strength of an early twentieth-century navy was measured—by the number of modern battleships it possessed. The American Navy enjoyed an inflated reputation among its citizenry and in Congress: the defeat of Spain's inadequate navy had seemed so easy. But none of America's battleships in service in 1901 displaced more than 11,500 tons or had a top speed of more than sixteen knots. Most of America's battleships were deemed suitable for "coastal defense" and were designed with less armor, speed, ordnance, and cruising range than the best British, German, and French battleships. T.R. intended to replace the coastal defense ships with ocean-going battleships. Accordingly, during his first years in office, the president obtained appropriations for ten battleships, as well as four armored cruisers, and seventeen miscellaneous vessels. In 1904 T.R. examined the plans of the proposed battleship *New Hampshire* and recommended to the Naval Board of Construction that the ship's battery be changed to all 11– or 12–inch guns rather than the hodgepodge of guns in the design. By making this recommendation (which the board did not adopt), Roosevelt was anticipating the revolutionary *Dreadnought* a year before the British began its construction. With these new ships built or building, T.R thought he had the basis for his modern battlefleet. Then in 1906 Britain launched the

Dreadnought, which displaced eighteen thousand tons, was capable of twenty-one knots, and mounted ten 12-inch guns. *Dreadnought*'s size, speed, and revolutionary all big-gun battery outclassed America's battleships afloat and under construction. U.S. battleships were obsolete, except for use against a lesser naval power, such as Spain. To keep up technologically with Britain (but not in numbers of ships), Germany, and France, America would have to engage in a construction program more expensive and advanced than that which T.R. had just put through Congress. Between 1906 and 1909, Roosevelt asked Congress to provide for ten more battleships, during years when he had anticipated that one per year would be satisfactory. Congress approved funding for six of the ships.

In 1901 the ships of the U.S. Navy were scattered in small squadrons at several stations around the world. Following general guidelines on fleet concentration laid down by Alfred Thayer Mahan, T.R. began his reorganization plan, withdrawing ships from the European and South Atlantic Stations and combining them with the North Atlantic Squadron to form the Atlantic Fleet. Additional cruisers reinforced the Asiatic Squadron, which was redesignated the Asiatic Fleet. Plans were made to form a Pacific Fleet. Thus, the battleships would be concentrated in the Atlantic ready to oppose the fleet of any potential enemy. When T.R.'s Panama Canal was completed, battleships could pass through from one ocean to another.

During his seven and one-half years in office, T.R. pursued a policy that led Congress to more than double the number of enlisted men in the Navy. The enlisted strength went from 18,800 in 1901 to 44,100 in 1909. Roosevelt obtained better food and higher pay for sailors. The number of officers also increased, going from 1,700 in 1901 to more than 2,500 in 1909. Many of these new officers came from the expanded classes at the U.S. Naval Academy at Annapolis, but T.R.'s plan to involuntarily retire older line officers to create faster promotions for younger officers was less than a complete success. Increasing the number of modern ships in service was encouraging to energetic junior and midlevel officers, including Roosevelt's naval aide, William Sowden Sims.

In December 1907 the Great White Fleet started on its 'round-the-world-voyage under the command of Robley Dunglison Evans. Roosevelt ranked this controversial martial display as one of the most important acts of his presidency, saying that the voyage was intended to give the sixteen white-painted battleships experience at fleet training, call Congress' attention to the need for additional naval appropriations, and impress the Japanese government. Japanese officials had been making bellicose remarks because of the mistreatment of Japanese immigrants in California. Relations with Japan were eased by the "Gentlemen's Agreement" (1907), in which T.R. promised that Japanese settlers would receive fair treatment, and the Root-Takahira Agreement (1908), in which both nations agreed to continue the Open-Door Policy in China and respect the integrity of each other's territory in the Pacific. On the other hand, some Japanese leaders may have been inspired by the Great White Fleet to push plans for a stronger

Japanese Navy. The voyage of the battlefleet was a typical showmanlike gesture on Roosevelt's part, but the cruise was more than a bravura performance. Men and machines were tested. More Americans saw the need for having a two-ocean navy. A big Pacific base and new naval facilities on the West Coast were obviously necessary.

Politics played a major part in the location of American naval yards and bases. Twenty installations were located on the Atlantic Coast, two on the Gulf of Mexico, and only two on the Pacific. In 1903 T.R. arranged for a ninety-nine year lease for Guantanamo Bay, Cuba. But would the location of a primary American military base in the Pacific be in the Philippines or Hawaii? In 1908 T.R. finally chose Pearl Harbor, Hawaii, and Congress appropriated funds for the base. This decision left the Philippines—which T.R. called "America's Achilles heel in the Pacific"—without adequate defenses.

During his presidency, Roosevelt had significantly increased the size and efficiency of the U.S. Navy. The fleet was top-heavy with battleships at the expense of cruisers and other ships, but T.R.'s objective was to get the big ships on line first. By 1909 America had become the world's number three naval power, behind Britain and Germany.

Many men who met Roosevelt or who wrote about him later mistook his unquenchable enthusiasm for immaturity. (Sir Cecil Spring Rice, a British diplomat, once remarked, "You must always remember that the President is about six.") T.R. was militaristic; he said that "a thousand rich bankers cannot leave such a heritage as Farragut left." Probably he was the most belligerent man ever to receive the Nobel Peace Prize. But in T.R.'s view a militarily unprepared nation was weak and thus tempted an attack by stronger nations. During the seven and one-half years of his administration, the United States was not involved in a general war.

Born in the Victorian era, Teddy Roosevelt became a man of the technological twentieth century. He was a multitalented, dynamic leader. Through the steps he took to enlarge and modernize the Navy, Roosevelt made his mark on American military developments. More than most presidents, he understood the close connection between military power and statecraft.

BIBLIOGRAPHY

Beale, Howard K. *Theodore Roosevelt and the Rise of America to World Power*. Baltimore: Johns Hopkins University Press, 1956.
Braisted, William R. *The United States Navy in the Pacific, 1897–1909*. Austin: University of Texas Press, 1958.
Harbaugh, William H. *The Life and Times of Theodore Roosevelt*. New York: Oxford University Press, 1975.
Jones, Virgil C. *Roosevelt's Rough Riders*. New York: Doubleday, 1971.
Marks, Frederick W., III. *Velvet on Iron: The Diplomacy of Theodore Roosevelt*. Lincoln: University of Nebraska Press, 1979.

Morison, Elting E. *Admiral Sims and the Modern American Navy*. Boston: Houghton Mifflin Company, 1942.

O'Gara, Gordon G. *Theodore Roosevelt and the Rise of the Modern Navy*. Princeton, N.J.: Princeton University Press, 1943.

JOSEPH G. DAWSON III

ROSECRANS, William Starke (b. Delaware County, Ohio, September 6, 1819; d. near Los Angeles, Calif., March 11, 1898), Army officer, public official. Rosecrans was a senior Union officer in the Western Theatre during the Civil War.

William S. Rosecrans came from one of the pioneer families that settled in Ohio. His father was a farmer-merchant of modest means, and Rosecrans received only a sporadic education in public schools. He was a voracious reader, however, and was able to educate himself. He secured an appointment to the U.S. Military Academy at West Point, New York, in 1838. Rosecrans performed well while at the Academy, graduating number five in a class of fifty-one. Because of his academic performance, he was rewarded with a commission as brevet second lieutenant, Corps of Engineers, as of July 1, 1842. An assignment to the Engineers was usually given only to the best Academy graduates. After working for a year on fortifications at Hampton Roads, Virginia, Rosecrans returned to West Point for the next four years as an assistant professor of engineering.

For the next several years Rosecrans was engaged in a number of different Army engineering projects until he resigned as of April 1, 1854, to enter business as an architect and civil engineer in Cincinnati, Ohio. He then moved to western Virginia to serve briefly as president of the New Coal River-Slack Water Navigation Company, resigning in 1857 to refine kerosene in Cincinnati. That year, he was severely burned by an explosion of a "safety" kerosene lamp on which he was working, taking many months to recover. In early 1861 his company was just beginning to be profitable.

On the outbreak of the Civil War, Rosecrans served as a volunteer aide to Major General George Brinton McClellan,* organizing and training new troops from April 19 until June 10, when he was appointed colonel of the 23d Ohio Volunteer Infantry Regiment. As a promising officer and a Catholic and a Democrat, Rosecrans was an ideal choice for a Republican administration seeking broad support. President Abraham Lincoln approved his commission as a brigadier general in the Regular Army, ranking from May 16. He commanded a brigade in McClellan's operations in western Virginia, and he won the Battle of Rich Mountain, July 11. Rosecrans succeeded McClellan in command of the Department of the Ohio before being assigned to command the Department of Western Virginia from September 21 to April 7, 1862.

Rosecrans was transferred west to command a division of the Army of the Mississippi and participated in the siege of Corinth, Mississippi, May 22–30. He commanded the Army of the Mississippi from June 11 until October 20. Rosecrans, under the command of Major General Ulysses Simpson Grant,* fought in the Battle of Iuka, Mississippi, September 19, but failed to trap the retreating Confederate forces as Grant had planned. This was the beginning of the friction that developed between the two men. The following day, Rosecrans learned that he had been promoted to major general to rank from March 21. In the Battle of Corinth, October 3–4, Rosecrans was attacked, and after a brief penetration by the Confederate forces into Corinth, he repulsed them while inflicting heavy losses. Rosecrans, however, delayed pursuing the disorganized Confederates for a day, allowing them to escape with most of their equipment which further annoyed Grant. Even so, Rosecrans had demonstrated considerable skill in his handling of the troops during the actual engagement.

With these two partial successes to his credit, Rosecrans was placed in command of the Army of the Cumberland in middle Tennessee on October 27 to face the Confederate Army of the Tennessee under Braxton Bragg.* Late in December, after building up his supplies in Nashville, Rosecrans advanced on Bragg, meeting him in the Battle of Murfreesboro (Stone's River), December 31. Bragg's aggressive attack was a tactical success, and his army inflicted more than thirteen thousand Union casualties while suffering only nine thousand of their own. Rosecrans was in a vulnerable position, but Bragg did not renew the assault. The Confederate force withdrew toward Tullahoma, Tennessee, on January 3, allowing Rosecrans to claim victory by virtue of having possession of the battlefield.

Rosecrans spent the next six months planning, organizing, and equipping his army. While his army grew stronger, Bragg's was shrinking. This fact was obvious to Rosecrans' superiors who constantly urged him to act while he had the advantage. Finally, on June 24, Rosecrans opened a brilliant campaign, and, by September 9, he had maneuvered Bragg out of Chattanooga without a fight. But help was on the way for Bragg's depleted army in the form of reinforcements from Mississippi and a corps from the Army of Northern Virginia under James Longstreet.* In the Battle of Chickamauga, Georgia, September 19–20, Rosecrans made a serious error by moving a division and leaving a gap in his line which the attacking Confederates exploited with disastrous effects. Apparently defeated by Bragg, he left the battlefield before the battle was over. The heroic stand of Major General George Henry Thomas* saved the army from complete annihilation. Rosecrans retreated to Chattanooga with his disorganized forces and was besieged, inexplicably allowing Bragg to occupy the high ground around the city. Cut off from significant resupply, Rosecrans faced a grim situation. He began planning for the reopening of his supply lines but had not acted when Thomas relieved him by Grant's orders on October 19.

Rosecrans' last active command was the Department of the Missouri from January 28 to December 9, 1864. He became alarmed about an alleged conspiracy uncovered in the state. Predicting an uprising, he constantly called for reinforcements for a relatively inactive military theater at a time when Union armies elsewhere needed every available soldier. These constant calls dismayed Grant, leading him to observe that Rosecrans would make similar calls if he were "stationed in Maine." After his removal from command in Missouri, Rosecrans was either awaiting orders or on leave of absence, until his resignation as of March 28, 1867.

After his resignation, Rosecrans served briefly as the U.S. minister to Mexico until Grant was elected president. He then pursued various mining, manufacturing, and railroad interests in California and Mexico, and served in the U.S. House of Representatives as a Democrat (1881–1885). As chairman of the House Committee on Military Affairs, Rosecrans was one of the few people in the country to oppose Grant's restoration to general after he had suffered severe financial reverses and was dying from cancer.

Rosecrans' reputation as a military commander is mixed. An intelligent man, an excellent planner and organizer, he sometimes lacked aggressiveness in executing his plans. His early successes in western Virginia demonstrated his organizational abilities and a marked ability to work with volunteer troops—an essential ingredient for success during the Civil War. He was personally brave under fire, but he had a tendency to get excited and give too many orders which were confusing to his commanders during the heat of battle. And, at times, he demonstrated flashes of strategic genius as he did during the summer of 1863.

Rosecrans bitterly denounced Grant's version of the battles of Iuka and Corinth, but the record indicates that Rosecrans was slow to move at crucial moments. This slowness was costly, allowing Confederate forces to escape from precarious situations without further molestation. And this slowness to move was even more costly after the Battle of Murfreesboro. Rosecrans evidently believed that it was unwise for the country to fight more than one major battle at a time, which may explain his delay in attacking Bragg when the Confederate Army of Tennessee was vulnerable. Had Rosecrans moved on Bragg earlier when Confederate forces were occupied at Vicksburg and in Pennsylvania, he might have been able to inflict a fatal blow to the Confederacy. Rosecrans' campaign of maneuver in the summer of 1863 was brilliantly executed. But it occurred at a time when Bragg could not afford to fight until help could arrive from the east and west after July 1863. Without this help, there would not have been a Battle of Chickamauga. During this battle Rosecrans lost his head and fled from the battlefield in despair at a time when he should have been doing all in his power to reorganize his shattered army.

Embittered by his relief at Chattanooga, Rosecrans developed a life-long hatred for Grant, blaming him for many of the things that had befallen him. It is true that Grant developed a healthy dislike for Rosecrans and refused to consider him for any important field command. But no amount of hatred, or making of excuses, could undo the consequences of that day at Chickamauga.

BIBLIOGRAPHY

Bearss, Edwin. *Decision in Mississippi*. Jackson, Miss.: Mississippi Commission on the War between the States, 1962.

Catton, Bruce. *Grant Moves South*. Boston: Little, Brown and Company, 1960.
Lamers, William M. *The Edge of Glory: A Biography of General William S. Rosecrans*. New York: Harcourt, Brace and World, 1961.
McDonough, James L. *Stone's River*. Knoxville: University of Tennessee Press, 1980.
Tucker, Glenn. *Chickamauga*. Indianapolis, Ind.: Bobbs-Merrill, 1961.

DAVID L. WILSON

SAMPSON, William Thomas (b. Palmyra, N.Y., February 9, 1840; d. Washington, D.C., May 6, 1902), naval officer. Sampson was commander in chief of the North Atlantic Squadron at the time of the defeat of Admiral Pascual Cervera's squadron in the Spanish-American War.

William T. Sampson was the oldest child of Presbyterian Scotch-Irish immigrant parents who settled in Palmyra, New York. An excellent student, young Sampson won an appointment to the U.S. Naval Academy in 1857. He was an outstanding student at the Naval Academy and was especially interested in ordnance. He was first in his class in his last three years and earned a reputation at the Academy for modesty and scholarship.

As a graduate in the spring of 1861, Sampson helped to defend the Naval Academy grounds against unfriendly local citizens while the underclassmen were transferred to Newport, Rhode Island. At the end of April he reported to Commander John Adolphus Bernard Dahlgren, the famous gun inventor, at the Washington Navy Yard. The capital was in a state of tension in those early weeks of the Civil War, and Sampson found himself concerned with cut telegraph lines, damaged or destroyed rail bridges, and attacks on Potomac steamers. In May Sampson served a brief stint aboard the sloop *Pocahontas*, and in June he reported to the *Potomac*, now an acting master, for nine months' duty in the Gulf of Mexico.

In 1862 Sampson was promoted to lieutenant and began his first assignment as an instructor at the Naval Academy, temporarily established at Newport. His great interest in armor, steam engines, and ordnance led him to accept the wartime teaching post without protest. In 1863 he served on a practice cruise to England and France aboard the frigate *Macedonia*. Sampson's midshipmen included most of his future captains and the leading naval officers of the Spanish-American War.

In 1864 Sampson was ordered to the South Atlantic Blockading Squadron as executive officer in the new monitor, *Patapsco*. He won praise for his coolness and composure when the *Patapsco* was sunk by a Confederate torpedo. In July 1866, amidst sharp cuts and economies in the Navy, he was promoted to lieutenant commander.

After the Civil War, Sampson's assignments were varied. He served for two years as a watch officer aboard the screw frigate *Colorado* of the European Squadron. In 1868 he began three energetic years of service as head of the new Department of Physics and Chemistry at the Naval Academy. He was then assigned as executive officer in the frigate *Congress* on European Station from

1871 to 1874. In was a time of embarrassment for U.S. naval officers as they witnessed a dramatic decline in every area of their nation's naval establishment. Sampson returned to the Naval Academy in 1874 where he introduced advanced scientific studies in several areas. Sampson's first command was aboard the screw gunboat *Swatara* in 1882. His next assignment was as assistant to the superintendent of the Naval Observatory in Washington for two years under four different superintendents; in effect, he headed the observatory. From 1884 to 1886 Sampson was inspector of ordnance and head of the Torpedo Station in Newport, where, with Commodore Stephen Bleeker Luce, he urged the creation of the Naval War College. Commander Sampson returned to Annapolis in September 1886 for three years as superintendent of the Naval Academy. As superintendent he presided over meetings of the U.S. Naval Institute during a period of vigorous technical activity. Sampson was promoted to captain in March 1889.

Captain Sampson left the Academy in the summer of 1890 to supervise the final technical installations aboard the new cruiser, *San Francisco*. On March 31, 1891, with Rear Admiral George Brown aboard, the *San Francisco*, commanded by Sampson, left for observation patrol off strife-torn Chile. In June 1892 Sampson became superintendent of the naval gun foundry in Washington and then served as chief of the Bureau of Ordnance, 1893–1897. Placed in command of the new battleship *Iowa* in June 1897, Sampson impressed Assistant Secretary of the Navy Theodore Roosevelt* as talented, level-headed, and dependable during fleet drills off the Virginia capes.

Sampson presided over the board of inquiry on the *Maine* disaster in Havana and, in recognition of his outstanding record, was appointed commander in chief of the North Atlantic Squadron on the eve of war with Spain. On April 21, 1898, he hoisted the pennant of rear admiral aboard his flagship, *New York*, and began to move his forces to a blockade of northern Cuba. He unsuccessfully sought from the Navy Department a clarification of operations between himself and Commodore Winfield Scott Schley* of the Flying Squadron. Schley, though two numbers senior to Sampson, was finally placed under Sampson's orders on May 24 by Secretary of the Navy John D. Long.

After an eastward cruise to Puerto Rico in search of Admiral Pascual Cervera's fleet, Sampson returned first to Key West and a meeting with Schley (May 18) and then to a blockade of Cuban waters. Sampson established that Cervera was in Santiago and ordered Schley (May 25) to proceed there at once and blockade the harbor. He returned to Key West to convoy Army units and learned that Schley had not moved directly into blockade position. He went there himself and arrived on June 1 and met with Schley. Sampson established an effective month-long close blockade of Santiago with searchlights fixed at night on the narrow harbor entrance. He seized Guantanamo Bay, supervised operations in support of the Army, directed all minor operations, bombardments, and reconnaissance, and was in command of more than one hundred vessels.

On the morning of July 3 Sampson had sailed seven miles to the east for a conference with General William Rufus Shafter* when Cervera's squadron came out of Santiago and under the guns of the blockading force. Every Spanish vessel was captured or destroyed, with only minimal U.S. casualties. However, the press deserted Sampson and made Schley the hero of the successful action against the Spanish, though Sampson was defended by the service and the Navy Department.

Although in poor health, Sampson continued in command of the North Atlantic Station for one more year. He became commandant of the Boston Navy Yard at the end of 1899, but his health continued to decline. On May 6, 1902, he died in Washington.

Sampson was a distinguished naval leader whose reputation has suffered from controversies inspired by sensational newspaper stories in an age noted for journalistic excesses. His meticulousness at every stage of his service at the Naval Academy helped the institution make a difficult transition into the age of advanced technology and scientific education. His thorough knowledge of armor plate metallurgy was of considerable value in the advancement of the American steel industry and the design and construction of modern naval vessels.

In the Spanish-American War Sampson successfully bore primary responsibility for preventing attacks on American coastal cities by locating and confining the Spanish Squadron. He provided the Army with transportation and supplies under difficult circumstances, and carried on effective reconnaissance and communications operations over an extensive range with limited equipment. His knowledge of armor and gunnery, and his experience with the men and ships under his command enabled him to construct an effective blockade which ultimately forced the enemy into a desperate attempt to escape. His effective gunnery drills, fleet exercises, and blockade plans prior to the battle all contributed to the American victory off Santiago. With pride he reported to Washington: "The fleet under my command offers the nation as a Fourth of July present the whole of Cervera's fleet."

At first, all the acclaim and admiration for the victory in Cuba went to Sampson; then within a few days the brilliance of his fame faded. He was criticized for minimizing Schley's accomplishments, for stealing a victory that was not his. Circumstances had drawn him off the battleline that morning and had delayed his return to action. The press divided into pro-Schley and pro-Sampson factions, and the Congress fueled the controversy by refusing to confirm the Navy Department's August 10, 1898, recommendation that Sampson be advanced eight numbers and Schley six. Finally, both men were made rear admirals by the Personnel Act of 1899, but Sampson never properly gained the recognition from his countrymen which he so properly deserved for his exemplary service and achievements.

BIBLIOGRAPHY

Azoy, A.C.M. *Signal 250! The Sea Fight Off Santiago*. New York: David McKay Company, 1964.
Herrick, Walter R., Jr. *The American Naval Revolution*. Baton Rouge: Louisiana State University Press, 1966.
Karsten, Peter. *The Naval Aristocracy: The Golden Age of Annapolis and the Emergence of Modern American Navalism*. New York: Free Press, 1972.
West, Richard S. *Admirals of American Empire*. New York: Bobbs-Merrill Company, 1948.

PHILIP Y. NICHOLSON

SCHLEY, Winfield Scott (b. Frederick County, Md., October 9, 1839; d. New York City, N.Y., October 2, 1909), naval officer. Schley is known for his command of the Flying Squadron at the victorious Battle of Santiago, July 3, 1898, in the Spanish-American War.

Winfield Scott Schley was born in his father's manor house, "Richfields," in Frederick County, Maryland. He won appointment to the U.S. Naval Academy in 1856 through the assistance of Representative H. W. Hoffman. Though not known for his scholarship, he loved the work and the camaraderie of his two practice cruises.

His first post was aboard the steam frigate *Niagra* in June 1860. At the outset of the Civil War the *Niagara* was placed on blockade duty off Charleston. Schley's first command was the delivery of the captured prize *General Parkhill* to the admiralty court in Philadelphia. Subsequently, Schley twice won distinction for hazardous volunteer duty under fire in small boats during a year's blockade duty off Mobile Bay. Promoted to lieutenant in 1862, he was made executive officer of the steam gunboat *Winona* in the squadron of Admiral David Glasgow Farragut* at Mobile Bay. He was navigator in the steam sloop *Richmond* and acted in command of the large ship on the occasional absences of the captain and executive officer. He was in command during the May 26, 1863, bombardment of Port Hudson, Louisiana, and won praise from Farragut for his fighting spirit. After his marriage to Annie Rebecca Franklin in September 1863, he was assigned to the Bureau of Ordnance. Later, Schley became executive officer in the double-ender *Wateree* for a futile search mission in the Pacific for the Confederate raider *Shenandoah*.

Twenty years of stagnation and decline characterized the U.S. Navy after the Civil War, but Schley remained popular with his associates and was on the fringes of that group of officers who gained the best assignments. He was acting assistant professor of Spanish at the Naval Academy from 1867 to 1869, and became friendly with George Dewey* who, along with William Thomas Sampson,* came to Annapolis at the same time. As executive officer aboard the screw cruiser *Benicia* (1869–1873), Schley saw action in a punitive expedition in Korea in June 1871. He added four more years at Annapolis as chairman of the Modern Languages Department, and from 1876 to 1879 Commander Schley was skipper of the frigate *Essex* in the South Atlantic. Next he was posted to Boston for four years as an inspector in the Lighthouse Service. Schley worked closely with Secretary William E. Chandler as chief of the apprentice system in the Bureau of Equipment and Recruiting in 1883. Schley gained national attention in 1884 for his successful and hazardous command of the *Thetis* and *Bear* in the rescue expedition that returned Army Lieutenant Adolphus W. Greely and six other survivors from near death in the Arctic Ocean north of Greenland. In recognition of his achievement, Schley, though a commander, was made chief of the Bureau of Equipment and Recruiting, where he served from 1884 to 1889.

Schley was promoted to captain in 1887 and was given command of the new cruiser *Baltimore* in July 1889. In 1891 he persuaded Secretary Benjamin F. Tracy to send him to Chile with the *Baltimore* during the diplomatic crisis there. Schley's action in cutting the telegraph cable from the rebel-held city of Iquique increased the Chileans' hostility toward the United States and focused that hostility most sharply on the *Baltimore* and her crew. A fight in the True Blue Saloon in Valparaiso resulted in the death of two of Schley's sailors; others were injured and thirty-six arrested. These troubles provoked sharp diplomatic reaction and the threat of war for several months. After his return from Chile, Schley moved to New York where he served as inspector for the Third Lighthouse District from 1892 to 1895.

In October 1895, after brief service on the Board of Inspection and Survey, Schley took command of the armored cruiser *New York*, the flagship of Admiral F. M. Bunce's Atlantic Squadron. He was named commodore in March 1898 and placed in command of the fast cruiser *Brooklyn*, the flagship of the Flying Squadron. His orders were to protect the coastal cities of the United States, an assignment, wrote Secretary of the Navy, John Long, that "was especially desirable, and one to which any one of his seniors might have felt entitled."

The declaration of war with Spain in April 1898 and the discovery of Admiral Pascual Cervera's squadron near Martinique sent Schley and his squadron to join Admiral Sampson and the Atlantic Squadron. Their object was to blockade the Spaniards in Cuba. Schley was indirectly placed under Sampson's command and sent to blockade the southern railroad port of Cienfuegos where Cervera was believed to have gone. Schley seemed to hesitate there, remaining in place from May 22 to 24 in spite of urgings to go to Santiago. His slow journey to Santiago where he first failed to establish a close blockade, then his peculiar retrograde movement toward Key West, and finally his leisurely return at about seven knots to Santiago earned him sharp criticism. (After the war President Theodore Roosevelt* convened a special naval court of inquiry to investigate the charges raised about his conduct. Admiral George Dewey presided, and in late 1901 the court of inquiry found Schley's actions prior to June 1, 1898, to be characterized by "vacillation, dilatoriness, and lack of enterprise.")

From June 1 to July 3, 1898, Schley's squadron joined Sampson's forces in a carefully controlled blockade of Santiago. When Cervera's ships made an attempt to escape, Schley's *Brooklyn* led in the attack which resulted in a complete victory over the Spanish. Sampson had withdrawn aboard the *New York* to confer with General William Rufus Shafter* seven miles east of the battle, and by the time Sampson had returned, the Spanish had been beaten. This prompted some public resentment over crediting the victory to Sampson. A subsequent Sampson-Schley controversy was carried on in the press and by their staffs, though Schley publicly acknowledged Sampson's right to the victory as the commander of U.S. naval forces at the time of the battle.

Schley was welcomed as a hero in New York and Washington in August 1898. He was promoted to rear admiral in 1899, and in November of that year was named commander in chief of the South Atlantic Station where he served until shortly before his retirement on October 9, 1901, at the statutory age limit of sixty-two. He traveled widely, speaking frequently as an honored and popular figure, and in 1904 he published his autobiography, *Forty-Five Years under the Flag*.

Undoubtedly, Schley was a controversial officer. In the Chilean crisis of 1891, he vigorously defended his sailors and won their warmest praise in return. He maintained that they had not been drunk or provocative; rather, they had been victims of premeditated attacks by Valparaiso's populace, aided by officials and police.

As chief of the Bureau of Equipment, Schley instigated important changes beneficial to sailors. On his urging the Navy adopted the practice of issuing standardized clothing to sailors. He established the first school to train Navy cooks and urged the use of a pension system for sailors comparable to that avialable to soldiers of the U.S. Army.

Schley's caution during the uncertain period prior to the exact location of Cervera's squadron in Santiago was said to have been due to a "passion for full bunkers." (Apparently, his rescue of Lieutenant Greely in the Arctic Ocean strongly impressed upon Schley the need for proper coal reserves.) Schley was known to regularly subtract from his coal reserves the amount needed to return to Key West, a possible contingency, though never really a necessity.

The court of inquiry that criticized his cautious actions before June 1, 1898, praised Schley for his coolness in battle. He was said to have "encouraged in his own person, his subordinate officers and men to fight courageously." His old friend, Admiral Dewey, dissented from the criticism of the majority. Dewey believed that Schley had been "in absolute command, and is entitled to the credit due to such a commanding officer for the glorious victory which resulted in the total destruction of the Spanish ships." In spite of controversy, Schley's reputation rests on his outstanding capabilities and achievements as a naval commander.

BIBLIOGRAPHY

Azoy, A.C.M. *Signal 250! The Sea Fight off Santiago*. New York: David McKay Company, 1964.

Herrick, Walter R., Jr. *The American Naval Revolution.* Baton Rouge: Louisiana State University Press, 1966.
Schley, Winfield Scott. *Forty-Five Years under the Flag.* New York: D. Appleton and Company, 1904.
West, Richard S., Jr. *Admirals of American Empire.* New York: Bobbs-Merrill, 1948.

PHILIP Y. NICHOLSON

SCOTT, Winfield (b. Laurel Branch, Va., near Petersburg, Dinwiddie County, June 13, 1786; d. West Point, N. Y., May 29, 1866), general, military theorist, diplomat, candidate for the American presidency.

Winfield Scott was sprung from a warrior clan. His grandfather, James Scott, fled to America after surviving the massacre at Culloden in 1746, and his father, William Scott, served in the American Revolution as a captain. His elder brother, James, was a regimental commander in the War of 1812. When Winfield was six years old, his father died, and his mother, Ann Mason Scott, followed her husband eleven years later. Ann Scott's grandfather was John Winfield, a very wealthy colonial planter. From this source, young Winfield was the recipient of an adequate, if somewhat limited, patrimony.

The U.S. Military Academy at West Point came into existence in 1802, but inasmuch as that school was in its infancy, and also because he had not yet determined to become a soldier, Scott entered William and Mary College in 1805. He disliked the college, in part because of a campus religious controversy, and he left it the same term as he entered, whereupon he traveled to Petersburg and read law in David Robinson's office.

Shortly following the *Chesapeake-Leopard* affair in 1807, Scott enlisted in the cavalry, and he immediately distinguished himself by seizing a British boat and its eight occupants, among whom were two officers. By May 1808, Scott was designated a captain of light artillery. His next duty assignment was in 1809 in New Orleans. He was so unimpressed by the quality of the officers there that he determined to quit the service and to reenter the law. At this time, in his youthful exuberance, he had somewhat less than privately censured his departmental commander, General James Wilkinson, as a traitor and an accomplice in the Burr Conspiracy. Wilkinson proffered charges against Scott, who, in turn, was relieved of his commission for a year. In the face of this brazen assault, Scott's mind again turned to the law, but with Congress' declaration of war in 1812, he received the rank of lieutenant colonel. In October Scott distinguished himself at the Battle of Queenstown Heights, where he was captured. Paroled, he next found action at Fort George, where he was wounded. He was then attached to the command of his old enemy, Wilkinson. Despite his unhappy situation, he busied himself with the training of the soldiery, and his successes gained the attentions of President James Madison and Secretary of War James Monroe.

By March 1814 Scott was raised to brigadier general, and the following July he distinguished himself at the spectacular Battle of Chippewa. He also fought at Lundy's Lane, where, once again, he was badly wounded. This time his brilliant service merited his superiors' attentions, and he was given medals by both Virginia and Congress and brevetted to the rank of major general.

At the war's conclusion, Scott wrote the new U.S. Infantry drill manual and then went to Europe, where he continued his military studies with which he had become fascinated. Upon his return to America in 1817, he married Maria D. Mayo of Richmond, Virginia. He made practical use of his knowledge through his office as the repeated president of the Army's Board of Tactics, and in 1834–1835, after yet one more trip to Europe, he expanded and honed the three-volume *Infantry Tactics*, which was published in 1835.

When Major General Jacob Jennings Brown died in 1828, Major General Alexander Macomb was elevated to the position of commanding general of the Army. Miffed at what he considered to be a slight, Scott tendered his resignation which was refused. In 1832 he was again commanding troops in the Black Hawk War, but his participation in that conflict was limited when he fell victim to cholera. Recovering, in 1835 he was sent to carry on a war against the Indians in Florida. While on a campaign against the Creeks, Andrew Jackson,* who had a distrust of Scott, first relieved him for dilatoriness and then had the conduct of his campaign examined by a court of inquiry, which in turn dismissed the charges, and in fact commended Scott's efforts. In 1838 he was actively engaged in various efforts in diplomacy with the British, Canadians, and Cherokees.

When General Macomb died in 1841, Scott rose to the command of the U.S. Army. He was a particularly active commander, and his reforms in uniform dress, temperance, military prisons, and education were widely noted. During this period, he made a serious blunder and an even greater indiscretion. He publically endorsed Henry Clay for the presidency. This ineptness earned deserved difficulties with the Democratic administration of President James K. Polk (1845–1849).

Upon the outbreak of the Mexican War, General Zachary Taylor* performed creditably against the Mexicans in northern Mexico, but it was strategically infeasible to win in that theater alone. With some reluctance, Polk sent Scott on an expedition into Mexico's interior via the Gulf coast and Vera Cruz. It is in this role that Scott's reputation as a major military captain rests. In a brilliant campaign, the likes of which has never before or since been witnessed in American military annals, Scott, despite great weaknesses in logistics and troops, overcame a more numerous enemy, who enjoyed the advantage of interior lines. Throughout, his campaign was conducted with intelligence and humanity, and even managed to earn the admiration of the Mexicans themselves. It was also in Mexico that Scott's temperament again ran afoul of civilian leadership, and he was the victim of another court of inquiry, this one seeded with his political and professional enemies. Nevertheless, his signal achievements could not be denied, and he was saved by a grateful Congress and once more rewarded with another gold medal struck in that body's name. Ultimately, he was elevated to the rank of lieutenant general, the first American to hold that exalted rank since

George Washington.* In 1852 Scott was nominated to the presidency by the Whig party, but he was overwhelmingly defeated by Franklin Pierce of New Hampshire, a former subordinate of his in the late war.

In 1860, on the eve of the American Civil War, Scott urged President James Buchanan to aid Fort Sumter and other important Federal military installations in the South. Buchanan ignored his advice. When Abraham Lincoln became president, the situation had so badly deteriorated that success in such a venture was virtually impossible. Though aged and infirm, Scott still proposed a plan, which with variations, was to be the general strategic concept of the United States in the Civil War. The Anaconda Plan, as it was known, called for seizure of the Mississippi River and blockade of southern ports. He hoped that this effort would strangle the Confederacy and diminish the use of invading Federal troops. As it was perceived by President Abraham Lincoln and General Ulysses Simpson Grant,* however, the employment of attacking columns was necessary.

Scott retired from the army on All Hallow's Eve in 1861. Although a Virginian, he supported the Union, and his resignation prompted the strongest praise from Lincoln. He was nearly eighty when he died, and he was buried at West Point amidst honors and kudos.

Winfield Scott was one of the greatest field commanders in modern military history. His praises are recorded by numerous military figures, including both Arthur Wellesley, the duke of Wellington, and the Baron Antoine Henri Jomini. He was a commander who often fought under severe handicaps, but whose genius overcame the most imposing obstacles. In this respect, he resembles John Churchill, the duke of Marlborough: neither ever lost a battle, and Scott's relations with Polk and Congress are reminiscent of the duke's with Queen Anne and Parliament. In addition, by force of his personality, integrity, and ability, he molded American military thought into the best European examples and advanced theories. In recent times, it has become fashionable to deny the influences of Jomini on American military development and to denigrate Scott's personal influence. Such is the whim of historical writing and the pervasive influence of the age of twentieth-century total war on the historical community. But to the end, Jomini's influence on Scott was unmistakable, and Scott's influence on the American Army profound. *Vis fortisimme in aetate tractabile erat.*

BIBLIOGRAPHY

Bauer, K. Jack. *The Mexican War, 1846–1848.* New York: Macmillan Company, 1974.
Elliott, Charles Winslow. *Winfield Scott: The Soldier and the Man.* New York: Macmillan Company, 1937.
Johnston, Robert Matteson. *Leading American Soldiers.* New York: Henry Holt, 1907.
Mansfield, Edward Deering. *The Life and Military Services of Lieut.-General Winfield Scott.* New York: N. C. Miller, 1862.
Sabin, Edwin Legrand. *Into Mexico with General Scott.* Philadelphia: J. B. Lippincott, 1920.

Scott, Winfield. *Memoirs of Lieut.-General Scott.* 2 vols. New York: Sheldon, 1864.
Smith, Arthur D. Howden. *Old Fuss and Feathers: The Life and Exploits of Winfield Scott.* New York: Greystone Press, 1937.
Smith, Justin H. *The War with Mexico.* New York: Macmillan Company, 1919.
Wright, Marcus Joseph. *General Scott.* New York: D. Appleton, 1894.

JAMES W. POHL

SEMMES, Raphael (b. Charles County, Md., September 27, 1809; d. Mobile, Ala., August 30, 1877), naval officer. Semmes is noted for his command of the Confederate commerce raider *Alabama* during the Civil War.

Raphael Semmes was the eldest son of Richard Thompson Semmes and his wife Catherine (Middleton) of French ancestry. His parents died early in his childhood, and he was raised by an uncle in Georgetown, District of Columbia. In April 1826 he was appointed a midshipman in the U.S. Navy by President John Quincy Adams, probably through the influence of another uncle, Benedict J. Semmes, an influential Maryland planter.

Eleven years passed before Semmes was promoted to lieutenant. This was not because of a poor record; he stood second in his class in 1832 at a naval school, and according to scattered references his performance at sea was satisfactory. The problem was that throughout the period promotion was extremely slow. During these years he served successively in the naval sloops *Lexington* and *Erie*, the frigate *Brandywine*, the schooner *Porpoise*, and the frigate *Constellation* on the Mediterranean, West India, and the South Atlantic Stations, and along the Florida coast during the Seminole War. Between tours of sea duty Semmes spent lengthy periods on shore. In 1832 he was placed in charge of the Navy's chronometers and became so fascinated by them that they became a lifetime hobby. He also spent some time on hydrographic surveys, studied and practiced law, and married Anne Elizabeth Spencer in May 1837. His marriage occurred three months after he was promoted to lieutenant.

During the next decade his professional career followed a normal peacetime routine of sea and shore duty. When the Mexican War broke out, Semmes was assigned to command the brig *Somers* deployed on blockade duty along the eastern coast of Mexico. Semmes was in command of this unlucky ship when she foundered during a sudden squall with the loss of more than half of her crew. The court of inquiry exonerated him of blame. He continued in active service during the war as flag-lieutenant to Commodore David Conner, with the shore-based naval artillery at the bombardment of Vera Cruz and the expedition against Tuxpan, and accompanied the army of General Winfield Scott* to Mexico on special duty.

The war ended in 1848, and Semmes, like many others, discovered that there were more officers than ships available. During his final years as a U.S. naval officer, he was on awaiting-orders status much of the time. While on active service, he commanded two small vessels, the schooner *Flirt* and the storeship *Electra*; was inspector of clothing and provisions at the Pensacola Naval Station in Florida; and served on court-martial and lighthouse duty. He was promoted to commander in 1855. Semmes resigned his commission in the U.S. Navy on February 15, 1861. At that time he was stationed in Washington, D.C., as chairman of the Lighthouse Board.

In 1841 Semmes had established legal residence in Alabama and considered Mobile his home. His resignation followed his state's secession and the creation of the Confederacy. In March he was appointed a commander in the Confederate States Navy. Even before this date Semmes had performed his first service for the new government by purchasing munitions, ordnance, machinery, and vessels in the North. After that he was made chief of the Lighthouse Bureau, but in April 1861 he was appointed to command the *Sumter*, the first Confederate commerce raider.

Semmes commanded the *Sumter* approximately a year—from her fitting out in New Orleans until she was blockaded by Union warships at Gibraltar and subsequently sold. Although the *Sumter* was too small and slow to be an effective commerce raider, she nevertheless captured eighteen prizes. Perhaps most important was the experience Semmes gained and the reputation he began to acquire as the beau ideal of a commerce destroyer.

At Nassau on the way home Semmes received orders to take command of the *Alabama* or *Enrica*, as she was christened at her launching in Liverpool. The vessel left England under British papers, and near the Azores took on her armament and was commissioned as a Confederate man-of-war. After a brief shakedown cruise, the *Alabama* captured and burned several whaling vessels in mid-Atlantic, took a number of vessels off the Newfoundland Banks, sailed for the Caribbean where coal and provisions were taken on board ship, and then sank the Union steamer *Hatteras* in a short and brisk action off Galveston, Texas. News of his promotion to captain as well as the thanks of Congress reached Semmes during his sortie in the Gulf of Mexico. After drifting down the coast of Brazil, the *Alabama* spent the summer months of 1863 cruising in the South Atlantic. Two months were spent in the vicinity of Capetown, South Africa, with negligible results (one vessel captured) before proceeding on an extended cruise through the Indian Ocean into the China Sea, reaching Singapore just before Christmas 1863. The ship then returned to European waters via the Indian Ocean and the South Atlantic, arriving at Cherbourg, France, on June 11, 1864. Since commissioning, the *Alabama* had sailed approximately seventy-five thousand miles and had taken sixty-four prizes. Three days after the Confederate warship anchored in the French harbor, the Union screw sloop *Kearsarge* took up station off the port.

Despite the *Alabama*'s poor condition, Semmes decided to fight the Union vessel. On Sunday, June 19, with thousands of people watching from the cliffs, the two warships engaged each other outside French waters, beyond the three-mile limit. The action lasted just over an hour with the two protagonists firing broadsides as they steamed in slowly narrowing circles. At the beginning of the eighth circle, when the warships were approximately four-hundred yards apart, the *Alabama* sank. Semmes along with a large number of his crew were picked up by the English yacht *Deerhound* and carried to England.

After a period of rest and relaxation in England and on the Continent, Semmes returned to the Confederacy by way of Mexico. He was promoted to rear admiral and in January 1865 was given command of the James River Squadron. This final naval command lasted less than three months. On April 2, General Robert Edward Lee informed President Jefferson Davis that Richmond must be abandoned. That night the ironclads and wooden vessels of the James River Squadron were set afire and scuttled or blown up. The squadron's personnel were evacuated by train, and in Danville, Virginia, they were formed into a naval brigade under Semmes' command as brigadier general. The brigade retreated to Greensboro, North Carolina, where as a part of the army of General Joseph Eggleston Johnston,* it surrendered. Semmes was paroled, went to his home in Mobile, but was later arrested. After being held for three months, charges were dropped and he returned home.

During the postwar years Semmes served as a probate judge for a brief period, as a professor at Louisiana State Seminary (now Louisiana State University), and as editor of a newspaper. He also practiced law. In 1869 he published *Memoirs of Service Afloat During the War Between the States*. This was the second of his autobiographical works. The first, *Service Afloat and Ashore During the Mexican War*, was published in 1852. He died in 1877 and was buried in Mobile.

Semmes was a competent and respected naval officer, but something of a loner and a maverick. He was unpopular with both superiors and subordinates. According to Rear Admiral Charles Wilkes in his autobiography, these traits were apparent even as a midshipman. Because of his martial bearing, waxed mustaches, and imperial-style chin whiskers, sailors nicknamed him "Old Beeswax," "Old Bim," and "Marshall Pomp."

Semmes unquestionably was the ablest and most successful of the Confederate commerce raiders. As commander of the *Sumter* and the *Alabama*, he took eighty-two prizes (by far more than any other raider commander) and caused considerable damage to the American merchant marine. Because of these exploits he is the best known of the Confederate naval officers.

BIBLIOGRAPHY

Boykin, E. C. *Ghost Ship of the Confederacy: The Story of the Alabama and Her Captain, Raphael Semmes*. New York: Funk and Wagnalls, 1957.

Dalzell, George W. *The Flight from the Flag: The Continuing Effect of the Civil War upon the American Carrying Trade*. Chapel Hill: University of North Carolina Press, 1940.

Delaney, Norman C. *John McIntosh Kell of the Raider Alabama*. University: University of Alabama Press, 1973.

Roberts, W. Adolphe. *Semmes of the Alabama.* Indianapolis, Ind.: Bobbs-Merrill Company, 1938.

Summersell, Charles G. *The Cruise of C.S.S. Sumter.* Tuscaloosa, Ala.: Confederate Publishing Company, 1965.

WILLIAM N. STILL

SHAFTER, William Rufus (b. Kalamazoo County, Mich., October 16, 1835; d. Bakersfield, Calif., November 13, 1906), Army officer. Shafter commanded the U.S. Army in Cuba during the Spanish-American War.

Shafter's parents moved from Vermont to Michigan where his father, Hugh, engaged in farming. Young Shafter attended school in Galesburg, Michigan, and later taught school and worked on his father's farm. Shafter sought further education and was attending Prairie Seminary in Richland County when the Civil War came.

Shafter enlisted as a first lieutenant in the 7th Michigan Volunteer Infantry Regiment and saw his first action of the Civil War in the Federal disaster at Ball's Bluff on the Potomac River (October 1861). He participated in the Peninsula Campaign of General George Brinton McClellan* during May-July 1862. Shafter was wounded and refused to leave the field at Seven Pines (Fair Oaks) on May 31-June 1, 1862, and was brevetted lieutenant colonel for gallantry in action. (Subsequently, on June 12, 1895, he was awarded the Congressional Medal of Honor for his role in this engagement.) On September 5, 1862, he was promoted to major, 19th Michigan Volunteer Infantry. (During a brief leave of absence, he married Harriet Amelia Grimes of Athens, Michigan. One daughter graced this long and happy union.) In June 1863 he was promoted to lieutenant colonel and one year later was named colonel, 17th U.S. Colored Infantry. This marked the beginning of a long association with black troops and provided invaluable experience in the post-Civil War period. Shafter was prominent in the action at Nashville, December 15-16, 1864, won the respect of General George Henry Thomas,* and on March 13, 1865, was promoted to brevet brigadier general of volunteers.

The end of the Civil War brought a drastic reduction in the armed forces, but Shafter wished to remain in the service. With the enthusiastic support of General Thomas, he was assigned to the 24th Infantry. This was a new regular regiment, one of four, composed of black troops with white officers and was regarded as an experiment in the use of blacks as regular troops. All four regiments, the 24th and 25th Infantry and the 9th and 10th Cavalry, were assigned to the turbulent Texas frontier.

For a decade Shafter served along the Rio Grande and in West Texas where conditions bordered on anarchy. His campaigns against hostile Indians—including Kiowas, Comanches, Apaches, and Kickapoos, the Kickapoos residing in Mexico—were all characterized by swift, aggressive, and effective action. In the summer of 1875 Shafter was ordered to explore, map, and evaluate the flora, fauna, water, and fuel resources of the Staked Plains of Texas, as well as to drive from that mysterious region any Indians found there. With a command composed of units of his own regiment and six troops of the black 10th Cavalry ("Buffalo soldiers"), he made a dogged and thorough sweep of this North American "Sahara." The command covered more than twenty-five hundred miles under the most trying conditions and provided the first reliable information about this vast tableland for oncoming settlers. Shafter earned a reputation in the frontier army as an able and imaginative officer, although he was often volatile and abusive with his troops. His staff found him warm and humorous when relaxed and totally dedicated to the Army.

Shafter's service in the Southwest came to an end in 1879 when he was promoted to colonel, 1st Infantry Regiment, and transferred to the Department of the Columbia. For nineteen years Shafter served in the Departments of the Columbia and California. These were times of comparative quiet with little opportunity for distinction or promotion.

With the outbreak of the war with Spain in April 1898, however, Shafter was promoted to major general of volunteers and was given command of the expeditionary force to Cuba with headquarters at Tampa, Florida. The nation was eager but ill-prepared for war, and the task of assembling, organizing, equipping, and supplying the army at Tampa proved an almost overwhelming one. Shafter, now nearing sixty-three years of age, weighed more than three hundred pounds and suffered intensely in the humid heat of a Florida summer. Nevertheless, he managed to bring some order out of chaos and to embark about sixteen thousand soldiers on thirty-two transports and to sail for Cuba on June 14, 1898.

The expeditionary force landed at Daiquiri on June 22, took Siboney the next day, and defeated the Spanish at Las Guasimas on June 24. Shafter then launched his main attack on the port city of Santiago de Cuba. Heights surrounding the city on its land side were stormed and taken without heavy loss, but Shafter hesitated to assault the formidable fortifications guarding the entrances to Santiago. His hesitancy brought a barrage of criticism from many of his officers and men and a tidal wave of complaint in the United States. Shafter's cause was made infinitely worse by his poor relations with numerous war correspondents who had flocked to the fighting front. Never sensitive about public relations, Shafter had alienated the correspondents by his gruff manner, corpulence, and untidy dress. The end result was a steady stream of uncomplimentary articles that were published in the newspapers and became, particularly in the Hearst and Pulitzer newspapers, little short of venomous.

Shafter ignored his critics and focused his attention on his army. His soldiers were falling victim to malaria, yellow fever, and dysentery. Shafter needed reinforcements, and an attack on the city would certainly produce heavy casualties; he had never believed in a large "butcher bill." Therefore, with considerable skill, he undertook negotiations leading to the surrender of the Spanish forces under General Jose Velasquez Toral. After the Spanish fleet had fled the harbor of Santiago and been destroyed by the American blockading fleet (under the command of Winfield Scott Schley*), Shafter was able to conclude terms of surrender with Toral on July 17, 1898. Shafter's invasion of Cuba had accomplished its objective with a minimum loss of life, but he did not emerge from the war as a popular hero. The savage attacks on him had done much to destroy his reputation and shunted him into relative obscurity.

With the war at an end, he was assigned to command the Department of California with headquarters at San Francisco. On October 16, 1899, he retired as a brigadier general, but remained in command of the department under his volunteer rank of major general until June 30, 1901. The next day he was advanced to the grade of major general on the retired list.

Shafter's place in American military history has suffered primarily because of criticism of his conduct of the Cuban Campaign, and much of this was unfair. Never one to court publicity and contemptuous of his critics, Shafter never attempted to answer the attacks made on him. Actually, many of the problems that arose during the Spanish-American War were not of his making. Given the state of unpreparedness coupled with unrealistic expectations, Shafter had done well by any standard. Nevertheless, the campaign remains one of the most criticized in U.S. military history.

His Civil War record was outstanding and appreciated by his superiors, but he never attracted public attention to the degree of other young officers such as George Armstrong Custer,* Ranald Slidell Mackenzie, Wesley Merritt, or George Crook.* It is equally true that Shafter never received appropriate recognition for his service in the Southwest. His dedication, energy, and aggressiveness contributed materially to peace along that tortured frontier, and his campaign on and exploration of the Staked Plains spurred settlement of that region.

Shafter's forty years of service were marked by unswerving loyalty and devotion to his country, and he performed ably in his assigned tasks. He merits a more prominent place in our military history than he has received.

BIBLIOGRAPHY

Holbrook, Stewart H. *Lost Men of American History*. New York: Macmillan Company, 1946.
Leckie, William H. *The Buffalo Soldiers: A Narrative of the Negro Cavalry in the West*. Norman: University of Oklahoma Press, 1967.
Millis, Walter. *The Martial Spirit*. New York: Houghton Mifflin Company, 1931.
Trask, David F. *The War with Spain in 1898*. New York: Macmillan Company, 1981.

WILLIAM H. LECKIE

SHERIDAN, Philip Henry (b. Albany, N.Y., March 6, 1831; d. Nonquitt, Mass., August 5, 1888), Army officer. Sheridan commanded the Federal Army of the Shenandoah during the Civil War.

Sheridan sprang from Irish Catholic parents. Philip's father settled his family in Somerset, Ohio, where he toiled as a construction worker and raised a brood of six. Philip obtained an appointment to the U.S. Military Academy when the first appointee failed to qualify. He was graduated in 1853 finishing thirty-fourth in a class of fifty-two. Sheridan had not been a prize pupil; in fact, he had been suspended from the Academy for one year after he lunged at an upperclassman with a bayoneted rifle. When the Civil War began in 1861, Phil Sheridan was an obscure lieutenant of infantry serving in Oregon.

During the early months of the war, Captain Sheridan held administrative positions until he became quartermaster on the staff of Henry Wager Halleck* during the campaign against Corinth, Mississippi (April 1862). Sheridan wrangled the colonelcy of the 2d Michigan Cavalry Regiment. Next, he got command of a cavalry brigade and led it on a successful raid against Booneville, Mississippi. He was promoted to brigadier general of volunteers and given command of an infantry division. In a defensive role, Sheridan's division repulsed Confederate attacks ordered by Braxton Bragg* at the battles of Perryville, Kentucky (October 1862) and Stones River, Tennessee (December 31, 1862-January 3, 1863). William Starke Rosecrans* favorably cited Sheridan's tenacity, and "Little Phil" was promoted to major general of volunteers.

At the Battle of Chicamauga, Tennessee (September 19–20, 1863), Sheridan learned stern lessons in tactics. While his division was maneuvering, it took the brunt of an unexpected attack by troops under James Longstreet.* Sheridan's men broke, suffered heavy casualties, and shared the ignominy of the rest of the Federal right wing, which all but disintegrated.

Sheridan rebounded in the battles around Chattanooga. Under Ulysses Simpson Grant,* Union forces attacked Bragg's Confederates, who occupied defensive works on Missionary Ridge. In a concerted Union attack (November 25, 1863), Sheridan's soldiers were ordered to expel Confederates from positions at the foot of the ridge. This they did, but after taking fire from Confederates on the crest, the soldiers themselves began an unordered but unstoppable advance up Missionary Ridge. Sensing victory, Sheridan joined his men in routing the Confederates.

Five months later Grant was general in chief of all Union armies, traveling with General George Gordon Meade* and the Army of the Potomac. Grant wanted a new commander for the army's cavalry and picked Sheridan, who reorganized the corps. Over Meade's objections, Sheridan got Grant's permission to lead his horse soldiers on a raid. The Richmond Raid (May 9–24, 1864) was a controversial exploit. Taking his ten thousand troopers, Sheridan rode toward Richmond, drawing James Ewell Brown Stuart* with him, and engaged in several skirmishes. Then Sheridan's force collided with Stuart's five thousand cavalrymen and killed the South's cavalier-hero at Yellow Tavern. Despite criticisms that the Richmond Raid had accomplished little, Sheridan set out with his men again (June 7–28). At Trevilian Station Sheridan suffered a reverse, but his second raid gained him favorable publicity in the North, and the rampaging Federal cavalry was disconcerting to the Southern government.

In July 1864 Jubal Anderson Early* led his army of doughty Confederates out of the Shenandoah Valley, threatening Washington and distracting Grant as he grappled with the Army of Northern Virginia under Robert Edward Lee.* Consequently, Grant ordered Sheridan to take command of the army of the Shenandoah (about forty thousand men), destroy Early's army (about twenty thousand men), and lay waste to the Valley, Lee's supply source. In August Sheridan moved cautiously into the Valley where several Union generals had come to grief. Marching over Opequon Creek, Sheridan attacked Early on September 19 in his defensive positions outside Winchester. The assault was carried by Rutherford Hayes' brigade of the VIII Corps under George Crook.* Sheridan was victorious and sent Early "whirling through Winchester." Three days later Sheridan confronted Early again at Fisher's Hill, turning the Confederate left, with Hayes again in the van. Had Sheridan's cavalry blocked Early's retreat, the Confederate Army might have been annihilated. Sheridan was promoted to brigadier general in the Regular Army.

Believing that Early was defeated, Sheridan posted his army in poorly chosen positions along Cedar Creek and went to Washington to confer with Halleck. Meanwhile, Early received reinforcements and planned a surprise attack. Before dawn on October 19, 1864, in a well-executed assault, Early's Confederates, led by John Brown Gordon, struck the poorly disposed Federals, routing Crook's VIII Corps. But Horatio Wright of the VI Corps was able to establish a defensive line. About midmorning Wright expected Early to deliver the *coup-de-grace*; it never came. Early hoped that his daybreak success would be enough to win the field. Then, Sheridan returned.

The sound of the guns had awakened Sheridan in Winchester, where he had stopped on his way from Washington. He gathered his staff and made haste to Cedar Creek. Stragglers lined the roads, and scattered squads and wayward companies had stopped to boil coffee. They evidenced no interest in returning to Cedar Creek. Sheridan called to his soldiers, promising that they would win the day yet. Incredibly, they responded to his call. Once-beaten soldiers and faltering officers turned around and followed their little general back into battle. Arriving at Wright's line, Sheridan planned a counterattack, which he sent in at 4:00 PM. This stroke drove Early from the field and ruined his army, which suffered nearly three thousand casualties, lost twenty-five guns, and left most of its supply wagons behind. Sheridan was supreme in the Shenandoah.

During February and March of 1865, after his troops had ravaged the Valley, Sheridan launched the Northern Virginia Raid, with the objective of capturing the rail center at Lynchburg. The raid resulted in the destruction of several miles of railroad, but Sheridan turned away from Lynchburg when reports indicated that it might be too strongly held for his cavalry to take. After resting for less than a week, Sheridan, under Grant's orders, applied almost continual pressure on Lee's retreating army. At Five Forks (April 1), he won a victory that blocked Lee's escape. On April 9 Sheridan was present for Lee's surrender at Appomattox.

Sheridan assumed important commands after the Civil War. In charge of the Division of the Gulf (1865–1866), he used demonstrations along the Rio Grande to persuade Napoleon III's French Army to end its occupation of Mexico in May 1866. Then Sheridan turned to Reconstruction, and President Andrew Johnson appointed him commander of the Fifth Military District (Texas and Louisiana). Sheridan sternly administered the district and supported the Radical Republicans, which prompted the conservative Johnson to order him to the Indian frontier. Promoted to lieutenant general in 1869, Sheridan commanded the Division of the Missouri, virtually the whole West between the Mississippi and the Rockies. Using the vainglorious George Armstrong Custer,* Sheridan saw to the defeat of all major Indian tribes in the region by 1878. He was commanding general of the Army from 1884 until his death in 1888. He had been promoted to full general just before he died.

Sheridan, like Grant, had the good fortune to serve in the West and to hold a series of increasingly responsible commands before being ordered to revitalize the Army of the Potomac's Cavalry Corps. During his career, Sheridan never fit any idealized picture of the professional Army officer—coincidentally, another trait he shared with Grant. Sheridan was short (he stood only five feet–five inches), swarthy, and long-armed. He had receding hair and a ragged mustache. But he was a skilled rider, and on the back of his horse, Sheridan's long torso and broad shoulders made him appear tall. Sheridan had a ferocious temper and wielded one of the most profane vocabularies in the Army. The most controversial display of Sheridan's temper occurred late in the war, at Five Forks, where he removed Gouverneur Warren for delivering a tardy and poorly directed attack.

Sheridan showed more restraint when he argued with his superior, General Meade, over how the Cavalry Corps should be used—as wagon guards or as mounted juggernaut. Sheridan's raiders sapped the spirit of Lee's cavalry, ripped up rail tracks, threatened Richmond, killed Jeb Stuart, disrupted supply lines, and caused doubts about Confederate defenses and capabilities.

In the Shenandoah, Sheridan had his greatest successes. Yet his command in the Valley, like the value of his raids, has been criticized. Supposedly, he won cheap victories against inferior Confederate forces. Actually, Sheridan was a winner where other Federal commanders had been losers. Nathaniel Banks, James Shields, and John Charles Frémont had been baffled in the Valley by Thomas Jonathan ("Stonewall") Jackson,* though the Union generals led forces that were numerically superior to Jackson's. Jube Early was no Stonewall Jackson, but Federal victories were not predestined by virtue of numbers alone. Twice Sheridan struck Early hard and refused to be defeated at Cedar Creek where all signs seemed to point to a Union rout. Other Union commanders might have yielded the field to Early; instead, Sheridan counterattacked and crippled Early's army. In the process, Sheridan won a signal victory, became a Northern hero, and sparked the reelection of President Abraham Lincoln.

Despite the fact that Sheridan refused to attack the rail center at Lynchburg, he demonstrated a consistent offensive spirit and repeatedly sought out the enemy army and brought it to combat. In the post-Civil War West, Sheridan showed the same offensive spirit, organizing an extraordinary winter campaign (1868–1869), and ruthlessly pushed his subordinates in the Red River War (1874–1875), the last major Indian war in Texas and Indian Territory. Eventually his subordinates, including Ranald Slidell Mackenzie, followed Sheridan's example and devastated the Indians' supplies in campaigns reminiscent of his Shenandoah Valley campaign.

Sheridan was determined in defense and relentless in attack. He envisioned the Union victorious, and he helped to make that vision a reality. Sheridan deserves to be ranked as the third most important Union general (behind Grant and William Tecumseh Sherman*) and was among the best combat commanders of the U.S. Army in the nineteenth century.

BIBLIOGRAPHY

Catton, Bruce. *A Stillness at Appomattox*. Garden City: Doubleday and Company, 1953.
Dawson, Joseph G., III. *Army Generals and Reconstruction: Louisiana, 1862–1877*. Baton Rouge: Louisiana State University Press, 1982.
Fuller, J.F.C. *The Generalship of Ulysses S. Grant*. New York: Dodd, Mead, and Company, 1929.
O'Connor, Richard. *Sheridan the Inevitable*. Indianapolis, Ind.: Bobbs-Merrill, 1953.
Williams, T. Harry. *Hayes of the Twenty-third: The Civil War Volunteer Officer*. New York: Alfred A. Knopf, 1965.

JOSEPH G. DAWSON III

SHERMAN, William Tecumseh (b. Lancaster, Ohio, February 8, 1820; d. New York City, N.Y., February 14, 1891), Army officer. Sherman is especially noted for his Atlanta Campaign and is notorious for his devastating marches through Georgia and South Carolina in the Civil War.

The sixth of eleven children of Charles and Mary Sherman, "Cump" was named for Tecumseh, the great Shawnee statesman and warrior whom his father particularly admired. When Judge Sherman died of a sudden fever in 1829, "Cump" was reared with the family of Thomas Ewing, his father's closest friend and a rising star in national politics. Senator Ewing appointed Sherman to the U.S. Military Academy in 1836, and he was graduated four years later sixth in a class of forty-three.

Commissioned second lieutenant in the artillery, Sherman spent eighteen months with the 3d Artillery in Florida during the final stages of the second Seminole War (1836–1842). In February 1842 his company was transferred to Fort Morgan near Mobile, and six months later it was sent to occupy Fort Moultrie, South Carolina, where it remained until the Mexican War. Sherman spent the war years on recruiting service and later on staff duty in California, where he observed the height of the Gold Rush in 1849. Returning to Washington the next year, he married Ellen Ewing, a daughter of his "second" father. The couple had eight children. After being promoted to captain, Sherman served briefly at St. Louis and New Orleans before resigning his commission in 1853 to become a banker.

Lacking "sense enough to keep out of such disreputable business," Sherman's branch bank in California failed and he lost his own fortune repaying funds he had invested on behalf of Army friends. He was by his own admission "a dead cock in the pit" when he was named superintendent of a new military institution in Louisiana in 1859. An obvious success, he resigned one year after the school (now Louisiana State University) opened because Louisiana had voted to secede and Sherman was unconditional in his loyalty to the Constitution.

Commissioned colonel in June 1861, he commanded a brigade at the First Battle of Bull Run (July 21), where his men fought "disorganized but not scared." He next was assigned to the Department of the Cumberland where his ultimate reponsibility as commander was the defense of Kentucky. Sherman's private assertion that two hundred thousand troops would be needed for any offensive action (he had but twenty thousand) was publicized out of context and led to so much public ridicule that in November 1861 he asked to be relieved. Many officers and politicians at this time thought Sherman insane; he considered himself a failure.

The efforts of Thomas Ewing and his own brother, Senator John Sherman, saved him for the Army. From a training command in St. Louis he went to Paducah, Kentucky, where he forwarded the men and supplies needed by Ulysses Simpson Grant* in his Fort Donelson Campaign, and in March 1862 Sherman's newly organized division was with the expeditionary force moving up the Tennessee to sever Confederate railroad communications between Memphis and the East. He fought well at Shiloh (April 6–7), although Sherman had ignored all reports of approaching Confederates and did not order his men to intrench. Following the siege of Corinth, Sherman was given command of the District of West Tennessee, and in December 1862 he led an expedition of thirty-thousand men down the Mississippi to attack Vicksburg while Grant pressed overland along the Mississippi Central Railroad against the main Confederate forces. When a cavalry strike against his supply bases forced Grant to give up his first attempt to take Vicksburg, Sherman was left to his own devices near the city. On December 29 he suffered a severe repulse at the hands of Stephen Dill Lee in attempting to storm Confederate fortifications at Chickasaw Bluffs. He subsequently served with John Alexander McClernand in the capture of Arkansas Post.

Sherman's XV Corps played a prominent and often an independent role in Grant's repeated attempts to take Vicksburg, and his main responsibility during the siege was to hold off a relieving Confederate army under Joseph Eggleston Johnston.* Subsequently, when Grant was ordered to relieve Chattanooga, he intended to make his main attack with Sherman's corps against the Confederate right, but the terrain made progress difficult and the battle was won by a "simultaneous" attack against the Confederate center atop Missionary Ridge. Sherman later returned to Vicksburg to lead two divisions 150 miles into the interior to destroy the arsenal, supply depots, and intersecting railroads at Meridian.

After Grant went east in March 1864 to assume overall command of the Union armies, Sherman was given the Military Division of the Mississippi. His mission in Grant's strategy in 1864 was "to move against Johnston's army, to break it up, and to get into the interior of the enemy's country . . . inflicting all the damage [possible] . . . against their war resources." The first step was Atlanta, one hundred miles distant and protected by mountain ranges and rivers running at right angles to Sherman's obvious line of advance, the Western and Atlantic Railroad. Coordinating the three armies of the Tennessee, the Cumberland, and the Ohio, Sherman adroitly maneuvered Johnston out of successive defensive positions. Although repulsed at Kennesaw Mountain (June 27), two months from the day that Union armies everywhere began their advance Sherman was within sight of Atlanta. After John Bell Hood* replaced Johnston, Sherman's armies beat back a series of fierce counterattacks and the noose around Atlanta gradually tightened. Disdaining a regular siege, Sherman inched his way southward to cut off the only remaining railroad feeding Atlanta, and on September 2 he announced the capture of "the Gate City of the South."

Leaving his good friend George Henry Thomas* behind to defend Tennessee, Sherman destroyed Atlanta and then cut loose from his own supply line to march sixty thousand men through Georgia to the sea, destroying the war potential of the area and much private property in the process. His troops stormed Fort McAlister near Savannah on December 13, and Savannah was captured in time for Sherman to present the city to Abraham Lincoln "as a Christmas gift."

Three weeks later he was on the move again, marching northward through the Carolinas and a possible juncture with Grant's army at Petersburg. A desperate Confederate attack against Sherman's left wing at Bentonville, North Carolina (March 19–21) failed to deter him, and after he was joined at Goldsboro by thirty thousand additional troops that had marched inland from the coast, Johnston, who had been returned to command, had no choice but to surrender. Sherman's initial terms were too widesweeping and generous to be palatable to the Radical Republicans in control after Lincoln's assassination, but the two generals finally came to reasonable terms on April 26, 1865, near Durham, North Carolina. The Civil War was virtually over.

After the war Sherman commanded one of three territorial divisions, embracing the lands between Ohio and the Rockies, in which capacity he directed small campaigns against the Indians and gave "continuous active aid" to the completion of the Union Pacific Railroad in 1869. When Grant was elected president, Sherman was promoted full general and was made general in chief of the Army. He tried to centralize the Army by bringing the bureau chiefs of the War Department under his direct control, but Grant supported his secretary of war in this bureaucratic battle. In disgust, Sherman moved Army headquarters to St. Louis. His continued interest in military lessons of the war, which he wrote about at length in his *Memoirs* originally published in 1875, prompted him to support the tactical reforms of Emory Upton.* Sherman also encouraged Upton to undertake his more celebrated studies of armies abroad and military policy at home. In 1881 Sherman founded the School of Application for Infantry and Cavalry at Fort Leavenworth (now the U.S. Army Command and General Staff College) so that the entire Army could "keep up with the rapid progress in the science and practice of war." Sherman's outspoken *Memoirs* continued to feed old controversies and contributed to the harsh view of him that was growing in the South. He retired from the Army in 1884 and died seven years later, one of the most venerated Union leaders in the war.

Sherman was an indispensable member of that team of Union generals that engineered the final Union victory. His Atlanta Campaign is the only Civil War campaign universally regarded as a masterpiece of *both* offensive and defensive maneuver, and his March to the Sea and subsequent sweep through the Carolinas, which he regarded as "by far" his "most important in conception and execution," contributed heavily to the material and psychological collapse of the Confederacy. A cautious tactician—"fighting is the least part of a general's work," he would insist—Sherman lacked the killer's instinct of striking for the jugular. But from the first he clearly understood the nature and scope of the conflict and the direction military operations must take. Never did he underestimate the will of the South to resist, but he was no less determined that the Union should control the Mississippi. Sherman fought the war with a single eye rare even for that generation. "Let every thought of the mind, every feeling of the heart, every movement of a human muscle, be directed to one sole object—successful war and consequent peace," and he never forgot that "the legitimate object of war is a more perfect peace." Grant's Vicksburg Campaign convinced Sherman that an army could free itself from its communications, and this knowledge, coupled with his conviction that the Civil War differed from European wars in that "we are not only fighting armies, but a hostile people," found its ultimate expression in his celebrated and controversial March to the Sea. A daring and imaginative strategist, Sherman excelled in logistics, and his skillful management of the railroads attracted the attention of soldiers abroad.

Defining strategy as "common sense applied to the art of war" in a day when most generals still obeyed the formal, time-honored maxims of Baron Antoine Henri Jomini, Sherman was as pragmatic as his Prussian contemporary Helmuth von Moltke, who similarly viewed strategy as "a system of expedients." B. H. Liddell Hart has elevated Sherman's system of expedients into a formal system called the "Strategy of Indirect Approach." More than any other general from history, Sherman contributed to the evolution of Liddell Hart's theories, which in turn directly influenced the concept of *blitzkrieg*. In European military circles no Civil War commander has had a greater following than Sherman.

BIBLIOGRAPHY

Barrett, John G. *Sherman's March Through the Carolinas*. Chapel Hill: University of North Carolina Press, 1956.

Lewis, Lloyd. *Sherman: Fighting Prophet*. New York: Harcourt, Brace and Company, 1932.
Liddell Hart, B. H. *Sherman: Soldier, Realist, American*. New York: Dodd, Mead and Company, 1929.
Merrill, James M. *William Tecumseh Sherman*. Chicago: Rand McNally and Company, 1971.
Sherman, William T. *Memoirs of Gen. W. T. Sherman*. 2 vols. New York: Charles L. Webster and Company, 1891.
Turner, George E. *Victory Rode the Rails: The Strategic Place of the Railroads in the Civil War*. Indianapolis, Ind.: Bobbs-Merrill, 1953.

JAY LUVAAS

SHORT, Walter Campbell (b. Fillmore, Ill., March 30, 1880; d. Dallas, Tex., September 3, 1949), soldier, business executive. Short was a principal figure in the Pearl Harbor controversy.

Walter Short, son of Scotch-Irish parents, Dr. Hiram Spait Short (a physician) and Sarah Mineriva Stokes Short, graduated with a Phi Beta Kappa key from the University of Illinois (B.A., 1901). Although appointed a second lieutenant in February 1901, he taught mathematics at Western Military Academy before accepting his commission in March 1902. There followed a successful, if largely unremarkable, military career: Short was stationed at the Presidio in San Francisco (April 1903) and then transferred to the 25th Infantry at Fort Reno, Oklahoma (1903–1907). Following a brief tour of duty in the Philippines (1907–1908), he joined the 6th Infantry in Nebraska. Other assignments took him to Alaska, California (1913), and Fort Sill, Oklahoma, where Short became the secretary of the School of Musketry and commander of the 12th Infantry. At this time (November 1914), he married Isabel Dean of Oklahoma City. They had one child, Walter Dean Short, a future colonel in the U.S. Army. His next tour of duty was with the 16th Infantry attached to General John Joseph Pershing's* expeditionary force in Mexico (March 1916). Four months later he was promoted to captain. During World War I, Short served as a small-arms training officer in Georgia. In June 1917 he went to France with the 1st Division. His administrative experience included staff positions with the I Corps automatic weapons school and the II Corps infantry weapons school. Now a lieutenant colonel (a temporary rank), he was attached to the training section of the General Staff (April-November 1918). His professionalism won him the Distinguished Service Medal for "conspicuous service in the inspecting and reporting upon frontline conditions" and for his efficiency in training machine gun crews.

Short saw combat during the battles of Aisne-Marne, St. Mihiel, and the Meuse-Argonne. During the occupation of Germany, he became the assistant chief of staff in charge of training for the Third Army. In 1919 he returned to the United States to serve as an instructor at the General Services Schools at Fort Leavenworth, Kansas. (Simultaneously, he attended the School of the Line, graduating in 1921.) In August 1919 Short reverted to the rank of captain and reported for duty with the 6th Division in Illinois as assistant chief of staff for operations and supply. Promoted to major in July 1920, Short was assigned to the War Department General Staff. For the next three years, he was with the Far Eastern Section of the Military Intelligence Division.

In 1922, Short published a textbook entitled *Employment of The Machine Gun*. His co-invention of an improved machine gun carrier also reflected his interest in automatic weapons. A lieutenant colonel in 1923, he attended the Army War College and then served with the 65th Infantry at San Juan, Puerto Rico. From August 1928 until September 1930 Short was an instructor at the Command and General Staff School at Fort Leavenworth, and the following years served as assistant to the chief of insular affairs and with the 6th Infantry at Jefferson Barracks, Missouri. He was then assigned to the Infantry School at Fort Benning, Georgia, as assistant commandant. In December 1936 he became a brigadier general and in February 1938 the commander of the 2d Infantry Brigade at Fort Ontario, New York. From there Short assumed command (June 1938) of the 1st Infantry Brigade at Fort Wadsworth, and in 1939 he became commander of the 1st Division at Fort Hamilton. Promoted to major general (1940), he was ordered to Columbia, South Carolina.

On February 8, 1941, General George Catlett Marshall* chose him to command the Hawaiian Department with the temporary rank of lieutenant general. The forty-three thousand air and ground forces under Short were assigned, in conjunction with the Navy, the defense of Oahu and the base at Pearl Harbor.

Following the Japanese attack on December 7, 1941, Short was demoted in rank to major general and was relieved of his command on December 17, 1941. Under pressure, Short applied for retirement. This became effective on February 28, 1942. He retired on three-quarters pay. The War Depatment never gave Short the opportunity to defend himself before a military court.

During his retirement, Short worked for the Ford Motor Company as a traffic manager in Dallas, Texas. He remained with Ford until 1946. He died in 1949 of a chronic heart ailment complicated by emphysema. He was buried at Arlington National Cemetery.

Was Walter Short guilty of dereliction of duty? Of bad judgment? Of errors in judgment? Had he failed as a commander? On the other hand, was Walter Short a scapegoat? Was he a good soldier thrown to the wolves to divert public attention from mistakes made in Washington? Was he a sacrificial victim in the coverup of some nefarious plot? An "American Dreyfus"?

No one should doubt that Short was a competent officer, industrious and conscientious. Possessing tactical skill, command and administrative experience, and an advanced military education, he was an assured military manager. It was not his career that came into question after December 7, 1941, but the decisions he made as the commander of the Hawaiian Department in the eleven months preceding the Japanese attack.

Eight separate investigations sought to find the reasons for the Pearl Harbor debacle. During these inquiries Short's role in the fiasco was of major concern. The first investigation (authorized by the president and headed by Supreme Court Justice Owen Roberts) issued a report in January 1942 that accused Short and his naval counterpart, Admiral Husband Edward Kimmel,* of bad judgment and dereliction of duty. The Army Pearl Harbor Board (which concluded its investigation in October 1944) also held Short responsible but concluded that the chief of staff, George C. Marshall,* and his chief of War Plans Division, General L. T. Gerow, shared in the responsibility for the disaster. In an addendum to the report, Secretary of War Henry Lewis Stimson insisted that Short had received adequate warning and that the circumstances of the attack did not excuse the Hawaiian commander's mistakes.

A joint congressional panel also conducted an inquiry into the attack. The majority report concluded that the Hawaiian commanders had failed to respond adequately to warnings from Washington, to prepare a unified defense system, to maintain an effective reconnaissance, to prepare to meet all possible attacks, and to employ their forces in such a way as to minimize damage in the event of an attack. The minority Republican report placed emphasis on the mistakes made in Washington.

A brief in Short's defense, however, would include the following points. First, the civilian and military leaders, including Short, expected the Japanese to attack somewhere in Southeast Asia—not at Pearl Harbor. Second, the chief of staff (on November 27, 1941) instructed Short to take measures to prevent sabotage but to avoid alarming the local civilian population. This Short did. Since neither Marshall nor Gerow responded to Short's report on his preparations (a report that indicated the base was not on full alert and that left out an effective defense against air attack), the War Department tacitly approved measures that inadvertently left Oahu vulnerable. Third, the authorities in Washington were in possession of vital information concerning a possible attack. The War Depatment withheld this information, acquired through the decoding of Japanese secret messages, from the local commanders. Fourth, the warnings sent to Hawaii were often incomplete, misleading, and confusing.

In addition, there is a Devil Theory of the Pearl Harbor debacle which, if it were true, would help exonerate Short: President Franklin Roosevelt withheld information from the local commanders, intentionally exposing the U.S. Pacific Fleet to attack. Since Hitler had given the United States no cause to enter the war on the Allied side, the president sought to entice the Japanese to strike, thus bringing America into the war through the back door. Afterwards, Roosevelt sought to cover up the affair by shifting the blame to the local commanders. The fleet and, incidentally, the career of an honorable soldier were sacrificed to further Roosevelt's political and diplomatic ambitions.

Yet, there is a less sinister interpretation of what went wrong: The American defeat at Pearl Harbor was a military defeat; the Army and Navy commanders in Washington and Pearl Harbor failed to gauge correctly the enemy's intentions and capabilites. It was not a unique failure; military history is replete with instances where the enemy surprised their opponents. Nor was it the result of evil designs or gross incompetence. Short, Kimmel, and the General Staff (as well as the civilian leaders) were looking the wrong way when the Japanese delivered a strategic left hook.

In the belief that the war would begin somewhere else, Short emphasized training and antisabotage precautions (the American planes were parked wingtip to wing-tip in neat rows on the morning of the attack) over reconnaissance and constant radar surveillance. This was not carelessness but miscalculation. Nevertheless, it was not Short's duty to reason where the Japanese Imperial forces would strike, nor was it necessary for him to be privy to all the information possessed in Washington. He was an outpost commander, responsible locally for the defense of his men and equipment.

The eight battleships sunk or damaged, the 247 planes wrecked, and the 2,330 men killed and 1,145 wounded were violent testimony to these errors in judgment. To be fair, Short was not the only one to make mistakes to misread the enemy's intentions. But he and no one else commanded the Hawaiian Department. The Pearl Harbor defeat occurred because good men like Short made the wrong decisions. They believed an attack on Pearl Harbor improbable and, therefore, ignored, out of a mass of intelligence reports, those signals that in retrospect pointed to an impending attack. Pearl Harbor was a tragedy of errors. It was a tragedy for the men who died that awful Sunday morning in 1941 and for their commander, Walter Campbell Short.

BIBLIOGRAPHY

Beard, Charles A. *President Roosevelt and the Coming of the War, 1941*. New Haven, Conn.: Yale University Press, 1948.

Melosi, Martin V. *The Shadow of Pearl Harbor: Political Controversy Over the Surprise Attack, 1941–1946*. College Station, Tex.: Texas A&M University Press, 1977.

Prange, Gordon. *At Dawn We Slept*. New York: McGraw Hill, 1981.

Report of the Joint Committee on the Pearl Harbor Attack. Washington, D.C.: U.S. Government Printing Office, 1946.

Wohlstetter, Roberta. *Pearl Harbor: Warning and Decision*. Stanford, Calif.: Stanford University Press, 1962.

FRANK J. WETTA

SMITH, Holland McTyeire (b. Hatchechubbee, Ala., April 20, 1882; d. San Diego, Calif., January 12, 1967), Marine Corps officer. Smith was a pioneer in amphibious warfare techniques before and during World War II.

Holland Smith, son of a prominent Alabama lawyer, was graduated in 1901 from Alabama Polytechnic Institute (now Auburn University) and from the University of Alabama Law School in 1903. He was admitted to the bar but disliked the practice of law and soon sought a commission in the Army. Finding no immediate opening in that service, he turned to the Marines, passed a competitive examination, and was commissioned a second lieutenant in the Marine Corps in

March 1905. After training at the School of Application, Annapolis, he reported to the Marine Brigade in the Philippine Islands. Subsequently, he was assigned to various posts in the United States, returned to the Philippines, and served aboard a cruiser in the Far East. In 1909 he participated in an expedition to Nicaragua and, in 1916, in another to Santo Domingo, where he came under fire for the first time.

During World War I Smith was among the first Americans to sail for France. He attended the Army Staff College at Langres, joined the staff of the Marine Brigade, 2d Division, and was awarded the *Croix de Guerre* for courage displayed during the Battle of Belleau Wood. He was then specially chosen as a Marine officer to serve on the staff of the I Corps, First Army, where he participated in the Aisne-Marne, St. Mihiel, Oise, and Meuse-Argonne offensives.

In 1920–1921 Smith attended the Navy War College and was then appointed as the first marine to serve on the Joint Army-Navy Planning Committee, a small group that formulated long-range war plans. He spent an uneventful year in Haiti in 1925 and completed the Marine Corps Field Officers' Course in 1927. In 1937, after various assignments ashore and afloat, he was appointed to the staff of the commandant of the Marine Corps as director of operations and training and in 1939 became assistant commandant.

Late in 1939 Smith was promoted to brigadier general and was given command of the 1st Marine Brigade at Quantico, Virginia. He immediately moved the brigade to Cuba and directed a period of such demanding training that he acquired the nickname "Howlin' Mad." In 1941 the brigade was expanded into the 1st Marine Division which shortly afterward was combined with an Army division to form the I Corps (Provisional) Atlantic Fleet. Smith was promoted to major general and, as the choice of Admiral Ernest Joseph King,* was named to command the I Corps. Although originally intended as an expeditionary force, the I Corps became a training command and until June 1943, Smith directed the training of the Army and Marine divisions preparing for landings in both the Atlantic and Pacific theaters.

In June 1943 Smith was appointed to command the V Amphibious Corps, a joint Army-Marine expeditionary force to be used by Admiral Chester William Nimitz* in his drive across the Central Pacific. In November 1943 the V Corps opened the drive by seizing Makin and Tarawa atolls in the Gilbert Islands. Early in 1944 V Corps troops captured several atolls in the Marshalls, including Kwajalein and Eniwetok. In June they struck the Marianas, first securing Saipan and then seizing Tinian and Guam. In August 1944 Smith, now a lieutenant general, was named to command the newly formed Fleet Marine Force, Pacific, and early in 1945 commanded three Marine divisions in the assault on Iwo Jima—the most desperate battle in the Marine Corps history.

In July 1945 Smith returned to San Diego as commanding general, Marine Training and Replacement Command, and in August 1946 he retired with the rank of general. He settled in La Jolla, California, and in 1948 published his controversial autobiography, *Coral and Brass*, which was highly critical of the conduct of the Pacific War.

Although he was popularly known as "Howlin' Mad," Smith has more appropriately been called the Father of Amphibious Warfare. He was a leader in the development of the amphibious techniques that made possible the landings in both the Atlantic and Pacific during World War II. When he took command of the 1st Marine Brigade in 1939, little actual training in amphibious techniques had been done, but because of the outbreak of war in Europe, Smith received support that had been unavailable to his predecessors. During intense training in Cuba and the Caribbean, he and his staff developed methods and techniques for landing on a hostile shore.

An early and crucial problem encountered was the lack of special landing craft. The ordinary ship's boats then used were inadequate, and Smith demanded better. He experimented with a shallow-draft boat, originally developed for Prohibition-era rum-runners, which could run up on the beach, rapidly discharge its cargo, and pull back under its own power. He tested and improved an amphibian tractor, originally designed for rescue work in the Everglades, which could function either as a boat at sea or as a tractor ashore. Through his efforts, both of these vital craft were adopted and were available for wartime landing operations.

Other basic problems of amphibious warfare included: organizing and equipping troops for rapid debarkation; devising a method for the rapid transfer of troops from ship to landing craft; "combat loading" vessels to ensure that needed supplies were unloaded first; controlling landing craft during the movement from ship to shore; and providing naval gunfire and air suport to the assault troops. By the time the United States entered the war, Smith had devised solutions to these problems, developed a doctrine of amphibious warfare, and established himself as the leading authority on amphibious operations. It was natural, then, for him to have been chosen to train, not only Marines, but a number of Army divisions as well. His work laid the foundation for the success of American landing operations during the war.

As a commander in the Central Pacific, Smith demanded hard-driving, relentless assaults that kept continual pressure on the enemy. He was not callous, but he believed that a swift assault shortened the battle and saved lives in the long run. Many believed that his fighting spirit, imparted to Marines at all levels, significantly shortened the island battles and may have provided the margin of victory on bitterly contested Iwo Jima. Smith considered himself a special spokesman for the Marines and was noted for his vehement arguments with his Navy colleagues about the proper conduct of amphibious operations. Prior to Tarawa, for example, he insisted upon the allotment of additional amphibious tractors, and at Tinian, he insisted that the landing be made across beaches which his naval superior considered unusable. In both instances his judgment was correct. The landing at Tarawa could easily have failed without the additional tractors, and the landing at Tinian was a nearly perfect operation. At Iwo Jima, Smith was unsuccessful in his argument for extending the length of the pre-invasion bombardment from three to ten days. Later, he and other Marines charged that the failure to lengthen the bombardment was a major reason for the heavy casualties suffered on Iwo Jima.

On Saipan, Smith relieved the unaggressive commander of an Army division. Such a relief of an Army general by a Marine was unprecedented, and it precipitated a controversy that seriously threatened interservice cooperation in the Pacific. The Army commander in the area charged that Smith was blindly prejudiced against Army units and urged that no Army troops ever again be placed under his command. Historians have generally agreed that the relief was justified, but Smith was embittered by the incident and its aftermath, in which he was portrayed as a butcher who recklessly threw away the lives of his men. In his autobiography, *Coral and Brass*, Smith attempted to vindicate himself, but the book was so marred by hindsight, second-guessing, and criticism of his colleagues that it actually harmed his reputation. Unfortunately, the relief incident and the allegations in *Coral and Brass* have come to overshadow Smith's pivotal role in the development of amphibious warfare and his contributions to victory in the Pacific.

BIBLIOGRAPHY

Dyer, George C. *The Amphibians Came to Conquer: The Story of Admiral Kelly Turner*. 2 vols. Washington, D.C.: U.S. Government Printing Office, 1972.

Heinl, Robert D., Jr. *Soldiers of the Sea: The United States Marine Corps, 1775–1962*. Annapolis, Md.: Naval Institute Press, 1962.

Hough, Frank O., et al. *History of U.S. Marine Corps Operations in World War II*. 5 vols. Washington, D.C.: U.S. Government Printing Office, 1956–1971.

Isely, Jeter A., and Philip A. Crowl. *The U.S. Marines and Amphibious War*. Princeton, N.J.: Princeton University Press, 1951.

Morison, Samuel E. *History of U.S. Naval Operations in World War II*. 15 vols. Boston: Atlantic, Little, and Company, 1947–1962.

NORMAN V. COOPER

SMITH, Oliver Prince (b. Menard, Tex., October 26, 1893; d. Los Altos, Calif., December 25, 1977), Marine Corps officer. Smith led the epic Marine Corps breakout from the Chosin Reservoir during the Korean War.

Oliver Prince Smith was born into a family that had settled in Virginia in 1740. His father died when Smith was young. His mother, a devout Christian Scientist, moved her family to Santa Cruz, California, in 1903. Smith remained a Christian Scientist all his life. He did not drink or swear, and he was considered to be a deeply religious person. He worked his way through the University of California at Berkeley, graduating in 1916. He was a member of the university Reserve Officer's Training Corps (ROTC). After graduation, Smith worked for the Standard Oil Company for a year. When the United States entered World War I in April 1917, he applied for a Marine Corps Reserve commission under a program for the direct commissioning of college graduates with ROTC experience. The Marine Corps accepted his application, and Smith was commissioned a second lieutenant in the reserves on May 4, 1917. He planned to stay in the Marine Corps only as long as the war lasted.

He was almost immediately ordered to the Marine Barracks on Guam to free a more experienced officer for duty in France. While sailing to Guam, Smith was one of a group of young lieutenants who invited Army Captain Benjamin Oliver Davis, a Negro, to sit at the head of their table in the wardroom after Davis refused the ship's quartermaster's request that he eat in his stateroom. While on Guam, Smith transferred to the regular Marine Corps. His college girlfriend, Esther King, came to Guam, and they were married on the island.

During the next two decades, Smith held a variety of assignments. In May 1919 he returned to the United States at Mare Island Marine Barracks, San Francisco. Ordered to sea duty in 1921, he served as commanding officer of the Marine detachment aboard the battleship *Texas* until 1924. Smith then began a four-year tour in the personnel section at Marine Corps Headquarters, Washington, D.C. In 1928 Smith went to Port-au-Prince, Haiti, to work as assistant chief of staff to the commandant of the *Garde d'Haiti* (formerly the *Gendarmerie d'Haiti*), a combined army and police force established by a Haitian treaty with the United States. Most of its officers were enlisted or commissioned U.S. Marines, while its enlisted personnel were Haitians. Smith held the rank of captain in the *Garde*, which was also his Marine Corps rank at that time. After three years in Haiti, Smith was ordered to the field officers' course at the Army Infantry School, Fort Benning, Georgia. Among the instructors at the school were George Catlett Marshall* and Omar Nelson Bradley,* and two of Smith's classmates were Walter Bedell Smith and Terry de la Mesa Allen, both of the Army. In June 1932, after graduation, Smith was sent to teach at the company officers' course at the Marine Corps facility at Quantico, Virginia. The next year he was assigned as assistant operations officer of the 7th Marine Regiment, also at Quantico. In 1934 Captain Smith and his family began a two and one-half year stay in France, where he took a course of study of the *Ecole Supérieure de Guerre* in Paris. In 1936 he returned to the schools at Quantico to teach amphibious operations. It might have been during this period that Smith received his nicknames of "the student general" and "the professor" from his contemporaries. Having been promoted to major while in France, Smith was promoted to lieutenant colonel in 1938. In July 1939 Smith was assigned as operations officer of the Fleet Marine Force, the combat arm of the Marine Corps, for duty at Marine Corps Base, San Diego.

In June 1940 he became commanding officer of the 1st Battalion, 6th Marine Regiment. In May 1941 he sailed with his regiment for Iceland where he remained for almost a year. Then Smith became executive officer of the Division of Plans and Policies at Marine Corps Headquarters.

Smith was ordered to join the 1st Marine Division in January 1944, while it was engaged in action on New Britain. On March 1 he took command of the

5th Marine Regiment. He had until March 6 to plan a landing on the Willaumez Peninsula behind Japanese lines and to capture what was believed to be their withdrawal center at Talasea. Smith received the Bronze Star with combat "V" for that operation. He was promoted to brigadier general and was made assistant division commander. The division was brought back to Pavuvu in the Russell Islands May 1944. Smith was in charge of planning the division's landing on Peleliu and related islands in the Palau Operation. Smith, operating from an antitank ditch, commanded the operations on shore during the first day of the Peleliu landing that September. In November he became the Marine deputy chief of staff to Army Lieutenant General Simon Bolivar Buckner, commanding the Tenth Army for the Okinawa operation. He served on the Tenth Army staff throughout the Okinawa Campaign.

In July 1945 Smith returned to the United States to command the Marine Corps Schools at Quantico. The following year the commandant of the Marine Corps, General Alexander Archer Vandegrift,* appointed him to a board of three generals to study the influence of the new atomic weapons on the future of amphibious warfare. That board recommended development of the helicopter as the future solution to the twin problems of the need to disperse the naval force over a wide area while having to concentrate the landing force at the place of the assault. In late 1948 Smith, then a major general and assistant commandant of the Marine Corps and chief of staff, was asked by the commandant, General Clifton B. Cates, to head a second board to examine measures which the Marine Corps should take to meet its responsibilities for leadership in amphibious warfare. The Smith Board recommended (1) that until major advances were made in helicopter technology, few advanced tactics could be developed, and (2) that the time was rapidly approaching when helicopter squadrons should be organized to support the Fleet Marine Force. Smith could soon put into practice those observations on the use of the helicopter.

Shortly before the outbreak of the Korean War, in July 1950, Smith was ordered to Camp Pendleton, California, to command the 1st Marine Division. He had less than twenty days from receipt of the directive to prepare the bulk of the division to move out to the Far East. Smith did the planning for and then led his division in three of the most difficult campaigns of the war. That September, Smith's division led the surprise landing at Inchon, behind the enemy's lines, in a move designed to trap and destroy the invading North Korean forces. Smith's immediate superior, X Corps commander, Army Major General Edward Mallory Almond,* did not understand the specialized requirements of an assault landing in a narrow harbor with exceptionally high tides. Smith and Rear Admiral James H. Doyle, however, were able to successfully plan this complicated landing without too much interference from higher levels. *Time* magazine put Smith on the cover of its September 25, 1950, issue for this achievement.

Under pressure from Almond to capture Seoul exactly three months from the date of the North Korean invasion, Smith was able to secure the South Korean capital adequately for the ceremony General Douglas MacArthur* staged, with

Smith present, turning the city back to the South Koreans. The 1st Marine Division then returned to Inchon and landed on the east coast of Korea for the attack north to the Yalu River to complete the conquest of North Korea.

Near the end of October 1950 the division began its march to the Chosin Reservoir. At one time, Smith's battalions were strung out over a two hundred mile line as they went north. He was careful not to divide his forces any more than he had to and to secure his main supply route. Throughout this period, as in the Inchon and Seoul campaigns, Smith used his helicopters for the purposes envisioned in the reports he had helped write earlier. They were used in reconnaissance, evacuations, resupply, and other capacities. Only the assault role was missing. On November 2 the Chinese Communist forces attacked units of the division in great strength. The northern advance of the Marines was over. On December 11 Smith was able to complete the fighting seventy-eight-mile withdrawal of his division to safety. In below-zero weather against eight Chinese Communist Army divisions, Smith first regrouped his forces and then organized the advance back to the sea, bringing his wounded and his equipment with him. Supported by Marine, Navy, and Air Force aircraft, the Marines reached the coast with forty-four hundred battle casualties and innumerable cases of frostbite and pneumonia. The Chinese Communists lost an estimated twenty-five thousand killed.

In early December, while Smith was planning his withdrawal, he gave an interview to a journalist which probably resulted in a famous quotation that is popularly attributed to him, but which Smith denied saying (he was famous in the Marine Corps for not drinking or swearing). Smith is alleged to have said upon being asked if the Marines were retreating under fire, "Retreat Hell, we're just attacking in another direction." In trying to explain that because the Marines, and their supporting forces, were surrounded and under attack from all sides and, thus, would have to fight no matter in which direction they moved, he might have said, as one obituary worded it, "We are not retreating—we are just attacking in a different direction." But his denials were unable to stop the circulation of the first version of that quotation.

After a period of rest and recuperation, Smith's division again was in combat. As part of the IX Corps, he was engaged in the February 1951 counteroffensive when Army Major General Bryant E. Moore suddenly died and Lieutenant General Matthew Bunker Ridgway* ordered Smith to take command of IX Corps. In one of the rare episodes when a Marine Corps general commanded a joint Army-Marine Corps division or corps, Smith commanded IX Corps from February 24 to March 5, 1951, when an Army general arrived to take over the corps.

In April 1951 Smith was assigned to command Camp Pendleton. He was promoted to lieutenant general in 1953 and took command of Fleet Marine Force, Atlantic, which consisted of the bulk of Marine Corps combat strength oriented towards the Atlantic Ocean. Subsequently, Smith headed another board to consider the requirements for small and medium helicopters in the Marine Corps.

His board recommended extensive use of the medium helicopter. Smith retired on September 1, 1955, and was promoted to general at that time.

Smith was a student and teacher of military science. He participated in campaigns on New Britain, Peleliu, and Okinawa during World War II. After the war, he helped prepare the Marine Corps for potential nuclear warfare with his participation on study boards that developed the use of the helicopter by the Marine Corps. During the Korean War, he directed the 1st Marine Division in the difficult surprise landing at Inchon that changed the course of the war. His finest hour came when the Chinese Communists entered the war and eight of their divisions attacked his at Chosin Reservoir. His careful planning and refusal to spread out his regiments enabled the Marines to withstand the assault. His leadership and planning for the fighting withdrawal enabled the Marines to maintain their tactical integrity and to destroy the eight enemy divisions as combat forces. That in turn enabled X Corps to evacuate the North Korean coast and to stay in the war as a tactical formation. Smith's withdrawal against heavy odds (Almond had told him to abandon his equipment) sustained the morale of the American and other United Nations forces at a critical time in the Korean War.

Smith was a scholar of warfare, a planner of amphibious operations, and a combat leader, and he excelled at those aspects of twentieth-century military life.

BIBLIOGRAPHY

Heinl, Robert D., Jr. *Victory at High Tide: The Inchon-Seoul Campaign.* Philadelphia: J. B. Lippincott Company, 1968.

Montross, Lynn, et al. *U.S. Marine Operations in Korea.* 5 vols. Washington, D.C.: U.S. Government Printing Office, 1954–1972.

Rawlins, Eugene W. *Marines and Helicopters, 1942–1962.* Washington, D.C.: U.S. Government Printing Office, 1976.

Shaw, Henry I., et al. *History of U.S. Marine Corps Operations in World War II.* 5 vols. Washington, D.C.: U.S. Government Printing Office, 1958–1971.

MARTIN K. GORDON

SPAATZ, Carl Andrew (b. June 28, 1891, Boyerstown, Pa.; d. Washington, D.C., July 13, 1974), Army officer, Air Force officer. Spaatz was one of the main disciples of William ("Billy") Mitchell* and was the first chief of staff of the U.S. Air Force.

Spaatz was one of five children of a Pennsylvania Dutch family who added an extra "A" to their last name in 1937 to assure proper pronunciation. His father was a printer and a Democrat state senator. At West Point, Spaatz acquired the nickname "Tooey" because of his resemblance to an upperclassman, and graduated into the infantry in 1914. After service at Schofield Barracks, he learned to fly at San Diego and transferred to the Air Service of the Signal Corps. He served with the Punitive Expedition under John Joseph Pershing's* command that pursued Pancho Villa deep into Mexico. As a major with the American

Expeditionary Force in France, Spaatz was assigned to training duties but went "AWOL to the front." He flew with a British unit while on leave and downed two German planes in a single action, narrowly escaping capture when he nearly ran out of gas. His extracurricular successes gained him a Distinguished Service Cross—and direct orders to return to his training duties.

In the 1920s and early 1930s Spaatz was a strong supporter of Billy Mitchell, and like many officers of that period spent a long time in grade, in his case fifteen years as a major. Taciturn and blunt, Spaatz served as a defense witness at the Mitchell court-martial. As a result of that symbolic defeat, air power enthusiasts in the Air Service/Air Corps undertook a series of publicity-making flights, inadvertently aided by Charles Lindbergh's dramatic transatlantic flight in 1927. Spaatz served as part of a "flying circus" demonstration team and won the Distinguished Flying Cross when he made an endurance refueling flight in the first week of January 1929, staying in the air almost 151 hours with Ira Clarence Eaker, who was then a major, and Elwood Quesada, then a lieutenant, both of whom became major commanders in the U.S. Army Air Force in World War II.

Spaatz reluctantly attended the U.S. Army Command and General Staff College in 1935–1936, commenting that he had never seen a happy general. In that period, most Air Corps officers saw Leavenworth as less desirable an assignment than a flying command or attendance at the Tactical School at Maxwell Field.

In 1940, Spaatz went with an observer team to the United Kingdom and was chief of the Army Air Forces Materiel Division at the time of Pearl Harbor. In May 1942 he went to England to command the Eighth Air Force, which began operations against targets in Europe in August 1942. Three months later, Spaatz became Allied Air Forces commander under Dwight David Eisenhower,* during Operation TORCH, the invasion of North Africa, and remained in the Mediterranean until early 1944. In spite of his bluff manner, Spaatz got along well with the British and became an advocate of systematic analysis of weapons effects of the type carrried out by Sir Solly Zuckerman, when others were not at all interested. The Spaatz-Zuckerman relationship led to a bombing of the Island of Pantellaria along lines suggested by scientific analysis which led to surrender of the garrison before a scheduled landing took place.

In the spring of 1944, Spaatz returned to Britain to command the newly formed U.S. Strategic Air Forces in Europe, where he argued for a redirection of the air offensive against vulnerable points in the German war network, moving away from attacks on specific aircraft-related industries to key arteries and nodes, the transportation system, and synthetic oil production facilities. Spaatz faced not only resistance from the Royal Air Force's Sir Arthur "Bomber" Harris, who wanted area attacks, but also a diversion of the Allied Air Forces to supporting the ground forces before, during, and after Operation OVERLORD, the major invasion of France. In the early summer of 1944 the Allied air forces again struck at transportation and oil, a tactic that proved dramatically successful. The starvation of German air and tank forces of fuel and lubricant blunted their effectiveness in such cases as the Battle of the Bulge and the defense of Budapest, and blocked the Germans' ability to bring their jet fighter force into full play. Spaatz shared one article of faith with Harris, the belief that air power properly applied could have eliminated the need for the D-Day invasion, an assertion that continues to be a main item of debate in respect to air power in World War II.

In June 1945, a month after Germany's downfall, Spaatz went to Guam to command U.S. Strategic Air Forces in the Far East, presiding over Curtis Emerson LeMay's* program of area firebomb raids, as well as the dropping of atomic bombs on Hiroshima and Nagasaki.

In the postwar period, Spaatz, who had attended all the main surrender ceremonies, became a strong publicist of air power. In 1947 he succeeded General Henry Harley ("Hap") Arnold* as chief of the U.S. Army Air Forces and then became the first U.S. Air Force chief of staff, with the creation of an independent American air element resulting from the National Security Act of 1947. After retirement in 1948, Spaatz became national security affairs correspondent for *Newsweek* magazine. He also served as chairman of the Civil Air Patrol and the International Reserve Committee, as well as a member of the committee that chose Colorado Springs as the Air Force Academy site. He is buried there.

Spaatz remains a somewhat enigmatic figure, in spite of his role as the major American commander of strategic air power in World War II, and his extensive comments in the popular press during the Cold War. A biography of substance is overdue, particularly since he and George Churchill Kenney showed the least tendency to get hung up on tactical method and dogma, to seek for success by alternatives within the general framework of air power, and not let too many chips ride on one number. In looking at Spaatz, one feels that, in spite of a certain amount of stylized bluster and pugnacity, he resembles Douglas MacArthur,* a first-class mind unchallenged in his environment by frequent contact with other first-class minds. In any event, his star has faded far out of proportion to his importance in the shaping of air power in World War II and the early Cold War.

BIBLIOGRAPHY

DuPre, Flint O. *U.S. Air Force Biographical Dictionary*. New York: Franklin Watts, 1965.
Craven, Wesley Frank, and James Lea Cate, eds. *The Army Air Forces in World War II*. 7 vols. 1948–1954.
Zuckerman, Sir Solly. *From Apes to Warlords*. London: Hamish Hamilton, 1978.

ROGER BEAUMONT

SPRUANCE, Raymond Ames (b. Baltimore, Md., July 3, 1886; d. Pebble Beach, Calif., December 13, 1969), naval officer. Spruance was the principal American naval commander in the Central Pacific during World War II and victorious commander at Midway.

Before the war, Spruance seemed an unlikely candidate for a future fleet commander. He was reared by women—at times by a domineering mother and at times by three young and adoring maiden aunts. His father was a recluse whom he hardly knew. As a teenager he wrote and published poetry that displayed his sensitivity and imagination. Spruance attended the Naval Academy with the class of 1907 because he could not afford to pay for his own university education. He was unhappy there because of the discipline, the hazing, and the sterile curriculum. Yet he was an excellent student, but so inconspicuous that few of his classmates knew him well. He was described in his yearbook as a shy young man, open and innocent, who would hurt nothing and no one, except in the line of duty.

Shortly after graduation, Spruance sailed around the world with the Great White Fleet, which was initially under the command of Robley Dunglison Evans. Spruance so enjoyed the experience that it was then that he decided to be a career naval officer. In 1909 he studied advanced electrical engineering for a year at the General Electric Company in Schenectady, New York, and became one of the Navy's finest technical experts. Consequently, Spruance received a number of engineering assignments and could have chosen to become a limited-duty specialist. He decided, however, to remain an unrestricted line officer.

He received his first of six commands in the Philippines, the primitive destroyer *Bainbridge*, in March 1913. He was promoted to lieutenant commander in August 1917 shortly after the United States entered World War I and began to mobilize the fleet. However, he never saw action owing to shipyard assignments in the United States. After the war his sea duty tours followed the normal peacetime routine, including command of the destroyers *Aaron Ward, Percival, Dale* and *Osborne*. His sixth—and major—command was the battleship *Mississippi* (1938). Spruance was regarded as a superb shiphandler and a quiet, conscientious, competent skipper.

Spruance supported not only his own family, but his mother and aunts as well. After World War I he became discouraged with his low pay and very nearly resigned his commission, but he remained in the service because his father-in-law told him he was too honest to be a successful businessman. Spruance believed that the only meaningful duty for promotion was at sea, and there he remained as long as he could. Even though he often became seasick, he was a stoic who would not admit to physical discomfort. Shore duty was for relaxation, and when he came ashore he sought comfortable quarters and pleasant surroundings; he neither worked overtime nor brought work home. He sought neither favors nor friends in high places nor duty in Washington to advance his career. He once told his close friend William Frederick Halsey, Jr.,* that he was simply trying to be a good naval officer. Spruance's last three tours of shore duty were at the Naval War College as a student and then as a staff officer. It was there that he learned the fundamentals of strategy and operational planning.

Selected for rear admiral in the fall of 1940, Spruance found that his assignment was to establish the Tenth Naval District Headquarters in San Juan, Puerto Rico.

Spruance subsequently supervised the construction of numerous bases and airfields in the Caribbean as a result of the general mobilization for war. In September 1941 Spruance took command of Cruiser Division Five in Pearl Harbor and was surface screen commander for Halsey's carrier task force in the early months of World War II. After his ships protected the task force which carried the Army aircraft that flew in the famous attack on Tokyo led by James Harold Doolittle, Spruance relieved Halsey, who was seriously ill. Spruance took command of the American carrier force that sank four Japanese carriers in the victory at the critical Battle of Midway (June 1942). Coupled with the Battle of the Coral Sea (May 1942, under Admiral Frank Jack Fletcher*), Midway blocked the expansion of the Japanese and actually put them on the defensive. Furthermore, the loss of four aircraft carriers, as well as losing the battle itself, was a tremendous psychological blow to the Japanese Navy. Spruance's ship disposition and use of available aircraft were brilliant. Midway was one of the most decisive battles of World War II.

Spruance then came ashore as chief of staff to Admiral Chester William Nimitz,* commander in chief, Pacific, at Pearl Harbor. A year later Spruance returned to sea as commander of the Fifth Fleet, leading American forces across the Pacific to the very shores of Japan. These campaigns included the seizures of major islands and island groups, including the Gilberts, Marshalls, Marianas, Iwo Jima, and Okinawa. Another of Spruance's famous fights was the Battle of the Philippine Sea; although Japan lost more than 450 aircraft in one day in the "Marianas Turkey Shoot," the Japanese fleet escaped. Afterwards Spruance was criticized for his passive defense off the shores of Saipan. Spruance claimed he had carried out his primary mission of protecting the troops ashore.

After the war Spruance ended his active duty as president of the Naval War College, although Fleet Admiral Ernest Joseph King* considered Spruance as well qualified to be the next chief of naval operations. Called out of retirement to become ambassador to the Philippines in 1952, Spruance and the Central Intelligence Agency worked together to ensure the election of Ramon Magsaysay as president under circumstances that seemed acceptable then under the threat of communision but that are subject to criticism today. Spruance retired again in 1955 and spent his remaining years at his home in Pebble Beach.

Because he abhorred publicity, Spruance was not well known by his fellow Americans. To his colleagues and subordinates he seemed rather an austere, remote, almost mysterious figure. In reality, he was a superb combination of fighter and intellectual. In Samuel Eliot Morison's words, Spruance was "secure within, a modest and a great man who should have been given a fifth star."

His intellectualism was not the kind associated with philosophy, science, or advanced degrees, and he disliked writing and speeches. He had superior mental power and relied solely upon his intellect—and never his emotions—when he fought the Japanese. He respected the Japanese as fighters and did not allow hatred to distort his judgment. War to him was an intellectual challenge that stimulated his mind. Spruance pragmatically accepted the notion that war meant killing and that many people would have to die. But he did everything in his power to reduce American casualties, primarily through meticulous planning and use of violent, overwhelming force, swiftly applied. In his judgment it would have been proper to use poison gas on Iwo Jima; American lives would have been spared, and no civilians were on the island. Spruance pitied the civilians who suffered in war, and he deplored the B–29 fire raids against Japan.

Spruance encouraged initiative in combat by telling his subordinates what he wanted done, giving them the necessary resources and then leaving the tactical direction entirely to the commanders at the scene. His operations orders were famous for their precision and clarity. Once the fighting started, Spruance would neither interfere nor offer advice, but he would make major decisions and issue general directives when necessary. His mind was always fresh and rested because of his splendid health and aloofness from details. His avoidance of long working hours seemed like laziness to some, but it was Spruance's way of conserving his health through a long war.

His moral courage was manifested by his incorruptible integrity. He spoke the truth, and he did what was morally right regardless of the possible consequences to his own career. At the height of the war Spruance spoke in California and publicly criticized the unjustified imprisonment of Japanese-American citizens in concentration camps. Immediately after the war, he argued publicly against the punitive confiscation of Japanese territory and recommended a drastic reduction in the size of the postwar American Navy because there were no more enemy naval powers in the near future.

Spruance's physical courage was unbelievable, and he was apparently fatalistic. Throughout the war his flagship was often attacked, yet he seemed oblivious to personal danger. He would gaze serenely at bombers diving upon him from above and was indifferent to projectiles from shore batteries bracketing his ship. Transcending his other virtues, however, was his fighting spirit: his eagerness and desire to come to grips with the enemy, to press on with vigor and determination against all obstacles, and to keep fighting until the battle was won. A complex and fascinating man, he was an enigma to everyone. Above all, he was a master of the art of naval warfare.

Morison wrote the words that provide the best brief description of Raymond Spruance: "Power of decision and coolness in action were perhaps Spruance's leading characteristics. He envied no one, regarded no one as rival, won the respect of everyone with whom he came in contact, and went ahead in his quiet way, winning victories for his country."

BIBLIOGRAPHY

Buell, Thomas B. *The Quiet Warrior: A Biography of Admiral Raymond A. Spruance.* Boston: Little, Brown and Company, 1974.
Forrestel, Emmet P. *Admiral Raymond A. Spruance, USN: A Study in Command.* Washington, D.C.: U.S. Government Printing Office, 1966.

Lord, Walter. *Incredible Victory*. New York: Harper and Row, 1967.
Morison, Samuel E. *History of U.S. Naval Operations in World War II*. 15 vols. Boston: Atlantic, Little, Brown and Company, 1947–1962.
Reynolds, Clark G. *The Fast Carriers: The Forging of an Air Navy*. New York: McGraw-Hill, 1968.

THOMAS B. BUELL

STEUBEN, Frederic William Ludolf Gerhard Augustin, "Baron von," (b. Magdeburg, Prussia, September 17, 1730; d. near Remsen, N.Y., November 28, 1794), professional soldier and inspector general of the Army of the United States. Steuben's signal accomplishment was to train the Continental Army as regular infantry of the line capable of standing up to the British in the field.

Steuben's father was an officer of engineers in the Prussian and Russian armies, and from his first days at Magdeburg, a key Prussian fortress, the future baron was exposed to guns, parades, and military trappings. Frederick William entered the Prussian Army in 1746 as a lance corporal. By the time the Seven Years' War broke out in 1756, he was a first lieutenant in the crack Lestwitz Regiment. Determined that the war would see him "either in Hades, or at the head of a regiment," Steuben attained neither, although he was twice wounded at Prague (1757) and again at Kunersdorf (1759). He spent a year on detached duty with a Free Battalion, as light infantry was then called, and for a time served as a general staff officer. Captured by the Russians in 1761, it was Steuben, probably while on parole, who was among the first to inform Frederick the Great of the death of his sworn enemy, the Empress Elizabeth, in 1762, causing Russia to change sides and then to drop out of the war altogether. In 1763 Steuben was one of fifteen officers selected to be taught the art of war under the personal supervision of Frederick, but soon after the war, probably because he was not of the hereditary nobility, he was retired from the Army.

Steuben spent the next decade at the court of a petty and bankrupt German principality, meanwhile trying in vain to find employment in the armies of France, the Empire, Sardinia, and even the East India Company. Not until the outbreak of the American Revolution was there a need for his talents. Recruited initially as a technical advisor to help train the American soldiers to look after arms and equipment that the French were sending surreptitiously before openly concluding a formal alliance, Steuben reached George Washington's* encampment at Valley Forge in February 1778. The Americans desperately lacked food, clothing, shelter, training, and discipline, and Washington, who was painfully aware that he needed a competent professional to hammer his army into shape, named Steuben acting inspector general.

In this capacity Steuben, working through a special company formed from the different regiments, taught the shivering Continentals the simplified rudiments of Prussian drill. By spring Washington's men knew how to bear arms, to march, to quickly form from column into line, and to fire with precision and at command. Above all they had learned how to use the bayonet. At Monmouth (June 28,

1778) those who saw the regiments of Washington's left wing wheel systematically into line under fire with the poise and precision of veterans, beat back a furious British assault and then counterattack with the bayonet, were impressed with what had been accomplished. When Congress officially created the Inspector General's Department the following February, Steuben became responsible for training all American troops.

Writing from memory, he salvaged whatever seemed essential from the Prussian regulations that could be adapted to a system based upon British organization and in a situation where soldiers were motivated by devotion to the cause and their leader rather than the harsh discipline and fear that kept Frederick's troops in line. By March 1779 he had produced his own *Regulations for the Order and Discipline of the Troops of the United States*, which by act of Congress became official doctrine. Steuben's Blue Book, as it was called, was reprinted more than seventy times before it was replaced in 1812 by a manual based upon French drill.

Steuben's accomplishments as inspector general have obscured his other services. When West Point was threatened in June 1780, Washington sent him to give "advice and assistance" to the commanding officer. Steuben also sat as a member of the court-martial that sentenced Major John André for his role in the plot to deliver this strategic stronghold to the British. Later that year Steuben went to Virginia to raise and equip reinforcements for Nathanael Greene* in the Carolinas. After surviving temporary setbacks when the British seized Richmond and later his own depot, Steuben rejoined Washington to command one of his three divisions before Yorktown. His previous experience in Europe was indispensable in helping to guide the Continentals in the intricacies of eighteenth-century siegecraft. Steuben saw no further action before he retired from the Army in 1784.

Although he remained in the United States, his hopes for a generous settlement from Congress for his services were never realized. A good disciplinarian but a bad manager of funds, Steuben could not even realize profit from the sixteen thousand acres in the Mohawk Valley given him by the state of New York. "In this country," he complained, "the laborers are barons and the barons are beggers." He continued to write on military affairs, and in his recommendations for a Swiss militia system to supplement the small Regular Army, for the harbor defenses of New York, and for the establishment of a military academy, Steuben continued to contribute to the military needs of the young republic. And as one of the founders of the Society of the Cincinnati he helped to keep alive the ideals of the Revolution. A confirmed bachelor, Steuben died on his Mohawk Valley estate without ever having found Eldorado: but if he was still in debt, he left his adopted nation even more in his debt.

Steuben was not an aristocrat. The prefix *von* signifying nobility had been inserted by a grandfather anxious to do well by his descendants, and he awarded himself the title of baron shortly before the American Revolution. Probably to cultivate the support of Frederick the Great, he also changed his last three christened names to August Henry Ferdinand, which "happened" also to be the names of Frederick's brothers, and just before leaving for America Steuben promoted himself in rank from captain to lieutenant general!

The *ersatz* baron, however, quickly became a genuine patriot, and herein lies the secret of his accomplishments. Any Prussian drill sergeant might have instructed the troops at Valley Forge, but Frederick himself could not have adapted the Prussian system to new and such radically different conditions. This required a mental retooling of the basic assumptions that lay behind all military training, which is why Steuben stressed the need for officers to cultivate the affection of their troops by treating the men "with every possible kindness and humanity." Fear and discipline would not motivate the American volunteer. Steuben's *Regulations*, it has been said, ran second only to the Bible on the reading list of American officers.

Many have paid tribute to the memory of Steuben and to his distinctive contributions to the cause of American independence, but of all testimonials the old general probably would have most preferred the "Creed adopted by the Officers of the American Army at Verplanck's Point" in 1792, particularly that portion of the "Apostle's Creed" affirming:

> We believe that George Washington is the only fit man in the world to head the American Army . . . that Nathaniel Greene was born a general . . . (and) that Baron Steuben has made us soldiers, and that he is capable of forming the whole world into solid column, and deploying it from the center. We believe in his *Blue Book*. We believe in General Knox and his artillery. And we believe in our bayonets. Amen!

BIBLIOGRAPHY

Busch, Noel F. *Winter Quarters. George Washington and the Continental Army at Valley Forge*. New York: Liveright, 1974.

Cronau, Rudolf. *The Army of the American Revolution and Its Organizer*. New York: Rudolf Cronau, 1923.

Kapp, Friedrich. *Life of Frederick William von Steuben*. New York: Mason Brothers, 1859.

Palmer, John McAuley. *General von Steuben*. New Haven, Conn.: Yale University Press, 1937.

Riling, Joseph R. *Baron von Steuben and his Regulations. Including a Complete Facsimile of the Original Regulations for the Order and Discipline of the Troops of the United States*. Philadelphia: Ray Riling Arms Books Company, 1966.

JAY LUVAAS

STILWELL, Joseph Warren (b. Palatka, Fla., March 19, 1883; d. San Francisco, Calif., October 12, 1946). Commander of U.S. Forces in the China-Burma-India Theater in World War II.

Joseph W. Stilwell was the older son of the four children born to Benjamin and Mary (Peene) Stilwell. Although born in Florida, Joseph spent his early years in Great Barrington, Massachusetts, and Yonkers, New York. Believing that the youth needed more discipline, his father arranged for Joseph to enter the U.S. Military Academy in 1900. Joseph graduated four years later, ranking thirty-second in a class of 124.

The 12th Infantry in the Philippines provided Stilwell with his first assignment. He stayed there for fourteen months, engaging in anti-guerrilla activities, before returning to West Point as an instructor in the Department of Modern Languages. Before 1917 he would alternate one more tour with the 12th Infantry in the Philippines (1911–1913) and with the faculty at West Point (1913–1917). While on leave in 1911, he made his first visit to China.

With the American entry into World War I Stilwell received a temporary promotion to major and an assignment as brigade adjutant in the 80th Division at Fort Lee, Virginia. In December 1917 he left for France, where he served as chief intelligence officer for the IV Corps.

During the war, Stilwell also saw staff service with the British 58th Division and the French XVII Corps (at Verdun). He returned to the American intelligence staff in April 1918, in time to help prepare plans for the offensive against St.-Mihiel. The explosion of an ammunition dump near Belrupt almost cost Stilwell his eyesight and severely impaired his vision. After the Armistice, Stilwell took part in the occupation duties assigned to the IV Corps. His wartime experiences earned for him not only the Distinguished Service Medal but also temporary promotions to lieutenant colonel and colonel.

Having been returned to the United States and the rank of captain, Stilwell volunteered to become a language officer for China. This assignment took him first to the University of California to study the Chinese language and then, with the new rank of major, to Peking by August 1920. While studying in California, Stilwell purchased land at Carmel, where he and his family eventually built a home.

Before Pearl Harbor, Stilwell served three separate tours in China, totaling ten years. From 1920 to 1923 he performed general duties as a student at the North China Union Language School, as a road engineer, and as an intelligence agent. Prior to his second assignment in China, Stilwell attended Infantry School at Fort Benning, Georgia (1923–1924) and Command and General Staff School at Fort Leavenworth, Kansas (1925–1926). The second China tour (1926–1929) placed Stilwell as a battalion commander in the 15th Infantry at Tientsin. The executive officer, George Catlett Marshall,* was impressed by Stilwell's performance. Stilwell eventually became acting chief of staff, and, while in China, he also earned a promotion to lieutenant colonel. Stilwell left China in 1929, proudly holding the title of handball champion of the Far East.

From 1929 to 1932 Stilwell taught at the Fort Benning Infantry School. He acquired the nickname "Vinegar Joe" there. An unhappy student, who had suffered one of Stilwell's notorious tongue-lashings, drew a caricature of Stilwell's head atop a bottle of vinegar. After a two-year stint training the organized reserves in San Diego, Stilwell returned to China for the third time (1935–1939). Promoted to colonel, he received orders to be the military attaché in China.

In 1939 George C. Marshall,* the new army chief of staff, recommended Stilwell for promotion to brigadier general. With his first star, Stilwell assumed command of the 3d Brigade of the 2d Division at Fort Sam Houston, Texas. He merited a certain measure of fame by telling an inquiring cavalry officer that the only role for a horse in the fighting in China was "good eating, if you're hungry." In July 1941 Stilwell was named commanding officer of the III Corps with headquarters at the Presidio of Monterey, California. By then he had earned a second star and had commanded the 2d Division at Ford Ord, California.

Soon after Pearl Harbor, Marshall summoned Stilwell to Washington. Although originally slated to command a proposed invasion of North Africa, Stilwell, now with three stars, was subsequently appointed chief of staff to Generalissimo Chiang Kai-shek on March 10, 1942. Concurrently, Stilwell received two other challenging assignments: commanding officer of all American forces in the China-Burma-India Theater (CBI) and selection by Chiang Kai-shek to command the 5th and 6th Chinese armies. Traveling throughout CBI, Stilwell immediately became entangled in the Allied loss of Burma. Only a courageous "walkout" to India in May 1942 by Stilwell and over one hundred people averted his own capture by the Japanese.

Following the Burma debacle, Stilwell set out to revitalize the CBI and, specifically, to train and equip Chinese troops so that they could play a key role in the defeat of Japan. In 1943 he took on yet another difficult responsibility, becoming deputy commander to Lord Louis Francis Mountbatten for the new South East Asia Command. During 1944 Stilwell participated in the Chinese military efforts that reclaimed northern Burma. Friction with Chiang Kai-shek and other influential Chinese leaders gradually led to a crisis later that year. The U.S. government proposed that Chiang appoint General Stilwell (he had received a fourth star on August 1, 1944) to command all Chinese forces. The ensuing political and military deadlock grew more intense, and, eventually, Washington had to acquiesce in Chiang's demand that Stilwell be recalled.

Stilwell departed for the United States on October 21, 1944, under strict orders to maintain silence about his situation. In January 1945 he received an assignment to supervise the training of American ground forces, and, in June, he became commanding officer of the Tenth Army in Okinawa. The Japanese surrender cut short plans to have the Tenth Army participate in the invasion of Japan. Ironically, Stilwell might have been involved with the liberation forces destined for China, but Chiang Kai-shek insisted that Stilwell not be allowed to go to China. Stilwell attended the surrender ceremony aboard the U.S.S. *Missouri*, and on September 7, he presided over the surrender ceremony at Okinawa.

In October 1945 Stilwell returned to the United States. He was assigned temporarily as president of the War Equipment Board. Three months later, he earned an appointment as commanding officer of the Sixth Army in charge of

Western Defense Command with headquarters in San Francisco. During 1946 his serious medical condition, heretofore undiscovered, was diagnosed as cancer of the stomach with severe deterioration of the liver. Joseph W. Stilwell died on October 12, 1946, in San Francisco. He left his wife, Winifred (Smith), whom he married in 1910, and five children.

Despite a long and successful Army career prior to December 1941, Stilwell is best remembered for his role in World War II. Controversy surrounds his war record. Some critics believe that he was hopelessly out of his league, trying to contend with Chinese politics and coalition diplomacy, while others think that he performed heroic duty, trying to carry the fight against the Japanese in what was supposed to be a key theater of the war.

In fact, Stilwell was thrust into an impossible situation. President Franklin D. Roosevelt, Secretary of War Henry Lewis Stimson, and Army Chief of Staff George C. Marshall* expected Stilwell not only to command all American forces in the CBI but also to serve as chief of staff to the Generalissimo. These two major responsibilities carried several other demanding duties, such as the administration of Lend Lease in China, command of the Chinese forces in India, command of the Chinese armies in Burma, and supervision of the Chinese Training and Combat Command. Each, of course, was a full-time job. Moreover, with the creation of the South East Asia Command (SEAC) in 1943, a third major responsibility fell to Stilwell, who was appointed deputy commander of SEAC.

His superiors in Washington repeatedly voiced their confidence to Stilwell that he was the best man for these difficult missions. Stimson, and especially Marshall, assured him that they understood his complex situation. Yet, Stilwell suffered the consequences of an eccentric organizational structure. Lord Mountbatten, Supreme Allied commander of South East Asia Command (SACSEA), pointed out that Stilwell could not possibly fulfill his three chief responsibilities because "only the Trinity could carry out his duties which require him to be in Delhi, Chungking and the Ledo Front simultaneously." Like a circus performer, Stilwell tried to wear three hats and juggle the attendant responsibilities of each, all at the same time. Questions of priorities and allegiance had to be resolved. Mountbatten thought that Stilwell, despite his title as deputy SACSEA, did not pursue the best interests of SEAC. Similarly, Chiang Kai-shek criticized his chief of staff for not sufficiently championing the Chinese cause in the politics of coalition diplomacy.

Another obstacle in Stilwell's path stemmed from the low supply priority allocated to CBI. The lack of equipment and the general shortage of supplies nourished a deep sense of frustration in Stilwell. He complained bitterly, "Peanut [Chiang Kai-shek] and I are on a raft, with one sandwich between us, and the rescue ship is headed away from the scene." Paradoxically, it is impossible to analyze Stilwell's performance without keeping in mind the relatively high strategic value placed on China. Future plans called for China to provide the base of operations for the final assault on Japan.

Stilwell was, above all, an excellent soldier. He made the military his career, and he knew his profession. In addition, his long experience in China before the war rendered him uniquely qualified for combat service there. He combined his expertise with an unshakable conviction that the Chinese soldier, if properly trained and equipped, was the equal of any soldier in the world. His confidence earned a certain confirmation when Chinese forces under his command reclaimed much of northern Burma during the first half of 1944. He devoted himself to breaking down the Chinese "defensive" psychology, especially that of the Kuomintang leadership under Chiang. His efforts, however, brought him only frustration. In fact, Stilwell courted controversy by expressing a desire to lead the Chinese Communist forces, who, in his opinion, earnestly wanted to fight the enemy.

Upon leaving China, Stilwell candidly acknowledged his "glaring deficiencies as a diplomat." He seemed to know his own strengths and weaknesses far better than anyone else. To the extent that each party caught in a personality clash bears a measure of responsibility for the problem, Stilwell must, consequently, be accorded some blame for the deteriorating relationship with Chiang Kai-shek. Stilwell disparagingly called him "Peanut" and made little effort to hide his strong dislike for the Generalissimo and the Kuomintang leadership. And this unfolded in a country where "face" and style are all-important. It is of little solace that he upheld the image of "Vinegar Joe" at the cost of damaged relations within the coalition and detraction from the war effort.

Nevertheless, Stilwell did realize some success in his assignments. His leadership contributed to Chinese military victories in Burma, which restored some confidence and self-esteem for the Chinese. Moreover, despite dark days, China did stay in the war against Japan. In addition, Stilwell's plans for the reorganization of the Chinese Army seemed to hold promise, at least at the time of his recall, for a brighter, more stable future in China.

Much of the criticism of Stilwell really should be directed against the central direction of the war in Washington. Heaping one impossible task after another on Stilwell, the American leaders simply deluded themselves with confident assurances about his considerable capabilities. Stimson later explained, "We knowingly gave him the toughest task in this war and it proved even harder than we anticipated."

Ironically, the crisis leading to his recall sprang from an attempt to give Stilwell yet another difficult assignment, namely, commander of all Chinese forces. No one man could handle all those responsibilities. His integrity, courage, and expertise were the equal to those of any man; nonetheless, somehow more was required in this impossible situation. Laden with hopeless tasks and conflicting responsibilities, Stilwell performed individual efforts that must be admired as among the greatest in World War II. The evolution of coalition warfare, however, had come to stress corporate management and institutionalized effort over rugged individualism. Perhaps his own words most effectively sum up his style and his wartime experience in China: "I've done my best and stood up for American interests. To hell with them."

BIBLIOGRAPHY

Belden, Jack. *Retreat with Stilwell*. New York: Alfred A. Knopf, 1943.
Dorn, Frank. *Walkout with Stilwell in Burma*. New York: Thomas Y. Crowell Company, 1971.
Romanus, Charles F., and Riley Sunderland. *Stilwell's Command Problems*. Washington, D.C.: Office of the Chief of Military History for the Department of the Army, 1956.
———. *Stilwell's Mission to China*. Washington, D.C.: Office of the Chief of Military History for the Department of the Army, 1953.
Tuchman, Barbara W. *Stilwell and the American Experience in China, 1911–1945*. New York: Macmillan Company, 1970.
White, Theodore H., ed. *The Stilwell Papers*. New York: William Sloane Associates, 1948.

JOHN J. SBREGA

STUART, James Ewell Brown ("Jeb"), (b. Laurel Hill Plantation, Patrick County, Va., February 6, 1833; d. Richmond, Va., May 12, 1864), Army officer. Stuart commanded the Cavalry Corps, Army of Northern Virginia, during the Civil War.

Stuart was the son of Archibald and Elizabeth Pannill Stuart; the family, of Scottish descent, settled in Virginia in 1738. After an early education at home and in Wytheville, Virginia, and two years at Emory and Henry College, he was appointed to the U.S. Military Academy and graduated thirteenth of forty-six in the class of 1854. Brevetted second lieutenant in the Regiment of Mounted Rifles, he was commissioned in that rank on October 31, 1854, and in March 1855 he was transferred to the 1st Cavalry Regiment. On November 14, 1855, at Fort Leavenworth, Kansas, he married Flora, daughter of Colonel Philip St. George Cooke. Three children (one of whom died in infancy) were born of the marriage. In Stuart's five years with the 1st Cavalry, it kept the peace in "Bleeding Kansas" and carried out expeditions, in one of which he was wounded, against hostile Indians. In October 1859, while on leave, Stuart volunteered as aide to Robert Edward Lee* and with him participated in the capture of John Brown at Harper's Ferry.

In January 1861 Stuart applied for "a position" in the Southern army which he expected to be formed; on May 3, following the secession of Virginia and his own promotion to captain, he resigned from the U.S. Army. Commissioned in the state forces of Virginia on May 6, 1861, he was assigned in June to the command of the 1st Virginia Cavalry, as colonel from July 16. While training his regiment, he also screened the army of Joseph Eggleston Johnston* at Winchester, Virginia, when the Federal army of Robert R. Paterson moved against it. Stuart distinguished himself in the Battle of Bull Run by the manner in which he protected the left flank of the brigade comanded by Thomas Jonathan ("Stonewall") Jackson.* On September 21 Stuart was promoted to brigadier general, Confederate States Army, and given command of a five-regiment cavalry brigade.

In the spring of 1862 Stuart attracted national attention. Sent by General Lee to locate the right flank of the Union Army on the Peninsula, he circled the army instead of returning the way he had come. This "brilliant exploit," as Lee called it, made Stuart the cavalryman par excellence of the Confederacy.

After the Seven Days' battles, in which Stuart covered Jackson's approach and protected his flanks, he was promoted to major general and given command of the cavalry of the Army of Northern Virginia, organized as a three-brigade division. In the Second Bull Run Campaign, he led a raid around the flank of the Union Army and captured papers belonging to General John Pope, which led to Lee sending Jackson's corps on its epic march to Pope's rear and thus set the stage for the Battle of Second Bull Run. Occupied mainly in scouting and screening in the ensuing Maryland Campaign, in the Battle of Antietam Stuart's cavalry and artillery, in a flank position, assisted materially in checking the Federal assaults on Jackson. After the battle, and the retreat of the army to Winchester, Stuart led a raid (October 9–12) to Chambersburg, Pennsylvania; riding around the Union Army, he outdistanced pursuit and recrossed the Potomac with twelve hundred captured horses, and with the loss of one man wounded. As the Union and Confederate armies moved east toward Fredericksburg, Stuart clashed repeatedly with the Federal cavalry, notably at Barbee's Cross Roads (November 5). In the three months following the Battle of Fredericksburg, his cavalry engaged in constant harassment of the Federal lines of communication.

After reporting to General Lee the advance of the Union Army toward Chancellorsville, Stuart brought him word on the evening of May 1, 1863, that the Federal right flank was "in the air." This led to Jackson's flank march and successful attack on the XI Corps. When Jackson and Ambrose Powell Hill* were wounded on the evening of May 2, Stuart took command of the corps, and the next morning, in some of the heaviest fighting of the war, drove the Federal infantry out of Chancellorsville.

The cavalry subsequently was given a month's rest, but at dawn on June 9, at Brandy Station, it was attacked by General Alfred Pleasanton's Federal cavalry in full strength. Stuart was saved from a damaging defeat by his own determined leadership (lacking on the other side), the valor of his men, and a great deal of luck. He was severely criticized by Southern newspapers for having been taken by surprise; there is little doubt that the criticism influenced his actions in the ensuing campaign.

Following Brandy Station, Stuart had the task of keeping the Federal cavalry away from the gaps through the Blue Ridge, thus protecting the march of the Confederate infantry northward to Pennsylvania. On June 17, 19 and 21, the two cavalry forces fought at Aldie, Middleburg, and Upperville, respectively. Tactically defeated in the last two of these engagements, Stuart nevertheless prevented the Federals from reaching the gaps. General Lee's orders to Stuart

(June 23) for his march into Maryland lacked precision; Stuart interpreted them as authorizing a circuit of the Union Army, and the crossing of the Potomac well to the east of the mountains. The intent of Lee's orders, and the validity of Stuart's interpretation, remain the subject of controversy. The result was that for seven days (June 25–July 1) Stuart and his three best brigades were out of touch with their army. Lee was to state that his movements were "much embarrassed" by their absence.

Stuart's march, slowed by the 125 supply wagons he captured on June 28 and by a fight with Judson Kilpatrick's cavalry at Hanover on June 30, took him north to Carlisle, Pennsylvania, where he learned that the army was at Gettysburg. He arrived there on July 2, with an exhausted command. The next day, at Cress's Ridge, he attacked the cavalry brigades of J. B. McIntosh and George Armstrong Custer,* with the evident objective (contrary to his claim) of breaking through to the rear of the Union position on Cemetery Ridge, as it was being charged frontally by George Edward Pickett.* The attack failed, and Stuart was himself driven back with loss. On the retreat to the Potomac, he protected the left flank and rear of the army, and in a series of combats with the Federal cavalry, kept it away from Lee's position at Williamsport until the army was able to recross the river.

In August Stuart's command was reorganized into a corps of two divisions, but he was not promoted to lieutenant general, the rank of officers commanding corps of infantry. In the Bristoe Campaign, at Liberty Mills (September 23), he was attacked front and rear by the divisions of Kilpatrick and John Buford, but extricated himself with a vigorous counterattack. At Brandy Station (October 11), the situation was reversed; he had Buford and Kilpatrick surrounded, but they were able to break through to safety. At Buckland Mills (October 19), Stuart routed Henry E. Davies, Jr.'s, cavalry brigade. Except for the brief interruption of the Mine Run Campaign (November 26–December 1), the winter was uneventful, Stuart's chief concern being the steady deterioration of the condition and numbers of his horses.

In March 1864 Philip Henry Sheridan* was given command of the Cavalry Corps of the Army of the Potomac. On the night of May 3 the Union Army advanced into the Wilderness. Until the arrival of Lee's infantry, Stuart harried the Federal advance, and on May 5 and 6, posted on the right of the army, he had a series of hard fights with Federal cavalry.

On May 9, authorized to cut loose from the army in order to "whip Stuart," Sheridan started toward Richmond with his corps of about ten thousand. Stuart started after him, but with only three of his six brigades, numbering about four thousand. Stuart's conduct of the operation was faulty in the extreme. On May 11, when he offered battle at Yellow Tavern, all the advantage lay with Sheridan's Federals, and Stuart was decisively defeated. In the thick of the fight, Stuart was mortally wounded; removed to Richmond, he died on the evening of the next day.

Stuart's place in the Confederate pantheon, beside Lee and Jackson, is secure; he owes it as much to his impact on the imagination as to his military achievements. Faced with the disciplinary problems that plagued all Confederate commanders, he created the Confederate cavalry in the East and made it in his own image, an extension of his high spirits and aggressiveness. He led by example, and had the trust and devotion of his men. Stuart had his faults; his boisterousness, flamboyance, vanity, and craving for admiration repelled many. He was only twenty-eight years old when he became a major general, however, and his faults were those of youth and of the high mettle which in a cavalryman was a virtue. Underlying them were a deep religious faith and an unquestioning dedication to the cause for which he fought. It was no common man who gained the affection and admiration of Jackson and Lee.

As a cavalryman, Stuart's greatest skill was that of an outpost officer, locating and identifying the enemy and ascertaining his intentions. When news of Stuart's death was brought to Lee, he said, "He never brought me a piece of false information." In a postwar conversation, Lee spoke of him as his "ideal of a soldier . . . always cheerful . . . always ready for any work, and always reliable."

Stuart's tactics were in the light cavalry tradition; he was devoted by instinct to the "cavalry spirit," the aggressive movement, the headlong charge with the saber. There were no subtleties, no novelties, in his battle tactics. Only when the character of the terrain inhibited mounted action did he resort to dismounted tactics. Commanding an auxiliary force, he did not make strategic decisions, nor did his talents lie in that direction. Stuart can be faulted for his addiction to showy raids, which, apart from their impact on morale, had minimal military value; he can be faulted also for the excessive demands he often made on the stamina of his men and animals. But, with all his weaknesses and strengths, human and military, he was unique. There was only one Jeb Stuart, and he had no successor.

BIBLIOGRAPHY

Blackford, William W. *War Years with Jeb Stuart*. New York: Charles Scribner's Sons, 1945.
Borcke, Heros von. *Memoirs of the Confederate War for Independence*. Edinburgh and London: W. Blackwood and Sons, 1866; reprinted, New York, 1938.
McClellan, Henry B. *I Rode with Jeb Stuart*. Bloomington: Indiana University Press, 1958 (original edition, 1885).
Starr, Stephen Z. *The Union Cavalry in the Civil War*. 2 vols. Baton Rouge: Louisiana State University Press, 1979–.
Thomason, John W., Jr. *Jeb Stuart*. New York: Charles Scribner's Sons, 1941.

STEPHEN Z. STARR

TAYLOR, Maxwell Davenport (b. Keytesville, Mo., August 26, 1901; d. Washington, D.C., April 19, 1987), Army officer. Taylor commanded the 101st Airborne Division in World War II and helped to shape U.S. policy during the Vietnam War.

Taylor grew up in small-town Missouri, the only child of a railroad attorney. Taylor's maternal grandfather, a Confederate veteran who had lost an arm in the Civil War, imbued the boy with the romance of military service. At the age of five, Taylor notified his parents that he intended to go to West Point.

World War I was ending as Taylor entered the U.S. Military Academy. At the time, the faculty contained several figures destined for prominence in World War II, including Joseph Lawton Collins,* Matthew Bunker Ridgway,* and Omar Nelson Bradley.* The superintendent was Douglas MacArthur,* then a brigadier general. Taylor had an enviable career at West Point: captain of cadets, captain of the tennis team, and fourth in his graduating class (1922).

During the 1920s Lieutenant Taylor served with engineering units in Maryland and Hawaii, and later he attended the Field Artillery School at Fort Sill, Oklahoma (1932–1933). Through his recognized facility with languages, Taylor drew several special assignments. To perfect his skill in French, the Army sent him to Paris in 1927. After teaching French and Spanish at West Point, he was assigned to the U.S. Embassy in Tokyo to learn Japanese (1935). He had attended the Command and General Staff School at Fort Leavenworth, Kansas (1933–1935), and later went to the Army War College (1939–1940). In 1940, because of his expertise in Spanish, Taylor was selected to participate in a mission to Latin America which determined the military equipment needs of eight hemispheric nations in view of the threat posed by Nazi Germany.

Taylor followed the Latin American mission with a one-year stint as commander of the 12th Field Artillery Battalion of the 2d Infantry Division, San Antonio, Texas. In July 1941 he was assigned to the military secretariat of the Army Chief of Staff, General George Catlett Marshall.* Taylor served in that post until the spring of 1942 when he was appointed chief of staff and artillery commander of General Ridgway's 82d Infantry Division, Camp Claiborne, Louisiana.

The fall of Crete to German parachute and glider forces caused the U.S. Army to take an immediate interest in creating airborne divisions. The 82d Infantry was ordered to Fort Bragg, North Carolina, where, supplemented by preexisting parachute elements, it was split into the 82d and 101st Airborne Divisions. Ridgway retained Taylor as artillery commander of the 82d. Following reorganization and training, the 82d was ordered to Morocco in 1943 to prepare for the assault on Sicily, which occurred in July. Taylor helped to plan but did not participate in the actual airborne operations in Sicily, which were calamitous to the point where the Army wavered on any future division-size airborne operations. Taylor conducted his artillery forces in the Sicilian Campaign with distinction.

Prior to the invasion of Italy, Taylor was chosen for a daring mission behind enemy lines. The Italians had overthrown Mussolini and replaced him with Marshall Pietro Badoglio as prime minister. Badoglio proposed an armistice, followed by Italy's switch to the Allied side in the war, with one condition: Allied troops must be provided immediately to defend Rome. The assault on

Rome would divert German forces from the main invasion point at Salerno, and General Dwight David Eisenhower* agreed to commit the 82d Airborne. But Taylor, Ridgway, and other officers had doubts about the Italians' ability to provide support for the division. To resolve the doubts, Taylor and an Air Corps colonel were sent on a secret mission to Rome. Traveling by British PT boat, Italian corvette, and ambulance, and clothed in regular American uniforms, Taylor and his companion determined that the landing would be a disaster and aborted it just as the first planes left the ground.

Taylor did not participate with the 82d in the assault on Salerno, for he was ordered to join an Allied mission to the Badoglio "government in exile." Taylor was selected because of his fluency in the language and his skill at diplomacy. At the end of 1943, the 82d was transferred to Northern Ireland to prepare for Operation OVERLORD, the Allied invasion of France, and Taylor was reassigned to the division. In February 1944 Taylor was selected as the new commander of the 101st Airborne "Screaming Eagle" Division.

In the darkness before dawn on D-Day (June 6, 1944), Major General Taylor parachuted with his men into Normandy, becoming the first American general to fight in France in World War II. His objective was to secure four elevated causeways which provided the only possible routes inland for the invasion forces from Utah Beach. Heavy German antiaircraft fire and poor visibility resulted in poor dispersion of the paratroopers. Nevertheless, Taylor rallied those of his troops he could find and captured the all-important causeways. Following the capture of Cherbourg, the 101st, having sustained casualties totaling one-third of the division, was withdrawn to England.

The division next saw action in the invasion of Holland (Operation MARKET-GARDEN), the largest airborne assault in history. Taylor jumped with his division on September 17, 1944, and succeeded in capturing several assigned bridges. But poor weather, bad planning, and unexpectedly heavy German resistance prevented the British 1st Division from securing the key bridge at Arnhem, dooming the operation to failure. Although MARKET-GARDEN failed in its prime objective of a Rhine crossing, it did create a major salient in the German line.

Early in December 1944 Taylor was ordered to Washington to discuss a reorganization of airborne divisions. While he was away, German forces surrounded the 101st at Bastogne in the famed Battle of the Bulge. Brigadier General Anthony McAuliffe, commanding in Taylor's absence, became a symbol of American tenacity by his refusal to surrender. Taylor rejoined his division on December 27. The 101st, along with other units, was able to eliminate the Bulge on January 17, 1945. This was the last major engagement of the war for the division.

As World War II ended, Taylor was named the fortieth superintendent of West Point. He revised and updated the course of study significantly. In particular, he increased the number of courses in the humanities and social studies. Furthermore, he initiated an intercollegiate student forum which brought in civilian participants. "The cadets," Taylor believed, "should not live in a mental cloister."

In 1949, after more than three years at West Point, Taylor was sent back to Germany, where he held important command positions. In 1951 he returned to Washington to serve as assistant chief of staff.

In 1953 Taylor was named commander of the Eighth Army in Korea. The war was winding down and ended a few months after he assumed command. In November 1954 Taylor, by now a four star general, was assigned to Japan to take charge of all U.S. Army forces in the Far East Command.

President Eisenhower made Taylor chief of staff, replacing General Ridgway, on June 30, 1955. For the next four years Taylor argued the Army's case against the "New Look" and massive retaliation doctrines which held sway during the Eisenhower administration. By his own admission, Taylor was not particularly successful. But his views on defense, particularly the doctrine of flexible response, were advocated by John F. Kennedy in his successful campaign for the presidency in 1960. Following his retirement in July 1959, Taylor served briefly as chairman of the board of a utilities company.

Kennedy called Taylor to Washington late in April 1961 to head the Cuba Study Group, charged with studying the Bay of Pigs debacle and making recommendations on policy relative to guerrilla warfare. Impressed with his efforts, Kennedy appointed Taylor to a new position, "Special Military Representative of the President." In this role Taylor led a mission to South Vietnam to recommend courses of action that the United States might take relative to the escalating activities of communist insurgents. In his report, Taylor recommended that a U.S. military presence in Vietnam should function primarily as a "logistical task force" and as an "emergency reserve in a military crisis."

At the request of President Kennedy, Taylor replaced General Lyman Lemnitzer as chairman of the Joint Chiefs of Staff (JCS) on October 1, 1962. The new chairman received a baptism of fire, for the Cuban missile crisis erupted just two weeks into his tenure. During the hectic thirteen days that followed, he opposed the eventual strategy (a naval "quarantine") in favor of strikes that would destroy the missile sites in Cuba.

Following Kennedy's assassination, Taylor stayed on as chairman under President Lyndon Johnson. Taylor took the lead in forming the JCS recommendation that American efforts in Vietnam be twofold: "an intensified counterinsurgency campaign in the south and selective air and naval attacks against targets in North Vietnam." When it became necessary in June 1964 to replace Henry Cabot Lodge, an aspirant for the Republican nomination, as ambassador to South Vietnam, Johnson chose Taylor. As ambassador, he continued to have influence on military policy, and the president also made him responsible for the entire military program in Vietnam. Consequently, Taylor was closely associated with the U.S. military commander, General William Childs Westmoreland.* Taylor resigned at the end of the year he had agreed to serve in Saigon. Johnson promptly appointed him as special counsel to the president, and he held this post until

1969. Taylor was also chairman of the President's Foreign Intelligence Advisory Board.

Maxwell Taylor was in the vanguard of those advocating the use of division-size airborne units in vertical envelopments. His (and Ridgway's) persistent arguments in favor of this technique, even after the poor initial showing in Sicily, helped make a success of the Normandy invasion. His decision to abort the airborne assault on Rome during the war was correct, in view of the paucity of Italian logistical support and the resistance Allied forces met in their drive toward Rome.

As superintendent of West Point, Taylor initiated reforms in the curriculum that are worthy of note. Academy graduates since his tenure have had a broader education that better prepares them for military leadership in a complex world.

As Army chief of staff, Taylor fought against the massive retaliation doctrine favored by the Eisenhower administration. He had (with contributions from Ridgway and James Maurice Gavin*) devised a sound rationale for the doctrine of flexible response. Although he was not successful with Eisenhower, his arguments were heard and accepted by John Kennedy and became the policy of that administration following the 1960 election.

President Kennedy followed Taylor's recommendation regarding a limited commitment of U.S. forces to South Vietnam for counterinsurgency purposes. That this strategy failed, as did every other strategy later pursued, was due to a complex of circumstances both military and political.

The belief that nuclear conflict was both unthinkable and unlikely was best expressed by Taylor in his book *The Uncertain Trumpet* (1959). Taylor was convinced that the conflicts with which America would most likely be confronted would be "wars of national liberation." Such unconventional warfare, he believed, would require forces-in-being trained in counterinsurgency. Subsequent events have served more to confirm than to repudiate his judgment.

BIBLIOGRAPHY

Halberstam, David. *The Best and the Brightest*. New York: Random House, 1969.
Ridgway, Matthew B. *Soldier*. New York: Harper, 1956.
Taylor, Maxwell D. *Swords and Plowshares*. New York: W. W. Norton and Company, 1972.
———. *The Uncertain Trumpet*. New York: Harper, 1960.

RICHARD F. HAYNES

TAYLOR, Zachary (b. Orange County, Va., November 24, 1784; d. Washington, D.C., July 9, 1850), major general, 12th president of the United States. Taylor was one of the two principal American commanders in the 1846–1848 War with Mexico.

Although he was born in Virginia and elected president from Louisiana, Zachary Taylor's most significant identification was with pioneer Kentucky. Brought to a farm on the edge of Louisville at the age of eight months, he literally grew up with the state, lived there constantly until he entered the Army at twenty-three, and frequently returned. As would be expected in a frontier and near-frontier environment, his formal education was slight.

Commissioned a first lieutenant of infantry in 1808, Taylor became a captain two years later. In September 1812, when things had been going badly for U.S. outposts in the Old Northwest, he gallantly defended Fort Harrison on the Wabash River in Indiana Territory. For this he received the brevet of major.

In 1814, at Credit Island in the Mississippi River, Major Taylor was less fortunate. Overmatched by British and Indian firepower, he retreated for the only time in his life. In 1832, during the Black Hawk War, Taylor—now a colonel—participated in the Battle of the Bad Axe in what is now Wisconsin. In 1837 he defeated Seminole and Mikasuki Indians on the north shore of Lake Okeechobee, Florida. Brevetted brigadier general in recognition of that achievement, he remained in Florida two and a half years in command of the peninsula.

Still not widely known, Taylor was sixty years old in mid–1845 when the annexation of Texas made warfare with Mexico possible. At issue were disputed stretches of land between the Nueces River and the Rio Grande, and President James K. Polk placed Taylor at the head of American Army units at Corpus Christi.

Taylor continued at that Gulf site until early 1846, when with his small force he was ordered to the Rio Grande's east bank opposite Matamoros. In April Mexican detachments crossed the river and inflicted casualties. Taylor then marched eastward to secure his supply base at Point Isabel. Returning, he found a Mexican army—led by Mariano Arista—confronting him.

Palo Alto on May 8, 1846, was the first battle of the Mexican War. Taylor limited it mainly to an artillery duel in which he had a decided advantage. The next day at Resaca de la Palma, infantry and cavalry were also committed. The result was undoubted: the Mexicans fled across the Rio Grande to Matamoros and beyond. Throughout the United States, overnight, Taylor was acclaimed a hero.

War having been declared in Washington, the first target in Mexico was Monterey where Pedro de Ampudia awaited the Americans. The action took place on September 21–23, when Taylor split his force in two and made substantial advances into the strongly fortified city. Victory, however, eluded him. Being a long way from his base of supplies, he agreed to an armistice. This involved the departure of Ampudia's army, a temporaray cessation of hostilities, and Monterrey's occupation by Taylor's men.

While many Americans viewed the Monterrey development as a Taylor triumph, the unauthorized armistice displeased Polk. The president now assigned Winfield Scott* to land at Vera Cruz and thence push on to Mexico City, confining Taylor's activities to a holding operation in the north.

Taylor was irate upon learning that most of his seasoned soldiers, including virtually all his regulars, would immediately be transferred to Scott's column.

General Antonio López de Santa Anna, getting wind of the depletions, launched a campaign against Taylor and attacked him on Buena Vista's rugged terrain where Taylor—again unauthorized—had recently advanced.

The Battle of Buena Vista occurred on February 21–23, 1847, a few miles south of Saltillo. Santa Anna had twenty thousand men and Taylor fewer than five thousand, many of them green and only 10 percent of them regulars. The outcome, long in doubt, was the most spectacular victory of Taylor's military career. It had more than anything else to do with his elevation to the White House.

At its national convention in June 1848, the Whig party made Taylor its presidential nominee. The number-one question before the country was whether slavery would be permitted in the vast area ceded to the United States by Mexico in the Treaty of Guadalupe Hidalgo.

Both Taylor and Lewis Cass, his Democratic opponent, dodged the issue. Not so Martin Van Buren, candidate of the fledgling Free Soil party. Van Buren's presence in the race enabled Taylor to win in pivotal New York. Taylor carried half the states, eight in the South, seven in the North. In the electoral college, he defeated Cass 163 to 127.

When one thinks of Taylor's brief presidency, the sectional abrasiveness of 1850 looms large. Would slavery be extended west and southwest, or would the institution be contained within the fifteen states where it was legal?

Democrats, Whigs, and Free Soilers in Congress debated the problem for nine months. A Senate committee proposed a compromise, based chiefly on California's admission as a free state and on applying the expedient of popular sovereignty to other Western areas.

No one in the House or Senate opposed such a compromise more adamantly than Taylor. Although Taylor welcomed the free-state California concept, he wanted New Mexico to be a free state too. He was incensed by threats that the slave state of Texas, claiming part of New Mexico, might dispatch a militia expedition against U.S. troops at Santa Fe.

The crisis in Washingon was acute. Charges and countercharges heated the blood. Congressmen went armed to Capitol Hill. There was danger of civil war. It was even reported that, in the event of overt challenges to federal authority, Taylor intended to take the field in person against any and all disunionists.

At the peak of the crisis, Taylor suddenly died. His successor, Millard Fillmore, favored an adjustment incorporating the popular sovereignty provision. With the prospect of a presidential veto no longer a factor affecting their procedures, congressmen in September enacted the Compromise of 1850.

Most of Taylor's military service, which lasted nearly forty years, occurred in periods of tranquility. Stationed mainly in the Northwest and Southwest, usually in command of frontier forts, he maintained peace with Indian tribes and guarded pioneer settlements.

When the hour of combat came, he demonstrated courage and resourcefulness. Prior to Mexico, these qualities were clearest in Florida Territory where he experienced greater success than any contemporary in connection with the Seminoles.

In the Mexican War, Taylor's personality for the first time was a subject of national scrutiny. Utterly natural, unpretentious, rarely wearing a uniform, he strongly appealed to the soldiers who served under him, though some West Pointers and other officers found him deficient in the science of arms.

Especially at Monterrey and Buena Vista, it was evident to all that Taylor gave no thought to his personal safety. Both before and after times of triumph, he was characterized by genuine modesty.

Taylor became a major general soon after Resaca de la Palma. This was his highest military grade. He saw no action after Buena Vista, returning in December 1847 to Louisiana where throughout the following year he commanded the Army's southern division.

Because Taylor planted cotton and owned over a hundred slaves, both Southerners and Northerners were surprised when in the presidential chair he so sternly opposed slavery's expansion. Taylor's resolution in this regard fundamentally reflected his Western background and the convictions he formed as an officer in the West. Growing to manhood in Kentucky, a state at least as much Western as Southern, he was deeply influenced by his Army years in the Northwest and Southwest alike. These reinforced the westernness of his youth and made him a nationalist through and through.

Understanding Taylor contributes importantly to clear comprehension of his times. Belying sectionalistic stereotypes and theories of economic determinists, "Old Rough and Ready" in his straightforward way was as undeviatingly devoted to the Union as Andrew Jackson* and Abraham Lincoln were.

BIBLIOGRAPHY

Bauer, K. Jack. *The Mexican War, 1846-1848*. New York: Macmillan, 1974.
Dyer Brainerd. *Zachary Taylor*, Baton Rouge: Louisiana State University Press, 1946.
Hamilton, Holman. *The Three Kentucky Presidents: Lincoln, Taylor, Davis*. Lexington: University Press of Kentucky, 1978.
———. *Zachary Taylor*. 2 vols. Indianapolis, Ind.: Bobbs-Merrill, 1941, 1951. Reissued in Hamden, Conn.: Archon Books, 1966.
Henry, Robert S. *The Story of the Mexican War*. Indianapolis, Ind.: Bobbs-Merrill, 1950.
Singletary, Otis A. *The Mexican War*. Chicago: University of Chicago Press, 1960.
[Taylor, Zachary.] *Letters of Zachary Taylor, from the Battle-fields of the Mexican War*. Rochester, N.Y.: Genesee Press, 1908. Reissued in New York: Kraus Reprint Company, 1970.

HOLMAN HAMILTON

THOMAS, George Henry (b. Southampton County, Va., July 31, 1816; d. San Francisco, Calif., March 28, 1870), Army officer, Union Commander in the West during the Civil War.

George Henry Thomas, whose ancestors settled in America in the midseventeenth century, was of English, Welsh, and French Huguenot ancestry. Born in the midst of slave territory, at age fifteen he fled with his family from Nat Turner's Rebellion. After receiving a local education, he studied law and served as deputy to his uncle, clerk of the Southampton County court, who later helped secure his appointment to West Point. There Thomas showed an aptitude for many subjects, particularly artillery and cavalry tactics. He was graduated twelfth in the forty-two-man class of 1840 and was posted to the 3d Artillery Regiment.

For two decades he did garrison duty in the South and Northeast, finally attaining the lieutenant colonelcy of the 2d Cavalry (in place of Robert Edward Lee,* resigned) at the outbreak of the Civil War. During that period he also taught tactics at the Military Academy (1851–1854) and fought the Seminoles in Florida (1840–1842, 1849–1850) and other Indians in Texas (1856–1860). His most extensive combat service, however, was in the Mexican War, in which he won brevets for gallantry at Monterrey and Buena Vista.

When Texas seceded, the 2d Cavalry was sent to Carlisle Barracks, Pennsylvania, where Colonel Thomas reorganized and reequipped it. In June 1861 he joined an army that invaded his native state via the Shenandoah Valley. Leading a brigade of regulars and volunteers in the July 2 skirmish at Falling Waters, he precipitated the retreat of Confederates under Thomas Jonathan ("Stonewall") Jackson.*

When the Valley Campaign closed, Thomas went west as a brigadier of volunteers. He received a division in the Army of the Ohio under Brigadier General Don Carlos Buell. In January 1862 Thomas led a dozen regiments against as many Rebels seeking to invade Bluegrass territory, routing them at Mill Springs.

Despite winning the Union's first decisive victory, Thomas was passed over for praise and promotion by the War Department, reportedly at the direction of Abraham Lincoln. The government held him suspect because of his heritage, his pro-Southern views on politics and slavery, his efforts to become commandant of cadets at the Virginia Military Institute, and his slow, if steady, approach to warfare. In the months ahead he would receive tardy recognition for services rendered and would be overslaughed by several junior officers.

In February Thomas participated in a movement culminating in the occupation of Nashville. Two weeks later, leading Buell's reserves, he arrived too late to fight at Shiloh. On April 25, when transferred to command the right wing of Union forces under Major General Henry Wager Halleck* for the siege of Corinth, he received the major generalship of volunteers he had truly won at Mill Springs.

Reassigned to Buell's army in June, Thomas joined the withdrawal to Nashville, occasioned by another Confederate foray in Kentucky, this one by General Braxton Bragg* and Major General Edmund Kirby Smith. Distressed by the retreat, the War Office ordered Thomas to supersede his superior. He refused, believing that Buell had been unfairly treated. In October at the Battle of Perryville, as Buell's second-in-command, Thomas helped stymie Bragg. Afterwards, however, Buell was compelled to step down, and Thomas accepted a division under Major General William Starke Rosecrans,* Thomas's former junior. Though stung by the affront, Thomas tenaciously held the center of the Army of the Cumberland's line at Stones River in December and January. By persuading Rosecrans to remain on the field despite initial setbacks, he ensured the withdrawal of Bragg's Army of the Tennessee.

During the next eight months, Thomas figured prominently in Rosecrans' successful campaign to maneuver Bragg into Georgia. On September 19, 1863, however, Bragg unexpectedly struck the Union Army along Chickamauga Creek. The next day, the Federal right and center broke and fled north to Chattanooga. Only Thomas's XIV Corps—twenty thousand men, later reinforced—held its position on the left. Having covered his comrades' retreat, Thomas withdrew in good order after midnight. By the time he rejoined Rosecrans, he had earned the rosbriquet ''Rock of Chickamauga.''

Rosecrans' defeat led to his relief and Thomas' elevation to command the Army of the Cumberland. Despite Bragg's heavy siege, which threatened the army with starvation, Thomas held Chattanooga until troops from Virginia under Joseph Hooker* and Vicksburg under Ulysses Simpson Grant* arrived to reopen its supply lines. With Grant as overall commander, the Union forces moved against Bragg late in November, and Thomas' army secured his advancement to brigadier general of regulars by an amazing feat of arms. On November 25 it attacked supposedly impregnable positions atop Missionary Ridge, southeast of Chattanooga, succeeding beyond Grant's expectations—and orders. Again Bragg was driven into Georgia and lost his command.

Due in part to Grant's coolness toward Thomas, another of Thomas' juniors, Major General William Tecumseh Sherman,* received command of the combined Federal forces in the West after Grant went to Virginia as general in chief in March 1864. During the Atlanta Campaign, Thomas led three infantry corps and three cavalry divisions, two-thirds of Sherman's army. His sixty-five thousand men were engaged at Dalton, Resaca, Cassville, Dallas, Pine and Kenesaw Mountains, Ruff's Station, Peach Tree Creek, and Jonesboro. At Jonesboro, August 31–September 1, they helped capture Atlanta's southern flank and the ''Gate City'' itself. This revived sagging Union fortunes and helped ensure Lincoln's reelection.

In October, planning his March to the Sea, Sherman returned Thomas to Nashville to organize an army to resist a new advance by the Army of the Tennessee, which was now under Lieutenant General John Bell Hood.* Laboring under severe handicaps against a fast-approaching deadline, Thomas collected seventy thousand castoffs from Chattanooga, St. Louis, and elsewhere and formed them into a cohesive force. His advance units slowed Hood's northward march at Columbia and Franklin, November 26–30, until Nashville could be made impregnable.

Originally scheduled for early December, Thomas' movement against Hood's new position below Nashville was delayed several days by a snowstorm and eleventh-hour preparations. From Virginia, Grant demanded he attack at once, fearing Hood's ability to outflank him and push unopposed into Union territory. Finally, Grant prepared to go west and personally relieve Thomas. In the interim the weather cleared and the army advanced. On December 15 and 16 Thomas vindicated his thorough planning, inflicting on his enemy the most decisive defeat of the war. Utterly routed, Hood hastened into Alabama, pressed by a vicious pursuit. The triumph won Thomas the thanks of Congress and of the Tennessee Assembly and a major generalship in the Regular Army.

Still lacking Grant's complete faith, Thomas played no active role in the 1865 campaign, his army being fragmented and sent to other theaters. He held garrison and departmental command at Nashville and Louisville for four years, when transferred to California. He administered the Military Division of the Pacific until his death from a stroke at age fifty-three, leaving a widow but no children.

Thomas' painful decision to subordinate his state to his nation cost him the love of his sisters, who disowned and shunned him, while Virginia's secession left him stateless until Tennessee adopted him as a citizen in 1865. A formidable looking man, Thomas was characterized by one subordinate as "six feet tall, of Jove-like figure, impressive countenance, and lofty bearing." Due perhaps to his girth (he weighed over two hundred pounds), probably to a spinal injury suffered in an 1860 railroad mishap, and certainly to his natural inclination, he seemed always to move at a moderate pace. His troops affectionately called him "Old Slow Trot" and "Old Pap." Of the Union's many prudent, deliberate, conservative commanders, he was by far the most successful because, once resolved to act, he did so decisively, with great confidence and vigor. Moreover, he alone enjoyed experience in and mastery of the tactics of all three combat arms.

Because of his unyielding principles of warfare, his sometimes eccentric behavior, his plainspokenness, and his inability to conceal resentment over slights dealt him and his colleagues by civilian and military superiors, he alienated some who might have promoted his career. Early in the Chattanooga Campaign as well as at Nashville, he impressed Grant as dilatory and lacking in strategic perception. These facts, plus the circumstances that led officials in Washington to doubt his loyalty for so long, denied him timely promotions, the opportunity to command an army, and a place on center stage at war's finale.

BIBLIOGRAPHY

Cleaves, Freeman. *Rock of Chickamauga: The Life of General George H. Thomas*. Norman: University of Oklahoma Press, 1948.
Horn, Stanley F. *The Decisive Battle of Nashville*. Baton Rouge: Louisiana State University Press, 1956.

McKinney, Francis F. *Education in Violence: The Life of George H. Thomas and the History of the Army of the Cumberland.* Detroit, Mich.: Wayne State University Press, 1961.

O'Connor, Richard. *Thomas: Rock of Chickamauga.* New York: Prentice-Hall, 1948.

Tucker, Glenn. *Chickamauga: Bloody Battle in the West.* Indianapolis, Ind.: Bobbs-Merrill Company, 1961.

Van Horne, Thomas B. *The Life of Major-General George H. Thomas.* New York: Charles Scribner's Sons, 1882.

EDWARD G. LONGACRE

TRUSCOTT, Lucian King, Jr. (b. Chatfield, Tex., January 9, 1895; d. Washington, D.C., September 12, 1965), Army officer. Division, Corps, and Army commander in the Mediterranean during World War II.

Among the few chosen for top combat command in the U.S. Army in World War II was Lucian King Truscott, Jr., who rose in rank from colonel to general through successive battle commands of regiment, division, corps, and field army, a unique record. No other officer in the U.S. Army in World War II duplicated this feat.

Truscott was the son of Lucian King Truscott, a country doctor, and Maria Temple (Tully) Truscott. He was of Irish descent on his mother's side and English on his father's. When he was six his family moved to Oklahoma, where he attended grammar and normal schools in Norman, Oklahoma. For six years he taught school during the winters and studied at various teachers' institutes during the summers.

Truscott was attending the Cleveland Teachers' Institute when war broke out in 1917. He enlisted in the Army, was selected for officer training, and was assigned to the Officers Training Camp at Fort Logan H. Roots, Arkansas. On August 15, 1917, he was commissioned a second lieutenant of cavalry in the Officers Reserve Corps and was assigned to the 17th Cavalry at Douglas, Arizona. In December 1917 he became a first lieutenant.

In March 1919 Truscott accompanied the 17th Cavalry to Hawaii, where he spent the next two and a half years. In the summer of 1921 he was reassigned to the United States. His unit was transferred to Marfa, Texas, where he spent the next three years.

In October 1925 he was assigned to the Cavalry School at Fort Riley, Kansas, where he attended both the Troop Officers and the Advanced Equitation courses, and was retained as an instructor for four years. Truscott's next assignment was to the 3d Cavalry at Fort Myer, Virginia, where he commanded a troop for three years. In August 1934 he entered the Command and General Staff School at Fort Leavenworth, Kansas. Upon completing the course, he was retained as an instructor for four years. While at Leavenworth, Truscott was promoted to major, having served nineteen years as a company grade officer.

After duty at Fort Knox, Kentucky, and Fort Lewis, Washington, Truscott, then a colonel, was selected by General George Catlett Marshall* for assignment to Admiral Louis Mountbatten's Combined Operations Headquarters in London. Truscott's survey of the British Commandos led to the formation of American Ranger units, whose name he suggested to commemorate Robert Rogers' Rangers.

Promoted to brigadier general in 1942, Truscott participated in the Dieppe raid. The following month he reported to General George Smith Patton, Jr.* to command sub-task force "Goal Post" of the Western Task Force in the landings on the West Coast of Africa. On November 8, 1942, his reinforced regiment secured Port Lyautey in Morocco. For his part in the North African landings, Truscott was awarded the Distinguished Service Medal and was promoted to major general. His citation mentioned both his planning and organizational skills, as well as his brilliant battlefield leadership.

In late 1942, General Dwight David Eisenhower* named Truscott his field deputy at his Advanced Command Post at Constantine, to provide timely information on the situation along the distant Tunisian front. As the Tunisian Campaign ended, Truscott assumed command of the 3d Infantry Division, where he instituted a rigorous training campaign in preparation for the invasion of Sicily. His "Truscott Trot," an accelerated pace over extended distances, paid off. The 3d Division spearheaded the Seventh Army landing, drove north to capture Palermo, and then east to Messina, covering some three hundred miles in thirty-eight days, over rugged, mountainous terrain against a determined enemy. *Life Magazine* referred to this operation as "a classic in military annals for speed and success." His battlefield leadership won him Patton's praise and the Distinguished Service Cross for gallantry in action. Among the many American division commanders in Sicily, Truscott was outstanding.

In September 1943 the 3d Division landed on the Salerno beachhead in Italy and continued up the peninsula with the Fifth Army forces to the Volturno River and the first winter line. In January the division was pulled out of the line to make an amphibious landing at Anzio, just south of Rome, as part of the VI Corps. In March Truscott was named VI Corps commander. General Mark Wayne Clark* said of Truscott, "I selected Truscott to become the new VI Corps commander because of all the division commanders... in the Anzio bridgehead... he was the most outstanding. He inspired confidence in all with whom he came in contact."

Truscott's VI Corps repulsed heavy enemy attacks and in May broke out of the beachhead to enter Rome on June 4. After the fall of Rome, the VI Corps was withdrawn from combat to plan and train for the invasion of southern France.

The VI Corps landing in southern France on August 15, 1944, was the culmination of Truscott's considerable experience in such matters and a masterpiece of execution. His subsequent pursuit and destruction of enemy forces up the Rhone Valley was noteworthy for speed and decisiveness. He considered the Battle of Montélimar his greatest tactical achievement. General Jean de Lattre, French Army "B," described the scene: "Over tens of kilometers there was nothing but an inextricable tangle of twisted steel frames and charred corpses—

the apocalyptic cemetery of all the equipment of the Nineteenth (German) Army, through which only bulldozers would be able to make a way." In nineteen days the VI Corps captured Lyon and shortly thereafter linked up with elements of the XV Corps to the north, opening a badly needed line of communications for General Eisenhower's forces driving toward Germany.

Truscott's successful leadership of the VI Corps resulted in his promotion to lieutenant general and selection to command the Fifth Army in Italy, succeeding General Clark. There he confirmed the confidence in which he was held by his superiors. The Fifth Army burst out of its winter line in the spring of 1945, pushed across the Po Valley to the foothills of the Alps, and secured the first German surrender in Europe in May 1945.

In 1954 Truscott was promoted to the rank of general by special act of Congress. He died in Washington, D.C., on September 12, 1965, and was buried in Arlington National Cemetery.

Truscott's military success derived from two basic factors, his preparation for a military career and his ability to apply in war what he had learned in peacetime. He survived the rugged physical demands of his early service, where he learned the importance of mental and physical durability and where he developed a strong motivation for a military career. Another factor in Truscott's prewar formation was his intellectual capacity. Perceptual acuity, decisiveness, and self-confidence were founded on twelve years of military school experience.

Truscott's military ability was based more on personal character than on academic learning. Generals Marshall, Eisenhower, and Clark all observed in him the primary ingredients of a combat leader; that is, personal integrity, courage, and loyalty. Moreover, his leadership style was straightforward. He was open, direct, and forceful without guile or dissemblance. One of his close colleagues during World War II described him this way: "He had Patton's charisma, Bradley's soundness, and Eisenhower's diplomacy." Another said of him, "He was a tough, outspoken, aggressive soldier almost universally admired by his men and superiors." Another said, "His knowledge of men, skill in conditioning and training them and interest in their well-being brought high morale to his command. He was a great soldier who contributed measurably to the success of the Allied effort in World War II."

On the basis of his strong character and his unsurpassed combat record, Truscott deserves a firm place in history. In the opinion of many of those with whom he served, he was the outstanding combat commander of American Army forces in World War II.

BIBLIOGRAPHY

Blumenson, Martin. *Anzio: The Gamble That Failed*. Philadelphia and New York: J. B. Lippincott Company, 1963.

Clark, Mark W. *Calculated Risk*. New York: Harper and Brothers, 1950.
Truscott, L. K., Jr. *Command Missions: A Personal Story*. New York: E. P. Dutton and Company, 1954.

THEODORE J. CONWAY

TRUXTUN, Thomas (b. Long Island, N.Y., February 17, 1755; d. Philadelphia, Pa., May 5, 1822), naval officer. Truxtun was one of the first six captains appointed upon the establishment of the Navy in 1794.

Thomas Truxtun was the son of an English barrister practicing in New York. When his father died in 1765, the ten-year-old Truxtun came under the guardianship of John Troup of Jamaica, Long Island. Two years later, Truxtun embarked upon a seafaring career, sailing with Captains Joseph Holmes and James Chambers in the London trade. Taken off a merchant ship at the age of fifteen, Truxtun was pressed into service in the Royal Navy. On board the British warship *Prudent* (64–guns), he so impressed his British commanding officer with his natural abilities that the man offered Truxtun his aid in securing a midshipman's warrant in the Royal Navy. Truxtun, however, declined and gained his release from British service through the good offices of influential friends. He returned to merchant service and, by age twenty, rose to command of the *Andrew Caldwell*. By that time, 1775, relations between the colonies and Great Britain had begun to deteriorate, and Truxtun participated in the military preparations at Philadelphia by running huge quantities of gunpowder into the city. He continued those activities until later in the year when his ship was seized by the British warship *Argo* near St. Kitts in the Leeward Islands.

Truxtun managed to make it back to Philadelphia by the summer of 1776 when events in the colonies had reached the point of a complete rupture with Great Britain. There he signed on as a lieutenant in the *Congress*, the first privateer to be fitted out for service against the British. During the last part of the year, he took part in the capture of several prizes while cruising off the coast of Cuba. In 1777 Truxtun took command of and fitted out his first command, *Independence*, and sailed her to the Azores. After taking three prizes in the vicinity of the Azores, he returned home, fitted out *Mars*, and commanded her on a highly successful cruise of the English Channel. Following that, he commanded the *Independence* once more and then captained the privateers *Commerce* and *St. James*.

Truxton's activities during the Revolution went beyond privateering. His ships also carried precious cargoes of military stores into the beleaguered colonies. At the end of one voyage in the *St. James*, Truxtun landed the most valuable such cargo brought into Philadelphia during the conflict. It is said that in lauding him at a dinner in his honor, General George Washington* declared Truxtun's services to be worth that of a regiment. On another occasion, also during his command of the *St. James*, his ship carried the American consul-general to France. During the voyage, he encountered a 32–gun British ship and, after a sharp fight, managed to disable his opponent.

Truxtun returned to mercantile service after the successful conclusion of the Revolution and served as master for several East Indiamen in the late 1780s and early 1790s. In 1794 Congress established the Navy Department and authorized the construction of six new frigates. To command them, six captains were selected. Truxtun received his appointment as one of the six on June 4, 1798, and put to sea in his new command, the 36–gun frigate *Constellation*, later that month to prosecute the undeclared naval war between the United States and Revolutionary France. He returned to one of his old hunting grounds, the seas between St. Kitts and Puerto Rico, at the head of a squadron of smaller ships. On February 9, 1799, Captain Truxtun scored the first of his two most celebrated victories. After a fight of about an hour, the *Constellation* overwhelmed the French frigate *Insurgente*, killing twenty-nine and wounding forty-four of the Frenchmen's crew. He brought *Insurgente* into St. Kitts where she was refitted and commissioned in the U.S. Navy as the *Insurgent* under the command of Captain John Rodgers.*

Truxtun resumed his patrols of the West Indies and, almost a year after the *Insurgente* battle, joined his second, and most spectacular, scrape with a French man-of-war. On February 1, 1800, the 36–gun *Constellation* encountered the 50–gun frigate *La Vengeance* and gave chase. The pursuit lasted the entire day and into the evening. Finally, at around eight that evening, the *Constellation* ovehauled her adversary. For the next five hours, Truxtun used superior American gunnery and heavy seas to his advantage, overcoming the French ship's initial broadside advantage by 1:00 AM on February 2. Later reports indicate that the French warship had struck her colors several times during the engagement, but Truxtun could not see this because of darkness, weather, and the action itself. Consequently, the battle continued until every gun on board *La Vengeance* fell silent. At that point she sheered off to flee. Truxtun tried to follow; however, *Constellation* lost her main mast over the side as the result of the rigging being completely shot away. With the *Constellation* unable to follow, *La Vengeance* made good her escape. Truxtun refitted his ship at Jamaica and returned to Norfolk in March 1800.

Between the summer of 1800 and May of 1801, Truxtun cruised the West Indies once more, this time in the 44–gun frigate *President*. Upon his return home, he was appointed commodore of a squadron fitting out for an expedition against the Tripolitan pirates. Through a misunderstanding engendered by his request to have a captain appointed to command his flagship, the 38–gun frigate *Chesapeake*, Truxtun's unintended resignation was accepted by President Thomas Jefferson. He retired first to Perth Amboy, New Jersey, and thence to Philadelphia.

Throughout the remainder of his life, Thomas Truxtun participated actively in local politics in Philadelphia. In 1809 he led the agitation there against the Embargo and, the following year, made an unsuccessful bid for a seat in Congress as a member of the Federalist party. From 1816 to 1819 he served as the sheriff of Philadelphia. Commodore Truxtun died at Philadelphia on May 5, 1822, and was interred there at Christ Church.

Truxtun's place in the history of the U.S. Navy rests with his role in laying down the foundation of naval tradition by helping to win American independence as a privateer and in being one of the first six captains in the new Navy of 1794. While in command of the *Constellation*, he sought out the enemy actively and, even when confronted by the seemingly overwhelming odds presented by the 50–gun *La Vengeance*, charged to the attack with the 36–gun *Constellation* and emerged the victor. The dogged determination he exhibited has inspired Navy men to fight courageously against seemingly impossible odds. One needs only to look at the battle such as that fought off Samar in October 1944, when contemporary American sailors fought under Admiral Thomas Cassin Kinkaid against similar odds and won a victory where defeat seemed more probable.

BIBLIOGRAPHY

Allen, Gardner W. *A Naval History of the American Revolution*. 2 vols. Boston: Houghton Mifflin Company, 1913.
———. *Our Naval War with France*. Boston: Houghton Mifflin Company, 1909.
Clark, William B. *Ben Franklin's Privateers: A Naval Epic of the American Revolution*. Baton Rouge: Louisiana State University Press, 1956.
Ferguson, Eugene S. *Truxtun of the Constellation: The Life of Commodore Thomas Truxtun, U.S. Navy, 1775–1822*. Baltimore: Johns Hopkins University Press, 1956.
Nash, Howard P. *The Forgotten Wars: The Role of the U.S. Navy in the Quasi War with France and the Barbary Wars, 1789–1805*. New York: A. S. Barnes and Company, 1968.

RAYMOND A. MANN

UPTON, Emory (b. near Batavia, N.Y., August 27, 1839; d. San Francisco, Calif., March 15, 1881), tactician, Army reformer. Upton's *Military Policy of the United States* was the first systematic, critical synthesis of American military history and has been the most influential statement of the case for a professional army as the cornerstone of national defense.

Upton grew up in the Burned-Over District of New York, the center of early nineteenth-century religious revivalism and related reform movements. His family was of New England Puritan background, turned Methodist, and was deeply involved in moral reform, especially temperance and abolitionism. His father, Daniel Upton, a farmer, was an acquaintance of the revivalist Charles G. Finney; from Finney, who became president of Oberlin College, Daniel secured scholarships to Oberlin for several of his sons. Emory matriculated there in 1854. Emory's ambition, however, was to attend the U.S. Military Academy, and he won an appointment in 1856. He graduated eighth in a class of forty-five on May 6, 1861. He retained his abolitionism, a rarity in the Army, and fought

Cadet Wade Hampton Gibbes of South Carolina with swords over it. An intensity of moral commitment always marked everything Upton undertook.

Commissioned a second lieutenant in the 4th Artillery on graduation, Upton was promoted to first lieutenant in the 5th Artillery eight days later; the Civil War had begun. His entire class had already been ordered to Washington to help train volunteers. As aide de camp to Brigadier General Daniel Tyler, Upton aimed and fired the opening gun of First Bull Run. Soon wounded in the left side and arm, he nevertheless carried messages for Tyler throughout the day. He recovered to command Battery D, 2d Artillery in the Peninsula Campaign, distinguishing himself to earn command of the Artillery Brigade of the 1st Division, VI Corps, in time for the Maryland Campaign. Upton had found that he relished battle, and to avoid an assignment as instructor at West Point, he used his New York connections to be able to fill a vacancy as colonel of the 121st New York Infantry. His regiment was involved only in skirmishing at Fredericksburg, but he led it in a costly and unsuccessful charge near Salem Church in the Chancellorsville Campaign. At Gettysburg, he led the 2d Brigade, 1st Division, VI Corps, which participated in the long march of the corps on July 2, 1863, to help pin down Little Round Top by nightfall. On November 7, Upton first won wide notice at the Battle of Rappahannock Station, where he wiped out a Confederate bridgehead, capturing sixteen hundred prisoners, eight colors, two thousand stand of arms, and the enemy pontoon bridge.

Upton's units were distinguished by their precise, careful training and discipline. From the attack near Salem Church onward, Upton felt deeply concerned that these qualities were not enough to carry positions against rifled firepower. Assigned on May 10, 1864, to lead an attack on the Mule Shoe—the later Bloody Angle—at Spotsylvania, Upton added to his command's assets meticulous preparation. Forming his task force in four lines of three regiments each, he conducted every regimental commander through a personal reconnaissance and explanation of what he intended. He personally placed the assault troops and the supporting artillery. The assault troops were not to pause to fire before they penetrated the enemy lines. Each of Upton's lines had a precise role to play. Upton broke the enemy defenses and captured over a thousand prisoners; but lack of followup by other troops finally compelled him to withdraw. This kind of experience left him critical of American officership as well as troubled over tactical problems. Cold Harbor did not improve his opinion of most of his seniors.

At the Battle of the Opequon on September 19, 1864, Upton succeeded David A. Russell in command of the 1st Division, VI Corps, and mounted a successful attack, only to have a femoral artery torn open by a shell fragment. Returning to active duty on December 13 as a major general of volunteers, he led the 4th Cavalry Division in the Selma Campaign of 1865. He emerged from the war a brevet major general of regulars.

His permanent rank was captain of the 5th Artillery (February 22, 1865), although he soon reached lieutenant colonel of the 25th Infantry (July 28, 1866; transferred to the 18th Infantry, March 15, 1869). He commanded cavalry of the District of East Tennessee from July to August 1865, and then the District of Colorado. By now he was laboring on an improved tactical system to try to cope with modern firepower. In January 1866 he requested permission to travel to Washington to submit his system to a board of general officers. On June 5 the War Department appointed a board to meet at West Point and study Upton's system, and Upton himself was ordered to West Point. For the next year, he met with the board and instructed cadets. In 1867, both the original board and the new one recommended adoption of Upton's tactics, which occurred August 1.

In November 1867 Upton took a year's leave, which he dedicated with his usual intensity to courtship and marriage of Emily Martin of Willowbrook, New York, and with a tour of Europe. Emily's health was precarious, and she died in Nassau, the Bahamas, in March 1870 while Upton was on duty at Atlanta. Thereafter Upton was yet more intense and humorless. From July 1870 to July 1875 he was a rigorous commandant of cadets at West Point. The commanding general of the Army, William Tecumseh Sherman,* sponsored a world tour for him in late 1875 and most of 1876, to observe foreign armies as a basis for still further American reforms. Out of the tour came *The Armies of Asia and Europe* (1878), which was largely devoted, implicitly where not explicitly, to Upton's ideas for reform not only in tactics now but also in organization and policy. Upton corresponded with other officers sympathetic to military reforms while he was superintendent of the Artillery School of Practice at Fortress Monroe beginning in March 1877, strongly influencing Sherman's and other senior officers' testimony before the Burnside Committee of Congress in 1878. Upton turned to the writing of another book, a critique of U.S. military policy presented through a study of American military history.

In July 1880 Upton received command of the 4th Artillery, with headquarters at the Presidio of San Francisco. The book was still incomplete, its narrative carried only to 1862, when increasingly frequent and extremely painful headaches grew so severe that Upton feared he no longer had the proper capacity to command. On March 15, 1881, he resigned his commission and shot himself through the head with his Colt .45.

Psychological depression was likely involved in the causes of his extreme physical pain and almost certainly contributed to Upton's suicide. Deeply dedicated to the improvement of the Army, he thought that the most fundamental reforms he advocated were unlikely to gain public and congressional acceptance. He had adapted tactics to rifled weapons, and his system of maneuvering by groups of four soldiers was to influence American tactics well into the next century. He advocated improved tactical organization, such as a three-battalion infantry regiment in place of the regiment of a single battalion; this kind of change might win approval in time, and did. But much more fundamental, and with much less chance to prevail, was Upton's prescripion for readying the Army for war in time of peace. This was the expansible Army plan, advocated earlier by Secretary of War John Caldwell Calhoun among others, whereby the entire staff and the basic regimental organization of a war army would exist during peace. When war came, there would be, in words Upton borrowed from Calhoun, "nothing either to new model or to create."

No peacetime army that any Congress foreseeable in Upton's day would approve could be expansible enough to build a war army with nothing either to "new model or to create." Any peacetime army acceptable to Congress would be swamped as badly in war as the Regular Army of 1861 had been. This was one cause of Upton's depression. His tours had left him impressed above all with the German Army. His version of an American expansible army was an adaptation of the German system of cadres around which war formations were built by conscription. Conscription was implicit in his plan: the "truly democratic doctrine...that every American citizen owes his country military service." But Congress was even less likely to vote conscription than to build an adequately expansible army.

Upton admired German military organization in general. He also admired the German system of an autonomous military, subject to minimal civilian control. "The disasters which ensued [in the Civil War]," he said, "...must...be credited to the defective laws which allowed the President to dispense with an actual General in Chief and substitute in his stead a civil officer." His opinion of close congressional scrutiny of military policy was no higher. Distrustful of civilian control, Upton was fundamentally distrustful of democracy itself. He doubted that American democracy could compete militarily with the great powers. "Whenever Congress has shown a disposition to adopt the principle of military organization observed in continental armies, it has been dissuaded from its purpose by the demagogic admonition that foreign organizations are dangerous to liberty."

The manucript of Upton's *Military Policy* circulated widely in the Army, and its ideas became well known in the officer corps before Secretary of War Elihu Root arranged for its publication in 1904. Peter Smith Michie's biography also disseminated Upton's ideas. In the small army of the late nineteenth century, among officers frustrated by slow promotion, Upton's pessimistic attitudes found a receptive audience. Upton had set a model of excellence as a battle captain and a tactical reformer. His ability to combine an outstanding career as a practical soldier with the thought and writing of a military intellectual commands admiration. His deepest impact, however, was a tendency to alienate American soldiers from the democratic politics and society they served.

BIBLIOGRAPHY

Ambrose, Stephen E. *Upton and the Army*. Baton Rouge: Louisiana State University Press, 1964.
Brown, Richard C. "Emory Upton, The Army's Mahan." *Military Affairs* 17 (Summer 1953): 125–31.
Cooling, Benjamin Franklin. "The Missing Chapters of Emory Upton: A Note." *Military Affairs* 37 (February 1973): 13–15.

Michie, Peter Smith. *Life and Letters of General Emory Upton*. New York: Appleton, 1885.

Morris, Schaff. *The Spirit of Old West Point, 1858–1862*. Boston: Houghton Mifflin Company, 1909.

Weigley, Russell F. *Towards an American Army: Military Thought from Washington to Marshall*. New York: Columbia University Press, 1962.

RUSSELL F. WEIGLEY

VANDEGRIFT, Alexander Archer (b. Charlottesville, Va., March 13, 1887; d. Bethesda, Md., May 8, 1973), Marine Corps officer. Vandegrift successfully led the 1st Marine Division at Guadalcanal in World War II and was the eighteenth commandant of the Corps.

Archer Vandegrift, the son of a business contractor in Charlottesville, was descended from Dutch farmers who came to America in the eighteenth century and from a long line of Virginia magistrates and judges. He pursued a college education at the University of Virginia from 1905 to 1908. The legends of his grandfather's heroic service in the Civil War and the advice of his family's physician, Dr. Wilson Randolph, persuaded Vandegrift to embark upon a military career. He therefore left the university, attended Swaveley preparatory school in Washington, D.C., and passed the Marine Corps entrance examination.

On January 22, 1909, Vandegrift received his commission as a second lieutenant in the Marine Corps at the Washington Marine Barracks. After attending the Marine Officers' School at Fort Royal, South Carolina, Vandegrift was detailed to the Marine Barracks at Portsmouth, New Hampshire. From there he engaged in a number of combat roles in the Caribbean. Between 1909 and 1923, Vandegrift participated in Marine operations in Nicaragua, Panama, Mexico, and Haiti. His outstanding actions during the period included the Battle of Coyotepe in Nicaragua where Vandegrift served under both Colonel Smedley Darlington Butler and Colonel Joseph Henry Pendleton. While in Haiti in 1915, he became Butler's adjutant and helped train the Haitian gendarmerie to protect that nation from the depredations of the Caco bandits. On his second stint in Haiti in 1919, Vandegrift personally led a spirited pursuit that resulted in the capture and execution of the Caco chieftain Charlemagne M. Peralté.

Upon his return from Haiti in 1923, Vandegrift went to Quantico, Virginia, to become General Butler's aide and a battalion commander. In 1925 he served briefly as Butler's assistant chief of staff at the Marine Barracks in San Diego. Moving with Butler to San Francisco in 1926, Vandegrift helped organize the Western Mail Guards to protect deliveries of the U.S. mails against armed robbery.

In 1927 Vandegrift again went overseas, this time to China, to defend the International Settlements at Shanghai from threats by Chiang Kai-Shek's Nationalist Army. He also assisted in the occupation of Tientsin under Smedley Butler as his operations officer.

At the end of 1928 Vandegrift returned to Washington to represent the Marine Corps in the Federal Co-ordinating Service whose job it was to prevent duplication of material requirements and procurement among the military services. He remained in that relatively quiet position for five years. In that time he managed to make some important contacts and made himself thoroughly familiar with the Washington scene. This experience would help him years later as commandant.

In 1933 Vandegrift returned to Marine duties as personnel officer for Brigadier General Charles Lyman, whose East Coast Expeditionary Force was stationed at Quantico, Virginia. Attached to the Marine Corps Schools at Quantico, Vandegrift ably assisted in the drawing up of the Marines' *Tentative Manual of Landing Operations*, the first formal expression of the amphibious doctrine that would guide marine operations in the Pacific during World War II. He also participated in the maneuvers at Culebra, Puerto Rico, which sought to put these new amphibious doctrines to the test.

For the next two years (1935 to 1937), Vandegrift served as executive officer and then commanding officer of the American Embassy Detachment at Peking. He had by then become a colonel. While in Peking, Vandegrift concentrated on drilling his men in marksmanship and equestrian training. He also learned a great deal about international diplomacy, associating daily with his British, French, and Japanese counterparts.

In early 1937 Vandegrift was recalled to Washington to serve as military secretary to the new commandant of the Marine Corps, Major General Thomas Holcomb. Later in 1940, as a sign of Holcomb's pleasure with his work, Vandegrift was elevated to assistant to the commandant. During this crucial transition period for both Vandegrift and the Marines, he was involved in such high-level staff duties as preparing budget presentations for Congress. He worked very closely with both Holcomb and the quartermaster, Seth Williams, to manage and control the Marine Corps' spiralling growth in the period 1937–1941.

In November 1941 Vandegrift joined the 1st Marine Division, which was then stationed at the New River, North Carolina, training center. He inherited command of the division in March 1942 upon the retirement of General Philip Torrey. This command took Vandegrift and his division to the forefront of the battle in the Pacific. In June 1942 Vandegrift received word that his division was to spearhead landing operations on Guadalcanal in the Solomon Islands in an attempt to stem the Japanese tide of victory. His main objective was to seize and hold the airfield on Guadalcanal which would enable American air power to punish Japanese bases and shipping. Vandegrift and his men succeeded in their mission despite heavy odds. Vandegrift was decorated with the Medal of Honor for his valor and courage in the four-month long seige against tenacious Japanese onslaughts. In December 1942 Vandegrift and his bone-weary men were finally relieved by the Army under General Alexander McCarrell Patch* commanding the 25th Infantry Division and the 2d Marine Division.

From Guadalcanal, Vandegrift proceeded to the Southwest Pacific Area, under the command of General Douglas MacArthur.* Vandegrift and his men got much needed rest and rehabilitation in Melbourne, Australia. In the middle of 1943 Vandegrift was elevated to commanding general of the 1st Marine Amphibious Corps in the South Pacific Area. Although he was slated to go back to Washington to assume the post of commandant of the Marine Corps, the unexpected death of General Charles Barrett forced him to remain for the landing operations at Bougainville in November 1943.

After turning this command over to General Roy Stanley Geiger,* Vandegrift left for Washington where he spent the next four years as the eighteenth commandant. During four very eventful and tumultuous years, he guided the Marines with a steady hand. The Corps increased in size (eventually containing more than five hundred thousand men) and conducted heroic actions at Okinawa and Iwo Jima, among others. In April 1945 Vandegrift became the first active duty Marine to attain the rank of four star general. Finally came the painful adjustments of postwar demobilization. In 1947 there was even an attempt to dismantle the Marine Corps which Vandegrift and his close aides were able to defuse. After leaving active service on December 31, 1947, he spent his retirement years in travel and charitable work.

Vandegrift's performance at Guadalcanal deserves greater attention from historians. On August 7, 1942, he landed his Marine forces on the northern coast of Guadalcanal in what became known as Operation SHOESTRING. His first tactic was to capture and hold the nearly completed Japanese airstrip, which the Marines dubbed Henderson Field (named after Major Lofton P. Henderson). Seizing and then fiercely defending the airfield in the months to come proved of immeasurable value to American operations in the area; for it was from Henderson Field that marine aviators were able to build up their so-called Cactus Air Force which provided crucial firepower to offset superior Japanese numbers. The main thrust of the campaign, however, was not just the holding of the airfield and its perimeter, but also the dogged determination which Vandegrift and his Marines showed in the face of mounting Japanese pressure and disease-ridden living conditions.

Command problems at the outset threatened to scuttle the entire Guadalcanal operation. Facing imminent Japanese attack, Vice Admiral Frank Jack Fletcher,* whose Task Force 62 brought the Marines to Guadalcanal, ordered his ships to sortie before the unloading of valuable supplies was complete. To make up for this loss, Vandegrift was constantly asking Washington for reinforcements and supplies. These requests largely went unheeded because the Battle of the Atlantic took precedence over campaigns in the Pacific. Finally, in November 1942 President Franklin D. Roosevelt broke the log jam and ordered the much needed supplies sent out quickly to Vandegrift. This relief enabled him to break out of his narrow perimeter around Henderson Field and defeat the very large concentrations of Japanese on the island. All told, Vandegrift, his talented staff, and his Marines conducted themselves with great perseverance in the Guadalcanal fight, making the first American offensive in the Pacific War a successful one.

BIBLIOGRAPHY

Asprey, Robert B., and Alexander Archer Vandegrift. *Once a Marine: The Memoirs of General A. A. Vandegrift, USMC.* New York: W. W. Norton, 1964.
Foster, John T. *Guadalcanal General: The Story of A. A. Vandegrift, U.S.M.C.* New York: William Morrow and Company, 1966.
Griffith, Samuel B. *The Battle for Guadalcanal.* Philadelphia: J. B. Lippincott, 1963.
Isley, Jeter A., and Philip A. Crowl. *The U.S. Marines and Amphibious War.* Princeton, N.J.: Princeton University Press, 1951.
Heinl, Robert D., Jr. *Soldiers of the Sea: The United States Marine Corps, 1775–1962.* Annapolis, Md.: Naval Institute Press, 1962.
Morison, Samuel E. *History of United States Naval Operations in World War II*: Vol. 5. *The Struggle for Guadalcanal, August 1942-February 1943.* Boston: Little, Brown and Company, 1949.

GIBSON BELL SMITH

WASHINGTON, George (b. Westmoreland County, Va., February 22, 1732; d. Fairfax County, Va., December 14, 1799), first president of the United States.

Born into a family with seventeenth-century roots in Virginia, Washington had minimal education and suffered the loss of his father at age eleven. Although the Washingtons were only marginally members of the planter aristocracy, they had influential friends, and their status was enhanced by the marriage of George's half-brother Lawrence into the prestigious Fairfax clan. It was Lawrence, a veteran of the British Cartagena Expedition, who first aroused in Washington serious military ambition; and it was Washington who, through his brother's connections, succeeded Lawrence as an adjutant of militia in 1752.

Washington's intense desire for military recognition was evident in the French and Indian War, which had its immediate origins in his volunteering to carry a warning letter to French forces encroaching on English claims in the Ohio Valley in 1753. Soon after the French rejected Washington's message, he was commissioned a lieutenant colonel and sent back into the disputed area, where on May 27, 1754, he surprised and defeated a French party near Great Meadows, Pennsylvania. Washington himself was compelled by a superior enemy force to surrender his own nearby post, Fort Necessity, on July 4.

Later, his "inclinations" still "strongly bent to arms," he served as a volunteer aide on the staff of British General Edward Braddock. Although he failed to get the royal military commission he desperately wanted, he distinguished himself in Braddock's defeat on the Monongahela River. Now a seasoned veteran at age twenty-three, he accepted a militia colonel's commission and served as commander of Virginia's frontier defenses from 1755 to 1758. This was a difficult, often frustrating assignment which he carried out effectively, and it helped prepare him for his larger role in the American Revolution.

For seventeen years prior to 1775 Washington apparently never donned a military uniform, except when he posed for Charles Wilson Peale's portrait in 1772, a sign perhaps that he still fancied himself a military man, or at least an indication that he felt his greatest achievements were in soldiering. If those peacetime years were devoid of military activity, they still helped to prepare him for his role in the Revolution, for he gained valuable administrative experience as the master of Mount Vernon, where he took his new wife, Martha Custis, to live in 1759. He also added to his record of public service by occupying continuously, beginning that same year, a seat in the Virginia House of Burgesses.

Long critical of British commercial policies, a factor in his resolution to switch from growing tobacco to wheat, which did not have to be exported to the mother country, Washington vigorously opposed British efforts to tax the colonies after 1763. He took a more active political role than previously, especially in the nonimportation movement against English manufacturers. Chosen to command several independent militia companies, he was also a Virginia delegate to the First and Second Continental Congresses in 1774 and 1775. There he impressed colleagues with his knowledge of military affairs, and he served on important committees concerned with the defense of the colonies. Moreover, he hailed from an influential colony, crucial to the war effort. For all these reasons he was appointed commander in chief of the Continental armies on June 15, 1775.

Assuming direct command at Cambridge, Massachusetts, on July 3, 1775, Washington spent the next few months organizing the American forces and containing the British in Boston, which General William Howe evacuated on March 17, 1776. That year Washington subsequently moved to New York City and prepared it against Howe's anticipated invasion. Washington had doubts about the feasibility of defending the city, but from the beginning he steadfastly followed the orders of Congress, ever committed to the concept of civil control of the military. In a series of skirmishes and battles between August and November, Washington suffered defeat on Long Island, fell back north of Manhattan Island, and lost his forts on the lower Hudson River. Finally, with Howe in close pursuit, Washington withdrew his dwindling regiments across New Jersey and over the Delaware River into Pennsylvania in December. Howe settled his army into winter quarters in a series of posts through New Jersey and in New York City.

If Washington recognized the need to preserve his army at all costs, he was nonetheless an aggressive warrior by nature, willing to take risks when the stakes were high, when the cause needed a psychological uplift. So it was at the end of December 1776 when he suddenly swept back across the Delaware and in a lightning week of campaigning picked off the British garrisons at Trenton and Princeton—taking many prisoners and valuable supplies—before finding a sanctuary in the hills about Morristown for the winter.

The campaign of 1777, which opened in the summer, found Washington determined to stay close to Howe's army while the American Northern army, commanded by Philip Schuyler and later Horatio Gates,* sought to block British General John Burgoyne's advance from Canada down the Lake Champlain-Hudson waterway. Howe found Washington to be a dogged, persistent adversary, perhaps so much a thorn in his side that he mainly ignored Burgoyne's army. Washington, aware of Howe's desire to take Philadelphia, prepared to harass Sir William's every step if the Briton moved overland toward the American capital. Instead, Howe traveled by sea, landing below the city only to find Washington sitting across his path. Although Washington experienced defeat at Brandywine Creek on September 11, 1777, and although Howe then occupied Philadelphia, Washington, as was his custom, lashed back, this time against Howe's major base at Germantown on October 3–4, 1777. After heavy losses on both sides, Washington withdrew to spend the now-famous winter of 1777–1778 at nearby Valley Forge.

Those were dark days for Washington, not only because of his failure to save Philadelphia and because of expiring enlistments—the severity of the winter weather itself has been exaggerated—but also owing to the so-called Conway Cabal to replace Washington as commander in chief. Washington's setbacks in Pennsylvania contrasted sharply with Gates' victory over Burgoyne at Saratoga, and Gates' admirers and Washington's critics were often one and the same. But contrary to the opinion of Washington's loyal followers, there appears to have been no well-organized effort to oust the commander in chief.

Spring of 1778 brought less talk of conspiracies and more optimism because of the new French alliance and the improved condition of the Continental Army, thanks in part to its drilling under Baron Frederic William von Steuben.* Proof of Washington's improving fortunes was seen in the British withdrawal across New Jersey and Washington's strong showing against the British at Monmouth, New Jersey, on June 28, 1778, when he took a heavy toll of the enemy before allowing Sir Henry Clinton's royal forces to continue on to New York City.

For the next three years Washington stayed encamped close by the enemy in New York City, but he lacked the forces and equipment to dislodge them. He did detach General John Sullivan on a successful raiding expedition against the Iroquois tribes of western New York, and he tried to assist as best he could American forces in the South.

The arrival of French military and naval units led Washington to seize the initiative when the opportunity availed itself. Washington consulted with French General Jean Baptiste de Rochambeau in Rhode Island, and the result was a plan to attack New York City, a plan that was soon changed in favor of cornering Lord Charles Cornwallis in Virginia. The Franco-American leaders had received word that French Admiral François de Grasse was sailing from the West Indies to Chesapeake Bay. With skill and boldness Washington raced to Virginia, where he besieged Cornwallis at Yorktown, while de Grasse's fleet cut off the British route of escape. Cornwallis' surrender on October 19, 1781, brought large-scale fighting in America to an end. Two years later, following the treaty of peace recognizing American independence, Washington resigned his commission after eight and a half years service as commander in chief.

During the postwar years Washington continued to express an interest in military affairs. In 1783 he had authored "Sentiments on the Peace Establishment," an essay urging that congressional jurisdiction be strengthened in the military sector, which included central government control over militia training. Likewise, as presiding officer at the Constitutional Convention of 1787, he supported those clauses of the new national charter that beefed up the federal government's authority to meet the nation's defensive needs. Even so, as the first president of the United States he found antimilitary sentiment still pervasive. His program to organize the militia according to federal standards met with only limited success, as did his desires to build a small but effective army and navy in response to Indian attacks and threats from the belligerents in Europe after the outbreak of war between England and France in the 1790s. Later, during President John Adams' administration Washington emerged from retirement to head a provisional army that was to be raised when the country seemed on the verge of war with France in 1798 following the XYZ Affair. But Adams managed to reduce Franco-American tensions, with the result that Washington never actually returned to the field as a military commander. He continued all the while to reside at Mount Vernon, where he died in 1799.

When one looks at Washington's military career in the American Revolution, the Virginian appears as a competent soldier but hardly exceptional as a tactician or strategist. But he showed the capacity for growth, and as one campaign followed another his mistakes became fewer and fewer. Fortunately for Washington, his military background of militia service was not the extreme limitation that it would have been in later wars. British officers in the eighteenth century were hardly specialists in the modern sense. Military schools were virtually nonexistent, and much military theory was romantic in nature, such as the idea of the "born general."

One of the greatest attributes of generalship is that nebulous thing called character, and the Virginian had it in abundance. Persistent, dogged, determined, he never knew when he was beaten; he always bounced back when a lesser man might have become dispirited to the point of resignation. Recognizing the importance of holding his army together at all costs—it was the most tangible, meaningful symbol of the Revolution and emerging American nationalism—he nonetheless was hardly a Fabius, a commander who preferred to retire rather than fight. For it was Washington who sought battle at Long Island, Trenton, Princeton, Brandywine, Germantown, Monmouth, and Yorktown.

Deeply committed to the Revolutionary cause, Washington inspired confidence in civilians and soldiers alike. Hotheaded and inordinately ambitious in his youth, he learned the virtue of patience, and he was unfailingly deferential to Congress. He angrily denounced the so-called Newburgh conspirators in 1783, officers who wished to threaten Congress with fire and sword if the Army's grievances over pay and other benefits were not immediately remedied.

In fact, in a broad sense, Washington the statesman stood above Washington the narrow soldier. The Virginia planter, the former militia officer, and the ex-legislator understood the unique requirements of waging an American war, a conflict in which his diplomatic skills counted greatly with the Congress, the state governments, the Continental troops, the local militias, and the civilian population. Favoring the use of legal processes against the Loyalists, he wanted no hangman's harvest. He opposed a predominantly guerrilla war on the grounds that it might irreparably destroy the fabric of society. A respecter of private property, he took stern precautions against plundering, which might turn the American people against their own army. Truly a military statesman, he grasped the Revolution in its totality: the relationship between the homefront and the battlefront, and the relationship between the war years and the forthcoming years of peace.

BIBLIOGRAPHY

Cunliffe, Marcus. *George Washington: Man and Monument*. Boston: Little, Brown, 1958.
Flexner, James T. *George Washington*. 4 vols. Boston: Little, Brown, 1965–1972.
Freeman, Douglas S. *George Washington: A Biography*. 6 vols. New York: Charles Scribner's, 1948–1954.
Knollenberg, Bernard. *Washington and the Revolution*. New York: Macmillan Company, 1940.
———. *George Washington: The Virginia Period*. Durham, N.C.: Duke University Press, 1964.
Morris, Richard B. *Seven Who Shaped Our Destiny*. New York: Harper and Row, 1973.
Nettels, Curtis. *George Washington and American Independence*. Boston: Little, Brown, 1951.
Palmer, Dave. *The Way of the Fox: American Strategy in the War for America*. Westport, Conn.: Greenwood Press, 1975.

R. DON HIGGINBOTHAM

WAYNE, Anthony (b. Waynesborough, Pa., January 1, 1745; d. Presque Isle, Pa., December 15, 1796), Revolutionary War general; commander in chief, U.S. Army, 1792–1796.

Anthony Wayne was born into a prominent family of some wealth in Chester County, Pennsylvania. He was the only son of Isaac Wayne, an assemblyman and militia officer who owned the largest tannery in the province. His grandfather was Anthony Wayne, an officer under William III and the Duke of Marlborough who emigrated to America and founded Waynesborough in 1724. Little is known of Wayne's early life; he attended the Academy in Philadelphia but did not graduate, instead becoming a surveyor. He attempted to establish a colony in Nova Scotia for a Philadelphia land syndicate, but the venture failed and Wayne returned to the family homestead to pursue a career in farming and the tanning business in partnership with his father. As a success in commerce and with many friends in Philadelphia society, Wayne gained local and then provincial recognition. By the eve of the War for Independence, he was a leader in the agitation against Britain, serving on various local and provincial committees for defense and nonimportation and sitting a term in the Pennsylvania Assembly. When fighting broke out, he recruited a regiment in Chester County. On January 3, 1776, he became colonel of the 4th Pennsylvania battalion in the new Continental Army authorized by Congress.

Wayne participated in most of the major campaigns of the Revolutionary War, achieving fame as a superior tactician and as perhaps the most aggressive battlefield commander in the Army. In 1776 he commanded troops sent to reinforce the effort to conquer Canada. His first major action was at Three Rivers, where he extricated his men from the swamp in which the American Army was caught, and then through his coolness and iron discipline helped in the withdrawal back into New York. After the winter in command at Fort Ticonderoga, Wayne joined the main army at Morristown, New Jersey, where as senior Pennsylvania brigadier he took command of his state's eight regiments.

During the campaigns of 1777, his division skirmished with British forces near New Brunswick and then moved with George Washington's* forces to defend Philadelphia. In September in the Battle of Brandywine, Wayne helped hold the center of the American line at Chad's Ford long enough for the rest of the army to escape the British envelopment. Ten days later, detached from the main army to attack the British baggage train, the brusque Pennsylvanian was surprised and nearly overwhelmed in a night raid by three British regiments. In this so-called Paoli Massacre, Wayne lost perhaps a quarter of his fifteen hundred men; a court of inquiry was held, and a subsequent court-martial exonerated him of any malfeasance. In October at Germantown he hurled his men at the center of the British line, but hearing firing to his rear and believing that the rest of John Sullivan's division (to which he was attached) was in trouble, Wayne wheeled about and in the confusion of the morning fog fired on other American units.

In the next two years, however, Wayne finally established the reputation he always sought. At the Battle of Monmouth in June 1778, after General Charles Lee* ordered the American retreat, Wayne directed the makeshift force that held off the British while the rest of the army regrouped. Then, with five regiments at the orchard in front of the American line, he withstood three separate British assaults before a fourth forced his withdrawal. After being replaced in 1779 as head of the Pennsylvania line by Major General Arthur St. Clair, the senior general from the state, Wayne formed a new corps of light infantry of units from different states. That July, in a night assault by bayonet alone, Wayne's men stormed the British garrison at Stony Point on the Hudson River, capturing over five hundred of the enemy and valuable ordnance and equipment. The victory was Wayne's own completely, a feat of extraordinary leadership and daring for which he gained great public acclaim.

The light infantry was soon disbanded, and for the rest of the war, Wayne fought in various theaters: with the main army around New York in 1780 (including a quick march at night to reinforce the troops at West Point in the wake of Benedict Arnold's* treason); with the Marquis de Lafayette's* forces in Virginia in 1781; and at Yorktown. In 1782, as part of Nathanael Greene's* Southern army, Wayne held an independent command in Georgia, battling the British, Indians, and Tories in an effort to return the state to American control.

What distinguished Wayne from his contemporaries in the winning of independence was his effectiveness as a commander: his ability to discipline a combat force and inspire them in battle, his continued advice in councils of war to take the offensive, and his dependable aggressiveness in pressing home the attack on the battlefield. Wayne was fearless, personally and as a leader. Wounded on several occasions, he always insisted on remaining on the field of battle. Twice he interposed himself physically before mutinying troops. He faced down at gunpoint a company at Ticonderoga in 1777; and when the Pennsylvania line revolted in January 1781, he tried initially to stop the men by himself, and then remained with them on the march to Philadelphia to prevent violence and to act as an intermediary. Wayne was not reckless or irresponsible, however. He always prepared himself and his men carefully for battle. The title "Mad Anthony" was apparently pinned on him in 1781 by a private, a Chester County neighbor, whom Wayne refused to free from arrest for desertion.

In many respects Wayne also typified the American generals in the Revolution. Egotistical and ambitious for fame and glory, he was extremely sensitive about his prerogatives and rank, and sulked at any slights to his dignity. (He carried on a running feud over rank with his senior, St. Clair, throughout the war.) Increasingly estranged from his wife after 1775, Wayne was a lonely man, mercurial, a martinet with a fiery temper, who alternated between gloom and enthusiasm and often acted in a testy and unreasonable manner. He could rage at the lack of civilian support for the war effort and at congressional tampering with the Army, voicing the same disgust for politicians that others at the head of the Continental Army often expressed.

Like many other general officers, Wayne was not particularly successful in business or politics after the war. Elected to the Pennsylvania Council of Censors in 1783 and the Pennsylvania Assembly in 1784 and 1785, he had always intended to work the Georgia land granted him by that legislature when the fighting ended. But mounting debts plagued his efforts, and the plantations never flourished. By the end of the 1780s, restless and bored, his property in Pennsylvania and Georgia in danger of confiscation, and he himself under threat of imprisonment for debt, Wayne sought federal office for the immunity it promised if for nothing else. Georgians sent him to the 2d Congress in 1791, and he finally cleared all his debts by abandoning almost all of his Georgia holdings, but within a few months the House unseated him for irregularities in his election.

At that low point, Wayne gained an opportunity for a second military career, and with it gained lasting historical recognition. Less than a month after Wayne's expulsion from Congress, President Washington named him to command the new five thousand man force authorized after two disastrous defeats by the Indians in the Ohio region annihilated the national army. Neither Washington nor the cabinet had great confidence in Wayne. "Open to flattery, vain," and perhaps "addicted to the bottle," noted Washington; "brave and nothing else," recorded Secretary of State Thomas Jefferson, a leader who might "run his head against a wall where success was both impossible and useless." But Wayne was the most experienced general officer from the Revolution available and physically able, and he wanted the position badly.

In two years, by his energy and the force of his personality, he transformed raw recruits into the first reliable national army after independence. He purged incompetent officers; he arranged for efficient logistical support; he instituted daily firing practice; he trained by means of full field maneuvers; he practiced savage, sometimes inconsistent, discipline. When the administration finally allowed him to attack in the fall of 1793, he moved slowly, using his espionage network and carefully fortifying his nightly encampments. The following year, when the Indians dissipated their strength in a futile attempt to overrun Fort Recovery, the most distant fort on the line of posts north from Cincinnati, Wayne moved decisively. His army stormed into the Maumee Valley, defeated the tribes at the Battle of Fallen Timbers (August 20, 1794), and burned Indian crops and towns. In a single campaign Wayne stifled British influence and broke the Indian domination of the Old Northwest. Equally important, he erased the strain of defeat on the Army, established pride and confidence in the officers and men, and gave the Army a cohesion and a tradition on which to build a permanent, peacetime frontier constabulary.

In the next two years, Wayne negotiated the Treaty of Greenville, which finally opened the Northwest Territory to peaceful white settlement. He also lobbied in Congress on behalf of the administration to keep the Army from being reduced in strength, now that the Indian War had ended, and tension with Great Britain had eased with the signing of Jay's Treaty. Less successfully, he fought off the effort of his subordinate, James Wilkinson, to discredit Wayne's leadership, gain the fidelity of the officers corps, and replace Wayne in the command. On December 15, 1796, at Presque Isle near the end of an inspection trip to Detroit and other Northwest posts, the salty commander, age fifty-one, died of sickness—still battling his enemies and working to strengthen American military power.

BIBLIOGRAPHY

Knopf, Richard C. *Anthony Wayne, A Name in Arms, Soldier, Diplomat, Defender of Expansion Westward of a Nation: The Wayne-Knox-Pickering-McHenry Correspondence.* Pittsburgh, Pa.: University of Pittsburgh Press, 1960.

Kohn, Richard H. "American Generals of the Revolution: Subordination and Restraint." In *Reconsiderations on the Revolutionary War: Selected Essays.* Edited by Don Higginbotham. Westport, Conn.: Greenwood Press, 1978, pp. 104–23, 188–200.
———. *Eagle and Sword: The Federalists and the Creation of the Military Establishment in America, 1783–1802.* New York: Free Press, 1975.
Rankin, Hugh F. "Anthony Wayne: Military Romanticist." In *George Washington's Generals.* Edited by George Athan Billias. New York: William Morrow and Company, 1964, pp. 260–90.
Stille, Charles J. *Major General Anthony Wayne and the Pennsylvania Line in the Continental Army.* Philadelphia, 1893. Reprinted, Port Washington, N.Y.: Kennikat Press, 1968.
Wildes, Harry Emerson. *Anthony Wayne: Trouble Shooter of the American Revolution.* New York, 1941. Reprinted, Westport, Conn.: Greenwood Press, 1969.

RICHARD H. KOHN

WESTMORELAND, William Childs (b. Spartanburg County, S.C., March 26, 1914), Army officer; commander, U.S. Forces in Vietnam, 1964–1968; Army chief of staff, 1968–1972.

The son of a textile plant manager, William C. Westmoreland attended public schools in Spartanburg, South Carolina, and after a year at The Citadel secured an appointment to West Point. While at the Academy, he displayed signs of the ambition and drive that would characterize his career. He was active in athletics, won the coveted Pershing Award for military proficiency and leadership, and during his final year was first captain of cadets. Unable to pass the rigorous eyesight tests required for flight training, he entered the artillery and held prewar assignments at Fort Sill, Oklahoma, in Hawaii, and at Fort Bragg, North Carolina.

Westmoreland served with distinction in the North African and European campaigns of World War II, establishing a reputation for combat leadership that would mark him for future top positions in the Army. A lieutenant colonel at the age of twenty-eight, he commanded the 34th Field Artillery, 9th Infantry Division, in North Africa, getting his artillery into position in time to prevent a German breakthrough at the Kasserine Pass. Following combat in Sicily, he served as executive officer of the 9th Infantry and participated in the landing on Utah Beach. Promoted to colonel, he became chief of staff of the 9th Infantry in July 1944. His combat record from France to the Elbe won plaudits from such future luminaries as James Maurice Gavin* and Maxwell Davenport Taylor.*

Remaining with the occupation forces in Germany after V-E Day, Westmoreland returned to the United States in 1946, took paratroop training, and was given command of the 504th Paratroop Infantry Regiment. He subsequently became chief of staff of the 82d Airborne Division at Fort Bragg. During the interval between World War II and Korea, he also taught at the Command and General Staff College at Fort Leavenworth and at the Army War College in

Carlisle, Pennsylvania. He commanded the 187th Airborne Regimental Combat Team in Korea, the only paratroop unit to see action in the war.

Intense, ambitious, and hardworking, Westmoreland advanced rapidly in the years after Korea. He returned to the United States in 1953 to become deputy assistant chief of staff for manpower control. After attending the advanced management program at the Harvard Graduate School of Business Administration, he was appointed secretary to the General Staff, serving under Army Chief of Staff Maxwell Taylor. The youngest major general in the Army, he assumed command of the 101st Airborne Division, the famous "Screaming Eagles," in 1958, where he achieved public notice by jumping with his men in training exercises, sometimes jumping ahead of them to test wind conditions. Superintendent of West Point from 1960 to 1963, he fought vigorously for and eventually won presidential commitment to double the size of the corps. He returned to Fort Bragg in 1963 to command the XVIII Airborne Corps.

Westmoreland was an obvious choice to succeed General Paul Donal Harkins in Vietnam in 1964. Considered one of the top three generals in the Army, he had a deserved reputation for efficiency and excellence in command. Strikingly handsome, hard working, and supremely confident, he seemed the ideal person for a most difficult position. He was close to Taylor, then chairman of the Joint Chiefs of Staff and soon to become ambassador to South Vietnam. Appointed deputy to Harkins in January 1964, he succeeded to the command in June.

Almost from his arrival in Saigon, Westmoreland urged an increased American military commitment. Supported by North Vietnamese regulars, the Vietcong had exploited the political chaos that followed the overthrow of Ngo Dinh Diem by drastically stepping up military operations. Westmoreland was certain by early 1965 that the embattled South Vietnamese Army could not stand up to the Vietcong by itself. Warning Washington that there was no solution but to "put our own finger in the dike," he pressed vigorously for the bombing of North Vietnam and subsequently for the deployment of American combat forces. In July 1965 President Lyndon B. Johnson gave him one hundred thousand ground troops and a free hand in their use.

Given three hundred thousand additional men between 1965 and 1967, Westmoreland waged a devastating war of attrition against the enemy. Relying on superior air power, firepower, and mobility, he dispatched American units across South Vietnam on large-scale operations to search out and destroy Vietcong and North Vietnamese regulars. The infusion of American military power and Westmoreland's aggressive strategy staved off what had appeared near certain defeat in 1965 and resulted in huge enemy losses.

In 1967 Westmoreland engaged Washington in a strategic debate that would last for over a year and would eventually lead to his recall. Persuaded that he was making steady progress, he requested an additional two hundred thousand troops and authority to pursue the enemy into his sanctuaries in Laos and Cambodia and across the demilitarized zone in order to speed up the timetable of victory. Johnson rejected his requests. Many of the president's civilian advisors had concluded that the search and destroy strategy could produce no better than a bloody stalemate. Johnson himself feared that expansion of the war might provoke Chinese or Soviet intervention. By 1967 the war had aroused widespread protest at home, and the president was unwilling to risk the political consequences of a major escalation.

The debate over strategy erupted anew after the Tet Offensive of 1968. Although caught off guard by the all-out Vietcong assault on South Vietnam's cities, U.S. forces quickly recovered, recouping early losses and inflicting devastating casualties on the attackers. Interpreting Tet as a major U.S. victory, Westmoreland urged that the advantage be exploited, and he reopened his request for additional troops and expansion of the war. The early enemy successes had produced profound shock in the United States, however, and after weeks of deliberation, Johnson decided upon a basic change of policy. He not only turned down Westmoreland's proposals but also withdrew from the presidential race and sought a negotiated settlement of the war. Westmoreland was called home to become Army chief of staff, a position he retained until 1972.

Upon retirement, Westmoreland returned to his native South Carolina and ran unsuccessfully for the Republican gubernatorial nomination of 1974. In his memoirs, *A Soldier Reports*, and in numerous speeches, he actively involved himself in the postwar debate on Vietnam.

Westmoreland has been sharply criticized for his conduct of the war; he has even been held responsible for the disaster that befell the United States in Vietnam. The search and destroy strategy, it has been argued, represented a futile attempt to apply traditional U.S. Army concepts of warfare in a situation where they could not work. The strategy was enormously destructive, moreover, doing permanent ecological damage to the landscape of South Vietnam and producing huge numbers of civilian casualties and refugees. By disrupting the already tattered social fabric of South Vietnam and turning the people against a government already lacking in support, U.S. military operations, in the eyes of many critics, were counterproductive. Westmoreland has also been criticized for his reports of progress, which, if not deliberately deceptive, reflected a poor understanding of the war he was fighting; for his failure to anticipate the devastating attacks of Tet; and for his alleged attempt to cover the failure by expanding the war.

The general has responded vigorously to his critics. Given the political decay in South Vietnam and the number and strength of enemy forces, he argued, he had no choice but to seek out and destroy the adversary. There could be no political stability until the military threat had been removed. While carefully avoiding a direct attack on President Johnson, Westmoreland has placed responsibility for the American failure on the civilians in Washington, particularly Secretary of Defense Robert Strange McNamara and his civilian advisors. The civilians' insistence on a graduated bombing campaign against North Vietnam nullified the effectiveness of American air power. The search and destroy strategy would have brought victory if he had been given the troops and the authority to pursue the enemy into the sanctuaries. Westmoreland conceded that his command misread the intelligence before Tet, but, he argued, the United States rebounded to inflict a decisive defeat on the Vietcong. Had the media and the civilians in Washington not been consumed by defeatism, the war could have been won. The principal lesson of Vietnam, Westmoreland has concluded, is that gradualism and partial measures do not work. Once engaged in war, the United States must employ its military power decisively.

It remains difficult to arrive at a balanced assessment of Westmoreland's generalship. He handled superbly the massive logistical buildup of 1965–1966. Despite the wretched conditions under which the war was fought and the ambiguity of American objectives, U.S. troops fought well under his command and morale remained high. American military power saved South Vietnam from certain collapse in 1965 and at least held the line in the face of the furious enemy offensive of 1968. As a strategist, on the other hand, Westmoreland is vulnerable to criticism. He may be correct in arguing that the situation he faced in 1965 left him few choices. It is difficult to see, for example, how the so-called enclave strategy advocated by James Gavin could have produced better results. Ultimate responsibility for the strategic failure in Vietnam rests with the leadership in Washington, which never gave Westmoreland strategic guidance or devised a viable grand strategy. Nevertheless, it is still clear that the strategy of attrition could not have worked in Vietnam. North Vietnam had an inexhaustible reservoir of manpower and the determination to prevail at any cost. The sanctuaries permitted them to control their losses and to retain the strategic initiative. Whether the United States could have achieved its goals in Vietnam under any circumstances will long be debated. If this was to be done, it would have required an ingenious politico-military strategy adapted to the peculiar nature of the war and the restrictions imposed by Washington. Westmoreland was not the man to perform such feats. Methodical rather than imaginative, an organizer rather than a creative genius, he applied with relentless precision the accumulated experience of thirty years in an army geared for conventional warfare. Formal and courtly, as "cleancut as Tom Mix," he struck observers as out of place in Vietnam, and in many ways he was. His failure as a strategist reflects in the broadest sense the inapplicability of traditional American methods of warfare in the alien and inhospitable environment of Vietnam.

BIBLIOGRAPHY

Furguson, E. B. *Westmoreland: The Inevitable General*. Boston: Little, Brown and Company, 1968.

Halberstam, David. *The Best and the Brightest*. New York: Random House, 1972.

Lewy, Guenter. *America in Vietnam*. New York: Oxford University Press, 1978.

Palmer, Dave Richard. *Summons of the Trumpet: U.S.-Vietnam in Perspective*. San Rafael, Calif.: Presidio Press, 1978.

The Senator Gravel Edition: The Pentagon Papers. Boston: Beacon Press, 1971. Vols. 3, 4.

Westmoreland, William C. *A Soldier Reports.* New York: Doubleday and Company, 1976.

GEORGE C. HERRING

WHEELER, Joseph (b. Augusta, Ga., September 10, 1836; d. Brooklyn, N.Y., January 25, 1906), Army officer. Wheeler was the principal Southern cavalry commander in the western theater during the Civil War.

Joseph Wheeler was born to New England parents who had migrated to Georgia. His maternal grandfather was General William Hull, a veteran of the American Revolution and War of 1812. After Wheeler's mother died in 1842, he went to Connecticut to live with her sisters and attend Cheshire Academy. In 1854, at age seventeen, he secured an appointment to the U.S. Military Academy at West Point, which at that time required five years for graduation. Wheeler finished fourth from the bottom in a class of twenty-two. Although he received his poorest grades in cavalry tactics, in 1859 he was brevetted a second lieutenant and sent to cavalry school at Carlisle Barracks, Pennsylvania, for special training.

In 1860 the War Department raised Wheeler to full rank and assigned him to duty with the Regiment of Mounted Riflemen at Fort Craig, New Mexico Territory. While en route to the Southwest with a wagon train, Wheeler earned the nickname "Fightin' Joe" in a skirmish with hostile Indians. Except for isolated incidents, however, Indians caused the Army relatively little concern in New Mexico during Wheeler's brief stint there, and he and the numerous other Southerners stationed at Fort Craig had ample time to ponder the threat of war and secession which loomed over the nation.

When Georgia left the Union in January 1861, Wheeler resigned his commission in the U.S. Army and accepted an appointment as lieutenant in the forces of his native state. Assigned to Fort Barrancas, Florida, he expertly supervised the remounting of spiked Union guns and won the admiration of influential Alabama officers who persuaded the Confederate War Department to promote him. Thus at age twenty-four, Wheeler, who stood only five feet-five inches tall and weighed about 120 pounds, became a full colonel and commander of the 19th Alabama Infantry, part of the Gulf Coast defense force under General Braxton Bragg.*

In February 1862 Wheeler's regiment was among the Confederate units that concentrated near Corinth, Mississippi, to stop the advance of Federal forces up the Tennessee River toward the Mobile and Ohio railroads. In April Wheeler saw his first action, at Shiloh, and won considerable praise for successfully covering the Confederate withdrawal, a task he performed time and again during the next three years. Wheeler succeeded quickly to command of an infantry brigade, and in July 1862 Bragg put him in charge of the cavalry of the Army of the Mississippi.

In August and September 1862, Wheeler accompanied Bragg and General Edmund Kirby Smith on the ill-fated campaigns through middle Tennessee into Kentucky. Federal troops under Don Carlos Buell repulsed the Confederates at Perryville, and both Bragg and Smith placed all their cavalry under Wheeler and instructed him to protect their retreat. Wheeler and his men felled trees to obstruct roads and fought on horseback and on foot for a week, while the two Confederate armies escaped without losing a single wagon or gun to the Federals. For these efforts Wheeler was commissioned a brigadier general and made chief of cavalry in the newly formed Army of the Tennessee.

Eventually, Wheeler rose to lieutenant general, but except for occasionally harassing communications behind Union lines, he spent the rest of the war fighting rearguard actions. After brilliantly circling the Federal Army of the Cumberland led by General William Starke Rosencrans* south of La Vergne, Tennessee, and destroying hundreds of Federal supply wagons, Wheeler covered Bragg's withdrawal from Murfreesboro, Tennessee, in January 1863. In September of that same year Wheeler carried out mop-up operations after Bragg won a tactical victory at Chickamauga, Georgia, below Chattanooga. Between early May and late July 1864, the gritty little Georgian covered the retreat of General Joseph Eggleston Johnston* from Chattanooga to Atlanta, and between November 1864 and April 1865 Wheeler provided almost the only significant resistance to General William Tecumseh Sherman* on his famous march through Georgia and the Carolinas. Federal troops finally captured Wheeler in May 1865, while he was trying to prevent the capture of Confederate President Jefferson Davis in Georgia.

Wheeler spent two months in a Federal prison before being paroled. Afterward, he lingered a short time in his native Augusta and then entered the hardware business in New Orleans. In 1866 Wheeler married a wealthy young widow he had met during the war. Four years later they moved near her home in Lawrence County, Alabama, where he became a successful planter. During his spare time Wheeler studied law and passed the bar, and in 1880 leading northern Alabama Democrats persuaded him to run for Congress. After an abortive first attempt, in 1883 Wheeler won a seat in the 47th Congress, where he pursued a middle course between Bourbonism and Populism. The voters of his district returned him to Congress seven times.

Through membership on the House Military Affairs Committee, Wheeler maintained his interest in the Army. When hostilities with Spain seemed imminent in 1898, he offered his services to the War Department. Following the American declaration of war on April 25, 1898, President William McKinley commissioned Wheeler a major general of volunteers, and the War Department gave him command of the cavalry forces in the invasion of Cuba. On June 24, 1898, he launched an unauthorized but successful attack against the Spanish at Guásimas and removed the first obstacle to the American advance on Santiago. Illness kept Wheeler from taking part in the Battle of San Juan Hill, but afterward he was active until the end of the Cuban Campaign.

Following an unsuccessful effort to resume his seat in Congress, Wheeler wrangled an assignment as brigadier general of volunteers in the Philippines in June 1899. He saw only limited action in the insurrection there and returned to the United States in January 1900. A short time later McKinley commissioned him a brigadier general in the Regular Army and made him commander of the Department of the Lakes. Wheeler retired in September 1900 and spent much of the rest of his life traveling. He died in Brooklyn, New York, while visiting his sister.

Wheeler is remembered primarily as the principal Confederate cavalry officer in the western theater during the Civil War. As chief of cavalry first in the Army of the Mississippi and later in the Army of the Tennessee, Wheeler carried out every major rearguard operation from Shiloh to Perryville to Atlanta. He lacked the flare of his somewhat more famous contemporaries, John Hunt Morgan and Nathan Bedford Forrest,* but he equaled them in aggressiveness and exceeded them in reliability and devotion to discipline and training. Much of Wheeler's personal success, as well as that of his commands, resulted from his patience, persistence, and ability to carry out orders. He was most effective when performing routine duties, such as covering Bragg's or Johnson's front or flanks and disrupting communications behind Union lines; he was least effective when attempting large-scale independent missions, such as trying to take Kingston, Tennessee, during the campaign against Knoxville in December 1863 and sweeping through middle Tennessee in September 1864.

In keeping with his reputation for discipline and training, during the spring of 1863 Wheeler wrote a Confederate cavalry manual. It was one of the first that unhesitatingly favored mounted infantry over heavy cavalry. Entitled *A Revised System of Cavalry Tactics for the Use of the Cavalry and Mounted Infantry, C.S.A.*, the manual reflected Wheeler's experience with the Regiment of Mounted Riflemen in New Mexico and his success in covering Bragg's and Smith's withdrawal from Kentucky in 1862. Wheeler contended that mounted infantry performed especially well in broken and wooded terrain.

After the war Wheeler came to symbolize the restoration of traditional white rule in the Southern states and political reconciliation between the South and the North. Elected to Congress by Bourbon Democrats, he maintained a paternal attitude toward blacks, opposed civil rights legislation, and called upon Southerners to forget the Civil War and devote their energies to industrialization. In 1898 President William McKinley decided to commission several ex-Confederates, including Fitzhugh Lee and Wheeler, to help heal sectional differences, make the Spanish-American War a national effort, and provide additional support for his administration.

BIBLIOGRAPHY

Cosmas, Graham A. *An Army for Empire: The United States Army in the Spanish-American War*. Columbia: University of Missouri Press, 1971.

Dubose, John W. *General Joseph Wheeler and the Army of Tennessee*. New York: Neale Publishing Company, 1912.
Dyer, John P. *"Fightin' Joe" Wheeler*. Baton Rouge: Louisiana State University Press, 1941.
Horn, Stanley F. *The Army of Tennessee: A Military History*. Indianapolis, Ind.: Bobbs-Merrill Company, 1941.
Lee, Fitzhugh, and Joseph Wheeler. *Cuba's Struggle Against Spain*. New York: American Historical Press, 1899.

GEORGE R. ADAMS

APPENDIX

Chronology of American Military Developments

This chronology is intended to assist the general reader and by no means pretends to comprehensiveness. For a fuller accounting of the developments listed here, the reader's attention is invited to R. Ernest and Trevor Dupuy, *The Encyclopedia of Military History from 3500 B. C. to the Present* (New York: Harper and Row, 1970); Richard B. Morris, editor, *The Encyclopedia of American History* (New York: Harper and Row, 1971); Charles Van Doren and Robert McHenry, editors, *Webster's Guide to American History* (Springfield, Mass.: G. & C. Merriam Company, Publishers, 1971); and Bernard and Fawn Brodie, *From Crossbow to H-Bomb* (Bloomington, Ind.: Indiana University Press, 1973), works from which this chronology has been drawn. Finally, because the course of American military history has often been influenced by developments abroad, some of these are noted here in order to provide a modicum of perspective.

AMERICAN MILITARY DEVELOPMENTS		DEVELOPMENTS ABROAD	
1607	Jamestown established.		
1609–14	First Powhatan uprising in Virginia.		
1613	Virginians raid Mount Desert Island, Maine, a rival French settlement.		
1614	Virginians raid Port Royal, Nova Scotia, a rival French settlement.		
		1615	Le Bourgeoys, French gunsmith, invents flintlock musket.
		1616	Thirty Years War begins in Europe.
1620–21	Founding of Plymouth colony. Peace agreed between		

AMERICAN MILITARY DEVELOPMENTS		DEVELOPMENTS ABROAD	
	Governor William Bradford and Massasoit, Narragansett headman.		
1622–32	Second Powhatan uprising in Virginia.		
1635	English establish Fort Saybrook on Connecticut River.		
1637	The Pequot War in Connecticut.		
1638	First American military unit formally established in Boston: the Ancient and Honorable Artillery Company.		
1641–45	Algonquin War against Dutch and English settlements in New York.		
		1642	English Civil War begins.
1643	New England Confederation formed for common defense against Dutch, French, and Indians.		
1644–46	Third Powhatan uprising in Virginia.		
		1648	Treaty of Westphalia concludes Thirty Years War.
		1649	Execution of King Charles I of England.
		1649–60	Protectorate of Oliver Cromwell in England.
		1650s	British naval officers argue use of formal, line-of-battle tactics versus melee tactics.
		1652–54	First Anglo-Dutch War.
		1660	Restoration of King Charles II of England.
		1662–64	Second Anglo-Dutch War.
1664	English forces capture New Amsterdam (New York).		
		1672–74	Third Anglo-Dutch War.
1676	King Philip's War in New England.		
	Bacon's rebellion in Virginia.		
1687	Revolt of the Yamassee Indians in Georgia and Florida.		

CHRONOLOGY OF AMERICAN MILITARY DEVELOPMENTS 355

AMERICAN MILITARY DEVELOPMENTS **DEVELOPMENTS ABROAD**

		1688	War of the League of Augsburg begins in Europe.
1689	King William's War (War of the League of Augsburg) begins in America.		
	French and Indian allies attack English settlements in New England.		
	Iroquois alliance with English colonists.		
	Leisler's Rebellion in New York.		
1690	French and Indian allies attack Schenectady, New York.		
	English seize Port Royal, Nova Scotia, from the French.		
1691	Jacob Leisler executed in New York.	1691	British Navy adopts "Fighting Instructions" in order to encourage cohesive combat doctrine throughout the Fleet.
1696	English and Indian allies attack French Quebec.		
	Treaty of Ryswick concludes King William's War in America and the War of the League of Augsburg in Europe.		
		1701	The War of Spanish Succession begins in Europe.
1702	Queen Anne's War (War of Spanish Succession) begins in America.		
	English attack Saint Augustine, Spanish Florida.		
1704	French and Indian allies attack Deerfield, Massachusetts.		
	English attack Port Royal.		
1706	Franco-Spanish fleet unsuccessfully attacks Charleston in the Carolinas.		
1707	English colonists attempt expedition against French Acadia.		
1708	French and Indian allies raid Haverhill, Massachusetts.		
1710	British naval force and Eng-		

AMERICAN MILITARY DEVELOPMENTS		DEVELOPMENTS ABROAD	
	lish colonists attack and seize Port Royal.		
1711	Failure of English colonial campaign against Montreal.		
	Tuscarora War begins in Carolina with massacre of 150 settlers.		
1712	Carolina militia retaliates against Tuscaroras at Neuse River.		
1713	Tuscarora War ends.		
	Queen Anne's War (and War of Spanish Succession in Europe) ends with Treaty of Utrecht.		
		1739–43	War of Jenkins' Ear.
		1740s–50s	Frederick the Great, King of Prussia, improves field (light) artillery.
1740	James Oglethorpe leads unsuccessful expedition against Saint Augustine.	1740	War of Austrian Succession begins in Europe.
	Combined British-colonial expedition against Cartagena, the West Indies, and Santiago, Cuba.		
1741	British attack on Santiago.		
1742	Battle of Bloody Marsh (Saint Simon's Island, Georgia) between Spanish and Oglethorpe's militia.		
1743	Oglethorpe invades Spanish Florida once more.		
1744	King George's War (War of the Austrian Succession) begins in America.		
	French attack Annapolis Royal (formerly Port Royal).		
1745	New Englanders seize the fortress at Louisbourg.		
	French and Indian allies invade New York.		
1746	French expedition against Cape Breton and Nova Scotia fails.		

AMERICAN MILITARY DEVELOPMENTS

1748	Treaty of Aix-la-Chapelle ends King George's War (and the War of the Austrian Succession in Europe).
1754	July. Battle of Great Meadow between Virginia militia and French Canadian militia begins the French and Indian War.
1755	June. British colonial expedition against French outposts on the Bay of Fundy, Canada.
	July. General Braddock's army of British regulars and colonial militia routed by French at the Battle of the Wilderness.
	August-September. British colonial expedition seizes Crown Point at Lake George, New York. British colonial expedition seizes Fort Niagara.
	September. Battle of Lake George.
	British War Office authorizes raising the first British regiments in America, the Royal Americans, now the King's Royal Rifle Corps.
1756	August. Marquis de Montcalm begins French offensive against Forts Oswego and Ticonderoga in New York.
1757	June-September. British expedition against the Fortress of Louisbourg fails.

DEVELOPMENTS ABROAD

1756–60s	Several European armies experiment with "light" infantry for skirmishing in advance of their main body of troops.
1756	Britain formally enters the Seven Years' War.

AMERICAN MILITARY DEVELOPMENTS **DEVELOPMENTS ABROAD**

	August. French and Indians besiege and massacre British garrison at Fort William Henry.
1758	May-July. French surrender Louisbourg to British under Amherst and Wolfe.
	July. Battle of Ticonderoga.
	July-November. British expedition against Fort Duquesne.
	August. British take Fort Frontenac, Lake Ontario.

1759   June-July. British campaigns along the Mohawk River to Niagara and against Ticonderoga. General Wolfe's campaign against Quebec begins in June.   1759   In France Duke de Broglie combines infantry and artillery regiments into divisions.

September. Battle of the Plains of Abraham outside Quebec.

1760   April. French counterattack against Quebec fails.

September. British campaign against Montreal. French surrender Canada to the British.

1763   February. Treaty of Paris concludes French and Indian War (and in Europe, the Seven Years' War).

May-November. Revolt of Pontiac against British western outposts.

August. Battle of Bloody Ridge breaks Pontiac's uprising. Fort Pitt, besieged by Indians, is relieved.

1765   June (?). Formation of the Sons of Liberty in British colonies to combat British enforcement of the Stamp Act.   1765   Jean Baptiste de Gribeauval, French officer, experiments with field artillery, improving upon Frederick the Great's innovations.

CHRONOLOGY OF AMERICAN MILITARY DEVELOPMENTS 359

	AMERICAN MILITARY DEVELOPMENTS	**DEVELOPMENTS ABROAD**
1768	October. Two regiments of British troops posted to Boston to enforce public order.	
1770	January. Battle of Golden Hill in New York between Sons of Liberty and British regulars.	
	Boston Massacre.	
1771	January-June. War of the Regulators in North Carolina.	
	May. Battle of Alamance, North Carolina.	
1773	December. Boston Tea Party.	
1774	September-October. 1st Continental Congress calls for formation of American militia units.	
	October. "Minute Men" formed in Massachusetts. Battle of Point Pleasant, Virginia.	
	September-October. Lord Dunmore's War (Shawnee uprising in western Virginia).	
1775	April. Battles of Lexington and Concord begin American Revolution.	
	April. Siege of Boston by colonial militia begins.	
	May. Americans seize Fort Ticonderoga.	
	June. 2d Continental Congress appoints George Washington commander of the Continental Army. Battle of Bunker Hill.	
	July. Washington assumes command of the Continental Army.	
	August-November. American expedition against Montreal fails.	

	AMERICAN MILITARY DEVELOPMENTS	DEVELOPMENTS ABROAD
	November 10. Congress authorizes formation of the Continental Marines (forerunners of the U.S. Marine Corps).	
	December. Benedict Arnold's expedition against Quebec fails.	
1776	February. American Commodore Esek Hopkins' raid on the Bahamas. Battle of Moores Creek Bridge, North Carolina.	
	March. Congress authorizes naval privateering. British troops evacuate Boston.	
	June. Battle of Trois Rivieres, Canada.	
	June-July. Americans retreat from Canada.	
	July. American Declaration of Independence. France and Spain pledge assistance to Americans.	
	August. Battle of Long Island.	
	September. Americans use first submarine, "The American Turtle," in warfare. Americans retreat from New York. Battle of Harlem Heights.	
	October. Battle of White Plains. Battle of Valcour Island on Lake Champlain, New York.	
	November. British capture Forts Washington and Lee.	
	November-December. Americans retreat through New Jersey.	
	December. Battle of Morristown. Battle of Trenton.	
1777	January. Battle of Princeton.	

AMERICAN MILITARY DEVELOPMENTS	DEVELOPMENTS ABROAD
	July. British seize Fort Ticonderoga.
	August. Battle of Oriskany, New York. Battle of Bennington, Vermont.
	September. Battle of Freeman's Farm, New York. Battle of the Brandywine, Pennsylvania. British take Philadelphia.
	October. Battle of Bemis Heights. British force under General Burgoyne surrenders at Saratoga, New York. Battle of Germantown, Pennsylvania.
	Winter of 1777–78. Continental Army bivouacs at Valley Forge.
1778	February. Franco-American Alliance. Baron von Steuben begins Prussian-style training in the Continental Army.
	April-May. John Paul Jones raids British waters in *Ranger*.
	June. France and England declare war. British troops evacuate Philadelphia for New York. Battle of Monmouth, New Jersey.
	July. French fleet under Comte d'Estaing arrives in American waters.
	August. Franco-American expedition against Newport, Rhode Island, fails.
	December. British forces capture Savannah, Georgia.
1779	January. British forces seize Augusta, Georgia.
	February. Battle of Port Royal, South Carolina.

AMERICAN MILITARY DEVELOPMENTS

DEVELOPMENTS ABROAD

Battle of Kettle Creek, South Carolina.

March. Battle of Briar Creek, Georgia.

June. Battle of Stono Ferry, Georgia.

September. John Paul Jones' *Bonhomme Richard* defeats Britain's HMS *Serapis*.

September-October. Franco-American siege of Savannah.

December. British force under General Clinton leaves New York for Southern Campaign.

1780 Treason of General Benedict Arnold.

February-May. British successfully besiege Charleston.

May-August. Guerrilla warfare in South Carolina.

July. French forces under General Rochambeau arrive at Newport, Rhode Island.

August. Battle of Camden, South Carolina.

October. Battle of King's Mountain, South Carolina.

1781 January. Battle of the Cowpens, South Carolina.

January-February. American retreat northward to the Dan River, North Carolina.

March. Battle of Guilford Courthouse, North Carolina. First Battle of the Virginia Capes between French and British fleets.

May. Captain John Barry's *Alliance* raiding in the

AMERICAN MILITARY DEVELOPMENTS		DEVELOPMENTS ABROAD
	North Atlantic. British General Cornwallis arrives in Virginia.	
	May-June. Americans besiege Fort Ninety-Six in South Carolina.	
	August. French Admiral de Grasse sails from the West Indies for American waters. Washington begins to move the Continental Army toward Virginia.	
	September. Second Battle of the Virginia Capes. Battle of Eutaw Springs, South Carolina.	
	September-October. Franco-American army besieges British at Yorktown, Virginia.	
	October. General Cornwallis surrenders the British forces at Yorktown.	
		1782 February-September. Anglo-French naval actions off the coast of India.
		April. Naval battle of Saints, West Indies.
1783	April 15. Treaty of Paris ratified by Congress, concluding the American Revolution.	
	November. British forces under Clinton evacuate New York City.	
		1784 British Army Lieutenant Henry Shrapnel invents the exploding artillery shell.
1786	August-February. Shays' Rebellion in Massachusetts.	
1789	August. Congress creates the War Department.	1789 French Revolution begins with the storming of the Bastille in Paris.

AMERICAN MILITARY DEVELOPMENTS		DEVELOPMENTS ABROAD	
	September. Henry Knox named first secretary of war.		
1790	Maumee Indian uprising in the American Northwest Territories.		
	October. Indians defeat General Harmar's expeditionary column in the Northwest Territory.		
		1790s	British Admiral Horatio Nelson adopts "melee" naval tactics.
1791	November. Indians defeat General St. Clair's expeditionary column in the Northwest Territory.		
1792	Congress passes the Militia Act.	1792	War of the First Coalition against Revolutionary France.
	Congress creates the Legion of the United States with General Anthony Wayne as commander.		
1794	May. Congress passes the Navy Act.	1794	French Minister of War Lazare Carnot adds cavalry to French Army divisional organizations.
	July-November. Whiskey Rebellion in Pennsylvania.		
	August. Battle of Fallen Timbers breaks Indian uprising in the Northwest Territory.		
1795	Treaty of Greenville concludes hostilities in the Northwest Territory.	1795	Napoleon Bonaparte takes command of French Army in Italy.
1797	First of the "Humphreys Frigates" launched.		
1798	"Quasi-War" with France.	1798–1800	War of the Second Coalition against Revolutionary France.
	Eli Whitney begins manufacturing muskets using interchangeable parts at his works in New Haven, Connecticut.		
	May. Congress establishes Navy Department.		

CHRONOLOGY OF AMERICAN MILITARY DEVELOPMENTS 365

AMERICAN MILITARY DEVELOPMENTS		DEVELOPMENTS ABROAD	
1799	American naval actions against French fleet in the western Atlantic and the West Indies.		
		1800	Napoleon becomes first consul of France. Napoleonic armies develop the infantry "attack column," stress use of massed artillery, and depot logistics. General Jean Moreau, commander of the French Army of the Rhine, first organizes corps.
		1800–15	Napoleonic Wars. British Colonel Sir William Congreve experiments with military rockets.
1801–5	Tripolitan War.		
1801	July. U.S. naval expedition sent to western Mediterranean to combat piracy.	1801	April. British fleet under Horatio Nelson victorious over Danes at Copenhagen.
1802	July. U.S. Military Academy opens at West Point, New York.	1802	British Royal Military College established at Sandhurst.
1803–6	Lewis and Clark explorations in the Trans-Mississippi West.		
1803	August. Commodore Edward Preble polices western Mediterranean against Barbary pirates. October. USS *Philadelphia* captured by the Tripolitans.		
1804	February. USS *Philadelphia* scuttled at Tripoli by U.S. naval raiders.	1804	Baron Antoine Henri Jomini publishes *Treatise on Great Military Operations*.
1805	Zebulon Pike's explorations of the West. April. U.S. naval force captures Derna in Tripolitania. August. U.S. Navy forces peace with Tunisian pirates.	1805	October. Naval Battle of Trafalgar, off Spain. December. Battle of Austerlitz.

AMERICAN MILITARY DEVELOPMENTS		DEVELOPMENTS ABROAD	
		1806	October. Battle of Jena.
1807	June. Naval action between HMS *Leopard* and USS *Chesapeake*.	1807	British Army makes first use of division organization.
		1808	French School of War opens at St. Cyr.
		1809–14	British Army under Wellington campaigns in the Peninsula (Spain and Portugal).
		1810	Prussian War Academy opens in Berlin.
1811	Shawnee uprising in the Northwest under Tecumseh. May. Naval action between HMS *Little Belt* and USS *President*. November. Battle of Tippecanoe, Indiana.		
1812	June. Congress declares war on Great Britain, beginning the War of 1812. July. British forces capture Fort Mackinac. August. British forces capture Fort Dearborn (Chicago). Naval action between USS *Constitution* and HMS *Guerriere*.	1812	June. Napoleon invades Russia.
			September. Battle of Borodino.
	October. Battle of Queenston, Canada. Naval action between USS *Wasp* and HMS *Frolic*. Naval action between USS *United States* and HMS *Macedonian*. November. American campaign on Lake Champlain. December. Naval action between USS *Constitution* and HMS *Java*.		December. Napoleon's Russian Campaign ends with French Army retreat.

CHRONOLOGY OF AMERICAN MILITARY DEVELOPMENTS 367

	AMERICAN MILITARY DEVELOPMENTS	**DEVELOPMENTS ABROAD**
1813	January. Battle of the Raisin River (Frenchtown), Michigan.	1813
	February. Naval action between USS *Hornet* and HMS *Peacock*.	
	April. American forces attack and burn York (Toronto).	
	May. Battles of Fort George and Stoney Creek near Niagara. Battle of Sackets Harbor, New York.	
	June. Naval action between HMS *Shannon* and USS *Chesapeake*.	
	July. Creek Indians ally with British.	
	August. Naval action between HMS *Pelican* and USS *Argus*.	
	September. Naval action between USS *Enterprise* and HMS *Boxer*. American naval forces win control of Lake Erie. American naval and land forces expel British from Detroit.	
	September-November. American campaign against Montreal fails.	
	October. Battle of the Thames River, Canada. Battle of Chateaugay River, Canada.	October. Battle of Leipzig.
	November. Battle of Chrysler's Farm, Canada. Battle of Talladega, Alabama.	
1814	February-March. Americans resume Canadian offensive.	1814
	March. British defeat Americans at Battle of La Colle Mill, Canada. Battle of	

AMERICAN MILITARY DEVELOPMENTS	DEVELOPMENTS ABROAD
Horseshoe Bend, Alabama. USS *Essex* taken by British warships in Pacific after commerce raiding cruise around the Horn begun in October 1812.	
April. Naval action between USS *Peacock* and HMS *Epervier*. General Jacob Brown takes command on the Niagara Front.	April. Napoleon abdicates.
June. Commerce raiding by USS *Wasp* in the English Channel.	
July. American offensive on the Niagara Front. Battle of Chippewa, Canada. Battle of Lundy's Lane, Canada.	
August. British invasion of New York begins. Treaty of Fort Jackson ends Creek involvement in the war. British land raiding force near Washington, D.C. Battle of Bladensburg, Maryland. Washington, D.C., sacked and burned by British troops.	
September. British attack on Baltimore repulsed. Battle of Plattsburgh, New York. Battle of Lake Champlain.	
November. U.S. forces under General Andrew Jackson invade Florida and take Pensacola. Jackson's forces march to defend New Orleans against British. British fleet departs Jamaica for invasion at New Orleans.	
1815 January. American forces un-	

	AMERICAN MILITARY DEVELOPMENTS		DEVELOPMENTS ABROAD
	der Jackson defeat British at the Battle of New Orleans. USS *President* taken by British warships. February. Congress ratifies the Treaty of Ghent, concluding the War of 1812. Naval action between USS *Constitution*, HMS *Cyane*, and HMS *Levant*. Congress orders demobilization of U.S. Army to 10,000 men. March. Naval action between USS *Hornet* and HMS *Penguin*. March-June. U.S. naval expedition against Algerian pirates in the Mediterranean.		June. Battle of Waterloo.
1818	April-May. First Seminole War. Punitive expedition by U.S. forces takes Pensacola.		
		1820s	French artillery officer Henri-Joseph Paixhans develops light, shell-firing cannon for naval use.
		1831	Prussian War Academy posthumously publishes Karl von Clausewitz's *On War*.
1832	April-August. Black Hawk War, Illinois frontier. August. Battle of Bad Axe, Wisconsin.		
1835-37.	Second Seminole War.		
1835	December. Dade Massacre by Seminoles in Wahoo Swamp, Florida.		
1836	January-May. Texas Revolution.	1836	Antoine Henry Jomini publishes his *Summary of the Art of War*.

AMERICAN MILITARY DEVELOPMENTS		DEVELOPMENTS ABROAD	
1837	December. Seminoles defeated at the Battle of Lake Okeechobee, Florida.		
1842	May. Dorr Rebellion in Rhode Island.	1840s	Working independently, Joseph Whitworth of England and Giovanni Cavalli of Italy develop accurate, breech-loading, rifled cannons.
1844	America launches USS *Princeton*, first screw-type naval steamer.		
1844–45	Lieutenant Thomas J. Rodman develops a method of cooling cast iron cannon barrels from the inside out, thus strengthening barrels.		
1845	March. Mexico threatens war as U.S. annexes Texas. July. U.S. forces under General Zachary Taylor ordered to Corpus Christi, Texas. October. Secretary of the Navy George Bancroft establishes the Naval School at Annapolis, forerunner of the U.S. Naval Academy (1850).		
1846	March. U.S. forces under Taylor take positions along the Rio Grande River in disputed territory. April. Mexican and U.S. cavalry clash along the Rio Grande. May. Battle of Palo Alto. Battle of Resaca de la Palma. U.S. declares war on Mexico. U.S. forces invade Mexico. June. Commodore John Sloat occupies Monterey, California.		

AMERICAN MILITARY DEVELOPMENTS		DEVELOPMENTS ABROAD	
	June-December. U.S. forces march from New Mexico to occupy California.		
	September. Battle of Monterrey, Mexico.		
	November. U.S. forces under General John Wool take Saltillo, Mexico.		
	December. Battle of San Pascual, California.		
1847	January. Battle of San Gabriel, California.		
	February. Battle of Buena Vista, Mexico. Battle of the Sacramento River, Mexico.		
	March. U.S. forces under General Winfield Scott make amphibious landings near Vera Cruz, Mexico. U.S. forces occupy Vera Cruz.		
	April. Battle of Cerro Gordo, Mexico.		
	April-September. U.S. forces march on Mexico City.		
	August. Battle of Contreras, Mexico. Battle of Churubusco, Mexico.		
	August-September. Armistice.		
	September. Battle of Molino del Rey, Mexico. Battle of Chapultepec, Mexico City. Mexico City surrenders to Scott's forces.		
	September-October. Mexican forces besiege Puebla.		
1847	Dennis Hart Mahan publishes *Outpost*.		
1848	Treaty of Guadalupe Hidalgo concludes Mexican War.		
1849–50s	Navy Lieutenant John Dahlgren engineers a new basic heavy cannon which the Navy adopts—the "Dahlgren gun."	1849	French Captain E. E. Minie adapts a cylindro-conoidal bullet tested by the British in the 1820s, eventually called the "Minie ball."

AMERICAN MILITARY DEVELOPMENTS		DEVELOPMENTS ABROAD	
1850	U.S. Navy outlaws flogging. U.S. Naval Academy opens at Annapolis, Maryland.		
1850s	Inventor Samuel Colt experiments with rapid-fire weapons.	1850s	French Army tests a machine gun, the Mitraillouse, and a 12-pounder, smoothbore field gun, dubbed "the Napoleon" after Emperor Napoleon III.
1850–65	Irregular warfare on the Western frontier. More than thirty significant armed conflicts between the Army and Indian tribes.		
		1853–56	The Crimean War.
1856	"Bleeding Kansas." Depredations along the Kansas-Missouri border by pro- and antislavery gangs.		
1857-58	Mormon expedition under A. S. Johnston and Joseph E. Johnston.	1858	British Army adopts breech-loading, rifled field gun introduced by English engineer William Armstrong.
1859	October. John Brown's raid on Harper's Ferry.	1859	British Navy Captain Cowper Coles devises ship's revolving gun turret. French launch the armored warship *Gloire*.
1860	After several experiments, Robert Parrott manufactures a small rifled cannon—the "Parrott Gun."	1860	British launch the armored warship *Warrior*.
1861	Inventor John Ericcson designs revolving gun turret for USS *Monitor*. January-April. Prelude to Civil War. Southern States secede from the Union. February 8. Confederate States of America provisionally formed. April 12–14. Confederate forces under General		

CHRONOLOGY OF AMERICAN MILITARY DEVELOPMENTS 373

AMERICAN MILITARY DEVELOPMENTS	DEVELOPMENTS ABROAD
	P.G.T. Beauregard bombard Fort Sumter, South Carolina.
	April 23. Confederate naval officer Matthew F. Maury begins experiments with "torpedoes" (underwater mines).
	May. Union naval blockade of the South begins.
	July 21. Confederates defeat Federals at the first Battle of Bull Run. Confederate reinforcements arrive on battlefield by railroad.
	August 10. Battle of Wilson's Creek, Missouri.
	August 27. Naval action at Hatteras Inlet, North Carolina.
	October 21. Battle of Ball's Bluff, Virginia.
	November 7. Union forces seize Port Royal, South Carolina.
1862	Dr. Richard Gatling carries out test on a machine gun, the "Gatling Gun."
	February. General U. S. Grant begins Union campaign against Forts Henry and Donelson, Tennessee. Union offensive against New Madrid and Island Number 10 begins the Mississippi River Campaign.
	February 7. Union naval expedition captures Roanoke Island, Virginia.
	March 7–8. Battle of Pea Ridge, Arkansas.
	March 8–9. Naval action between armored ships *Monitor* and *Merrimac* at Hampton Roads, Virginia.

AMERICAN MILITARY DEVELOPMENTS	DEVELOPMENTS ABROAD
March 23. Battle of Kernstown, Virginia.	
April 5. General George B. McClellan begins siege of Yorktown, Virginia.	
April 6–7. Battle of Shiloh, Tennessee.	
April 11. Union takes Fort Pulaski, Georgia, improving blockade.	
April 16. Confederacy institutes first conscription act.	
April 24. Union naval squadron forces passage by Confederate forts below New Orleans.	
April 28. CSS *Florida* arrives in Bahamas and prepares to raid Northern shipping.	
May. Confederate campaign begins in the Shenandoah Valley under "Stonewall" Jackson.	
May 1. Union forces take New Orleans.	
May 5. Battle of Williamsburg, Virginia.	
May 8. Battle of McDowell, Virginia.	
May 9. Confederates evacuate naval base at Norfolk.	
May 25. First Battle of Winchester, Virginia.	
May 31–June 1. Battle of Seven Pines.	
June 1. General Robert E. Lee assumes command of the Army of Northern Virginia.	
June 6. Battle of Memphis, Tennessee.	
June 8. Battle of Cross Keys, Virginia.	
June 9. Battle of Port Republic, Virginia.	

AMERICAN MILITARY DEVELOPMENTS

DEVELOPMENTS ABROAD

June 12-15. General J.E.B. Stuart's raid around the Army of the Potomac.

June 17. Federal Congress authorizes the enlistment of black troops.

June 25-July 1. In Virginia, the Seven Days' Battles: Mechanicsville (June 25); Gaines' Mill (June 27); and Malvern Hill (July 1).

July 29. CSS *Alabama* leaves England to raid on Union shipping.

August 5. Battle of Baton Rouge, Louisiana.

August 9. Battle of Cedar Mountain, Virginia.

August 29-30. Second Battle of Bull Run, Virginia.

September 4. Army of Northern Virginia crosses the Potomac River to campaign in Maryland.

September 14. Battle of South Mountain, Maryland.

September 17. Battle of Antietam, Maryland.

September 18. Army of Northern Virginia retreats across the Potomac to Virginia.

September 22. President Lincoln issues Preliminary Emancipation Proclamation.

October 3-4. Battle of Corinth, Mississippi.

October 8. Battle of Perryville, Kentucky.

November. Beginning of the Fredericksburg Campaign. Beginning of the Vicksburg Campaign.

December 13. Battle of Fredericksburg.

AMERICAN MILITARY DEVELOPMENTS	DEVELOPMENTS ABROAD
	December 29. Battle of Chickasaw Bluffs, Mississippi.
	December 31. Battle of Murfreesboro, Tennessee.
1863	March 3. Union institutes conscription.
	April. Chancellorsville Campaign begins.
	April 7. Union naval expedition under Admiral S. F. DuPont repulsed at Charleston.
	April 17. Colonel B. F. Grierson begins raid through Mississippi.
	May 1–4. Battle of Chancellorsville, Virginia.
	May 7–19. Big Black River Campaign in Mississippi.
	May 16. Battle of Champion's Hill, Mississippi.
	May 19-July 4. Siege of Vicksburg, Mississippi.
	May 22. Federal War Department establishes Bureau of Colored Troops.
	June-July. Gettysburg Campaign.
	June 9. Largest cavalry battle of the war at Brandy Station, Virginia.
	June 13–14. Second Battle of Winchester.
	June 23-July 2. Tullahoma Campaign in Tennessee.
	July-December. Siege of Charleston.
	July 1-3. Battle of Gettysburg.
	July 4. Surrender of Vicksburg.
	July 8. Port Hudson, Louisiana, surrenders, giving control of Mississippi River to the Union.
	September 19–20. Battle of Chickamauga, Georgia.

AMERICAN MILITARY DEVELOPMENTS	DEVELOPMENTS ABROAD
September-October. Siege of Chattanooga, Tennessee.	

October 5. Confederate torpedoboat, *David*, attacks Union ship in Charleston Harbor.

November-December. Siege of Knoxville, Tennessee.

November 24–25. Battle of Chattanooga.

1864　March-May. Red River Campaign, Louisiana.

March 9. General U. S. Grant takes command of Union Army.

May 4, Opening of the Wilderness Campaign.

May 5. Atlanta Campaign opens.

May 5–6. Battle of the Wilderness, Virginia.

May 5–16. Bermuda Hundred Campaign, Virginia.

May 8–18. Battle of Spotsylvania, Virginia.

May 11. Battle of Yellow Tavern, Virginia.

May 15. Battle of New Market, Virginia.

May 16. Battle of Drewry's Bluff, Virginia.

June. Siege of Petersburg begins.

June 3–12. Battle of Cold Harbor, Virginia.

June 10. Battle of Brice's Cross Roads, Mississippi.

June 15–18. Battle of Petersburg, Virginia.

June 19. Naval action between USS *Kearsarge* and Confederate raider *Alabama*.

June 27. Battle of Kennesaw Mountain, Georgia.

July 9. Battle of the Monocacy, Maryland.

AMERICAN MILITARY DEVELOPMENTS	DEVELOPMENTS ABROAD
July 14–15. Battle of Tupelo, Mississippi.	

July 20. Battle of Peachtree Creek, Georgia.

July 22. Battle of Atlanta.

August 5. Naval battle of Mobile Bay.

August–October. General Phil Sheridan's Shenandoah Valley Campaign.

September 19. Third Battle of Winchester.

September 22. Battle of Fischer's Hill, Virginia.

October 19. Battle of Cedar Creek, Virginia.

November 16. Sherman and Union Army begin "March to the Sea."

November 30. Battle of Franklin, Tennessee.

December 9–21. Union investment of Savannah, Georgia.

December 15–16. Battle of Nashville, Tennessee.

1865 January 19. Sherman and Union Army begin march from Savannah, Georgia, through South Carolina.

February 7. Confederates evacuate Charleston.

February 22. Main port of Confederacy at Wilmington, North Carolina, falls to Union forces.

March 19–20. Battle of Bentonville, North Carolina.

March 25. Battle of Fort Stedman, Petersburg, Virginia.

March 29–31. Battle of Dinwiddie Courthouse, Virginia.

April 1. Battle of Five Forks, Virginia.

	AMERICAN MILITARY DEVELOPMENTS		DEVELOPMENTS ABROAD
	April 2. Battle of Selma, Alabama. Confederates evacuate Petersburg.		
	April 6–7. Battle of Sayler's Creek, Virginia.		
	April 9. Battle of Appomattox, Virginia. General Lee surrenders Confederate forces at Appomattox Court House.		
	April 12. Confederates surrender at Mobile, Alabama.		
	April 14. President Lincoln is assassinated.		
	April 26. General Joseph E. Johnston surrenders to General Sherman at Durham Station, North Carolina.		
	May 26. Confederates in Trans-Mississippi Department surrender at New Orleans.		
	May 29. Formal conclusion of Civil War; President Andrew Johnson grants amnesty.		
	November 6. Commerce raider CSS *Shenandoah* surrenders flag in Great Britain.		
1865–68	Intermittent campaigning by U.S. Army against Indians in Far West and Northwest.		
1866	December. Fetterman massacre in Wyoming.	1866	June-August. Austro-Prussian War.
1867–75	Intermittent campaigning by U.S. Army against Indians in the Central Plains and Southwest.		
		1870–71	Franco-Prussian War.
1872–73	The Modoc War, California.		
1873	Army campaigns against the Apaches in the Southwest.		

AMERICAN MILITARY DEVELOPMENTS		DEVELOPMENTS ABROAD	
1876	February-June. Big Horn Campaign in Montana and Wyoming.		
	March. Battle of Slim Buttes.		
	June 17. Battle of the Rosebud.		
	June 25. Battle of the Little Big Horn.		
	November. Battle of Crazy Woman Fork.		
1877	January. Battle of the Wolf Mountains.		
	June. Nez Perce War begins. Battle of White Bird Canyon.		
	July-August. Battles of the Clearwater and Big Hole Basin.		
	October. Battle of Eagle Creek.		
1878	Bannock War, Northwest Territories.		
1878–79	Army campaigns against Northern Cheyennes.		
1881	Army establishes School of Application for Infantry and Cavalry at Fort Leavenworth, Kansas.		
1882	March. Navy establishes Office of Naval Intelligence.		
1885–86.	Army campaigns against Geronimo's Apaches.	1885	Sir Hiram Maxim develops a machine gun that loads, fires, and ejects shells using its own recoil.
1886	U.S. Naval War College opens at Newport, Rhode Island.		
1890	May. A. T. Mahan publishes *The Influence of Sea Power upon History*.		
1895	Inventor John M. Browning develops an air-cooled machine gun that utilizes gas pressure for its operation.		

CHRONOLOGY OF AMERICAN MILITARY DEVELOPMENTS

	AMERICAN MILITARY DEVELOPMENTS		**DEVELOPMENTS ABROAD**
1898	February 15. USS *Maine* explodes in Havana Harbor.		
	April 25. U.S. declares war on Spain.		
	May 1. Admiral George Dewey's fleet defeats Spanish at Manila Bay, Philippines.		
	May-July. U.S. naval blockade of Santiago Bay, Cuba.		
	June. U.S. forces land at Santiago.		
	July 3. Battle of Santiago Bay.		
	July 17. U.S. forces capture Santiago.		
	July 25. U.S. forces land in Puerto Rico.		
	August. U.S. forces capture Manila.		
	December. Treaty of Paris concludes Spanish-American War.		
1899	January. Filipino insurgents declare independence of the Philippines.		
	February. Filipino insurgency against U.S. occupation begins.		
1902–5	U.S. forces campaign against insurgents on Luzon and Moros on Mindinao.		
1903	Secretary of War Elihu Root sponsors reform of U.S. Army, creating a General Staff and a War College.		
		1904–5	Russo-Japanese War.
		1906	First modern battleship, HMS *Dreadnought*, constructed in Great Britain.
1907–9	Voyage of U.S. Navy's "Great White Fleet."		
1910	U.S. Marine Corps establishes the Advanced Base School for amphibious assault training.		

AMERICAN MILITARY DEVELOPMENTS		DEVELOPMENTS ABROAD	
		1911	Chinese Revolution begins.
1912	U.S. intervention in Honduras and Nicaragua. Admiral Bradley Fiske develops techniques for aerial torpedo launching.		
1914	U.S. expedition occupies Vera Cruz, Mexico.	1914	August. World War I begins in Europe.
		1915	May. German submarine sinks British liner *Lusitania*.
1916	U.S. sends Punitive Expedition against Villistas in northern Mexico.	1916	January-December. German Zeppelin raids on London. February-December. Battle of Verdun. May-June. Naval battle of Jutland.
1917	January. Germany declares unrestricted submarine warfare. March. German submarines sink four American merchant ships. April 6. U.S. declares war on Germany. May 19. Congress passes Selective Service Act. June. General John J. Pershing becomes commander, American Expeditionary Force. U.S. 1st Infantry Division arrives in France.	1917	March. Russian Revolution begins as Czar Nicholas II abdicates. April-May. Mutinies in the French Army. November. Petrograd revolt begins Bolshevik Revolution. British use first major tank formations in Battle of Cambrai.
		1917–18	German aircraft attacks on England.
		1917–22	Russian Civil War.
1918	May. Battle of Cantigny (first U.S. action on the Western Front). May-June. Battles of Chateau Thierry and Belleau Wood. July-August. Second Battle of the Marne. September. U.S. forces lead	1918	September. British put the air-

CHRONOLOGY OF AMERICAN MILITARY DEVELOPMENTS

	AMERICAN MILITARY DEVELOPMENTS		DEVELOPMENTS ABROAD
	offensive against the Saint-Mihiel salient. September-November. Meuse-Argonne Offensive. November 11. Armistice.		craft carrier *Argus* to sea, the first of its kind with a full-length flight deck. October. British researchers develop "asdic" sounding device to locate submarines.
1918–19	Allied forces (including U.S.) intervene in Russia.		
1919	Reserve Officers Training Corps (ROTC) established in National Defense Act of 1919.	1919	Treaty of Versailles ends World War I.
1920	Congress passes National Defense Act of 1920, reflecting ideas of General J. M. Palmer.	1920s-30s	British military theorists J.F.C. Fuller and B. H. Liddell Hart develop and proselytize views on combined arms warfare later called *blitzkrieg*.
1920–21	Washington Naval Conference.		
1922–27	U.S. Navy experiments with the aircraft carrier *Langley*, a converted collier.		
1925	December. Court-martial of Colonel William Mitchell.		
1928	U.S. Navy puts aircraft carriers *Lexington* and *Saratoga* into service.	1928	Many nations of the world sign Kellogg-Briand Pact to outlaw offensive war.
		1929	Allied forces evacuate the Rhineland.
1931	U.S. Naval Research Laboratory begins studies of "radar" (radio detection and ranging) device.	1931	Mukden incident begins Japanese seizure of Manchuria.
1933–35	U.S. Army participates in Civilian Conservation Corps activities.	1933	Establishment of Nazi dictatorship in Germany.
		1935–36	Italo-Ethiopian War.
1936	April. Rudimentary radar developed by U.S. Naval Research Laboratory.	1936	Germany reoccupies the Rhineland.
		1936–39	Spanish Civil War.
1937	U.S. Navy commissions aircraft carrier *Yorktown*.	1937	Sino-Japanese War begins.

	AMERICAN MILITARY DEVELOPMENTS		DEVELOPMENTS ABROAD
1938	U.S. Navy commissions carrier *Enterprise*.	1938	Germany annexes Austria.
		1938–39	Russo-Japanese hostilities in Manchuria.
1939	Radars installed on U.S. ships. September. United States declares neutrality.	1939	Germany invades Poland. World War II begins.
		1939–40	Russo-Finnish War.
		1940	April-June. German conquest of Norway and Denmark. May-June. German conquest of the Low Countries and France. British share knowledge of radar with United States. August-November. Battle of Britain.
1940	September. Anglo-American "destroyers for bases" agreement is made. Selective Service Act passed by Congress.		
			September. Italians invade Egypt. October. Italians invade Greece.
1941		1941	January. British offensive in North Africa begins.
	March. U.S. Lend Lease aid begins. April. United States stations forces in Greenland.		March. German offensive in North Africa begins. April. Germans invade Greece. German Army besieges Tobruk in North Africa. May. The battle for Crete. June. British offensive in North Africa. German invasion of Russia.
	July. United States stations forces in Iceland.		July. Japanese Navy approves plans and training for attack on Pearl Harbor.
	August. Atlantic Conference. September. Selective Service Act extended. U.S. con-		November-December. British Army launches offensive in North Africa. Defense

AMERICAN MILITARY DEVELOPMENTS

voy escorts begin in North Atlantic.

September-December. American Volunteer Group ("The Flying Tigers") is formed in China.

December 7. Japanese launch surprise attack against American Pacific Fleet at Pearl Harbor, Hawaii.

December 8. Japanese launch surprise attack on Americans at Clark Field, the Philippines.

December 10. Japanese attack American base on Guam.

December 22. Japanese launch invasion of Luzon, the Philippines.

December 22–January 14. Arcadia Conference.

1942 January. Battle of the Atlantic begins against German submarine "wolfpacks."

January 7–26. Defense of Bataan, the Philippines.

January 23. Naval battle of the Macassar Strait, off Borneo.

February-August. Battle for Guadalcanal.

February 1. U.S. naval attack on Gilbert and Marshall Islands.

February 4. Naval battle of the Madoera Strait, Dutch East Indies.

February 27. Naval battle of the Java Sea.

April 18. First American air raid on Tokyo (The Doolittle Raid).

DEVELOPMENTS ABROAD

of Moscow and Russian counteroffensive.

December 10–31. Japanese launch offensive in Malaya.

December 25. Japanese capture Hong Kong.

1942 January-February. Japanese invade Netherlands East Indies. Air battles for Rangoon, Burma.

January 12–29. Japanese invade Burma.

February 8–15. Singapore Campaign.

February 19. Japanese launch air raids on Darwin, Australia.

February 29–March 9. Battle for Java.

April 10–19. Battle of Yenangyaung, China.

April-May. Japanese invest and finally take U.S. forces on Corregidor.

AMERICAN MILITARY DEVELOPMENTS

May 7–8. Battle of the Coral Sea (first naval engagement fought entirely by aircraft of opposing carriers).

June 3–7. Japanese Aleutian Offensive.
June 4–6. Naval Battle of Midway.

September-November. Allied campaigns against Buna and New Guinea.
October 11–13. Battle of Cape Esperance, off Guadalcanal.
November 12–15. Naval battle for Guadalcanal.

1943 January-December. The Solomons Campaign.
January 14-23. Casablanca Conference.
February 7. Japanese forces evacuate Guadalcanal.
February 14. Battle of Kasserine Pass, Tunisia.

March 2–4. Battle of the Bismarck Sea.
May 3–13. Battle of Tunisia.
July 2–August 25. Allied landing on New Georgia, Solomon Islands.

DEVELOPMENTS ABROAD

May. Allied retreat from Burma.
May 30–31. RAF Bomber Command's first thousand-plane raid against Germany launched from England.
May-June. Battle of Gazala in North Africa.
June 28–July 7. German summer offensive in Russia.
June-September. Japanese offensive against Port Moresby, New Guinea.
August 24-December 31. Battles for Stalingrad.
August 31. Battle of Alam Halfa, North Africa.

October 23-November 4. Battle of El Alamein, North Africa.
November. Allies land on Moroccan coast (Operation TORCH).

1943

February-April. Allies launch first Chindit Raid into Burma.
February 3. German Army surrenders at Stalingrad.
February-March. German counteroffensive begins at Kharkov, Russia.

July. Russian Army goes on the offensive.
July 5–16. Battle of Kursk,

CHRONOLOGY OF AMERICAN MILITARY DEVELOPMENTS

AMERICAN MILITARY DEVELOPMENTS	DEVELOPMENTS ABROAD
July 9–10. Allied landings on Sicily.	Russia. Largest tank battle of the war. July 24. Mussolini deposed in Italy. July 26–29. Air Battle of Hamburg, Germany.
August 1. Allied air forces raid oilfields at Ploesti, Rumania.	
September 3. Armistice in Italy. Allied landings at Salerno, Italy.	
October 12-November 14. The Volturno River Campaign, Italy.	
October 14. Allied air raid on Schweinfurt, Germany.	
October 19–30. Allied leaders meet for Moscow conference.	
October-December. Battle for Bougainville, Solomon Islands.	
November. General Dwight D. Eisenhower named supreme commander, Allied Expeditionary Force, Europe. Battle of Tarawa, Gilbert Islands.	November-December. Air Battle of Berlin. December-February 1944. Arakan Campaign in Burma.
December. Allied forces under General Joseph Stilwell launch offensive into Burma.	
1944 January-March. The New Britain Campaign.	1944 January 15–19. Liberation of Leningrad.
January-May. Allied bomber offensive against Germany.	January-February. Russian winter offensive continues.
January 15-25. The Rapido-Cassino battles in Italy.	
January 22. Allies make landings at Anzio, Italy.	
January 29-February 1. Battle of Kwajalein, Marshall Islands.	

AMERICAN MILITARY DEVELOPMENTS

DEVELOPMENTS ABROAD

March-July. Allies launch second Chindit raid into Burma.
March-September. Imphal-Kohima Campaign, India.

April. Battles of Aitape and Hollandia, New Guinea.

June. Russian summer offensive begins.

May 17–18. Allies launch assault and siege of Myitkyina, Burma.
June. Rome taken by Allied forces.
June-August. The Marianas Campaign.

July. Russian Army drives into Poland.

June 6. D-Day. Allies land in Normandy.
June 15. First strike of Allied strategic bombing offensive against Japanese mainland.
June 15-July 13. Battle of Saipan, Marianas Islands.
June 19–21. Battle of the Philippine Sea.
July 21. Battle of Guam begins.
July 25-31. Allies begin breakout from Normandy beachhead. Operation COBRA.
August 13–19. Battle of the Falaise-Argentan gap, France.
August 15. Allied landings in Southern France (Operation ANVIL-DRAGOON).
August-September. Vosges Mountain Campaign, France.
September 17–26. Allied invasion of Belgium (Operation MARKET-GARDEN).
September-December. Stilwell's offensive in China.
October. General Stilwell is relieved of command.

CHRONOLOGY OF AMERICAN MILITARY DEVELOPMENTS

AMERICAN MILITARY DEVELOPMENTS   **DEVELOPMENTS ABROAD**

October 20–22. Allies invade Leyte Island, the Philippines.
October 23–25. Naval Battle of Leyte Gulf.
October-November. Battle for the Scheldt Estuary, Holland.
November-December. Battles of the Huertgen Forest, Germany.
November 16-December 15. The Lorraine Campaign. The Alsace Campaign.
December-January 1945. German counteroffensive in the Ardennes.
December 26-January 2, 1945. The defense of Bastogne.

1945   January-February. Reduction of the Colmar Pocket by Allied forces, Alsace.   1945
January-August. The Luzon Campaign, Philippines.
January 9. Allies land at Lingayen Gulf, Luzon, Philippines.
January 27. Allies reopen the Burma Road.
February-March. The Rhineland Campaign. Allies liberate Manila.
February-August. Allies campaign in Mindinao, the Philippines.
February 13–14. Allied air forces firebomb Dresden, Germany.
February 19-March 24. Battle of Iwo Jima.
March 7. Allied forces seize the Remagen Bridgehead across the Rhine River.
March 9–21. Battle of Mandalay, Burma.

AMERICAN MILITARY DEVELOPMENTS	DEVELOPMENTS ABROAD
March 9–10. Allied Air Forces firebomb Tokyo.	
March 14-June 22. Battle of Okinawa.	
March 15-August 15. Philippine Mountain Campaign.	
April. Po Valley Campaign, Italy.	
May 2. Allied forces liberate Rangoon, Burma.	
May 7-8. Germany surrenders.	
July 16. First explosions of the atomic bomb at Alamagordo, New Mexico.	
August 6. First atomic bomb used in warfare dropped on Hiroshima, Japan.	
August 9. Second atomic bomb used in warfare dropped on Nagasaki, Japan.	August 9. Russia enters war against Japan with an invasion of Manchuria.
August 10. Japanese cabinet tenders offer to surrender.	
August 15. Warring powers agree to a ceasefire in Asia.	
August 28. American occupation forces arrive in Japan.	
September 2. Japan formally surrenders, concluding World War II.	

1946
March 5. Prime Minister Winston Churchill makes his "Iron Curtain" speech in Fulton, Missouri, warning of Soviet expansionist policies.

November 20, 1945-October 1, 1946. Nuremberg War Crimes Trials.

June 3, 1946-November 12, 1948. Tokyo War Crimes Trials.

AMERICAN MILITARY DEVELOPMENTS		DEVELOPMENTS ABROAD	
1947	March 12. President Truman enunciates his "containment doctrine" against communism and Soviet expansion.		
	June 5. Truman approves Marshall Plan for the economic reconstruction of Europe.		
	July. "The Sources of Soviet Conduct" by "Mr. X" (George Kennan) is published in the journal *Foreign Affairs*.		
	July 26. National Security Act creates National Military Establishment, a secretary of defense, and the U.S. Air Force as a separate military service.		
	October 3–27. The "Revolt of the Admirals."		
1948	March. Key West Conference between military service chiefs determines postwar military roles and missions.	1948	Israeli War of Independence.
	June 21. Congress passes new Selective Service Act.		
	June 24–May 12, 1949. Berlin Blockade and Airlift.		
1949	April 4. Establishment of North Atlantic Treaty Organization (NATO).		
	August 10. Congress passes National Security Act, creating Department of Defense.		
1950	April 7. NSC–68 promulgated, articulating national military policy of deterrence.		
	May. President Truman orders desegregation of armed forces.		
	June 25. North Korean troops begin invasion of South Korea.		

AMERICAN MILITARY DEVELOPMENTS	DEVELOPMENTS ABROAD
June 27. U.N. member states begin to send armed forces to the aid of South Korea. Korean War effectively begins.	
July 20. United States partially mobilizes for the Korean War.	
August 6-September 15. Battle of the Pusan Beachhead.	
September 15. U.N. troops land at Inchon.	
September 26. U.N. troops take Seoul.	
October 20. U.N. troops take Pyongyang.	
October 26. China intervenes in the Korean War. Chinese troops cross the Yalu River.	
November 25-26. Communist forces launch counteroffensive against U.S. Eighth Army.	
November 27-December 9. U.S. X Corps withdraws to Hungnam perimeter.	
December 5-December 15. X Corps evacuates to Pusan.	

1951
- January 4. U.N. troops evacuate Seoul.
- March. U.N. counteroffensive retakes Seoul.
- April 11. President Truman relieves General Douglas MacArthur of U.N. command.
- April-May. General Communist offensive in Korea.
- May. U.N. forces launch counteroffensive and retake line north of 38th parallel.

AMERICAN MILITARY DEVELOPMENTS **DEVELOPMENTS ABROAD**

July. Negotiations begin for Korean armistice.

November 12. Peace talks open at Panmunjom, Korea.

1952 Military stalemate continues on 38th parallel while peace talks are held. Active raiding and counter-raiding by combatants.

November. U.S. tests first hydrogen bomb at Eniwetok Island in the Pacific Ocean. Warring powers sign armistice in Korea.

1953 July 27. Korean Armistice formally signed.

August. The Sequoia Conference: U.S. service chiefs agree upon the politico-military doctrine of "massive retaliation."

United States begins military aid to France in Indochina.

1954 January 22. President Eisenhower announces a "new look" in American military policy.

1954 August. Soviet Union tests its first hydrogen bomb.

January 25. Secretary of State Dulles articulates policy of "massive retaliation."

May 7. French stronghold of Dienbienphu falls to Vietminh forces.

September 8. Southeast Asia Treaty Organization (SEATO) is formed.

September 30. U.S. Navy launches the first nuclear-powered submarine, USS *Nautilus*.

AMERICAN MILITARY DEVELOPMENTS	DEVELOPMENTS ABROAD
1954–55 Tension between United States and China over Nationalist Chinese occupation of Quemoy, Matsu, and other offshore islands.	
1955 January 20. United States begins direct military aid to South Vietnam. June. U.S. Air Force Academy opens at Colorado Springs, Colorado.	
1956 May. "The Colonels' Revolt." Public dispute between Army and Air Force staff officers over primacy of air power in national security policy.	**1956** October. Hungarians revolt against Russian occupation. October-November. Suez Crisis. Second Arab-Israeli War.
1957 January 5. The Eisenhower Doctrine: United States will aid Middle East countries threatened by Communist subversion or invasion.	
1958 May. President Eisenhower proposes reorganization of U.S. military command structures. July-October. America intervenes in Lebanon. August 6. Congress passes Defense Reorganization Act.	
1960 Presidential candidate Kennedy proposes that "flexible response" replace "massive retaliation" as cornerstone of national security policy. December 15. United States announces aid to Laos.	

CHRONOLOGY OF AMERICAN MILITARY DEVELOPMENTS

AMERICAN MILITARY DEVELOPMENTS	**DEVELOPMENTS ABROAD**

1961   February. United States tests first intercontinental ballistic missile (ICBM).

April 15-20. U.S.-sponsored army of Cuban exiles attempts invasion of Cuba at the Bay of Pigs.

August 13. East Germans begin construction of the Berlin Wall. U.S. forces put on alert.

1962   February 8. U.S. Military Assistance Command, Vietnam (MACV) is established in Saigon.

September-November. Cuban Missile Crisis.

October 5. U.S. military advisors withdrawn from Laos.

1963   January. In the Battle of Ap Bac, Vietcong defeat several regiments of the South Vietnamese Army.

November 1. South Vietnam government of Ngo Dinh Diem overthrown by military coup. Diem is assassinated.

1964   January 29. Young South Vietnamese officers led by General Nguyen Khanh take control of government.

August 1. North Vietnamese patrol boats reportedly attack USS *Maddox* in the Gulf of Tonkin.

August 4. USS *Maddox* and USS *C. Turner Joy* reportedly attacked by North Vietnamese patrol boats in the Gulf of Tonkin.

August 7. Congress passes the Gulf of Tonkin Resolu-

AMERICAN MILITARY DEVELOPMENTS	DEVELOPMENTS ABROAD
tion, authorizing the use of force for the protection of U.S. units. (In the absence of a formal declaration of war, this resolution is generally regarded as marking the beginning of the war in Vietnam.) December 24. Vietcong sappers bomb U.S. officers' billet in Saigon.	

1965
January. First North Vietnamese Army regiment reportedly enters South Vietnam.
February 6. Vietcong attack on U.S. base at Pleiku.
February 7. President Johnson orders commencement of air operations against North Vietnam. Operation ROLLING THUNDER begins on March 2.
March 6. President Johnson orders two battalions of Marines to South Vietnam.
April 28-June 28. United States intervenes in the Dominican Republic.
June 9. United States begins construction of port at Cam Ranh Bay.
June 18. United States begins B–52 strikes against suspected Vietcong enclaves, known as ARC LIGHT.
June 27. U.S. troops initiate first major offensive in War Zone D, South Vietnam.
July 28. President Johnson announces reinforcement of U.S. forces in Vietnam to 125,000.

CHRONOLOGY OF AMERICAN MILITARY DEVELOPMENTS

AMERICAN MILITARY DEVELOPMENTS	DEVELOPMENTS ABROAD
October-November. Battle of the Ia Drang Valley.	
1966 February 6–8. Honolulu Conference: President Johnson and Premier Ky of South Vietnam confer on conduct of the war.	1966
	March 31. France withdraws from NATO.
May 1. First targets hit in Vietcong sanctuaries in Cambodia.	
June 11. United States announces increase in troop strength in Vietnam to 285,000.	
June 29. United States makes first air attacks on oil installations at Hanoi and Haiphong, North Vietnam.	
November 24. Operation ATTLEBORO: 22,000 U.S. and South Vietnamese troops sweep War Zone C (Tay Ninh Province).	
1967 January 6. U.S. and South Vietnamese armies launch offensive in the Mekong Delta.	1967
January 8. Operation CEDAR FALLS, a combined offensive in the "Iron Triangle" northwest of Saigon.	
February 23-May 15. Operation JUNCTION CITY: largest allied operation of the year.	
	June. Fourth Arab-Israeli War.
July 15. Massive Vietcong mortar attack on U.S. base at Da Nang.	
September 27. Battle of Con Thien begins, lasting more than a month and a half.	

AMERICAN MILITARY DEVELOPMENTS	DEVELOPMENTS ABROAD
November 23. Battle for Dak Tho.	

1968
- January 21-April 5. The siege of Khe Sanh. Operation PEGASUS relieves Khe Sanh on April 8.
- January 23. Seizure of USS *Pueblo* off North Korean coast.
- January 30. The Tet Offensive
- March 11. U.S. counteroffensive in the "Iron Triangle."
- March 31. United States announces temporary cessation of air war against North Vietnam.
- April 21. Operation DELAWARE in the A Shau Valley.
- May 13. Peace talks begin in Paris.
- June 19. General Westmoreland leaves Vietnam to be Army chief of staff. General Abrams takes command of U.S. Military Assistance Command, Vietnam on July 3.
- June 27. U.S. forces abandon base at Khe Sanh.
- December-May 1969. In the Mekong Delta's dry season, Operation SPEEDY EXPRESS begins.

1969
- May 10–28. Battle of the A Shau Valley.
- July 8. First U.S. troops depart Vietnam as part of withdrawal schedule.
- October 4. In the United States, a Gallup Poll shows 58 percent of Americans think involvement in Vietnam is a mistake.

September 3. Ho Chi Minh dies in Hanoi.

AMERICAN MILITARY DEVELOPMENTS		DEVELOPMENTS ABROAD
	October 9. Secretary of Defense Melvin Laird confirms American policy to "Vietnamize" the war.	
	November 12. Army announces investigation of the My Lai massacre.	
1970	April 29-June 30. U.S. and South Vietnamese forces invade Cambodia.	
	May 4. National Guard troops kill four students during antiwar protest at Kent State University, Ohio.	
1971	January 30-April 3. Operation LAM SON 719 (NVA) drives into Laos to interdict North Vietnamese Army supply routes into South Vietnam.	
	June 13. *The New York Times* begins to publish the "Pentagon Papers."	
1972	April 1. Last units of U.S. Navy depart South Vietnam.	
	April 15. Americans turn over Da Nang to South Vietnam.	
	May 9. Cam Ranh Bay Air Base turned over to South Vietnam.	
	August 11. The last U.S. ground combat units in South Vietnam, the 3d battalion, 21st Infantry, is ordered to stand down.	
1973	January 23. The United States and North Vietnam agree on ceasefire in South Vietnam. Accord is formally signed on January 27.	
	March 29. U.S. Army, Vietnam, is formally disestablished.	

	1974	December–April 1975. Fall of South Vietnam.
		December. North Vietnamese begin offensive against South Vietnam by attacking Phuoc Long.
1975	1975	January 7. NVA takes Phuoc Binh.
		March 10. Ban Me Thuot falls to NVA.
		March 19. Quang Tri falls to NVA.
		March 20. An Loc falls to NVA.
		March 24. Tan Ky falls to NVA.
		March 25. Quang Ngai falls to NVA.
		March 29. Da Nang falls to NVA.
		April 1. Qui Nhon falls to NVA.
		April 3. Nha Trang falls to NVA.
		April 4. Dalat falls to NVA.
		April 20. Xuan Loc falls to NVA.
April 29. Americans remaining in Saigon are evacuated.		April 30. Saigon falls to NVA.

Index

Abrams, Creighton W., Jr., 1–4
Admirals' Revolt, 30
Aguinaldo, Emilio, 52
Air Corps Tactical School, 4, 171
Aisne-Marne Offensive, 4, 28, 224
Alger, Russell, 211
Allen, Ethan, 8
Allen, Henry Tureman, 19
Almond, Edward M., 4–7, 296
America, 142
Americal Division, 225, 227
American Expeditionary Force (AEF), 28, 29, 64, 177, 195, 196, 202, 213, 224, 228, 234–35, 288, 299
American Historical Association, 190
American Revolution, 140, 190, 240, 338–41
Amphibious warfare, 69, 72, 293, 295
Anaconda Plan, 274
André, John, 152, 305
Antietam, battle of, 41, 111, 117, 120, 133, 179, 186, 205, 209, 312. *See also* Sharpsburg
Appomattox Campaign, 44, 62, 81, 97, 179, 207, 282
Armies of Europe and Asia, 332
Army Air Corps, 12
Army Air Forces, 12
Army Air Service, 11, 12, 213
Army and Navy Club, 19

Army Ground Forces, 49
Army of Northern Virginia, 97, 282
Army of the Potomac, 41, 44, 97, 105, 184, 185, 187, 206–7, 281
Army of the Republic of South Vietnam, 3
Army of the Tennessee, 25, 80, 96
Army of the West, 55
Army Pearl Harbor Board, 290
Army School of the Line, 212. *See also* Command and General Staff College
Army War College, 2, 4, 18, 19, 27–28, 32, 38, 47, 64, 77, 91, 107, 167, 169, 174, 202, 345
Arnold, Benedict, 7–11, 84, 143, 218
Arnold, Henry, 11–14, 214, 300
Atlanta Campaign, 118, 139, 286–87, 350
Atlantic, battle of the, 149
Atlantic Charter Conference, 12
Atomic bomb, 247
Atomic Energy Commission, 247

Bainbridge, William, 73, 241
Baker, Newton, 195, 197, 235
Ball's Bluff, battle of, 278
Banks, N. P., 96, 133
Barbary Wars, 154, 155
Barnett, George, 71, 167, 168
Battle of the Bulge, 3, 22, 23, 67, 115, 229, 300, 316

Bay of Pigs, 317
Beauregard, P. G. T., 14–17, 24, 62, 136, 137, 238
Bell, James Franklin, 202
Belleau Wood, battle of, 292
Bemis Heights, battle of, 9, 84
Berlin Crisis, 2, 22, 172, 204
Bikini Island, 91
Black Hawk War, 135, 137, 273, 319
Black Hills, 45
Black Kettle, 45
Blanc Mont Ridge, battle of, 71
Bliss, Tasker H., 17–20
Blitzkrieg, 49, 82
Blue Book, 305
Bonhomme Richard, 141
Boston, siege of, 100, 159, 338
Boston Tea Party, 159
Bougainville, battle of, 91
Braddock Expedition, 218, 337
Bradley, Omar N., 20–23, 40, 113, 114, 250
Bragg, Braxton, 23–26, 80, 130, 179, 264, 281, 323
Brandy Station, battle of, 312
Brandywine, battle of the, 100, 151, 153, 342
Brice's Crossroad, battle of, 81
Brown, Jacob J., 129, 273
Brown, John, 132, 163, 311
Buchanan, Franklin, 76
Buchanan, James, 274
Buckner, Simon B., 296
Buell, Don Carlos, 105, 136, 322, 350
Buena Vista, battle of, 24, 320
"Buffalo Soldiers," 279
Buford, John, 206
Bullard, Robert, 19, 26–29
Bull Run, First battle of, 120, 132, 137, 178, 185, 285, 311, 331. *See also* Manassas
Bull Run, Second battle of, 133, 179, 312. *See also* Manassas
Buna, battle of, 65
Burgoyne, John, 84, 218, 339
Burke, Arleigh, 29–32, 217
Burma Campaign, 310

Burnside, Ambrose E., 120, 133, 163, 186, 205
Burr Conspiracy, 272
Butler, Benjamin F., 15, 238
Butler, Smedley D., 334

Cactus Air Force, 91, 92, 336
Calhoun, John C., 128, 333
Cambodia, invasion of, 3
Camden, battle of, 85, 86–87, 100
Cantigny, battle of, 28, 234
Cape Engano, battle of, 109
Cape Gloucester campaign, 245
Cape St. George, battle of, 30
Carleton, Guy, 8
Carrier battles, 78
Cartagena Expedition, 337
Castro, Fidel, 69
Catherine the Great, 142
Cedar Creek, battle of, 283
Central Intelligence Agency (CIA), 59, 60, 68, 302
Cervera, Pascual, 266, 270, 271
Chancellorsville, battle of, 61, 62, 112, 120, 122, 133, 163, 165, 179, 205, 206, 209, 312, 331
Chapultepec, battle of, 14, 95, 237
Chateau-Thierry, battle of, 176
Chattanooga, battle of, 25, 96, 99, 122, 281, 285, 323
Chesapeake-Leopard affair, 155–56
Chiang Kai-shek, 308, 309, 334
Chickamauga, battle of, 25, 26, 41, 80, 118, 179, 264, 265, 281, 323, 350
Chief Joseph, 209
Chief of Naval Operations (CNO), 31, 148
Chilean Crisis, 270, 271
China-Burma-India Theater (CBI), 308
Chippewa, battle of, 272
Chosin Reservoir, 6, 245, 297, 298
CHROMITE, 6. *See also* Inchon
Churchill, Winston, 203
Citadel, The, 33, 34
Civilian Conservation Corps (CCC), 12, 170, 203
Clark, Mark, 32–34, 326
Clark, William, 34–37
Clausewitz, Karl von, 136

INDEX

Clinton, Sir Henry, 10, 198, 339
COBRA, 40
Collins, J. Lawton, 37–40, 116
Colmar Pocket, 48, 226
Combined Chiefs of Staff, 13
Command and General Staff College, 2, 4, 12, 38, 47, 64, 65, 88, 91, 225, 287, 299, 307, 315, 325, 345
Confederate Naval Brigade, 277
Conner, David, 275
Constellation, 329
Containment, 68
Continental Army, 54, 84, 153
Continental Congress, 8, 9
Continental Navy, 140
Conway Cabal, 84, 86, 151, 153, 218
Cooke, Philip St. George, 311
Coolidge, Calvin, 58, 213
Coral Sea, battle of the, 78, 79, 302
Corinth, battle of, 16, 105, 263–64
Cornwallis, Lord Charles, 54, 85, 101, 153, 199, 200, 219, 339
Council on Foreign Relations, 19
Cowpens, battle of, 101, 200, 219
Coyotepe, battle of, 334
Craig, Malin, 64, 203
Crazy Horse, 42
Creek War, 130
Crimean War, 185
Crook, George, 40–43, 45, 209, 211
CSS *Alabama*, 275, 276–77
CSS *Sumter*, 276
Cuba, 18
Cuban Missile Crisis, 31, 172, 317
Culebra Maneuvers, 167
Custer, George A., 42, 43–47, 209, 283

Danbury Raid, 8
Daniels, Josephus, 53, 168
Davis, Benjamin O., 295
Davis, Jefferson, 15, 16, 25, 81, 117, 135, 138, 140, 163, 209, 350
D-Day, 228, 316. *See also* Normandy Invasion
Decatur, Stephen, 155, 241
De Grasse, Françoise, 339
De Kalb, Johannes, 152
De Rochambeau, Jean Baptiste, 339

Devers, Jacob, 47–50
Dewey, George, 50–53, 257, 269, 270
Dickman, Joseph T., 176
Diem, Ngo Dinh, 346
Dieppe Raid, 326
Doniphan, Alexander W., 53–57
Donovan, William J., 57–60
Doolittle, James H., 108, 216, 302
Doubleday, Abner, 206
Dragon, 226
Dreadnought, 53, 268
Drewry's Bluff, battle of, 15
Dulles, Allen, 59

Eaker, Ira C., 299
Early, Jubal, 41, 44, 60–63, 120, 163, 282
Easter Offensive, 2
Eastern Solomons, battle of the, 78
Ecole Supérieure de Guerre, 295
Eichelberger, Robert L., 63–66
82d Airborne Division, 21, 88, 89, 250, 252, 315
Eisenhower, Dwight David, 21, 22, 33, 48, 66–69, 89, 115, 197, 228, 251, 299, 316, 326
Elements of the Military Art and Science, 103, 106
Ellis, Earl, 69–73, 92, 169
El Paso, battle of, 55
"Embalmed Beef Controversy," 211
Empress Augusta Bay, battle of, 30
European Recovery Act (Marshall Plan), 204
Eutaw Springs, battle of, 102, 200
Evans, Robley D., 144

Falaise Gap, battle of, 21
Fallen Timbers, battle of, 34, 344
Farragut, David G., 51, 73–77, 269
Fast Carrier Task Force 58, 30
Fisher's Hill, battle of, 41, 63
Fiske, Bradley A., 51, 53
Five Forks, battle of, 97, 238, 239, 282
Fleet Marine Force, Pacific, 292
Fletcher, Frank Jack, 77–79, 302, 336
"Flexible response," 89–90, 253, 318
Flying Squadron, 267–91
Forrest, Nathan Bedford, 79–83

Forrestal, James, 150
Fort Benjamin Harrison, 64
Fort Benning, 21, 88, 113. *See also* Infantry School
Fort Bliss, 1
Fort Donelson, 80, 95, 98, 105, 106, 136, 285
Fort Henry, 95, 98, 105, 106, 136. *See also* Fort Donelson
Fort Knox, 2, 48
Fort Leavenworth, 35, 201, 311. *See also* Command and General Staff College
Fort Mims massacre, 127
Fort Pillow, 81
Fortress Monroe, 17
Fort Stanwix, 8
Fort Sumter, 120, 209
Fort Ticonderoga, 8, 84, 343
42d Division, 181
Foulois, Benjamin D., 213
Franklin, battle of, 118
Fredericksburg, battle of, 112, 120, 121, 133, 163, 179, 205, 209, 238
Frederick the Great, 304
Freeman's Farm, battle of, 84
Fremont, John C., 104, 133
French and Indian War, 99, 198, 337
Fuller, J. F. C., 136, 164

Gaines' Mill, battle of, 117, 238
Garde d'Haiti, 295. *See also Gendarmerie d'Haiti*
Gates, Horatio, 9, 83–87, 100, 199, 218, 219
Gavin, James M., 87–90, 251, 318, 348
Geiger, Roy S., 90–94, 336
Gendarmerie d'Haiti, 243
General Services Schools, 288–89. *See also* Command and General Staff College
George III, 158
Germantown, battle of, 100, 339, 342
Geronimo, 27, 42, 209
Gettysburg, battle of, 44, 61, 62, 112, 117, 122, 164, 179, 180, 205, 206, 207, 208, 237, 238, 240, 313, 331
Goethals, George W., 196
Grant, Ulysses Simpson, 15, 24, 25, 75, 80, 94–99, 105, 122, 135, 138, 164, 207, 263, 264, 265, 274, 281, 285, 323
Great Meadows, battle of, 337
Great White Fleet, 107, 144, 261, 301
Greely, Adolphus W., 270
Greene, Nathanael, 85, 99–103, 200, 219, 305, 343
Green Mountain Boys, 8
Green Springs, battle of, 154
Guadalcanal, battle of, 38, 78, 91, 108, 216, 225, 244, 334, 335
Guam, battle of, 92
Guantanamo Bay, 267
Guardia Nacional (Nicaragua), 244
Guilford Court House, battle of, 101
"Gun Club," 30

Hague Peace Conference, 189
Halleck, Henry Wager, 16, 95, 103–7, 120, 186, 206, 281, 322
Halsey, William F., Jr., 77, 93, 107–10, 123, 301
Hamilton, Alexander, 104
Hammelburg Raid, 229
Hancock, W. S., 45, 206, 208, 209
Harkins, Paul D., 346
Harlem Heights, battle of, 100
Harris, Sir Arthur, 299
Harrison, William Henry, 231
Hart, B. H. Liddell, 236
Hart, T. C., 123
Heligoland Bight, battle of, 145
Henderson Field, 245. *See also* Cactus Air Force; Guadalcanal
Hewitt, Henry Kent, 146
Hill, A. P., 110–13, 131, 163, 179
Hiroshima, 109, 300
Hitler, Adolph, 237
HMS *Serapis*, 141
HMS *Shannon*, 156–57
Hodges, Courtney, 21, 113–16
Holcomb, Thomas, 335
Hollandia, 66
Hood, John Bell, 81, 116–19, 139, 286, 323
Hooker, Joseph, 61, 119–23, 163, 205–6
"Horse Marines," 244
Horseshoe Bend, battle of, 127, 129

INDEX

Hotchkiss, Jedediah, 133, 134
Howard, Oliver O., 122, 209
Howe, Sir William, 153, 160, 338
Hue, battle of, 2
Huertgen Forest, battle of the, 115

Inchon, 5, 22, 184, 296, 298
Infantry School, 21, 32, 113, 202, 244, 295, 307. See also Fort Benning
Infantry Tactics, 273
Influence of Sea Power upon History, 189, 190
Ingersoll, Royal E., 123–26
Italian Campaign, 32–33, 315, 326
Iuka, battle of, 264
Iwo Jima, battle of, 293

Jackson, Andrew, 126–31, 237, 273
Jackson, Thomas J., 61, 121, 131–34, 163, 164, 165, 205, 312, 322
Japan, occupation of, 182
Jefferson, Thomas, 241, 344
Johnson, Lyndon B., 2, 346
Johnston, Albert Sidney, 15, 24, 80, 96, 117, 134–37, 162
Johnston, Joseph E., 14, 96, 118, 132, 137–40, 163, 179, 186–87, 277, 285, 311
Joint Army and Navy Board, 20, 52
Joint Army and Navy Planning Committee, 292
Joint Chiefs of Staff, 13, 22, 52, 149, 150, 184
Jomini, Antoine Henri, 16, 104, 190, 193, 274, 287
Jones, John Paul, 140–44
Jones, William, 255

Kassarine Pass, battle of, 67, 228, 345
Kearny, Stephen W., 55
Kennedy, John F., 317
Kenney, George C., 300
Kimmel, Husband E., 144–48, 222, 291
King, Ernest J., 124, 147, 148–51, 222, 223, 292, 302
Kinkaid, Thomas K., 108
Kipling, Rudyard, 226

Korean War, 2, 5, 30, 33, 39, 172, 182, 204, 245, 251–52, 296

Lafayette, Marquis de Marie, 151–54, 343
Lake Erie, battle of, 230–32
Las Guasimas, battle of, 350
Lawrence, James, 154–57
Lee, Charles, 151, 157–62, 342
Lee, Henry, 101, 162, 199
Lee, Robert E., 15, 97, 105, 111, 117, 120, 122, 132, 135, 138, 162–66, 206, 238, 314
Lee, Stephen D., 285
Lejeune, John A., 70–71, 166–70
LeMay, Curtis E., 170–73, 300
Lewis and Clark Expedition, 35–36
Lexington, battle of, 7
Leyte Gulf, battle of, 108, 110, 216
Libby Prison, 41
Liggett, Hunter, 173–78, 202, 237
Liman Campaign, 143
Lincoln, Abraham, 104, 120, 185, 206, 263, 283, 322
Lincoln, Benjamin, 85, 198
Lindbergh, Charles, 299
Little Big Horn, battle of, 42, 45–46
Little Rock riots, 68
London Naval Conference, 124
Long, John B., 52
Long Island, battle of, 338
Longstreet, James B., 25, 62, 111, 122, 133, 164, 178–81, 206, 238, 281
Looking Glass, 209
Lopez de Santa Anna, Antonio, 320
Louisiana State University, 285
Louisiana Territory, 35
Luce, Stephen B., 188, 267
Lundy's Lane, battle of, 273
Luzon, invasion of, 182

MacArthur, Arthur, 181, 195
MacArthur, Douglas, 5, 108, 114, 181–84, 204, 222, 223, 251–52, 296, 300, 336
McCarthy, Joseph, 204, 251
McClellan, George B., 44, 106, 120, 131, 132, 136, 163, 184–88, 205, 209, 263
MacKay Trophy, 11, 12
MacKenzie, Ranald S., 284

McKinley, William, 120, 211, 257, 350
McNair, Lesley J., 226
McNamara, Robert S., 172, 347
Madison, James, 36, 127, 272
MAGIC, 147
Magsaysay, Ramon, 302
Mahan, Alfred Thayer, 51, 53, 188–91, 193, 256, 257, 261
Mahan, Denis Hart, 103, 188, 191–95
Mahan, Milo, 190
Manassas, First battle of, 14, 16, 61, 62, 111. *See also* Bull Run, First battle of
Manassas, Second battle of, 61, 111, 163, 186, 205. *See also* Bull Run, Second battle of
Manila Bay, battle of, 52, 53, 195, 257
March, Peyton, 195–98, 235
March Field, 12
March to the Sea, 323
Marine Corps Amphibious Base Force, 70, 167, 169
Marion, Francis, 102, 198–201, 220
MARKET-GARDEN, 88–89, 251, 316
Marshall, George C., 6, 11, 21, 33, 48, 67, 113, 115, 150, 176, 197, 201–5, 245, 250, 289, 290, 295, 307, 308, 315, 325
Massachusetts Committee of Safety, 7–8
Mayo, Henry T., 148
Meade, George G., 97, 164, 205–8, 281
Meredith, James M., 2
Meuse-Argonne Offensive, 4, 28, 176, 177, 224, 228, 235, 236
Mexican War, 14, 25, 55–56, 60–61, 95, 111, 119, 120, 122, 131, 135, 137, 162, 178, 185, 273–74, 275, 318–20, 322
Micronesia Plan, 73, 170
Midway, battle of, 78, 79, 108, 216, 223, 300, 302
Miles, Nelson A., 42, 43, 208–12, 259
Military-Industrial Complex, 69
Military Policy of the United States, 330
Military Service Institution, 19
Missionary Ridge, battle of, 281, 285
Missouri Territory, 35
Mitchell, William, 12, 181, 212–15, 299
Mitscher, Marc A., 30, 215–18
Mobile Army Division, 18
Mobile Bay, battle of, 76

Molino del Rey, battle of, 95
Monmouth, battle of, 100, 128, 151, 161, 304, 339, 342
Monroe, James, 129, 152, 232
Monroe Doctrine, 259–60
Montelimar, battle of, 326
Monterrey, battle of, 24, 95, 205, 319
Montgomery, Bernard Law, 21, 23, 40, 67, 114, 115, 251
Montgomery, Richard, 8
Morgan, Daniel, 84, 101, 200, 218–20
Morgan's Riflemen, 218
Morman Rebellion (1857), 135
Morman War (1838), 54
Morrow Board, 213
Mosquito Fleet, 74
Mountbatten, Lord Louis, 308, 326
Murfreesboro, battle of, 25, 26, 80, 264–65. *See also* Stone's River

Nagumo, Chiuchi, 79
Naktong River offensive, 183
Napoleon, 193–94
Napoleon Club, 193
Nashville, battle of, 81, 118, 278, 324
National Defense Act of 1920, 202
National Security Act of 1947, 59, 300
Naval Observatory, 267
Naval War Board, 189
Naval War College, 17, 70, 77, 91, 107, 124, 145, 188, 189, 190, 221, 222, 260, 292, 301, 302
Naval War of 1812, The, 256
Navy Act of 1916, 168
Navy Department, 329
Navy Flying School, 90
Navy General Board, 30, 50, 52, 78
New Caledonia Campaign, 225
New Georgia Campaign, 38
"New Look," 31, 68, 89, 252, 317
"New Navy," 51
New Orleans, battle of (1862), 74–75, 128
Nez Perce, 209
Nimitz, Chester W., 78, 79, 107, 123, 146, 220–24, 244, 247, 292, 302
92d Infantry Division, 6
Nixon, Richard M., 248

Normandy Invasion, 1, 114, 203, 250. *See also* D-Day
North African Campaign, 21
North Atlantic Treaty Organization (NATO), 22, 39, 68, 204, 252
NSC 68, 22
Nullification Crisis, 129

Office of Strategic Services (OSS), 58–59
Okinawa, battle of, 91, 93, 296, 308
101st Airborne Division, 316
Open Door Policy, 261
Opequon, battle of the, 331
Ostfriesland, 213
Out-Post, 192
OVERLORD, 21, 67, 299. *See also* Normandy Invasion

Pacification, 3
Palo Alto, battle of, 319
Panama Canal, 256, 261
Panamanian Revolution, 167
Papuan Campaign, 182
Paris Peace Conference, 124
Patch, Alexander M., 224–27, 335
Patrick, Mason M., 213
Patton, George S., Jr., 1, 2, 21, 67, 113, 130, 226, 227–30, 326
Pearl Harbor, 13, 30, 38, 65, 77, 107, 146–47, 204, 222, 289
Peleliu, battle of, 92, 245
Pemberton, John C., 96, 138
Pendleton, A. S., 134
Pendleton, Joseph H., 70, 334
Perry, Oliver Hazard, 230–33
Perryville, battle of, 25, 281, 322, 350
Pershing, John J., 28, 57, 67, 168, 175, 196, 202, 228, 233–37, 288
Pershing Rifles, 234
Petersburg Campaign, 15–16, 97, 112
Philippines, 5, 11, 18, 27, 53, 63, 65, 108, 175, 195, 201, 302
Philippine Sea, battle of the, 216, 302
Pickett, George E., 237–40
Pickett's Charge, 179, 238 39
Pillow, Gideon, 120
"Plan Orange," 124
PLAN 712, 71

Plattsburg Training Camp Movement, 259
Pleasanton, Alfred, 44, 312
Polaris program, 31, 248
Pope, John, 186
Porter, David, 73
Porter, David Dixon, 51, 75, 96
Port Gibson, battle of, 98
Port Hudson, battle of, 96
Potsdam Conference, 203
Pratt, William V., 124
Preble, Edward, 155, 240–43, 254
Princeton, battle of, 338
Puerto Rican Campaign, 17
Puller, Lewis B., 93, 243–46
Punitive Expedition, 228, 234, 288, 298

Quasi-War, 154, 241, 254
Quebec, battle of, 8
Queenstown Heights, battle of, 272
Quesada, Elwood, 299

Rabaul, 108
Rainbow Division, 57
Randall, James G., 208
Rappahannock Station, battle of, 331
RECKLESS Task Force, 65
Reconstruction, 105, 180
Red River War, 209, 284
Regensburg Raid, 171
Remagen Bridgehead, 114
Reynolds, John F., 206
Richardson, James O., 145
Richmond Campaign, 132
Rich Mountain, battle of, 263
Rickover, Hyman G., 246–49
Ridgway, Matthew B., 249–53, 297
Ridgway Report, 253
Rodgers, John, 253–56
Roosevelt, Franklin Delano, 12, 48, 58, 144, 145, 149, 168, 214, 309, 336
Roosevelt, Theodore, 51, 181, 210, 256–63, 267, 270
Root, Elihu, 18, 106, 210, 211, 236, 258, 333
Root Reforms, 259
Root-Takahira Agreement, 261
Rosebud, battle of the, 42

Rosecrans, William S., 25, 26, 96, 263–66, 323, 350
Rough Riders, 257–58
Ruhr Pocket, 251
Rupertus, William, 243
Russo-Japanese War, 195, 258

St. Mihiel, battle of, 168, 176, 202, 213, 307
Saipan, battle of, 92, 294
Salem Church, battle of, 121
Salerno, battle of, 67, 88, 316. *See also* Italian Campaign
Sampson, William T., 266–69
Sandino, Augusto, 244
San Juan Hill, battle of, 258
Santa Fe Trail, 55
Santiago Bay, battle of, 211, 267, 268, 279
Saratoga, battle of, 8, 10, 218, 339
Savannah Campaign, 198
Schley, Winfield S., 267–68, 269–72
Schofield, John M., 17
Schuyler, Philip, 84, 339
Scott, Hugh Lenox, 18, 195
Scott, Winfield, 14, 56, 95, 119, 162, 237, 272–75, 319
Selective Service Act, 203
Seminole War (1818), 24, 128, 130, 275
Seminole War (1837), 60, 111, 119, 137, 205, 284
Semmes, Raphael, 275–78
"Sentiments on a Peace Establishment," 340
Seven Days', battle of the, 111, 120, 133, 163, 179, 186, 187, 312
Seven Pines (Fair Oaks), battle of, 138, 140, 163, 186, 209, 238, 239, 278
7th Cavalry Regiment, 44
Seven Years' War, 158, 304
Shafter, William R., 259, 271, 278–80
Sharpesburg, battle of, 163. *See also* Antietam
Sheridan, Philip H., 41–46, 97, 106, 209, 216, 238, 280–84, 313
Sherman, William T., 15, 81, 104, 105, 118, 139, 193, 209, 284–88, 323, 332, 350

Shenandoah Valley Campaign, 61, 62, 132, 134, 283
Shiloh, battle of, 15, 24, 80, 96, 98, 105, 106, 136, 285, 322, 349
Shippen, Margaret, 9–10
SHOESTRING, 336
Short, Walter C., 147, 288–91
Sicilian Campaign, 21, 67, 88, 228, 250, 315, 326
Siegfried Line Campaign, 114, 115, 229
Sitting Bull, 210
Smith, Edmund Kirby, 350
Smith, Holland M., 92, 94, 291–94
Smith, Joseph, 54
Smith, Oliver P., 294–98
Smith, Robert, 242
Smith Board, 296
Society of the Cincinnati, 305
Soloman Islands Campaign, 216
Southeast Asia Command (SEAC), 309
South Mountain, battle of, 120, 186
Spaatz, Carl A., 170, 173, 214, 298–300
Spanish-American War, 11, 27, 51, 148, 167, 174, 210, 234, 266, 278–79, 350
Spanish Civil War, 58
Spotsylvania, battle of, 331
Spruance, Raymond A., 78, 108, 110, 217, 300–4
Squire, George O., 213
Stanton, Edwin M., 105, 122, 186
Stark, Harold R., 124, 149
Steuben, Frederick W., 101, 103, 304–6, 339
Stilwell, Joseph W., 94, 306–11
Stimson, Henry, 290, 310
Stony Point, battle of, 342
Strategic Air Command, 170, 172, 173
Strategic bombing, 13
Stuart, J. E. B., 44, 281, 311–14
Student, Karl, 250
Sullivan, John, 342
Sumter, Thomas, 200
Supreme War Council, 19–20

Taft, William Howard, 18, 258
Tampico Expedition, 168
Tarleton, Bannastre, 199, 219
Task Force 11, 77

INDEX 409

Task Force 17, 77
Taylor, Maxwell D., 314–18, 346
Taylor, Zachary, 56, 95, 119, 135, 273, 318–21
Terry, Alfred, 45
Tet Offensive, 2, 347–48
Texas Brigade, 117–19
Thames, battle of the, 232–33
Thayer, Sylvanus, 104, 183, 188, 191
37th Tank Battalion, 1
Thomas, George H., 25, 81, 96, 118, 264, 278, 321–25
Three Rivers, battle of, 342
Ticonderoga, battle of, 86
Tokyo Raid, 108. *See also* Doolittle, James H.
TORCH, 299
Tracy, Benjamin F., 270
Treaty of Greenville, 344
Treaty of Guadalupe Hidalgo, 320
Trenton, battle of, 100, 338
Trevilian Station, battle of, 281
Tripolitan Wars, 155, 240, 241, 254
Truman, Harry S., 23, 30, 59, 68, 183, 204, 252
Truscott, Lucian K., Jr., 325–28
Truxton, Thomas, 328–30
Tullahoma Campaign, 41
25th Infantry Division, 38

ULTRA, 115
United Nations, 204, 222
United Nations Command, 33, 182
U.S. Air Force Academy, 300
U.S. Military Academy, 24, 27, 32, 37, 38, 39, 41, 44, 47, 60, 64, 65, 66, 87, 88, 94, 103, 111, 113, 116, 119, 131, 135, 137, 162, 173, 178, 181, 183, 185, 195, 205, 221, 224, 227, 233, 237, 249, 250, 263, 272, 281, 284, 298, 307, 311, 315, 316, 318, 322, 330, 332, 345, 349. *See also* West Point
U.S. Military Advisory Command-Vietnam, 2, 3
U.S. Naval Academy (Annapolis), 29, 50, 51, 77, 107, 123, 143, 144, 148, 166, 188, 191, 215, 221, 246, 261, 266, 267, 268, 269, 301

U.S. Naval Institute, 267
U.S.S. *Constitution*, 241
U.S.S. *Lexington*, 148
U.S.S. *Maine*, 51, 257, 267
U.S.S. *Missouri*, 109, 222, 308
U.S.S. *Nautilus*, 248
U.S.S. *Philadelphia*, 155, 241
Upton, Emory, 287, 330–34
Utah Beach, 250. *See also* Normandy Invasion; D-Day

Valley Forge, 100, 151, 304, 306
Vandegrift, Alexander A., 92, 296, 334–37
Vandenberg, Hoyt S., 172
Venezuelan Crisis, 52
Vera Cruz Expedition, 181
Verdun, battle of, 307
Vicksburg, siege of, 74, 75, 96, 98, 138–39, 285
Vietnam War, 1, 2, 4, 39, 314, 317, 345–48
Virginia Military Institute, 4, 6, 131–32, 168, 192, 201, 243

Wake Island, battle of, 77, 79, 146
War of 1812, 36, 41, 73, 127, 130, 154–55, 231, 255, 272–73, 319
War Plans Division, 203, 250
Washington, George, 8, 84, 100, 151, 153, 161, 304, 328, 337–41, 342, 344
Washington College, 165
Washita River, battle of the, 45
Wayne, Anthony, 34, 219, 341–45
Weapons Systems Evaluation Group, 88
Western Flotilla, 75
Western Sea Frontier, 125–26
Westmoreland, William C., 3, 317, 345–49
Westover, Oscar, 12
West Point, 1, 10, 11, 14, 17, 20. *See also* U.S. Military Academy
Wheeler, Joseph, 41, 349–52
Whiskey Rebellion, 219
Wilderness Campaign, 61, 97, 112, 164, 179, 207, 209
Wilkinson, James, 84, 127, 272
Williams, T. Harry, 136

Williamsburg, battle of, 120
Wilson, James H., 17
Wilson, Woodrow, 19
Winchester, battle of, 41, 132, 282
Wood, Leonard, 19
Wool, John E., 56
Wounded Knee massacre, 210
Wright Brothers, 11

Yalta Conference, 13
Yellowstone Expedition, 45
Yellow Tavern, battle of, 44, 281, 313
Yorktown, battle of, 54, 102, 152, 154, 200, 305, 339, 343

Zuckerman, Sir Solly, 299

Contributors

GEORGE R. ADAMS is Director of the Education Division of the American Association for State and Local History.

JAMES B. AGNEW (1930–1980), Colonel, U.S. Army, was Director of the U.S. Army Military History Institute.

STEPHEN E. AMBROSE is Professor of History at the University of New Orleans.

WAYNE AUSTERMAN is a Historian with the U.S. Air Force.

DONALD L. BAUCOM, a Lieutenant Colonel, U.S. Air Force, and a former editor of *Air University Review*, now serves at the Office of Air Force History.

K. JACK BAUER was Professor of History at Rennselaer Polytechnic Institute.

EDWIN C. BEARSS is a Historian with the U.S. National Park Service.

ROGER BEAUMONT is Professor of History at Texas A&M University.

HARRY R. BOROWSKI, Lieutenant Colonel, U.S. Air Force, is on the faculty of history at the U.S. Air Force Academy.

JAMES C. BRADFORD is Associate Professor of History at Texas A&M University and editor of *The Papers of John Paul Jones*.

WILLIAM R. BRAISTED, now retired, was Professor of History at the University of Texas.

RALPH ADAMS BROWN is Emeritus Professor of History, State University of New York at Cortland.

THOMAS B. BUELL, Commander, U.S. Navy, is now retired from active service.

JOHN L. BULLION is Associate Professor of History at the University of Missouri, Columbia.

JACK J. CARDOSO is Professor of History, State University of New York at Buffalo.

PHILANDER D. CHASE is Assistant Editor of *The Papers of George Washington*.

DAVID CHILDRESS is Associate Professor of History at Jacksonville (Alabama) State University.

EDWARD M. COFFMAN is Professor of History at the University of Wisconsin.

THEODORE J. CONWAY, General, U.S. Army, retired, is now an Adjunct Professor of History at the University of South Florida.

NORMAN V. COOPER is Adjunct Professor of History at the University of Alabama, Birmingham.

ROBERT J. CRESSMAN is a Historian with the U.S. Marine Corps Historical Center.

VAN M. DAVIDSON, JR., former Major, U.S. Army, is an attorney in Lake Charles, Louisiana.

JEFFERY M. DORWART is Professor of History at Rutgers University, Camden.

EDWARD J. DREA is a Supervisory Historian at the U.S. Army Center of Military History.

WILLIAM S. DUDLEY is the Senior Historian at the U.S. Naval Historical Center.

EDWARD K. ECKERT is Associate Professor of History at Saint Bonaventure University.

THOMAS R. ENGLISH is Professor of History at Delaware County Community College, Media, Pennsylvania.

CONTRIBUTORS

UZAL W. ENT, Colonel, U.S, Army, is now retired as Historian of the 28th Infantry Division.

JOHN FERLING is Associate Professor of History at West Georgia College.

MARTIN K. GORDON is a Historian with the U.S. Army Office of the Chief of Engineers.

HOLMAN HAMILTON (1910–1980) was Emeritus Professor of History at the University of Kentucky.

WARREN W. HASSLER, JR., is Professor Emeritus of History at Pennsylvania State University.

RICHARD F. HAYNES is Professor of History at Northeast Louisiana University.

GEORGE C. HERRING is Professor of History at the University of Kentucky.

R. DON HIGGINBOTHAM is Professor of History at the University of North Carolina.

JOSEPH P. HOBBS is Professor of History at North Carolina State University.

JOHN T. HUBBELL is Professor of History at Kent State University, editor of *Civil War History*, and Director of the Kent State University Press.

ALFRED F. HURLEY, Brigadier General, U.S. Air Force, retired, is President of the University of North Texas.

JOHN W. HUSTON is Professor of History at the U.S. Naval Academy.

PAUL A. HUTTON is Associate Professor of History at the University of New Mexico.

D. CLAYTON JAMES is Biggs Professor of Military History at the Virginia Military Institute.

PHILIP D. JONES is Associate Professor of History at Bradley University.

THOMAS L. KARNES is Professor of History at Arizona State University.

BROOKS E. KLEBER, retired, was Assistant Chief of Military History, U.S. Army.

RICHARD H. KOHN is Chief of the Office of Air Force History.

WILLIAM M. LEARY, JR., is Professor of History at the University of Georgia.

WILLIAM H. LECKIE, retired, was Vice President for Academic Affairs and Professor of History at the University of Toledo.

E. B. LONG (1919–1981) was Professor of American Studies at the University of Wyoming.

EDWARD G. LONGACRE is a Historian with the U.S. Air Force Strategic Air Command.

JOHN L. LOOS is Emeritus Professor of History, Louisiana State University.

MARK M. LOWENTHAL is an Analyst in National Defense, Congressional Research Service, at the Library of Congress.

JOHN B. LUNDSTROM is a Historian at the Milwaukee Public Museum, Milwaukee, Wisconsin.

JAY LUVAAS is Professor of Military History, the U.S. Army War College.

ARCHIE P. McDONALD is Professor of History at Stephen F. Austin State University.

JAMES LEE McDONOUGH is Professor of History at Auburn University.

CHRISTOPHER McKEE is Professor of History at Grinnell College.

RAYMOND A. MANN is a Historian at the U.S. Naval Historical Center.

EDWARD J. MAROLDA is a Historian at the U.S. Naval Historical Center.

JAMES KIRBY MARTIN is Professor of History at the University of Houston.

JAMES M. MERRILL, retired, was Professor of History at the University of Delaware.

FRANK C. MEVERS is State Archivist at the Division of Archives, Concord, New Hampshire.

ALLAN R. MILLETT is Professor of History at Ohio State University.

JAMES L. MOONEY is a Historian at the U.S. Naval Historical Center.

PAUL D. NELSON is Professor of History at Berea College.

TIMOTHY K. NENNINGER is a Senior Historian with the National Archives.

PHILIP Y. NICHOLSON is Professor of History at Nassau Community College.

WALTER E. PITTMAN is Professor of History at the Mississippi University for Women.

FORREST C. POGUE, retired, was Director of the Dwight D. Eisenhower Institute for Historical Research at the Smithsonian Institution.

JAMES W. POHL is Professor of History at Southwest Texas State University.

JOSEPH C. PORTER is Curator of Western Art, the Joselyn Museum, Omaha, Nebraska.

E. B. POTTER is Emeritus Professor of History at the U.S. Naval Academy.

MARTIN REUSS is a Historian with the U.S. Army Office of the Chief of Engineers.

CLARK G. REYNOLDS is Professor Emeritus of History at the College of Charleston.

CHARLES P. ROLAND is Professor Emeritus of History at the University of Kentucky.

DAVID ALAN ROSENBERG is Professor of Strategy at the Naval War College.

JOHN J. SBREGA is Chairman of the Department of Social Sciences at Tidewater Community College.

THOMAS E. SCHOTT is a Historian with the U.S. Air Force, Oklahoma City, Oklahoma.

ROBERT SEAGER II is Professor of History at the University of Kentucky.

JAMES E. SEFTON is Professor of History at California State University, Northridge.

RICHARD K. SHOWMAN is editor of *The Papers of Nathanael Greene*.

CHARLES R. SHRADER, Lieutenant Colonel, U.S. Army, is now retired from active service and is a professional historical consultant.

JACK SHULIMSON is a Historian at the U.S. Marine Corps Historical Center.

B. MITCHELL SIMPSON III, Lieutenant Commander, U.S. Navy, retired, is now associated with the law firm of Callahan and Sayer, Newport, Rhode Island.

GIBSON BELL SMITH is an Archivist at the National Archives.

DONALD SMYTHE, S. J., was Professor of History at John Carroll University.

STEPHEN Z. STARR was a noted Civil War historian and former Director of the Cincinnati Historical Society.

WILLIAM N. STILL is Professor of History at East Carolina State University.

RICHARD G. STONE, JR., is Professor of History at Western Kentucky University.

ROY TALBERT is Associate Vice Chancellor at Carolina Coastal College.

JACK W. THACKER is Professor of History at Western Kentucky University.

HARRY M. WARD is Professor of History at the University of Richmond.

RUSSELL F. WEIGLEY is Professor of History at Temple University.

JOHN M. WERNER is Professor of History at Western Illinois University.

FRANK J. WETTA is Assistant Dean and Professor of History at Galveston College.

GERALD E. WHEELER is Professor of History at San Jose State University.

DAVID L. WILSON is Associate Editor of the U.S. Grant Association and Assistant Professor of History at Southern Illinois University.

ALAN WILT is Professor of History at Iowa State University.

ROBERT E. WOLFF is a student of American military history.

About the Editors

ROGER J. SPILLER is Professor of Combined Arms Warfare and Deputy Director of the Combat Studies Institute at the U.S. Army Command and General Staff College, Fort Leavenworth, Kansas. He is the author of *"Not War But Like War": The American Intervention in Lebanon*, and was the Editor of the original *Dictionary of American Military Biography* (Greenwood Press, 1984). His articles have appeared in *Military Affairs*, *Military Review*, the *Journal of the Royal United Services Institution*, *The Public Historian*, *The South Atlantic Quarterly*, and *American Heritage Magazine*.

JOSEPH G. DAWSON III is Associate Professor of History at Texas A&M University. He is the author of *Army Generals and Reconstruction: Louisiana, 1862–1877* and was Associate Editor of the original *Dictionary of American Military Biography* (Greenwood Press, 1984). His articles have appeared in *Civil War History*, *Southern Studies*, *Louisiana History*, the *Red River Valley Historical Review*, and the *Dictionary of Literary Biography*.

72735
178